JOHN DONNE

The Satires, Epigrams
AND
Verse Letters

JOHN DONNE

The Satires, Epigrams

AND

Verse Letters

EDITED WITH

INTRODUCTION AND COMMENTARY

BY

W. MILGATE

READER IN ENGLISH
THE AUSTRALIAN NATIONAL UNIVERSITY

OXFORD

AT THE CLARENDON PRESS

1967

Oxford University Press, Ely House, London W. 1

GLASGOW NEW YORK TORONTO MELBOURNE WELLINGTON
CAPE TOWN SALISBURY IBADAN NAIROBI LUSAKA ADDIS ABABA
BOMBAY CALCUTTA MADRAS KARACHI LAHORE DACCA
KUALA LUMPUR HONG KONG TOKYO

67- 111041

PRINTED IN GREAT BRITAIN
AT THE UNIVERSITY PRESS, OXFORD
BY VIVIAN RIDLER
PRINTER TO THE UNIVERSITY

PREFACE

THIS edition of the Satires, Epigrams, and Verse Letters of Donne has been designed to accompany the editions of the Divine Poems and of the Love Poems by Helen Gardner (in 1952 and 1965, respectively). Its purposes were to examine the text in the light of manuscripts not available to Sir Herbert Grierson for his great edition of 1912, to test the evidence for the existence of different versions and possible authentic revisions of the poems, to provide a fuller commentary, and generally to gather together the results of half a century of scholarly and critical work on the poems since Grierson's edition appeared.

The text which has resulted from my scrutiny of the manuscripts does not differ greatly from that of Grierson, and I have found evidence in every direction that confirms the general soundness of his methods. Miss Gardner's work on the manuscripts, and more especially her demonstration of the nature of the text in the first edition of 1633, make it possible, however, to improve the text in a good many places, and to provide a more consistent and more accurate presentation of what seem to have been the poet's intentions. I have reached the conclusion that, of the poems in this volume, only the first four regular Satires show signs of revision by the author. The evidence for the existence of authentic versions and suggestions as to their possible dates are set out in the Textual Introduction; here also will be found an account of the traditions of the text and (in the last section) a statement of the methods I have adopted in handling the text and compiling the textual apparatus. The poems are printed in what I hope will be found a more logical and more convenient order than that adopted by Grierson. To the canon of Donne's work in these genres which Grierson accepted in 1912 are added the letter to the Countess of Huntingdon ('That unripe side of earth'), the letter 'written by Sir H. G. and J. D. *alternis vicibus*', an epigram in English ('Manliness'), and two (surviving in Donne's handwriting) in Latin.

In the Commentary matters relating to text are dealt with first and are separated from the general note on sources, date, and the like, so that readers not interested in textual concerns can avoid them. The Commentary on each poem typically begins with a list of the manuscripts in which it is found, an account of any peculiarities of the basic text and of my departures from it, and an indication of the differences between my text and Grierson's. Many scholars have mentioned the need for as full a commentary as possible; and there has been a great volume of helpful comment in publications over more than fifty years. Against the temptations to length and fullness must, however, be set the reasonable limits of space. I have tried to avoid enlarging upon the obvious, and to comment briefly, and as accurately as possible, on real difficulties; for, as Donne says, 'darke texts need notes'. At the other extreme, although I have tried to do full justice to Donne's wit, intelligence, and originality, I have had in mind his ironic glance at the over-ingenious and over-solemn reader: 'For in those things which the *Poets* writ, though they themselves did not beleeve them, we have since found many truths, and many deep mysteries.'

This edition was first proposed while I was in Oxford as the holder of a Nuffield Foundation Travelling Fellowship in Humanities in 1949; and with the greatest generosity the Foundation extended my tenure of the Fellowship for a year to enable me to do the basic collation and gathering of material. I acknowledge with gratitude the kindness of the Warden and Fellows of Merton College in admitting me to membership of the College with special privileges, although (in the terms of my Travelling Fellowship) I was not reading for a degree, and the warm hospitality extended to me by members of the Common Room. I hold in especially grateful memory the late Professor F. P. Wilson, not only because as my supervisor he helped me in every way and made available to me the rich resources of his scholarship and wise counsel, but also because, with Mrs. Wilson, he made me warmly welcome as guest and friend.

Heavy pressure of professional work, and resulting ill health, held up my progress with this edition for many years. My thanks are due to the Research Committee of the University of Sydney for providing me with a research secretary during a period when I was able to give this work some attention. It is proper also that I should express my appreciation of the patience (sorely tried) of the Delegates and officers of the Clarendon Press, who, understanding my difficulties, have given me every assistance in trying to surmount them.

My greatest debt is to Miss Helen Gardner. She has given me advice and criticism throughout my work, has helped me with the loan of photostats and with information about manuscripts which the needs of the case did not require me to see, and in the final stages has read through the whole typescript and made many valuable suggestions as to improvements in interpretation and presentation. In addition, I had the privilege of using proofs of her edition of the Love Poems in preparing this book for the press. It would be difficult fully to express, perhaps impossible to over-estimate, what I owe to her guidance and example.

My debt to other editors of Donne, especially to Grierson, and to many scholars and critics whose published work I have used, will, I trust, be obvious. It is a great sadness that so many with whom I was able to talk about Donne, with great pleasure and profit to myself, have been lost by death to the world of scholarship: I gratefully record the names of Evelyn M. Simpson, Ruth C. Wallerstein, R. C. Bald, H. W. Garrod, and J. B. Leishman.

Professor G. A. Wilkes, of Sydney University, has given me assistance on a number of points, and has taken a friendly interest in this book. I thank also Mr. M. Van Wyk Smith, of the University of Kansas, whom I was fortunate enough to meet in Oxford as he was completing a thesis on Donne's *Metempsychosis*, and who generously directed me to useful material and to subtleties in the poem which I should otherwise have missed.

To the Librarians of Christ Church, St. John's, Wadham, and Worcester Colleges in Oxford I express my gratitude for arranging for me to use copies of the edition of 1633. I am grateful also to the authorities and Librarians of the following, for the use of manuscripts in their care and for willing regard for my needs and my convenience: the Bodleian Library, Oxford; the Cambridge University Library; the Queen's College, Oxford; Trinity College, Dublin; the Library of St. Paul's Cathedral. The late Wilfred Merton kindly allowed me to use the Dowden manuscript while it was on deposit in the

British Museum, and the late Richard Jennings generously allowed me free access to the John Cave manuscript. I am indebted to Mr. W. Park, Keeper of Manuscripts in the National Library of Scotland, for allowing me to use the Hawthornden manuscripts and for answering questions on doubtful points. I have had to study manuscripts in the United States of America by means of photographs, and I am grateful to officers of the Huntington Library, the Houghton Library (Harvard University), and the Folger Shakespeare Library for supplying them through the Clarendon Press. I have to thank Dr. Gordan, Curator of the Henry W. Berg and Albert A. Berg Collection in the New York Public Library, for permission to use photostats of the Westmoreland manuscript in Miss Gardner's possession for the purposes of this edition. The only manuscript in Britain that I have been unable to see is the recently discovered Dolau Cothi manuscript, and I am grateful to the Librarian of the National Library of Wales for supplying microfilms of it.

To Sir Geoffrey Keynes I owe special thanks, for allowing me free (and frequent) use of the Leconfield and Luttrell manuscripts, and for permission to print the Latin epigram on Scaliger written by Donne in a book now owned by Sir Geoffrey. In addition, he has made me welcome in his library and his home with a hospitality far in excess of any ordinary bounds of courtesy. I am grateful also to the Duke of Bedford for allowing me to reproduce the portrait of the Countess of Bedford at Woburn Abbey, and to the Very Rev. the Dean of St. Paul's Cathedral for permission to reproduce the portrait of Donne in the Deanery.

It will be apparent that, so assisted and encouraged, I can claim full credit for little in this book save the errors and inadequacies that may be found in it.

W. M.

Canberra, A.C.T.
Australia

CONTENTS

PLATES

REFERENCES AND
ABBREVIATIONS

QUOTATIONS from Donne's poems, other than those included in this volume, are taken from the following texts: the *Divine Poems*, and the *Elegies and the Songs and Sonnets*, from the editions by Helen Gardner (1952 and 1965, respectively); the remainder from *The Poems of John Donne*, edited by H. J. C. Grierson, 2 vols. (Oxford, 1912). These are referred to as

Grierson

Gardner, *Divine Poems*

Gardner, *Elegies etc.*

Quotations from the *Sermons*, *Essays*, and *Devotions* are taken from the following modern editions: *The Sermons of John Donne*, edited by G. R. Potter and Evelyn M. Simpson, 10 vols. (University of California Press, 1953–61); *Essays in Divinity*, edited by Evelyn M. Simpson (Oxford, 1952); *Devotions upon Emergent Occasions*, edited by John Sparrow (Cambridge, 1923). For the *Paradoxes and Problems* I have used the edition by Sir Geoffrey Keynes (1923). These are referred to as

Sermons

Simpson, *Essays*

Sparrow, *Devotions*

Keynes, *Paradoxes and Problems*

Quotations from Donne's other prose works are taken from the original editions, to which reference is made as follows:

Pseudo-Martyr   *Pseudo-Martyr.* 1610

Letters   *Letters to Severall Persons of Honour.* 1651

Tobie Mathew Collection   *A Collection of Letters, made by Sr Tobie Mathews K^t.* 1660

Other references:

Bennett   *The Complete Poems of John Donne*, edited by Roger E. Bennett. Chicago, 1942

Chambers   *The Poems of John Donne*, edited by E. K. Chambers (The Muses' Library). 2 vols. 1896

Gosse   *The Life and Letters of John Donne*, by Edmund Gosse. 2 vols. 1899

Grolier   *The Poems of John Donne*, edited by J. R. Lowell and C. E.
                         Norton (The Grolier Club, New York). 2 vols. 1895

Grosart   *The Complete Poems of John Donne, D.D., Dean of St.
                         Paul's*, edited by A. B. Grosart (Fuller Worthies
                         Library). 2 vols. 1872

Hayward   *John Donne Dean of St. Paul's Complete Poetry and Selected
                         Prose*, edited by John Hayward (Nonesuch Press). 1929

Keynes   *A Bibliography of Dr. John Donne*, by Geoffrey Keynes,
                         third edition. Cambridge, 1958

Alden   *The Rise of Formal Satire in England under Classical In-
                         fluence*, by R. M. Alden, 1899

Burton, *Anatomy*   Robert Burton, *The Anatomy of Melancholy*, edited by
                         H. Jackson (Everyman's Library). 3 vols. 1932

Castiglione   *The Book of the Courtier by Count Baldassare Castiglione, done
                         into English by Sir Thomas Hoby* (Everyman edition)

Chamberlain, *Letters*   *The Letters of John Chamberlain*, edited by N. E.
                         McClure. 2 vols. 1939

Jonson, *Works*   *Ben Jonson*, edited by C. H. Herford and Percy and
                         Evelyn Simpson. 11 vols. Oxford, 1925–52

Linthicum   *Costume in the Drama of Shakespeare and his Contemporaries*,
                         by Miss M. C. Linthicum, 1936

Middleton, *Works*   *The Works of Thomas Middleton*, edited by A. H. Bullen.
                         8 vols. 1885–6

Migne, *P.G., P.L.*   J. Migne, *Patrologia Graeca* and *Patrologia Latina*. (The
                         references are given to volume and column.)

Nashe, *Works*   *The Works of Thomas Nashe*, edited by R. B. McKerrow,
                         revised by F. P. Wilson. 5 vols. Oxford, 1958

Shakespeare   I have followed Professor Peter Alexander's edition of
                         1951 in using the line references of Clark and
                         Wright's Cambridge edition

Tilley   *A Dictionary of the Proverbs in England in the Sixteenth and
                         Seventeenth Centuries*, by M. P. Tilley, 1950

Walton, *Lives*   Unless specific reference is made to another edition,
                         quotations are taken from the reprint of the edition
                         of 1675 in the World's Classics Series

                         *   *   *

A.V.; V.   The Authorized Version, and the Vulgate text, res-
                         pectively, of the Bible. Scriptural texts are quoted
                         from the *A.V.*, and other versions are referred to
                         only if there are relevant differences in readings.

C.S.P.D.	*Calendar of State Papers — Domestic Series*
D.N.B.	*The Dictionary of National Biography*
E.L.H.	*A Journal of English Literary History*
H.L.Q.	*The Huntington Library Quarterly*
J.E.G.P.	*Journal of English and Germanic Philology*
M.L.N.	*Modern Language Notes*
M.L.R.	*Modern Language Review*
M.P.	*Modern Philology*
N. and Q.	*Notes and Queries*
O.E.D.	*Oxford English Dictionary*
P.M.L.A.	*Publications of the Modern Language Association of America*
P.Q.	*Philological Quarterly*
R.E.S.	*Review of English Studies*
S.N.	*Studia Neophilologica*
S.Q.	*Shakespeare Quarterly*
T.L.S.	*Times Literary Supplement*

GENERAL INTRODUCTION

I. DONNE AS SATIRIST

ALEXANDER POPE 'commended Donne's Epistles, Metempsychosis, and Satires, as his best things'.[1] Although the grounds of this opinion can be understood, nobody nowadays is likely to share it. Pope's own brilliance stands in the way of our appreciation of earlier satiric and epistolary poetry, for his writing has enlarged our sense of what is possible in satire and verse epistle in English, and has given new dimensions to the idea of the 'imitation' of classical authors. Donne himself has turned our attention from his satires and verse letters and has caused us sometimes to undervalue them, because of the superior literary achievement, and the more seminal quality of style, in his love lyrics and his religious poetry. To consider the poems in this volume as far as possible apart from these distractions, however, is to see many of them as better things than we had perhaps thought. They are not merely the by-products or aberrations of a metaphysical lyrist.

In the poetry he wrote before 1600 Donne often looked to classical models as at least points of departure in the composition of elegy, epigram, and satire. In elegy and epigram he was, perhaps, more basically experimental in extending the range of the genres—in elegy by fusing Ovidian effects with those of the continental writers of Paradoxes, in epigram by sometimes grafting upon the neatness and wit the musical and emotional qualities of the song. In the *Satires*, however, although he made them equally his own, Donne's manner shows less the confounding or extension of poetical 'Kinds'; here for the first time in English is a sustained 'imitation' of a Latin genre, the consistent adoption of the techniques and tones of Roman satire.[2] Here are the stock subjects; the blending of moral reflection, narrative and direct denunciation; the humour and the

[1] Joseph Spence, *Anecdotes*, ed. S. W. Singer, 1820, p. 144.
[2] See H. F. Brooks, 'The "Imitation" in English Poetry, especially in Formal Satire, before the Age of Pope', *R.E.S.*, 1949, and *The Poems of Joseph Hall*, ed. A. Davenport, 1949, pp. xxiv ff.

scorn; the terse vigour; the 'dark' and 'harsh' style; the urban setting; the uncompromising realism; and the mixture of conversational directness and ironic allusiveness. The methods not only of Horace, but of Juvenal and Persius too, have been thoroughly exploited for Donne's purposes; yet it is rarely possible to put a finger on specific lines in the Latin satirists which Donne is referring to or copying. Rather we have to a striking degree the absorption of the general methods of Roman satire into an essentially original and individual way of writing; Donne validates anew the modes of approach and the techniques of the ancient satirists.

If a list is made of the subjects treated in his satires, nothing could seem more trite or, in the worst sense, imitative: poetasters, wards, widows, spendthrift heirs, fortune-hunters, flatterers; modern degeneracy as compared with older times, religion without the spirit, waste and riot in the city as compared with the blessedness of a well-managed country life, fraud, vanity, obsequiousness, and the rest—these are the stock-in-trade of Roman satire, and indeed of sermons, homilies, and moral writings through the ages. It could be answered that these follies and vices were none the less real in Donne's day for being familiar. John Chamberlain tells us how, in 1600, Lord Keeper Egerton drew the attention of the Star Chamber to a list of abuses in the commonwealth that reads like part of a summary of the subjects of his secretary's *Satires*; he

made a very grave speach in nature of a charge to the Judges to looke to the overgrowinge ydle multitude of justices of peace; to maintainers and abettors of causes and suites, to sollicitors and pettifoggers, to gentlemen that leave hospitalitie and housekeping and hide themselves in Cities and Borough-townes, to the vanitie and excesse of womens apparell, to forestallers and regraters of markets, to drunckards and disorderly persons, to masterles men and other companions that make profession to live by theyre sword and by theyre wit, to discoursers and medlers in Princes matters, and lastly to libellers...[1]

We do not need, however, to rely on external information to prove that Donne's subjects flourished in reality all about him. The sharp-

---

[1] Chamberlain, *Letters*, i. 97.

ness of his observation and the swift, terse language in which he hit off what he observed make the sins and follies of the day convincingly plain to us. No one, we feel, could be so intensely involved with mere chimeras. What Donne describes has the unmistakable air of the contemporaneous, the up to date. All his fools and knaves are up and doing, vividly active before our eyes; and (in this respect like Pope's dunces) they are cheerfully and complacently unaware of their moral plight. Donne has in large measure the capacity of Dryden and Pope to make it seem that the things he sees going on about him were put there expressly for the purposes of his satire; it is only necessary to contemplate them until the right pithy expression of their eccentricity is found to show them up for what they are. It is not only a busy world and a corrupt world in the *Satires*, moreover, but it is also a crowded world, almost as full and various as that in Jonson's comedies; it ranges from kings to kitchen-maids, from the patriotic ape to the treacherous officer of state, from pursuivants to poets. As the large canvas is filled, the comprehensiveness of the whole adds weight and conviction to each detail. The authenticity of the subject-matter is much enhanced, too, by the dramatic and anecdotal means of presentation. You have only to step outside your door, it would seem, to be plunged into this welter of evil and stupidity. Snatches of dialogue, lively personal encounters, the vivid registering of city life as it beats upon the sensibilities of a wandering observer—these catch and hold the reader's attention and convey the world of the *Satires* to him with the reality almost of his own.

The fullness of this world is increased by Donne's frequent use of a device found occasionally in the Roman satirists, very rarely in the English—the use of ironic or illustrative allusion to things not strictly relevant to the main subject of satire. Often the allusion is introduced as an image. Donne turns the device to original use by almost invariably making the minor term of the image, or the thing to which reference is made, itself an object of satire or an emblem of corruption.

> For as a thrifty wench scrapes kitching-stuffe,
> And barrelling the droppings, and the snuffe,
> Of wasting candles, which in thirty yeare

(Relique-like kept) perchance buyes wedding eare;
Peecemeale he gets lands, and spends as much time
Wringing each Acre, as men pulling prime.

The poor quality of candles, the poverty of servants (and the decay
of moral sense in a community that allows both), the keeping of
relics, and obsessive gambling with cards, are all used to illustrate
and sharpen the attack on legal malpractice in the land-grabbing
frauds of the time; but they themselves also suffer satiric disparage-
ment. No other satirist approaches Donne in the frequency and
resource with which this device is employed. In his exposure of vice
and folly he must, of course, exhibit 'all signes of loathing' and, like
preachers and moralists of other ages, he must bring to his denunciation images of corruption that express a proper degree of disgust;
such images Donne introduces chiefly by the technique just illustrated. To list them out of their context[1] (coffins, 'itchie lust',
catamites, pestilence, vomit, excrement, botches, pox, 'carted
whores', and the like) is, however, to exaggerate the frequency
with which they occur, and to falsify the actual effect of such things
in their place in the poem, where they are usually given a more
subtle and complex satiric bite by the wit and humour of the
treatment.

Most general accounts of late sixteenth-century satire make so
much of the harsh, 'snarling', obscure, prurient and uncouth
quality aimed at, and all too often achieved, that it is perhaps
necessary to point out how much wit and humour—how much
sheer fun—can in fact be found in Donne's *Satires*. These are obvious
enough in, for example, the sustained farce of Coscus's wooing in
'Satire II'. It is easy to miss, however, the more sly but admirably
sustained caricature in the comparisons and allusions in the opening
twenty-four lines of the same poem. Donne's images often achieve
at once a neat brevity and a humorous satiric exaggeration, whether
pictorial (as in the account of the fop who 'like light dew exhal'd'
whisks away from his companion, or in the lines admired by Pope
which describe how the remarks of the bore issue relentlessly 'as
a Still, which staies/A Sembriefe, 'twixt each drop'), or more subtly

---

[1] Cf. C. S. Lewis, *English Literature in the Sixteenth Century*, 1954, pp. 469–70.

witty, as in the description of the 'ideot actors' inspired by the over-worked playwright—

> As in some Organ, Puppits dance above
> And bellows pant below, which them do move.

Only when Donne is forcing himself to write against the grain does his humorous touch falter, either deserting him altogether in the fifth Satire, or becoming rather juvenile in the lines on Coryate's *Crudities*.[1] In the main, however, the wit and humour add to the dispassionateness and to the judicial quality of Donne's satiric writing (a quality which led Coventry Patmore to the somewhat startling conclusion that the *Satires* are 'the best in the English language').[2] The humorous poise and the absence of hysteria are due in part, no doubt, to Donne's realization that however violently the satirist writes he cannot really correct vice and folly; it is the preachers, not the poets, who have the means of cleansing society (IV. 237–41). For this reason the satirist's necessary pose of moral superiority is always in danger of appearing only an unwarranted and rather repellent superciliousness. Humour, Donne knew, could save his satire from so crippling a fault, without diminishing the sense of earnestness and moral gravity that underlie, and indeed justify, the satirist's denunciation.

It has been suggested that this earnestness is indeed a pose, and that, like the other satirists of the fifteen-nineties, Donne wrote to attract the attention of the Court and 'probably neither felt nor reflected any serious discontent with the age'.[3] It is impossible to 'prove' from the *Satires* themselves that Donne was vitally concerned in his denunciation. One cannot deny, however, that the *persona*, the voice speaking in the poems, is well controlled to persuade us of a genuine moral fervour in the speaker. The explosive openings suggest a man whose exasperation can no longer be contained; the pungent and incisive comments that follow give us a continual

---

[1] Yet Pope perhaps learned something even from this poem of a type of humour useful in satirizing the dunces:

> Infinite worke, which doth so farre extend,
> That none can study it to any end.

See J. Peter, *Complaint and Satire in Early English Literature*, 1956, p. 134.

[2] *Lowe's Edinburgh Magazine*, February 1846.

[3] J. Wilcox, 'Informal Publication of Late Sixteenth-Century Verse Satire', *H.L.Q.*, 1950.

impression of powerful indignation only held in check by the good sense and compassion of the satirist. This is the voice of a man who inspires confidence; he knows his times through and through, if we can judge by the comprehensiveness of the description and commentary; he ranges as widely in his reading as he does in the study of mankind (Aristotle, the Chroniclers, Ariosto, Luther, Rabelais, Dante, Dürer, and the like are at his fingertips); he comes down unerringly on the side of traditional and established moral values against the corruption and follies of the time; he is stoical, grave, and modest in his 'course attire'; he has humour and generosity of spirit. If much of this 'character' was suggested by Latin models, Donne has revitalized and deepened it in a way peculiarly his own. The speaker in his *Satires* is much concerned with religion: he 'confers' with God as well as with the Muses, and there are a multitude of images and allusions taken from religious controversies or from scriptural and ecclesiastical sources.[1] There are constant reminders throughout the poems that the authority for the judgements made of morals and manners is of the highest; the speaker serves two mistresses, 'faire Religion' and 'Truth', and knows that even princes are responsible to God. Here is the norm against which what he sees about him is measured. And although this satiric voice has less range and variety than Pope's, it is a convincing voice—that of the Moral Man who can rise at times to the heroic and dare greatly: to speak, for instance, of those who

> to'every suitor lye in every thing,
> Like a Kings favorite, yea like a King.

Dramatic conviction is given to this voice by the style of utterance which Donne has devised for it. The rhythms, the intonation, the nerve of conversational English are exploited in every possible way to give dramatic immediacy and liveliness to the satire. Dr. F. R. Leavis has shown, in a striking passage,[2] how the interplay of metrical beat with the movement of everyday speech is controlled by Donne to make the pauses and the stresses imitate, and as it were

---

[1] Miss M. M. Mahood, *Poetry and Humanism* (1950), pp. 103–4, notes their prevalence especially in 'Satire II'. It was perhaps this quality in the poems to which Dryden was referring when he said, in 1693, that Donne 'affects the metaphysics . . . in his satires'.

[2] *Revaluation*, 1936, Chapter 1.

enact, what is being said. His use of language in this way concerns quite small details, as in the simile quoted above, of the still which stays 'A Sembriefe, 'twixt each drop', where the cluster of consonants between 'Sembriefe' and ''twixt' makes the voice itself 'stay'; it concerns also the larger rhetorical effects seen at their best in the third Satire. Donne seems to have interpreted the imitation of the supposed obscurity and harshness of Persius and Juvenal as an opportunity for testing out the language to the full, to achieve density and compactness as well as energy and vigour. There is a constant tendency to aphorism and to epigram. Donne will try out even what seemed to be viable of the current attempts to Latinize English:

> but unmoved thou
> Of force must one, and forc'd but one allow;
> And the right; aske thy father which is shee,
> Let him aske his.

He handles the couplet with a sensitiveness to rhetorical utterance and a freedom (not to say a licence) which dramatists did not attempt in blank verse until later. One of the most useful qualities of Roman satire was the shifting tone of the writing, so that it could move from stern denunciation of the wicked to a lighter scorn or banter of the foolish. Few of Donne's contemporaries can match him in portraying changing moods through sustained speech, and the practice of verse satire undoubtedly helped him to develop this skill. In his lyrics he can present the speaker in the poem caught up, mind and emotions alike, in an intense dramatic experience, and yet able to observe critically with one part of his mind the ironies and even the humour of the situation. The spirit of satire is never very far away in any of Donne's poetry;[1] his keen perception of any falseness of attitude, of the difference between the pretension and the reality, enable him to achieve an unusual psychological realism and subtlety.

In the *Satires* Donne's use of a single dramatic *persona*, whose voice is heard in passionate witty monologue, is the main means by which the multifarious material is held together. The great defect of so-called formal satire is that it is not a form at all, but a mode of

[1] See A. Stein, 'Donne and the Satiric Spirit', *E.L.H.*, 1944.

approach; the satirist is encouraged to stray at random from one topic to another. Thus in 'Satire I', as C. S. Lewis points out, there is no necessary connexion (ll. 36–40) between obsequiousness and lechery; it is rather by sleight of hand that they are brought together under the general heading of man's sin. Donne does his best to overcome this looseness of structure. Sometimes he establishes a sequence of congruent imagery through the poem, like the references to clothes in 'Satire I', and in 'Satire V' the images from bridges and water. He gives some sort of finality to each poem by a clinching epigrammatic couplet. Nevertheless the second and fourth Satires fall apart badly, and the fifth seems to keep going at all only by a series of spasmodic efforts. The third Satire, in this respect as in most others superior to the rest, is saved by the happy chance that the possible sources of truth in religion are limited to three, and this fact is neatly reflected in the triple structure of the whole poem; there is, moreover, a limited area of subject-matter to be treated, and a consistent particular theme dominates the whole.

It must be confessed that Donne's experimental approach to satire sometimes leaves us with an impression of haste, of impatience, even of some unsettlement in the usually confident voice that speaks from his pages. Although I do not think that Donne was much influenced by the idea of satire as 'satyr-like', hairy, licentious, savage, and rough,[1] there is no doubt that the harshness thought to be apparent in Roman satire gave him the excuse, even after revision, to leave blemishes in his satiric poems that seem pointlessly careless and gauche. Perhaps he felt that he had drained the genre of any virtues it might have had; in the first four Satires he certainly seems to have said all that he had to say, and had reached the limits of what he could achieve in this style. The fifth Satire, to which he turned to please his patron, though it probably expresses Donne's own convictions fairly enough, exhibits a rather pathetic attempt to achieve his old verve and forthrightness, and falls back on material repeated from the other Satires. We may be thankful that he did not stretch out his material over greater length. For the popularity of the first four Satires, however, there were excellent reasons. Witty contemporaneity, pungent and memorable phrasing, skilful carica-

---

[1] See J. Peter, 'This Word Satyre', *R.E.S.*, n.s. vi, 1955.

ture of familiar types and practices, the re-creation in modern terms of yet another ancient genre, and at the same time an appeal to the intellect and to religious decorum—all these would be especially ingratiating to the Inns-of-Court wits and the adventurers to Cadiz and the Islands, with whom Donne primarily shared his verses.

II. *THE PROGRESS OF THE SOUL*

In August 1601 Donne hit upon what seems to have been an exciting idea for a satiric poem of quite a new type. In great high spirits he wrote a preliminary epistle hinting at the general scheme, but implying that he had not yet a detailed plan, for he did not know how his stock of material would hold out. The poem would probably be published (either in the printing-house or by manu-script circulation) for the benefit of sophisticated readers (not such as he could teach); it was dedicated, in a mock-grandiose gesture, to infinity; and before it he would place his 'picture', either an actual portrait, or more probably the delightfully ironic picture he actually gives of his plain, flat, and transparent mind. Allowing for the humour of this preface, it looks as if Donne thought that he had a very promising idea for a long satiric poem.[1]

In it he proposed to trace the history of the soul of the apple from the Tree of Knowledge which Adam and Eve ate. He adopted for the purposes of the poem a form of the theory of metempsychosis: that a soul is able to move indifferently into the bodies of plants, birds, fish, animals, women, and men, as each of its previous bodies dies. In the Epistle we are told that the soul can remember what happened to it in each of its incarnations, in the poem (ll. 506 ff.) that it keeps some character, and hence some moral attributes, of each incarnation also. The soul in the poem was to be placed 'in most shapes' (ll. 3, 29–30); it was to live significantly at all the high points of history and when 'every great change' occurred (ll. 3–8, 67–69); it was to be finally incarnated in England (l. 57, 'home';

---

[1] The most helpful studies of the poem are: D. C. Allen, 'The Double Journey of John Donne', in *A Tribute to George Coffin Taylor*, ed. A. Williams, 1952; W. A. Murray, 'What was the Soul of the Apple?', *R.E.S.*, 1959; and H. W. Janson, *Apes and Ape Lore in the Middle Ages and the Renaissance* (Studies of the Warburg Institute, xx), 1952.

l. 60, 'Thames') in the body of a man ('hee,[1] whose life you shall finde in the end of this booke'), who powerfully influenced the lives of Donne and his contemporaries (ll. 61–63), and who was to 'relate' the soul's story, as the Epistle says, to Donne himself. In earlier incarnations the soul was to become Mahomet and Luther (ll. 66–67).

Ben Jonson's account of the poem does not altogether match what Donne has in fact given us. 'The conceit of Dones transformation or μετεμψύχοσις', he told Drummond, 'was that he sought the soule of that Aple which Eva pulled, and therafter made it the soule of a Bitch, then of a sheewolf & so of a woman. his generall purpose was to have brought in all the bodies of the Hereticks from the soule of Caine & at last left it in the body of Calvin. of this he never wrotte but one sheet.'[2] Apart from a small slip in respect of the wolf, the first and last of these sentences accurately describe the completed part of the poem. The references to Cain and to Calvin, however, must be wrong. For the one inescapable fact about a soul is that it cannot, except in a highly mystical sense not exploited in this poem, be in two bodies at once. Donne does his best with the limited gymnastics possible, playing variations on the idea of one living being containing another (ll. 241–2, 292–8, 395–9). By no stretch of the imagination, however, could the soul of Themech be the same as that of Cain; and if the soul, as the poem says, was to be Luther's, it could not also have been Calvin's. Any man who, so far as we know, could fit the description in ll. 61–63 is ruled out by the fact that his life overlapped that of Luther.[3]

Even to bring the soul from Eden to its last certain abode in the body of Luther would have involved Donne in a poem of tremendous scope. For it he accordingly adopts a kind of epic form. He makes the traditional opening gestures—a statement of the main action,

[1] Only one manuscript, the highly sophisticated O'Flaherty MS., reads 'Shee' for 'hee'· This reading was adopted from O'F into the edition of 1635 and stood in all subsequent seventeenth-century editions. The Grolier editors, Chambers, and Grierson all rightly restored 'hee'. The reading 'Shee', like other readings peculiar to O'F (and to O'F and its parent, the Luttrell manuscript), is plainly an attempt to make sense of what seemed an error ('shee is hee, whose life . . .'), and has no authority whatever.

[2] 'Conversations with Drummond', Works, i. 136.

[3] The suggestion by Gosse and others that the soul was to end its progress in the body of Queen Elizabeth, as well as being ruled out by the statement in the Epistle that the soul's contemporary incarnation was to be masculine, is made impossible by the fact that her life also overlapped Luther's.

with the ritual phrase 'I sing', and the address to the inspiring spirit
(l. 111). The surviving canto (or 'song') is about the length of an
epic 'book'. The imagery befits the decorum of epic, being mostly
descriptio or *translatio*: 'loose-rein'd careere', 'steepe ambition',
'spungie confines', 'gummie blood', 'Plyant aire', 'gulfe-like throat',
and the like. The epic hero is a 'deathlesse' soul, who lives on from
age to age, but is conditioned and controlled by matter, by fate, by
the temporary and the mean; this hero is both immortal and short-
lived.[1] The larger action is the story of the progressive corruption
of a soul; but each episode brings in single varieties of evil and folly
which are treated satirically. What Donne attempts, therefore, is a
kind of anti-epic with incidental, but continual, satiric comment.
Here he ventures upon another confusion of the traditional poetic
'Kinds' such as had never before been devised. To the Renaissance
poet the epic, which elevated man's achievement in the high style,
was incompatible with satire, which exposed men's folly and vice in
the low style. Of the two methods possible for combining epic
sweep with satiric intent, that of Byron in *Don Juan* was neither
available nor suitable; it is to the other, the mock-epic, that Donne
is feeling his way (and both Dryden and Pope might have found his
experiments suggestive). The grandeur of his opening stanzas is a
mock-grandeur; witness, for example, the preposterous gravity of
his claim for a poem of this kind—that it would outlast Seth's priceless pillars and rank next to the Bible. To complete his gargantuan
labours he would like a guarantee of thirty uninterrupted years of
poetic concentration. Ordinary epic poets address only their inspiring Muse (and perhaps their patron also); Donne apostrophizes
with greater variety—the Sun, Noah, Destiny as well. Touches of
mock-heroic appear from time to time throughout the poem: the
most delightful example, perhaps, being the description—pathetic,
vivid, grotesque—of the growth of that 'young Colossus' the mandrake.

Of so much, concerning the scheme and method of the poem, we
can be reasonably certain. There were, however, difficulties in
Donne's conception that would prevent the completion of his poem
—difficulties so crippling, one would have thought, that he could

[1] D. C. Allen, op. cit.

hardly for very long have remained unaware of them, and so basic that (although Jonson's statement, and Donne's reference to Luther, might suggest that he intended to finish it) he must soon have realized that this was an 'epic' for which no ending could seriously be contemplated; and the suspicion crosses one's mind that, however the poem began, it turned into a parody of a grand Renaissance design that could never have been carried out. For example, on the mere level of mechanics the soul's progress was limited by the fact that it could be in only one identifiable body at any one time. In the darker ages of the world's history the sequence of bodies inhabited by the soul could be freely managed, but when dates were known it would be very difficult to find a new quickening at the time of the death of any significant figure in history (such as Mahomet or Luther). It may be, of course, that the melon and the spider mentioned in the Epistle were to have been introduced at awkward spots along the way.[1] This, however, would either have made the soul's progress meaningless by breaking the sequence of accumulated evils, or have created moral chaos by the equation of the vegetal, sensible, and rational souls (a result which provoked one of the chief Christian objections to the theory). It was possible to get the soul as a moral entity into the body of Themech only because the rational soul subsumed and controlled the lower faculties. In its progress, moreover, the soul climbs in regular order through the links of the Chain of Being (through bodies progressively 'of more worth', l. 245): from the apple it passes to the mandrake (a link with higher forms, preferred, for its 'human' qualities, to the fungus, or 'Mucheron', mentioned in the Epistle); then to a bird, and through the world of fishes to the greatest of them, the whale; and through the world of beasts to the ape, the animal most like man; and so to the woman Themech. Donne would hardly have repeated this carefully devised cycle; and even without further incidents involving short-lived creatures it would have taken a huge number of cantos, through any plausible sequence of human incarnations, to bring the

---

[1] Several easily accessible forms of the theory of metempsychosis allowed for a regression of the soul from man to beasts, etc., whether haphazardly, as in Lucian's *Dream, or the Cock*; through the soul's moral 'sympathy' with an appropriate beast, as in Macrobius's *Commentary on the Dream of Scipio* (trans. and ed. W. H. Stahl, 1952, p. 125, etc.); or for purgation and punishment (Pythagoras's idea, as presented, e.g., by Primaudaye in *The French Academy*, trans. by T. B., 1594, pp. 507–8).

soul from Themech down to the modern age. Furthermore, though the soul would accumulate corruption, it could never become a very interesting dramatic object because it could not really accumulate individuality. The evils accumulated in the soul would far have exceeded the compatible moral experiences that can possibly be experienced by one soul or dramatized in one poem about it. The poem as we have it already shows how impossible it was to demonstrate the growing depravity of this soul within the tiny area of each episode. If the wolf-dog and the ape are somewhat more complex and sophisticated in their villainy, this is because Donne has attributed to them some of the human quality of the possessor of a rational soul (e.g., ll. 445–6), not because they are really any more wicked than the sparrow or the mouse. If the poem had proceeded, perhaps in Canto II with the race of Cain, the difficulty of finding an increasingly complex corruption in each person in the dismal sequence would have been insurmountable. Nor does the poem show (nor perhaps could it show) a growing subtlety or increasing indignation or depth in the incidental satiric comment, in the handling of emblems of vice (the sparrow of lechery, the swan of pride, and so on) or in moral condemnation. In neither way does Donne achieve a true 'progress'. The doctrine of metempsychosis itself does not yield up any deeper unifying meaning in the poem, being no more than a *datum*, a comic contrivance to keep the action moving. Nor does there seem to be any real significance in the soul's first having been placed in the apple on the Tree of Knowledge.[1] This idea serves as an amusing ironic overture to the soul's adventures and as a neat way of introducing strictures on Eve as the source of man's fall; but the essential purposes of the poem would have been as well served by any other vegetable soul.

The writer of epic was supposed to represent in his poem all the

---

[1] Mr. W. A. Murray, in the article cited, attempts to show from Philo Judaeus's allegories of the Book of Genesis that the 'soul of the apple' is the power of moral choice; of the corruption of this power the poem is an account. This theory seems to me untenable, for in the account he gives of the soul's adventures Donne insists over and over again that the soul is completely at the command of Destiny or Fate. If the soul *is* the power of rational moral choice, it is hard to see why Donne mentions the qualities of the souls of sense and of growth—the sub-rational faculties—at all (ll. 181, 204, 455). Philo is interpreting Eden as a static emblem of the qualities of fallen Man, and in working out his allegory he says that *all* the plants, not only the Tree of Knowledge, 'are endowed with soul or reason bearing the virtues for fruit, and besides these insight and discernment'.

forms of human wisdom and learning; and accordingly, Donne includes references to all kinds of miscellaneous and fascinating lore—
often more interesting than the adventures of the soul itself, and
hence at times a distraction from the main preoccupations of the
poem. Much of this information seems, to the modern reader, more
esoteric than it really was—Adam's children, Seth's pillars, the
mode of respiration in fish, and so on. I agree with Miss Gardner's
suggestion[1] that the poem shows the influence of Donne's explora-
tions in the works of authors quite unlike the Roman writers who
had hitherto been a main source of his inspiration; his interest was
now being caught by neo-Platonic, cabbalistical, rabbinical, and
neo-Pythagorean speculation. It may be doubted, however, whether
during his busy life as Egerton's secretary he had gone much
further than catching an experimental excitement and a mood of
defiant unorthodoxy from his reading. He did, it is true, take from
it a small amount of out-of-the-way detail; but in the main his
method in the poem is to exploit familiar material in an unorthodox
way, to achieve an askewness, an ironic perverseness, which looks
more fundamental than it really is. Thus the familiar doctrine of
metempsychosis is pushed awry by the idea (so far as I can discover,
an idea of Donne's own) that, since the soul remembers its past
incarnations, it remembers and is indeed marked by its accumulated
sins. The role of Destiny in the world is expressed in startling terms,
without being clearly related to God's Providence; yet the power of
Destiny is really exerted fully, when we look more closely at the poem,
only on the irrational faculties of the soul. Everybody else would use
the moon (Diana, Cynthia) as a symbol of Queen Elizabeth; Donne
would use it as an image to describe an influential man. Even such
trivial and commonplace bits of natural 'history' as the elephant's
fear of the mouse and the properties of the mandrake are wrested
out of the orthodox groove. When Donne looks most defiant and
'libertine', for example in questioning God's justice in His dealings
with Adam, Eve, and the Serpent, or in describing sexual freedom
before the giving of the Law, he is using material almost wearisomely
familiar in commentaries on Genesis. Part of the 'wit' of the poem
throughout, however, lies in this twisting and colouring of the

---

[1] *Elegies etc.,* pp. lviii–lix.

material to bring out its sinister, or ironic, or grotesque facets, and to suggest the gulf between human pretensions and practice.[1]

The satiric expression of this disparity, like the mock-heroic elevation, is not everywhere well sustained. The writing wavers from a true poetic grandeur—'the fervent and gloomy sublimity' that De Quincey found in the poem[2]—to the bathos of

> Is any kinde subject to rape like fish?

At times the style, partly because of the exigencies of Donne's original stanza-form, becomes forced or flat; at others it relaxes into the delightful movement of lines like

> The free inhabitants of the Plyant aire

or rises into rotund and melodious utterance:

> I launch at paradise, and saile toward home.

In Donne's grasp of detail, however, there is no weakness. No poem of his illustrates better the power of natural description, which he has often been said to lack; a conspicuous example is his account of the hatching of the sparrow, which is at once accurate, closely observed, and tender. In another vein he can describe with the utmost lucidity and with imaginative vividness the formation of the human embryo. The great fish of the ocean absorb him, and he is able to realize for us, not only the thresher and the swordfish as he read of them in cold print, but also the magnificent heraldic whale, suggested no doubt by the monsters depicted in maps wallowing in unexplored seas. Donne is completely at home in the world of Genesis, and he handles its details with unerring sureness: Siphatecia's 'kidskinne apron', Adam's fishing-net, Abel's sheep-dog, and the like, bring to life the primitive world in a way hardly ever to be found in the dull commentaries from which Donne learned much of his information. His assurance is reflected in the grotesque fun and the sardonic humour with which he presents both the oddities of

---

1 It was perhaps the memory of the askew and unorthodox overtones of the poem that prompted Jonson's use of the idea of 'heresy'. There seems to be no evidence in the poem that the soul was to be embodied only in heretics; and it is most unlikely that in 1601 Donne would think of Luther as a heretic at all.

2 'Massy diamonds compose the very substance of [Donne's] poem on the Metempsychosis, thoughts and descriptions which have the fervent and gloomy sublimity of Ezekiel and Aeschylus. . .'. *Blackwood's Magazine*, xxiv, 1828, 892–3.

the first days of mankind and the latter-day follies and vices of a mankind even more obviously fallen.

The failure to perceive how much verve and high-spirited fun the poem contains has led, I believe, to much misrepresenting of its relation to Donne's genuine beliefs and personal circumstances; De Quincey's epithet 'gloomy' has had an undue influence. Thus I cannot see any evidence for Grierson's idea[1] that the poem shows Roman Catholic sympathies. Nor does there seem to be any special reference to the execution of Essex six months before the poem was begun; there is no evidence that Donne was really close to the Earl or was much affected by his downfall.[2] The reflections on tyrants, favourites, and officers in the poem are generalized and unemotional, and seem to have more connexion with such poems as Spenser's *Visions of the World's Vanity* than with any special event in history. If Donne is cynical about courtiers, he finds the antics of lovers far more hilarious. He was probably already acquainted with, and attracted to, Ann More, though the love which swept him into an indiscreet and illegal marriage to her does not seem to have ripened till Ann came to London two and a half months after the poem was begun. The strictures on women (related to the consistently askew notion that Eve, not Adam, brought death into the world and all our woe) are not to be regarded as any more evidence of bitterness than the strictures on courtiers. Donne was becoming enslaved to one of the former, and himself, with a seat in Parliament (on 1 October) already in the offing, was an increasingly successful example of the latter. It is strange that there should have been seen in the poem evidence of Hamlet-like brooding or portentously solemn despair at Donne's lack of faith in man and in God.[3]

If anything, Donne can be accused of not having taken his poem seriously *enough* as a poetic work, of not having embodied in it more clearly its basic 'conceit', and not having made it more consistently a parody, a mock-epic, or a witty episodic satire. Evidently, although he must have allowed copies to be taken, he had no lasting satisfaction in the poem. From it, on clarifying some of the insights it was

[1] ii, pp. xviii–xix.
[2] See R. E. Bennett, 'John Donne and the Earl of Essex', *Modern Language Quarterly*, 1942.
[3] Cf. M. M. Mahood, *Poetry and Humanism*, p. 106.

probably meant to convey, he salvaged two ideas. One, the satire on 'heretics' who were responsible for 'every great change'—of innovators—issued ten years later in *Ignatius his Conclave*. The other, the idea of a spiritual journey, re-imagined and fully realized, emerged as *The Second Anniversary*, 'Of the Progress of the Soul'.[1]

III. DONNE AS MORALIST—THE VERSE LETTERS

Donne's part in the revival of the old classical poetic forms is now in no danger of being underestimated, nor are the originality and experimental ingenuity with which he tested their limits and the possibilities of fusing them into modes of expression answering more to the interests and tensions of contemporary life. He was almost certainly the first to write an Ovidian 'book' of Elegies in English; his first two Satires, and possibly the third, anticipated those published by Lodge in *A Fig for Momus* (1595). Just as Hall, perhaps ignorant of Donne's satires, and ignoring Lodge's, claimed priority in publishing (perhaps also in writing) regular classical satire in English,[2] so Lodge claimed to be the first Englishman to publish verse epistles.[3] Lodge was right in thinking that the verse letter was something of an innovation, and honest in saying that his own letters were the first 'publiquely' written (for privately Donne and perhaps some of his friends had written some earlier). Hitherto the verse epistle in English had mostly meant commendatory or dedicatory verses prefixed to works of other kinds. Donne's own earliest attempts (pretty certainly his earliest surviving poems), like 'All haile sweet Poët', suggest that his use of the form began with short commendations of his friends' writings, expanded into the more general discussion of his and their writing

---

[1] The re-use of this title shows that Donne had definitely abandoned the *Metempsychosis*, and had given up all thought of printing it.

[2] *Virgidemiarum* (1597), Prologue to Book I, ll. 3–4:

    I first adventure: follow me who list,
    And be the second English Satyrist.

The discussion of Hall's priority, inevitably inconclusive, began in J. P. Collier's *Poetical Decameron* (1820) and was taken as far as it has ever gone by Alden, pp. 102 ff.

[3] 'For my *Epistles*, they are in that kind, wherein no Englishman of our time hath publiquely written. . . .' *A Fig for Momus*, 1595, 'To the Gentlemen Readers whatsoever', sig. A3–4.

and other pursuits, and grew (probably on his initiative) into an exchange of poetic correspondence and the writing of fully fledged verse letters. The form has been little studied, probably because of its amorphousness; place into any satire, verse essay, or lyric an address to some person, and one can claim to have written a verse epistle. From Horace, the chief exemplar in classical literature, Donne learned something in his *Satires* (especially in the third), but it is only in the mature letters to his men friends that we first hear unmistakable Horatian tones in his verse epistles proper. The early letters rise with considerable originality out of Donne's pursuits and his relations with others, as documents of 'my second religion, friendship'.

His first attempts, it is true, are tentative enough, and are sufficiently gauche to be recognizable as the experiments of a young poet in a novel form. Like most young poets Donne writes a good deal about the writing of poetry;[1] he is preoccupied also with the proper use of his other talents, and the activities in which he and his friends engage, or should engage. Beneath the experiments with imagery (sometimes with strained and even blasphemous religious imagery) and with verse form, beneath the disillusioned vignettes of the London scene and the elaborate compliments, there is a good deal of uncertainty about the direction of the writer's life and the position he will occupy in the world.

About 1597, with 'The Storm', 'The Calm', and the fine letter to Woodward beginning 'Like one who'in her third widdowhood', Donne's writing of verse letters takes on new dimensions; his early themes are caught up in wider and deeper considerations of personal and public morality, and his command of form is immeasurably improved. His descriptions of the storm and the calm brilliantly register sights and sounds in the startling and realistic manner perfected in the earlier satires and elegies. Designed to shock the reader into wide-eyed realization, the descriptive conceits are for the most part highly effective, and their ingenuity is lost in the preternatural vividness with which the situations are brought home to our imagination. Donne shows great skill in suggesting the impact

---

[1] Donne's remarks about poetry are interestingly assembled by L. Jonas, in *The Divine Science*, 1940.

of these experiences upon the sensibility of a man undergoing them.[1]
It is no surprise when in the second poem a description of the 'bed-
ridde' ships is followed (as if in reply to the question now coming to
the surface of the mind—'Why am I here, in this predicament?'),
with apparent abruptness, by

> Whether a rotten state, and hope of gaine,
> Or to disuse mee from the queasie paine
> Of being belov'd, and loving, or the thirst
> Of honour, or faire death, out pusht mee first,
> I lose my end.

The thought then leads to another question—'What are wee then?';
and this inquiry is never absent in one form or another from Donne's
verse letters. They are never mere expressions of cordiality or only
neat compliments; their writer is always concerned not only with,
or about, his friend or patron, but also with moral issues.

As in the *Satires*, Donne's main attention is turned upon being
and seeming. One aspect of this subject appears mainly in his letters
to men friends—the whole integrity of mind and soul, and the need
to cultivate (in the metaphor from husbandry Donne often uses) all
one's moral and spiritual sensibilities, and to direct them into the
paths of virtue under God's guidance. The other aspect appears in
all his work after about 1597—the use of 'discretion', which is the
knowledge of how to relate virtue thus cultivated to one's conduct
in the sight of men. The letter to Woodward announces these basic
moral themes:

> If our Soules have stain'd their first white, yet wee
> May cloth them with faith, and deare honestie,
> Which God imputes, as native puritie.

> There is no Vertue, but Religion:
> Wise, valiant, sober, just, are names, which none
> Want, which want not Vice-covering discretion.

> Seeke wee then our selves in our selves; . . .

> Manure thy selfe then, to thy selfe be'approv'd.

[1] See the interesting study of the poems by B. F. Nellist, 'Donne's "Storm" and "Calm"
and the Descriptive Tradition', *M.L.R.*, 1964.

In the succeeding letters (as printed in this volume) will be found the elaboration of these ideas. Self-examination, self-cultivation, the control of the sub-rational 'beasts' of the human personality, the striving (so far as man's fallen nature will allow) for 'white integritie' and for honour—these are the main concerns of the letters to Wotton and Edward Herbert. They prompt also the beautiful letter to Goodyer, where they are handled with a certainty and conviction conveyed in a poetic form of unusual strength and grace; no one wrote better in this stanza before Gray, and not even Jonson achieved so well the Horatian weight and manly lucidity[1] of Donne's epistolary style at its best in these letters to men.

In the verse letters to great ladies Donne faced a different relationship, in which he was, in fact as in courtly convention, the inferior in status. The theme of virtue was ideally suited to dignified flattery; it could be related to the conventional attribution of beauty, grace, honour, and talent to the lady addressed; her possession of virtue warranted praise which could not (therefore) be supposed merely trivial and false; and it could be imaged and described in many properly poetic ways. Donne, however, extended the conventions, and rooted his compliments deeply in genuine moral conviction. He took from Plato[2] an idea connected with one which we have already mentioned—the notion that virtue itself has integrity, is one and entire, and cannot be divided up into separate virtues; for a person 'is not vertuous, out of whose actions you can pick an excellent one'.[3] To express this idea Donne uses not only Plato's own image—gold—but also ideas associated with gold and the philosophers' stone by the Paracelsians—the 'virtue', 'balsam', 'tincture', which is the indivisible essence and power of a substance. Furthermore, a person's virtue must be shown in his 'actions'. A 'milde innocence' is no doubt praiseworthy, but it is 'active good' (as Donne makes clear in the letter to the Countess of Huntingdon, 'Man to Gods image') that is the real mark of virtue. In his prose letters, and in his sermons also, he insists on the importance of practising virtue. He does his best to remove from the spirits of his congregations and of his friends that 'diffidence' (a stultifying lack

---

[1] See J. B. Leishman, *The Monarch of Wit*, 5th ed., 1962, pp. 137 ff.
[2] See L. Stapleton, 'The Theme of Virtue in Donne's Verse Epistles', *S.P.*, 1958.
[3] *Letters*, p. 97.

of confidence) that stifles or freezes up the outward expression of
virtue; he urges upon them the need for 'holy alacrity and cheereful-
nesse'.[1] There is a kind of 'retirednesse' which gives time for reflection and issues in fruitful and creative activity; but 'cloysterall' men
and those who shun the world do not reach the heart of virtue. As
early as the first letter to 'Mr I. L.' Donne speaks of the 'duties of
Societies'; and in all his later work, and very frequently in his
sermons, he stresses the importance, in man's 'meteorique' nature
(partaking of earth as well as of heaven), of the active exercise of
goodness in daily affairs.[2] To withdraw from these obligations
out of fearfulness or false humility is to deprive oneself of the full
measure of virtue, since 'ignorance of vice, makes vertue lesse'; it is
not virtue to flee the choice between good and evil; and, as Donne
says at an agonizing time of inactivity in his own life, 'to chuse,
is to do: but to be no part of any body, is to be nothing'.[3]

For Donne, of course, there is no virtue but religion; and the
Christian reconciliation of the claims of God with the claims of
human society rested partly in the relation of faith to good works
(for, as the Homily of Faith stated,[4] 'a true faith cannot be kept
secret, but when occasion is offered, it will break out and shew itself
by good works'), and partly in the exercise of discretion. To the
latter subject Donne recurs again and again. On the strength of texts
like Proverbs iii. 21, 'keep sound wisdom and discretion', discretion
was traditionally associated with wisdom (*sapientia*); it is one of the
gifts of the Spirit (1 Cor. xii. 8); it is the power to discern what is,
and what is not, sin; it is, Donne says, 'the mother of all vertues';[5]
all goodness, even humility itself,[6] requires the exercise of discretion. It is an error to take Donne's remark in *The First Anniversary*,[7] 'Wicked is not much worse than indiscreet', as if it were part

---

[1] See, for example, *Sermons*, v. 273, and *Letters*, pp. 46–47.
[2] For example: 'Every man hath a *Politick life*, as well as a *natural life*; and he may no more
take himself away from the world, then he may make himself away out of the world. For he
that dies so, by withdrawing himself from his calling, from the labours of mutual society in his
life, that man *kills himself*, and God calls him not.' *Sermons*, i. 209–10.
[3] *Letters*, p. 51.
[4] *Homilies*, ed. G. E. Corrie (1850), i. 34.
[5] *Sermons*, v. 199.
[6] Compare *A Litany*, ll. 149–51, where there is a prayer to be delivered 'From indiscreet
humilitie,/Which might be scandalous,/And cast reproach on Christianitie'; and see the
editor's notes, Gardner, *Divine Poems*, p. 89.
[7] l. 338.

of a repartee in a Restoration comedy. For besides being a matter of spiritual wisdom and choice, discretion is also letting one's light so shine before men that they may see one's good works and glorify God; it is not cunning prudential ostentation that is in question, but Christian witness, and not to show virtue is almost as bad as not to have it.

This pattern of thought underlies and dignifies all Donne's letters to great ladies. Merely to express it is to turn courtly compliment into an example of the discretion which he advocates:

> Discretion is a wisemans Soule, and so
> Religion is a Christians, and you know
> How these are one; . . .
>
> If either ever wrought in you alone
> Or principally, then religion
> Wrought your ends, and your wayes discretion.

His greatest praise, '*Beeing* and *seeming* is your equall care', is of the kind that dignifies the praiser and the praised. Once having laid this serious moral foundation, however, Donne entertains and also flatters the ladies by the playful wit, the intellectual fantasy, sometimes (almost) the mild engaging idiocy with which he elaborates the basically simple thought and imagery from which he begins. The main images are taken from courtly convention: the lady is a sun, a star, a saint; she is a divinity with her own saints, temples, and devotees; her virtue and beauty are shining lights. But there is certainly nothing either conventional or simple in Donne's development of both thought and image; the ingenuity and lively fancy with which he pursues the basic analogy to the remotest paradox or the most refined abstraction, the resource of mind which summons all sorts of apparently unrelated but fascinating detail to the imaging of the thought—these command our admiration even when (occasionally) they seem too far-fetched and inappropriate. When they succeed the result is a kind of complimentary verse that was truly of Donne's own invention, poetry in which the sheer wit and elaborate play of mind and fancy become an oblique expression of respect and affection. The 'valters sombersalts' of intellect which the lady is supposed to be able to appreciate are no less flattering to her

powers of mind than the genuine moral ardour of Donne's references
to virtue and beauty are to her character; no poet, we may suppose,
would put forth all this effort of mind and imagination for anyone
whom he did not really admire. Even the greatest hyperbole of
compliment, moreover, has some justification; Donne establishes
terms of reference which remind us that every spark of beauty and
goodness on earth must be of God and so divine, so that when he
calls a Countess 'divinity' there is an other-world in which it is
true.

Serious as this sense of a spiritual dimension is, however, it does
not provoke solemnity. The very hyperboles themselves can be
made to impart a touch of comic caricature to the occasion; and
at times, as in the satire of the veneration of saints at the beginning
of the letter to Lady Carey and her sister, or in the absurd caricature
of his own 'lowness', Donne is able to keep his tone poised in the
right degree of regard and respect by making fun of the very images
and conventions that are the vehicle of his compliment.

Like all his other poems, these verse letters show his command of
the colloquial and conversational style in poetry. It is usually a
reasoning mind whose words we hear, and the poems are kept in
motion by the tightly logical progress of the thought[1] no less than
by the dramatic colouring of the speaking voice. Gravely or play-
fully, wittily or fancifully, the speaker proceeds: 'What though',
'But', 'And, that', 'But when', 'Yet when', 'Then as', 'And then',
'Yet maist', 'And since', 'Perchance' (the examples come from thirty
lines of the letter to 'Mrs M. H.'); and thus what might have become a monotonous catalogue of qualities, a static reiteration of
compliments, becomes a true progression of thought and feeling,
and turns complimentary rhetoric into poetry.

If we will take these poems on their own terms we shall not, I
think, be troubled by thoughts of a cringing poet sacrificing sincerity
and artistry alike in the mercenary pursuit of a patron.[2] The dignity
of the tone seldom seriously lapses, and when it does so it is Donne's
handling of this difficult genre that falters, not his self-respect. A

---

[1] See J. B. Leishman, *The Monarch of Wit*, in one of the few extended critiques so far
attempted of these verse letters, pp. 122–44.

[2] For a different opinion see P. Thomson, 'The Literature of Patronage 1580–1630',
Essays in Criticism, 1952.

reader alert to the changes of tone, with a proper ear for dignity and levity, for serious thought and feeling, and for the witty and humorous play of mind, can enjoy these letters as a legitimate kind of complimentary and moral writing. There is no essential falseness in Donne's addresses to his friends, whether patrons or not. It would be strange if a poet who so persuasively and shrewdly wrote of the need for, or existence of, integrity in others should ever have abjectlv surrendered his own.

TEXTUAL INTRODUCTION

AN edition of any considerable part of Donne's poetry must take as its foundation the theory of the texts put forward by Sir Herbert Grierson in 1912 and developed by Miss Helen Gardner in her editions of the *Divine Poems* (1952) and of the *Elegies and the Songs and Sonnets* (1965). It has been established that the only edition which has any authority is the first (*1633*), but that this is not homogeneous in text. Its editor used manuscripts of two of the main extant Groups as the chief sources of his text, and hence the authority of *1633*'s readings varies with the source for the moment being employed. He also appears to have corrected the text of one manuscript by comparing it with that of the other, and by referring to another source to make good certain deficiencies in his two main manuscripts; and he took some care to alter readings, apparently on his own authority, in order (as he thought) to improve the meaning and the rhythm. We cannot therefore rely solely upon this text, but must go to the surviving manuscripts which were copied before most of the poems were printed. In addition to the two Groups (I and II) from an exemplar of each of which the editor of *1633* mainly worked, other manuscripts (called by Grierson 'Group III') embody a tradition, or traditions, differing in some ways from those in the two main and clearly identifiable groups. Of the larger manuscript collections, moreover, some have many, or all, of the qualities of *1633* itself; there is not only much evidence of sophistication and conflation, but also we find that in gathering Donne's work together compilers took poems or groups of poems now from this tradition of the text, now from that. Some poems and groups of poems, therefore, present special problems within the general theory of the texts. This is certainly true of the *Satires* and of the *Metempsychosis*; for in the transmission of these poems certain manuscripts have acquired a version different from that in others to which they are elsewhere closely related in text and contents. In addition to this lack of homogeneity (and as part of its cause), the textual problems are complicated by the existence of manuscripts containing only the regular

Satires (or these accompanied by two or three other poems) or the
Metempsychosis, and by the relationship of these to the larger
collections grouped by Miss Gardner.

I. THE MANUSCRIPTS

A. The *Satires*

(I)

The five manuscripts of Group I (*C 57*, *D*, *H 49*, *Lec* and *SP*)[1]
preserve a collection of Donne's poems contained in a common
ancestor of the group, which Miss Gardner called *X*. Their general
relationship can be summarized by the following stemma:

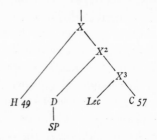

All five contain the *Satires* copied as a group of poems, in the order
of all the editions from *1633* onwards, except that *H 49* lacks
the fifth.[2]

But, whereas in all the other poems they include the five manuscripts are textually very close to one another, in the first four
Satires *C 57* and *Lec* have a text distinct from that in *D* and *H 49*,
but agreeing closely with that found in manuscripts otherwise
distinguished from those of Group I. In 'Satire V', however, missing

---

[1] For a key to sigla, shelf-marks, and present location of manuscripts, see the list on
pp. lxxv–lxxvii. The Group I manuscripts are described by Gardner, *Divine Poems*, pp. lvii–lxvi,
and *Elegies etc.*, pp. lxiv–lxv; for an analysis of their make-up see Margaret Crum, 'Notes
on the Physical Characteristics of some Manuscripts of the Poems of Donne and of Henry
King', *The Library*, June 1961.

[2] With these manuscripts must be grouped a fragment bound into *A 23* (Additional MS.
23229, among the Conway papers in the British Museum, beginning at f. 95; see Grierson,
ii, p. lxxxii, and Gardner, *Divine Poems*, p. lxxvii). This contains the fourth Satire from l. 203
and the whole of the fifth. Comparison with *Lec* shows that the scribe of *Lec* wrote *A 23* also,
and that he was making a second transcript (possibly of the *Satires* only) either from the same
original, or from one of the copies (*A 23* or *Lec*) which he had himself made. The fragment
constantly agrees with *Lec* even in trivial details, and the only differences in wording, three in
number, are shown by a comparison with *C 57* to be mere slips in copying.

from *H 49*, the text of *D* is that found in *C 57* and *Lec.*[1] There is thus no single 'Group I text' of the *Satires*. It would seem that *X* must have contained only the first four, and that the compiler of *X²*, or more probably the compiler of *D*, added the fifth Satire to the four that *D*, like *H 49*, derived from *X*. The compiler of *X³*, on the other hand, instead of completing the set from another source, substituted for the four Satires in *X* a complete set of five from another manuscript.

(II)

The four manuscripts of Group II (*A 18*, *N*, *TCC*, and *TCD*)[2] preserve an even larger collection of Donne's poems than that found in the manuscripts of Group I, contained in a common ancestor of the group which Miss Gardner called *Υ*. Of the four manuscripts *A 18* is a copy of *TCC*, and *N* is a copy of *TCD*.[3] Some poems in *TCD* have been added to those which it derived, like *TCC*, from *Υ*; but *Υ* itself seems clearly to have been of composite origin. This is shown by comparison of *TCC* and *TCD* with another manuscript, *L 74*,[4] which preserves a smaller collection from which the collection in *Υ* seems to have grown by accretion. There is throughout, both in the text and at times in the order of the poems common to *L 74* and Group II, a striking similarity. The text of *L 74* is very close to that of Group II, but is free from the characteristic errors of the Group, and is on the whole rather better. It is in the opening pages of *L 74* and *TCD*, containing the *Satires* among other poems, that we find the greatest similarity in the order of the contents.[5] The nine poems

[1] The variants in the text of 'Satire V' in the manuscripts of all Groups are so trivial that it would be misleading to think of a 'Group I text' of this Satire; one can, however, establish the relationship of the text in *D* with certainty.

[2] For descriptions of these manuscripts see Gardner, *Divine Poems*, pp. lxvi–lxviii.

[3] For this reason, Group II readings can be indicated by the siglum *TC*, which, following Grierson, I use for readings in which *TCC* and *TCD* agree.

[4] Lansdowne MS. 740, described by Grierson, ii, pp. civ–cv, and more fully in Gardner, *Elegies etc.*, pp. lxviii–lxix.

[5] Omitting poems by other writers, the sequence in *L 74* is: *Satires* (III, IV, V, II), 'The Bracelet', 'Satire 6' ('Sleep, next Society'), 'Satire I', 'The Comparison', 'The Perfume', 'Change', 'Loves War', 'Going to Bed', 'The Autumnall', 'The Storm', 'The Calm', 'The Anagram', letters to Rowland Woodward ('Like one who'in her third widdowhood') and Wotton ('Here's no more newes'). The opening poems in *TCD* are: *Satires* (I, III, IV, V, 6, II), 'The Bracelet', 'The Storm', 'The Calm', 'The Anagram' (*TCC* begins here), the same letters to Woodward and Wotton, 'The Comparison', 'The Perfume', 'Change', 'Tutelage', 'The Autumnall'. From this it seems certain that the opening poems in *TCD* were in *Υ*, and that nine were lost from *TCC* (on the first leaves) before *A 18* was copied.

with which *TCD* begins, however, including the *Satires*, are missing from *TCC*, so that in discussing the text of these poems we have only *TCD* to consider in relation to *L 74*.

In the *Satires TCD* and *L 74* have the same close relationship in text evident in the other poems which they share. Their version of the *Satires* is that found also in *C 57* and *Lec*; the four manuscripts agree against all others (except, occasionally, manuscripts with a contaminated text) in more than eighty significant readings, and,

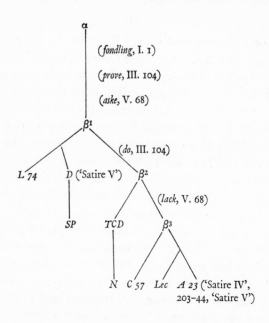

while disagreements among them show that none is the direct source of the others, all must have derived their version ultimately from the same copy. The text in all these manuscripts is carefully transcribed, and there are comparatively few readings that indicate their precise relationship to one another. It would seem, however, that *L 74* (and 'Satire V' in *D*) must have been copied from a manuscript which was not the direct source of *TCD*, *C 57*, *Lec* (or of the fragment in *A 23*). Certain readings in which these manuscripts disagree with *L 74* show that they descend from a nearer common original. Further, the divergences of *C 57*, *Lec*, *A 23*, from *TCD* suggest that they were not copied from the same text as *TCD*, but that another manuscript intervened upon which *C 57*, *Lec*, and *A 23* closely depend; *C 57* and *Lec* are clearly copied from the same original (and neither from the other), while *A 23*, the work of the scribe of *Lec*, is either another copy of the same original, or the scribe has made a copy of his own work. The relationships of all these manuscripts to their common original, which I shall call α, can be summarized in the stemma on p. xliv.

(III)

The other manuscript collections of Donne's poems were described by Grierson as constituting 'Group III'; they do not derive from a single large collection, but may be loosely considered as a group because (with partial exceptions, in the *Satires* as elsewhere) they contain a text different from that in Groups I and II. Group III manuscripts vary very greatly in the number and arrangement of poems (even of the *Satires*) which they contain, and there is usually much evidence of contamination both within the group and (in the *Satires*) sometimes with manuscripts of other groups. It will be useful to consider along with them two collections of a more miscellaneous kind, *Ash* and *HN*, since in the Satires they contain they have the type of text found in manuscripts of Group III. In accumulating their collections, the compilers of these manuscripts might sometimes have added single poems,[1] but in the main Donne's poems seem to have circulated in groups. This is certainly true of the *Elegies*, and the evidence of the texts shows, I believe, that the *Satires* too circulated as a set of poems, and that the absence of one or more Satires from a collection is due either to accident or to conscious selection by the copyist. Selection, for example, accounts

---

[1] Tanner MS. 306 in the Bodleian Library includes a sheet (f. 375) containing a seventeenth-century poem (not by Donne) on the back of which is written, in a contemporary hand, 'Entred into my book'. The notion of fragmentary assemblage can, however, be pushed too far, and appearances can be deceptive. Miss Gardner's study of *H 40* (*Elegies etc.*, pp. lxv–lxvi) suggests that scribes sometimes worked from collections already assembled in the form of quires and loose sheets, and inserted these into already existing collections. Group I, as Miss Crum suggests, descends from such a collection of loose papers, and the order of poems in *L 74* and Group II makes it possible that at some stage in the accretion of the large Group II collection a similar assemblage of loose sheets and leaves was used. *O* and *P*, to be discussed later, seem clearly to derive from such a collection, the quires and sheets being copied in a different order by each scribe.

for the presence of only two Satires in *HN*, for in transcribing the fourth and second (in that order) Drummond of Hawthornden prefixed to 'Satire IV' the following note: 'This Satyre (though it heere have the first place because no more was intended to this booke) was indeed the Authors fourth in nomber & order; he having wreten five in all to which this caution will sufficientlie direct in the rest.'[1]

It is convenient first to discuss *W* (Westmoreland MS.), which stands apart from the rest of the Group III collections, and which has high extrinsic and intrinsic authority.[2] The manuscript was copied by one scribe (now identified as Rowland Woodward) about 1620 (since the sonnet on the death of Ann Donne, which *W* includes, dates probably from 1619), and consists of three sections, the whole being apparently a fair copy of poems of Donne in Woodward's possession. The first part consists of early poems: the five *Satires* in the accepted order (which are followed by a blank page as if they were copied from a separate 'book'), the *Elegies*, verse letters to men friends, and the 'Lincoln's Inn Epithalamion'. The second part contains '*La Corona*' and the nineteen Holy Sonnets (a sonnet 'To E. of D.', here called 'To L. of D.', having strayed from its appropriate set of Holy Sonnets into the first part of the manuscript); and the third part contains Paradoxes and Problems, the *Epigrams* and one lyric, 'A Jet Ring Sent'. It is the first part of *W* that especially interests us here. It contains familiar letters not found elsewhere,[3] including one not written by Donne but addressed to him. Apart from 'To E. of D.' there is no poem in this section of *W* known to be later than 'Satire V' (1598); and letters to Wotton are addressed to 'Mr', not to 'Sir', 'H. W.', so that it seems certain that the poems were taken from early copies.[4] Everything about the manuscript

---

[1] Drummond's gift to the Library of the University of Edinburgh of 'A Satyre. MS.' by Donne is recorded in *Auctarium Bibliothecae Edinburgenae, sive Catalogus Librorum quos Gulielmus Drummondus ab Hawthornden D.D.Q. Anno. 1627*, Edinburgh, 1627. The manuscript has been missing from the Library for many years, if indeed it was ever actually handed over. It might, of course, have been a copy of the *Metempsychosis*.

[2] For descriptions see Gardner, *Divine Poems*, pp. lxxviii–lxxxi, and *Elegies etc.*, p. lxxii.

[3] There is, however, a single leaf (f. 132) bound into *A 23* which must have come from a manuscript that was practically a duplicate of *W*. It contains six short verse-letters. See below, p. lxv, n. 2.

[4] See Grierson, ii, pp. lxxxi–lxxxii. Mrs. Simpson showed that in the Paradoxes *W* has a text of which the only other known representative was *Bur*, Wotton's commonplace book ('More Manuscripts of Donne's "Paradoxes and Problems" ', *R.E.S.*, 1934).

suggests that it is close to Donne's own papers; and it is safe to assume that *W* has a text of the *Satires* which was in existence by about 1598, and also that this text is of great authority.

In the first four Satires it is, in fact, the text of *D* and *H 49*, manuscripts belonging to Group I. These manuscripts share some readings with *W* alone, and others with *W* and a small number of other manuscripts; but the crucial resemblance is the omission from *W*, *D*, and *H 49* alone of l. 46 of 'Satire II', an error which could hardly be made by two scribes independently. *D* and *H 49* are closer to each other than either is to *W* and derive from a nearer common original (*H 49* omitting III. 40, and each manuscript making smaller errors of its own). Their agreements against *W* are mostly due to scribal errors in the text from which they derive, though a few may be due to conscious substitution (for example, in IV. 199, where *D* and *H 49* read 'As the Queenes Presence', *W* 'As the Presence'). It is clear, however, that *W*, *D*, and *H 49* descend from a common source, perhaps at several removes, and represent a tradition of the text different from that most often found in Group III.

(IV)

The five Satires are found as part of a larger collection of Donne's poems in the following Group III manuscripts: *A 25*, *B*, *Dob*, *D 17*, *JC*, *K*, *Lut*, *O*, *O'F*, *P*, *S*, and *S 962*. In addition, *Cy* has the first four in the accepted order, and *S 96* has three, in the order II, I, IV. *Ash* contains the fourth Satire,[1] and *HN* the fourth and second. Three other manuscripts seem to have been intended as collections only or primarily of the *Satires* (arranged in the accepted order): *H 51*, which has the first three; and *Q* and *D 16*, which have all five, followed by 'The Storm' and 'The Calm', to which *Q* adds 'The Curse', here called 'Dirae'. Since in *A 25* we can see a 'book' like that exemplified in *Q* and *D 16* being absorbed into a larger collection, and since it is reasonable to suppose that such 'books' contain a text of the *Satires* in their earliest form, or at least descending from early copies, it seems appropriate to begin with these.

---

[1] *Bur* (Burley MS.) also contained only the fourth Satire, which was not included in a copy of parts of the manuscript made before its destruction by fire.

Q, *D 16*, and *A 25* contain a version of the *Satires* which is homogeneous and, except to some extent in *A 25*, not certainly contaminated. *Q* (in the Library of the Queen's College, Oxford) is a small manuscript of three sheets in quarto, bound up with a number of other documents in MS. 216. Some of the other papers bear dates from 1636 to 1674, but the manuscript containing Donne's work has no date and gives no sign of its provenance. It is headed 'Mr John Dunnes Satires', and may therefore be held with some probability to be, or to have descended from, a manuscript antedating the granting of the degree of D.D. to Donne in 1615. The scribe has written 'Finis' at the end of the last poem ('The Curse'). *D 16* is a similar complete manuscript in the Dyce Collection, uniformly transcribed in secretary hand, containing the *Satires*, 'The Storm', and 'The Calm'.[1] A certain P. Neve has annotated the manuscript in a much later hand, 'Poems written about the Year 1616; and believed to be unprinted'. The comment does not suggest that Neve was well informed, but there is a slight possibility that his information preserves the approximate date of transcription. As Chambers suggested, these two manuscripts are of the kind very probably seen by Thomas Freeman, who printed among his epigrams in 1614 the following:

To John Dunne.

The *Storme* describ'd, hath set thy name afloate,
Thy *Calme*, a gale of famous winde hath got:
Thy *Satyres* short, too soone we them o'relooke,
I prethee *Persius* write a bigger booke.[2]

A 25[3] is a large folio collection of seventeenth-century poetry by

---

[1] *Q* and *D 16* are discussed by Grierson, ii, pp. lxxix–lxxx.

[2] Epigram 84 in *Runne and a great Cast*, *The Second Bowle* (being Part II of *Rubbe, and a great Cast*, 1614), discussed by Chambers, i, pp. xxxv–xxxvi; the epigram was first noted by J. P. Collier, *Poetical Decameron* (1820), i. 157–8. It is reasonable to suppose that 'books' of the *Satires* were circulating fairly freely by 1614. Probably in 1608, Francis Davison noted that he had lent 'John Duns Satyres' to 'my br. Christopher' (MS. Harley 298, British Museum, f. 159). For other early references to the *Satires*, see Keynes, pp. 233–6.

[3] British Museum, Add. MS. 25707, described by Grierson, ii, pp. cvii–cviii, clii–cliii, and by Gardner, *Elegies etc.*, pp. lxxviii–lxxix. A copy of parts of *A 25* exists in *C* (in the Baumgartner Collection, Cambridge University Library); the text shows that the writer has selected poems or portions of poems from *A 25*, transcribing them in the same order. A comparison made with the aid of photostats leads me to question Grierson's suggestion (ii, p. clii) that the hand in *A 25* which he designates 'A' is that of the scribe of *C*. The name 'Edward Smyth' occurs in *C*,

various authors written in more than a dozen hands on paper with differing water-marks. The original copyists left blank pages and spaces at the foot of others, which have been filled up with poems, many by Henry King, in a hand that may be Philip King's.[1] If we ignore these additions, the first sixty-five leaves are devoted to poetry chiefly by Donne, written out by five scribes. The collection of Donne's work includes no poem by him later than 1614 (the date of 'Obsequies to the Lord Harrington', copied in the hand of the scribe whose work comes first in the manuscript); it was obviously put together from a variety of sources as material was obtained. The section of the manuscript which concerns us here (ff. 48–56) is in the hand called 'C' by Grierson, and contains a sequence of the five *Satires* in the accepted order, 'The Storm' and 'The Calm', after which the scribe left three blank pages. The possibility at once arises that these seven poems were copied from a manuscript like *Q* and *D 16* (and at about the same date), and that for a time there was no other material available for copying.

The text of *Q*, *D 16*, and *A 25* turns this possibility into certainty. The version of the seven poems they share is like that of the manuscripts loosely assigned to Group III, but where these divide, *Q*, *D 16*, and *A 25* usually agree in their readings, some of them striking (e.g. 'Sleydan' for 'Surius', IV. 48); and they share interesting readings found in no other manuscript. No one of them can, however, have been copied directly from another, since each has errors and omissions not found in the other two. *Q* and *D 16* are more closely connected with each other than either of them with *A 25*, and could have been copied from the same original, each scribe making some errors to which the agreement of the other manuscript with *A 25* is generally a safe guide.[2] *A 25* makes a number of errors of its own;

---

probably that of the owner; it seems to be a more carefully written signature of the Edward Smith who wrote his name at the end of *H* (Harley MS. 3998, containing the *Metempsychosis*); he was perhaps a collector of Donne's verse, and his failure to cause to be copied from *A 25* the *Satires*, 'The Storm', and 'The Calm' might be due to his already having a 'book' like *Q* and *D 16*.

[1] See Margaret Crum, *The Library*, June 1961.

[2] The readings in one not found in the other are obvious slips in copying, with one interesting exception, in IV. 216. I give full details of this reading, since it illustrates some of the processes by which the textual state of the Group III manuscripts has been complicated. Most manuscripts of all groups, including *D 16* and *A 25*, read 'Pursevant'. *Q* reads 'Topclief'. In *Lut* the scribe wrote 'Pursevant', but underlined the word and put 'Topcliff' in the margin, presumably as correction rather than as gloss; the scribe of *O'F* accepted the

but on other occasions it is a matter of doubt whether it has been contaminated by another version or whether it properly records the reading of the ancestor of Q, D 16, and A 25 itself.[1] As a group, however, these three manuscripts seem to preserve parts at least of a distinct tradition of the text of the *Satires*.[2]

Three other manuscripts, *Lut*, *O'F*, and *S 962*,[3] are clearly related in the *Satires* to Q, D 16, and A 25. *S 962* has the five *Satires* in the same order as *Lut* and *O'F* (II, I, III, IV, V), and shares with them a number of readings found in no other manuscript. Its text shows it to be a late copy, probably at several removes, of a large Group III collection from which *Lut* and (sometimes independently) *O'F* derived most of their contents; but it is full of errors and there is much evidence of sophistication. Although textually of little importance, however, it suggests that the original of *Lut*, *O'F*, and *S 962* was closer than any of its descendants to the original of Q, D 16, and A 25. *O'F* is basically a copy of *Lut*, with additions from other sources.[4] In both manuscripts there is a constant effort to 'improve' the text. In the *Satires* they share a considerable number of the characteristic readings of Q, D 16, and A 25 (e.g. 'Sleydan' in IV. 48); they disagree with these three manuscripts so often, however, that the attempt to work out a textual relationship in any detail seems hopeless. Apart from obvious sophistication, there is

correction and copied 'Topcliff' into his text, but the 'first corrector' (see Gardner, *Divine Poems*, p. lxxii n.), who may or may not have been the scribe, has underlined the word and written 'Pursevant' above. In *JC* the original reading was 'Topcliffe', but it has been altered to 'Pursivant'; *D 17* has copied the original reading, 'Topcliffe'. *Dob* has 'Pursuivant', but the word has been underlined and 'Topcliff' has been written in the margin (probably in a different but contemporary hand). *Ash* reads, with characteristic simplicity, 'Toplife'.

[1] Contamination seems the more likely explanation for such readings as that in IV. 84, where *Q* and *D 16* read 'One S^r', while *A 25* agrees with the great majority of other manuscripts in reading 'one Frenchman'.

[2] The text of 'The Storm' and 'The Calm' confirms the relationship of the three manuscripts, except that, owing to the relative absence of complication in the text of these two poems, *A 25* offers no evidence of possible contamination.

[3] Miss Gardner, who was the first editor to use *Lut* (Luttrell MS.) and *S 962* (Stowe MS. 962), discusses *Lut* and *O'F* (O'Flaherty MS.), *Divine Poems*, pp. lxix ff., and *S 962*, p. lxxvi n.; see also Gardner, *Elegies etc.*, pp. lxxiii–lxxv, lxxxi.

[4] One such source was a Group II MS. from which *O'F* took the *Metempsychosis*, and some lines in verse letters to the Countess of Salisbury and to Goodyer, not found in *Lut*. The compiler of *Lut* had already used material ultimately from Donne's own papers : a verse letter ('No want of duty') with the subscription 'Yo^r obedient sonne/Jo : Donne'; 'A letter' ('Thou sendst me prose & rimes'), which in *W* is addressed to Donne; and the fragment 'Resurrection'. *O'F* adds to these another fragment, addressed to the Countess of Bedford ('Though I be dead and buried'). The compiler went back to a Group III MS. for four lines (85–88) omitted from 'Satire III' by the scribe of *Lut* as he turned over to begin a new page.

evidence of contamination not only within the Group III tradition, but also with a manuscript of Group II (with a text of the *Satires* like that in *TCD* and *C 57*). Nevertheless it is very probable that a text like that in *Q*, *D 16*, *A 25*, lies ultimately behind *Lut*, *O'F*, and *S 962*.

(v)

The remaining manuscripts of Group III are in such a state of corruption in the text of the *Satires* that not a great deal can be learned from them. We can, however, distinguish three, which have some relation to the text represented in *W*, *D*, and *H 49*, from the rest, in which we see a progressive deterioration of the version represented by *Q* and *O'F* and the manuscripts associated with them. These three are *HN*, *H 51*, and *B*.

HN[1] is a small collection (forty leaves) in William Drummond's handwriting of poems by Donne, Pembroke, Rudyerd, Roe, and Hoskins, with a few trifles perhaps by other writers; it includes Donne's fourth and second Satires. No poem in it is known to have been composed later than 1609; and certainly the earlier poems seem to derive from early copies, since, for example, the verse letters to Wotton in *HN* are both addressed to 'M^r', not to 'Sir', 'H. W.', and presumably descend from a text antedating the conferring of Wotton's knighthood in 1603. At first sight, indeed, the manuscript seems to bring us close to Donne himself, for on the second leaf is written 'Thirre poems belonginge to Jhon Don Transcribed by William Drummond'. The inscription is in a hand different from that in which Drummond copied the poems, and unfortunately we do not know with what authority this statement is made; there is some doubt, therefore, whether the collection does indeed derive from copies in Donne's possession of poems by himself and others. Furthermore, against 'Satire II' Drummond has written 'after C. B. coppy'; and if this statement does not flatly contradict the general description of the poems as copies belonging to Donne, it can only mean that Donne kept a transcript of the Satire identifiable as one sent, or lent, to C. B. The text of the two Satires in *HN* does not

---

[1] This collection is part of MS. 2067 (Hawthornden MSS., vol. xv) in the National Library of Scotland. It is described by Grierson, ii. 104–5, 203, 242; cf. also Gardner, *Elegies etc.*, pp. xxxvii–xxxviii.

enable us to resolve these doubts. The transcript of the fourth Satire exhibits exactly the same qualities as that of the second, so that the virtues of C. B.'s copy may be reasonably attributed to the text of both. Of the readings peculiar to *HN* (nine in 'Satire II' and twenty in 'Satire IV') none seems of any importance. When the Group III manuscripts seriously disagree, *HN* in most cases follows *W*. Most (though not all) of the readings in which it disagrees with *W* could be the result of faulty copying from a common source, but *HN* contains l. 46 of 'Satire II', missing from *W*. Yet it is possible that *HN* and *W* descend ultimately from a common original, if in a few places we allow the possibility of contamination (more probably in the closer source of *HN*).

H 51[1] is a small 'book' containing the first three Satires in the accepted order. The first scribe wrote out the first Satire, and began the second with a version of ll. 1–6 which he later discarded and corrected before going on to the end and writing the title of the third Satire in the margin. A second scribe transcribed 'Satire III', and a third hand has made good an omission in 'Satire I' (hazarding 'roome' for the omitted word 'state' in l. 70). On the first leaf (which at one time, as water-stains show, was as Grierson describes it,[2] at the back of the manuscript) are the words, 'Jhon Dunne his Satires / Anno Domini 1593', written possibly by the first scribe, in the italic script which he uses for other headings.[3] The date 1593 as applied to all three poems makes one doubtful whether the writer was in touch with authoritative information; it could, however, have been the date prefixed to the copy of the first Satire from which the scribe was working. We cannot safely assume that *H 51* descends from a copy of the *Satires* when there *were* only three, or that the intention was to produce a 'book' of *Satires* like that in *Q* and *D 16*. The first scribe tired of his labours, and the second might have done the same; we do not know how much more

---

[1] Harley MS. 5110, in the British Museum, contains this MS. as the sixth (ff. 95–100) of eight miscellaneous documents. It consists of loose sheets with two different water-marks, in folio, cut and hinged for binding. There is no clue as to its origin, and the other documents are quite unrelated; among them are dates from 1613 to 1645. *H 51* was first discussed by J. P. Collier, in his *Poetical Decameron* (1820), i. 153 ff.

[2] ii. 100.

[3] Mr. T. C. Skeat allows me to say that there seems to him to be no reason why this scribe should not have written the inscription, but that there is too little evidence for a positive opinion one way or the other.

material, if any, there was to be copied; and other copies of the remaining Satires might have already been in the possession of the first owner of *H 51*. We are therefore driven to the text in order to determine the value of the manuscript as a witness. The copy, except in punctuation, has been carefully made; excluding the curious version of ll. 1–6 first adopted and then discarded,[1] there are only six readings peculiar to the manuscript. The text is farthest from that in *O'F* (among the Group III manuscripts) and has none of the characteristic readings of *Q*. Although it resembles *HN* in these ways, it is not positively connected with *HN* in the only Satire (II) common to the two manuscripts. Nevertheless *H 51* has the same tendency as *HN* to follow *W* when the Group III manuscripts divide, and it differs from *W* rather less often than *HN*; when it does so, it nearly always agrees with *B*.

B (Bridgewater MS.)[2] is a collection of as much of Donne's poetry in existence by about 1620 as the compiler could assemble, together with a collection of his Paradoxes and Problems, and a good number of poems not accepted as Donne's; the poet was 'Dr. Donne' when it was compiled. It bears on its first leaf the signature of John, first Earl of Bridgewater, the son of Donne's patron, Egerton. It is rather a chaotic collection, though most of the Divine Poems are grouped at the end, and the five *Satires* (II, I, III, IV, V) occur as a group in the middle. The scribe of *B* makes many errors in the *Satires* as elsewhere. No surviving manuscript shares the omission of V. 15–18, or any of the smaller omissions;[3] on the other hand, *B* cannot have been copied from any surviving manuscript. Its closest connexions are with *H 51* in the first three Satires, and with *W* in all five; and when the Group III manuscripts conflict among themselves, *B*, like *H 51*, most often follows *W*.

It is disappointing that these three manuscripts, *HN*, *H 51*, and *B*, each of which either by its provenance or by its form gives promise of authoritative help in determining the text of the *Satires*, should turn out to be of comparatively little use. They might

---

[1] Traces of this version are otherwise found only in *S 96* and in manuscript notes in the copy of *1633* in the Library of St. John's College, Oxford.

[2] *B* is described in Gardner, *Divine Poems*, pp. lxxii–lxxiii, and *Elegies etc.*, p. lxxx.

[3] Except that an omission of some words in IV. 143–4 is made also in *S 962*. Although the order of the Satires is the same in *B* as in *S 962*, the texts are so far apart that the omission, obviously due to eye-slip, must have been made by the two scribes independently.

represent copies issued by the poet with some emendations preserved and added to in *W*; or, much more probably, they might descend from the original of the text represented by *W*, *D*, and *H 49*, perhaps at some removes, being variously contaminated in the process of copying.

Among the remaining Group III mauscripts Miss Gardner was able to make some finer discriminations on the basis of the text of the Love Poems. In the text of the *Satires*, however, such sub-groups break down. Four manuscripts, *Lut*, *O'F*, *S 96*, and *Dob*, in respect of the Love Poems, can more properly be designated a 'Group' because the texts can be shown to have had a common original.[1] *S 96* (Stowe 961), in the three Satires which it contains and with which it begins (II, I, IV), does show some connexion with *Lut* and *O'F*. But although, amongst a multitude of unique and obviously erroneous readings, there are to be found others that represent the text of this sub-group, most of the characteristic readings of *O'F* (and of *Q*) in the *Satires* have been lost. *Dob* (Dobell MS.) sometimes agrees with *Lut* and *O'F*; but it disagrees with these, and indeed with all other, manuscripts so often that it can hardly be said, in the narrower sense, to belong to any group. While most of the 'improvements' and some of the errors might have been made by the scribe of *Dob* independently, the text indicates a thorough process of contamination within, and sometimes from without, the Group III traditions.

Another sub-group, *HK 2*, *Cy*, *O*, *P*,[2] breaks down even more decisively in the text of the *Satires*. *HK 2* does not contain them. *Cy* has only the first four Satires, which occur in the accepted order as a set near the beginning; they may derive from early copies, since the first two are said to be Satires of 'M^r. John Donne' (the other two being initialed 'J. D.'). Their origins are, however, obscured by errors, sophistications, and contamination from within, and in a few places from without, Group III. *O* and *P* have a text more like that in *S 96* than that in *Cy*. One hesitates to say even

---

[1] See Gardner, *Elegies etc.*, pp. lxxii–lxxv.

[2] Cf. Gardner, *Elegies etc.*, pp. lxxv–lxxvii. I have not seen *HK 2* or *O*, but have relied upon Miss Gardner's report of them, which convinced me that full collation of their texts was unnecessary. *O* is very close in text to *P*; it omits two poems (not by Donne) found in *P*, and has four of Donne's poems not in *P*, including a verse letter to 'T.W.' ('At once, from hence'). *P* is described by Grierson, ii. c–ci.

this of *O* and *P*, since the text of the *Satires* of which they are both copies contained many errors (including some that suggest writing from dictation), and was clearly contaminated from other Group III copies. Further, though the text is basically like that in *S 96*, it has absorbed some thirty-two readings, nearly all of them striking, which are peculiar to, or characteristic of, the version in *C 57* and *TCD* (and which are not found in *Cy*). It is difficult to imagine a more variously corrupted text.

The few remaining manuscripts have no clear affiliations with those already discussed that would enable us to fit them into a line of descent; we can say only that they belong loosely to Group III. *JC* (John Cave MS.) opens with an admiring poem by John Cave, its first owner, 'Upon Mr Donns Satires', signed 'Jo. Ca. Jun. 3. 1620'. A copy of Cave's manuscript in the Dyce Collection (*D 17*) is dated 1625, so that *JC* must have been written between these dates.[1] The collection is in three parts with separate title-pages; (*a*) the *Satires*, 'Litany', 'The Storm', 'The Calm'; (*b*) 'Elegies and Epigrammes' (though there are no Epigrams); and (*c*) a miscellaneous collection of lyrics and other poems. The five *Satires* occur in the accepted order, and have been corrected by a later hand from a text of which *D* is the closest extant exemplar. The original text is a rather careless rendering of a typical Group III version, but unfortunately *JC* differs from all Group III manuscripts so frequently in important readings that it is impossible to establish any clear relationship. Equally valueless as a witness is *S* (Stephens MS.),[2] which bears the date 19 July 1620. The five canonical *Satires* in the regular order, with 'Satyra Sexta' ('Sleep, next Society'), were apparently copied as a group, since they are preceded by eight blank pages and followed by six more. The manuscript, however, is full of careless blunders, and the affiliations of its text of the *Satires* vary almost from line to line. It is contaminated not only from within Group III but also from other traditions of the text, including that represented in *C 57* and *TCD*. In no respect, therefore, can *S*

---

[1] In and after 1615 Donne could have been (and in *D 17* is) called 'Doctor Donne', and Cave shows that he was aware that Donne was a Doctor of Divinity. His reference to 'Mr. Donne' suggests that we should be cautious in building too much on such titles in the dating of manuscripts. For *JC* and *D 17*, see Gardner, *Elegies etc.*, p. lxxix.

[2] For descriptions see Gardner, *Divine Poems*, pp. lxxiv–lxxv, and *Elegies etc.*, pp. lxxx–lxxxi.

be regarded as trustworthy. This can be said even more emphatic-
ally of K,[1] a manuscript which in contents and text has a close
relation with S; it is even more corrupt than S, however, and considerably later in date, and I have not thought it worth detailed
collation. In the only Satire which it contains (the fourth), Ash[2] is
also very unreliable. The manuscript is late and the text very poor,
and in this Satire, as elsewhere,[3] gives evidence of oral transmission.
Of its unique readings, which abound, and are mostly absurd
blunders, the only one which has any attractiveness (and which was
adopted by Grierson) is the use of the singular in the rhyme-words
of IV. 205–6, 'trye' and 'thyge' (*sic*). Otherwise its text is generally
like that in the worst of the Group III manuscripts. One cannot say
that it has a Group III text, since, as should be clear from this survey
of the manuscripts, no 'Group III text' of the *Satires* can be shown to
exist.

(VI)

Any attempt to decide the authenticity and probable date of the
versions of the *Satires* must obviously remain to some degree
tentative. Yet the versions themselves are reasonably clear. The
text of manuscripts containing all five Satires (and of D in the four
Satires it shares with H 49) is invariably homogeneous. Of the
fifth Satire there seems to have been only one version, existing in
two main copies with few variant readings, none of which is of any
importance. There is no reason why scribes should have been more
careful or responsible in transcribing this Satire than in transcribing
the rest of the set; and the fewness and unimportance of the variants
in 'Satire V' is a strong argument for the authenticity of striking
variant readings found throughout the other four Satires, for which
it is difficult or impossible to account as due to accidents of transmission. Since the available evidence suggests that the *Satires* circulated as a set of poems, and were absorbed as a group into larger
collections, it is reasonable to look for the earliest version in manu-

---

[1] The King MS., first described in Gardner, *Divine Poems*, p. lxxv.
[2] MS. Ashmole 38, discussed by R. Dunlap, *Poems of Thomas Carew* (1949), pp. lxx ff.,
and by J. A. W. Bennett and H. R. Trevor-Roper, *Poems of Richard Corbett* (1955), p. lxiii.
[3] Cf. Gardner, *Divine Poems*, p. 109.

scripts which are complete in themselves and consist primarily of a 'book' of Satires.

Q̲, *D 16*, and the portion of *A 25* derived from a similar manuscript, contain readings that seem authentic and that also seem to have been removed in Donne's own revision of the text. About the reading 'Sleydan' for 'Surius', in IV. 48, there can hardly be reasonable doubt; only Donne could have substituted the name of a particular Catholic historian, Surius, for that of the Protestant Sleidan. By the time he was Egerton's secretary, and therefore professedly an Anglican, Donne could hardly have wished Sleidan's name to appear in his work as a type of lying historian; it seems incredible that 'Sleydan' should have been the revised reading. Where there are such readings as these, it is at least very probable that other readings in the version of *Q̲* also record Donne's 'first thoughts'. In *Lut* and *O'F* we seem to meet this version at a later stage of copying, when, although still recognizable, it is already beginning to be submerged by scribal interference and carelessness. A progressively deteriorating text of this kind is that found in Group III generally; and although manuscripts like *Cy*, *Dob*, *O*, *P*, and *S* are not of much positive help in reconstructing the earliest version of the *Satires*, they do at times show how error has occurred and make it less likely that we should take a corruption of the text for a genuine early reading.

The version which seems to have its most reliable representative in *W* has less striking characteristic readings than that in *Q̲* ; indeed, those recorded in the apparatus as peculiar to this version (represented there by *W* and *H 49*) would hardly seem to amount to a different authentic text of the *Satires* at all. That it is very probably such a text is indicated by two main considerations: firstly, by the great authority of *W* itself, and the less, though still considerable, authority of the Group I manuscripts containing this text, *D* and *H 49*; and secondly, by the disappearance, presumably by revision, of the characteristic readings of the version in *Q̲* , and by the absence of the many improvements in phrasing found in the version of *C 57* and *TCD*. Apart from readings changed from those of *Q̲* and readings not yet changed to those of *C 57*, *TCD*, one might consider that an intelligent copyist could have hit upon readings in

which *W*, *H 49* differ significantly from other versions; yet there is
never any discernible reason why at these particular places a scribe
should either have misread his copy or have felt that emendation was
needed. The readings seem to be of the kind that might occur to a
poet writing out his poems some time after their composition (without the intention of thoroughgoing revision) as variations, for the
moment an improvement, which he might later discard. *HN*, *H 51*,
and even *B*, might possibly descend from such copies. But there is
another possibility (which I consider more likely)—that, like *D*
and *H 49*, these manuscripts are less accurate copies than *W* of a
text of the *Satires* prepared by Donne for a specific occasion. Such an
occasion, I suggest, might have arisen when Donne addressed to his
patron and employer, Lord Keeper Egerton, the fifth Satire, written
not many months after he entered Egerton's service in late 1597 or
early 1598. It is possible that Donne was then asked for a copy of his
other four Satires. We learn from Walton that he was a favourite in
the Lord Keeper's family, and it is not improbable that his poetry
would arouse their warm interest; to one of the daughters of Egerton's third wife (Elizabeth, later Countess of Huntingdon), indeed,
he wrote two verse letters. Such a theory would suggest a reason
for the presence of only the first four Satires (and in this version) in
H 49 and presumably in the archetype of Group I; it is difficult
otherwise to see why, in so authoritative a collection, the fifth
Satire should have become detached from the others. (The compiler of *D*, as we have seen, had to complete his set of the *Satires*
with a text of the fifth taken from another source.) Some support
might be found for the suggestion that this text of the *Satires*
originated in an occasion of which only close friends of the poet
would have known, when we recall that *HN* has some claim to be
connected with copies 'belonging' to Donne or to one of his friends,
Christopher Brooke; and *W* was copied by Rowland Woodward.
Although, as Chamberlain tells us,[1] Egerton showed concern in
1600 about many of the abuses satirized in the work of his secretary,
Donne could hardly, as a responsible employee of a high officer of
State, have prepared a new version of the *Satires*, even for manuscript
circulation, after the banning of published satires in June 1599. It

[1] See *ante*, p. xviii.

is possible, therefore, that *W* and the related manuscripts contain a version made in 1598;[1] it was apparently not widely known outside the poet's circle, since very few other manuscripts are contaminated with its readings.

Little doubt can, I think, be felt about the authenticity of the many variant readings in another version of the *Satires*, that found in *C 57*, *TCD*, and *L 74*. The alteration of 'changeling' (the reading of the *Q* and *W* versions) in I. 1 to 'fondling' is a typical example of what I believe to be the author's revisions; others even more striking are found in a short space in a passage in 'Satire III' (ll. 79 ff.). Few of the more than eighty characteristic readings of this version can reasonably be ascribed to accidents of copying or to scribal inter-ference. I suggest that this, the text of the *Satires* containing Donne's final revisions, was that of a copy prepared for the Countess of Bedford. Ben Jonson wrote an epigram 'To Lucy, Countesse of Bedford, with M. Donnes Satyres', in which he says that she 'desired' them; and, probably in 1608, Francis Davison included in a list of 'Manuscripts to gett'[2] the item: 'Satyres, Elegies, Epigrams &c. by John Don. q^{re}. some from Eleaz. Hodgson, Ben: Johnson', which implies that Davison thought (or knew) it was possible that Jonson would have a copy of the *Satires*. Donne met the Countess, so far as we know, late in 1607, in which year relations between Donne and Jonson were sufficiently close for Donne to pay an exceptional compliment by supplying a Latin epigram on *Volpone*, printed in front of the play. It is interesting that the Satire most heavily revised in this version was the third, on religion. Donne's special interest in improving it would have been both appropriate to the tastes of his new patroness (for the Countess was a religious woman) and in accord with his own problem in 1607. In that year Thomas Morton had vainly suggested to Donne, in tempting terms,

---

[1] The *Satires* occur in that part of *W* which, as we have seen (with one explicable exception), contains no poem known to have been composed after 'Satire V', 1598. In *Skialetheia*, attributed to Edward Guilpin, there are echoes of the *Satires*, and the fifth of Guilpin's Satires in this work is a close imitation of Donne's 'Satire I'. Guilpin's phrasing suggests that he was using a version like that in *Q* or that in *W* (we cannot be more precise); his book was published in 1598.

[2] Harley MS. 298, British Museum, f. 159^v; a list of French books on f. 160, compiled by Davison about the same time, includes Régnier's works (1608); see editions of Davison's *Poetical Rhapsody* by N. H. Nicholas (1826), i, pp. xlii–xlv, and by A. H. Bullen (1890), i, pp. l–lv; cf. Grierson, ii, p. lvii.

that he should take holy orders;[1] and although Donne refused, evidence of his self-examination may be found in passages in his private letters of this period, especially in one to Sir Henry Goodyer, probably written in 1608, in which although the idea is different from that in 'Satire III' the general subject-matter is the same: 'You know I never fettered nor imprisoned the word Religion; not straightning it Frierly, *ad Religiones factitias*, . . . nor immuring it in a *Rome*, or a *Wittemberg*, or a *Geneva*. . . .'[2] The poems of the years 1607–14 are also more concerned with religious and moral subjects; and they include eight verse letters addressed to the Countess of Bedford, and (in this period) three funeral poems mourning her friends or relatives. It seems probable that the final version of the *Satires* was the outcome both of the first challenge to Donne to consider taking orders, and more immediately of the acquisition of a patroness in that courtiers' world in which he had first tried to make a career. The appearance of this version in *L 74* suggests that it was in existence, like the other poems in that manuscript, by 1610 or (if Walton's account of the occasion of 'A Valediction: forbidding Mourning' is accepted) 1611. The substitution of this version of the *Satires* for that in *H 49* in the transmission of the Group I collection might be due, not only to the lack of the fifth Satire in the archetype, but also to the knowledge that the text of *C 57* and *Lec* was that of the author's final version. This theory of the date and occasion of its making, though speculative, would also account for the fact that there is no evidence, as there is in the text of some other poems,[3] that *TCD* contains any revisions by the poet beyond those found in *C 57* and *Lec*; in the *Satires* the revisions had been completed some years before.

(VII)

The theory of the transmission of versions of the *Satires* put forward above can be represented by a stemma; some doubtful relations are suggested by hatched lines, but for some of the Group

---

[1] See Walton, *Lives*, pp. 32–35, and R. B[addily], *The Life of Dr. Thomas Morton* (1669), pp. 98–99.
[2] *Letters*, p. 29.
[3] Cf. Gardner, *Divine Poems*, p. lxviii.

III manuscripts it is impossible even to suggest any very clear relationship.

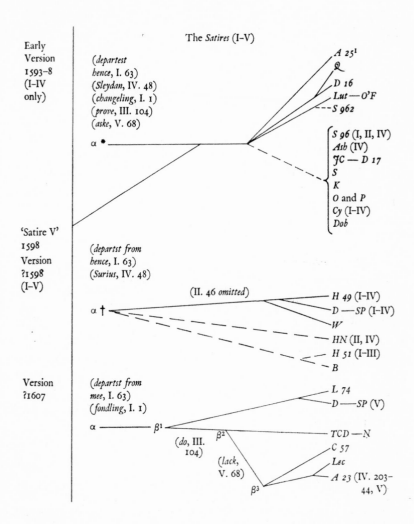

B. *Metempsychosis*

Donne's *Metempsychosis*, or *The Progress of the Soul*, is preserved in two 'books' containing only this poem, *G* (Gosse MS.) and *H* (Harley MS. 3998); in the manuscripts of Group II, *TCD* (and its copy, *N*) and *TCC* (and its copy, *A 18*); in one manuscript of Group I, *C 57*; and in one manuscript of Group III, *O'F*. The texts in *C 57* and *O'F* are closely related to those in *TCD* and *TCC*. All four depend ultimately on a common source, a copy of the poem that was in some ways defective and that could not have been the source of either *G* or *H*.[1] *C 57* is closer to *TCC* and *TCD* than to *O'F*, but it cannot depend upon their common source, since it is free of their common errors, nor can it be that source, since it has distinctive errors of its own. Hence the source of *C 57* and the common original of *TCD* and *TCC* must be a manuscript superior to all three, but inferior in some respects to the source of *O'F*. *O'F* itself cannot have been the source of any of the other manuscripts, since its text contains nearly sixty readings not found elsewhere, about half of which are errors of transcription, the rest being certainly or probably sophistications. On the other hand, *O'F* has some important correct readings where Group II and *C 57* are wrong or deficient. Hence the text of *O'F* must derive from a source earlier in the tradition, a manuscript which did not contain the errors found only in *C 57*-*TCC*-*TCD* or only in *O'F*, but which had other errors and defects common to all these manuscripts.

In the correction of the deficiencies in the large collections, *G* and *H* are of great value. *G*[2] is a quarto manuscript, beautifully written in italic script, containing 'Dr: Donne's Μετεμψύχωσις with, Certaine select Dialogues, of Lucian, and The Tale of the Fauorite'. The copy of Donne's poem is made with only reasonable care. In

---

[1] They share five important omissions (e.g. of 'Rivulets', the reading of *G* and *H*, at the end of l. 94, though the original scribe of *O'F* invented the reading 'Nothing letts' to fill the blank); they alone have the heading 'First Song' after the preliminary Epistle; all have difficulty with corrupt copy in ll. 180, 383, and 427; and they alone share seven significant readings, five of them errors.

[2] The manuscript was acquired by Sir Edmund Gosse from the Phillipps collection, and was sold from his library in May 1929 to the Folger Shakespeare Library. On a blank leaf at the beginning is the name of a former, perhaps the original, owner, Roger Bradon. Gosse, who first described the manuscript (i. 140–1), notes that the date 16 August 1601 (attached to the poem in *C 57*, Group II and *O'F*) is missing from *G*. Grierson (ii, p. lxxxii) was the first editor to use the manuscript.

l. 137, however, G alone preserves the correct reading. Twenty other readings G shares only with H, of which most are certainly right, and none can be proved wrong.

H is a copy of the poem bound as the eleventh of the miscellaneous manuscripts in Harley MS. 3998 in the British Museum.[1] It is written in a clear Italian hand, and is entitled 'Infinitati Sacrum, Poema Satiricum, Metempsycosis'. The preliminary Epistle breaks off in mid sentence at the words 'None writes so ill that he', and the last stanza (LII) is missing; apparently the copy from which the scribe was working was defective.[2] The text in H is rather carelessly copied; of some seventy-five readings not found elsewhere, only two are certainly correct, and about sixty are certainly, or very probably, errors. On the other hand the significant readings which H shares with G against the other texts point to a common origin, and are the more significant for having been preserved amidst so much that is erroneous. Four other readings H shares only with G and O'F, and six only with O'F.

These facts suggest that the relationship of the surviving manuscripts of the *Metempsychosis* can be explained as follows: G and H descend from a common original which contained the significant readings peculiar to the two manuscripts; the other manuscripts all descend from a copy in which these readings were lost; O'F was copied from this, and preserved correct readings lost in the further transmission of the text. C 57 was copied at a later point in the tradition, and then, independently, the original of the Group II manuscripts, which in the text of this poem maintain their normal relationships to one another. This theory of the transmission of the text of the poem can be shown by the following stemma:

---

[1] *H* was first described by H. J. L. Robbie, 'Two More Undescribed Manuscripts of John Donne's Poems', *R.E.S.*, 1928. It was first used by Mr. John Hayward in *Donne—Complete Verse and Selected Prose*, 1929, and by Grierson in his one-volume edition of the poems in the same year. The dates on certain documents bound with *H* range from 1576 to 1657. The name 'Edward Smith' occurs at the beginning and end of the poem (see p. xlviii, n. 3). The manuscript has suffered considerable damage, and some readings must remain doubtful.

[2] Mr. Robbie suggested that *H* represented the original form of the poem, and that Donne added the last stanza after revising the text later. While the last stanza might have been, in a sense, an afterthought, the variants in *H* do not, on the whole, support the contention that they derive from an unrevised version; but I have included the readings most likely to be considered authentic in my apparatus. The fact that part of the Epistle is omitted from *H* as well as the last stanza seems to point to a defective exemplar. Compare *Cy*, which breaks off in the middle of a poem.

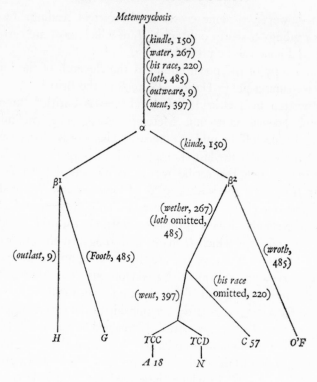

c. The *Epigrams*

No epigrams are included in the Group I manuscripts. The Group II manuscripts contain thirteen; the closely related *DC*[1] has seven of these, and also two others ('Disinherited' and 'Ralphius') not in Group II. It seems certain, from the text and order of the epigrams, that at least the six that begin the Group II collection also preceded the nine in *DC* on a leaf now missing from the manuscript. Of the epigrams in the Group II manuscripts ten appear in the miscellaneous collection *S 962*, with a text that shows them to have been derived from Group II. Of the Group III manuscripts, *O'F* has eighteen, *HN* fourteen, *Dob* twelve, *B* ten, *O* and *P* five, *Cy* four, and *S 96* one. The fullest collection of all is found in *W*; its text is here essentially the same as that in Group III; and at least *O'F* and

---

[1] The Dolau Cothi MS. in the National Library of Wales, first described in Gardner, *Elegies etc.*, pp. lxx–lxxi.

B took the text from a collection like that in *W*.[1] Thus there seem to be only two traditions of the text of the *Epigrams*, that in Group II (and *S 962*) and that in Group III and *W*. When these traditions disagree, it is seldom doubtful which is in error. Those who find epigrams memorable often have faulty memories, and many variations in the manuscripts can be ascribed to this cause.[2] Fortunately the manuscript containing the largest collection, *W*, is a good safeguard against such aberrations; it provides an authoritative check upon Group II readings, and the best guidance as to the order in which the epigrams should be arranged.[3]

D. Verse Letters

Thirty-six verse letters (including the Latin letter to Andrews) have been accepted into the canon of Donne's poetry,[4] and one other, that 'written by Sir H. G. and J. D. *alternis vicibus*', should, I think, be added.

The nineteen written by the end of 1598, with the surprising exception of 'The Calm', are included in the authoritative collection in *W*. Four, indeed (three to 'Mr R. W.' and that to 'Mr E. G.'), are found only there;[5] but the other fifteen (including 'The Calm') formed part also of the basic Group II collection.[6] From a Group II manuscript, eight of these were copied into *Lut* (and *O'F*) to

---

[1] The *Epigrams* are among the poems added in *O'F* to those in *Lut*, which has no epigrams.

[2] This seems to be especially true of *HN*. John Manningham entered in his diary, obviously from memory, a version of 'A lame begger' (31 March 1603; Harley MS. 5353). Some of the epigrams are occasionally found in commonplace books and miscellanies; I mention in the Commentary any in which I have encountered them. A few other epigrams are found ascribed explicitly or by implication to Donne; they are trivial and uncharacteristic and cannot be ascribed to him on the evidence of one manuscript or miscellany alone.

[3] The *Epigrams* probably circulated, to some extent, in groups. Group II has its thirteen and *DC* its nine in the same order as they are in *W*, if the extra epigrams in *W* are removed. Six of the ten in *B* are in the same order as in *W*, and there is almost as close a resemblance in the order in *O'F*.

[4] Five of the poems included by Miss Gardner in her edition of the *Divine Poems* might also be classified as verse letters: 'To Mrs. Magdalen Herbert: of St. Mary Magdalen', 'To E. of D. with six holy Sonnets', 'To Mr. Tilman after he had taken orders', 'To Mr. George Herbert, with my seal, of the Anchor and Christ', and 'The Cross' (which, as Miss Gardner suggests, pp. xxi, 92, is more a verse letter than a divine poem). The 'Epitaph' is added to the letters in my text, making the total thirty-eight.

[5] There is, however, a leaf in *A 23* which once formed part of a duplicate of the whole, or a part, of *W*; it contains six short letters, including two of these three to 'Mr R. W.' *W* supplies our only copy of ll. 5–6 in 'To T. W.' ('Hast thee harsh verse') and of ll. 11–12 in 'To Mr I. L.' ('Blest are your North parts').

[6] They are all found in *TCD* and in *DC* with practically the same text; 'The Storm' and 'The Calm', now missing from *TCC*, were once included in it (see p. xliii, n. 5).

supplement the Group III collection. The other seven occur now
and then in other Group III manuscripts, and all of them in *Lut* and
O'F; while six are found in manuscripts of Group I. All these are
letters to Donne's men friends. Of the later letters, that to Wotton
fighting in Ireland was preserved only in *Bur*.[1] The letter written
jointly by Donne and Goodyer is found only in *A 25*; the letter to
Wotton as he left for Venice occurs in Group II (and *DC*), *Lut*, *O'F*
(and two other manuscripts, the miscellanies *La* and *HK 2*); but
those to Goodyer and Edward Herbert were much more widely
copied.

The largest collection of letters to ladies is found in *TCD* and in
the part of *DC* most closely connected with Group II.[2] The basic
Group II collection (*Υ*), however, contained only the letter 'To Mrs
M. H.', and possibly also that to the Countess of Bedford beginning
'You that are she and you'.[3] In *TCD* the collection in *Υ* was enlarged
by the addition of five letters to the Countess of Bedford and those
to Lady Carey, the Countess of Huntingdon ('Man to Gods image'),
and the Countess of Salisbury. The last two, and two to Lady
Bedford ('T'have written then' and 'This twilight of two yeares'),
are found outside Group II only in *Lut* and *O'F*, and are among the
poems taken by the compilers of these manuscripts from a Group II
collection; another letter to the Countess of Bedford appears also
in *Dob*, *S 96*, in *B*, and in *HK 1*. The other three letters added by
TCD, like the letter to 'Mrs M. H.' and 'You that are she and you',
were much more widely circulated.[4]

A study of the text of verse letters that occur in more than one
of the main groups of manuscripts (taking *W* and its partial copy,
A 23, as a separate group) suggests that the traditions of the text

[1] The Burley MS., since destroyed by fire, is described in L. Pearsall Smith's *Life and
Letters of Sir Henry Wotton* (1907), ii. 489–90; see also Grierson, ii, pp. cx–cxi, and Simpson,
Prose Works, pp. 300 ff., 307, 319–20.

[2] Each manuscript has one letter to the Countess of Bedford which the other lacks, *TCD*
omitting the unfinished letter 'begun in France', and *DC* omitting 'You that are she and you'.
The texts of the manuscripts are very close to one another, and the order of the whole collection of letters is the same, except that the letters to the Countess of Salisbury and to Lady
Carey appear earlier in *DC*, and two letters to Wotton appear earlier in *TCD*.

[3] The omission of this letter (probably by accident), and of a verse letter not by
Donne which immediately follows, breaks the run of poems in *TCC* which it shares with
TCD.

[4] The two remaining letters addressed to great ladies, one 'To the Countess of Huntington'
('That unripe side of earth'), and the 'Epitaph' addressed to the Countess of Bedford, raise
special problems, discussed in the Commentary and in Appendix D.

ERRATA

p. lxvii, *note 2, l. 6, read* 'HK 2.'

p. 5, *2nd line from bottom, read* 'me'and]

p. 31, *4th line from bottom, read* 'uncorrected'

p. 54, *2nd line from bottom, read* 'castrat^e'

p. 67, *4th line from bottom, read* 'Lethe', *1633*'

p. 90, *last line, read* 'of *Dob*'

p. 105, *3rd line from bottom, read* 'La: Co: of C:'

p. 115, *l. 24, read* 'then').'

p. 131, *l. 29, for* 'pinot' *read* 'point'

p. 202, *ll. 26–27, for* 'Lincoln's Inn' *read* 'the Court'

p. 203, *l. 20, for* 'Anne' *read* 'Ann'

p. 224, *l. 29, for* 'forti' *read* 'fortis'

p. 235, *l. 24, for* '1628' *read* '1627'

derive from one copy, or (probably at most) two copies, taken from the original; these copies were variously corrupted in the course of transmission, those in *W*, in *TCD-DC*, and in Group I being generally much more sound than other copies used in compiling Group III manuscripts. In these last there is much carelessness and a good deal of sophistication; even in the letters added in *Lut* and *O'F* from Group II to those normally found in Group III there is a certain amount of 'improvement' of the text.[1] The occurrence of letters in the different groups, among the members of each group, and in the order of contents in many manuscripts, seems to be largely accidental, and the textual history of any one letter is not necessarily the same as that of another. At times, copies of one or more letters seem to have been made by selection from a larger group in the exemplar, or according to the chance of their having become available; even within some collections there is evidence that the letters each contains are not all from the same tradition.[2]

Some letters at least, however, were transmitted as a group. A number of early verse letters to men friends seem to have been copied from the same original into *W*, and into an ancestor of Group II (thence into *Lut, O'F*). Again, the Countess of Bedford seems to have allowed copies to be taken, probably on more than one occasion, of all or some of the letters (and other poems) sent to her by Donne;[3] most of these appear to have been transmitted through (and some only through) Group II collections, eventually reaching the fullest collection of all, *O'F*. Only one other small group of poems seems to have been brought together early in the process of copying. 'The Storm' and 'The Calm' (as in *Q̲ , D16, A 25*) became attached

---

[1] I believe that in the verse letters we are dealing with good and less good copies of the same original text, and not, as Grierson suggested (ii, pp. cxix n., 154, 173), with copies of an original and of a revised authentic version.

[2] In most letters the variants are too few or too trivial to allow firm deductions as to textual relationship. Nevertheless, among the manuscripts loosely called Group III by Grierson, the sub-groups observed by Miss Gardner in the text of the Love Poems also hold in the text of the verse letters shared by members of each sub-group: namely, a more precisely defined Group III—*Dob, Lut, O'F, S 96* (eleven letters); and a group consisting of *Cy, O, P* (sharing nine letters) and (in five letters) *HK 2, A 25, B, JC*, and *S* are unclassifiable, having all derived their texts from a variety of sources. It is fair to say that the texts of verse letters in all manuscripts are generally much better than the text of the *Satires*. In the four, and three, letters which they respectively contain, *H 40* and *RP 31* show the same relationship to each other and to Group I evident in the text of the love lyrics.

[3] Donne does not seem normally to have kept copies of his verse letters since, when he thought of publishing his poems, he speaks of the difficulty of getting hold of copies. See *Letters*, p. 197.

to the *Satires*; but they also occur, in many manuscripts, with two letters to Wotton ('Sir, more then kisses' and 'Here's no more newes'), often associated with a letter to Woodward ('Like one who'in her third widdowhood'), either as a run, or in close proximity. It would seem that, having been composed at about the same time, they remained together among Donne's, or a friend's, papers long enough for one or more copies to be taken of them as a set.

II. THE EDITIONS

The first (posthumous) edition of Donne's collected poems was published in 1633.[1] The main sources of the text were, as Grierson showed, a manuscript of Group I, supplemented by a manuscript of Group II, and by reprints of the 'Elegy on Prince Henry' and the two *Anniversaries*. From his Group I manuscript the printer took the *Satires*, *Metempsychosis*, and eleven verse letters. Seventeen other letters, inserted between the ninth and tenth of these, were taken from the Group II manuscript, and another letter from it called 'Elegie to the Lady Bedford' ('You that are she and you') occurs by itself 180 pages further on. The *Epigrams* also come from the Group II text; but the edition prints three more epigrams than are found in *TCD*, the fullest extant Group II manuscript. Either the Group II manuscript used had some extra poems, or the 'editor' of *1633* found these three epigrams, along with a few other poems not in our extant manuscripts of Groups I and II, in some other source.

Study of the text of *1633* reveals that the Group I manuscript used was very close to *C 57*, and that the Group II manuscript, though like *TCD*, was even closer to *DC*, which sometimes agrees with *1633* against the surviving Group II manuscripts. The text of *1633* is, however, superior to that in any surviving single manuscript of either group, and evidence from the text of poems in this volume supports Miss Gardner's conclusions from her study of the Love Poems. It is now clear that *1633* was very carefully edited. Readings from the Group II manuscript were imported into poems primarily based on the Group I manuscript. Deficiencies in the copy not remediable in this way were made good by reference

---

[1] Other seventeenth-century editions appeared in 1635, 1639, 1649, 1650, 1654, and 1669.

to some other source. And when all else failed, the editor of *1633* did a certain amount of emending, on his own authority, to adjust both meaning and rhythm to his own satisfaction.

The text of the *Satires* in *1633* is that of the version in *C 57*, *Lec*, *L 74*, and *TCD*, though none of these manuscripts can have provided the printer's copy. The printed text is closest to *C 57*, sharing nineteen readings with *Lec* and *C 57* against *L 74* and *TCD*, but avoiding errors made in *Lec* but not in *C 57*; it is also closer to *C 57* in spelling than to any other manuscript. In certain readings the printer's copy was superior to *C 57*, and some of these could have been obtained from a Group II manuscript with a text like that in *TCD*.[1] On the other hand, *1633* makes a number of errors of its own; indeed, whenever it goes against the combined authority of the manuscripts containing this version it is wrong, except for three obvious emendations not beyond the powers of the editor. On the whole the text of *1633* is not so strikingly superior in the *Satires* as it is elsewhere to the text one could construct from the surviving manuscripts. This is very probably due to the delay in receiving permission to print the *Satires*,[2] and the consequent haste with which their text was set up in the last formes of the volume. The *1633* text is, however, at least as good as that in any surviving manuscript, and provides far better than any of them the accidents of the text. Since *1633* also, I believe, has the text of Donne's final revision, I take it as the copy-text for the *Satires*.

The text of the *Metempsychosis* in *1633* is also closest to *C 57* among the surviving manuscripts, and, like *C 57*, *1633* begins with this poem. Efforts were made to correct the text as the copy went through the press, but a study of uncorrected formes shows that the manuscript from which the poem was originally set up had not only all (except perhaps one) of the errors and defects of the original of Group II and *C 57*, but also others found elsewhere only in the text of *C 57* (e.g. the omission of 'his race', l. 220). The printer's copy was occasionally subjected to editorial emendation (e.g. the insertion of 'leagues o'erpast' to complete l. 296) and was corrected

---

[1] *DC* inexplicably omits the *Satires*.

[2] The entry in the Stationers' Register recording permission to print the book (13 September 1632) 'excepts' the 'five *satires*'; they were allowed in an entry of 31 October 1632.

(sometimes as the book went through the press) either from conjecture, or from the supplementary manuscript which the editor used elsewhere.[1] Apart from these remediable faults, *1633* offers the modern editor a better copy-text than any manuscript extant.

In the *Epigrams* and verse letters which it contains *1633* similarly commends itself as the appropriate copy-text. The editor has worked over the text with consistent care; one is never left in much doubt about his procedures, and his work can be checked and, where necessary, corrected with the aid of the manuscripts.

In the second edition of Donne's poems, in 1635, a rearrangement of the contents was made under the headings devised in *Lut* and copied in *O'F*. The Epistle introducing the *Metempsychosis* was left at the beginning, but the poem itself was placed 300 pages later; the *Epigrams* were inserted between the *Songs and Sonnets* and the *Elegies*; and the *Satires* were moved to a position after the *Elegies* and marriage poems, and immediately before the verse letters, these last being all collected under the title 'Letters to severall Personages'. Twenty-eight poems were added to those taken from *1633*, including a verse letter to the Countess of Huntingdon ('That unripe side of earth') and the Latin letter to Dr. Andrews, and also two forms of the 'Epitaph', one among the funeral poems and one among the *Divine Poems*. For these *1635* serves as the best copy-text.[2] The poems taken from *1633* were not simply reprinted in *1635*, but were revised with the help of *O'F*; in these poems, as Miss Gardner showed,[3] the *1635* text is a rather haphazard conflation of *1633* and *O'F*. This has meant that, in the text of the *Satires*, not only two textual traditions, but two authentic versions also, have been confused. While *1635* is sometimes helpful in improving the punctuation of *1633*, it cannot, in the poems shared by the two editions, be thought to have any independent authority.

The only other seventeenth-century editions that are of interest here are those of 1649 and 1650. In the first the lines on Coryate's

---

[1] His Group II manuscript was of little use in correcting the copy in his Group I manuscript, since it shared the main deficiencies of the Group I manuscript.

[2] I use the accidentals of *1635* also for some lines prudentially omitted from the *Satires* in *1633*.

[3] *Divine Poems*, pp. lxxxvii–xc. See also below, Appendix A.

Crudities (excluding the macaronic quatrain) were reprinted from Coryate's book (1611); the second added a reprint of Donne's Latin epigram to Jonson on *Volpone*, and also the first surviving text of the translation from Gazaeus.

III. CONCLUSIONS

(1)

Apart from poems not included in the collected editions in the seventeenth century, the copy-text for each poem is the first printed text. For the great bulk of the poems this will be the text of *1633*. While this edition is superior to any single manuscript, however, it must be corrected from the manuscripts. It must be corrected where it misprints or has obviously misread the manuscript that it is following. In addition, readings in which *1633* follows *C 57* and *Lec* against the other manuscripts of Group I must be regarded as errors derived from the Group I manuscript used in compiling *1633*, and must be corrected. Further, any readings in *1633* that do not have manuscript support must be regarded as editorial emendations and (unless the reasons that would appear to have swayed the first editor are still valid)[1] must be rejected. In the *Satires 1633* must be emended primarily from within the group of manuscripts containing the same version, where the printed text fails properly to present it. In some places the result of an attempt to establish different versions of the *Satires* obliges an editor to accept as the final version a reading poetically inferior to that of an earlier version. But although all the texts containing the *1633* version are relatively careful, it is unlikely that there were no primitive errors in this tradition, and in a few places it has seemed better to assume the presence of such error and emend from another version. There must clearly be a strong argument to justify such a step, and any such readings are discussed in the Commentary. In the *Metempsychosis* the manuscript used for *1633* comes fairly well down in the line of descent; *a priori H, G,* or even *O'F* is as likely to give the correct reading at any point. The careful printing of *1633*, however, makes it the most suitable copy-text; but emendation

---

[1] As in 'To the Countess of Bedford' ('T'have written then'), l. 59.

must be made where *G* and *H*, or *G*, *H*, *O'F* agree against *1633*. Readings peculiar to *G* or *H* must also be considered when other manuscripts and *1633* seem to be corrupt or to give inferior sense; but readings peculiar to *O'F* must be treated with scepticism because of the scribe's carelessness on the one hand, and his readiness to sophisticate the text on the other. Where *G* or *H* differs from the other texts and is not demonstrably wrong, however, I record its reading in the apparatus. Of the more widely copied epigrams and verse letters Group III manuscripts offer a text which seems much further from Donne's originals than that in Groups I and II, and which must be rejected when *1633* has the support of Groups I and II. When Groups I and II differ, or when in the less widely copied poems the better manuscripts disagree among themselves, I have accepted or emended *1633* on my own judgement of the evidence.

Four English and two Latin epigrams, and six verse letters, not included in seventeenth-century editions, are printed from the best (in some cases, the only) manuscript copy.

In poems from editions I follow the spelling and usually the punctuation of the copy-text, but abandon long *ſ* and the ligatured *ɛt*; printers' contractions have been expanded; the use of *I, J, U,* and *V* has been modernized; and in titles the typography has been regularized. The punctuation has been emended sparingly; for the changes I have made there is nearly always warrant in one or more of the more careful manuscripts or in editions later than *1633*. For a few suggestions, however, I am indebted to Grierson, whose tact for making the punctuation of *1633* consistent within its own terms was admirable, and some of whose emendations have been confirmed by the punctuation of manuscripts that have come to our knowledge since he wrote. The use of elision-marks by the editor of *1633* is careful, though not consistent throughout the volume; he has thrown an obligation upon his successors to be at least as painstaking. Only in the text of the *Satires* does this become a serious problem. Permission to print them came late, and the text in *1633* shows signs of haste; the use of elision-marks, particularly, is sparing and rather erratic. It has been possible, however, to insert such marks in at any rate the more obvious places without unduly cluttering the apparatus. I have also marked genuine contractions where *1633* clearly fails to follow its usual practice.[1] In poems printed from manuscripts I have silently expanded contractions (e.g. *yᵗ* to *that*); and here (as in quotations from older texts, in the Commentary and elsewhere) I have also normalized the use of *i, j, u,* and *v* (to agree with *1633*, which follows modern usage in the lower case).

In the textual apparatus I name the copy-text for each poem, and the manuscripts from which readings are given. These manuscripts have been chosen to represent the groups in which the poem is found, or the main traditions of the text.[2] Where a manuscript has been corrected by someone after the scribe had finished his copying I give the original reading, adding '(*b.c.*)', that is, 'before correction'. *O'F* has been corrected twice, however, and in this case '(*b.c.*)' means 'before its correction to the reading of *1633*'. Readings quoted as being shared by the manuscripts representing a group or a version of the poem are normally those of all the manuscripts having that type of text; if not, the fact will be indicated by differences in the readings of the representative manuscripts. I have adopted Grierson's convenient siglum *TC* to show that the reading of *TCD* is also that of *TCC*; when they differ I quote each separately. In quoting variants I give the spelling of the first manuscript named (normalizing the use of *u* and *v*), unless the reading is adopted into the text, when it is made to conform to the style of *1633*; and differences in spelling among the manuscripts are ignored, unless there is some point in recording them.

The apparatus records all variations from the copy-text. Its more interesting, and perhaps more important, function, however, is to record, in the form of group readings, any variation in the text which could possibly be authentic (and in the *Satires* the changes that Donne might have made in revising his work). To this end it has been pruned of readings that can be proved wrong, and as far as possible of scribal errors and sophistications. An editor cannot, of course, be dogmatic about such things, and, although I do not think that a good many of the variants recorded are authentic, I

---

[1] See the note on versification prefixed to the Commentary.
[2] A list of all manuscripts in which I have encountered the poem begins the commentary upon it.

have included all those that might possibly be so. Readings of old editions later than the first are not given, having been based upon *1635*, the nature of whose text is shown in Appendix A. I quote readings from Grierson's edition of 1912, however, where it differs from mine.

I have collated eleven copies of *1633*[1] for press variants, and those I have discovered are noted in the apparatus. I print from the corrected state, except for the editorial sophistications in *Metempsychosis*, ll. 17 and 137 and in the letter 'To Mr T. W.' ('All haile sweet Poët'), ll. 14–15. Any titles given in the manuscripts are recorded, sometimes (to avoid over-burdening the apparatus) in the Commentary.

(ii)

I have printed the poems in an order which will, I hope, seem more logical than that in former editions (except R. E. Bennett's), for which there was no particular authority. The *Satires* are followed by the other satirical poems in chronological sequence. The *Epigrams* come next, printed in the order of *W*, the only manuscript in which they all occur, and which might be as authoritative in this respect as in others. Then follow 'The Storm' and 'The Calm', which, though not strictly verse letters, are normally grouped with them, and which in Groups I and II and in some Group III manuscripts begin the collection of letters. The letters to men follow, the majority in the order of *W*, and then the letters to ladies grouped according to the recipients. In the whole series as printed there is perhaps not much dislocation, except in a few obvious places, in the order of their composition. The Latin poems and the translation from Gazaeus are placed in a separate section.

---

[1] British Museum (2), Bodleian Library (2), Victoria and Albert Museum (2; one each in the Dyce and Forster collections); Christ Church, Corpus Christi, St. John's, Wadham, and Worcester Colleges, Oxford.

LIST OF SIGLA

Classified List of Manuscripts of the Satires, Epigrams, *and* Verse Letters

(i) MSS. containing collections of Donne's poems

GROUP I

C 57 Cambridge University Library, Add. MS. 5778.

D Dowden MS. Bodleian Library, MS. Eng. Poet. e 99 (formerly in the library of Mr. Wilfred Merton).

H 49 British Museum, Harleian MS. 4955.

Lec Leconfield MS. In the library of Sir Geoffrey Keynes.

SP St. Paul's Cathedral Library, MS. 49 B 43.

H 40 British Museum, Harleian MS. 4064.

GROUP II

A 18 British Museum, Add. MS. 18647.

N Norton MS. Harvard College Library, MS. Eng. 966/3 (formerly MS. Nor. 4503).

TCC Trinity College, Cambridge, MS. R 3 12.

TCD Trinity College, Dublin, MS. G 2 21.

L 74 British Museum, Lansdowne MS. 740.

DC National Library of Wales, Dolau Cothi MS.

GROUP III

A 25 British Museum, Add. MS. 25707.

B Bridgewater MS. Huntington Library, MS. EL 6893.

C Cambridge University Library, Add. MS. 29.

Cy Carnaby MS. Harvard College Library, MS. Eng. 966/1 (formerly MS. Nor. 4502).

Dob Dobell MS. Harvard College Library, MS. Eng. 966/4 (formerly MS. Nor. 4506).

D 17 Victoria and Albert Museum, Dyce Collection, MS. D 25 F 17.

JC John Cave MS. George Arents Tobacco Collection, New York Public Library. (Formerly in the library of Mr. Richard Jennings.)

K   King MS. In the library of Mr. James Osborn, Yale University. (Raphael King, Catalogue 51, Item 73.)

Lut   Luttrell MS. In the library of Sir Geoffrey Keynes.

O'F¹   O'Flaherty MS. Harvard College Library, MS. Eng. 966/5 (formerly MS. Nor. 4504).

O   Osborn MS. In the library of Mr. James Osborn, Yale University.

P   Phillipps MS. Bodleian Library, MS. Eng. Poet. f 9.

S   Stephens MS. Harvard College Library, MS. Eng. 966/6 (formerly MS. Nor. 4500).

S 96   British Museum, Stowe MS. 961.

IV

W   Westmoreland MS. Berg Collection, New York Public Library.

(ii) MSS. with copies of single poems, or limited or fragmentary collections

(*a*) *MSS. of* 'The Progress of the Soul' ('Metempsychosis')

G   Gosse MS. In the Folger Shakespeare Library.

H   British Museum, Harleian MS. 3998.

(*b*) *MS. collections wholly, or mainly, of the* Satires

D 16   Victoria and Albert Museum, Dyce Collection, MS. D 25 F 16.

H 51   British Museum, Harleian MS. 5110.

Q   The Queen's College, Oxford, MS. 216.

(*c*) *Fragmentary MSS.*

A 23   British Museum, Harleian MS. 23229.

(iii) MSS. containing Donne's poems with those of other authors

A 10   British Museum, Add. MS. 10309.

A 30   British Museum, Add. MS. 30982.

A 34   British Museum, Add. MS. 34744.

Ash   Bodleian Library, MS. Ashmole 38.

Ash 47 Bodleian Library, MS. Ashmole 47.

---

¹ *O'F* (*b.c.*): O'Flaherty (before correction). This indicates that the reading cited has been corrected to the reading of *1633*.

Bur   Burley MS., destroyed; partly preserved in transcript, Bodleian Library.

D 54   Bodleian Library, MS. Don c 54.

E 22   British Museum, Egerton MS. 2230.

H 39   British Museum, Harleian MS. 3910.

HK 1   Haslewood-Kingsborough MS., first part. Huntington Library MS. HM 198.

HK 2   Haslewood-Kingsborough MS., second part. Huntington Library, MS. HM 198.

HN   Hawthornden MS. National Library of Scotland, MS. 2067.

La   Edinburgh University Library, Laing MS. iii 493.

RP 117(1) Bodleian Library, Rawlinson Poetical MS. 117, first part.

RP 31   Bodleian Library, Rawlinson Poetical MS. 31.

S 962   British Museum, Stowe MS. 962.

TCD(2) Trinity College, Dublin, MS. G 2 21, second part.

Wy   Wyburd MS. Bodleian Library, MS. Don b 9.

The editions of Donne's poems from 1633 to 1669 are cited under their dates, as *1633*, *1635*, etc.

The Poems of John Donne, ed. H. J. C. Grierson, 2 vols. (Oxford, 1912), is cited as *Gr*.

TCC and *TCD*, when they agree, are cited as *TC*; when they disagree, they are cited separately.

The symbol Σ is used in the apparatus and the Commentary when the great majority of manuscripts agree in a reading, and applies to all named in the apparatus but those specifically excepted.

JOHN DONNE
From the portrait in the Deanery of St. Paul's Cathedral, by
kind permission of the Very Reverend the Dean

SATIRES
EPIGRAMS
AND
VERSE
LETTERS

SATYRES

Satyre I

A WAY thou fondling motley humorist,
Leave mee, and in this standing woodden chest,
Consorted with these few bookes, let me lye
In prison, and here be coffin'd, when I dye;
Here are Gods conduits, grave Divines; and here   5
Natures Secretary, the Philosopher;
And jolly Statesmen, which teach how to tie
The sinewes of a cities mistique bodie;
Here gathering Chroniclers, and by them stand
Giddie fantastique Poëts of each land.   10
Shall I leave all this constant company,
And follow headlong, wild uncertaine thee?
First sweare by thy best love in earnest
(If thou which lov'st all, canst love any best)
Thou wilt not leave mee in the middle street,   15
Though some more spruce companion thou dost meet,
Not though a Captaine do come in thy way
Bright parcell gilt, with forty dead mens pay,
Nor though a briske perfum'd piert Courtier
Deigne with a nod, thy courtesie to answer,   20
Nor come a velvet Justice with a long
Great traine of blew coats, twelve, or fourteen strong,
Wilt thou grin or fawne on him, or prepare
A speech to court his beautious sonne and heire.
For better or worse take mee, or leave mee: 25

SATYRES. *Text from 1633, with paragraphing and with quotation marks and terminal punctuation for direct speech supplied. Readings are given from representative MSS. named in the apparatus. For variants in titles see Commentary.*

Satyre I. *MSS.: C 57, L 74, and TCD; H 49 and W; O'F and Q.*   1 fondling]
changeling *H 49, W, O'F, Q*   5 conduits, . . . Divines;] conduits; . . . Divines, *1633*
6 Philosopher;] Philosopher. *1633*   16 dost] do *W, Q*   19 Nor *Σ*: Not *1633, C 57,*
Q, Gr   20 courtesie] Courtsies *O'F, Q*   answer,] answer. *1633*   23 Wilt]
Shalt *H 49, W, O'F, Q*   24 court] Court *1633*   heire.] heire? *1633*   25 or worse]
and worse *H 49, W*

To take, and leave mee is adultery.
Oh monstrous, superstitious puritan,
Of refin'd manners, yet ceremoniall man,
That when thou meet'st one, with enquiring eyes
Dost search, and like a needy broker prize   30
The silke, and gold he weares, and to that rate
So high or low, dost raise thy formall hat:
That wilt consort none, untill thou have knowne
What lands hee hath in hope, or of his owne,
As though all thy companions should make thee   35
Jointures, and marry thy deare company.
Why should'st thou (that dost not onely approve,
But in ranke itchie lust, desire, and love
The nakednesse and barenesse to enjoy,
Of thy plumpe muddy whore, or prostitute boy)   40
Hate vertue, though shee be naked, and bare?
At birth, and death, our bodies naked are;
And till our Soules be unapparrelled
Of bodies, they from blisse are banished.
Mans first blest state was naked, when by sinne   45
Hee lost that, yet hee'was cloath'd but in beasts skin,
And in this course attire, which I now weare,
With God, and with the Muses I conferre.
    But since thou like a contrite penitent,
Charitably warn'd of thy sinnes, dost repent   50
These vanities, and giddinesses, loe
I shut my chamber doore, and 'Come, lets goe.'
But sooner may a cheape whore, that hath beene
Worne by as many severall men in sinne,
As are black feathers, or musk-colour hose,   55
Name her childs right true father, 'mongst all those:

---

27 monstrous] monster *H 49, W*   29 eyes] eyes; *1633 uncorrected*   32 raise]
vaile *W, O'F, Q*   hat] hate *1633 uncorrected*   37–40 thou (that . . . boy)] thou that
. . . boy *1633*   39 barenesse *H 49, W, O'F, Q*: barrennesse *1633, C 57, L 74, TCD*
40 Of] of *1633 uncorrected*   41 bare?] bare: *1633*: bare, *1633 uncorrected*   45 blest]
best *O'F, Q*   46 hee'was] hee was *1633*   47 I now] now I *W, O'F, Q*   weare,]
weare *1633*   50 warn'd] warm'd *1633 uncorrected*   52 'Come, lets goe.'] come,
lets goe, *1633*   53 that *Σ*: who *1633, O'F, Gr*   55 musk-colour] muske-
colourd *O'F, Q*   56 right true father, 'mongst] true father amongst *O'F, Q*

Sooner may one guesse, who shall beare away
Th'Infant of London, Heire to'an India:
And sooner may a gulling weather-Spie
By drawing forth heavens Scheame tell certainly　　　60
What fashion'd hats, or ruffes, or suits next yeare
Our subtile-witted antique youths will weare;
Then thou, when thou depart'st from mee, canst show
Whither, why, when, or with whom thou wouldst go.
But how shall I be pardon'd my offence　　　65
That thus have sinn'd against my conscience?
　　Now we are in the street; He first of all
Improvidently proud, creepes to the wall,
And so imprison'd, and hem'd in by mee
Sells for a little state his libertie;　　　70
Yet though he cannot skip forth now to greet
Every fine silken painted foole we meet,
He them to him with amorous smiles allures,
And grins, smacks, shrugs, and such an itch endures,
As prentises, or schoole-boyes which doe know　　　75
Of some gay sport abroad, yet dare not goe.
And as fidlers stop low'st, at highest sound,
So to the most brave, stoops hee nigh'st the ground.
But to a grave man, he doth move no more
Then the wise politique horse would heretofore,　　　80
Or thou O Elephant or Ape wilt doe,
When any names the King of Spaine to you.
Now leaps he upright, joggs me,'and cryes, 'Do'you see
Yonder well favour'd youth?' 'Which?' 'Oh, 'tis hee
That dances so divinely.' 'Oh,' said I,　　　85

58 Th'] The *1633*　Infant] infant *1633*: Infanta *O'F, Q, Gr*　to'an] to an *1633*　India:]
India, *1633*　　59 weather-Spie] weather Spie *1633 uncorrected*　　60 Scheame *H 49,
W, O'F, Q*: Scheames *L 74*: Sceanes *1633, C 57, TCD*　　61 fashion'd] fashioned *1633*
62 subtile-witted *H 49*: subtile wittied *1633, C 57, L 74, TCD*: supple-witted *W, O'F, Q*
63 depart'st from mee] departst from hence *W*: departest from hence *H 49*: departest hence
O'F, Q　canst *TCD, W, O'F, Q*: can *1633, Σ*　　64 when] where *Q*　　65 my] mine
O'F, Q　　66 conscience?] conscience. *1633*　　69 imprison'd] imprisoned *1633*
70 his *MSS.*: high *1633*　libertie;] libertie, *1633*　　73 them *MSS.*: then *1633*
77 low'st] lowest *1633*　　78 stoops *H 49, W, O'F, Q*: stoopt *1633, C 57, L 74, TCD*
nigh'st the] nighest *H 49, W, Q*　　81–82 *From MSS.: omit 1633*　　83 joggs]
Joggs *1633*　me,'and] me, and *1633*　Do'you] Do you *1633*　　84 favour'd] favoured
1633　youth?] yo uth; *1633 uncorrected*　Oh] yea *W, Q*

'Stand still, must you dance here for company?'
Hee droopt, wee went, till one (which did excell
Th'Indians, in drinking his Tobacco well)
Met us; they talk'd; I whisper'd, 'Let us goe,
'T may be you smell him not, truely I doe.'   90
He heares not mee, but, on the other side
A many-colour'd Peacock having spide,
Leaves him and mee; I for my lost sheep stay;
He followes, overtakes, goes on the way,
Saying, 'Him whom I last left, all repute   95
For his device, in hansoming a sute,
To judge of lace, pinke, panes, print, cut, and plight,
Of all the Court, to have the best conceit.'
'Our dull Comedians want him, let him goe;
But Oh, God strengthen thee, why stoop'st thou so?'   100
'Why? he hath travail'd.' 'Long?' 'No, but to me'
(Which understand none,) 'he doth seeme to be
Perfect French, and Italian.' I reply'd,
'So is the Poxe.' He answer'd not, but spy'd
More men of sort, of parts, and qualities;   105
At last his Love he in a windowe spies,
And like light dew exhal'd, he flings from mee
Violently ravish'd to his lechery.
Many were there, he could command no more;
He quarrell'd, fought, bled; and turn'd out of dore   110
    Directly came to mee hanging the head,
    And constantly a while must keepe his bed.

89 Met us;] Met us, *1633*   whisper'd, 'Let] whispered, let *1633*   90 'T may] May *H 49*, *W*, *O'F*, *Q*   92 colour'd] coloured *1633*   94 on] in *W*, *Q*   95 Him] him *1633*   all *Σ*: s'all *1633*, *C 57*, *L 74*   97 print, cut, and plight] Cutt, Print, or Plight *H 49*, *W*, *O'F*, *Q*   101 'Why? he hath travail'd.' 'Long?' 'No] Why, he hath travailed long? no *1633*   102 (Which . . . none,)] Which . . . none, *1633*; *see note*   103 reply'd] replyed *1633*   104 answer'd] answered *1633*   105 and] of *Q*   108 lechery. *MSS.*: liberty; *1633*

Satyre II

SIR; though (I thanke God for it) I do hate
Perfectly all this towne, yet there's one state
In all ill things so excellently best,
That hate, towards them, breeds pitty towards the rest.
Though Poëtry indeed be such a sinne   5
As I thinke that brings dearths, and Spaniards in,
Though like the Pestilence and old fashion'd love,
Ridlingly it catch men; and doth remove
Never, till it be sterv'd out; yet their state
Is poore, disarm'd, like Papists, not worth hate.   10
One, (like a wretch, which at Barre judg'd as dead,
Yet prompts him which stands next, and cannot reade,
And saves his life) gives ideot actors meanes
(Starving himselfe) to live by'his labor'd sceanes;
As in some Organ, Puppits dance above   15
And bellows pant below, which them do move.
One would move Love by rimes; but witchcrafts charms
Bring not now their old feares, nor their old harmes:
Rammes, and slings now are seely battery,
Pistolets are the best Artillerie.   20
And they who write to Lords, rewards to get,
Are they not like singers at doores for meat?
And they who write, because all write, have still
That excuse for writing, and for writing ill.
But hee is worst, who (beggarly) doth chaw   25
Others wits fruits, and in his ravenous maw
Rankly digested, doth those things out-spue,
As his owne things; 'and they are his owne, 'tis true,

Satyre II. *MSS.*: *C 57, L 74 and TCD*; *H 49 and W*; *O'F and Q.*   4 towards them
Σ: toward . . . *1633, L 74, Gr*   rest.] rest; *1633*   6 dearths *C 57, L 74, TCD, W*:
dearth *1633, H 49, O'F, Q*   7 and] or *H 49, W, O'F, Q*   8 Ridlingly it] It ridlingly
W, Q: It riddinglye *H 49, O'F*   10 hate.] hate: *1633*   12 cannot] could not *W, H 49,
O'F, Q*   14 by'his] by his *1633*   sceanes;] sceanes. *1633*   15 Organ] Organes
H 49, W, Q   17 rimes] *spelt* rithmes *1633*   witchcrafts] witchcraft *H 49, O'F, Q*
18 harmes:] harmes. *1633*   22 singers at doores] Singers at dore *O'F*: boyes singing at
dores *W, H 49, Q* (at a doore)   24 excuse] 'scuse *O'F*: scuse *H 49, W, Q*   ill.] ill; *1633*
27 Rankly] Rawly *W (corrected from* Rankly), *H 49*   28 'and] and *1633*

For if one eate my meate, though it be knowne
The meate was mine, th'excrement is his owne.   30
But these do mee no harme, nor they which use
To out-doe Dildoes, and out-usure Jewes;
To'out-drinke the sea, to'out-sweare the Letanie;
Who with sinnes all kindes as familiar bee
As Confessors; and for whose sinfull sake   35
Schoolemen new tenements in hell must make:
Whose strange sinnes, Canonists could hardly tell
In which Commandements large receit they dwell.
　　But these punish themselves; the insolence
Of Coscus onely breeds my just offence,   40
Whom time (which rots all, and makes botches poxe,
And plodding on, must make a calfe an oxe)
Hath made a Lawyer, which was (alas) of late
But a scarce Poët; jollier of this state,
Then are new benefic'd ministers, he throwes   45
Like nets, or lime-twigs, wheresoere he goes,
His title'of Barrister, on every wench,
And wooes in language of the Pleas, and Bench:
'A motion, Lady.' 'Speake Coscus.' 'I'have beene
In love, ever since *tricesimo*'of the Queene,   50
Continuall claimes I'have made, injunctions got
To stay my rivals suit, that hee should not
Proceed.' 'Spare mee.' 'In Hillary terme I went,
You said, If I returne next size in Lent,
I should be in remitter of your grace;   55
In th'interim my letters should take place
Of affidavits—': words, words, which would teare
The tender labyrinth of a soft maids eare,

30 owne.] owne: *1633*   32 out-doe] outswive *H 49*, *W*, *O'F*   Dildoes *From MSS.*: omit (*with semi colon before* and) *1633*   33 To'out-drinke] To out-drinke *1633*   to'out-sweare] to out-sweare *1633*: outsweare *H 49*, *W*, *Q*   Letanie *From MSS.*: omit *1633*   34 all *Σ*: of all *1633*, *C 57*   36 Schoolemen] Schoolemen, *1633*   40 just] greate *H 49*, *W*, *O'F*, *Q*   43 Lawyer,] Lawyer; *1633*   (alas)] alas *1633*   44 a scarce *Σ*: scarce a *1633*, *C 57*, *O'F*   Poët;] Poët, *1633*   46 *Omit H 49*, *W*   wheresoere *Σ*: wheresoever *1633*, *Gr*: where ere *Q*   47 title'of] title of *1633*   49 Lady.] Lady, *1633*   I'have] I have *1633*   50 *tricesimo*'of] *tricesimo* of *1633*   51 I'have] I have *1633*   53 Proceed.] Proceed, *1633*   Spare] spare *1633*   54 returne] Returne *1633*: return'd *H 49*, *W*, *O'F*, *Q*, *Gr*   next] this *H 49*, *W*, *Q*   57 affidavits—] affidavits *1633* 58 eare,] eare. *1633*

More, more, then ten Sclavonians scolding, more
Then when winds in our ruin'd Abbeyes rore.   60
When sicke with Poëtrie,'and possest with muse
Thou wast, and mad, I hop'd; but men which chuse
Law practise for meere gaine, bold soule, repute
Worse then imbrothel'd strumpets prostitute.
Now like an owlelike watchman, hee must walke   65
His hand still at a bill, now he must talke
Idly, like prisoners, which whole months will sweare
That onely suretiship hath brought them there,
And to'every suitor lye in every thing,
Like a Kings favorite, yea like a King;   70
Like a wedge in a blocke, wring to the barre,
Bearing like Asses, and more shamelesse farre
Then carted whores, lye, to the grave Judge; for
Bastardy'abounds not in Kings titles, nor
Symonie'and Sodomy in Churchmens lives,   75
As these things do in him; by these he thrives.
Shortly ('as the sea) hee'will compasse all our land;
From Scots, to Wight; from Mount, to Dover strand.
And spying heires melting with luxurie,
Satan will not joy at their sinnes, as hee.   80
For as a thrifty wench scrapes kitching-stuffe,
And barrelling the droppings, and the snuffe,
Of wasting candles, which in thirty yeare
(Relique-like kept) perchance buyes wedding geare;
Peecemeale he gets lands, and spends as much time   85
Wringing each Acre, as men pulling prime.
In parchments then, large as his fields, hee drawes
Assurances, bigge, as gloss'd civill lawes,
So huge, that men (in our times forwardnesse)
Are Fathers of the Church for writing lesse.   90
These hee writes not; nor for these written payes,

60 rore.] rore; *1633*   61 Poëtrie,'and] Poëtrie, and *1633*   63 gaine, . . .
soule,] gaine; . . . soule *1633*   69-70 *From MSS.: omit 1633*   74-75 *From MSS.:*
omit 1633   75 'and] and *MSS.*   77 'as] as *1633*   hee'will] hee will *1633*   our
land *Σ*: the land *1633, Q*   79 luxurie] Gluttonye *H 49, W, O'F (b.c.)*   80 will]
would *Q*   84 Relique-like *Σ*: Reliquely *1633, C 57*   87 parchments *H 49, W,*
Q: parchment *1633, C 57, L 74, TCD, O'F*

Therefore spares no length; as in those first dayes
When Luther was profest, he did desire
Short *Pater nosters*, saying as a Fryer
Each day his beads, but having left those lawes,   95
Addes to Christs prayer, the Power and glory clause.
But when he sells or changes land, he'impaires
His writings, and (unwatch'd) leaves out, *ses heires*,
As slily'as any Commenter goes by
Hard words, or sense; or in Divinity   100
As controverters, in vouch'd Texts, leave out
Shrewd words, which might against them cleare the doubt.
Where are those spred woods which cloth'd hertofore
Those bought lands? not built, nor burnt within dore.
Where's th'old landlords troops, and almes? In great hals   105
Carthusian fasts, and fulsome Bachanalls
Equally'I hate; meanes blesse; in rich mens homes
I bid kill some beasts, but no Hecatombs,
None starve, none surfet so; But (Oh) we'allow
Good workes as good, but out of fashion now,   110
    Like old rich wardrops; but my words none drawes
    Within the vast reach of th'huge statute lawes.

Satyre III

K INDE pitty chokes my spleene; brave scorn forbids
    Those teares to issue which swell my eye-lids;
I must not laugh, nor weepe sinnes, and be wise,
Can railing then cure these worne maladies?
Is not our Mistresse faire Religion,   5
As worthy'of all our Soules devotion,

93 he] He *1633*   98 *heires,] heires 1633*   99 slily'as] slily as *1633*   by] by, *1633*
102 doubt.] doubt: *1633*   104 Those] these *TCD, H 49, W*   105 Where's] Where
H 49, W, O'F, Q   almes? In great hals *H 49, W, Q*: almes, great hals? *1633*: Almes, Great
Halls; *C 57*: almes? Great Halls *TCD*: Almes in Halls *L 74*: Almes? In halls *O'F*
107 Equally'I hate;] Equally I hate, *1633*   108 no] not *H 49, W, O'F, Q*   109
we'allow] we allow, *1633*

    Satyre III. *MSS.: C 57, L 74* and *TCD; H 49* and *W; O'F* and *Q*.   2 Those]
These *H 49, W, Q*   eye-lids;] eye-lids, *1633*   3 not] nor *W, O'F*   sinnes] sin *H 49,
W*   4 Can] May *H 49, W, O'F, Q*   6 worthy'of] worthy of *1633*

As vertue was to the first blinded age?
Are not heavens joyes as valiant to asswage
Lusts, as earths honour was to them? Alas,
As wee do them in meanes, shall they surpasse   10
Us in the end, and shall thy fathers spirit
Meete blinde Philosophers in heaven, whose merit
Of strict life may be'imputed faith, and heare
Thee, whom hee taught so easie wayes and neare
To follow, damn'd? O if thou dar'st, feare this;   15
This feare great courage, and high valour is.
Dar'st thou ayd mutinous Dutch, and dar'st thou lay
Thee in ships woodden Sepulchers, a prey
To leaders rage, to stormes, to shot, to dearth?
Dar'st thou dive seas, and dungeons of the earth?   20
Hast thou couragious fire to thaw the ice
Of frozen North discoveries? and thrise
Colder then Salamanders, like divine
Children in th'oven, fires of Spaine,'and the line,
Whose countries limbecks to our bodies bee,   25
Canst thou for gaine beare? and must every hee
Which cryes not, 'Goddesse,' to thy Mistresse, draw,
Or eate thy poysonous words? courage of straw!
O desperate coward, wilt thou seeme bold, and
To thy foes and his (who made thee to stand   30
Sentinell in his worlds garrison) thus yeeld,
And for forbidden warres, leave th'appointed field?
Know thy foes: The foule Devill, whom thou
Striv'st to please, for hate, not love, would allow
Thee faine, his whole Realme to be quit; and as   35
The worlds all parts wither away and passe,

7 to L 74, H 49, W, O'F, Q: in 1633, C 57, TCD   blinded] blinde H 49, W, Q
9 honour] honors H 49, W   13 be'imputed] be imputed 1633   14 so easie
wayes and] wayes easye and H 49, W, Q: wayes so easy and O'F   15 this;] this.
1633   16 is.] is; 1633   17 and dar'st] darest (or darst, durst) W, H 49, O'F, Q
22–23 discoveries?... Salamanders,] discoveries,... Salamanders? 1633   24 'and] and
1633   28 words?] words, 1633   31 Sentinell] Souldier H 49, W, O'F, Q   his]
this O'F, Q   32 forbidden] forbid W, O'F   33 foes: W: foes; H 49, O'F, Q:
foe, 1633, C 57, TCD: foe; L 74   Devill W, H 49, Q: devill h'is 1633, C 57: divell is
L 74: Devill, his TCD: Divell, hee O'F   34 Striv'st] Strivest 1633   please,] please:
1633   35 quit] ridde H 49, W, O'F, Q

So the worlds selfe, thy other lov'd foe, is
In her decrepit wayne, and thou loving this,
Dost love a wither'd and worne strumpet; last,
Flesh (it selfes death) and joyes which flesh can taste,   40
Thou lov'st; and thy faire goodly soule, which doth
Give this flesh power to taste joy, thou dost loath.
  Seeke true religion. O where? Mirreus
Thinking her unhous'd here, and fled from us,
Seekes her at Rome; there, because hee doth know   45
That shee was there a thousand yeares agoe,
He loves her ragges so, as wee here obey
The statecloth where the Prince sate yesterday.
Crants to such brave Loves will not be inthrall'd
But loves her onely, who'at Geneva's call'd   50
Religion, plaine, simple, sullen, yong,
Contemptuous, yet unhansome; As among
Lecherous humors, there is one that judges
No wenches wholsome, but course country drudges.
Graius stayes still at home here, and because   55
Some Preachers, vile ambitious bauds, and lawes
Still new like fashions, bid him thinke that shee
Which dwels with us, is onely perfect, hee
Imbraceth her, whom his Godfathers will
Tender to him, being tender, as Wards still   60
Take such wives as their Guardians offer, or
Pay valewes. Carelesse Phrygius doth abhorre
All, because all cannot be good, as one
Knowing some women whores, dares marry none.
Graccus loves all as one, and thinkes that so   65
As women do in divers countries goe
In divers habits, yet are still one kinde,
So doth, so is Religion; and this blind-
nesse too much light breeds; but unmoved thou

39 wither'd] withered *1633* 40 *omit H 49* selfes *Σ*: selfe *1633* 41 lov'st]
lovest *1633* 42 loath.] loath; *1633* 44 here] her *1633* 45 Rome;]
Rome, *1633* 47 her *Σ*: the *1633*, *C 57*, *L 74*, *TCD* 49 inthrall'd] inthralled
1633 50 who'at Geneva's] who at Geneva is *1633* 51 sullen] solemne *O'F, Q*
52 unhansome;] unhansome. *1633* 53 that] which *H 49*, *W*, *O'F, Q* 54 drudges.]
drudges: *1633* 57 bid *Σ*: bids *1633*, *C 57*, *L 74*, *TCD* 67 kinde,] kinde; *1633*

Of force must one, and forc'd but one allow;   70
And the right; aske thy father which is shee,
Let him aske his; though truth and falshood bee
Neare twins, yet truth a little elder is;
Be busie to seeke her, beleeve mee this,
Hee's not of none, nor worst, that seekes the best.   75
To'adore, or scorne an image, or protest,
May all be bad; doubt wisely; in strange way
To stand inquiring right, is not to stray;
To sleepe, or runne wrong, is. On a huge hill,
Cragged, and steep, Truth stands, and hee that will   80
Reach her, about must, and about must goe;
And what th'hills suddennes resists, winne so;
Yet strive so, that before age, deaths twilight,
Thy Soule rest, for none can worke in that night.
To will, implyes delay, therefore now doe: 85
Hard deeds, the bodies paines; hard knowledge too
The mindes indeavours reach, and mysteries
Are like the Sunne, dazling, yet plaine to'all eyes.
Keepe the truth which thou'hast found; men do not stand
In so'ill case here, that God hath with his hand   90
Sign'd Kings blanck-charters to kill whom they hate,
Nor are they Vicars, but hangmen to Fate.
Foole and wretch, wilt thou let thy Soule be ty'd
To mans lawes, by which she shall not be try'd
At the last day? Will it then boot thee   95
To say a Philip, or a Gregory,
A Harry, or a Martin taught thee this?
Is not this excuse for mere contraries,
Equally strong? cannot both sides say so?

---

75 that] which *H 49, W*   76 To'adore] To adore *1633*   77 wisely;] wisely, *1633*
78 stray] stay *H 49, Q*   79 is. On] is : on *1633*   huge] high *H 49, W, O'F, Q*
80 Cragged *L 74, TCD*: Cragg'd *1633*, *C 57*: Ragged *H 49, W, O'F*: Rugged *Q*   stands]
dwells *H 49, W, O'F, Q*   81 her] it *H 49, W, Q*   about must goe] about goe *MSS.*;
see note   82 th'hills] the hills *1633*   84 Soule] mynde *H 49, W, O'F, Q*   night.]
night, *1633*   85 doe:] doe *1633*   86 too] to *1633*   88 like] as *H 49, W,
O'F, Q*   to'all] to all *1633*   eyes.] eyes; *1633*   89 thou'hast] thou hast *1633*
90 so'ill] so ill *1633*   case here] *Σ*: case *1633, C 57, TCD*   93 ty'd] tyed *1633*
94 mans] mens *H 49, W*   try'd] tryed *1633*   95 Will] Oh will *H 49, W, Q, Gr*: Or
will *O'F*   boot] serve *H 49, W, O'F, Q*   97 thee] me *W*   99 strong?] strong *1633*

That thou may'st rightly'obey power, her bounds know;   100
Those past, her nature and name's chang'd; to be
Then humble to her is idolatrie;
As streames are, Power is; those blest flowers that dwell
At the rough streames calme head, thrive and prove well,
But having left their roots, and themselves given   105
To the streames tyrannous rage, alas, are driven
Through mills, and rockes, and woods,'and at last, almost
Consum'd in going, in the sea are lost:
   So perish Soules, which more chuse mens unjust
   Power from God claym'd, then God himselfe to trust.   110

Satyre IV

WELL; I may now receive, and die; My sinne
   Indeed is great, but I have beene in
A Purgatorie, such as fear'd hell is
A recreation to,'and scant map of this.
My minde, neither with prides itch, nor yet hath been   5
Poyson'd with love to see, or to bee seene,
I had no suit there, nor new suite to shew,
Yet went to Court; But as Glaze which did goe
To'a Masse in jest, catch'd, was faine to disburse
The hundred markes, which is the Statutes curse,   10
Before he scapt, So'it pleas'd my destinie
(Guilty'of my sin of going,) to thinke me
As prone to'all ill, and of good as forget-
full, as proud, as lustfull, and as much in debt,
As vaine, as witlesse, and as false as they   15
Which dwell at Court, for once going that way.

100 may'st rightly'obey] mayest rightly obey *1633*   101 name's changed; to be]
name is chang'd to be, *1633*   103 is;] is, *1633*   that] which *H 49, W, Q*
104 prove *Σ*: do *1633, C 57, TCD, Gr*   106 alas,] alas *1633*   107 and rockes]
Rockes *H 49, W, O'F, Q*   'and at] and at *1633*
    Satyre IV. *MSS.: C 57, L 74 and TCD: H 49 and W; O'F and Q.*   4 recreation
to, *Q*: recreation, *1633, Σ; see note*   'and] and *1633*   scant] scarse *Q, Gr*   5 neither
1633, L 74, TCD: neithers *C 57*: nor *H 49, W, Q*: not *O'F*   9 To'a *Σ*: To
1633, C 57, O'F, Q   10 curse,] curse; *1633*   12 Guilty'of] Guilty of *1633*
13 to'all] to all *1633*   14 as lustfull] lustfull *H 49, W, O'F*   16 at *Σ*: in *1633, C 57*

Therefore I suffer'd this; Towards me did runne
A thing more strange, then on Niles slime, the Sunne
E'r bred; or all which into Noahs Arke came;
A thing, which would have pos'd Adam to name;   20
Stranger then seaven Antiquaries studies,
Then Africks Monsters, Guianaes rarities.
Stranger then strangers; One, who for a Dane,
In the Danes Massacre had sure beene slaine,
If he had liv'd then; And without helpe dies,   25
When next the Prentises 'gainst Strangers rise.
One, whom the watch at noone lets scarce goe by,
One, to'whom th'examining Justice sure would cry,
'Sir, by your priesthood tell me what you are.'
His cloths were strange, though coarse; and black, though
        bare;   30
Sleevelesse his jerkin was, and it had beene
Velvet, but 'twas now (so much ground was seene)
Become Tufftaffatie; and our children shall
See it plaine Rashe awhile, then nought at all.
This thing hath travail'd, and saith, speakes all tongues, 35
And only know'th what to all States belongs;
Made of th'Accents, and best phrase of all these,
He speakes one language; If strange meats displease,
Art can deceive, or hunger force my tast,
But Pedants motley tongue, souldiers bumbast,   40
Mountebankes drugtongue, nor the termes of law
Are strong enough preparatives, to draw
Me to beare this: yet I must be content
With his tongue, in his tongue, call'd complement:
In which he can win widdowes, and pay scores,   45
Make men speake treason, cosen subtlest whores,
Out-flatter favorites, or outlie either

17 suffer'd] suffered *1633*   19 bred;...came;] bred,...came:*1633*   20 name;]
name,*1633*   22 rarities.] rarities,*1633*   28 to'whom th'examining] to whom, the
examining *1633*   35 tongues,] tongues *1633*   36 know'th] knoweth *1633*: knowes
H 49, *W*, *O'F*, *Q*   what to all States] to all States what *O'F*, *Q*   belongs;] belongs,*1633*
37 th'...of all] the...of *H 49*, *O'F*, *Q*   38 one] no *Q*, *Gr*   42 enough pre-
paratives] preparatives enough *O'F*, *Q*   43 this:] this,*1633*   44 With his
tongue,] With his tongue:*1633*   47 or] and *H 49*, *W*, *O'F*, *Q*

Jovius, or Surius, or both together.
He names mee,'and comes to mee; I whisper, 'God!
How have I sinn'd, that thy wraths furious rod,   50
This fellow chuseth me?' He saith, 'Sir,
I love your judgement; Whom doe you prefer,
For the best linguist?' And I seelily
Said, that I thought Calepines Dictionarie;
'Nay, but of men, most sweet Sir?' Beza then,   55
Some Jesuites, and two reverend men
Of our two Academies, I nam'd; There
He stopt mee,'and said, 'Nay, your Apostles were
Good pretty linguists, and so Panurge was;
Yet a poore gentleman, all these may passe   60
By travaile.' Then, as if he would have sold
His tongue, he prais'd it, and such wonders told
That I was faine to say, 'If you'had liv'd, Sir,
Time enough to have beene Interpreter
To Babells bricklayers, sure the Tower had stood.'   65
He adds, 'If of court life you knew the good,
You would leave lonenesse.' I said, 'Not alone
My lonenesse is. But Spartanes fashion,
To teach by painting drunkards, doth not tast
Now; Aretines pictures have made few chast;   70
No more can Princes courts, though there be few
Better pictures of vice, teach me vertue.'
He, like to'a high stretcht lute string squeakt, 'O Sir,
'Tis sweet to talke of Kings.' 'At Westminster,'
Said I, 'The man that keepes the Abbey tombes,   75
And for his price doth with who ever comes,
Of all our Harries, and our Edwards talke,
From King to King and all their kin can walke:

48 Surius] Sleydan *O'F* (*b.c.*), *Q*   49 mee,'and] mee, and *1633*   55 Sir?] Sir.
1633   56 Some] Some other *Gr* (*from HN*)   57 nam'd] named *1633*   58 'and]
and *1633*   said,] said; *1633*   59 Good pretty] Pretty good *O'F, Q*   Panurge *H 49, W*:
Panirge *1633, C 57, L 74, TCD*: Panurgus *O'F, Q*   60 gentleman, all] gentleman;
All *1633*   62 prais'd] praised *1633*   wonders *Σ*: words *1633, C 57, L 74* (*b.c.*), *TCD*
65 the] that *H 49, W*   67, 68 lonenesse *H 49, W, O'F, Q*: lonelinesse *1633, C 57,
L 74, TCD*   67 lonenesse.] lonelinesse; *1633*   Not] not *1633*   68 is. But] is,
but *1633*   69 tast *O'F, Q*: last *1633, Σ, Gr*; *see note*   73 to'a high] to a high
1633: a to'high *W*

Your eares shall heare nought, but Kings; your eyes meet
Kings only; The way to it, is Kingstreet.'   80
He smack'd, and cry'd, 'He's base, Mechanique, coarse,
So'are all your Englishmen in their discourse.
Are not your Frenchmen neate?' 'Mine? as you see,
I'have but one Frenchman, looke, hee followes mee.'
'Certes they'are neatly cloth'd; I,'of this minde am,   85
Your only wearing is your Grogaram.'
'Not so Sir, I have more.' Under this pitch
He would not flie; I chaff'd him; But as Itch
Scratch'd into smart, and as blunt iron ground
Into an edge, hurts worse: So, I (foole) found,   90
Crossing hurt mee; To fit my sullennesse,
He to another key, his stile doth addresse,
And askes, 'What newes?' I tell him of new playes.
He takes my hand, and as a Still, which staies
A Sembriefe, 'twixt each drop, he nigardly,   95
As loth to'enrich mee, so tells many'a lie.
More then ten Hollensheads, or Halls, or Stowes,
Of triviall houshold trash he knowes; He knowes
When the Queene frown'd, or smil'd, and he knowes what
A subtle States-man may gather of that;   100
He knowes who loves; whom; and who by poyson
Hasts to an Offices reversion;
He knowes who'hath sold his land, and now doth beg
A licence, old iron, bootes, shooes, and egge-
shels to transport; Shortly boyes shall not play   105
At span-counter, or blow-point, but they pay
Toll to some Courtier;'And wiser then all us,
He knowes what Ladie is not painted; Thus

79 Kings] Kinge H 49, W, O'F   82 So'are] So are 1633   83 Mine? Σ: Fine,
1633, L 74 (b.c.): in mee TCD   84 I'have] I have 1633   Frenchman] frenchman 1633:
Sʳ O'F, Q   85 they'are . . . cloth'd; I,'of] they are . . . cloth'd. I, of 1633   86 is
your] is this H 49, W, O'F, Q   89 ground] grown'd 1633   90 (foole)] foole 1633
92 addresse,] addresse. 1633: dresse H 49, W, O'F, Q   93 What] what 1633
96 to'enrich . . . many'a] to enrich . . . many a 1633   lie.] lie, 1633   97 or . . .
or] and . . . and H 49, W   98 trash he] trash; He 1633   99 frown'd, or smil'd]
smilde, or frownd H 49, W   103 who'hath] who O'F, Q   104 bootes, shooes,
and] shooes, Bootes, or H 49, W, O'F, Q   106 span-counter, or blow-point] blow-
poynte, or span counter H 49, W, O'F, Q   they Σ: shall 1633, L 74   107 'And]
And 1633   108 what] which H 49, W, O'F, Q

He with home-meats tries me; I belch, spue, spit,
Looke pale, and sickly, like a Patient; Yet   110
He thrusts me more; And as if he'undertooke
To say Gallo-Belgicus without booke
Speakes of all States, and deeds, that have been since
The Spaniards came, to the losse of Amyens.
Like a bigge wife, at sight of loathed meat,   115
Readie to travaile: So I sigh, and sweat
To heare this Makeron talke: In vaine; for yet,
Either my humour, or his owne to fit,
He like a priviledg'd spie, whom nothing can
Discredit, Libells now 'gainst each great man.   120
He names a price for every office paid;
He saith, our warres thrive ill, because delai'd;
That offices are entail'd, and that there are
Perpetuities of them, lasting as farre
As the last day; And that great officers,   125
Doe with the Pirates share, and Dunkirkers.
Who wasts in meat, in clothes, in horse, he notes;
Who loves Whores, who boyes, and who goats.
I more amas'd then Circes prisoners, when
They felt themselves turne beasts, felt my selfe then   130
Becomming Traytor, and mee thought I saw
One of our Giant Statutes ope his jaw
To sucke me in; for hearing him, I found
That as burnt venom'd Leachers doe grow sound
By giving others their soares, I might growe   135
Guilty, and he free: Therefore I did shew
All signes of loathing; But since I am in,
I must pay mine, and my forefathers sinne
To the last farthing; Therefore to my power
Toughly'and stubbornly'I beare this crosse; But the'houre 140

109 tries] cloyes *O'F*   111 me *C 57, L 74, TCD*: on *1633, O'F, Gr*: omit *H 49,
W, Q*   he] he had *H 49, W, O'F, Q*: he'd *Gr*   113 that] which *H 49, W, O'F,
Q*   have Σ: hath *1633, C 57, L 74, TCD*   115 Like] Like to *H 49, W*   116 sigh]
belch *H 49, W*   117 this] his *L 74, TCD, W, O'F*   talke: In vaine; for] talke in
vaine: For *1633*   122 saith] sayes *H 49, W, O'F, Q*   130 turne] turnde *Q*   133 in;
. . . him,] in, . . . him. *1633*   134–6 That . . . free: *From MSS.*: omit *1633*
134 venom'd *MSS.*: venome *Gr* (*from 1635*)   140 Toughly'and stubbornly'I]
Toughly and stubbornly I *1633*

Of mercy now was come; He tries to bring
Me to pay'a fine to scape his torturing,
And saies, 'Sir, can you spare me?' I said, 'Willingly.'
'Nay, Sir, can you spare me'a crowne?' Thankfully I
Gave it, as Ransome; But as fidlers, still,   145
Though they be paid to be gone, yet needs will
Thrust one more jigge upon you: so did hee
With his long complementall thankes vexe me.
But he is gone, thankes to his needy want,
And the prerogative of my Crowne: Scant   150
His thankes were ended, when I, (which did see
All the court fill'd with more strange things then hee)
Ran from thence with such or more hast, then one
Who feares more actions, doth make from prison.

    At home in wholesome solitarinesse   155
My precious soule began, the wretchednesse
Of suiters at court to mourne, and a trance
Like his, who dreamt he saw hell, did advance
It selfe on mee; Such men as he saw there,
I saw at court, and worse, and more; Low feare   160
Becomes the guiltie, not th'accuser; Then,
Shall I, nones slave, of high borne, or rais'd men
Feare frownes? And, my Mistresse Truth, betray thee
To th'huffing braggart, puft Nobility?
No, no, Thou which since yesterday hast beene   165
Almost about the whole world, hast thou seene,
O Sunne, in all thy journey, Vanitie,
Such as swells the bladder of our court? I
Thinke he which made your waxen garden, and
Transported it from Italy to stand   170
With us, at London, flouts our Presence, for

141 mercy] redemp*t*ion *Q*   142 pay'a] pay a *1633*   143 Willingly] willingly
1633   144 me'a] me a *1633*   147 more jigge] Jigg more *L 74, TCD*
153 Ran] Run *W*   154 doth make *H 49, W*: makes *O'F, Q*: doth hast *1633, C 57,
L 74 (b.c.), TCD*   prison.] prison; *1633*   156 precious] Piteous *H 49, W, O'F, Q*
159 on] ore *H 49, W, O'F, Q*   mee;] mee, *1633*   Such] and such *H 49, W, O'F, Q*
161 th'accuser] the accuser *1633*   164 th' *Σ*: omit *1633, C 57, TCD*   huffing]
huffing, *1633*   Nobility?] Nobility. *1633*   166 whole] omit *C 57, TCD*   169 your]
yon *W, O'F* (yond), *Q*: the *H 49*   170 Transported] Transplanted *H 49, W, O'F*
171 Presence] Court here *H 49 W, Q*: Courtiers *O'F*

Just such gay painted things, which no sappe, nor
Tast have in them, ours are; And naturall
Some of the stocks are, their fruits, bastard all.
    'Tis ten a clock and past; All whom the Mues,   175
Baloune, Tennis, Dyet, or the stewes,
Had all the morning held, now the second
Time made ready, that day, in flocks, are found
In the Presence, and I, (God pardon mee.)
As fresh, and sweet their Apparrells be, as bee   180
The fields they sold to buy them; 'For a King
Those hose are,' cry the flatterers; And bring
Them next weeke to the Theatre to sell;
Wants reach all states; Me seemes they doe as well
At stage, as court; All are players; who e'r lookes   185
(For themselves dare not goe) o'r Cheapside books,
Shall finde their wardrops Inventory. Now,
The Ladies come; As Pirats, which doe know
That there came weak ships fraught with Cutchannel,
The men board them; and praise, as they thinke, well,   190
Their beauties; they the mens wits; Both are bought.
Why good wits ne'r weare scarlet gownes, I thought
This cause, These men, mens wits for speeches buy,
And women buy all reds which scarlets die.
He call'd her beauty limetwigs, her haire net;   195
She feares her drugs ill laid, her haire loose set.
Would not Heraclitus laugh to see Macrine,
From hat, to shooe, himselfe at doore refine,
As if the Presence were a Moschite,'and lift
His skirts and hose, and call his clothes to shrift,   200
Making them confesse not only mortall
Great staines and holes in them; but veniall

    173 are;] are, *1633*   180 their] the L *74*: th' H *49*, W   182 cry *1633*,
O'F: cryes Σ   the] his H *49*, W, O'F, Q   183 to the] unto the C *57*, TCD
184 seemes] thinkes O'F, Q   185 players;] players, *1633*   186 o'r] in O'F, Q
187 Inventory.] Inventory; *1633*   188 doe] did L *74*, H *49*, W, O'F
193 These] Those O'F, Q   194 scarlets] scarlett H *49*, W, O'F, Q   195 call'd]
calls O'F, Q   195-6 net; . . . set.] net. . . . set; *1633*   199 As if
the] as the L *74*, W, O'F, Q: As the Queenes H *49*   Moschite,'and] Moschite, and
1633

Feathers and dust, wherewith they fornicate;
And then by *Durers* rules survay the state
Of his each limbe, and with strings the odds tries   205
Of his neck to his legge, and wast to thighes.
So in immaculate clothes, and Symetrie
Perfect as circles, with such nicetie
As a young Preacher at his first time goes
To preach, he enters, and a Lady which owes   210
Him not so much as good will, he arrests,
And unto her protests protests protests
So much as at Rome would serve to have throwne
Ten Cardinalls into th'Inquisition;
And whisperd 'by Jesu', so'often, that A   215
Pursevant would have ravish'd him away
For saying of our Ladies psalter; But 'tis fit
That they each other plague, they merit it.
But here comes Glorius that will plague them both,
Who, in the other extreme, only doth   220
Call a rough carelessenesse, good fashion;
Whose cloak his spurres teare; whom he spits on
He cares not; His ill words doe no harme
To him; he rusheth in, as if 'Arme, arme,'
He meant to crie; And though his face be'as ill   225
As theirs which in old hangings whip Christ, yet still
He strives to looke worse, he keepes all in awe;
Jeasts like a licenc'd foole, commands like law.

   Tyr'd, now I leave this place, and but pleas'd so
As men which from gaoles to'execution goe,   230
Goe through the great chamber (why is it hung
With the seaven deadly sinnes?); Being among
Those Askaparts, men big enough to throw

203 wherewith] with which *H 49, W, O'F, Q*   fornicate;] fornicate. *1633*
204 survay] survayes *H 49, W, O'F (b.c.)*   205-6 tries . . . thighes] trye . . . thighe
Gr (from Ash)   209 his] the *O'F, Q*   211 he arrests] streight arrests *H 49, W,*
O'F: he straight arrests *Q*   214 th'] the *1633*   215 whisperd] whispers *O'F*
so'often] so often *1633*   216 Pursevant] Topcliff *O'F (b.c.), Q*   him] him quite*O'F, Q*
217 saying of] saying *H 49, W, O'F, Q*   our Ladies] Jesus *O'F*   223 not;] not, *1633*
224 Arme] arme *1633*   225 meant] came *H 49, W, O'F, Q*   be'as] be as *1633*
226 yet still] still *H 49, W, O'F, Q, Gr*   229 I] Ile *H 49, W*   230 men which
MSS.: men *1633*   232 sinnes?); Being] sinnes) being *1633*

Charing Crosse for a barre, men that doe know
No token of worth, but 'Queenes man', and fine   235
Living, barrells of beefe, flaggons of wine;
I shooke like a spyed Spie. Preachers which are
Seas of Wit and Arts, you can, then dare,
Drowne the sinnes of this place, for, for mee
Which am but a scarce brooke, it enough shall bee   240
To wash the staines away; Though I yet
With *Macchabees* modestie, the knowne merit
   Of my worke lessen: yet some wise man shall,
   I hope, esteeme my writs Canonicall.

Satyre V

THOU shalt not laugh in this leafe, Muse, nor they
   Whom any pitty warmes; He which did lay
Rules to make Courtiers, (hee being understood
May make good Courtiers, but who Courtiers good?)
Frees from the sting of jests all who'in extreme   5
Are wrech'd or wicked: of these two a theame
Charity and liberty give me. What is hee
Who Officers rage, and Suiters misery
Can write, and jest? If all things be in all,
As I thinke, since all, which were, are, and shall   10
Bee, be made of the same elements:
Each thing, each thing implyes or represents.
Then man is a world; in which, Officers
Are the vast ravishing seas; and Suiters,
Springs; now full, now shallow, now drye; which, to   15

234 that] which *H 49*, *W*, *O'F*, *Q*   236 Living,] Living *1633*   236–7 wine;
. . . Spie.] wine. . . . Spie; *1633*   238 Wit *Σ*: Wits *1633*, *C 57*, *H 49*   240 Which
am but a scarce brooke] Who ame a skant brooke *W*, *O'F*, *Q*: Who ame a shalowe brooke
H 49   241 the *1633*, *C 57*: these *L 74*, *TCD*: theyre *H 49*, *W*, *O'F*, *Q*   Though]
though *1633*, *Σ*: Although *O'F*, *Gr*   242 knowne merit] Merritt *L 74*, *H 49*, *W*
243 man] men *L 74*, *TCD*, *W*, *Q*
   Satyre V. *MSS.*: *C 57*, *D*, *L 74 and TCD*; *W*; *O'F and Q.*   5 who'in] who in
1633   6 wrech'd] wreched *1633*   12 implyes] *spelt* employes *1633*   represents.]
represents, *1633*   13 Officers] Officers, *1633*   14 ravishing] ravenous *O'F*, *Q*

That which drownes them, run: These selfe reasons do
Prove the world a man, in which, officers
Are the devouring stomacke, and Suiters
Th'excrements, which they voyd. All men are dust;
How much worse are Suiters, who to mens lust   20
Are made preyes? O worse then dust, or wormes meat,
For they do'eate you now, whose selves wormes shall eate.
They are the mills which grinde you, yet you are
The winde which drives them; and a wastfull warre
Is fought against you, and you fight it; they   25
Adulterate lawe, and you prepare their way
Like wittals; th'issue your owne ruine is.

    Greatest and fairest Empresse, know you this?
Alas, no more then Thames calme head doth know
Whose meades her armes drowne, or whose corne o'rflow: 30
You Sir, whose righteousnes she loves, whom I
By having leave to serve, am most richly
For service paid, authoriz'd, now beginne
To know and weed out this enormous sinne.

    O Age of rusty iron! Some better wit   35
Call it some worse name, if ought equall it;
Th'iron Age *that* was, when justice was sold; now
Injustice is sold dearer farre. Allow
All demands, fees, and duties; gamsters, anon
The mony which you sweat, and sweare for, is gon   40
Into'other hands: So controverted lands
Scape, like Angelica, the strivers hands.
If Law be in the Judges heart, and hee
Have no heart to resist letter, or fee,
Where wilt thou'appeale? Powre of the Courts below   45
Flow from the first maine head, and these can throw
Thee, if they sucke thee in, to misery,

· 19 Th'excrements] The excrements *1633*: . . . excrement *W, O'F, Q*   voyd. All]
voyd; all *1633*   dust;] dust, *1633*   21 preyes?] preyes. *1633*   22 do'eate] do eate *1633*
26 their] the *O'F, Q*   27 wittals; . . . is.] wittals, . . . is; *1633*   33 authoriz'd]
authorized *1633*   37 Th'iron] The iron *1633*   sold;] sold, *1633*   38 dearer
farre. Allow] deerer farre; allow *1633*   39 demands] claymd *W, O'F, Q*   40 sweat,
and sweare] sweare and sweat *W, O'F, Q*   41 Into'other] Into other *1633*: . . . others
O'F, Q   45 thou'appeale] thou appeale *1633*   Powre] powre *1633*

To fetters, halters; But if th'injury
Steele thee to dare complaine, Alas, thou go'st
Against the stream, when upwards: when thou'art most   50
Heavy'and most faint; and in these labours they,
'Gainst whom thou should'st complaine, will in the way
Become great seas, o'r which, when thou shalt bee
Forc'd to make golden bridges, thou shalt see
That all thy gold was drown'd in them before;   55
All things follow their like, only who have may'have more.
Judges are Gods; he who made and said them so,
Meant not that men should be forc'd to them to goe,
By meanes of Angels; When supplications
We send to God, to Dominations,   60
Powers, Cherubins, and all heavens Courts, if wee
Should pay fees as here, daily bread would be
Scarce to Kings; so 'tis. Would it not anger
A Stoicke, a coward, yea a Martyr,
To see a Pursivant come in, and call   65
All his cloathes, Copes; Bookes, Primers; and all
His Plate, Challices; and mistake them away,
And aske a fee for comming? Oh, ne'r may
Faire lawes white reverend name be strumpeted,
To warrant thefts: she is established   70
Recorder to Destiny, on earth, and shee
Speakes Fates words, and but tells us who must bee
Rich, who poore, who in chaires, who in jayles:
Shee is all faire, but yet hath foule long nailes,
With which she scracheth Suiters; In bodies   75
Of men, so'in law, nailes are th'extremities,
So Officers stretch to more then Law can doe,
As our nailes reach what no else part comes to.

48 th'injury] the injury *1633*   49 complaine,] complaine; *1633*   go'st] goest *1633*
50 thou'art] thou art *1633*   51 Heavy'and] Heavy and *1633*   these] those *W*,
O'F, Q   52 the] thy *W, O'F, Q*   56 only who have] only, who have, *1633*   may'
have] may have *1633; see note*   more.] more *1633*   58 not that] not *L 74, W, O'F*
61 Courts *L 74, W, O'F, Q* : Court *1633, C 57, D, TCD*   62 daily] Daily *1633*
63 'tis. Would] 'tis, would *1633*   68 aske *Σ* : lack *1633, C 57*   comming?]
comming; *1633*   72 but tells us who *W, O'F, Q* : tells who *1633, C 57, D, L 74, TCD*
76 men,] men; *1633*   so'in] so in *1633*   th'extremities *MSS.* : extremities *1633*

Why bar'st thou to yon Officer? Foole, Hath hee
Got those goods, for which erst men bar'd to thee? 80
Foole, twice, thrice, thou'hast bought wrong,'and now hungerly
Beg'st right; But that dole comes not till these dye.
Thou'had'st much, and lawes Urim and Thummim trie
Thou wouldst for more; and for all hast paper
Enough to cloath all the great Carricks Pepper. 85
Sell that, and by that thou much more shalt leese,
Then Haman, when he sold his Antiquities.
O wretch that thy fortunes should moralize
Esops fables, and make tales, prophesies.
    Thou'art the swimming dog whom shadows cosened, 90
And div'st, neare drowning, for what vanished.

INFINITATI SACRUM,

16 Augusti 1601.

Metempsychosis

Poêma Satyricon

Epistle

OTHERS at the Porches and entries of their Buildings set their
Armes; I, my picture; if any colours can deliver a minde so
plaine, and flat, and through light as mine. Naturally at a new
Author, I doubt, and sticke, and doe not quickly say, good. I
censure much and taxe; And this liberty costs mee more then others, 5
by how much my owne things are worse then others. Yet I would

79 bar'st] barest *1633*   80 which erst men *W, O'F, Q*: wch men erst *L 74*: which
men *1633, C 57, D, TCD*   bar'd] bared *1633*   81 thou'hast...'and] thou hast...and
1633   83 Thou'had'st] Thou had'st *1633*   87 when] if *W, O'F, Q*   90 Thou
'art] Thou art *1633*   the] that *W, O'F, Q*   91 And] Whoe *Q*: Which *O'F*   div'st
1633, TCD: div'dst *C 57, D, L 74, W*: div'd *O'F, Q*   what] what's *Gr (from N)*

INFINITATI SACRUM, etc. *1633. MSS.*: *C 57*; *TC (TCD with TCC)*; *O'F*; *G*; *H. Titles from
1633 (which spells* Metempsycosis*), C 57, TC, O'F*: Dr. Donne's Μετεμψύχωσις *G*: Infinitati Sacrum *only H*.
   4 quickly say *Σ*: say quickly *1633, C 57, Gr*

not be so rebellious against my selfe, as not to doe it, since I love it;
nor so unjust to others, as to do it *sine talione*. As long as I give them
as good hold upon mee, they must pardon mee my bitings. I forbid
10 no reprehender, but him that like the Trent Councell forbids not
bookes, but Authors, damning what ever such a name hath or shall
write. None writes so ill, that he gives not some thing exemplary,
to follow, or flie. Now when I beginne this booke, I have no purpose
to come into any mans debt; how my stocke will hold out I know
15 not; perchance waste, perchance increase in use; if I doe borrow any
thing of Antiquitie, besides that I make account that I pay it to
posterity, with as much and as good: You shall still finde mee to
acknowledge it, and to thanke not him onely that hath digg'd out
treasure for mee, but that hath lighted mee a candle to the place.
20 All which I will bid you remember, (for I would have no such
Readers as I can teach) is, that the Pithagorian doctrine doth not
onely carry one soule from man to man, nor man to beast, but
indifferently to plants also: and therefore you must not grudge to
finde the same soule in an Emperour, in a Post-horse, and in a
25 Mucheron, since no unreadinesse in the soule, but an indisposition in
the organs workes this. And therefore though this soule could not
move when it was a Melon, yet it may remember, and now tell
mee, at what lascivious banquet it was serv'd. And though it could
not speake, when it was a spider, yet it can remember, and now
30 tell me, who used it for poyson to attaine dignitie. How ever the
bodies have dull'd her other faculties, her memory hath ever been
her owne, which makes me so seriously deliver you by her relation
all her passages from her first making, when shee was that apple
which Eve eate, to this time when shee is hee, whose life you shall
35 finde in the end of this booke.

8 as to G, H: to *1633*, Σ, Gr   11 what ever] whatsoever O'F, H   12 he]
The Epistle breaks off here in H   14 debt;] debt, *1633*   17 still finde mee] find
me still G   20 you] yow to G   would *MSS.*: will *1633*, Gr   33 making,] making
1633   apple] aple *1633*   34 hee] Shee O'F

The Progresse of the Soule

First Song

I

I SING the progresse of a deathlesse soule,
Whom Fate, which God made, but doth not controule,
Plac'd in most shapes; all times before the law
Yoak'd us, and when, and since, in this I sing.
And the great world t'his aged evening, 5
From infant morne, through manly noone I draw.
What the gold Chaldee,'or silver Persian saw,
Greeke brasse, or Roman iron, is in this one;
A worke t'outweare *Seths* pillars, bricke and stone,
 And (holy writt excepted) made to yeeld to none. 10

II

Thee, eye of heaven, this great Soule envies not,
By thy male force, is all wee have, begot.
In the first East, thou now beginst to shine,
Suck'st early balme, and Iland spices there,
And wilt anon in thy loose-rein'd careere 15
At Tagus, Po, Sene, Thames, and Danow dine,
And see at night thy Westerne land of Myne,
Yet hast thou not more nations seene then shee,
That before thee, one day beganne to bee,
 And thy fraile light being quench'd, shall long, long out live
 thee. 20

III

Nor, holy *Janus*, in whose soveraigne boate
The Church, and all the Monarchies did floate;
That swimming Colledge, and free Hospitall

The Progresse . . . Song *1633*, *Σ*: *omit G*: Poema Satiricum / Metempsycosis *H*.
 5 t'his] to his *1633* evening,] evening; *1633* 7 Chaldee,'or] Chaldee, or *1633*
9 t'outweare] t'outlast *H* 10 writt *O'F, G*: writs *1633, Σ* 12 begot.] begot,
1633 13 East] east *1633 uncorrected* beginst *Σ*: begins *1633, C 57* 16 Danow
Σ: Danon *1633, C 57* dine,] dine. *1633* 17 Myne *MSS. and 1633 uncorrected*:
mine *1633* 21 Nor, holy *Janus*,] Nor holy *Ianus 1633*

Of all mankinde, that cage and vivarie
Of fowles, and beasts, in whose wombe, Destinie   25
Us, and our latest nephewes did install
(For thence are all deriv'd, that fill this All,)
Did'st thou in that great stewardship embarke
So diverse shapes into that floating parke,
    As have beene mov'd, and inform'd by this heavenly
        sparke.   30

IV

Great Destiny the Commissary of God,
That hast mark'd out a path and period
For every thing; who, where wee of-spring tooke,
Our wayes and ends seest at one instant; Thou
Knot of all causes, thou whose changelesse brow   35
Ne'r smiles nor frownes, O vouch thou safe to looke
And shew my story,'in thy eternall booke;
That (if my prayer be fit) I may'understand
So much my selfe, as to know with what hand,
    How scant, or liberall this my lifes race is spand.   40

V

To my sixe lustres almost now outwore,
Except thy booke owe mee so many more,
Except my legend be free from the letts
Of steepe ambition, sleepie povertie,
Spirit-quenching sicknesse, dull captivitie,   45
Distracting businesse, and from beauties nets,
And all that calls from this, and t'other whets,
O let me not launch out, but let mee save
Th'expense of braine and spirit; that my grave
    His right and due, a whole unwasted man may have.   50

27 For *G, H*: From *1633, Σ, Gr*   All,)] All) *1633*   30 mov'd] moved *1633*
31 Commissary] commissary *1633 uncorrected*   33 thing;] thing, *1633*   36 vouch
thou safe *MSS.*: vouch-safe thou *1633*   37 'in] in *1633*   booke;] booke. *1633*
47 t'other *Σ*: to others *1633, C 57, Gr*

VI

But if my dayes be long, and good enough,
In vaine this sea shall enlarge, or enrough
It selfe; for I will through the wave, and fome,
And shall, in sad lone wayes a lively spright,
Make my darke heavy Poëm light, and light.   55
For though through many streights, and lands I roame,
I launch at paradise, and saile toward home;
The course I there began, shall here be staid,
Sailes hoised there, stroke here, and anchors laid
    In Thames, which were at Tigrys, and Euphrates waide. 60

VII

For this great soule which here amongst us now
Doth dwell, and moves that hand, and tongue, and brow,
Which, as the Moone the sea, moves us; to heare
Whose story, with long patience you will long;
(For 'tis the crowne, and last straine of my song)   65
This soule to whom *Luther*, and *Mahomet* were
Prisons of flesh; this soule which oft did teare,
And mend the wracks of th'Empire, and late Rome,
And liv'd where every great change did come,
    Had first in paradise, a low, but fatall roome.   70

VIII

Yet no low roome, nor then the greatest, lesse,
If (as devout and sharpe men fitly guesse)
That Crosse, our joy, and griefe, where nailes did tye
That All, which alwayes was all, every where;
Which could not sinne, and yet all sinnes did beare;   75
Which could not die, yet could not chuse but die;
Stood in the selfe same roome in Calvarie,

54 shall,] shall *1633*   lone *O'F, H*: love *1633*, *Σ*   wayes . . . spright,] wayes, . . .
spright *1633*   57 saile *G, H*: I saile *1633, Σ, Gr*   toward *G, H*: towards *1633, Σ, Gr*
61 this *Σ*: the *1633, C 57, Gr*: that *O'F*   amongst] emong *H*   63 Which, . . .
us;] Which . . . us, *1633*   69 where *Σ*: when *1633, C 57, Gr*   74 where;]
where *1633*

Where first grew the forbidden learned tree,
For on that tree hung in security
    This Soule, made by the Makers will from pulling free.   80

                                    IX

Prince of the orchard, faire as dawning morne,
Fenc'd with the law, and ripe as soone as borne
That apple grew, which this Soule did enlive,
Till the then climing serpent, that now creeps
For that offence, for which all mankinde weepes,   85
Tooke it, and t'her whom the first man did wive
(Whom and her race, only forbiddings drive)
He gave it, she, t'her husband, both did eate;
So perished the eaters, and the meate:
    And wee (for treason taints the blood) thence die and
        sweat.   90

                                    X

Man all at once was there by woman slaine,
And one by one we'are here slaine o'er againe
By them. The mother poison'd the well-head,
The daughters here corrupt us, Rivulets;
No smalnesse scapes, no greatnesse breaks their nets;   95
She thrust us out, and by them we are led
Astray, from turning, to whence we are fled.
Were prisoners Judges, 'twould seeme rigorous,
Shee sinn'd, we beare; part of our paine is, thus
    To love them, whose fault to this painfull love yoak'd us.   100

                                    XI

So fast in us doth this corruption grow,
That now wee dare aske why wee should be so.
    Would God (disputes the curious Rebell) make

    83 enlive, G, H: enlive 1633, O'F: omit 1633 uncorrected, C 57, TC   87 her] whose H
93 poison'd] poisoned 1633   94 corrupt MSS.: corrupts 1633   Rivulets;
G, H (but unpunctuated): omit 1633, C 57, TC: Nothing letts O'F (b.c.)   95 breaks]
breake 1633 uncorrected   nets;] nets, 1633   96 thrust] thrusts 1633 uncorrected
97 fled.] fled, 1633 uncorrected   98 'twould] t'would 1633   99 beare; Σ: here,
1633, C 57, TC (heare,)

A law, and would not have it kept? Or can
His creatures will, crosse his? Of every man   105
For one, will God (and be just) vengeance take?
Who sinn'd? 'twas not forbidden to the snake
Nor her, who was not then made; nor is't writ
That Adam cropt, or knew the apple; yet
    The worme and she, and he, and wee endure for it.   110

XII

But snatch mee heavenly Spirit from this vaine
Reckoning their vanities, lesse is the gaine
Then hazard still, to meditate on ill,
Though with good minde; their reasons, like those toyes
Of glassie bubbles, which the gamesome boyes   115
Stretch to so nice a thinnes through a quill
That they themselves breake, doe themselves spill:
Arguing is heretiques game, and Exercise
As wrastlers, perfects them; Not liberties
    Of speech, but silence; hands, not tongues, end heresies.   120

XIII

Just in that instant when the serpents gripe,
Broke the slight veines, and tender conduit-pipe,
Through which this soule from the trees root did draw
Life, and growth to this apple, fled away
This loose soule, old, one and another day.   125
As lightning, which one scarce dares say, he saw,
'Tis so soone gone, (and better proofe the law
Of sense, then faith requires) swiftly she flew
T'a darke and foggie Plot; Her, her fate threw
    There through th'earths pores, and in a Plant hous'd
    her anew.   130

107 'twas] t'was *1633*   108 is't] i'st *1633*   112 the *G, H*: their *1633, Σ,*
Gr   114 minde; . . . reasons,] minde, . . . reasons *1633*   115 which] with *1633*
uncorrected   117 spill:] spill, *1633*   119 perfects] perfect *1633 uncrrected*
125 day.] day, *1633 uncorrected*   126 scarce dares] dare scarce *H*: dares scarse *O'F*
129 T'a] To a *1633*   fate *G, H*: fates *1633, Σ, Gr*   130 earths pores *MSS.*:
earths-pores *1633*: earth-pores *1633 uncorrected*   anew *MSS.*: a new *1633*

XIV

The plant thus abled, to it selfe did force
A place, where no place was; by natures course
As aire from water, water fleets away
From thicker bodies, by this root throng'd so
His spungie confines gave him place to grow:　　　　135
Just as in our streets, when the people stay
To see the Prince, and have so fill'd the way
That weesels scarce could passe, when she comes nere
They throng and cleave up, and a passage cleare,
　　As if, for that time, their round bodies flatned were.　140

XV

His right arme he thrust out towards the East,
West-ward his left; th'ends did themselves digest
Into ten lesser strings, these fingers were:
And as a slumberer stretching on his bed,
This way he this, and that way scattered　　　　　145
His other legge, which feet with toes upbeare.
Grew on his middle parts, the first day, haire,
To show, that in loves businesse hee should still
A dealer bee, and be us'd well, or ill:
　　His apples kindle, his leaves, force of conception kill.　150

XVI

A mouth, but dumbe, he hath; blinde eyes, deafe eares,
And to his shoulders dangle subtile haires;
A young *Colossus* there hee stands upright,
And as that ground by him were conquered
A leafie garland weares he on his head　　　　　155
Enchas'd with little fruits, so red and bright
That for them you would call your Loves lips white;

131 The] This *H*　　　134 throng'd] thronged *1633*　　　135 grow:] grow, *1633*
136 Just as . . . when] As . . . when as *H*　　　137 Prince *MSS. and 1633 uncorrected*:
Princesse *1633 corrected*; *see note*　　and have so fill'd *G*: and so fill'd *1633, C 57, TC*: and
so filld up *O'F*: so filled is *H*　　144 bed,] bed; *1633*　　146 upbeare.] upbeare; *1633*
150 kindle *G, H*: kinde *1633, Σ*

So, of a lone unhaunted place possest,
Did this soules second Inne, built by the guest,
   This living buried man, this quiet mandrake, rest.   160

XVII

No lustfull woman came this plant to grieve,
But 'twas because there was none yet but Eve:
And she (with other purpose) kill'd it quite;
Her sinne had now brought in infirmities,
And so her cradled child, the moist red eyes   165
Had never shut, nor slept since it saw light;
Poppie she knew, she knew the mandrakes might,
And tore up both, and so coold her childs blood;
Unvirtuous weeds might long unvex'd have stood;
   But hee's short liv'd, that with his death can doe most
      good.   170

XVIII

To an unfetterd soules quick nimble hast
Are falling stars, and hearts thoughts, but slow pac'd:
Thinner then burnt aire flies this soule, and she
Whom foure new comming, and foure parting Suns
Had found, and left the Mandrakes tenant, runnes   175
Thoughtlesse of change, when her firme destiny
Confin'd, and enjayld her, that seem'd so free,
Into a small blew shell, the which a poore
Warme bird orespread, and sat still evermore,
   Till her enclos'd child kickt, and peck'd it selfe a dore. 180

XIX

Outcrept a sparrow, this soules moving Inne,
On whose raw armes stiffe feathers now begin,
As childrens teeth through gummes, to breake with paine,
His flesh is jelly yet, and his bones threds,

159 guest,] guest *1633*   162 'twas] t'was *1633*   166 slept] sleept *1633*
light;] light, *1633*   167 might,] might; *1633*   180 enclos'd *G, H*: uncloath'd *1633*
C 57: encloth'd *TC, O'F (b.c.)*   peck'd *C 57, TC, O'F*: pick'd *1633*: prickt *G*: pok't *H*
811842   D

All a new downy mantle overspreads;   185
A mouth he opes, which would as much containe
As his late house, and the first houre speaks plaine,
And chirps alowd for meat. Meat fit for men
His father steales for him, and so feeds then
   One, that within a month, will beate him from his hen.   190

XX

In this worlds youth wise nature did make hast,
Things ripen'd sooner, and did longer last;
Already this hot cocke, in bush and tree,
In field and tent, oreflutters his next hen;
He asks her not, who did so tast, nor when,   195
Nor if his sister, or his neece shee be;
Nor doth she pule for his inconstancie
If in her sight he change, nor doth refuse
The next that calls; both liberty doe use;
   Where store is of both kindes, both kindes may freely
     chuse.   200

XXI

Men, till they tooke laws which made freedome lesse,
Their daughters, and their sisters did ingresse;
Till now unlawfull, therefore ill, 'twas not.
So jolly, that it can move, this soule is,
The body so free of his kindnesses,   205
That selfe preserving it hath now forgot,
And slackneth so the soules, and bodies knot,
Which temperance streightens; freely'on his she friends
He blood, and spirit, pith, and marrow spends,
   Ill steward of himself, himselfe in three yeares ends.   210

185 All a new downy *MSS.*: All downy a new *1633*   overspreads;] overspreads, *1633*
187 houre] howre *1633 uncorrected*   190 month] moneth *1633*   192 ripen'd]
ripened *1633*   193 cocke, . . . tree,] cocke . . . tree *1633*   194 tent, . . . hen;]
tent . . . hen, *1633*   195 tast] last *H*   196 be;] be, *1633*   199 calls; . . .
use;] calls, . . . use, *1633 uncorrected*   202 ingresse;] ingresse, *1633*   203 ill, . . .
not.] ill; . . . not *1633*   'twas] t'was *1633*   204 move, this soule is,] move this
soule, is *1633*: . . . soule; Is *1633 uncorrected*   208 freely'on] freely on *1633*

XXII

Else might he long have liv'd; man did not know
Of gummie blood, which doth in holly grow,
How to make bird-lime, nor how to deceive
With faind calls, hid nets, or enwrapping snare,
The free inhabitants of the Plyant aire.   215
Man to beget, and woman to conceive
Askt not of rootes, nor of cock-sparrowes, leave:
Yet chuseth hee, though none of these he feares,
Pleasantly three, then streightned twenty yeares
    To live, and to encrease his race, himselfe outweares.   220

XXIII

This cole with overblowing quench'd and dead,
The Soule from her too active organs fled
T'a brooke; A female fishes sandie Roe
With the males jelly, newly lev'ned was,
For they had intertouch'd as they did passe,   225
And one of those small bodies, fitted so,
This soule inform'd, and abled it to rowe
It selfe with finnie oares, which she did fit:
Her scales seem'd yet of parchment, and as yet
    Perchance a fish, but by no name you could call it.   230

XXIV

When goodly, like a ship in her full trim,
A swan, so white that you may unto him
Compare all whitenesse, but himselfe to none,
Glided along, and as he glided watch'd,
And with his arched necke this poore fish catch'd.   235
It mov'd with state, as if to looke upon
Low things it scorn'd, and yet before that one

212 grow,] grow *1633*   214 hid *G, H*: his *1633, Σ*   snare,] snare *1633*   220 his
race *Σ*: *omit 1633, C 57*   223 A] a *1633*   225 had intertouch'd *G, H*: inter-
touched *1633, C 57, O'F*: inter-touch'd *TC*   227 rowe] roe *1633*   228 fit:] fit,
1633   230 you could] cowld y^w *H*

Could thinke he sought it, he had swallow'd cleare
This, and much such, and unblam'd devour'd there
    All, but who too swift, too great, or well armed were.   240

XXV

Now swome a prison in a prison put,
And now this Soule in double walls was shut,
Till melted with the Swans digestive fire,
She left her house the fish, and vapour'd forth;
Fate not affording bodies of more worth   245
For her as yet, bids her againe retire
T'another fish, to any new desire
Made a new prey; For, he that can to none
Resistance make, nor complaint, sure is gone.
    Weaknesse invites, but silence feasts oppression.   250

XXVI

Pace with her native streame, this fish doth keepe,
And journeyes with her, towards the glassie deepe,
But oft retarded, once with a hidden net
Though with great windowes, for when Need first taught
These tricks to catch food, then they were not wrought   255
As now, with curious greedinesse to let
None scape, but few, and fit for use, to get,
As, in this trap a ravenous pike was tane,
Who, though himselfe distrest, would faine have slain
    This wretch; So hardly are ill habits left again.   260

XXVII

Here by her smallnesse shee two deaths orepast,
Once innocence scap'd, and left th'oppressor fast.
The net through-swome, she keepes the liquid path,
And whether she leape up sometimes to breath

238 swallow'd] swallowed *1633*   240 armed] arm'd *1633*   were.] were *1633*
251 her *Σ*: the *1633*: *omit C* 57   254 Need] need *1633*   257 use,] use *1633*
260 wretch; So . . . again] wretch, so . . . againe *1633 uncorrected*   262 th'oppressor]
the oppressor *1633*   fast.] fast; *1633*

And suck in aire, or finde it underneath,   265
Or working parts like mills or limbecks hath
To make the water thinne and airelike, faith
Cares not; but safe the place she's come unto
Where fresh, with salt waves meet, and what to doe
    She knowes not, but betweene both makes a boord or
      two.   270

XXVIII

So farre from hiding her guests, water is,
That she showes them in bigger quantities
Then they are. Thus doubtfull of her way,
For game and not for hunger a sea Pie
Spied through this traiterous spectacle, from high,   275
The seely fish where it disputing lay,
And t'end her doubts and her, beares her away:
Exalted she'is, but to th'exalters good,
As are by great ones, men which lowly stood.
    It's rais'd, to be the Raisers instrument and food.   280

XXIX

Is any kinde subject to rape like fish?
Ill unto man, they neither doe, nor wish:
Fishers they kill not, nor with noise awake,
They doe not hunt, nor strive to make a prey
Of beasts, nor their yong sonnes to beare away;   285
Foules they pursue not, nor do undertake
To spoile the nests industrious birds do make;
Yet them all these unkinde kinds feed upon,
To kill them is an occupation,
    And lawes make Fasts, and Lents for their destruction.   290

---

266 mills] mills, *1633*   267 water *O'F, G, H*: wether *1633, C 57, TC*   thinne
... airelike,] thinne, ... airelike *1633*   268 not;] not, *1633*   place] Place *1633*
270 two.] two *1633*   271 is,] is *1633*   277 away:] away, *1633*   278 th'exalters]
the exalters *1633*   280 It's] It *1633 uncorrected*   287 industrious] industruous *1633*
290 Fasts, and Lents] fasts, & lents *1633*

XXX

A sudden stiffe land-winde in that selfe houre
To sea-ward forc'd this bird, that did devour
The fish; he cares not, for with ease he flies,
Fat gluttonies best orator: at last
So long hee hath flown, and hath flown so fast   295
That many leagues at sea, now tir'd hee lyes,
And with his prey, that till then languisht, dies:
The soules no longer foes, two ways did erre,
The fish I follow,'and keepe no calender
   Of th'other; he lives yet in some great officer.   300

XXXI

Into an embrion fish, our Soule is throwne,
And in due time throwne out againe, and growne
To such vastnesse as, if unmanacled
From Greece, Morea were, and that by some
Earthquake uprooted, loose Morea swome,   305
Or seas from Africks body'had severed
And torne the hopefull Promontories head,
This fish would seeme these, and, when all hopes faile,
A great ship overset, or without saile
   Hulling, might (when this was a whelp) be like this
   whale.   310

XXXII

At every stroake his brazen finnes do take,
More circles in the broken sea they make
Then cannons voices, when the aire they teare:
His ribs are pillars, and his high arch'd roofe
Of barke that blunts best steele, is thunder-proofe: 315
Swimme in him swallow'd Dolphins, without feare,

      291 selfe] same *H*   295 flown . . . flown] flowen . . . flowen *1633*   296 many
leagues *G, H*: leagues *C 57, TC, O'F (b.c.)*: leagues o'er-past *1633*   297 dies:] dies, *1633*
299 follow,'and] follow, and *1633*   300 th'other] the other *1633*   301 our] this *H*
throwne,] throwne *1633*   303 vastnesse as,] vastnesse, as *1633*   306 body'had]
body had *1633*   311 take,] take *1633*   315 thunder-proofe:] thunder-proofe, *1633*
316 swallow'd] swallowed *1633*

And feele no sides, as if his vast wombe were
Some Inland sea, and ever as hee went
Hee spouted rivers up, as if he ment
 To joyne our seas, with seas above the firmament. 320

XXXIII

He hunts not fish, but as an officer
Stayes in his court, as his owne net, and there
All suitors of all sorts themselves enthrall;
So on his backe lyes this whale wantoning,
And in his gulfe-like throat, sucks every thing 325
That passeth neare. Fish chaseth fish, and all,
Flyer and follower, in this whirlepoole fall;
O might not states of more equality
Consist? and is it of necessity
 That thousand guiltlesse smals, to make one great, must
  die? 330

XXXIV

Now drinkes he up seas, and he eates up flocks,
He justles Ilands, and he shakes firme rockes.
Now in a roomefull house this Soule doth float,
And like a Prince she sends her faculties
To all her limbes, distant as Provinces. 335
The Sunne hath twenty times both Crab and Goate
Parched, since first lanch'd forth this living boate;
'Tis greatest now, and to destruction
Nearest; There's no pause at perfection;
 Greatnesse a period hath, but hath no station. 340

XXXV

Two little fishes whom hee never harm'd,
Nor fed on their kinde, two not throughly arm'd
With hope that they could kill him, nor could doe

---

321 officer] officer, *1633*: favorite *H* 322–3 Stayes . . . there All] Lies still
at Court, and is him selfe a nett Where *H* 322 as *Σ*: at *1633, Gr*: in *TCD*
330 thousand . . . smals] thousands . . . small *H* 336 Crab and Goate] crab and goate
1633 337 boate;] boate. *1633* 339 perfection;] perfection. *1633*

Good to themselves by'his death, (they doe not eate
His flesh, nor suck those oyles, which thence outstreat)   345
Conspir'd against him, and it might undoe
The plot of all, that the plotters were two,
But that they fishes were, and could not speake.
How shall a Tyran wise strong projects breake,
    If wreches can on them the common anger wreake?   350

XXXVI

The flaile-finn'd Thresher, and steel-beak'd Sword-fish
Onely attempt to doe, what all doe wish.
The Thresher backs him, and to beate begins;
The sluggard Whale yeelds to oppression,
And t'hide himselfe from shame and danger, downe   355
Begins to sinke; the Swordfish upward spins,
And gores him with his beake; his staffe-like finnes,
So well the one, his sword the other plyes,
That now a scoffe, and prey, this tyran dyes,
    And (his owne dole) feeds with himselfe all companies.   360

XXXVII

Who will revenge his death? or who will call
Those to account, that thought, and wrought his fall?
Th'heires of slaine kings, wee see are often so
Transported with the joy of what they get,
That they, revenge and obsequies forget,   365
Nor will against such men the people goe,
Because h'is now dead, to whom they should show
Love in that act; Some kings by vice being growne
So needy'of subjects love, that of their own
    They thinke they lose, if love be to the dead Prince
    shown.   370

344 by'his] by his *1633*   344–5 death, (they . . . outstreat)] death: they . . . outstreat, *1633*   344 doe *G, H*: did *1633, Σ, Gr*   345 outstreat] out-sweate *O'F, H*
351 flaile-finn'd] flaile-find *1633*: flatt fin'd *H*   358 well the *TC, O'F*: were the *1633,
C 57, G*: weareth *H*   363 Th'heires] The heires *1633*   365 they, revenge]
they, revenge, *1633*: they revenge, *1633 uncorrected*   368 act;] act. *1633*   Some]
And *H*   being] ar *H*   369 needy'of] needy of *1633*

XXXVIII

This Soule, now free from prison, and passion,
Hath yet a little indignation
That so small hammers should so soone downe beat
So great a castle. And having for her house
Got the streight cloyster of a wreched mouse,   375
(As basest men that have not what to eate,
Nor enjoy ought, doe farre more hate the great
Then they, who good repos'd estates possesse)
This Soule, late taught that great things might by lesse
    Be slain, to gallant mischiefe doth herselfe addresse.   380

XXXIX

Natures great master-peece, an Elephant,
The onely harmlesse great thing; the giant
Of beasts; who thought, no more had gone, to make one
    wise
But to be just, and thankfull, loth t'offend,
(Yet nature hath given him no knees to bend)   385
Himselfe he up-props, on himselfe relies,
And foe to none, suspects no enemies,
Still sleeping stood; vex't not his fantasie
Blacke dreames; like an unbent bow, carelesly
    His sinewy Proboscis did remisly lie: 390

XL

In which as in a gallery this mouse
Walk'd, and surveid the roomes of this vast house,
And to the braine, the soules bedchamber, went,
And gnaw'd the life cords there; Like a whole towne
Cleane undermin'd, the slaine beast tumbled downe;   395
With him the murtherer dies, whom envy sent

---

375 mouse,] mouse *1633*   383 thought . . . one *1633, G*: thought nor had gone, to
make one *C 57*: thought noe had gon, to make one *TC*: thought none had to make him
O'F: had beene King but yᵗ too *H*   384 But . . . thankfull] Hee was, just, thankfull, *H*   t'offend] to offend *1633*   385 Yet] For *H*   386 relies,] relies *1633*
389 dreames;] dreames, *1633*   390 lie:] lie. *1633*   395 downe;] downe, *1633*
396 dies,] dies *1633*

To kill, not scape, (for, only hee that ment
To die, did ever kill a man of better roome,)
And thus he made his foe, his prey, and tombe:
    Who cares not to turn back, may any whither come.   400

XLI

Next, hous'd this Soule a Wolves yet unborne whelp,
Till the best midwife, Nature, gave it helpe,
To issue. It could kill, as soone as goe.
Abel, as white, and milde as his sheepe were,
(Who, in that trade, of Church, and kingdomes, there   405
Was the first type) was still infested soe
With this wolfe, that it bred his losse and woe;
And yet his bitch, his sentinell attends
The flocke so neere, so well warnes and defends,
    That the wolfe, (hopelesse else) to corrupt her, intends.   410

XLII

Hee tooke a course, which since, succesfully,
Great men have often taken, to espie
The counsels, or to breake the plots of foes.
To Abels tent he stealeth in the darke,
On whose skirts the bitch slept; ere she could barke,   415
Attach'd her with streight gripes, yet hee call'd those,
Embracements of love; to loves worke he goes,
Where deeds move more then words; nor doth she show
Now much resist, nor needs hee streighten so
    His prey, for, were shee loose, she would not barke, nor
        goe.
                                        420

XLIII

Hee hath engag'd her; his, she wholy bides;
Who not her owne, none others secrets hides.

397–8 (for, . . . roome,)] for, . . . roome, *1633*   399 his foe, his] him for his *H*
403 goe.] goe, *1633*   405 Who, . . . trade,] Who . . . trade *1633*   406 soe]
soe, *1633*   411 course] way *H*   413 foes.] foes, *1633*   418 show] show, *1633*
419 Now much resist *TC, G, H*: Nor much resist *1633, C 57*: Resistance much *O'F*: Nor
⟨make⟩ resist *Gr*   420 not barke *Σ*: nor barke *1633, G, Gr*   421 wholy]
onely *O'F, G*   422 none] no *O'F, H* hides.] hides, *1633*

If to the flocke he come, and Abell there,
She faines hoarse barkings, but she biteth not,
Her faith is quite, but not her love forgot.   425
At last a trap, of which some every where
Abell had plac'd, ended his losse, and feare,
By the Wolves death; and now just time it was
That a quick soule should give life to that masse
    Of blood in Abels bitch, and thither this did passe.   430

XLIV

Some have their wives, their sisters some begot,
But in the lives of Emperours you shall not
Reade of a lust the which may equall this;
This wolfe begot himselfe, and finished
What he began alive, when hee was dead;   435
Sonne to himselfe, and father too, hee is
A ridling lust, for which Schoolemen would misse
A proper name. The whelpe of both these lay
In Abels tent, and with soft Moaba,
    His sister, being yong, it us'd to sport and play.   440

XLV

Hee soone for her too harsh, and churlish grew,
And Abell (the dam dead) would use this new
For the field. Being of two kindes made,
He, as his dam, from sheepe drove wolves away,
And as his Sire, he made them his owne prey.   445
Five yeares he liv'd, and cosen'd with his trade,
Then hopelesse that his faults were hid, betraid
Himselfe by flight, and by all followed,
From dogges, a wolfe; from wolves, a dogge he fled;
    And, like a spie to both sides false, he perished.   450

---

427 plac'd,] plac'd *1633 uncorrected*   ended *G, H*: End and *C 57, TCC*: ending *TCD*:
ends all *1633, Gr*: end all *1633 uncorrected*: ends both *O'F*   feare,] feare *1633 uncorrected*
432 lives of Emperours] life of Princes *H*   435 dead;] dead, *1633*   443 field.
Being] field, being *1633*   made] thus made *O'F, Gr*   446 cosen'd] cosened *1633*

XLVI

It quickned next a toyfull Ape, and so
Gamesome it was, that it might freely goe
From tent to tent, and with the children play.
His organs now so like theirs hee doth finde,
That why he cannot laugh, and speake his minde,   455
He wonders. Much with all, most he doth stay
With Adams fift daughter *Siphatecia*,
Doth gaze on her, and, where she passeth, passe,
Gathers her fruit, and tumbles on the grasse,
    And wisest of that kinde, the first true lover was.   460

XLVII

He was the first that more desir'd to have
One then another; first that ere did crave
Love by mute signes, and had no power to speake;
First that could make love faces, or could doe
The valters sombersalts, or us'd to wooe   465
With hoiting gambolls, his owne bones to breake
To make his mistresse merry; or to wreake
Her angers on himselfe. Sinnes against kinde
They easily doe, that can let feed their minde
    With outward beauty; beauty they in boyes and beasts
      do find.   470

XLVIII

By this misled, too low things men have prov'd,
And too high; beasts and angels have beene lov'd.
This Ape, though else through-vaine, in this was wise,
He reach'd at things too high, but open way
There was, and he knew not she would say nay;   475
His toyes prevaile not, likelier meanes he tries,
He gazeth on her face with teare-shot eyes,

---

453 play.] play, *1633*   459 fruit *G, H*: fruits *1633*, *Σ, Gr*   460 of] in *H*
468 angers *G, H*: anger *1633*, *Σ, Gr*   470 beauty;] beauty, *1633*   472 lov'd.]
lov'd; *1633*   475 would] could *H*

And up lifts subtly with his russet pawe
Her kidskinne apron without feare or awe
    Of nature; nature hath no gaole, though shee have law.   480

XLIX

First she was silly'and knew not what he ment:
That vertue, by his touches, chaft and spent,
Succeeds an itchie warmth, that melts her quite;
She knew not first, now cares not what he doth,
And willing halfe and more, more then halfe loth,   485
She neither puls nor pushes, but outright
Now cries, and now repents; when *Tethlemite*
Her brother, enters, and a great stone threw
After the Ape, who, thus prevented, flew.
    This house thus batter'd downe, the Soule possest a
        new.   490

L

And whether by this change she lose or win,
She comes out next, where th'Ape would have gone in.
Adam and *Eve* had mingled bloods, and now
Like Chimiques equall fires, her temperate wombe
Had stew'd and form'd it: and part did become   495
A spungie liver, that did richly'allow,
Like a free conduit, on a high hils brow,
Life-keeping moisture unto every part;
Part hardned it selfe to a thicker heart,
    Whose busie furnaces lifes spirits do impart.   500

LI

Another part became the well of sense,
The tender well-arm'd feeling braine, from whence,

480 have *TC, G, H*: hath *1633, C 57, Gr*: was *O'F (b.c.)*   481 silly'and] silly and *1633*
ment:] ment, *1633*   483 quite;] quite, *1633*   485 loth *H*: *omit C 57, TC*:
Tooth *1633*: Footh *G*: wroth *O'F*   487 *Tethlemite TC, O'F, H*: Tethlemit *G*:
Tethelemite 1633, C 57   488 enters *G, H*: entred *1633, Σ, Gr*   489 flew.] flew,
1633   492 th'Ape] the Ape *1633*   in.] in, *1633*   496 richly'allow] richly allow
1633   498 Life-keeping] Life keeping *1633*   part;] part, *1633*   502 well-
arm'd] well arm'd *1633*

Those sinowie strings which do our bodies tie,
Are raveld out; and fast there by one end,
Did this Soule limbes, these limbes a soule attend;   505
And now they joyn'd: keeping some quality
Of every past shape, she knew treachery,
Rapine, deceit, and lust, and ills enow
To be a woman. *Themech* she is now,
    Sister and wife to *Caine*, *Caine* that first did plow.   510

LII

Who ere thou beest that read'st this sullen Writ,
Which just so much courts thee, as thou dost it,
Let me arrest thy thoughts; wonder with mee,
Why plowing, building, ruling and the rest,
Or most of those arts, whence our lives are blest,   515
By cursed *Cains* race invented be,
And blest *Seth* vext us with Astronomie.
Ther's nothing simply good, nor ill alone,
Of every quality comparison,
    The onely measure is, and judge, opinion.   520

Upon Mr Thomas Coryats *Crudities*

O H to what heighth will love of greatnesse drive
    Thy leaven'd spirit, *Sesqui-superlative*?
Venice vast lake thou'hadst seen, and would'st seeke than
Some vaster thing, and foundst a Cortizan.
That inland Sea having discover'd well,   5
A Cellar-gulfe, where one might saile to hell
From Heydelberg, thou longdst to see; And thou
This Booke, greater then all, producest now.

504 out;] out, *1633*   505 attend;] attend, *1633*   511–20 *Omit H*
513 thoughts;] thoughts, *1633*   517 Astronomie.] Astronomie, *1633*

Upon Mr Thomas Coryats *Crudities*. *Text from* Coryats Crudities, *1611*, *with paragraphing
supplied. Title from 1649 :* Incipit Ioannes Donne *1611*.   1 heighth] heigth *1611*
2 leaven'd] leavened *1611*   3 thou'hadst] thou hadst *1611*   5 discover'd] discovered *1611*

Infinite worke, which doth so farre extend,
That none can study it to any end.   10
'Tis no one thing; it is not fruite, nor roote;
Nor poorely limited with head or foote.
If man be therefore man, because he can
Reason, and laugh, thy booke doth halfe make man.
One halfe being made, thy modesty was such,   15
That thou on th'other halfe wouldst never touch.
When wilt thou be at full, great Lunatique?
Not till thou'exceed the world? Canst thou be like
A prosperous nose-borne wenne, which sometime growes
To be farre greater then the Mother-nose?   20
    Goe then; and as to thee, when thou didst goe,
Munster did Townes, and *Gesner* Authors show,
Mount now to *Gallo-belgicus*; Appeare
As deepe a States-man, as a Gazettier.
Homely'and familiarly, when thou comm'st backe,   25
Talke of *Will* Conqueror, and *Prester Jacke*.
Goe bashfull man, lest here thou blush to looke
Upon the progresse of thy glorious booke,
To which both Indies sacrifices send;
The west sent gold, which thou didst freely spend,   30
(Meaning to see'it no more) upon the presse.
The east sends hither her deliciousnesse;
And thy leaves must embrace what comes from thence,
The Myrrhe, the Pepper, and the Frankinsence.
This magnifies thy leaves; But if they stoope   35
To neighbour wares, when Merchants doe unhoope
Voluminous barrels; if thy leaves doe then
Convay these wares in parcels unto men;
If for vast Tonnes of Currans, and of Figs,
Of Medcinall, and Aromatique twigs,   40
Thy leaves a better methode doe provide,
Divide to Pounds, and Ounces subdivide;

11 'Tis] T'is *1611*   18 thou'exceed] thou exceed *1611*   25 Homely'and]
Homely and *1611*   comm'st] commest *1611*   28 booke,] booke. *1611*   33, 35,
37, 41, 47, 67 leaves] leau's *1611*   37 barrels;] barrels, *1611*   38 men;] men,
1611   39 Tonnes] Tomes *1611*

If they stoope lower yet, and vent our wares,
Home-*manufactures*, to thicke popular faires;
If *omnipraegnant* there, upon warme stals   45
They hatch all wares for which the buyer cals;
Then thus thy leaves we justly may commend,
That they all kinde of matter comprehend.
Thus thou, by meanes which th'Ancients never tooke,
A Pandect mak'st, and Universall Booke.   50
   The bravest Heroes, for publique good
Scattred in divers lands, their limmes and blood.
Worst malefactors, to whom men are prize,
Doe publique good, cut in Anatomies;
So will thy Booke in peeces: For a Lord   55
Which casts at Portescues, and all the board,
Provide whole Books; Each leafe enough will be
For friends to passe time, and keepe companie.
Can all carouse up thee? No: thou must fit
Measures; and fill out for the half-pinte wit.   60
Some shall wrap pils, and save a friends life so,
Some shall stop muskets, and so kill a foe.
Thou shalt not ease the Critiques of next age
So much, at once their hunger to asswage.
Nor shall wit-pyrats hope to finde thee lie   65
All in one bottome, in one Librarie.
Some leaves may paste strings there in other books,
And so one may, which on another looks,
Pilfer, alas, a little wit from you,   * I meane from
But hardly* much; And yet, I thinke this true;   one page which
                                                     shall paste strings
As *Sybils* was, your booke is mysticall,   in a booke.
For every peece is as much worth as all.
   Therefore mine impotency I confesse;
The healths which my braine beares, must be farre lesse;
Thy Gyant-wit o'rethrowes me, I am gone,   75
And rather then reade all, I would reade none.

In eundem Macaronicon

QUOT, *dos haec,* **Linguists** perfetti, *Disticha* fairont,
    Tot cuerdos **States-men,** *hic* livre fara *tuus.*
Es *sat* **a my** l'honneur estre *hic* inteso; Car **I leabe**
L'honra, de personne nestre creduto, *tibi.*

Explicit Joannes Donne.

In eundem Macaronicon. Coryats Crudities, *1611.*

EPIGRAMS

Hero and Leander

BOTH rob'd of aire, we both lye in one ground,
Both whom one fire had burnt, one water drownd.

Pyramus and Thisbe

TWO, by themselves, each other, love and feare
Slaine, cruell friends, by parting have joyn'd here.

Niobe

BY childrens birth, and death, I am become
So dry, that I am now made mine owne tombe.

A Burnt Ship

OUT of a fired ship, which, by no way
But drowning, could be rescu'd from the flame,
Some men leap'd forth, and ever as they came
Neere the foes ships, did by their shot decay;
So all were lost, which in the ship were found,   5
They in the sea being burnt, they in the burnt ship
      drown'd.

EPIGRAMS. *Text from 1633 unless otherwise stated. Readings are given from the following representative MSS.: TC, W, B, Dob, HN, O'F. When an epigram is not found in one of these, the omission is noted.*

Hero and Leander. *B, Dob omit. Title from 1633, MSS.*   2 drownd] dround *1633 uncorrected*

Pyramus and Thisbe. *B, Dob omit. Title from 1633, MSS.*

Niobe. *B, Dob omit. Title from 1633, MSS.*   1 birth *MSS.*: births *1633, Gr*
2 made mine owne *W, O'F*: made my owne *HN*: mine owne *TC*: mine owne sad *1633, Gr*

A Burnt Ship. *B, Dob, HN omit. Title from 1633, TC*: De Nave Arsa *O'F*; Nave arsa *W.*
2 rescu'd] rescued *1633*

Fall of a Wall

UNDER an undermin'd, and shot-bruis'd wall
A too-bold Captaine perish'd by the fall,
Whose brave misfortune, happiest men envi'd,
That had a towne for tombe, his corps to hide.

A Lame Begger

I AM unable, yonder begger cries,
To stand, or move; if he say true, hee *lies*.

Cales and Guyana

IF you from spoyle of th'old worlds farthest end
To the new world your kindled valors bend,
What brave Examples then do prove it trew
That one things end doth still beginne a new.

Sir John Wingefield

BEYOND th'old Pillers many'have travailed
Towards the Suns cradle, and his throne, and bed.
A fitter Piller our Earle did bestow
In that late Iland; for he well did know
Farther then Wingefield no man dares to go.   5

Fall of a Wall. *Title from 1633, TC*: Caso d'un muro *W, O'F* (Caeso): Caso di muro *HN*: no title *B, Dob.*   4 corps *Σ*: bones *1633, TC, Gr*

A Lame Begger. *B omits. Title from 1633, TC*: Zoppo *W, O'F*: A beggar *HN*: *no title Dob.*

Cales and Guyana. *First printed in E. Gosse, Life and Letters of John Donne, 1899. Text from W. Also in O'F*: omit *Σ. Title from W* (Calez), *O'F*.   1 farthest] fardest *W*
2 bend,] bend *W*   4 beginne] begine *W*

Sir John Wingefield. *First printed in E. Gosse, Life and Letters etc., 1899. Text from W. Also in O'F*: omit *Σ. Title from Gr*: Il Cavalliere Gio: Wingef: *W*: On Cavallero Wingfeild *O'F.*

A Selfe Accuser

YOUR mistris, that you follow whores, still taxeth you:
'Tis strange she should confesse it, though'it be true.

A Licentious Person

THY sinnes and haires may no man equall call,
For, as thy sinnes increase, thy haires doe fall.

Antiquary

IF in his Studie Hammon hath such care
To'hang all old strange things, let his wife beware.

Manliness

THOU call'st me effeminat, for I love womens joyes;
I call not thee manly, though thou follow boyes.

Disinherited

THY father all from thee, by his last Will,
Gave to the poore; Thou hast good title still.

A Selfe Accuser. *TC omit. Title from 1633*: A mistrisse *HN: no title Σ.*   2 she *MSS.*:
that she *1633, Gr*   should *MSS.*: should thus *1633, Gr*   confesse it] confesse *B, Dob,
HN, O'F*

A Licentious Person. *B omits. Title from 1633, TC*: A Whorer *HN: no title Σ.*

Antiquary. *Title from 1633, TC, W*: Hammon *HN: no title Σ.*   1 Hammon hath
W, B, Dob, O'F: Hammon have *HN*: he hath *1633, Gr*: hee have *TC*   such *Σ*: so much
1633, TC, Gr   2 strange] *omit B, Dob, HN, O'F*

Manliness. *First printed in R. E. Bennett*, Complete Poems of John Donne, *1942. Text
from W. Also in HN: Σ omit. Title supplied by Bennett: no title W*: The Jughler *HN*.
1 for] that *HN*   joyes;] ioyes *W*: toyes *HN*

Disinherited. *TC omit. Title from 1633*: One disherited *HN: no title Σ.*   1 Will,] Will
1633

The Lier

THOU in the fields walkst out thy supping howers,
     And yet thou swearst thou hast supp'd like a king;
Like Nabuchadnezar perchance with grass and flowers,
A Sallet worse then Spanish dyeting.

Mercurius Gallo-Belgicus

LIKE *Esops* fellow-slaves, O *Mercury*,
     Which could do all things, thy faith is; and I
Like *Esops* selfe, which nothing; I confesse
I should have had more faith, if thou hadst lesse;
Thy credit lost thy credit: 'Tis sinne to doe,   5
In this case, as thou wouldst be done unto,
To beleeve all: Change thy name: thou art like
Mercury in stealing, but lyest like a *Greeke*.

Phryne

THY flattering picture, *Phryne*, is like thee,
     Onely in this, that you both painted be.

An Obscure Writer

PHILO, with twelve yeares study, hath beene griev'd
     To be'understood; when will hee be beleev'd?

The Lier. *First printed by J. Simeon, 1857; see note. TC omit. Text from W. Title from HN:*
no title W, Σ.   1 howers,] howres *W*   2 swearst] sayst *B, Dob, O'F*   supp'd]
supd *W*   3 grass and flowers,] gras & flowres *W*   grass] hearbes *Bur (cited Gr)*
4 Sallet] Sallet, *W*

Mercurius Gallo-Belgicus. *HN omits. Title from 1633, MSS. (B adds* Graecus).
8 but] and *W, B, O'F*

Phryne. *Title from 1633, TC, HN: no title Σ.*

An Obscure Writer. *HN omits. Title from 1633, TC: no title Σ.*   1 griev'd] griev'd,
1633   2 To be'] To'be *1633*   understood;] understood, *1633*   beleev'd?]
beleev'd. *1633*

Klockius

KLOCKIUS so deeply'hath vow'd, ne'r more to come
In bawdie house, that hee dares not goe home.

Raderus

WHY this man gelded *Martiall* I muse,
Except himselfe alone his tricks would use,
As *Katherine*, for the Courts sake, put downe Stewes.

Ralphius

COMPASSION in the world againe is bred:
Ralphius is sick, the broker keeps his bed.

Klockius. *Title from HN: no title 1633, Σ.*   1 Klockius] Rawlings *Bur (cited Gr)*
deeply'hath] deeply hath *1633*   so . . . more] hath sworne so deep never *HN*   vow'd
Σ: sworne *1633, TC, Gr*   more] *omit B, Dob, O'F*

Raderus. *B, Dob, HN omit. Title from 1633, Σ*: Martial: castrat' *W*.

Ralphius. *TC omit. Title from HN: no title 1633, Σ*.

VERSE LETTERS

The Storme

To Mr Christopher Brooke

THOU which art I, ('tis nothing to be soe)
   Thou which art still thy selfe, by these shalt know
Part of our passage; And, a hand, or eye
By *Hilliard* drawne, is worth an history,
By a worse painter made; and (without pride)   5
When by thy judgment they are dignifi'd,
My lines are such: 'Tis the preheminence
Of friendship onely to'impute excellence.

   England to whom we'owe, what we be, and have,
Sad that her sonnes did seeke a forraine grave   10
(For, Fates, or Fortunes drifts none can soothsay,
Honour and misery have one face and way.)
From out her pregnant intrailes sigh'd a winde
Which at th'ayres middle marble roome did finde
Such strong resistance, that it selfe it threw   15
Downeward againe; and so when it did view
How in the port, our fleet deare time did leese,
Withering like prisoners, which lye but for fees,
Mildly it kist our sailes, and, fresh and sweet,
As to a stomack sterv'd, whose insides meete,   20
Meate comes, it came; and swole our sailes, when wee
So joy'd, as *Sara*'her swelling joy'd to see.

VERSE LETTERS. *Text from 1633 unless otherwise stated. Readings are given from representative MSS. (except when there is a single manuscript source) named in the apparatus for each letter.*

The Storme. *MSS.: C 57, H 49; L 74, TCD; Dob, O'F, Q; W. Title from 1633, C 57, TCD* (Mr. C. B.): The Storme *H 49*: A Storme *L 74, Q*: To Mr. Christopher Brooke from the Island voyage with the E. of Essex / The Storme *O'F*: The Storme. / To Mr. Brooke . . . Earle of Essex *Dob.*   2 these] this *O'F*   3 passage] passadges *C 57, H 49*
4 an] a *Dob, O'F, W*   7 such:] such. *1633*   9 *No paragraph 1633*
11 soothsay] Southsay *1633*   12 and way] one way *Dob, O'F, Q*   19 fresh]
fresh, *1633*   20 As] As, *1633*   21 So joy'd] So joyd *1633*

But 'twas but so kinde, as our countrimen,
Which bring friends one dayes way, and leave them then.
Then like two mighty Kings, which dwelling farre   25
Asunder, meet against a third to warre,
The South and West winds joyn'd, and, as they blew,
Waves like a rowling trench before them threw.
Sooner then you read this line, did the gale,
Like shot, not fear'd till felt, our sailes assaile;   30
And what at first was call'd a gust, the same
Hath now a stormes, anon a tempests name.
Jonas, I pitty thee, and curse those men,
Who when the storm rag'd most, did wake thee then;
Sleepe is paines easiest salve, and doth fullfill   35
All offices of death, except to kill.
But when I wakt, I saw, that I saw not;
I, and the Sunne, which should teach mee'had forgot
East, West, Day, Night, and I could but say,
If the'world had lasted, now it had beene day.   40
Thousands our noyses were, yet wee 'mongst all
Could none by his right name, but thunder call:
Lightning was all our light, and it rain'd more
Then if the Sunne had drunke the sea before.
Some coffin'd in their cabbins lye,'equally   45
Griev'd that they are not dead, and yet must dye;
And as sin-burd'ned soules from graves will creepe,
At the last day, some forth their cabbins peepe:
And tremblingly'aske what newes, and doe heare so,
Like jealous husbands, what they would not know.   50
Some sitting on the hatches, would seeme there,
With hideous gazing to feare away feare.
There note they the ships sicknesses, the Mast
Shak'd with this ague, and the Hold and Wast
With a salt dropsie clog'd, and all our tacklings   55

23 'twas] 'twas, *1633*   24 Which] Who *O'F, Q*   30 fear'd] fear'd, *1633*
37 not;] not. *1633*   38 I] Yea *Q*   39 Day, Night] day, night *1633*   but *L 74,*
TCD, Dob, Q, W : omit *C 57, H 49* : onely *1633, Gr* : then but *O'F*   40 If the']
If the' *1633*   44 before.] before; *1633*   46 dye;] dye. *1633*   47 graves
MSS.: grave *1633*   49 tremblingly] trembling *Dob, O'F, Q*   50 Like] As *O'F, Q*
53 There *Σ*: Then *1633, C 57, H 49, Gr*   54 this] an *Dob, O'F*

Snapping, like too-high-stretched treble strings.
And from our totterd sailes, ragges drop downe so,
As from one hang'd in chaines, a yeare agoe.
Even our Ordinance plac'd for our defence,
Strive to breake loose, and scape away from thence.   60
Pumping hath tir'd our men, and what's the gaine?
Seas into seas throwne, we suck in againe;
Hearing hath deaf'd our saylers; and if they
Knew how to heare, there's none knowes what to say.
Compar'd to these stormes, death is but a qualme,   65
Hell somewhat lightsome, and the'Bermuda calme.
Darknesse, lights elder brother, his birth-right
Claims o'r this world, and to heaven hath chas'd light.
All things are one, and that one none can be,
Since all formes, uniforme deformity   70
Doth cover, so that wee, except God say
Another *Fiat*, shall have no more day.
So violent, yet long these furies bee,
That though thine absence sterve me,'I wish not thee.

The Calme

OUR storme is past, and that storms tyrannous rage,
    A stupid calme, but nothing it, doth swage.
The fable is inverted, and farre more
A blocke afflicts, now, then a storke before.
Stormes chafe, and soone weare out themselves, or us;   5
In calmes, Heaven laughs to see us languish thus.
As steady'as I can wish, that my thoughts were,
Smooth as thy mistresse glasse, or what shines there,
The sea is now. And, as those Iles which wee

59 Even] Yea, even *Dob, O'F*   64 knowes] knew *L 74, TCD, W*   66 and
the'Bermuda] and the Barmoodas *Dob, Q* : the Bermudas *O'F*   67 elder *Σ*: eldest *1633*,
C 57   68 Claims *MSS.*: Claim'd *1633*   this] the *Dob, O'F, Q*

The Calme. *MSS.*: *C 57, H 49*; *L 74, TCD*; *Dob, O'F, Q. Title from 1633, Σ*: A Calme
L 74, Q.   6 Heaven laughs] heavens laugh *O'F*   7 can wish, that] can wish *TCD* :
cold wish *Dob, O'F* : colde wish that *Q*   9 those *L 74, TCD, O'F, Q* : these *H 49, Dob* :
the *1633, C 57, Gr*

Seeke, when wee can move, our ships rooted bee.   10
As water did in stormes, now pitch runs out,
As lead, when a fir'd Church becomes one spout.
And all our beauty, and our trimme, decayes,
Like courts removing, or like ended playes.
The fighting place now seamens ragges supply;   15
And all the tackling is a frippery.
No use of lanthornes; and in one place lay
Feathers and dust, to day and yesterday.
Earths hollownesses, which the worlds lungs are,
Have no more winde then th'upper valt of aire.   20
We can nor left friends, nor sought foes recover,
But meteorlike, save that wee move not, hover.
Onely the Calenture together drawes
Deare friends, which meet dead in great fishes jawes:
And on the hatches as on Altars lyes   25
Each one, his owne Priest, and owne Sacrifice.
Who live, that miracle do multiply
Where walkers in hot Ovens, doe not dye.
If in despite of these, wee swimme, that hath
No more refreshing, then our brimstone Bath,   30
But from the sea, into the ship we turne,
Like parboyl'd wretches, on the coales to burne.
Like *Bajazet* encag'd, the shepheards scoffe,
Or like slacke sinew'd *Sampson*, his haire off,
Languish our ships. Now, as a Miriade   35
Of Ants, durst th'Emperours lov'd snake invade,
The crawling Gallies, Sea-gaoles, finny chips,
Might brave our Venices, now bed-ridde ships.
Whether a rotten state, and hope of gaine,
Or to disuse mee from the queasie paine   40
Of being belov'd, and loving, or the thirst
Of honour, or faire death, out pusht mee first,

---

11 out,] out *1633*   20 th'upper] the upper *1633*   21 left Σ: lost *1633*, *Dob*,
O'F, Q, Gr   29 these] this *L 74, TCD, Dob, O'F, Q*   30 our] a *Dob, O'F, Q*
33 shepheards] sheepheards *1633*   34 Or] And *L 74, TCD, Dob, Q*   37 Sea-
gaoles] Sea-goales *1633*   38 Venices] venices *1633*: Pinaces *O'F, Gr*   39 and] or
O'F, Q   40 Or] Or, *1633*

I lose my end: for here as well as I
A desperate may live,'and a coward die.
Stagge, dogge, and all which from, or towards flies,   45
Is paid with life, or pray, or doing dyes.
Fate grudges us all, and doth subtly lay
A scourge, 'gainst which wee all forget to pray;
He that at sea prayes for more winde, as well
Under the poles may begge cold, heat in hell.   50
What are wee then? How little more alas
Is man now, then before he was? he was
Nothing; for us, wee are for nothing fit;
Chance, or our selves still disproportion it.
Wee have no will, no power, no sense; I lye,   55
I should not then thus feele this miserie.

To Mr T. W.

ALL haile sweet Poët, more full of more strong fire,
    Then hath or shall enkindle any spirit,
    I lov'd what nature gave thee, but this merit
Of Wit and Art I love not but admire;
Who have before or shall write after thee,   5
Their workes, though toughly laboured, will bee
    Like infancie or age to mans firme stay,
    Or earely and late twilights to mid-day.

Men say, and truly, that they better be
    Which be envy'd then pittied: therefore I,   10
    Because I wish thee best, doe thee envie:

44 'and a] and a 1633: a Dob: and O'F   45 all] each Dob, O'F, Q   48 all
forget] all forgott L 74, TCD, Dob, Q: had forgot O'F   pray;] pray, 1633   50 poles] Pole
O'F, Q   52 was? he was] was, he was? C 57, H 49, O'F, Q (he was)   55 no will,
no power L 74, TCD: no will nor power O'F: nor will, nor power Dob, Q: no power, no
will 1633, C 57, H 49, Gr   no sense] nor sence Dob, O'F, Q

    To Mr T. W. MSS.: TC; Dob, O'F; W. Title from W: To M. I. W. 1633: To M. J. W.
TC: A letter. Incerto O'F (Incerto is changed to To Mr. J. W.): A lre. incog: Dob.
2 any] my dull Dob, O'F   3 lov'd] love Dob, O'F   this] thy O'F   4 Wit] wit
1633   5 have] hath Dob, O'F   8 and] or Dob, O'F (b.c.)   twilights] twilight Dob,
O'F (b.c.)   10 envy'd] envyed 1633

O wouldst thou, by like reason, pitty mee!
But care not for mee: I, that ever was
In Natures, and in Fortunes gifts, (alas,
   Before thy grace got in the Muses Schoole)   15
   A monster and a begger, am now a foole.

Oh how I grieve, that late borne modesty
   Hath got such root in easie waxen hearts,
   That men may not themselves, their owne good parts
Extoll, without suspect of surquedrie,   20
For, but thy selfe, no subject can be found
Worthy thy quill, nor any quill resound
   Thy worth but thine: how good it were to see
   A Poëm in thy praise, and writ by thee.

Now if this song be too'harsh for rime, yet, as   25
   The Painters bad god made a good devill,
   'Twill be good prose, although the verse be evill,
If thou forget the rime as thou dost passe.
Then write, that I may follow, and so bee
Thy debter, thy'eccho, thy foyle, thy zanee.   30
   I shall be thought, if mine like thine I shape,
   All the worlds Lyon, though I be thy Ape.

To Mr T. W.

HAST thee harsh verse, as fast as thy lame measure
  Will give thee leave, to him, my pain and pleasure.
I'have given thee, and yet thou art too weake,
Feete, and a reasoning soule and tongue to speake.

   12 mee!] mee, *1633*   13 mee:] mee, *1633*   ever] never *Dob, O'F (b.c.)*   14 Natures, and in Fortunes] . . . fortunes *1633*: Fortunes or in Natures *Dob, O'F*   15 Before thy grace . . . the Muses *Σ and 1633 uncorrected*: Before by thy grace . . . th'Muses *1633 corrected*: but by thy grace . . . *Dob, O'F (correcting* by *to* for)   16 am now *Dob, O'F, W*: am *1633, TC*   18 easie] all softe *Dob, O'F (b.c.)*   20–21 surquedrie, / For, but] surquedry. / But for *Dob, O'F (b.c.)*   22 nor] or *Dob, O'F*   23 worth *Σ*: worke *1633, TC*   27 evill,] evill. *1633*   28 passe.] passe, *1633*   29 that *Σ*: then *1633, TC*   30 thy'eccho, thy foyle] th'Eccho, the Foile *TC*: thy foyle, thy Eccho *Dob*: foyle, thy Eccho *O'F*

   To Mr T. W. *MSS.*: *TC*; *O'F*; *W. Title from W, O'F*: To M. T. W. *1633, TC.*
1 verse,] verse *1633*   2 him, . . . pain . . . pleasure.] him; . . . pain, . . . pleasure *1633* my] My *1633*   3 I'have] I have *1633*   4 Feete,] Feete *1633*

Plead for me,'and so by thine and my labour,   5
I'am thy Creator, thou my Saviour.
Tell him, all questions, which men have defended
Both of the place and paines of hell, are ended;
And 'tis decreed our hell is but privation
Of him, at least in this earths habitation: 10
And 'tis where I am, where in every street
Infections follow, overtake, and meete:
Live I or die, by you my love is sent,
And you'are my pawnes, or else my Testament.

To Mr T. W.

PREGNANT again with th'old twins Hope, and Feare,
Oft have I askt for thee, both how and where
Thou wert, and what my hopes of letters were;

As in our streets sly beggers narrowly
Watch motions of the givers hand and eye,   5
And evermore conceive some hope thereby.

And now thine Almes is given, thy letter'is read,
The body risen againe, the which was dead,
And thy poore starveling bountifully fed.

After this banquet my Soule doth say grace,   10
And praise thee for'it, and zealously imbrace
Thy love; though I thinke thy love in this case
    To be as gluttons, which say 'midst their meat,
    They love that best of which they most do eat.

5–6 *Only in W* (*which reads* me, and; thyne; *and* I ame)   14 And you'are] You ar
O'F   pawnes] *omit W*

To Mr T. W. *MSS.*: *TC*; *O'F*; *W*. *Title from W, O'F*: To M. T. W. *1633, TC.*
4 our] yᵉ *W*   5 Watch] Marke *W*   *and MSS.*: or *1633*   7 thine *MSS.*: thy
1633, Gr   12 Thy love;] Thy love, *1633*

To Mr T. W.

AT once, from hence, my lines and I depart,
   I to my soft still walks, they to my Heart;
I to the Nurse, they to the child of Art;

Yet as a firme house, though the Carpenter
Perish, doth stand: as an Embassadour   5
Lyes safe, how e'r his king be in danger:

So, though I languish, prest with Melancholy,
My verse, the strict Map of my misery,
Shall live to see that, for whose want I dye.

Therefore I envie them, and doe repent,   10
That from unhappy mee, things happy'are sent;
Yet as a Picture, or bare Sacrament,
   Accept these lines, and if in them there be
   Merit of love, bestow that love on mee.

To Mr R. W.

ZEALOUSLY my Muse doth salute all thee,
   Enquiring of that mistique trinitee
Wherof thou'and all to whom heavens do infuse
Like fyer, are made; thy body, mind, and Muse.
Dost thou recover sicknes, or prevent?   5
Or is thy Mind travail'd with discontent?
Or art thou parted from the world and mee
In a good skorn of the worlds vanitee?
Or is thy devout Muse retyr'd to sing
Upon her tender Elegiaque string?   10
Our Minds part not, joyne then thy Muse with myne,
For myne is barren thus devorc'd from thyne.

To Mr T. W. *MSS.*: H 49; TC; Dob, O'F; W. *In 1633, TC the poem follows (untitled)*
without break from the preceding. Title from W: An Old Letter H 49: A łre incog. Dob: Łre
O'F.   6 his] the Dob, O'F   7 Melancholy] Malancholy *1633*   14 of love,]
of love *1633*

To Mr R. W. *First printed in* E. Gosse, *Life and Letters of John Donne, 1899. Text and
title from* W.   1 thee,] thee W   6 travail'd] travaild W   9 retyr'd] retyrd
W   11 myne,] myne W

To Mr R. W.

MUSE not that by thy Mind thy body'is led:
For by thy Mind, my Mind's distempered.
So thy Care lives long, for I bearing part
It eates not only thyne, but my swolne hart.
And when it gives us intermission   5
We take new harts for it to feede upon.
But as a Lay Mans Genius doth controule
Body and mind; the Muse beeing the Soules Soule
Of Poëts, that methinks should ease our anguish,
Although our bodyes wither and minds languish.   10
Write then, that my griefes which thyne got may bee
Cur'd by thy charming soveraigne melodee.

To Mr C. B.

THY friend, whom thy deserts to thee enchaine,
Urg'd by this inexcusable occasion,
    Thee and the Saint of his affection
Leaving behinde, doth of both wants complaine;
And let the love I beare to both sustaine   5
    No blott nor maime by this division,
    Strong is this love which ties our hearts in one,
And strong that love pursu'd with amorous paine;
But though besides thy selfe I leave behind
    Heavens liberall, and earths thrice-fairer Sunne,   10
    Going to where sterne winter aye doth wonne,
Yet, loves hot fires, which martyr my sad minde,
    Doe send forth scalding sighes, which have the Art
    To melt all Ice, but that which walls her heart.

To Mr R. W. *First printed in Gr. Text and title from W.*   1 body'is] body is *W*
8 Body] body *W*   9 Poëts] Poets *W*   10 Although] Allthough *W*   11 Write]
Wright *W*

To Mr C. B. *MSS.: TC; O'F, W. Title from O'F, W:* To M. C. B. *1633, TC.*
2 inexcusable *MSS.*: unexcusable *1633, Gr*   10 liberall,] liberall *1633*   earths] the
earths *O'F*   thrice-fairer *Gr*: thrice fairer *W*: thrice-faire *1633*: thrice faire *TC, O'F*
11 sterne] sterv'd *O'F*

To Mr E. G.

EVEN as lame things thirst their perfection, so
   The slimy rimes bred in our vale below,
Bearing with them much of my love and hart,
Fly unto that Parnassus, wher thou art.
There thou oreseest London: Here I'have beene,   5
By staying in London, too much overseene.
Now pleasures dearth our City doth posses,
Our Theaters are fill'd with emptines;
As lancke and thin is every Street and way
As a Woman deliver'd yesterday.   10
Nothing wherat to laugh my spleene espyes
But bearbaitings or Law exercise.
Therfore Ile leave'it, and in the Cuntry strive
Pleasure, now fled from London, to retrive.
Do thou so too: and fill not like a Bee   15
Thy thighs with hony, but as plenteously
As Russian Marchants, thy selfes whole vessell load,
And then at Winter retaile it here abroad.
Blesse us with Suffolks Sweets; and as that is
Thy garden, make thy hive and warehouse this.   20

To Mr R. W.

IF, as mine is, thy life a slumber be,
   Seeme, when thou read'st these lines, to dreame of me,
Never did Morpheus nor his brother weare
Shapes soe like those Shapes, whom they would appeare,
As this my letter is like me, for it   5
Hath my name, words, hand, feet, heart, minde and wit;

To Mr E. G. *First printed in E. Gosse*, Life and Letters of John Donne, *1899. Text and title from W*.   3 hart,] hart *W*   5 I'have] I have *W*   beene,] beene *W* 6 staying] staing *W*   London,] London *W*   7 dearth] dirth *W*   posses,] posses *W* 8 emptines;] emptines. *W*   10 deliver'd] deliuerd *W*   13 leave'it] leaue it *W* 15 too] to *W*   19 that] it *Gr*

To Mr R. W. *MSS.*: *TC*; *O'F*; *W. Title from MSS.*: To M. R. W. *1633*. 3 brother] brethren *W*   6 hand] hands *TC, O'F*

It is my deed of gift of mee to thee,
It is my Will, my selfe the Legacie.
So thy retyrings I love, yea envie,
Bred in thee by a wise melancholy,   10
That I rejoyce, that unto where thou art,
Though I stay here, I can thus send my heart,
As kindly'as any enamored Patient
His Picture to his absent Love hath sent.

All newes I thinke sooner reach thee then mee;   15
Havens are Heavens, and Ships wing'd Angels be,
The which both Gospell, and sterne threatnings bring;
Guyanaes harvest is nip'd in the spring,
I feare; And with us (me thinkes) Fate deales so
As with the Jewes guide God did; he did show   20
Him the rich land, but bar'd his entry in:
Oh, slownes is our punishment and sinne.
Perchance, these Spanish businesse being done,
Which as the Earth betweene the Moone and Sun
Eclipse the light which Guyana would give,   25
Our discontinu'd hopes we shall retrive:
But if (as all th'All must) hopes smoake away,
Is not Almightie Vertue'an India?

If men be worlds, there is in every one
Some thing to'answere in some proportion   30
All the worlds riches: And in good men, this,
Vertue, our formes forme and our soules soule, is.

21 in:] in, *1633*   22 Oh *Σ*: Ah *W*: Our *1633*   sinne.] sinne; *1633*   23 these]
this *TC*   businesse] businesses *O'F, W*   26 discontinu'd] discontinued *1633*
27 all th'All] All th'All *1633*   30 to'answere] to answere *1633*]   31 this,]
this *1633*   32 soule,] soule *1633*

To Mr R. W.

KINDLY'I envy thy Songs perfection
  Built of all th'elements as our bodyes are:
  That litle of earth that'is in it, is a faire
Delicious garden where all Sweetes are sowne.
In it is cherishing fyer which dryes in mee   5
  Griefe which did drowne me: and halfe quench'd by it
  Are Satirique fyres which urg'd me to have writt
In skorne of all: for now I admyre thee.
And as Ayre doth fullfill the hollownes
  Of rotten walls; so it myne emptines,   10
Wher tost and mov'd it did begett this sound
Which as a lame Eccho of thyne doth rebound.
  Oh, I was dead: but since thy song new life did give,
  I recreated, even by thy creature, live.

To Mr S. B.

O THOU which to search out the secret parts
  Of th'India, or rather Paradise
  Of knowledge, hast with courage and advise
Lately launch'd into the vast Sea of Arts,
Disdaine not in thy constant travailing   5
  To doe as other Voyagers, and make
  Some turnes into lesse Creekes, and wisely take
Fresh water at the Heliconian spring;
I sing not, Siren-like, to tempt; for I
  Am harsh; nor as those Scismatiques with you,   10
  Which draw all wits of good hope to their crew;

To Mr R. W. *First printed in Gr. Text and title from W.*   1 Kindly'I] KindlyI *W*
10 emptines,] emptines. *W*   11 mov'd] movd *W*   13–14 Oh, . . . give, . . .
recreated, . . . creature,] *no commas W*

To Mr S. B. *MSS.: TC; O'F; W. Title from O'F; To M. S. B. 1633, TC, W.*
2 th'India] the India *1633*   9 Siren-like] Siren like *1633*   10 harsh;] harsh, *1633*

But seeing in you bright sparkes of Poëtry,
   I, though I brought no fuell, had desire
   With these Articulate blasts to blow the fire.

To Mr I. L.

O F that short Roll of friends writ in my heart
   Which with thy name begins, since their depart,
Whether in the'English Provinces they be,
Or drinke of Po, Sequan, or Danubie,
There's none that sometimes greets us not, and yet   5
Your Trent is Lethe; that past, us you forget.
You doe not duties of Societies,
If from the'embrace of a lov'd wife you rise,
View your fat Beasts, stretch'd Barnes, and labour'd fields,
Eate, play, ryde, take all joyes which all day yeelds,   10
And then againe to your embracements goe:
Some houres on us your frends, and some bestow
Upon your Muse, else both wee shall repent,
I that my love, she that her guifts on you are spent.

To Mr B. B.

I

I S not thy sacred hunger of science
   Yet satisfy'd? Is not thy braines rich hive
   Fulfil'd with hony which thou dost derive
From the Arts spirits and their Quintessence?
Then weane thy selfe at last, and thee withdraw   5
   From Cambridge thy old nurse, and, as the rest,
   Here toughly chew, and sturdily digest

12 seeing] seing *1633*; seene *TCD, O'F, W*; seeme *TCC*   Poëtry] Poetry *1633*

To Mr I. L. *MSS.*: *TC*; *O'F*; *W*. *Title from Gr*: To Mr J. L. *W*: To M. I. L. *1633*, *TC*:
To Mr T. L. *O'F*.   3 the'English] the English *1633*   6 Lethe;] Letho', *1633*
forget.] forget, *1633*   13 your] thy *W*   14 you] thee *W*   spent.] spent *1633*

To Mr B. B. *MSS.*: *TC*; *O'F*; *W*. *Title from O'F, W*: To M. B. B. *1633*, *TC*. *Numbering
of sonnets supplied.*

Th'immense vast volumes of our common law;
And begin soone, lest my griefe grieve thee too,
 Which is, that that which I should have begun   10
 In my youthes morning, now late must be done;
And I as Giddy Travellers must doe,
  Which stray or sleepe all day, and having lost
  Light and strength, darke and tir'd must then
   ride post.

11

IF thou unto thy Muse be marryed,
 Embrace her ever, ever multiply,
 Be far from me that strange Adulterie
To tempt thee and procure her widowhed.
My Muse, (for I had one,) because I'am cold,   5
 Divorc'd her selfe: the cause being in me,
 That I can take no new in Bigamye,
Not my will only but power doth withhold.
Hence comes it, that these Rymes which never had
 Mother, want matter, and they only have   10
 A little forme, the which their Father gave;
They are prophane, imperfect, oh, too bad
  To be counted Children of Poetry
  Except confirm'd and Bishoped by thee.

To Mr I. L.

BLEST are your North parts, for all this long time
 My Sun is with you, cold and darke'is our Clime;
Heavens Sun, which staid so long from us this yeare,
Staid in your North (I thinke) for she was there,
And hether by kinde nature drawne from thence,   5
Here rages, chafes, and threatens pestilence;

8 our] the *O'F* 12 I . . . Travellers] I, . . . Travellers, *1633* 13 stray] stay *W*
2 ever, ever] still: encrease & *W* 4 widowhed. *W*: widdowhood, *1633* 5 Muse
MSS.: nurse *1633* 6 selfe:] selfe, *1633*
  To Mr I. L. *MSS.*: *TC*; *O'F*; *W*. *Title from Gr*: To M. I.P. *1633*: To M. J. L. *TC*, *W*:
To Mr T. L. *O'F*. 6 rages, chafes,] rages chafes *1633*: rages, burnes, *W*

Yet I, as long as shee from hence doth staie,
Thinke this no South, no Sommer, nor no day.
With thee my kinde and unkinde heart is run,
There sacrifice it to that beauteous Sun: 10
And since thou art in Paradise and need'st crave
No joyes addition, helpe thy friend to save.
So may thy pastures with their flowery feasts,
As suddenly as Lard, fat thy leane beasts;
So may thy woods oft poll'd, yet ever weare   15
A greene, and when thee list, a golden haire;
So may all thy sheepe bring forth Twins; and so
In chace and race may thy horse all out goe;
So may thy love and courage ne'r be cold;
Thy Sonne ne'r Ward; Thy lov'd wife ne'r seem old;   20
But maist thou wish great things, and them attaine,
As thou telst her, and none but her, my paine.

To Mr Rowland Woodward

LIKE one who'in her third widdowhood doth professe
Her selfe a Nunne, ty'd to retirednesse,
So'affects my muse now, a chast fallownesse;

Since shee to few, yet to too many'hath showne
How love-song weeds, and Satyrique thornes are growne   5
Where seeds of better Arts, were early sown.

Though to use, and love Poëtrie, to mee,
Betroth'd to no'one Art, be no'adulterie;
Omissions of good, ill, as ill deeds bee.

11–12 *Only in W* (*which reads* needst *and* frind)   16 when thee list,] when thee list
1633, TC: when thou wilt *W*: (when shee list) *O'F*   20 lov'd] fair *W*: young *O'F*
22 her, ... her,] her ... her *1633*

    To Mr Rowland Woodward. *MSS.*: *C 57, H 49; L 74, TC; Dob, O'F; W. Title from 1633,*
C 57, H 49, L 74: To Rowland Woodward *Dob*: A łre to Rowland Woodward *O'F*: To Mr.
R. W. *W*: *no title TC*.   1 professe] professe, *1633*   2 ty'd] tyed *1633*: tired
TC, W   to] to a *L 74, TC, W*   3 fallownesse;] fallownesse. *1633*: holiness *Dob*
(*b.c.*), *O'F* (*b.c.*)   4 too] so *W*

For though to us it seeme,'and be light and thinne,   10
Yet in those faithfull scales, where God throwes in
Mens workes, vanity weighs as much as sinne.

If our Soules have stain'd their first white, yet wee
May cloth them with faith, and deare honestie,
Which God imputes, as native puritie.   15

There is no Vertue, but Religion:
Wise, valiant, sober, just, are names, which none
Want, which want not Vice-covering discretion.

Seeke wee then our selves in our selves; for as
Men force the Sunne with much more force to passe,   20
By gathering his beames with a christall glasse;

So wee, if wee into our selves will turne,
Blowing our sparkes of vertue, may outburne
The straw, which doth about our hearts sojourne.

You know, Physitians, when they would infuse   25
Into any'oyle, the Soule of Simples, use
Places, where they may lie still warme, to chuse.

So workes retirednesse in us; To rome
Giddily, and bee every where, but at home,
Such freedome doth a banishment become.   30

Wee are but farmers of our selves, yet may,
If we can stocke our selves, and thrive, uplay
Much, much deare treasure for the great rent day.

Manure thy selfe then, to thy selfe be'approv'd,
And with vaine outward things be no more mov'd,   35
But to know, that I love thee'and would be lov'd.

10 seeme,'and be] seeme but *O'F*   14 honestie] Integrity *Dob*, *O'F* (*b.c.*)
15 puritie.] puritie, *1633*   16 Religion:] Religion, *1633*   22 if] If *1633*   23 our]
the *L 74, TC*   25 infuse] infufe *1633*   26 Soule *MSS.*: Soules *1633*   28 To]
to *1633*   29 Giddily,] Giddily *1633*   31 farmers *MSS.*: termers *1633*   32 and
thrive] and there *C 57, H 49*: *omit L 74 (b.c.), TC*   33 deare] good *Dob, O'F*
36 lov'd] beloved *L 74, TC*

To Sir Henry Wotton

SIR, more then kisses, letters mingle Soules;
For, thus friends absent speake. This ease controules
The tediousnesse of my life: But for these
I could ideate nothing, which could please,
But I should wither in one day, and passe   5
To'a bottle'of Hay, that am a locke of Grasse.
  Life is a voyage, and in our lifes wayes
Countries, Courts, Towns are Rockes, or Remoraes;
They breake or stop all ships, yet our state's such,
That though then pitch they staine worse, wee must touch. 10
If in the furnace of the even line,
Or under th'adverse icy Poles thou pine,
Thou know'st two temperate Regions girded in,
Dwell there: But Oh, what refuge canst thou winne
Parch'd in the Court, and in the country frozen?   15
Shall cities, built of both extremes, be chosen?
Can dung and garlike be'a perfume? or can
A Scorpion and Torpedo cure a man?
Cities are worst of all three; of all three
(O knottie riddle) each is worst equally.   20
Cities are Sepulchers; they who dwell there
Are carcases, as if no such there were.
And Courts are Theaters, where some men play
Princes, some slaves, all to one end, and of one clay.
The Country is a desert, where no good,   25
Gain'd (as habits, not borne,) is understood.
There men become beasts, and prone to more evils;
In cities blockes, and in a lewd court, devills.

To Sir Henry Wotton. *MSS.*: *C 57, H 49*; *TC*; *Dob, O'F*; *W. Title* from *1633, Σ*: To
M^r. H. W. *W.*   6 bottle] botle *1633*   that] w^ch *Dob, O'F*   7 *No paragraph 1633*
lifes] lives *O'F*   11 even *MSS.*: raging *1633*   12 Poles *Σ*: pole *1633, TC*
16 cities, . . . extremes,] cities . . . extremes *1633*   17 dung] dung, *1633*   and] or *Dob,
O'F*   18 Scorpion] Scorpion, *1633*   and *H 49, TC, W*: or *1633, C 57, Dob, O'F*
21 who] w^ch *Dob, O'F*   22 no] none *Dob, O'F*   there *Σ*: they *1633*: then *TC*
25 no] the *Dob, O'F*   26 Gain'd (as habits,] Gain'd, as habits, *1633, Σ*: Gayn'd,
inhabits *O'F*   not borne,) is understood] not borne, is understood *1633, Σ*: borne, is not
understood *Dob, O'F*; *see note*   27 more *1633, C 57, W*: meere *H 49*: men *TC*: all
Dob, O'F

As in the first Chaos confusedly
Each elements qualities were in the'other three;   30
So pride, lust, covetize, being severall
To these three places, yet all are in all,
And mingled thus, their issue'incestuous.
Falshood is denizon'd. Virtue'is barbarous.
Let no man say there, Virtues flintie wall   35
Shall locke vice in mee,'I'll do none, but know all.
Men are spunges, which to poure out, receive,
Who know false play, rather then lose, deceive.
For in best understandings, sinne beganne,
Angels sinn'd first, then Devills, and then man.   40
Onely perchance beasts sinne not; wretched wee
Are beasts in all, but white integritie.
I thinke if men, which in these places live
Durst looke for themselves, and themselves retrive,
They would like strangers greet themselves, seeing then   45
Utopian youth, growne old Italian.
  Be then thine owne home, and in thy selfe dwell;
Inne any where, continuance maketh hell.
And seeing the snaile, which every where doth rome,
Carrying his owne house still, still is at home,   50
Follow (for he is easie pac'd) this snaile,
Bee thine owne Palace, or the world's thy Gaole.
And in the worlds sea, do not like corke sleepe
Upon the waters face; nor in the deepe
Sinke like a lead without a line: but as   55
Fishes glide, leaving no print where they passe,
Nor making sound, so, closely thy course goe;
Let men dispute, whether thou breathe, or no.
Onely'in this one thing, be no Galenist: To make
Courts hot ambitions wholesome, do not take   60

  32 these] those *Dob, O'F*   all are in all] are all, in all *Dob, O'F*   33 issue] yssue is
Dob: Issue's *O'F*   issue'incestuous] issue incestuous *1633*   34 Virtue'is] Virtue is *1633*
36 mee,'I'll] mee, I'll *1633*   44 for Σ: in *1633*: into *Dob, O'F*   47 then Σ:
thou *1633, C 57, Gr*   50 his] her *Dob, O'F*   home,] home. *1633*   51 easie *1633*,
H 49, W: easilye *C 57, TC, Dob, O'F (b.c.)*   52 Gaole.] goale; *1633*   57 sound,
. . . goe;] sound; . . . goe, *1633*   58 breathe] breath *1633*   no.] no: *1633*   59 one
thing] omit *Dob, O'F*   Galenist:] Galenist. *1633*

A dramme of Countries dulnesse; do not adde
Correctives, but as chymiques, purge the bad.
　　But, Sir, I'advise not you, I rather doe
Say o'er those lessons, which I learn'd of you:
Whom, free from German schismes, and lightnesse   65
Of France, and faire Italies faithlesnesse,
Having from these suck'd all they had of worth,
And brought home that faith, which you carried forth,
I throughly love. But if my selfe I'have wonne
To know my rules, I have, and you have   70

　　　　　　　　　　　　　DONNE.

To Sir Henry Wotton

HERE'S no more newes, then vertue:'I may as well
　　Tell you *Cales*, or St *Michaels* tale for newes, as tell
That vice doth here habitually dwell.

Yet, as to'get stomachs, we walke up and downe,
And toyle to sweeten rest, so, may God frowne,   5
If, but to loth both, I haunt Court, or Towne.

For here no one is from the'extremitie
Of vice, by any other reason free,
But that the next to'him, still, is worse then hee.

In this worlds warfare, they whom rugged Fate,   10
(Gods Commissary,) doth so throughly hate,
As in'the Courts Squadron to marshall their state:

If they stand arm'd with seely honesty,
With wishing prayers, and neat integritie,
Like Indians 'gainst Spanish hosts they bee.   15

63 *No paragraph 1633*   I'advise] I advise *1633*   64 you:] you. *1633*   69 selfe]
selfe, *1633*   70 DONNE.] donne : *1633*

　　To Sir Henry Wotton. *MSS.*: C *57*, H *49*; L *74*, TC; *Dob*, O'F; *W. Title from 1633*,
Σ: Jo. D: to Mr. H: W. TC: To Mr H. W. 20 July 15098 (*sic*) At Court. *W*.
　　I vertue:'I] vertue,'I *1633*   2 *Cales*] Calis *1633*   tale] tales *Dob*, O'F   for
newes] *omit* O'F   9 still, is worse] is still worsse L *74*, TC: 's still worse *Dob*, O'F
12 state:] state *1633*   14 wishing prayers] wishes pray'res O'F

Suspitious boldnesse to this place belongs,
And to'have as many eares as all have tongues;
Tender to know, tough to acknowledge wrongs.

Beleeve mee Sir, in my youths giddiest dayes,
When to be like the Court, was a playes praise,   20
Playes were not so like Courts, as Courts'are like playes.

Then let us at these mimicke antiques jeast,
Whose deepest projects, and egregious gests
Are but dull Moralls of a game at Chests.

But now 'tis incongruity to smile,   25
Therefore I end; and bid farewell a while,
At Court; though *From Court*, were the better stile.

H. W. in Hiber. Belligeranti

WENT you to conquer? and have so much lost
   Yourself, that what in you was best and most,
Respective frendship, should so quickly dye?
In publique gaine my share'is not such that I
Would lose your love for Ireland: better cheap   5
I pardon death (who though hee do not reap,
Yet gleanes hee many of our frends away)
Then that your waking mind should bee a pray
To letargies. Lett shott, and boggs, and skeines
With bodies deale, as fate bidds or restreynes;   10
Ere sicknesses attack, yong death is best;
Who payes before his death doth scape arest.
Lett not your soule (at first with graces fill'd,
   And since, and thorough crooked lymbecks, still'd

19 youths] youngst *Dob, O'F (b.c.)*   20 playes] players *O'F (b.c.)*   21 are] *omit*
O'F   26 Therefore] Wherefore *Dob*   27 *At Court*;] *At Court, 1633* From
Court] from Court *1633*

*H. W. in Hiber. Belligeranti. First printed in Gr. Text and title from Bur (as transcribed by
L. Pearsall Smith).*   2 most,] most *Bur*   3 frendship,] frendship *Bur*
4 share'is] share is *Bur*   5 lose] loose *Bur*   6 reap,] reap *Bur*   10 restreynes;]
restreynes *Bur*   11 attack,] attack *Bur*   best;] best *Bur*   13 first] first) *Bur*
fill'd] filld *Bur*   14 since,] since *Bur*   still'd] stild *Bur*

In many schools and courts, which quicken it,)   15
It self unto the Irish negligence submit.
I aske not labor'd letters which should weare
Long papers out: nor letters which should feare
Dishonest carriage: or a seers Art:
Nor such as from the brayne come, but the hart.   20

To Sir Henry Wotton, at his going Ambassador to Venice

AFTER those reverend papers, whose soule is
   Our good and great Kings lov'd hand and fear'd name,
By which to you he derives much of his,
   And (how he may) makes you almost the same,

A Taper of his Torch, a copie writ   5
   From his Originall, and a faire beame
Of the same warme, and dazeling Sun, though it
   Must in another Sphere his vertue streame:

After those learned papers which your hand
   Hath stor'd with notes of use and pleasure too,   10
From which rich treasury you may command
   Fit matter whether you will write, or doe:

After those loving papers, where friends send
   With glad griefe, to your sea-ward steps, farewel,
Which thicken on you now, as prayers ascend   15
   To heaven in troupes at'a good mans passing bell:

Admit this honest paper, and allow
   It such an audience as your selfe would aske;
What you must say at Venice this meanes now,
   And hath for nature, what you have for taske: 20

17 labor'd] labored *Bur*   19 Art:] Art *Bur*
   To Sir Henry Wotton, at his going Ambassador to Venice. *MSS.*: TC, O'F. *Title from MSS.*: To Sir H. W. at . . . Venice. *1633.*   10 pleasure *TCC, O'F*: pleasures *1633, TCD*   12 write,] write *1633*   14 sea-ward] Sea-ward *1633*   19 must] would *O'F*   20 taske:] taske. *1633*

To sweare much love, not to be chang'd before
    Honour alone will to your fortune fit;
Nor shall I then honour your fortune, more
    Then I have done your honour wanting it.

But 'tis an easier load (though both oppresse)   25
    To want, then governe greatnesse, for wee are
In that, our owne and onely businesse,
    In this, wee must for others vices care;

'Tis therefore well your spirits now are plac'd
    In their last Furnace, in activity;   30
Which fits them (Schooles and Courts and Warres o'rpast)
    To touch and test in any best degree.

For mee, (if there be such a thing as I)
    Fortune (if there be such a thing as shee)
Spies that I beare so well her tyranny,   35
    That she thinks nothing else so fit for mee;

But though she part us, to heare my oft prayers
    For your increase, God is as neere mee here;
And to send you what I shall begge, his staires
    In length and ease are alike every where.   40

A Letter written by Sir H. G. and J. D.
alternis vicibus

SINCE ev'ry Tree beginns to blossome now
    Perfuminge and enamelinge each bow,
Hartes should as well as they, some fruits allow.

---

24 honour wanting it *1633*: noble wanting it *TC*: noble-wanting-witt *O'F*
31 Warres] warres *1633*: tents *Bur (cited Gr)*
    A Letter written by Sir H. G. and J. D. *alternis vicibus. First printed in E. K. Chambers,*
Poems of John Donne, *1896. Text and title from A 25, with italics supplied for Goodyer's*
stanzas.   2 *bow,*] bow *A 25*

For since one old poore sunn serves all the rest,
You sev'rall sunns that warme, and light each brest   5
Doe by that influence all your thoughts digest.

And that you two may soe your vertues move,
On better matter then beames from above,
Thus our twin'd soules send forth these buds of love.

As in devotions men joyne both there hands,   10
Wee make our's doe one Act, to seale the bands,
By which w'enthrall our selves to your Commaunds.

And each for others faith, and zeale stand bound;
As safe as spirits are from any wound,
Soe free from impure thoughts they shalbe found.   15

Admit our Magique then by which wee doe
Make you appeere to us, and us to you,
Supplying all the Muses in you twoe.

Wee doe consider noe flower that is sweet,
But wee your breath in that exhaling meet,   20
And as true Types of you, them humbly greet.

Heere in our Nightingales, wee heere you singe,
Who soe doe make the whole yeare through a springe,
And save us from the feare of Autumns stinge.

In Ancors calme face wee your smoothnes see,   25
Your mindes unmingled, and as cleare as shee
That keepes untoucht her first virginitie.

Did all St. Edith Nunns descend againe
To honor Polesworth with their cloystred traine,
Compar'd with you each would confesse some stayne.   30

10 joyne] Joyne *A 25*   hands,] hands *A 25*   13 *bound;*] bound, *A 25*
22 singe,] singe *A 25*   25 *Ancors*] Auchos *A 25*   29 cloystred] Cloystre'd *A 25*
traine,] traine *A 25*

Or should wee more bleed out our thoughts in Inke,
Noe paper (though it would bee glad to drinke
Those drops) could comprehend what wee doe thinke.

For 'twere in us ambition to write
Soe, that because wee two, you two unite,   35
Our letter should as you, bee infinite.

To Sir Henry Goodyere

W HO makes the Past, a patterne for next yeare,
         Turnes no new leafe, but still the same things reads,
Seene things, he sees againe, heard things doth heare,
   And makes his life, but like a paire of beads.

A Palace, when 'tis that, which it should be,   5
   Leaves growing, and stands such, or else decayes:
But hee which dwels there, is not so; for hee
   Strives to urge upward, and his fortune raise;

So had your body'her morning, hath her noone,
   And shall not better; her next change is night: 10
But her faire larger guest, to'whom Sun and Moone
   Are sparkes, and short liv'd, claimes another right.

The noble Soule by age growes lustier,
   Her appetite, and her digestion mend,
Wee must not sterve, nor hope to pamper her   15
   With womens milke, and pappe unto the end.

Provide you manlyer dyet; you have seene
   All libraries, which are Schools, Camps, and Courts;
But aske your Garners if you have not beene
   In harvests, too indulgent to your sports.   20

31 *Inke,*] Inke *A 25*   33 *comprehend*] Comprehend *A 25*   34 'twere]
t'were *A 25*

   To Sir Henry Goodyere. *MSS.: C 57, H 49; TC; Dob, O'F. Title from 1633, Σ:* To Sr. H. G.
moveing him to Travell. *TC:* To Sr. Henry Goodyeere moving . . . travell. *O'F.*
2 things] thinge *Dob, O'F*   6 decayes:] decayes, *1633*   8 upward] upwards *TC*
fortune] fortunes *TC, O'F*   16 the] her *TC, Dob, O'F*   17 dyet;] dyet, *1633*
20 harvests] harvest *O'F*

Would you redeeme it? then your selfe transplant
   A while from hence. Perchance outlandish ground
Beares no more wit, then ours, but yet more scant
   Are those diversions there, which here abound.

To be a stranger hath that benefit,   25
   Wee can beginnings, but not habits choke.
Goe; whither? Hence; you get, if you forget;
   New faults, till they prescribe in us, are smoake.

Our soule, whose country'is heaven, and God her father,
   Into this world, corruptions sinke, is sent,   30
Yet, so much in her travaile she doth gather,
   That she returnes home, wiser then she went;

It payes you well, if it teach you to spare,
   And make you'asham'd, to make your hawks praise, yours,
Which when herselfe she lessens in the aire,   35
   You then first say, that high enough she toures.

Howsoever, keepe the lively tast you hold
   Of God, love him as now, but feare him more,
And in your afternoones thinke what you told
   And promis'd him, at morning prayer before.   40

Let falshood like a discord anger you,
   Else be not froward. But why doe I touch
Things, of which none is in your practise new,
   And Fables, or fruit-trenchers teach as much;

But thus I make you keepe your promise Sir,   45
   Riding I had you, though you still staid there,
And in these thoughts, although you never stirre,
   You came with mee to Micham, and are here.

23 no] not *H 49*, *TC*, *Dob*   27 Goe;] Goe, *1633*   Hence] hence *1633*   28 in]
to *Dob*, *O'F*   37 Howsoever *C 57*, *H 49*, *TC*: Howsever *Dob*: Howsoe're *O'F*: However *1633*, *Gr*   42 froward.] froward; *1633*   44 Fables *Σ*: Tables *1633*, *C 57*, *Gr*
or] and *Dob*, *O'F*   45 make] made *TC*   48 with mee to] to mee at *TC*

To Sir Edward Herbert, at Julyers

MAN is a lumpe, where all beasts kneaded bee,
Wisdome makes him an Arke where all agree;
The foole, in whom these beasts do live at jarre,
Is sport to others, and a Theater;
Nor scapes hee so, but is himselfe their prey: 5
All which was man in him, is eate away,
And now his beasts on one another feed,
Yet couple'in anger, and new monsters breed.
How happy'is hee, which hath due place assign'd
To'his beasts, and disaforested his minde!   10
Empail'd himselfe to keepe them out, not in;
Can sow, and dares trust corne, where they have bin;
Can use his horse, goate, wolfe, and every beast,
And is not Asse himselfe to all the rest.
Else, man not onely is the heard of swine,   15
But he's those devills too, which did incline
Them to a headlong rage, and made them worse:
For man can adde weight to heavens heaviest curse.
As Soules (they say) by our first touch, take in
The poysonous tincture of Originall sinne,   20
So, to the punishments which God doth fling,
Our apprehension contributes the sting.
To us, as to his chickins, he doth cast
Hemlocke, and wee as men, his hemlocke taste;
We do infuse to what he meant for meat,   25
Corrosivenesse, or intense cold or heat.
For, God no such specifique poyson hath
As kills we know not how; his fiercest wrath
Hath no antipathy, but may be good
At lest for physicke, if not for our food.   30
Thus man, that might be'his pleasure, is his rod,
And is his devill, that might be his God.

To Sir Edward Herbert, at Julyers. *MSS.*: *C 57, H 49*; *TC*; *Dob, O'F. Title from 1633,
C 57, H 49, O'F*: To Sr. Edward Herbert *Dob*: To Sr. E. H. *TC*.   4 Theater;]
Theater, *1633*   5 prey:] prey; *1633*   8 breed.] breed; *1633*   9 which] who *O'F*
10 minde!] minde? *1633*   24 taste;] taste. *1633*   28 we] men *Dob, O'F*

Since then our businesse is, to rectifie
Nature, to what she was, wee'are led awry
By them, who man to us in little show;   35
Greater then due, no forme we can bestow
On him; for Man into himselfe can draw
All; All his faith can swallow,'or reason chaw.
All that is fill'd, and all that which doth fill,
All the round world, to man is but a pill;   40
In all it workes not, but it is in all
Poysonous, or purgative, or cordiall,
For, knowledge kindles Calentures in some,
And is to others icy *Opium*.
As brave as true, is that profession than   45
Which you doe use to make; that you know man.
This makes it credible; you'have dwelt upon
All worthy bookes, and now are such a one.
Actions are authors, and of those in you
Your friends finde every day a mart of new.   50

To the Countesse of Huntington

THAT unripe side of earth, that heavy clime
  That gives us man up now, like *Adams* time
Before he ate; mans shape, that would yet bee
(Knew they not it, and fear'd beasts companie)
So naked at this day, as though man there   5
From Paradise so great a distance were,
As yet the newes could not arrived bee
Of *Adams* tasting the forbidden tree;
Depriv'd of that free state which they were in,
And wanting the reward, yet beare the sinne.   10

35 show;] show, *1633*   38 All;] All, *1633*   40 pill;] pill, *1633*   41–50 *Omit*
C 57   44 icy] jcy *1633*   47 credible;] credible, *1633*   you'have] you have *1633*
48 bookes,] bookes; *1633*   a *MSS*: an *1633, Gr*   49 those] these *Dob, O'F (b.c.)*

  To the Countesse of Huntington. *Text from 1635. MSS.:* TCD(2), P. *Paragraphing
supplemented. Title from 1635:* Sʳ Walter Aston to the Countesse of Huntington. *TCD:* Sʳ
Wal. Ashton to ... P.   2 man] men *P*

But, as from extreme hights who downward looks,
Sees men at childrens shapes, Rivers at brookes,
And loseth younger formes; so, to your eye,
These (Madame) that without your distance lie,
Must either mist, or nothing seeme to be,   15
Who are at home but wits mere *Atomi*.
But, I who can behold them move, and stay,
Have found my selfe to you, just their midway;
And now must pitty them; for, as they doe
Seeme sick to me, just so must I to you.   20

Yet neither will I vexe your eyes to see
A sighing Ode, nor crosse-arm'd Elegie.
I come not to call pitty from your heart,
Like some white-liver'd dotard that would part
Else from his slipperie soule with a faint groane,   25
And faithfully, (without you smil'd) were gone.
I cannot feele the tempest of a frowne,
I may be rais'd by love, but not throwne down.
Though I can pittie those sigh twice a day,
I hate that thing whispers it selfe away.   30
Yet since all love is fever, who to trees
Doth talke, doth yet in loves cold ague freeze.
'Tis love, but, with such fatall weaknesse made,
That it destroyes it selfe with its owne shade.
Who first look'd sad, griev'd, pin'd, and shew'd his paine, 35
Was he that first taught women, to disdaine.

As all things were one nothing, dull and weake,
Untill this raw disorder'd heape did breake,
And severall desires led parts away,
Water declin'd with earth, the ayre did stay,   40
Fire rose, and each from other but unty'd,
Themselves unprison'd were and purify'd:
So was love, first in vast confusion hid,

11 downward] downewards *P*: inward *TCD*   17 who] that *MSS*.   20 you.]
you, *1635*   21 neither] never *TCD*   22 nor] or *MSS*.   26 faithfully]
finially *P*   you smil'd] your smile *MSS*.   30 whispers] whisp*ered P*: vapours *TCD*
31 love is] love's a *P*   32 ague] Feaver *P*   35 paine,] paine. *1635*   36 women]
woman *TCD*   38 disorder'd] disordered *1635*   41 but] once *P*

An unripe willingnesse which nothing did,
A thirst, an Appetite which had no ease,   45
That found a want, but knew not what would please.
What pretty innocence in those days mov'd!
Man ignorantly walk'd by her he lov'd;
Both sigh'd and enterchang'd a speaking eye,
Both trembled and were sick, both knew not why.   50
That naturall fearefulnesse that struck man dumbe,
Might well (those times consider'd) man become.
As all discoverers whose first assay
Findes but the place, after, the nearest way:
So passion is to womans love, about,   55
Nay, farther off, than when we first set out.
It is not love that sueth, or doth contend;
Love either conquers, or but meets a friend.
Man's better part consists of purer fire,
And findes it selfe allow'd, ere it desire.   60
Love is wise here, keepes home, gives reason sway,
And journeys not till it finde summer-way.
A weather-beaten Lover but once knowne,
Is sport for every girle to practise on.
Who strives, through womans scornes, women to know,   65
Is lost, and seekes his shadow to outgoe;
It must bee sicknesse, after one disdaine,
Though he be call'd aloud, to looke againe.
Let others sigh, and grieve; one cunning sleight
Shall freeze my love to Christall in a night.   70
I can love first, and (if I winne) love still;
And cannot be remov'd, unlesse she will.
It is her fault if I unsure remaine,
Shee onely can untie, and binde againe.
The honesties of love with ease I doe,   75
But am no porter for a tedious woo.

47 mov'd!] mov'd? *1635*   48 by] w^th *P*   50 both] but *MSS.*   52 consider'd] considered *1635*   53–54 whose . . . Findes] who . . . find *P*   57 sueth,
or] sues and *P*   65 strives,] strives *1635*   womans] womens *P*   scornes, women]
scorne woman *TCD*   know,] know. *1635*   67 sicknesse,] sicknesse *1635*   69 sigh
MSS.: sinne *1635*   70 love] Love *1635*   74 and *P*: I *1635, TCD*   76 woo
TCD: wooe *P*: woe *1635*

But (madame) I now thinke on you; and here
Where we are at our hights, you but appeare,
We are but clouds you rise from, our noone-ray
But a foule shadow, not your breake of day.   80
You are at first hand all that's faire and right,
And others good reflects but backe your light.
You are a perfectnesse, so curious hit,
That youngest flatteries doe scandall it.
For, what is more doth what you are restraine,   85
And though beyond, is downe the hill againe.
We have no next way to you, we crosse to'it:
You are the straight line, thing prais'd, attribute;
Each good in you's a light; so many'a shade
You make, and in them are your motions made.   90
These are your pictures to the life. From farre
We see you move, and here your *Zani's* are:
So that no fountaine good there is, doth grow
In you, but our dimme actions faintly shew.

Then finde I, if mans noblest part be love,   95
Your purest luster must that shadow move.
The soule with body, is a heaven combin'd
With earth, and for mans ease, but nearer joyn'd.
Where thoughts the starres of soule we understand,
We guesse not their large natures, but command.   100
And love in' you, that bountie is of light,
That gives to all, and yet hath infinite;
Whose heat doth force us thither to intend,
But soule we finde too earthly to ascend,
'Till slow accesse hath made it wholy pure,   105
Able immortall clearnesse to endure.
Who dare aspire this journey with a staine,
Hath waight will force him headlong backe againe.

77 I now] now I *TCD*   78 hights] height *TCD*   79 clouds . . . from,]
clouds, . . . from *1635*   noone-ray] noone-ray, *1635*   81 right] bright *P*   83 a per-
fectnesse] all perfectnes *TCD*: all *perfections P*   84 youngest] the quaintest *TCD*
flatteries] flatterers *MSS*.   doe] *omit TCD*   86 though] whats *P*   87 to'it]
to it *1635*   88 attribute;] attribute, *1635*   89 many'a] many a *1635*
91 These] Those *TCD*   102 infinite;] infinite. *1635*   105 wholy] holy *MSS*.
107 dare] dares *MSS*.   108 waight] weights *MSS*.

No more can impure man retaine and move
In that pure region of a worthy love   110
Then earthly substance can unforc'd aspire,
And leave his nature to converse with fire:
Such may have eye, and hand; may sigh, may speak;
But like swoln bubles, when they'are high'st they break.

Though far removed Northerne fleets scarce finde   115
The Sunnes comfort; others thinke him too kinde.
There is an equall distance from her eye,
Men perish too farre off, and burne too nigh.
But as ayre takes the Sunne-beames equall bright
From the first Rayes, to his last opposite: 120
So able men, blest with a vertuous Love,
Remote or neare, or howsoe'r they move;
Their vertue breakes all clouds that might annoy,
There is no Emptinesse, but all is Joy.
He much profanes whom violent heats doe move   125
To stile his wandring rage of passion, *Love*:
Love that imparts in every thing delight,
Is fain'd, which onely tempts mans appetite.
Why love among the vertues is not knowne
Is, that love is them all contract in one.   130

To the Countesse of Huntingdon

MADAME,

M AN to Gods image, *Eve*, to mans was made,
   Nor finde wee that God breath'd a soule in her,
Canons will not Church functions you invade,
   Nor lawes to civill office you preferre.

109 impure] unpure *P*   110 love] love: *1635*   113 eye, and hand] eyes and
hands *MSS.*   114 they'are] they are *1635*   high'st they] highest *MSS.*   break.]
break *1635*   115 *Paragraph at 113 in 1635*   Though far removed] Through far re-
motenesse *P*   fleets] Iles *TCD*   116 comfort;] comfort· *1635*   119 ayre . . .
the] yᵉ aire . . . all *P*   120 first Rayes] rayes first *TCD*; rise first *P*   121 men
P: man *1635, TCD*   123 Their *P*: There *1635, TCD*   125 violent *MSS.*:
valiant *1635*   126 *Love*:] Love. *1635*   127 imparts] imports *TCD*   128 Is
fain'd, which onely tempts mans appetite *P (no comma)*: Is thought the Mansion of sweet
appetite *TCD*: Is fancied (*rest of line blank*) *1635*   130 Is, that] Is; 'cause *TCD*
contract in *P*: contracted *1635, TCD*
   To the Countesse of Huntingdon. *MSS.*: *TCD*; *O'F*. Title from *1633*, *O'F*: To the C. of
H. *TCD*.

Who vagrant transitory Comets sees,   5
  Wonders, because they'are rare; But a new starre
Whose motion with the firmament agrees,
  Is miracle; for, there no new things are;

In woman so perchance milde innocence
  A seldome comet is, but active good   10
A miracle, which reason scapes, and sense;
  For, Art and Nature this in them withstood.

As such a starre, the *Magi* led to view
  The manger-cradled infant, God below:
By vertues beames by fame deriv'd from you,   15
  May apt soules, and the worst may, vertue know.

If the worlds age, and death be argu'd well
  By the Sunnes fall, which now towards earth doth bend,
Then we might feare that vertue, since she fell
  So low as woman, should be neare her end.   20

But she's not stoop'd, but rais'd; exil'd by men
  She fled to heaven, that's heavenly things, that's you;
She was in all men, thinly scatter'd then,
  But now amass'd, contracted in a few.

She guilded us: But you are gold, and Shee;   25
  Us she inform'd, but transubstantiates you;
Soft dispositions which ductile bee,
  Elixarlike, she makes, not cleane, but new.

Though you a wifes and mothers name retaine,
  'Tis not as woman, for all are not soe,   30
But vertue having made you vertue,'is faine
  T'adhere in these names, her and you to show,

---

13 the *MSS.*: which *1633*   *Magi*] Magis *TCD*: Mages *O'F*   14 below:] below.
1633   16 may,] may *1633*   17 argu'd] argued *1633*   22 you;] you, *1633*
24 amass'd] a Mass *TCD*, *O'F* (*b.c.*)   25 Shee;] Shee, *1633*   26 you;] you, *1633*
28 makes,] makes *1633*

Else, being alike pure, wee should neither see;
    As, water being into ayre rarify'd,
Neither appeare, till in one cloud they bee,   35
    So, for our sakes you do low names abide;

Taught by great constellations, which being fram'd,
    Of the most starres, take low names, *Crab*, and *Bull*,
When single planets by the *Gods* are nam'd,
    You covet not great names, of great things full.   40

So you, as woman, one doth comprehend,
    And in the vaile of kindred others see;
To some you are reveal'd, as in a friend,
    And as a vertuous Prince farre off, to mee:

To whom, because from you all vertues flow,   45
    And 'tis not none, to dare contemplate you,
I, which doe so, as your true subject owe
    Some tribute for that, so these lines are due.

If you can thinke these flatteries, they are,
    For then your judgement is below my praise,   50
If they were so, oft, flatteries worke as farre,
    As Counsels, and as farre th'endeavour raise.

So my ill reaching you might there grow good,
    But I remaine a poyson'd fountaine still;
But not your beauty, vertue, knowledge, blood   55
    Are more above all flattery, then my will.

And if I flatter any, 'tis not you
    But my owne judgement, who did long agoe
Pronounce, that all these praises should be true,
    And vertue should your beauty,'and birth outgrow.   60

33 see;] see, *1633*   43 you *MSS*.: ye *1633*, *Gr*   44 mee:] mee. *1633*
47 doe so, *O'F* (*b.c.*): doe *TCD*: to you *1633*   48 due.] due, *1633*

Now that my prophesies are all fulfill'd,
  Rather then God should not be honour'd too,
And all these gifts confess'd, which hee instill'd,
  Your selfe were bound to say that which I doe.

So I, but your Recorder am in this,   65
  Or mouth, and Speaker of the universe,
A ministeriall Notary, for 'tis
  Not I, but you and fame, that make this verse;

I was your Prophet in your yonger dayes,
And now your Chaplaine, God in you to praise.   70

To Mrs M. H.

MAD paper stay, and grudge not here to burne
     With all those sonnes whom my braine did create,
At lest lye hid with mee, till thou returne
  To rags againe, which is thy native state.

What though thou have enough unworthinesse   5
  To come unto great place as others doe,
That's much; emboldens, pulls, thrusts I confesse,
  But 'tis not all; Thou should'st be wicked too.

And, that thou canst not learne, or not of mee;
  Yet thou wilt goe? Goe, since thou goest to her   10
Who lacks but faults to be a Prince, for shee,
  Truth, whom they dare not pardon, dares preferre.

But when thou com'st to that perplexing eye
  Which equally claimes *love* and *reverence*,
Thou wilt not long dispute it, thou wilt die;   15
  And, having little now, have then no sense.

64 that] thar *1633*   66 and *MSS*.: or *1633, Gr*   67 Notary] notary *1633*
    To Mrs M. H. *MSS*.: *TC*; *Dob, O'F. Title from O'F*: To M. M. H. *1633, TC*: *no title
Dob*.   2 whom] w^ch *Dob, O'F*   3 returne] returne. *1633*   4 is] was *Dob,
O'F*   7 much;] much, *1633*   8 'tis] thats *Dob, O'F*   all; Thou] all, thou *1633*
10 goe? Goe] goe, Goe *1633*   12 not] to *Dob, O'F (b.c.)*   14 *reverence,*]
reverence. 1633

Yet when her warme redeeming hand, which is
    A miracle; and made such to worke more,
Doth touch thee (saples leafe) thou grow'st by this
    Her creature; glorify'd more then before.   20

Then as a mother which delights to heare
    Her early child mis-speake halfe utter'd words,
Or, because majesty doth never feare
    Ill or bold speech, she Audience affords.

And then, cold speechlesse wretch, thou diest againe,   25
    And wisely; what discourse is left for thee?
From speech of ill, and her, thou must abstaine,
    And is there any good which is not shee?

Yet maist thou praise her servants, though not her,
    And wit, and vertue,'and honour her attend,   30
And since they'are but her cloathes, thou shalt not erre,
    If thou her shape and beauty'and grace commend.

Who knowes thy destiny? when thou hast done,
    Perchance her Cabinet may harbour thee,
Whither all noble'ambitious wits doe runne,   35
    A nest almost as full of Good as shee.

When thou art there, if any, whom wee know,
    Were sav'd before, and did that heaven partake,
When she revolves his papers, marke what show
    Of favour, she alone, to them doth make.   40

Marke, if to get them, she o'r skip the rest,
    Marke, if shee read them twice, or kisse the name;
Marke, if she doe the same that they protest,
    Marke, if she marke whether her woman came.

19 saples] shape-les *Dob*, *O'F* (*b.c.*)   22 mis-speake] mispeake *1633*   utter'd]
uttered *1633*   27 From *MSS.*: For, *1633*, *Gr*   her,] her *1633*   31 erre,] erre
1633   33 Who...destiny?] We knowe thy Destiny; *Dob*, *O'F*   35 noble'ambitious]
noble ambitious *1633*   41 o'r skip] do skipp *TC*: skips *Dob*: skipps o're *O'F*
42–45 *Omit Dob*

Marke, if slight things be'objected, and o'r blowne,   45
    Marke, if her oathes against him be not still
Reserv'd, and that shee grieves she's not her owne,
    And chides the doctrine that denies Freewill.

I bid thee not doe this to be my spie;
    Nor to make my selfe her familiar;   50
But so much I doe love her choyce, that I
    Would faine love him that shall be lov'd of her.

To the Countesse of Bedford

MADAME,

R EASON is our Soules left hand, Faith her right,
    By these wee reach divinity, that's you;
Their loves, who have the blessing of your sight,
    Grew from their reason, mine from far faith grew.

But as, although a squint lefthandednesse   5
    Be'ungracious, yet we cannot want that hand,
So would I, not to'encrease, but to expresse
    My faith, as I beleeve, so understand.

Therefore I study you first in your Saints,
    Those friends, whom your election glorifies,   10
Then in your deeds, accesses, and restraints,
    And what you reade, and what your selfe devize.

But soone, the reasons why you'are lov'd by all,
    Grow infinite, and so passe reasons reach,
Then backe againe to'implicite faith I fall,   15
    And rest on what the Catholique voice doth teach;

51 I doe] doe I *Dob, O'F, TCC*

To the Countesse of Bedford. *MSS.*: *C 57, H 49; L 74, TCD; Dob, O'F. Title from 1633, Σ*:
Another to the Countis of Bed. *L 74*: To the Countesse of B. *TCD*.   3 blessing *Σ*:
blessings *1633, C 57, H 49, Gr*   sight *MSS.*: light *1633, Gr*   4 far *C 57, H 49, Dob*;
faire *1633, L 74 TCD*: *omit O'F (b.c.)*   7 to'encrease] to encrease *1633*   13 by]
of Dob, O'F   16 voice *MSS.*: faith *1633*

LUCY, COUNTESS OF BEDFORD
From the portrait at Woburn Abbey, by kind permission of
His Grace the Duke of Bedford

That you are good: and not one Heretique
    Denies it: if he did, yet you are so;
For, rockes, which high top'd and deep rooted sticke,
    Waves wash, not undermine, nor overthrow.   20

In every thing there naturally growes
    A *Balsamum* to keepe it fresh, and new,
If 'twere not injur'd by extrinsique blowes;
    Your birth and beauty are this Balme in you.

But you of learning and religion,   25
    And vertue,'and such ingredients, have made
A methridate, whose operation
    Keepes off, or cures what can be done or said.

Yet, this is not your physicke, but your food,
    A dyet fit for you; for you are here   30
The first good Angell, since the worlds frame stood,
    That ever did in womans shape appeare.

Since you are then Gods masterpeece, and so
    His Factor for our loves; do as you doe,
Make your returne home gracious; and bestow   35
    This life on that; so make one life of two.
        For so God helpe mee,'I would not misse you there
        For all the good which you can do me here.

To the Countesse of Bedford

MADAME,

Y OU have refin'd mee, and to worthyest things
    (Vertue, Art, Beauty, Fortune,) now I see
Rarenesse, or use, not nature value brings;
    And such, as they are circumstanc'd, they bee.
        Two ills can ne're perplexe us, sinne to'excuse;   5
        But of two good things, we may leave and chuse.

18 so;] so. *1633*   19 high top'd and *1633*, *TCD*: high to Sun, and *L 74*: high to
some, & *C 57*, *H 49*: high to seeme, *Dob*: high to sence, *O'F*   25 But] But, *1633*
36 This *MSS.*: Thy *1633*
   To the Countesse of Bedford. *MSS.*: *C 57*, *H 49*; *TCD*; *Dob*, *O'F*. *Title from 1633*, *Σ*:
O'F adds Twitnam: To the Countess of B. *TCD.*   2 (Vertue ... Fortune,)] Vertue ...
Fortune, *1633*   5 ne're] nere *1633*

Therefore at Court, which is not vertues clime,
   (Where a transcendent height, (as, lownesse mee)
Makes her not be, or not show) all my rime
    Your vertues challenge, which there rarest bee;   10
      For, as darke texts need notes: there some must bee
      To usher vertue, and say, *This is shee.*

So in the country'is beauty; to this place
   You are the season (Madame) you the day,
'Tis but a grave of spices, till your face   15
    Exhale them, and a thick close bud display.
      Widow'd and reclus'd else, her sweets she'enshrines;
      As China, when the Sunne at Brasill dines.

Out from your chariot, morning breaks at night,
   And falsifies both computations so;   20
Since a new world doth rise here from your light,
    We your new creatures, by new recknings goe.
      This showes that you from nature lothly stray,
      That suffer not an artificiall day.

In this you'have made the Court th'Antipodes,   25
   And will'd your Delegate, the vulgar Sunne,
To doe profane autumnall offices,
    Whilst here to you, wee sacrificers runne;
      And whether Priests, or Organs, you wee'obey,
      We sound your influence, and your Dictates say.   30

Yet to that Deity which dwels in you,
   Your vertuous Soule, I now not sacrifice;
These are *Petitions*, and not *Hymnes*; they sue
    But that I may survay the edifice.
      In all Religions as much care hath bin   35
      Of Temples frames, and beauty,'as Rites within.

9 show)] show: *1633*   17 enshrines;] enshrines *1633*   21 light *1633*, *TCD*:
sight *C 57, H 49, Dob, O'F (b.c.)*   25 th'Antipodes] the Antipodes *1633*

As all which goe to Rome, doe not thereby
  Esteeme religions, and hold fast the best,
But serve discourse, and curiosity,
    With that which doth religion but invest,   40
      And shunne th'entangling laborinths of Schooles,
      And make it wit, to thinke the wiser fooles:

So in this pilgrimage I would behold
  You as you'are vertues temple, not as shee,
What walls of tender christall her enfold,   45
    What eyes, hands, bosome, her pure Altars bee;
      And after this survay, oppose to all
      Bablers of Chappels, you th'Escuriall.

Yet not as consecrate, but merely'as faire,
  On these I cast a lay and country eye.   50
Of past and future stories, which are rare,
  I finde you all record, all prophecie.
    Purge but the booke of Fate, that it admit
    No sad nor guilty legends, you are it.

If good and lovely were not one, of both   55
  You were the transcript, and originall,
The Elements, the Parent, and the Growth,
  And every peece of you, is both their All:
    So'intire are all your deeds, and you, that you
    Must do the same thing still: you cannot two.   60

But these (as nice thinne Schoole divinity
  Serves heresie to furder or represse)
Tast of Poëtique rage, or flattery,
  And need not, where all hearts one truth professe;
    Oft from new proofes, and new phrase, new doubts
      grow,   65
    As strange attire aliens the men wee know.

42 fooles:] fooles. *1633 uncorrected*   49 faire,] faire; *1633*   50 eye.] eye, *1633
uncorrected*   52 all prophecie *MSS.*: and prophecie *1633, Gr*   prophecie.] prophecie,
1633 uncorrected   57 Growth,] Growth *1633*   58 All:] All, *1633*   60 thing
Σ: things *1633, C* 57   66 aliens] alters *Dob, O'F*

Leaving then busie praise, and all appeale
To higher Courts, senses decree is true,
The Mine, the Magazine, the Commonweale,
The story'of beauty,'in Twicknam is, and you.   70
Who hath seene one, would both; As, who had bin
In Paradise, would seeke the Cherubin.

To the Lady Bedford

YOU that are she and you, that's double shee,
   In her dead face, halfe of your selfe shall see;
Shee was the other part, for so they doe
Which build them friendships, become one of two;
So two, that but themselves no third can fit,   5
Which were to be so, when they were not yet;
Twinnes, though their birth *Cusco*, and *Musco* take,
As divers starres one Constellation make;
Pair'd like two eyes, have equall motion, so
Both but one meanes to see, one way to goe.   10
Had you dy'd first, a carcasse shee had beene;
And wee your rich Tombe in her face had seene;
She like the Soule is gone, and you here stay,
Not a live friend; but th'other halfe of clay.
And since you act that part, As men say, here   15
Lies such a Prince, when but one part is there,
And do all honour, and devotion due
Unto the whole, so wee all reverence you;
For, such a friendship who would not adore
In you, who are all what both was before,   20
Not all, as if some perished by this,
But so, as in you all contracted is.

67 appeale] appeale, *1633*   70 story'of] story of *1633*

To the Lady Bedford. *MSS.*: *L 74, TCD*; *O'F. Title from O'F*: Elegie to the Lady Bedford.
1633: Elegie . . . La: Bedford *TCD*: An . . . *L 74*.   1 she and you,] she, and you *1633*
6 yet;] yet *1633*   7 take,] take *1633 uncorrected*   8 make;] make, *1633*
10 goe.] goe; *1633*   13 stay,] stay *1633*   14 th'other] thother *1633*   clay.]
clay; *1633*   16 there,] there; *1633*   17 honour,] honour: *1633*   due] due; *1633*
18 you;] you *1633 uncorrected*   20 was *1633*, Σ: were *O'F, Gr*   22 as] that
L 74, TCD   in you all *MSS*: all in you *1633, Gr*   is.] is; *1633*

As of this all, though many parts decay,
The pure which elemented them shall stay;
And though diffus'd, and spread in infinite,   25
Shall recollect, and in one All unite:
So madame, as her Soule to heaven is fled,
Her flesh rests in the earth, as in a bed;
Her vertues do, as to their proper spheare,
Returne to dwell with you, of whom they were: 30
As perfect motions are all circular,
So they to you, their sea, whence lesse streames are.
Shee was all spices, you all metalls; so
In you two wee did both rich Indies know.
And as no fire, nor rust can spend or waste   35
One dramme of gold, but what was first shall last,
Though it bee forc'd in water, earth, salt, aire,
Expans'd in infinite, none will impaire;
So, to your selfe you may additions take,
But nothing can you lesse, or changed make.   40
Seeke not in seeking new, to seeme to doubt,
That you can match her, or not be without;
But let some faithfull booke in her roome be,
Yet but of *Judith* no such booke as shee.

To the Countesse of Bedford

T'HAVE written then, when you writ, seem'd to mee
   Worst of spirituall vices, Simony,
And not t'have written then, seemes little lesse
Then worst of civill vices, thanklessenesse.
In this, my debt I seem'd loath to confesse,   5
In that, I seem'd to shunne beholdingnesse.
But 'tis not soe; *nothings*, as I am, may
Pay all they have, and yet have all to pay.

28 a bed *MSS.*: the bed *1633*, *Gr*   30 were:] were; *1633*: were, *1633 uncorrected*
32 are.] are; *1633*   34 know.] know; *1633*   36 dramme] dreame *1633 uncorrected*
42 can] can can *1633*   without;] without *1633 uncorrected*

   To the Countesse of Bedford. *MSS.*: *TCD*, *O'F*. Paragraphing supplied. Title from *1633*:
To ... of B. *MSS.*   5 debt *MSS.*: doubt *1633*   7 soe;] soe, *1633*   *nothings Gr*:
Nothings *O'F*: *nothing 1633*, *TCD*   may] may, *1633*

Such borrow in their payments, and owe more
By having leave to write so, then before.   10
Yet since rich mines in barren grounds are showne,
May not I yeeld (not gold) but coale or stone?
Temples were not demolish'd, though prophane:
Here *Peter*, *Joves*; there *Paul* hath *Dian's* Fane.
So whether my hymnes you admit or chuse,   15
In me you'have hallowed a Pagan Muse,
And denizend a stranger, who mistaught
By blamers of the times they mard, hath sought
Vertues in corners, which now bravely doe
Shine in the worlds best part, or all It; You.   20
I have beene told, that vertue'in Courtiers hearts
Suffers an Ostracisme, and departs.
Profit, ease, fitnesse, plenty, bid it goe,
But whither, only knowing you, I know;
Your (or you) vertue two vast uses serves,   25
It ransomes one sex, and one Court preserves.
There's nothing but your worth, which being true,
Is knowne to any other, not to you:
And you can never know it; To admit
No knowledge of your worth, is some of it.   30
    But since to you, your praises discords bee,
Stoop, others ills to meditate with mee.
Oh! to confesse wee know not what we should,
Is halfe excuse; wee know not what we would:
Lightnesse depresseth us, emptinesse fills,   35
We sweat and faint, yet still goe downe the hills.
As new Philosophy arrests the Sunne,
And bids the passive earth about it runne,
So wee have dull'd our minde, it hath no ends;
Onely the bodie's busie, and pretends;   40

14 *Peter*, *Joves*;] *Peter Ioves 1633*   hath *O'F*: have *1633*: *omit TCD (b.c.)*   *Dian's*]
Dian's 1633   20 all It; You. *Gr*: all it, you. *MSS.*: all, inyou. *1633*: all, inyou, *1633
uncorrected*   21 vertue'in] vertue in *1633 uncorrected*   25 Your (or you) vertue]
Your, or you vertue, *1633*   26 preserves.] preserves; *1633*   28 you:] you. *1633*
30 is *MSS.*: it *1633*   32 Stoop, *MSS.* (*no comma*): Stop *1633*   ills] ills, *1633*
34 excuse; ... would:] excuse, ... would. *1633*   36 hills.] hills; *1633*   37 Philo-
sophy] Phylosophy *1633 uncorrected*

As dead low earth ecclipses and controules
The quick high Moone: so doth the body, Soules.
In none but us, are such mixt engines found,
As hands of double office: For, the ground
We till with them; and them to heav'n wee raise;   45
Who prayer-lesse labours, or, without this, prayes,
Doth but one halfe, that's none; He which said, *Plough
And looke not back*, to looke up doth allow.
Good seed degenerates, and oft obeyes
The soyles disease, and into cockle strayes;   50
Let the minds thoughts be but transplanted so,
Into the body,'and bastardly they grow.
What hate could hurt our bodies like our love?
Wee (but no forraigne tyrans could) remove
These not ingrav'd, but inborne dignities,   55
Caskets of soules; Temples, and Palaces:
For, bodies shall from death redeemed bee,
Soules but preserv'd, not naturally free.
As men to'our prisons, new soules to us are sent,
Which learne vice there, and come in innocent.   60
First seeds of every creature are in us,
What ere the world hath bad, or pretious,
Mans body can produce; hence hath it beene
That stones, wormes, frogges, and snakes in man are seene:
But who ere saw, though nature can worke soe,   65
That pearle, or gold, or corne in man did grow?
We'have added to the world Virginia,'and sent
Two new starres lately to the firmament;
Why grudge wee us (not heaven) the dignity
T'increase with ours, those faire soules company?   70
    But I must end this letter; though it doe
Stand on two truths, neither is true to you.

---

42 body, Soules] body soules *1633 uncorrected*   45 raise;] raise *1633 uncorrected*
50 strayes;] strayes. *1633*   54 (but ... could)] but ... could *1633*   remove]
remove, *1633*   55 dignities,] dignities *1633*   58 not] borne *O'F*   free.] free; *1633*
59 new] now *MSS.*   60 vice *O'F*: it *1633, TCD*   63 produce;] produce, *1633*
66 That] That, *1633*   grow?] grow. *1633*   70 company?] company. *1633*
71 letter;] letter, *1633*

811842   H

Vertue hath some perversenesse; For she will
Neither beleeve her good, nor others ill.
Even in you, vertues best paradise,   75
Vertue hath some, but wise degrees of vice.
Too many vertues, or too much of one
Begets in you unjust suspition;
And ignorance of vice, makes vertue lesse,
Quenching compassion of our wrechednesse.   80
But these are riddles; Some aspersion
Of vice becomes well some complexion.
Statesmen purge vice with vice, and may corrode
The bad with bad, a spider with a toad:
For so, ill thralls not them, but they tame ill   85
And make her do much good against her will;
But in your Commonwealth, or world in you,
Vice hath no office, nor good worke to doe.
Take then no vitious purge, but be content
With cordiall vertue, your knowne nourishment.   90

To the Countesse of Bedford
At New-yeares Tide

THIS twilight of two yeares, not past nor next,
    Some embleme is of mee, or I of this,
Who Meteor-like, of stuffe and forme perplext,
    Whose *what*, and *where*, in disputation is,
    If I should call mee *any thing*, should misse.   5

I summe the yeares, and mee, and finde mee not
    Debtor to th'old, nor Creditor to th'new,
That cannot say, My thankes I have forgot,
    Nor trust I this with hopes, and yet scarce true
    This bravery is, since these times shew'd mee you.   10

74 ill.] ill, *1633*   75 you, MSS. (*no comma*): your *1633*   78 suspition;] suspition.
1633   86 will;] will, *1633*   87 Commonwealth,] Commonwealth *1633*   you,]
you *1633*   88 nor MSS.: or *1633*, Gr

To the Countesse of Bedford At New-yeares Tide. MSS.: TCD, O'F. *Title from MSS.*
(*which, however, read* B. *for* Bedford): To ... Bedford. On New-yeares day *1633*, Gr.
9 true] true, *1633*   10 is,] is *1633*   times MSS.: time *1633*

In recompence I would show future times
  What you were, and teach them to'urge towards such.
Verse embalmes vertue;'and Tombs, or Thrones of rimes,
  Preserve fraile transitory fame, as much
  As spice doth bodies from corrupt aires touch.   15

Mine are short-liv'd; the tincture of your name
  Creates in them, but dissipates as fast,
New spirits: for, strong agents with the same
  Force that doth warme and cherish, us doe wast;
  Kept hot with strong extracts, no bodies last: 20

So, my verse built of your just praise, might want
  Reason and likelihood, the firmest Base,
And made of miracle, now faith is scant,
  Will vanish soone, and so possesse no place,
  And you, and it, too much grace might disgrace.   25

When all (as truth commands assent) confesse
  All truth of you, yet they will doubt how I,
One corne of one low anthills dust, and lesse,
  Should name, know, or expresse a thing so high,
  And not an inch, measure infinity.   30

I cannot tell them, nor my selfe, nor you,
  But leave, lest truth b'endanger'd by my praise,
And turne to God, who knowes I thinke this true,
  And useth oft, when such a heart mis-sayes,
  To make it good, for, such a prayser prayes.   35

Hee will best teach you, how you should lay out
  His stock of *beauty, learning, favour, blood*;
He will perplex security with doubt,
  And cleare those doubts; hide from you,'and shew you good,
  And so increase your appetite and food;   40

12 such.] such, *1633*   16 short-liv'd] short liv'd *1633*   17 fast,] fast *1633*
uncorrected   18 spirits *MSS.*: spirit *1633*   20 last:] lasts. *1633 uncorrected*
27 I,] I *1633*   29 name, know,] name know *1633*   35 prayser *O'F*: prayer
1633, TCD   37 *blood*;] *blood,* *1633*   39 doubts;] doubts, *1633*

Hee will teach you, that good and bad have not
　　One latitude in cloysters, and in Court;
Indifferent there the greatest space hath got;
　　Some pitty'is not good there, some vaine disport,
　　On this side sinne, with that place may comport.　　45

Yet he, as hee bounds seas, will fixe your houres,
　　Which pleasure, and delight may not ingresse,
And though what none else lost, be truliest yours,
　　Hee will make you, what you did not, possesse,
　　By using others, not vice, but weakenesse.　　50

He will make you speake truths, and credibly,
　　And make you doubt, that others doe not so:
Hee will provide you keyes, and locks, to spie,
　　And scape spies, to good ends, and hee will show
　　What you may not acknowledge, what not know.　　55

For your owne conscience, he gives innocence,
　　But for your fame, a discreet warinesse,
And though to scape, then to revenge offence
　　Be better, he showes both, and to represse
　　Joy, when your state swells, *sadnesse* when 'tis lesse.　　60

From need of teares he will defend your soule,
　　Or make a rebaptizing of one teare;
Hee cannot, (that's, he will not) dis-inroule
　　Your name; and when with active joy we heare
　　This private Ghospell, then 'tis our New Yeare.　　65

To the Countesse of Bedford

HONOUR is so sublime perfection,
　　And so refinde; that when God was alone
And creaturelesse at first, himselfe had none;

42 Court;] Court, *1633*　　43 got;] got, *1633*　　45 side sinne,] side, sinne; *1633*
(he,] he *1633*　　47 Which *MSS.*: With *1633*　　65 New Yeare.] new yeare, *1633*
To the Countesse of Bedford. *MSS.*: *TCD*; *Dob*, *O'F*. *Title from 1633*, *Σ*: To . . . of B.
TCD.

But as of th'elements, these which wee tread,
Produce all things with which wee'are joy'd or fed,   5
And, those are barren both above our head:

So from low persons doth all honour flow;
Kings, whom they would have honour'd, to us show,
And but *direct* our honour, not *bestow*.

For when from herbs the pure parts must be wonne   10
From grosse, by Stilling, this is better done
By despis'd dung, then by the fire or Sunne.

Care not then, Madame,'how low your praysers lye;
In labourers balads oft more piety
God findes, then in *Te Deums* melodie;   15

And, ordinance rais'd on Towers, so many mile
Send not their voice, nor last so long a while
As fires from th'earths low vaults in *Sicil* Isle.

Should I say I liv'd darker then were true,
Your radiation can all clouds subdue;   20
But one, 'tis best light to contemplate you:

You, for whose body God made better clay,
Or tooke Soules stuffe such as shall late decay,
Or such as needs small change at the last day.

This, as an Amber drop enwraps a Bee,   25
Covering discovers your quicke Soule; that we
May in your through-shine front your hearts thoughts see.

You teach (though wee learne not) a thing unknowne
To our late times, the use of specular stone,
Through which all things within without were shown.   30

4 th'elements] the elements *1633*   8 honour'd] honoured *1633*   10 parts
MSS.: part *1633*, *Gr*   13 Madame] Lady *Dob*, *O'F*   praysers *Σ*: prayses *1633*:
prayer *Dob*   15 melodie;] melodie. *1633*   16 Towers,] Towers *1633*
20 subdue;] subdue, *1633*   21 you:] you. *1633*   27 front] face *Dob*, *O'F*
your hearts *MSS.*: our hearts *1633*

Of such were Temples; so,'and of such you are;
Beeing and *seeming* is your equall care,
And *vertues* whole *summe* is but *know* and *dare*.

But as our Soules of growth and Soules of sense
Have birthright of our reasons Soule, yet hence   35
They fly not from that, nor seeke presidence:

Natures first lesson, so, discretion,
Must not grudge zeale a place, nor yet keepe none,
Not banish it selfe, nor religion.

Discretion is a wisemans Soule, and so   40
Religion is a Christians, and you know
How these are one; her *yea*, is not her *no*.

Nor may we hope to sodder still and knit
These two, and dare to breake them; nor must wit
Be colleague to religion, but be it.   45

In those poore types of God (round circles) so
Religions tipes, the peeclesse centers flow,
And are in all the lines which all wayes goe.

If either ever wrought in you alone
Or principally, then religion   50
Wrought your ends, and your wayes discretion.

Goe thither stil, goe the same way you went,
Who so would change, do covet or repent;
Neither can reach you, great and innocent.

31 so,'and of such *TCD (no elision-mark)*: so and such *1633*, Σ   36 presidence:]
presidence. *1633*   40–42 *precede ll. 34–39 in MSS.*   42 one;] one, *1633*
yea, . . . *no.*] yea, . . . no. *1633*   48 all wayes *Dob*: alwayes *1633*, Σ   49 either
ever] ever either *TCD, Dob*   53 so] ere *Dob, O'F*

Epitaph on Himselfe

To the Countesse of Bedford

MADAME,

THAT I might make your Cabinet my tombe,
    And for my fame, which I love next my soule,
Next to my soule provide the happiest roome,
    Admit to that place this last funerall Scrowle.
        Others by Testament give Legacies, but I   5
        Dying, of you doe beg a Legacie.

Omnibus

MY Fortune and my choice this custome break,
    When we are speechlesse grown, to make stones
        speak,
Though no stone tell thee what I was, yet thou
In my graves inside see what thou art now: 10
Yet thou'art not yet so good, till us death lay
To ripe and mellow here, we'are stubborne Clay.
Parents make us earth, and soules dignifie
Us to be glasse; here to grow gold we lie.
Whilst in our soules sinne bred and pamper'd is,   15
Our soules become wormeaten carkases;
So we our selves miraculously destroy.
Here bodies with lesse miracle enjoy
Such priviledges, enabled here to scale
Heaven, when the Trumpets ayre shall them exhale.   20
Heare this, and mend thy selfe, and thou mendst me,
By making me being dead, doe good to thee,
And thinke me well compos'd, that I could now
A last-sicke houre to syllables allow.

*Epitaph on Himselfe. Text from 1635. MSS.: H 49, Dob, O'F. For title and form of the poem,
see note.*   2 fame,] fame *1635*   5 Testament *Σ*: testaments *O'F (changed to* wills):
Wills *1635*   7 choice] will *O'F*   8 speechlesse] sencelesse *O'F*   9 tell] tel
1635   10 see *Σ*: seest *1635, Dob*   11 thou'art] thou art *1635*   us death *MSS.*:
death us *1635*   12 here] there *Dob, O'F*   we'are] we are *1635*   14 lie.] lie; *1635*
22 to *MSS.*: for *1635*

To the Countesse of Bedford

Begun in France but never perfected

THOUGH I be *dead*, and buried, yet I have
　　(Living in you,) Court enough in my grave,
And oft as there I thinke my selfe to bee,
So many resurrections waken mee.
That thankfullnesse your favours have begot　　　　5
In mee, embalmes mee, that I doe not rot.
This season as 'tis Easter, as 'tis spring,
Must both to growth and to confession bring
My thoughts dispos'd unto your influence; so,
These verses bud, so these confessions grow.　　　　10
First I confesse I have to others lent
Your stock, and over prodigally spent
Your treasure, for since I had never knowne
Vertue or beautie, but as they are growne
In you, I should not thinke or say they shine,　　　　15
(So as I have) in any other Mine.
Next I confesse this my confession,
For, 'tis some fault thus much to touch upon
Your praise to you, where half rights seeme too much,
And make your minds sincere complexion blush.　　　　20
Next I confesse my'impenitence, for I
Can scarce repent my first fault, since thereby
Remote low Spirits, which shall ne'r read you,
May in lesse lessons finde enough to doe,
By studying copies, not Originals,　　　　25

Desunt caetera

To the Countesse of Bedford *Begun . . . perfected. MS.: O'F. Title from 1633, O'F.*
5 begot] forgot *1633 uncorrected*　　6 embalmes mee, . . . rot.] embalmes mee; . . . rot;
1633　　9 influence;] influence, *1633*　　10 grow.] grow; *1633*　　16 Mine.]
Mine; *1633*　　18 upon] upon, *1633*

A Letter to the Lady Carey, and Mrs Essex Riche

From Amyens

MADAME,

HERE where by All All Saints invoked are,
　　'Twere too much schisme to be singular,
And 'gainst a practise generall to warre.

Yet turning to Saincts, should my'humility
To other Sainct then you directed bee,　　　　　　5
That were to make my schisme, heresie.

Nor would I be a Convertite so cold,
As not to tell it; If this be too bold,
Pardons are in this market cheaply sold.

Where, because Faith is in too low degree,　　　10
I thought it some Apostleship in mee
To speake things which by faith alone I see.

That is, of you, who are a firmament
Of virtues, where no one is growne, or spent,
They'are your materials, not your ornament.　　15

Others whom wee call vertuous, are not so
In their whole substance, but, their vertues grow
But in their humours, and at seasons show.

For when through tastlesse flat humilitie
In dow bak'd men some harmelessenes we see,　20
'Tis but his *flegme* that's Vertuous, and not Hee:

A Letter to the Lady Carey, . . . *Amyens. MSS.*: *C 57, H 49*; *TCD*; *Dob, O'F. Title from 1633, C 57, H 49*; To the Lady Cary and her sist^r Mrs. Essex . . Amiens *O'F*: To the Lady Carey *Dob*: To the La: Co: of: *C TCD.*　　5 Sainct] saints *Dob, O'F*　　7 would] cold *Dob, O'F*　　13 are *MSS.*: is *1633*　　21 *flegme*] *flegme, 1633 uncorrected* Vertuous] *Vertuous 1633*

Soe is the Blood sometimes; who ever ran
To danger unimportun'd, he was than
No better then a *sanguine* Vertuous man.

So cloysterall men, who, in pretence of feare   25
All contribution to this life forbeare,
Have Vertue'in *Melancholy,*'and only there.

Spirituall *Cholerique* Crytiques, which in all
Religions find faults, and forgive no fall,
Have, through this zeale, Vertue but in their Gall.   30

We'are thus but parcel guilt; to Gold we'are growne
When Vertue is our Soules complexion;
Who knowes his Vertues name or place, hath none.

Vertue'is but aguish, when 'tis severall,
By'occasion wak'd, and circumstantiall.   35
True vertue'is *Soule*, Alwaies in all deeds *All*.

This Vertue thinking to give dignitie
To your soule, found there no infirmitie,
For, your soule was as good Vertue, as shee;

Shee therefore wrought upon that part of you   40
Which is scarce lesse then soule, as she could do,
And so hath made your beauty, Vertue too.

Hence comes it, that your Beauty wounds not hearts,
As Others, with prophane and sensuall Darts,
But as an influence, vertuous thoughts imparts.   45

But if such friends by th'honor of your sight
Grow capable of this so great a light,
As to partake your vertues, and their might,

26 contribution Σ: contributions *1633*, C *57*, Gr   27 Vertue'in *Melancholy,*'and]
Vertue in *Melancholy,*'and *1633*   28 which] who *Dob, O'F*   30 this Σ: their
1633, C *57*   31 Gold] Golds *1633 uncorrected*   35 By'occasion] By occasion *1633*
36 vertue'is] vertue is *1633*   46 th'honor] the honor *1633*

What must I thinke that influence must doe,
Where it findes sympathie and matter too,   50
Vertue, and beauty'of the same stuffe, as you?

Which is, your noble worthie sister, shee
Of whom, if what in this my Extasie
And revelation of you both I see,

I should write here, as in short Galleries   55
The Master at the end large glasses ties,
So to present the roome twice to our eyes,

So I should give this letter length, and say
That which I said of you; there is no way
From either, but by th'other, not to stray.   60

May therefore this be'enough to testifie
My true devotion, free from flattery;
He that beleeves himselfe, doth never lie.

To the Countesse of Salisbury

August, 1614

FAIRE, great, and good, since seeing you, wee see
     What Heaven can doe,'and what any Earth can be:
Since now your beauty shines, now when the Sunne
Growne stale, is to so low a value runne,
That his disshevel'd beames and scatter'd fires   5
Serve but for Ladies Periwigs and Tyres
In lovers Sonnets: you come to repaire
Gods booke of creatures, teaching what is faire;
Since now, when all is wither'd, shrunke, and dri'd,
All Vertue ebb'd out to a dead low tyde,   10

50 Where] When *Dob, O'F*   51 beauty'of] beauty of *1633*   57 our *1633,*
TCD, O'F: yor *C 57, H 49, Dob*   60 th'other,] the other *1633*   61 be'enough]
be enough *1633*

   To the Countesse of Salisbury *August 1614.* MSS.: *C 57, H 49: TCD; O'F. Title from*
1633, C 57, H 49: To . . . Salisbury *O'F:* To the Countess of S. *TCD.*   2 doe,'and]
doe, and *1633*   and what] what *TCD, O'F*   5 scatter'd] scattered *1633*
8 faire;] faire. *1633*   9 wither'd] withered *1633*   10 Vertue *C 57, H 49, O'F:*
Vertues *1633, TCD, Gr*

All the worlds frame being crumbled into sand,
Where every man thinks by himselfe to stand,
Integritie, friendship, and confidence,
(Ciments of greatnes) being vapor'd hence,
And narrow man being fill'd with little shares,   15
Court, Citie, Church, are all shops of small-wares,
All having blowne to sparkes their noble fire,
And drawne their sound gold-ingot into wyre,
All trying by a love of littlenesse
To make abridgments, and to draw to lesse,   20
Even that nothing, which at first we were;
Since in these times, your greatnesse doth appeare,
And that we learne by it, that man to get
Towards him that's infinite, must first be great;
Since in an age so ill, as none is fit   25
So much as to accuse, much lesse mend it,
(For who can judge, or witnesse of those times
Where all alike are guiltie of the crimes?)
Where he that would be good, is thought by all
A monster, or at best fantasticall;   30
Since now you durst be good, and that I doe
Discerne, by daring to contemplate you,
That there may be degrees of faire, great, good,
Through your light, largenesse, vertue understood:
If in this sacrifice of mine, be showne   35
Any small sparke of these, call it your owne.
And if things like these, have been said by mee
Of others; call not that Idolatrie.
For had God made man first, and man had seene
The third daies fruits, and flowers, and various greene,   40
He might have said the best that he could say
Of those faire creatures, which were made that day;
And when next day he had admir'd the birth
Of Sun, Moone, Stars, fairer then late-prais'd earth,

18 wyre,] wyre; *1633*   24 him] him, *1633*   that's] thats *1633*   great;] great.
1633   30 best] least *TCD, O'F*   fantasticall;] fantasticall: *1633*   40 greene,]
greene *1633*   42 day;] day: *1633*   43–46 *Omit C 57*

Hee might have said the best that he could say,   45
And not be chid for praising yesterday;
So though some things are not together true,
As, that another'is worthiest, and, that you:
Yet, to say so, doth not condemne a man,
If when he spoke them, they were both true than.   50
How faire a proofe of this, in our soule growes!
Wee first have soules of growth, and sense, and those,
When our last soule, our soule immortall came,
Were swallow'd into it, and have no name:
Nor doth he injure those soules, which doth cast   55
The power and praise of both them, on the last;
No more doe I wrong any; I adore
The same things now, which I ador'd before,
The subject chang'd, and measure; the same thing
In a low constable, and in the King   60
I reverence; His power to worke on mee:
So did I humbly reverence each degree
Of faire, great, good; but more, now I am come
From having found their *walkes*, to finde their *home*.
And as I owe my first soules thankes, that they   65
For my last soule did fit and mould my clay,
So am I debtor unto them, whose worth,
Enabled me to profit, and take forth
This new great lesson, thus to study you;
Which none, not reading others, first, could doe.   70
Nor lacke I light to read this booke, though I
In a darke Cave, yea in a Grave doe lie;
For as your fellow Angells, so you doe
Illustrate them who come to study you.
The first whom we in Histories doe finde   75
To have profest all Arts, was one borne blind:
He lackt those eyes beasts have as well as wee,
Not those, by which Angels are seene and see;

46 yesterday;] yesterday: *1633*   48 another'is] another is *1633*   51 growes!]
growes? *1633*   54 swallow'd] swallowed *1633*   name:] name. *1633*   61 mee:]
mee; *1633*   63 good;] good, *1633*   64 *home*] *hrme 1633 uncorrected*
77–78 *Omit* C 57, H 49

So, though I'am borne without those eyes to live,
Which fortune, who hath none her selfe, doth give,   80
Which are, fit meanes to see bright courts and you,
Yet may I see you thus, as now I doe;
I shall by that, all goodnesse have discern'd,
And though I burne my librarie, be learn'd.

79 borne] borne, *1633 uncorrected*

LATIN POEMS, AND A TRANSLATION

Ad Autorem

NON eget Hookerus tanto tutamine; Tanto
Tutus qui impugnat sed foret Auxilio.

J. Donne.

Ad Autorem

EMENDARE cupis Joseph qui tempora, Leges
Praemia, Supplicium, Religiosa cohors
Quod iam conantur frustra, Conabere frustra;
Si per te non sunt deteriora sat est.

J. Donne.

Amicissimo et meritissimo Ben. Jonson
In Vulponem

QUOD arte ausus es híc tuâ, POETA,
Si auderent hominum Deique iuris
Consulti, sequi aemularierque,
O omnes saperemus ad salutem.
His sed sunt veteres araneosi;   5
Tam nemo veterum est sequutor, ut tu
Illos quos sequeris novator audis.
Fac tamen quod agis; tuíque primâ
Libri canitie induantur horâ:

Ad Autorem / Non eget *etc. Text from autograph in Donne's copy of W. Covell, A . . . Defence of . . . Hooker, 1603; first printed by E. Gosse,* Life and Letters of John Donne, *1899.*

Ad Autorem / Emendare cupis *etc. Text from autograph in Donne's copy of J. Scaliger, De Emendatione Temporum, 1583; first printed by G. Keynes, T.L.S., 1958, p. 93.*

Amicissimo et . . . In Vulponem. *Text from Jonson,* Volpone, *1607;* In Vulponem **added** *to title in Jonson's* Workes, *1616.*   3 *sequi Ed:* veteres sequi *1607; see note*   7 *quos Ed:* quod *1607*

Nam cartis pueritia est neganda,   10
Nascantúrque senes, oportet, illi
Libri, queis dare vis perennitatem.
Priscis, ingenium facit, labórque
Te parem; hos superes, ut et futuros,
Ex nostrâ vitiositate sumas,   15
Quâ priscos superamus, et futuros.

                 J. D.

De Libro cum Mutuaretur Impresso;
Domi a pueris frustatim lacerato; et post reddito
Manuscripto.

Doctissimo Amicissimoque v.D.D. Andrews

PARTURIUNT madido quae nixu praela, recepta,
   Sed quae scripta manu, sunt veneranda magis.
Transiit in Sequanam Moenus; Victoris in aedes,
   Et Francofurtum, te revehente, meat.
Qui liber in pluteos, blattis cinerique relictos,   5
   Si modo sit praeli sanguine tinctus, abit;
Accedat calamo scriptus, reverenter habetur,
   Involat et veterum scrinia summa Patrum.
Dicat Apollo modum; Pueros infundere libro
   Nempe vetustatem canitiemque novo.   10
Nil mirum, medico pueros de semine natos,
   Haec nova fata libro posse dedisse novo.
Si veterem faciunt pueri, qui nuperus, Annon
   Ipse Pater Iuvenem me dabit arte senem?
Hei miseris senibus! nos vertit dura senectus   15
   Omnes in pueros, neminem at in Iuvenem.
Hos tibi servasti praestandum, Antique Dierum,
   Quo viso, et vivit, et juvenescit Adam.

De Libro...v. D. D. Andrews. *Text from 1635, which reads in title:* mutuaretur, Impresso,; frustratim; lacerato,.   1 *recepta,*] recepta; 1635   2 *manu, sunt*] manu sunt, 1635 4 *revehente,*] revehente 1635   5 *blattis*] blattis, 1635   6 *abit;*] abit, 1635 14 *Pater Iuvenem*] Pater, Iuvenem, 1635   *arte*] arte, 1635   15 *senibus!*] senibus; 1635

Interea, infirmae fallamus taedia vitae,
  Libris, et Coelorum aemulâ amicitiâ.   20
Hos inter, qui à te mihi redditus iste libellus,
  Non mihi tam charus, tam meus, ante fuit.

                                          I. D.

Translated out of Gazaeus, *Vota Amico facta*

GOD grant thee thine own wish, and grant thee mine,
  Thou, who dost, best friend, in best things outshine;
May thy soul, ever chearfull, nere know cares,
Nor thy life, ever lively, know gray haires.
Nor thy hand, ever open, know base holds,   5
Nor thy purse, ever plump, know pleits, or folds.
Nor thy tongue, ever true, know a false thing,
Nor thy word, ever mild, know quarrelling.
Nor thy works, ever equall, know disguise,
Nor thy fame, ever pure, know contumelies.   10
Nor thy prayers, know low objects, still Divine;
God grant thee thine own wish, and grant thee mine.

19 *infirmae*] *Infirmæ 1635*   21 *redditus*] *redditus, 1635*
Translated out of Gazaeus, *Vota Amico facta. Text from 1650, which adds to title*: fol. 160

COMMENTARY

Note on Versification

DONNE'S verse is not nearly as 'rough' as critics (except for sensitive readers like Coleridge and Patmore) once used to assert. It is in most types of poem regularly syllabic, but involves much use of elision and synalœpha. Syllables which are assimilated are not necessarily unpronounced, but they are not counted metrically and are 'like grace-notes in music', which do not disturb the time (Gardner, *Divine Poems*, p. 54). In *1633* the editor took care to indicate contracted forms, and also elisions between final and initial vowels where he thought they occurred; he did not, however, mark places where an unstressed medial syllable should be dropped or slurred. Donne's alertness to the movement of colloquial speech is shown in the great liberties he takes here, and he relies on his reader to sense the proper rhythm. Compare his treatment of the word 'reverence' in consecutive lines (61–62) in the letter to the Countess of Salisbury:

$$\overset{\times}{I} \overset{/}{rev} \mid \overset{\times}{er}\overset{/}{ence}; \mid \overset{\times}{His} \overset{/}{power} \mid \overset{\times}{to} \overset{/}{worke} \mid \overset{\times}{on} \overset{/}{mee}:$$
$$\overset{/}{So} \overset{\times}{did} \mid \overset{\times}{I} \overset{/}{humb} \mid \overset{\times}{ly} \overset{/}{rev} \mid \overset{\times}{'rence} \overset{/}{each} \mid degree.$$

The editor of *1633* had a good idea of Donne's practice, and I have tried to apply his principles consistently throughout. His carefulness is shown by the fact that in over 1,800 lines (excluding the five *Satires*) I have needed to supply or remove marks of contraction or elision only about sixty times (twenty-six of them in the *Metempsychosis*). He was attentive to these details even as the book was passing through the press (inserting a mark, for example, while correcting the sheet containing l. 21 of the letter to the Countess of Bedford, 'T'have written then'. In the 669 lines of the *Satires*, however, even a conservative policy requires the insertion of over ninety elision marks or signs of contraction. This is due not only to the deliberately experimental and daring 'roughness' appropriate to satire (which caused great uncertainty in those manuscripts where scribes marked elisions), but also to the delay in gaining approval for printing these poems and the consequent haste with which their text was set up in the last formes of the book; the editor did not have enough time to deal with the metrical problems of the *Satires*, in which there are about two and a half times as many elisions and contractions as there are (proportionately) in the *Songs and Sonnets* (see the useful study by M. F. Moloney, 'Donne's Metrical Practice', *P.M.L.A.*, 1950). The couplet permitted far more venturesome effects than could be attempted in Donne's lyrical stanza-forms without producing metrical chaos.

As elsewhere, Donne allows himself the regular freedom in English syllabic verse of an extra weak final syllable, the Chaucerian licence of a defective

first foot, and also the use (normally found only in dramatic verse) of a defective foot in the middle of the line, to mark a dramatic pause, as in 'Satire
III', l. 95:

$$\text{At the } | \text{ last day? } || \text{ Will } | \text{ it then } | \text{ boot thee.}$$

But, in addition, writing in the familiar style in satires and verse letters, he
goes beyond his usual practice and is willing, at times, to treat such mono-
syllables as 'a', 'and', 'as', 'the', and 'are' as metrically worthless, even
though elision cannot take place. The edition of 1633 puts an elision mark on
some of these occasions; and, following its example, I have supplied such
marks nine times.[1]

In suggesting the scansion of a line I mark feet with normal stress ×/, feet
with inverted stress /×, feet with level stress //, and feet with a very light
stress × x́. I mark this last because Donne clearly accepts the foot and requires
that we bear the basic metre in mind as we read.

The editor of 1633 also took trouble over the indenting and arrangement of
lines in poems written in stanzas, to draw attention to line-length and
rhyme-scheme. Neither in these poems nor in those written in couplets, however, was he thorough-going or consistent. In this volume, since nearly every
line is in ten-syllable iambic metre, I have been able to arrange the lines entirely according to rhyme-scheme (except in the *Metempsychosis*, where the
typographical results would have been too distracting). I do not follow the
editor of 1633 in indenting alternate lines of some poems in couplet to make
them look like 'elegiacs', e.g. in the letters to Edward Herbert and to the
Countess of Bedford ('T'have written then', 'You that are she and you'). In
longer poems, however, I have felt free to indent some lines, not to bring out
metrical qualities, but to indicate paragraphs where I think that this will
assist the reader.

SATIRES

MSS.: Group I (*C 57*, *D*, *H 49*, *Lec*, *SP*); Group II (*N*, *TCD*); *L 74*; Group III
(*A 25*, *B*, *Cy*, *Dob*, *D 16*, *D 17*, *JC*, *K*, *Lut*, *O'F*, *O*, *P*, *Q̣*, *S*); *W*.
Miscellany: *S 962*.

These twenty-four collections contain all five of the regular Satires, except
that *H 49* and *Cy* lack the fifth. If a satire is found elsewhere this fact is noted
at the beginning of the commentary upon it.

In 1633, which I take as copy-text, the *Satires* were printed from a manuscript to which *C 57* among surviving collections bears the closest resemblance.
The text in 1633 is fairly good, but needs correction when it is in error,

---

[1] See 'The Storm', ll. 40, 66; 'To Mr Rowland Woodward', l. 10; and letters to Wotton,
'Here's no more newes', ll. 4, 12, 21, and 'at his going Ambassador to Venice', l. 16, where
1633 marks elision where elision cannot take place; and 'Satire I', l. 46, 'Satire II', l. 28,
'Satire III', ll. 24 and 107, 'Satire IV', ll. 107 and 199, 'Satire V', l. 81, 'The Calm', l. 44,
and 'To Mr E. G.', l. 13, where I have supplied elision marks in similar circumstances.

either through misprints, misreading or sophistication of the manuscript source, or when this source is itself corrupt.

The version of the *Satires* in *1633* (and in *C 57*, *Lec*, *N*, *TCD*, and *L 74*) is, I believe, that resulting from Donne's final revision made late in 1607; it is represented in the apparatus by *C 57*, *L 74*, and *TCD* as well as by *1633* itself. There seems to be only one version of 'Satire V', but an intermediate version of the first four Satires (? 1598) is fairly certainly traceable in *W*, *D*, *H 49*, *SP*, and (in a debased form) in *B*; it is represented in the apparatus by *W* and *H 49*. The earliest version of Satires I–IV is, I believe, to be found in *A 25*, *D 16*, and *Q*, in *Lut*, *O'F*, and (in variously corrupt forms) in the other manuscripts loosely assigned to Group III; it is represented in the apparatus by *Q* and *O'F*. For a discussion of these versions, see Textual Introduction, pp. lvi–lx.

Donne did not give his satires special titles, and in most manuscripts each is called simply 'Satire' ('Satyre', 'Satira', etc.), often with a number according to its order in the set ('Satyre I', 'Iª', 'Prima', etc.). When there is any other title it is noted in the commentary on the satire concerned.

Paragraphing has been supplied. I have also employed quotation marks in passages of dialogue, and placed the appropriate stop, period or query, at the end of speeches where the edition merely divides speeches from each other by semicolons. Strictly, this is inadmissible in an old-spelling text; but the convenience of readers seems more important than strictness here. The seventeenth-century use of italic for direct speech would not assist readers to distinguish the speakers, and, particularly in 'Satire I', it is not always immediately clear that one speaker is interrupting the other.

Satyre I (p. 1)

MSS.: Also in *H 51* (with a text most like that in *W*) and in *S 96* (with a poor text of the version in *Q*, *O'F*).

The text in *1633* closely follows a Group I manuscript like *C 57*, except that in the edition ll. 81–82 are prudentially omitted. These lines are present in all manuscripts without significant variations, and were included in the second edition in 1635. I have thought it simplest to take the accidents here from *1635*.

I abandon eleven of the readings of *1633*: three errors peculiar to the edition (ll. 70, 73, 108), one reading found elsewhere only in three Group III manuscripts (l. 53), six readings in which manuscripts containing this version are also in error (ll. 39, 60, 62, 63, 78, 95—but in ll. 63 and 95 *TCD* is right), and one in which *C 57*, *Lec*, and some Group III manuscripts support the edition against the weight of manuscript evidence (l. 19). In three places (ll. 19, 53, 58) my readings differ from Grierson's.

The idea of a walk in the street with a wearisome companion was perhaps suggested by Horace, *Sat.* I. ix, but Donne's poem is a brilliantly original adaptation of the general methods of Roman satire. Alden (p. 153) first noted a close imitation of ll. 2–10 in *Skialetheia* (1598), attributed to Edward (or

Everard) Guilpin, to whom extracts from it are assigned in *England's Parnassus* (1600). (For Guilpin, see the commentary on 'To Mr E. G.', below, p. 216.) Guilpin's *Satyra Quinta* begins thus:

> Let me alone I prethee in thys Cell,
> Entice me not into the Citties hell;
> Tempt me not forth this *Eden* of content,
> To tast of that which I shall soone repent:
> Prethy excuse me, I am not alone
> Accompanied with meditation,
> And calme content, whose tast more pleaseth me
> Then all the Citties lushious vanity.
> I had rather be encoffin'd in this chest
> Amongst these bookes and papers I protest,
> Then free-booting abroad purchase offence,
> And scandale my calme thoughts with discontents.
> Heere I converse with those diviner spirits,
> Whose knowledge, and admire the world inherits:
> Heere doth the famous profound *Stagarite*,
> With Natures mistick harmony delight
> My ravish'd contemplation: I heere see
> The now-old worlds youth in an history:
> Heere may I be grave *Platos* auditor; etc.

Donne's satire seems, however, to have been written some five years earlier. On the title-page of *H 51* is written (probably by the first copyist to work in the manuscript): 'Jhon Dunne his Satires Anno Domini 1593'. I think it very likely that this was the date affixed to the first satire in the copy from which the scribe was working. References to current matters of interest are consistent with this date: to the performing horse (l. 80), to the similarly trained elephant and ape (l. 81), and even to the Infante, heir or heiress (l. 58); see the notes on these lines. As Grierson noted, similar references are made in some of the forty-five epigrams of Sir John Davies included in a Bodleian MS. (Rawlinson Poet. 212) dated 'An° 1594 in November'. Of these No. 30 ('In Dacum') refers to the horse and the ape, and (like No. 14, 'In Titum') to the elephant; it is clear that these, like the new 'water-worke' and 'my Lo. Chancellors Tombe' (Hatton had died in 1591), also mentioned in the epigram 'In Titum', were among the current 'sights' of the city. The alertness of Donne's critical observation of contemporary events would ensure, I believe, that his references to these phenomena would be among the earliest; his mention of the performing horse, for example, being contemporary with that of Nashe in 1593. This satire almost certainly belongs to that year, the second of Donne's residence in Lincoln's Inn.

Only two manuscripts expand the normal title: *Cy* ('A Satyre of Mr John Donnes') and *S 962*, which has 'Satyre 2: On the Humorist'.

l. 1. *fondling*: a 'fond' or foolish person. This is the reading of Donne's final version (and of *S*, a contaminated manuscript); the earlier reading, 'change-ling' (one given to change, a fickle or inconstant person, *O.E.D.*, sense 1), was presumably rejected because its meaning is already contained in 'humorist' and 'motley'.

motley: varying in character or mood, changeable.

humorist: a person subject to 'humours' or fancies, a fantastical or whimsical person, a faddist (*O.E.D.*, sense 1); 'a fribble' (Chambers).

l. 2. *this standing woodden chest*. Between 1587 and 1613 the Benchers of Lincoln's Inn rebuilt the greater part of the chambers (see *The Black Books*, ii, 1898, xiv–xvi, 90). Each chamber was divided into two, and each half-chamber seems to have consisted of a bedroom and a study divided off by wainscot partitions; two members of the Society occupied each chamber (op. cit., p. 65). Donne was admitted to Lincoln's Inn on 6 May 1592, and, according to Walton (*Lives*, p. 29), Christopher Brooke was his chamber-fellow. Donne seems to have been sensitive to the effects of closed spaces, and such a room might well appear to him like a chest 'standing' (i.e. on end).

chest: frequently spelt 'chist' (e.g. in *Lut* and *O'F*), and, as the word was then pronounced, a good rhyme here. 'Chest' often meant 'coffin'; hence 'coffin'd', l. 4.

Marvell found this passage suggestive; see *Fleckno*, ll. 9–14 (*Poems and Letters*, ed. H. M. Margoliouth, i. 83).

l. 5. *Gods conduits*: channels conveying God's Word.

l. 6. *Natures Secretary, the Philosopher*: Aristotle, to the Schoolmen always 'the Philosopher'. John of Salisbury, in his *Metalogicon*, has a chapter (iv. 7) explaining why Aristotle pre-eminently deserves the title (Migne, *P.L.* cxcix. 920). Suidas first called him 'Secretary of Nature', i.e. one acquainted with the secrets of nature; see *O.E.D.*, 'secretary', I. d. The rhythm seems to be:

$$\text{Natures | Secret | 'ry, the | Philos | opher.}$$

l. 7. *jolly Statesmen*. 'Jolly' (*O.E.D.* II. 6) means overweeningly self-confident, full of presumptuous pride, defiantly bold, arrogant, overbearing; so Nashe: 'Is thys the jollie fellow that shooke kingdoms?' (*Works*, i. 116). The reading of *1635, Lut, O'F, S 962*, 'wily', is an emendation, or a misreading of 'ioly'.

l. 8. *The sinewes of a cities mistique bodie*. The 'natural' body of a city is its physical existence as houses, streets, etc. Its 'mistique', or spiritual, body is its existence as a community of persons, the 'body politic'. The comparison of the 'body politic' to the human body is a commonplace, as is the metaphorical use of 'sinew' as 'the main strength, or chief support' of a society; cf. 'chivalrie is the fundation and sinewes of a commonweale' (Fleming's continuation of Holinshed, 1587, iii. 1343b), and 'Familiaritie and conference,/That were the sinewes of societies' (Nashe, *Works*, iii. 271).

The rhyme of 'tie' with 'bodie'—of a tenth accented syllable with an unaccented eleventh—is an example of what C. S. Lewis called 'Simpsonian' rhyme: see P. Simpson, 'The Rhyming of Stressed with Unstressed Syllables in Elizabethan Verse' (*M.L.R.* xxxviii, 1943). There is another example in 'The Storm', ll. 55–56.

l. 9. *gathering Chroniclers*: chroniclers who merely gather information, much of it 'triviall houshold trash'; cf. 'Satire IV', ll. 97–98.

l. 10. *Giddie fantastique Poëts of each land.* The poets come last. Cf. Bacon's division of learning, by which history is referred to memory, poetry to the imagination or fancy, and philosophy to reason. Bacon dismisses poetry with the words 'It is not good to stay too long in the theatre', as he passes to 'the judicial place or palace of the mind', reason (*Advancement of Learning*, II. iv. 1–5).

Speculation as to which poets stood on Donne's shelves is fruitless. He was certainly well read in Latin and Italian poetry, and in a letter to Buckingham in 1623, when the latter was in Spain, he says of his library 'I can turn mine eye towards no shelf, in any profession from the mistress of my youth, Poetry, to the wife of mine age, Divinity, but that I meet more authors of that nation than of any other' (Gosse, ii. 176).

l. 12. *headlong, wild.* The punctuation of *1633* (with a comma after 'headlong') correctly, I think, indicates that 'headlong' is an adverb. It is not impossible to take 'headlong' as an adjective (*O.E.D.* B. 4), meaning 'madly impetuous', and describing the 'humorist' ('thee'); but this meaning seems already to be contained in 'wild uncertaine'.

l. 13. This line lacks a syllable, unless the 'r' in 'earnest' is syllabic, and the word a trisyllable. The most reliable manuscripts of all types agree with *1633*. In *JC* (*D 17*), however, the line is 'mended' by writing 'sweare to mee by', and *Lut, O'F* sophisticate it to read 'sweare heare by' (changed in *1635* to 'sweare by thy best love, here'); evidently some contemporary readers found the line metrically deficient.

l. 15. *in the middle street.* A Latinism, *in media via.*

l. 18. *Bright parcell gilt, with forty dead mens pay.* Some 'dead pays' (that is, pay for men whose names were kept on the muster roll, though dead) were allowed to a captain of a company as a recognized perquisite. Matthew Sutcliffe writes (in *The Practice, Proceedings, and Laws of Arms,* 1593, p. 320) of the abuse of forging muster rolls, and wonders 'that those that should reforme it, in some places doe suffer captaines to have certeine dead payes, which is a meanes to mainteine it, and cover it'. Forty 'dead pays' would, of course, be grossly excessive. Grierson cites a letter to Sir John Norreyes (*Acts of the Privy Council,* 1592, p. 279) stating that there are '15 deade paies allowed ordynarily in every bande, which is paide allwaies and taken by the captaines'. References are frequent, and the swindle was too profitable to be quickly stamped out; there is a space of almost a century between the first example *s.v.* 'dead pay' in the *O.E.D.* (1565) and the last (1663).

parcell gilt: 'partly gilded'. Dekker fills out the picture of this captain:

'Captayns, some in guilt armor (unbattred,) some in buffe Jerkins, plated o're with massy silver lace, (rayzd out of the ashes of dead pay,) . . . ' (*News from Hell*, 1606, sig. E1ᵛ).

l. 20. The spelling 'Courtsies' in *O'F* suggests that the line is properly syllabic:

$$\acute{} \quad × \quad × \quad \acute{} \quad × \quad \acute{} \quad × \quad × \quad \acute{} \quad ×$$
Deigne with | a nod, | thy court | 'sie to | answer.

l. 22. *blew coats*: servants. Blue coats were the livery of lower retainers; see *O.E.D.*, 'blue', II. 5. c, and 'blue coat', 2. To appear in the streets with twelve or fourteen in one's retinue, probably in double file, would show extravagance and ostentation.

With the 'spruce' clothes of a possible companion (l. 16), the gilt armour and lace of the captain (l. 18), the velvet garb of the justice (l. 21), and the coats of servants, Donne is well embarked on the train of imagery from clothing which runs through the satire.

l. 23. *Wilt*. Since this reading occurs in all manuscripts containing the final version, and only there, it seems to be an alteration of Donne's own (from 'Shalt'), and matches 'wilt' in l. 15.

l. 24. The 'humorist', impressed by the judge's splendour, will think of cultivating his son and heir as a way into high society, or as a source of wealth (since the heir is possibly 'melting with luxurie', 'Satire II', l. 79), or as a potential ward: for any of these reasons, the heir would seem beauteous.

l. 26. The comma after 'take' in *1633* (and in several manuscripts) brings out the sense: 'to take me, and after that to leave me'.

l. 27. *monstrous*. The 'monster' of some manuscripts is the older form of the adjective (*O.E.D.* B. 1). It may have stood in at least one of Donne's own copies.

    superstitious: punctilious, over-scrupulous (*O.E.D.* 3).

    puritan: one who is, or affects to be, or is accounted extremely strict, precise, or scrupulous in religion or morals (*O.E.D.* 2).

l. 28. *ceremoniall*: addicted to ceremony or ritual, precise in observance of forms of politeness (*O.E.D.*, adj. 2; the first example given is from Fulke, 1579: 'a ceremoniall and superstitious man').

    The humorist is a 'monstrous' Puritan in his excessive scrupulosity over refined manners, and yet even more in being a 'ceremoniall man', since ceremonies were abhorrent to Puritans.

    This line has eleven syllables; the light second syllable of 'manners', coming before a marked medial pause, is treated as if it were an extra light syllable at the end of a line:

$$× \quad \acute{} \quad × \quad \acute{} \quad × \quad × \quad \acute{} \quad × \quad \acute{} \quad × \quad \acute{}$$
Of re | fin'd man | ners, || yet cer | emon | iall man.

For other examples cf. 'Satire II', l. 43; 'Satire IV', ll. 22, 65, 185, 210; 'Satire

V', ll. 39, 40, 59; 'The Progress of the Soul', ll. 150, 371, 374; 'Mercurius Gallo-Belgicus', l. 5; 'To Mr T. W.' ('All haile sweet Poët'), ll. 1, 16; 'To Mr I. L.' (p. 67), l. 6; 'To Sir Henry Wotton' ('Sir, more then kisses'), l. 20; 'To the Countess of Bedford' ('T'have written then'), l. 59.

ll. 29–34. Cf. Juvenal, *Sat.* iii. 140–2 (noted by Alden):

> De moribus ultima fiet
> Quaestio: quot pascit servos? quot possidet agri
> Jugera? quam multa, magnaque paropside coenat?

l. 30. *broker*: pawnbroker or second-hand clothes dealer.
prize: appraise.

l. 31. *silke, and gold.* These are an emblem, in the literature of the time, of extravagance and ostentation in dress. For at least two centuries the Crown had attempted to limit by statute the wearing of cloth of gold (one kind of which consisted of gold thread woven with silk), crimson cloth, velvet, etc. See Linthicum, p. 144.

l. 32. *raise.* Although this word is easily confused with 'vaile' in secretary hand, and the reading of the intermediate version of the satire (*W, D, H 49*) is doubtful, 'raise' seems to have been Donne's final choice. The two words were equally current. See *O.E.D.*, 'vail', I. 2; and cf. *Skialetheia, Sat.* I: 'Vayleth his cap to each one he doth meet'. The metaphor here is from 'vailing' or lowering the topsails in submission, or in courtesy, to another vessel. For the adjustment of this courtesy to the wealth or rank of the person greeted, compare Massinger's *Emperor of the East* (1632), I. ii. 187–92, where the 'master of the habit and maners' says:

> I have in a table
> With curious punctualitie set downe
> To a haires breadth, how low a new stamp'd courtier
> May vaile to a country Gentleman, and by
> Gradation, to his marchant, mercer, draper,
> His linnen man, and taylor.

formall: rigorously observant of forms, precise, ceremonious (*O.E.D.* A. 8). The epithet is transferred.

l. 33. *consort*: accompany (*O.E.D.* I, citing, e.g., Heywood, *Four Prentices of London*, 1615, sig. G3ʳ: 'Wilt thou consort me, beare me company').

have. A subjunctive, changed in all Group III manuscripts to 'hast'; the scribes have mistaken the construction for a false concord.

l. 36. *Jointures.* A jointure, 'strictly speaking, signifies a joint estate, limited to both husband and wife' (*O.E.D.* 4), though often extended to mean the sole estate of a wife. Donne's usage is strict, as befitted a student of Lincoln's Inn.

ll. 37–40. The brackets are not in *1633*, which is too lightly punctuated; they have warrant in *Q* and other manuscripts with the same version, and are in the editions 1650–69.

l. 38. *ranke*: 'lustful, licentious' (*O.E.D.*, sense 13; also sense 14, gross, loathe-some).

itchie: from 'itch', an uneasy or restless desire or hankering.

l. 39. *barenesse*. The manuscripts containing the final version, and *1633*, spell 'barrennes(s)(e)' (similarly *O*, *P*, *S*, *S 96*, *S 962*). The two words were not identical in sound, but 'bare' could be spelt 'barre', and the error was easy for a superficial reader to make. 'Nakednesse and barenesse' corresponds to 'naked, and bare' in l. 41.

l. 40. *muddy*: morally impure, 'dirty' (*O.E.D.* 7); with some reference, perhaps, to her complexion.

l. 42. 'Naked came I out of my mother's womb, and naked shall I return thither' (Job i. 21).

l. 43. *unapparrelled*: undressed, from the verb 'unapparrell', used in 'Obsequies to the Lord Harrington', l. 12.

For the metaphor, cf. 'to lay up the *garments* of your *soules*, your bodies, in the *wardrobe* the *grave* till you call for them, and put them on again, in the resurrection' (*Sermons*, vi. 87).

l. 45. *Mans first blest state was naked.* See Gen. ii. 25. Nearly all the Group III manuscripts read 'best', which seems to be an error; 'blest' includes 'best', catches up 'blisse' from the preceding line, and properly suggests exactly what was 'lost' by sin.

l. 46. 'Unto Adam also, and to his wife, did the Lord God make coats of skins, and clothed them' (Gen. iii. 21). In the state of innocence man was naked. When he lost that he was still clothed only in the skins of beasts. Hence all we need, or are entitled to wear, is 'course attire'.

ll. 53–62. The passage suggested to Alden the similar incidental irony of the illustrations in Juvenal, *Sat.* x. 219 ff.:

> Quorum si nomina quaeras,
> Promptius expediam quot amaverit Oppia moechos,
> Quot Themison aegros autumno occiderit uno,
> Quot Basilius socios, quot circumscripserit Hirrus
> Pupillos . . .

l. 55. *black feathers.* These appear to have been fashionable among gallants around 1593. Cf. Sir John Davies's *Epigrams*, 'Meditation of a Gull' (No. 47):

> But he doth seriously bethinke him whether
> Of the guld people he bee more esteem'd,
> For his long cloake, or his great blacke feather,
> By which each gull is now a gallant deem'd.

and 'Ad Musam' (No. 48):

> Besides this muse of mine, and the blacke fether
> Grew both together fresh in estimation,
> And both growne stale were cast away togither:
> What fame is this that scarse lasts out a fashion?

musk-colour. 'Musk', apparently a dark shade of brown, does not appear in Royal Wardrobe accounts until the Stuart period (Linthicum, p. 14).

l. 57. *beare away*: as a prize; 'win' as ward, or as wife.

l. 58. *Th'Infant of London, Heire to'an India*. The first version apparently read 'Infanta' (as in *Q*, *D 16*, *A 25*, *Lut*, *O'F*). The reference is not primarily to any particular person; the word means 'the wealthiest heiress (still a minor, and probably a ward) you can think of among the families of the merchant princes of the City'. Thus Chamberlain writes (7 July 1608) jocularly of Lord Norris's daughter as 'the Infanta Norreys' (*Letters*, i. 258).

'Infant' (or 'Infante') can mean either a princess or prince of Spain, and it is possible that Donne himself changed the specific feminine form of the first version ('Infanta') to make the satiric effect more general by including male heirs (cf. l. 24 above), who could be profitable as wards.

Grierson is probably right in seeing a secondary reference to the claim of the Infanta of Spain to the throne of England. A Bull of Sixtus V (1588) confirmed the deposition of Elizabeth and named Philip II of Spain King of England; in Roman Catholic circles the Infanta was recognized as the heir to the English crown.

For 'India' as signifying 'vast wealth' cf., for example, Middleton, *Anything for a Quiet Life*, IV. ii. 70–71 (*Works*, v. 312): 'Why, what ship has brought an India home to him, that he's so bountiful?'

l. 59. *gulling*: cheating, deceptive.
weather-Spie: weather prophet.

l. 60. *heavens Scheame*. A 'scheme' (*O.E.D.* 2) was a diagram showing the relative positions, either real or apparent, of the heavenly bodies. The astrologer divided the scheme of the heavens into twelve 'mansions', and from the relative positions of the heavenly bodies in each mansion, from the signs of the Zodiac and the 'aspects' of the planets, he arrived at his predictions. The spellings 'scheame' and (in *L 74*) 'Scheames' suggest the process by which the error 'Sceanes' (in *1633*, *C 57*, *Lec*, *TCD*) was brought about. Cf. the Elegy, 'The Bracelet', ll. 59–61.

l. 61. *suits*. A 'suit' was a matching ensemble of doublet, hose, coat, jerkin, mandilion or cloak (Linthicum, p. 212).

l. 62. *subtile-witted antique youths*. The reading 'supple-witted' (*W* and nearly all Group III manuscripts) may possibly have stood in Donne's first version, 'supple' meaning 'compliant'.

The 'antic youths' (that is 'fantastics', such as Lucio in *Measure for Measure*) are ironically credited with discriminating and penetrating intellects in their pursuit of fashions.

l. 63. *depart'st from mee*. The reading of *1633* and manuscripts containing the same version is superior to the readings of the two earlier versions of the line, because *both* satirist and 'humorist' are departing 'hence' or 'from hence'—i.e. from the poet's chamber into the street; 'from mee' is dramatically more appropriate, more exact, and less harsh.

canst. The reading of *1633*, 'can', is smoother, but it is not grammatical. The possibility of error in transcribing 'canst show' is considerable, and the error is made independently in manuscripts of all groups.

ll. 65–66. For the idea, cf. 'Satire IV', ll. 11–16.

l. 66. *conscience*. A trisyllable.

ll. 67–70. The 'humorist' furtively ('creepes') takes the place of honour, the wall side, given in politeness to one's superior. The Grolier editors quote Nashe's gibe at Gabriel Harvey, that he 'would make no bones to take the wall of *Sir Philip Sidney* and another honourable Knight (his companion) about Court yet attending' (*Works*, iii. 76). The outside position was the more hazardous, involving the risks of mire underfoot and of refuse thrown from the windows above. Care for his clothes as well as for his dignity ('state') prompted the humorist's sidling to the wall. But he acted 'improvidently' since his freedom of movement in catching the eye of courtiers, etc., was impeded.

l. 74. *smacks*: sc. his lips, as a sign of relish or anticipation.
itch: hankering.

l. 77. *And as fidlers*, etc. Cf. Gynecia's lines upon a lute in *Arcadia*, iii (Sidney's *Poems*, ed. W. A. Ringler, 1962, p. 81): 'And lowest stops doo yeeld the hyest sounde'.

l. 78. *brave*: finely dressed, resplendent.
stoops. Sequence of tenses requires the 'dramatic present'. Final 's' and final 't' are easily confused, and 'stoopt' seems to be a primitive error in the text of the final version.

l. 80. *the wise politique horse*. The bay gelding 'Morocco', owned by the horse-trainer Banks. Nearly all the many allusions to Banks and his horse were collected by S. H. Atkins, *N. and Q.*, 21 July 1934. The horse could indicate the number of coins in a purse, add up a throw of dice, dance, and so on; and 'By a sign given him, he would beck for the King of Scots and for Queen Elizabeth, and when ye spoke of the King of Spain, would both bite and strike at you . . .' (quoted by Atkins from Patrick Anderson's manuscript history of Scotland, 1596). The earliest clear reference to Morocco that can be dated occurs in Nashe's *The Unfortunate Traveller*, published in 1594, but finished (according to a note at the end) on 27 June 1593: 'Wiser was our Brother *Bankes* of these latter daies, who made his jugling horse a Cut' (*Works*, ii. 230; see also iii. 21). Banks's performances were no doubt affected by the periods of severe plague 1592–4; hence Nashe's phrase, 'of these latter daies', and Donne's 'heretofore'.
politique: sagacious, diplomatic.

ll. 81–82. The wise politique editor of *1633* omitted these two lines, perhaps fearing that they would give offence, by recalling the King's journey to Spain in 1623 as a prospective suitor of the Infanta. The lines were added in *1635*, probably from *O'F* (which similarly reads '6').

l. 81. *Elephant or Ape*. The performing elephant is mentioned in Davies's epigram 'In Dacum' (written in or before 1594; see introductory note above) and in Jonson's *Every Man out of his Humour*, IV. vi. 60–61. Joseph Hall writes (*Virgidemiarum*, IV. ii. 93–95) of 'some tricke / Of strange *Moroccoes* dumbe Arithmeticke, / Or the young Elephant'. Basse says (in ?1646, *Poetical Works*, ed. R. Warwick Bond, 1893, p. 336) that 'in our youths we saw the Elephant', and Sir Thomas Browne had seen an elephant 'not many years past', this being 'not the first that hath been seen in England' (*Vulgar Errors*, iii. 1). Donne is the only writer to refer to this response by the elephant to the name of the King of Spain.

The ape was also well known. In the Induction of Jonson's *Bartholomew Fair* (1614) we read of 'a Jugler with a wel-educated Ape to come over the chaine, for the *King* of *England*, and backe againe for the *Prince*, and sit still on his arse for the *Pope*, and the *King* of *Spaine*!' (*Works*, vi. 13). For an earlier reference, see Nashe, *Works*, iii. 37.

l. 83. *joggs*: nudges.

l. 88. *in drinking his Tobacco*. The manuscript *JC* is now in the George Arents Tobacco Collection (New York Public Library) on the strength of this passage—a latter-day tribute to Donne's quickness of social observation. While the tobacco plant was referred to (*O.E.D.*) as early as 1577, there are only two references definitely earlier than Donne's here to tobacco prepared for smoking (1588, 1589). 'Drink' is the usual word.

l. 90. *'T may*. The change from 'May', though trivial, may be authentic, since only manuscripts with the final version (and *Dob*) agree with *1633*.

l. 95. *all repute*. The curious reading 's'all repute' is shared by *1633*, *C 57*, *Lec*, and *L 74*. It is perhaps due to an early scribe's having mistaken 'all repute' for a parenthetical phrase, 'everybody says', and having added 'so' to make this clear.

repute: esteem, value.

l. 96. *device*: faculty of devising, inventiveness, ingenuity.

hansoming. From the verb to 'handsome' (*O.E.D.*), meaning to make handsome, or becoming, to beautify or adorn.

l. 97. *pinke*. A 'pink' was a hole or eyelet punched or cut in a garment for decorative purposes. Cf. Jonson, *Cynthia's Revels*, V. iv. 298: 'Is this pinke of equall proportion to this cut?' See Linthicum, pp. 153–4.

panes. These were strips of cloth joined to make one cloth, sometimes with lace or other trimming material inserted in the seams; or strips of the same cloth distinguished by colour or separated by lines of trimming; or strips made by slashing a garment lengthwise to expose fine lining or an undergarment: used often in sleeves and breeches. See Linthicum, pp. 172, 205.

print. Applied to the exact crimping, goffering, or set of the 'plaits' or pleats of the neck-ruffs then worn; used also of other pleated garments. 'To maintain a "spruce ruff" or one "starched in print" the wearer must carry his head straight and avoid damp' (Linthicum, p. 160).

cut: either 'fashionable shape' (*O.E.D.* III. 16) or, more probably, 'slash, incision into the edge of a garment for ornament' (*O.E.D.* IV. 19), as in *Much Ado*, III. iv. 19: 'Cloth o' gold, and cuts, and lac'd with silver'.

plight: pleat, either of ruffs, or of other garments, such as French breeches, which were 'made in panes, i.e. strips, or in pleats which parted slightly, showing a rich lining' (Linthicum, p. 205).

l. 98. *to have the best conceit*: to have the best notion or judgement. Such an expert would have been invaluable in advising on 'suits' and styles in those days of various and swiftly changing fashions. Cf. Chapman, *All Fools*, v. ii (the opening speech):

> A thing whose soul is specially employ'd
> In knowing where best gloves, best stockings, waistcoats
> Curiously wrought, are sold; sacks milliners' shops
> For all new tires and fashions, and can tell ye
> What new devices of all sorts there are . . .
>   and for these womanly parts
> He is esteem'd a witty gentleman.

l. 99. *Our dull Comedians want him.* The sartorial expert would be a godsend to actors. Cf. 'Satire IV', ll. 180–5, where courtiers sell their cast-off Court clothes to the Theatre.

l. 100. *stoop'st.* The humorist, as in l. 78, is bowing obsequiously, forgetting again the injunctions of the satirist (ll. 49–51); hence, 'God strengthen thee'.

l. 102. (*Which understand none,*). I follow Grierson in bracketing these words, since they seem to have no point unless they are a sarcastic interpolation, *sotto voce*, by the satirist: 'To you, who understand neither French nor Italian (languages and fashions), he appears perfectly French and Italian—but to no-one who is really acquainted with these languages and fashions.' Every satirist and epigrammatist of the period inveighs against the aping of continental fashions by Englishmen, especially by returned travellers. Compare Portia on her English suitor, *Merchant of Venice*, I. ii. 65–68: 'How oddly he is suited! I think he bought his doublet in Italy, his round hose in France, his bonnet in Germany, and his behaviour everywhere.' The clothing of Donne's 'traveller' was probably the only evidence of his acquaintance—if any—with France and Italy. Cf. 'An Affected Traveller', in *The Overburian Characters*, ed. W. J.

Paylor, 1936, p. 11: 'His attire speakes *French* or *Italian*, and his *gate* cryes *Behold mee.*'

l. 105. *of sort, of parts*: of rank and talents.

ll. 106–7. Guilpin imitates (*Skialetheia*, Sat. V, sig. D7ᵛ):

> There in that window mistres minkes doth stand,
> And to some copesmate beckneth her hand,
> In is he gone, Saint *Venus* be his speede.

l. 107. *flings*: dashes, rushes away. He evaporates like dew drawn off swiftly by the bright sun (his mistress).

ll. 107–10. Compare the character, 'A Humorist', in H(enry) P(arrot)'s *Cures for the Itch*, 1626 (B3ᵛ): 'Hee's of that quaint society and behaviour, as not enduring to stay long in company, leaves you abruptly, without taking leave: he finds not halfe so soone the cause of quarrell, as thereto proves occasioned without a cause.'

l. 109. *he could command no more.* His mistress was entertaining other lovers, and he was no longer in 'sole command'.

l. 112. *constantly a while.* A parting shot: the 'humorist' or 'inconstant' is at last constant in something (if only for a while).

Satyre II (p. 7)

MSS.: Also in *H 51*, *HN* (with a text nearest to that in *W*), and *S 96* (with a text corrupted from that in *Q₂*, *O'F*).

The editor of *1633* suppressed words in ll. 32 and 33, and the entire lines 69–70, 74–75, representing them by dashes. All the manuscripts agree among themselves and with *1635* in these places, and I have taken the accidents from *1635*.

The text of *1633* is otherwise good, and the nine variations I make from it are relatively minor; some of the errors are made independently in a few of the manuscripts. In four places the edition follows its Group I manuscript in error (ll. 34, 44, 84, 105); in three others *1633* is alone, or has only haphazard manuscript support (ll. 46, 4, 77); in l. 6 the weight of evidence is against the edition, but in l. 87 *1633*, with all the manuscripts containing the final version (and many others), seems to have made a minor error. I differ from Grierson in three readings.

There is no specific evidence as to the date of this Satire. It seems likely, however, that its composition was prompted, in some degree, by the appearance in 1594 of the anonymous series of sonnets, *Zepheria*. (This book also seems to have inspired two of the satirical sonnets in the *Gulling Sonnets* attributed with great probability to Sir John Davies; see vol. ii of his *Complete Works*, ed. A. B. Grosart, 1876.) The forty poems in *Zepheria* are mostly feeble efforts in the 'Petrarchan' style, distinguished from other collections of bad

Elizabethan poetry by the use throughout of atrocious new coinages; among his muse's 'hyperboliz'd trajections' the author includes words like 'Thesaurize', 'portionize', 'irrotulat', 'excordiat', etc. This oddity of style is pilloried neither by Davies nor by Donne, though it might have stimulated the use of 'imbrothel'd' (l. 64) and 'controverters' (l. 101), which for lack of previous examples may be taken as coinages of Donne's own. Three of the poems in *Zepheria*, however (nos. 20, 37, 38), are written in ludicrous legal conceits, and three or four others have a hint, or a sprinkling, of legal phraseology. Thus 'Canzon 37' begins:

> When last mine eyes dislodged from thy beautie,
> Though serv'd with proces of a parents writ,
> A Supersedeas countermanding dutie
> Even then I saw upon thy smiles to sit.

Whether such poems were meant to be taken seriously or not, it seems likely, as Grierson suggested, that they prompted Donne's conception of the lawyer-poet, and the terms of Coscus's wooing (ll. 49–57). Since Coscus has been 'of late' a poet (l. 43) this connexion with *Zepheria* suggests 1594 as the date of Donne's Satire (though *Zepheria* might have circulated earlier in manuscript). Nothing in the poem makes this date unlikely. Drummond of Hawthornden copied only two satires into his selection (*HN*) from Donne's poems, this one and 'Satire IV'; the date which he wrote against the latter, 1594, is impossible for that poem and may have been attached to the wrong satire.

'Satire II' is not mainly concerned with a specific poet, with a type of poet, or even with poetry in general; but the figure of Coscus enables Donne to give some appearance of unity to his satire of the abuse of poetry, and, more important, of the abuse of law. All evil things, he says, occur in one form that is so essentially evil that our hatred for this enables us to view the less heinous forms of the vice with pity (ll. 1–4). Poetry is such an evil, but one cannot hate helpless poets (ll. 5–10), whether they are playwrights (ll. 11–16), wooers (ll. 16–20), flatterers for a fee (ll. 21–22), fashionable scribblers (ll. 23–24), or plagiarists (ll. 25–30). All manner of other evil-doers are relatively harmless, too, for they punish themselves (ll. 31–39). Coscus was worse than these when he wrote poetry; but even then he was not beyond hope (ll. 39–62). He reached the 'excellently best' or purest form of evil, putting himself beyond the bounds both of pity and of hope, when he chose to practise law only for gain, by every shabby trick. The rest of the poem deals with this evil, for which only hatred can be felt.

In *Cy* the poem is entitled 'Another Satyre of M^r. John Donne'; in *O*, *P* it is copied separately as 'Law Satyre'; and in *S 962* it is called 'Satyre I: Agaynst Poets and Lawyers'.

l. 1. *Sir*. It is not impossible that, as Grierson suggests (ii. 111), the poem is addressed to Christopher Brooke, Donne's close friend and chamber-fellow at Lincoln's Inn, himself a writer. The only evidence, however, is very weak:

the note in Drummond's hand attached to the poem in *HN*, 'After C. B. Coppy'.

ll. 2–3.   *yet there's one state*
                             In all ill things so excellently best,

In *H 51* the scribe first wrote, 'yet in every state / There are some found so villanously best' (later inserting the reading of the normal text above it). The same words are written by an annotator of the copy of *1633* in the library of St. John's College, Oxford, near the printed text. In *S 96* the reading is: 'yet everie state / Hath in't some founde soe villanouslie bleste'. The text of which these traces remain seems to have been a gloss, or 'improvement', by someone who did not understand, or like, Donne's metaphysical paradoxes. He says here that there is a perfect or quintessential state of everything in which it is 'best' or purest; in this sense evil ('ill') itself can take a form which is 'best' and 'excellent'.

l. 4. *them*: the 'ill things' when they are in this 'excellently best' state.
   pitty. For the satirist's 'pity', modifying his scorn, anger, or hatred, cf. 'Satire III', ll. 1–4.

l. 6. Donne echoes, and gives precision to, the common Puritan charge that poetry, the nurse of idleness and effeminacy, takes men from fruitful labour and is the enemy of the military virtues. The *locus classicus* for these charges is Gosson's *School of Abuse* (1579).
   dearths. All manuscripts containing the final version have the plural, and enough of the other manuscripts have it to make it clear that 'dearth' (*1633*) is an error in any version. There had been a time of great scarcity in 1586, and another was developing in 1594 (lasting into 1598); each coincided with signs of a growing threat from Spain.

ll. 7–9. *Though like the Pestilence*, etc. Men become sick with poetry (cf. l. 61), with the plague, and (according to the old-style Petrarchan conventions) with love inexplicably, and can be cured only by starving out the ailment. The starving poet (ll. 14, 22) is a familiar figure in satires of classical, Renaissance, and Augustan times. On cures for the plague medical writers do not express themselves much or confidently. Walter Bruel, however, writes (*Praxis Medicinae*, 1585, translated by J. A., 1632, p. 400): 'They must eate sparingly in the beginning of the disease'; but (pp. 406–7) 'as they are forbidden to glut themselves, so they must not be altogether fasting'.
   As for love, loss of appetite was one of the symptoms. If, however, the emotion was still in the sanguine stage, it was necessary to reduce the amount of blood in the body and so reduce desire; hence a spare diet was recommended. Cf. *Measure for Measure*, IV. iii. 150–3, and Burton, *Anatomy*, part. 3, sect. 2, memb. 5, subsect. 1, who prescribes 'slender and sparing diet'.

l. 9. *their*: the poets'.

l. 10. *poore, disarm'd, like Papists.* By statute 27° Eliz. c. 2. (1584–5) Jesuits and seminary priests who refused to take the oath of supremacy were banished, and a fine was imposed, or imprisonment at the Queen's pleasure, upon any-one not disclosing to a J.P. or other such officer the presence of a priest in the kingdom (*Statutes of the Realm,* iv. 707). In *An Humble Supplication to Her Majesty* (1591) Robert Southwell gives moving accounts of the sufferings of Roman Catholics (see the edition by R. C. Bald, 1953, pp. 1, 40 ff.). Donne's brother had suffered and, indeed, died in 1593 as a result of his violation of the statute referred to.

l. 12. *reade.* An accused man could still, in Donne's day, claim benefit of clergy, i.e. clemency, if he could read the so-called 'neck-verse', usually the beginning of the 'Miserere' (Ps. 51), and so save his neck. 'If a man murder another in anger and the criminal can read, he is shown mercy in so far as his hands only are cut off, that he may be able to read, in the hope that he may yet perform some good, but if he cannot read, then he forfeits his life . . .' (*Thomas Platter's Travels in England, 1599,* translated and ed. Clare Williams, 1937, pp. 187–8). Cf. *Sermons,* i. 232.

l. 13. *ideot*: in its root meaning, 'one without special knowledge', hence 'ignorant', 'uneducated'.

ll. 15–16. *As in some Organ,* etc. This is the most original and wittily accurate of the images by which the poets and playwrights assert the dependence of the actors upon them. (J. B. Leishman collected such passages in his ed. of the *Parnassus Plays,* 1949, pp. 344–5.) Moving puppets or figures were attached to some contemporary organs, actuated or 'inspired' by air from the bellows which laboured ('pant') away unseen. Such figures (angels moving trumpets to and from their mouths, or waving their wings; suns, moons, and stars in motion; birds chirping, etc.) were common on Continental organs in the six-teenth century (see E. J. Hopkins and E. F. Rimbault, *The Organ; its History and Construction,* 2nd ed., 1870, pp. 87–88, and C. Sachs, *History of Musical Instruments,* 1940, p. 308). References to puppets on English organs are much later. 'Sabbath day, about the time of morninge prayer, we went to the [Hereford] Minster, where the pipes played and the puppets sange so sweetely that some of our soildiers could not forbeare dauncinge in the holie quire' ('Letters from a Subaltern Officer of the Earl of Essex's Army', 1642, *Archaeologia,* xxxv, 1853, p. 332). The old organ at Lynn, Norfolk, 'had on it a figure of King David playing on the harp cut in solid wood, larger than the life: likewise several moving figures which beat time, etc. This is an old prac-tice, and alluded to by Dr. Donne: *As, in some organs . . .* ' (W. L[udham], *Gentleman's Magazine,* xlii, 1772, p. 565 n.). There was in London in Donne's day an organ-builder, Thomas Dallam, eminently capable of such work; see W. L. Sumner, *The Organ,* 2nd ed., 1955, p. 110.

l. 17. *rimes*: incantations or spells.

ll. 17–18. *witchcrafts charms Bring not now their old feares*, etc. The rationalizing of the powers of the Devil, and hence of witches' powers also, had reached an advanced stage in Reginald Scot's *The Discovery of Witchcraft* (1584) and in the work of his followers, most recently in George Giffard's *A Dialogue concerning Witches and Witchcrafts* (1593). Giffard writes (*Shakespeare Association Facsimiles*, i, 1931, sigs. A2ᵛ–A3):

> The Devils would hurt and destroy with bodily harmes, both men and beastes and other creatures: but all the Divels in Hell are so chained up and brideled by this high providence [of God] that they can not plucke the wing from one poore little Wrenne, without speciall leave given them from the ruler of the whole earth. And yet the Witches are made beleeve that at their request . . . their spirites doe lame and kill both men and beastes. . . . God giveth him [the Devil] power sometimes to afflict both men and beastes with bodily harmes: If he can, he will doe it, as intreated and sent by Witches, but for us to imagin either that their sending doth give him power, or that he would not doe that which God hath given him leave to doe, unlesse they should request and send him, is most absurd . . .

There was an increasing tendency to ascribe the witches' conception of their powers to delusion. See L. Babb, *The Elizabethan Malady*, 1951, pp. 54 ff.

ll. 19–20.   *Rammes, and slings now are seely battery,*
                    Pistolets are the best Artillerie.

During Donne's lifetime there was a vigorous controversy over the relative virtues of the traditional English weapon, the long-bow, and 'Artillerie, or fire-shott' (see K. Muir, *S.Q.* x, 1959, p. 137). Humfrey Barwick in *A Brief Discourse concerning the force and effect of all manual weapons of fire and the disability of the Long-Bow* (?1594) says: 'What, shall we refuse the Cannon and fall to the Ram againe, or to knowne weapons more meeter for Savadge people then for puissant Princes' (sig. A4ʳ).

'Battering rams and slings are pitiable (*seely*) weapons of assault nowadays and of all artillery "pistolets" are the best.' Donne makes the same pinot, with the same pun (on 'pistolet', a small pistol, and 'pistolet', a Spanish coin, the *écu*), in 'The Bracelet' (ll. 31–32):

> Those unlick'd beare-whelps, unfil'd Pistolets,
> That, more then cannon-shot, availes or lets . . .

The most effective weapon against foreign countries is gold that buys information, corrupts officers of state, and foments rebellion. See Gardner, *Elegies etc.*, p. 115, for quotations illustrating the fear of the ubiquity of Spanish gold. Miss Gardner dates 'The Bracelet' *c.* 1593–4.

In love's war, charms and spells, and old-fashioned ways of wooing are weak weapons compared with money.

ll. 25–30. There is a possible echo of these lines in Marston's *The Scourge of Villainy*, xi. 74 ff., ending:

> O that this Eccho, that doth speake, spet, write
> Naught but the excrements of others spright . . .

Miss Gardner has suggested a possible echo of Donne's 'The Curse' in *The Scourge of Villainy*. See Marston, *Poems*, ed. A. Davenport, 1961, pp. 169–70 and commentary, and Gardner, *Elegies etc.*, pp. 164–5. Marston might have known Donne's *Satires* in manuscript through his friend Guilpin, who imitated them as early as 1598.

l. 27. *Rankly*: grossly, coarsely. The word has also the suggestion of luxuriance and rottenness. 'Rawly' ('swallowed with incomplete understanding and refinement') possibly stood in one of Donne's copies, since *W, D, H 49* (and *S, S 96*) share this reading.

l. 31. *use*: make it a practice or habit.

l. 32. *out-doe*: like 'out-swive', in the bawdy sense, = 'out-copulate'.
 Dildoes: artificial phalluses. Cf. 'The Anagram', l. 53.

l. 33. *out-drinke*. Analogous to 'out-doe', 'out-usure', and 'out-sweare', and therefore meaning 'outdo in drinking', 'drink more than the sea does' (sc. from the rivers that flow into it). See P. Legouis, *S.N.* xiv. 195–6.
 out-sweare the Letanie. This phrase was sufficiently dangerous to cause the omission of 'Letanie' from all editions until *1669*. Grierson refers to Warburton's note on Pope's version of this satire explaining Donne's phrase as 'a low allusion to a licentious quibble used at that time by the enemies of the English Liturgy; who disliking the frequent invocations in the *Letanie*, called them the *taking God's Name in vain*, which is the Scripture periphrasis for *swearing*' (Pope's *Works*, ed. of 1766, iv. 250).

l. 34. *sinnes all kindes*. I take 'sinnes' as a possessive plural, 'sins' '—'all the varieties of every sin', familiar to priests who hear them uttered in the confessional. The reading of *1633* is an error made independently in isolated manuscripts of all groups.

l. 36. *Schoolemen new tenements*, etc. Referring to the belief that all those convicted of a particular sin were consigned to the same region of Hell. In the Inferno, as represented by Dante, there are some twenty-four groups of unblest souls (heathen, heretics, flatterers, simonists, suicides, forgers, etc.), each group suffering in its own abiding-place ('tenement'). The places in or near Hell are discussed in *The Golden Legend*, ed. F. S. Ellis, 1900, vi. 109 ff. The number of 'tenements' depended upon the number, and the classification, of sins (beginning usually from Aristotle's basic division of evils into three classes). The new outlandish ('strange', l. 37) sins of London require new classifications, and hence new places of punishment in Hell. There is a satiric glance at the arrogance of the Schoolmen as they (and not God Himself) 'make' these places. Cf. Simpson, *Essays*, p. 27: 'Schoolmen, which have invented new things, and found out, or added Suburbs to Hell, will not be exceeded in this boldness upon words.'

l. 37. *Canonists*: canon-lawyers.

l. 38. *large receit*: broad scope.

l. 40. *my just offence*: the offence I justly feel. The reading 'just', which is confined to manuscripts containing the last version, seems to be a revised reading of Donne's own. The earlier reading, 'great', is weak, being less energetic than 'hate Perfectly' (ll. 1–2).

l. 41. *makes botches poxe*: makes pimples, as they develop, reveal themselves as the effects of serious disease.

ll. 42–43. Cf. *The Return from Parnassus*, Part 2, ll. 1664–5:

> When thou wert borne dame *Nature* cast her Calfe:
> Forrage and time hath made thee a great Oxe.

'A simple scholer, or none at all may be a lawyer. . . . If thou canst but have the patience to plod inough, talke, and make noise inough, be impudent inough, and 'tis inough' (Jonson, *Poetaster*, I. ii. 120 ff.).

l. 43. For the metre, see note to 'Satire I', l. 28.

l. 44. *a scarce Poët*. The reading of *1633* and of some manuscripts, 'scarce a Poët', is an error. Donne's use of 'scarce' in this way (like the Italian *scarso*, defined by Florio, *A World of Words*, 1598, as ' . . . sparing, miserable, scant') caused trouble to copyists also in 'Satire IV', l. 4 and l. 240. Donne is not saying that Coscus is scarcely a poet, but that he is a bad one.

jollier of this state: prouder of this (new) position in life. For 'jolly' in this sense, cf. 'Satire I', l. 7.

l. 46. *lime-twigs*: twigs smeared with bird-lime (a sticky substance made from hollybark) for catching small birds. Properly speaking, only the 'nets' are 'throwne'.

l. 48. *language of the Pleas, and Bench*: language of the Court of Common Pleas and the Queen's Bench. All the legal terms in Coscus's wooing precisely describe the actions by which one would claim possession of a contested piece of land. See Lucille S. Cobb, *Explicator*, xv, 1956, Item 8.

l. 49. *motion*: an application for a rule or order of the court, permitting the case to proceed. The judge (i.e. the lady) grants it ('Speake').

l. 50. tricesimo'*of the Queene*: 1588, the thirtieth year of Elizabeth's reign.

l. 51. *Continuall claimes*. A continual claim (*O.E.D.*, 'continual', I. c) is a claim formally reiterated within statutory intervals so that it might not be deemed to be abandoned. John Rastell, however, gives some livelier details relevant here (*An Exposition of Certain difficult and obscure words, and terms of the Laws* . . . , 1595): '*Continual claim* is where a man hath right to enter into certaine landes whereof another is seised in fee simple or fee tayle, and hee dare not enter for feare of death or beating, but approcheth as nigh as he dare, and maketh claime thereto within the yeare and day before the death of him that hath the landes', etc. Although his rival is rather forbidding, Coscus has pressed his suit during the last six years whenever the lady has let him approach 'nigh' enough.

l. 51. *injunctions.* Judicial processes, which could be issued by Chancery to 'stay' proceedings of the Common Law courts if the suit was unjust or had been brought on insufficient grounds (e.g. to harass the defendant), also to compel restitution to an injured party. The lady has from time to time admitted that she has been unjust to Coscus, and has ceased to listen to the pleas (both unfair and frivolous) made by his rival.

l. 53. *Spare mee*: excuse me, allow me to go; as in 'Satire IV', l. 143.

Hillary terme: kept at Westminster from 23 January to 12 February. Coscus has returned to the attack well within the year and a day allowed by law for the making of his claim.

l. 54. *size*: assize, sitting of the courts.

l. 55. *remitter*: 'is when a man hath two titles to anie land, and he commeth to the lande by the last title, yet he shall bee judged in by force of his elder title, and that shall bee saide to him a remitter' (Rastell). Coscus's present claim on the lady is based on her invitation to 'returne'; but the more valid claim is that his love for her antedated that of his rival—his right is that of first possession. While he has been absent (in the 'interim' of his pleadings) he has used the only other means possible to win his case—by sworn statements (affidavits) in his love-letters.

Cf. 'A Meere Common Lawyer' (*The Overburian Characters*, ed. W. J. Paylor, p. 31): 'His love letters of the last yeere of his Gentlemanship' (i.e. studentship at his Inn of Court) 'are stuft with *Discontinuances, Remitters,* and *Uncore prists.*'

ll. 59–60. Pope omits these lines from his 'versification' of the satire, but uses suggestions from l. 60 in *Windsor-Forest*, l. 68: 'The hollow Winds thro' naked Temples roar.'

l. 59. *Sclavonians scolding.* Sclavonia, or Slavonia, was, strictly speaking, the tract of country between the rivers Slav and Drau (Ortelius, *Theatrum Orbis Terrarum*, 1592, maps 87, 88); loosely applied, however, to regions in or near the old Roman province of Dalmatia (Munster, *Cosmographia*, 1572, p. 1067). When 'Sclavonian' is not merely a term of abuse (as in Nashe, *Works*, iii. 109; Henry Parrot, *Laquei ridiculosi*, 1613, sig. A3), it seems to mean chiefly 'one who speaks an outlandish, barbarous tongue'. Cf. *A Fair Quarrel*, by Middleton and Rowley, IV. i. 25–38, 82–84 (Middleton, *Works*, iv. 226, 228): 'tell me in what language I shall roar a lecture to you . . . the *Sclavonian, Parthamenian, Barmeothian*'; 'we could now roar in the Sclavonian language, but this practice hath been a little sublime . . .', etc.

l. 60. Cf. 'An hymn to the Saints, and to Marquess Hamilton', ll. 23–24:

> So fell our *Monasteries*, in one instant growne
> Not to lesse houses, but, to heapes of stone.

l. 61. *possest with muse.* The idea of poetic 'possession' comes from Plato's *Ion*, 533-4, and *Phaedrus*, 245. The use of 'muse' = 'inspiration' without an article or possessive adjective is unexampled in *O.E.D.*

l. 63. *bold soule.* A parenthesis, addressed to the poet's own soul, or to the 'Sir' of l. 1.

repute. An imperative: 'estimate'.

l. 65. *owlelike*: wakeful at night.

l. 66. *at*: holding.

bill: the watchman's familiar weapon, the halberd. There is also a pun on the legal meaning of 'bill', a written statement of a case. 'Look on our lawyers' bills, not one contains Virtue or honest drifts' (Chapman, *An Humorous Day's Mirth*, vii. 80-81).

l. 68. *suretiship*: responsibility taken by one person on behalf of another, as for payment of a debt (*O.E.D.*). This is a respectable reason for being sent to prison (since one is brought there by another's default and one's own generosity), and is too good a lie to give up easily (it is maintained for 'whole months').

l. 70. *Like a Kings favorite*, etc. A touch of Juvenal's loftier and more daring manner, as in *Sat.* iv. 72-75:

> Vocantur
> Ergo in consilium proceres, quos oderat ille,
> In quorum facie miserae magnaeque sedebat
> Pallor amicitiae.

It seemed too risky to the editor of *1633*, who omitted ll. 69-70.

ll. 71-72.   *Like a wedge in a blocke, wring to the barre,*
                    Bearing like Asses,

Coscus must work his way laboriously to the counsellors' bar (through the crowded court) like a wedge through a block of wood, pressing on with the dogged stupidity characteristic of asses, and (a practised liar, ll. 69-70) he must lie to the judge, etc. See Appendix B.

wring: writhe, labour, contend (*O.E.D.* 19). 'Brocke the lawier was lately dead by straining over violently at the chauncerie barre, wherby a rupture he had, burst out and in three or fowre days made an end of him' (Chamberlain, *Letters*, i. 318). For the crowded conditions of the courts, see the incident narrated in Chapman's *All Fools*, II. i. 324 ff.

l. 72. *Bearing*: pressing, moving with persistence. In his use of 'Asses' and 'whores' in relation to Coscus, Donne hovers between words and images expressing the characteristics now of the individual, now of the class.

more shamelesse. Cf. a passage translated by Lynn Thorndike from a manuscript *Liber de Similitudinibus et exemplis* (*Speculum*, xxxii, 1957, p. 791): 'So many hire lawyers to defend their property, but they consume it. Also note that lawyers are worse than whores, since whores sell the viler and worse parts of their body, but lawyers the nobler and better, forsooth the mouth and tongue.'

l. 73. *carted whores.* Convicted prostitutes were taken from the court in a cart to Bridewell, where they were whipped naked in public (*O.E.D.*, 'cart', vb. 2).

l. 75. *Symonie.* Traffic in church livings was sufficiently prevalent to warrant legislation, Stat. 31 Eliz., cap. 6, 4–5; but according to Stubbes, *Anatomy of Abuses*, Part II, 1583 (where there is much on the subject, sigs. L3–6), ways were found of evading the law.

Sodomy. This was a stock charge of the more vehement Protestants against monastic orders, especially in recounting 'revelations' during the dispossession of the monasteries by Henry VIII: 'read but Bale's catalogue of sodomites, at the visitation of abbeys here in England' (Burton, *Anatomy,* part. 3, sect. 2, memb. 5, subsect. 5).

l. 77. *compasse.* Compare: 'How easily could I overthrow such a wastfull young Man, and compasse his Land, if I had but Money, to feed his humours?' (*Sermons*, vi. 199). In *O.E.D.*, 'compass', vb. IV. 9, means to seize, lay hold of; but Pope's version of the line is quoted under sense 7, to encircle (as the sea), enclose.

ll. 77–78. *all our land; From Scots*, etc. He will gain possession of all Britain, from Scotland to the Isle of Wight, from Mount St. Michael (Land's End, Cornwall) to Dover shore: i.e. the length and breadth of the land.

l. 79. *luxurie.* Donne's first choice seems to have been 'Gluttony'; but 'luxurie' is 'by far the more general . . . ; for, heirs were not supposed to get rid of their estates by mere gluttony, a vice of older age, but by debauchery generally' (Grosart). 'Luxurie' implies lasciviousness, and 'melting' is therefore doubly appropriate since not only the heir's estate dwindles, but also his bodily substance. Cf. 'Where are thy goodly uplands, and thy down lands? all sunk into that little pit, lechery' (Middleton, *A Trick to Catch the Old One*, I. i. 3–4).

l. 82. *snuffe*: candle-end. Stubbes, speaking of chandlers, says (*The Second Part of the Anatomy of Abuses*, 1583, sig. G7ᵛ): 'as for the stuffe whereof they make their candles, I am ashamed to speake of it. For whereas they should make them of good liquor and sweet, they make them of all kind of kitchen stuffe, and other stinking baggage.'

l. 83. *yeare.* This is the Old English uninflected plural *géar.*

l. 84. *Relique-like.* This form of the word is much more characteristic of Donne than the 'Reliquely' of *1633* and odd manuscripts in all groups; the latter reading seems to be due to independent substitution. The kitchen-maid treasures her hoard as if it were a sacred relic; it does, in a way, like a relic, contribute to her future bliss.

l. 86. *Wringing*: wresting (from the self-indulgent heirs).

men pulling prime. The men are playing primero, a sort of poker much played by courtiers for high stakes; for descriptions see, e.g., Nares's *Glossary* (ed. 1888, ii. 687 ff.); *Archaeologia*, viii. 131–2, 148 ff. 'Prime' was the winning hand consisting of different suits; to 'pull for prime' was to draw for a card or cards which might make the player prime. Coscus takes no longer getting money out of each acre than a gamester does in pulling out a winning card.

l. 87. *parchments.* The plural suits 'fields' better, and it is unlikely that Donne would have changed it to the singular, even though *1633* and the manuscripts containing the final version all read 'parchment'. As Grierson says, final 's' could easily be misread as final 'e' (as, apparently, in a few unrelated manuscripts).

drawes: draws up.

l. 88. *Assurances, bigge,* etc. Assurances are documents securing the title to property. In Coscus's hands they become as large as the whole body of Civil Law with Commentary. Cf. Stubbes, *Anatomy of Abuses*, Part II, 1583, sig. E7ᵛ:

For whereas in times past when men dealt uprightly, and in the feare of God, sixe or seven lines was sufficient for the assurance of any peece of land whatsoever, now 40. 60. 100. 200. 500. nay a whole skin of parchment, and sometimes 2. or 3. skins will hardly serve. Wherin shalbe so many provisoes, particles, and clauses, and so many observances, that it is hard for a poore ignorant man to keep halfe of them: and if he fail in one of the lest, you knowe what followeth.

l. 89. *in our times forwardnesse*: in these advanced days.

l. 90. *Fathers of the Church.* The Fathers are notoriously bulky writers.

ll. 92–96. *those first dayes When Luther was profest,* etc. The doxology ('For Thine is the kingdom, the power and the glory' etc.), or the 'Power and glory clause', is not in the Vulgate scriptures, and so was not used by Luther while he was a young friar. It was taken by Erasmus from the Greek codices for his Latin version of the New Testament (1516). Luther, having in the meantime renounced the monastic laws, adopted it in his translation of the Testament into German (1521). In *The Courtier's Library*, ed. E. M. Simpson, 1930, p. 33, Donne includes as item 13 'M. Lutherus de abbreviatione orationis Dominicae'. His serious references to Luther are respectful, e.g. a 'man of infinite undertaking, and industry, and zeal, and blessings from the Highest' (Simpson, *Essays*, p. 9). Like Luther, Coscus has abandoned principles he once held; but the analogy is very loose when it concerns the point of 'writing at greater length'.

l. 101. *controverters*: controversialists.

vouch'd: brought forth as evidence or confirmation. Strictly speaking it is the theological arguments that are vouched *for* by the texts.

ll. 103–4. The woods are cut down, not for building or firewood needed on the estate, but for quick profit. Cf. Middleton's *Michaelmas Term*, II. iii. 372–4, where, as Easy signs a bond, Quomodo (who resembles Coscus) says: 'Now I begin to set one foot upon the land: methinks I am felling of trees already.'

l. 105. *Where's*. There are several other examples in Donne's verse of this idiomatic use of a singular verb with a plural subject following: e.g. 'The Bracelet', ll. 31–32.

th'old landlords troops, and almes: the crowds of relatives, guests, and servants in the young man's father's day, before the slick lawyer wrested the estate away, and the charity once dispensed to the needy by the master of the great house. For similar material cf. Juvenal, *Sat.* i. 92 ff., and Hall, *Virgidemiarum*, v. ii ('Houskeping's dead') with the notes in A. Davenport's edition of Hall's *Poems*. 'Where are the great Chines of staulled Beefe? the great blacke Jackes of doble Beere? the long Haull tables furnished with good victuals? and the multitude of good fellowes. . . . In a worde, they are all banyshed with the spirit of the Butterie, they are as rare in this age, as common in former times' (*The Servingman's Comfort*, 1598, Shakespeare Association Facs. 3, 1931, G4ᵛ; see also sigs. H2ᵛ–H4).

l. 106. *Carthusian fasts*. The Carthusians were an order of monks founded by St. Bruno in 1086, noted for the severity of their rule. 'The Carthusian Friers thought they descended into as low pastures as they could goe, when they renounced all flesh, and bound themselves to feed on fish onely' (*Sermons*, ii. 297–8).

fulsome: cloyingly or disgustingly excessive.

Bachanalls: licentious orgies, like those thought to characterize the ancient *Bacchanalia*, held in honour of Bacchus, god of wine.

l. 107. *meanes blesse*: middle ways (moderation, the avoidance of excesses) bring blessings. For 'means' (plural) in this sense, the *O.E.D.* instances Spenser, 'An Hymn in Honour of Love', ll. 85–86: 'tempering goodly well / Their contrary dislikes with loved meanes'. The blessings of a life 'seated in the mean' were advocated by Plato, *Repub.* x. 619 a, *Laws*, iii. 691 c, etc.; Aristotle took up the idea in his discussions of virtue, *Eth. Nic.* II. 6. 1107ᵃ. 2–3, *Eth.* ii. 7, and *Pol.* IV. xi. 3.

l. 108. *Hecatombs*. A 'hecatomb' is a great public sacrifice, properly of 'a hundred oxen', loosely of 'a great number of victims'.

l. 109. (*Oh*): a sigh, as the satirist contemplates the melancholy fact.

l. 110. *Good workes*. Article XI of the XXXIX Articles of Religion setting out Church of England doctrine states that we are justified before God by Faith only (Gal. ii. 16); but Article XII 'allows' that Good Works which are the fruit of Faith are 'pleasing and acceptable to God'. We are condescending enough to admit the desirability of good actions; unfortunately they are not in fashion.

l. 111. *old rich wardrops*. Donne seems to be thinking of an old-fashioned wardrobe containing valuable things now unusable because fashions have changed, just as the treasury of good works can no longer be displayed or 'worn' in public.

ll. 111–12. A final hit at the times. Lawyers and lawsuits abound, legislators swell the statute-books to enormous proportions; but no one can accuse the satirist of an offence against any law (cf. 'Satire IV', ll. 131–3): for all he says is true.

Satyre III (p. 10)

MSS.: Also in *H 51*.

There are two misprints in the text of *1633* (ll. 40, 44); I abandon also two spellings (ll. 80, 86) and readings in six other lines (ll. 7, 33, 47, 57, 90, 104) in which the edition follows the Group I manuscript in certain or probable errors. I differ from Grierson in two readings (ll. 95, 104).

It is not possible to date this poem very precisely. The historical allusions are not of much assistance, since they might be made to any one of several occurrences, or might be quite general in reference. Although we must be careful in attaching a precise autobiographical significance to what Donne says in his *persona* of satirist, it would be most unlikely that he would, or could, have written in this way had he still been a convinced Roman Catholic. He must have definitely renounced membership of the Roman Church by the time of his entering the employ of Egerton (probably late in 1597); and indeed, by going on the Cadiz Expedition in 1596, he was already committed to the service of a Protestant Queen against her Roman Catholic enemies. Donne's earliest definite statement that he was a Protestant occurs in a letter to Sir George More in February 1602. He says, however, in the Preface to *Pseudo-Martyr*, that he 'used no inordinate hast, nor precipitation in binding my conscience to any locall Religion'. We can believe Walton, therefore, when he implies that quite early in his career at the Inns of Court (1591–4) Donne was already questioning the Roman Catholic position: he 'began seriously to survey, and consider the Body of Divinity, as it was then controverted betwixt the *Reformed* and the *Roman Church*', and he 'did shew the then *Dean* of *Gloucester*' all the works of Cardinal Bellarmine 'marked with many weighty observations under his own hand' (*Lives*, pp. 25–26). The third and last volume of Bellarmine's *Disputations* appeared in 1593, so that it may have been only a few months after this that Donne was discussing controversial religious matters with a Protestant clergyman (see Appendix III in R. C. Bald's edition of Southwell's *An Humble Supplication*, 1958). This satire seems to imply some such background of earnest inquiry. If the *Satires* are, as Drummond says (p. xlvi above), 'in number and order' as Donne wrote them, this one must fall between 'Satire II', very probably written in 1594, and 'Satire IV', which belongs to 1597. I am inclined to take the references to 'fires of Spaine', etc. rather as due to anticipatory excitement that led Donne to join the Cadiz and

Islands Expeditions in 1596–7, than as the results of his experiences as a member of them, and to date this poem 1594 or 1595.

The central idea is found, more crudely stated, in an early prose composition, Problem 5: 'nor was [the Devill's] *Kingdome* ever so much advanced by *debating Religion* (though with some *aspersions of Error*) as by a *dull* and *stupid security*, in which many *grose things* are swallowed' (Keynes, *Paradoxes and Problems*, pp. 45–46). Donne attacks the paltry attitude of men to the finding of a religious faith, in contrast to the courage and energy they display in other concerns. The truth is there to be found, and it is man's first duty to seek it with diligence and by means of responsible inquiry; it must not be accepted on the authority of religious or political leaders or in obedience to man-made laws, but it must be pursued 'with all our soul's devotion' in the light of conscience and of our knowledge of the primitive tradition of our forefathers. For the place of the Satire in Donne's religious development, see Gardner, *Divine Poems*, pp. xvii–xix. Donne revised it with some care, as the variant readings will show.

The poem has three 'movements'. Since the pity and scornful laughter proper to a satirist are mutually destructive, a cure of the weakness and cowardice of men in respect of religion might be effected by railing (ll. 1–43). The properly 'satirical' part of the poem deals with the trivial reasons why men adopt a form of religion (ll. 43–69). The last section of the poem is in the grave and forceful style of Donne's verse letters to his men friends—an exhortation to an active pursuit of a personal faith.

'If you would teach a scholar in the highest forms to *read*, take Donne, and of Donne this satire' (*Coleridge's Miscellaneous Criticism*, ed. T. M. Raysor, p. 134).

The title is amplified only in *H 51* ('Of Religion') and in *S 962* ('Uppon Religion').

l. 1. *Kinde pitty*: the pity 'natural' to a well-disposed man (which chokes with grief the satirist's scornful laughter).

spleene. The spleen, in the physiology of the time, was thought to be the seat of laughter, but also of melancholy; hence it was associated with bitter laughter, scorn, ridicule. Cf. Persius, *Sat*. i. 11–12: '(nolo . . . sed sum petulanti splene) cachinno', and Hall, *Virgidemiarum*, IV. i. 74.

brave scorn: a 'fine show' of scorn (demanded of the satirist).

l. 3. *laugh*: laugh to scorn (*O.E.D.*, vb. 5).
weepe: lament with tears (*O.E.D.*, vb. II. 6).

l. 4. *worne*: stale and hackneyed.

l. 7. *blinded*: denied the light of revelation. 'Æmulate those men, and be ashamed to be outgone by those men, who had no light but nature' (*Sermons*, ix. 85). Donne is referring to 'the virtuous heathen', on whom cf. Browne, *Hydriotaphia*, iv.

l. 9. *them*: those who lived in the 'first blinded age', whose spur to virtue was fame on earth.

l. 12. *blinde*: = 'blinded', l. 7.

ll. 12–13. *blinde Philosophers in heaven*, etc. The Scriptures seem to allow the possibility of salvation to men of virtue who have not heard of Christ (cf. Acts xvii. 30, Rom. ii. 14–15). Donne refers to the question on some ten occasions in the *Sermons*; for example: 'Almost in every one of the ancient Fathers, you shall find some passages, wherein they discover an inclination to that opinion, that before Christ came in the manifestation of his Gospel (for, since that coming, every man is bound to see him there) many Philosophers, men of knowledge, and learning, were sav'd without the knowledge of Christ' (iv. 119). Cf. also Burton, *Anatomy*, part. 3, sect. 4, memb. 2, subsect. 6, and Browne, *Religio Medici*, i. 54.

ll. 12–13.   *whose merit*
                         Of strict life may be'imputed faith,

Luther taught that Justification was granted by God to men in response to the disposition of faith alone (*sola fides*), and that it brought with it the imputation to the sinner of the merits of Christ. Donne is impudently using the key Lutheran concepts of 'imputation', and faith as the *sine qua non* of salvation, to suggest what would have horrified Luther: that men can be saved by their own 'merit of strict life' and that this can be imputed to them as justifying faith.

l. 17. *mutinous Dutch*. The Low Countries had been in revolt against the Spanish conqueror since 1568, and the English had been giving them 'ayd' since 1586. Donne mentions the fact of their mutiny, but we cannot deduce that 'To the Catholic Donne the Dutch are still mutineers' (Grierson, *Metaphysical Lyrics*, 1921, p. 235). Official help to the Dutch was not accompanied by much lively sympathy with them on the part of the average Englishman; see notes to 'Love's War', ll. 5–6, in Gardner, *Elegies etc.*, p. 129.

The insertion of 'and' in the last form of this line removes a dramatic effect employed by Donne in the earlier versions—the dropping of a syllable after a medial pause. For other examples cf. ll. 33 and 95 below; 'Satire IV', ll. 2, 56, 222, 223, 241; 'Satire V', ll. 11, 66, 73, 84; 'The Storm', l. 39; 'The Progress of the Soul', ll. 117, 273, 443.

l. 18. *Sepulchers*. Cf. 'The Storm', l. 45 ('Some coffin'd in their cabbins lye'), and 'Love's War', ll. 26–27:

> And ships are carts for executions,
> Yea they are deaths.

l. 19. *leaders rage*. This may refer to the quarrels among the leaders of the Cadiz and Islands voyages, but, as Grierson says, it is too little to build on. The 'rage' of leaders is much more probably their 'warlike ardour' or 'fury', which is one of the hazards their men have to face (cf. *King John*, II. i. 265: 'shall we give the signal to our rage', and 'Satire V', l. 8, 'Officers rage').

l. 20. *dungeons*: mines, or caves.

l. 22. *frozen North discoveries*. Attempts to find a north-west passage to the Pacific were made by the Cabots (in and after 1497), Martin Frobisher (1576–8), John Davis (in each of the three years 1585–7), and most recently by the Dutchman, Barents (1594).

l. 23. *Colder then Salamanders*. The salamander (a lizard-like creature) was thought to be so cold by nature that contact with it could extinguish fire (Aristotle, *Hist. Animal.* v. 19, 552^b; Pliny, *Nat. Hist.* x. 86; etc.).

ll. 23–24. *divine Children in th'oven*. Shadrach, Meshack, and Abednego, the three children of God ('divine'), or 'servants of the most high God', survived unharmed the burning fiery furnace into which Nebuchadnezzar cast them. See Daniel iii. 11–30; and cf. 'The Calm', l. 28, and T. Bastard, *Chrestoleros*, 1598, Bk. iv, epig. 23 (p. 92), 'De tribus pueris in fornace ignea', l. 8 of which reads: 'Were they three Salamanders in the fire?' The three 'Children' were, significantly, to be punished for refusing to accept a religion (worshipping the golden image) at the command of a King; cf. below, ll. 89 ff.

l. 24. *fires of Spaine,' and the line*: the tropical heat of the regions of the Spanish Main and the equatorial line. Possibly by 'fires of Spaine' the fires of the Spanish Inquisition are intended: a danger attendant on being taken prisoner.

l. 25. *limbecks*: alembics, or stills. Our bodies sweat in these climes, in a process like distillation.

ll. 27–28. *draw, Or eate thy poysonous words*: 'fight a duel with you or swallow your insults'.

l. 28. *straw*. The *O.E.D.* 7, says that this word is 'often used as a type of what is of trifling value or importance'. The words 'seeme bold', however, shift the primary meaning to sense 2. e, 'counterfeit, sham, dummy', as in the phrase 'man of straw' (P. Legouis, *S.N.* xiv. 188–9).

l. 30. *his*: God's.

l. 31. *Sentinell in his worlds garrison*. 'Sentinell' is superior to the reading of earlier versions, catching up the idea of 'Soldier' and adding the idea of watchfulness. Grierson quotes John of Salisbury, *Policrat.* ii. 27 (Migne, *P.L.* cxcix. 471): 'Veteris quidem philosophiae principes Pythagoras et Plotinus prohibitionis huius non tam auctores sunt quam praecones, omnino illicitum esse dicentes, quempiam militiae servientem a praesidio et commissa sibi statione discedere, citra ducis vel principis iussionem. Plane eleganti exemplo usi sunt eo quod *militia est vita hominis super terram*' [Job vii. 1, *V.*].

l. 32. Contention with one's fellows in battle, love, or exploration 'for gaine' is, in the moral sphere, forbidden because sinful; 'to expose ourselves to these perils we abandon the moral warfare to which we are appointed' (Grierson).

l. 33. *Know thy foes.* The reading 'foe' must be wrong, since there are three foes, and the plural in l. 30 should be matched here. (Having made this mistake, the writer of the archetype of the final version further misunderstood his copy and inserted 'h'is' [he is]; *L 74*, 'is', and *TCD*, 'his', make things worse.)

'We are sent as so many soldiers into this world, to strive with it, the flesh, the devil; our life is a warfare, and who knows it not?' (Burton, *Anatomy*, part. 2, sect. 3, memb. 2). Donne deals with each in turn: 'The foule Devill' (ll. 33–35), the world (ll. 36–39), and 'last, Flesh' (ll. 39–42).

For the metre, see the note on l. 17 above.

ll. 33–35. 'The foul Devil, whom you strive to please, would be only too willing, out of hate not love, to grant you the whole of his kingdom of Hell to satisfy you.' The sentence is tangled and the sense of 'to be quit' is obscure. But the main sense is clear: Donne is expanding the injunction 'Know thy foes'. He presents the Devil sardonically as a monarch only too willing to grant favour in return for service, but doing it from hate, not love. 'To be quit' might mean 'to be rid of your importunity', or 'in full discharge of what he owes you'. In the same way, Donne goes on to anatomize the world and the flesh. The world is a strumpet, and the flesh has of itself no power to taste joy but owes all its power to the soul.

l. 36. *The worlds all parts wither away.* 'There is no certain future: for the things of this world pass from us; we pass from them; the world it self passes away to nothing' (*Sermons*, ix. 185).

l. 38. *In her decrepit wayne.* Donne often recurs to the contemporary belief that the world was in decay, the main theme of *The First Anniversary*. For a full account of the seventeenth-century controversy on the decay of nature, see Victor Harris, *All Coherence Gone*, University of Chicago, 1949.

l. 40. *Flesh (it selfes death).* The joys of the flesh bring destruction to the flesh— as in gluttony, drunkenness, lechery; even the exercise of the functions of the body impairs it.

ll. 41–42. *soule, which doth Give this flesh power.* Cf. Donne's statements of the function of the soul in the body in 'The Ecstasy', ll. 50 ff., and in 'The Progress of the Soul', l. 131.

l. 43. *Seeke true religion.* Donne everywhere insists that 'in all Christian professions there is way to salvation' (*Letters*, p. 100). The point of the satire in the succeeding lines is that the search for true religion (and salvation) will fail, wherever it is directed, if it is prosecuted with superficial, irresponsible, or cowardly motives.

Mirreus. The proper names seem to have little special appropriateness.

'Myrrheus' = perfumed with myrrh, suggests a rather feminine interest in the sensuous and decorative aspects of worship.

l. 47. *ragges*: ceremonial trappings (which are 'brave', resplendent, l. 49). They are *her* trappings, nevertheless; religion was once to be found beneath them. 'The' seems to be an error in manuscripts with the *1633* version rather than a revised reading.

ll. 47–48. *as wee here obey The statecloth*, etc. The state-cloth was the canopy over the chair of state. Fynes Moryson (*Itinerary*, ed. 1907–8, iv. 253) speaks of 'our English manner, who give reverence to that Chaire [of Estate], though our Princes be absent'. Donne writes to Mrs. Herbert: 'your memory is a State-cloth and Presence; which I reverence, though you be away' (Walton, *Lives*, p. 335); cf. Simpson, *Essays*, p. 6.

l. 49. *Crants*. There seems to be no need to adopt the spelling 'Crantz' to 'emphasize the Dutch character of the name' (Grierson) or to restrict the reference to the 'Schismaticks of Amsterdam' ('The Will', ll. 20–21). Calvin's work in Geneva inspired Presbyterianism, and some copyists of all groups write 'Grants' or 'Grant', the latter presumably to give a Scottish reference to the lines. In *Q* the name appears as 'Crates' (Greek, 'kratos' = strength)—an attempt to match this name with the others, which are of classical origin. 'Crants', however, seems to be what Donne wrote.

ll. 51–52. The contrast of the 'brave' religion of Rome and the 'plaine' religion of Geneva is drawn in several places in the *Sermons*, e.g., 'in a *painted Church*, on one side, or in a *naked Church*, on another' (vi. 284).

l. 51. *Religion*. Four syllables.
sullen: drab, dismal.

l. 53. *Lecherous humors*: the whims of the lecher.

l. 55. *Graius*: 'a Greek'. I cannot see any particular point in the choice of this name, or of 'Phrygius' (l. 62), 'a Phrygian'.

l. 56. *ambitious bauds*. They are 'bawds' presumably because they procure adherents, or prostitute their office, by making false claims for the English Church (i.e. that it is the only perfect Church), in order to curry favour with, and win promotion from, high officers in Church and State.

l. 57. *Still new like fashions*. A comment on the rapid succession of laws regulating beliefs, ceremonies, and penalties for recusancy, etc., that marked the growth of the English Church.

l. 60. *tender . . . tender*. The word-play heightens the contempt: 'offer to him while he is of tender years and insufficient judgement'.

l. 62. *Pay valewes*. A ward who refused a marriage arranged on his or her behalf had to pay the guardian a fine known as 'the value of the marriage'; cf. *O.E.D.*, 'value', sb. I. 1. c, and 'valour', 3. d. Graius accepts the English Church because his godfathers (the legislators, as well as his actual sponsors at baptism) so decide; then (like a ward refusing a pre-arranged marriage) he must pay a fine (under the Act of Uniformity, 1559) if he refuses to attend his parish church.

ll. 62–64. 'Never say, There is no Church without error: therefore I will be bound by none' (*Sermons*, ix. 75). Cf. Burton's remarks on those who 'infer, that if there be so many religious sects, and denied by the rest, why may they not all be false?' (*Anatomy*, part. 3, sect. 4, memb. 2, subsect. 1).

l. 65. *all as one*: all alike. The Gracchi were champions of democracy; there may be some faint appropriateness in giving the name to one who finds religions (as they did men) 'of equal worth'.

ll. 68–69. 'Too much light causes this blindness.' Finding the light of truth everywhere (in every sect), Graccus is blinded to true religion when he actually comes across it. Jonson seems to borrow Donne's phrase in *Volpone*, v. ii. 23 ('Too much light blinds 'hem, I thinke') and in *A Tale of a Tub*, I. i. 56–57.

blind-nesse. For other examples of violent enjambment cf. 'Satire IV', ll. 13–14, 104–5.

l. 69. *unmoved*: unswayed (by such frivolous considerations as move Phrygius and Graccus).

l. 70. *Of force must one, and forc'd but one allow*. Man must, of necessity, approve and follow one form of religion and, if forced, must approve as true one and one only. It is not easy to give an exact sense to 'forc'd', which probably includes the notion of being 'forc'd' by the law to declare oneself. The sense appears to be that one cannot be religious without 'having a religion', and that in the last resort one must give one's allegiance to one religion and only to one.

l. 71. *aske thy father*. Cf. Deut. xxxii. 7: 'Remember the days of old, consider the years of many generations: ask thy father, and he will shew thee; thy elders, and they will tell thee'; and Jer. vi. 16: 'Stand ye in the ways, and see, and ask for the old paths, where is the good way, and walk therein.' Donne seems to be taking the Protestant point of view, that the primitive purity of the Church must be restored; but, as he well knew, all parties in religious disputes of the time appealed to such texts, and the Roman was called 'the old religion'. Cf. Dryden, *The Hind and the Panther*, ii. 164–7.

ll. 72–73. *though truth and falshood bee Neare twins*, etc. Cf. Tertullian, *Adv. Praxeam* ii (Migne, *P.L.* ii. 157): 'Quo peraeque adversus universas haereses iam hinc praejudicatum sit, id esse verum, quodcumque primum; id esse adulterum, quodcumque posterius.' Quoting this, Samuel Bochart (*Opera*, 1712, ii, p. 2) adds: 'Necesse enim est ut veritas sit prior mendacio, cum mendacium nihil aliud sit quam corruptio veritatis.' I owe these references to

D. C. Allen (*M.L.N.* lx, 1945). Contrast Butler, *Satires &c.*, ed. R. Lamar, 1928, p. 184:

> Truth can be no older then
> The first original of men
> But Lying is much Antienter . . .

l. 75. *best*: best religion.

l. 76. *protest*: be a Protestant.

l. 77. Cf.

This very scruple was the voyce and question of God in him: to come to a doubt, and to a debatement in any religious duty, is the voyce of God in our conscience: Would you know the truth? Doubt, and then you will inquire: And *facile solutionem accipit anima, quae prius dubitavit*, sayes S. *Chrysostome*. As no man resolves of any thing wisely, firmely, safely, of which he never doubted, never debated, so neither doth God withdraw a resolution from any man, that doubts with an humble purpose to settle his owne faith, and not with a wrangling purpose to shake another mans (*Sermons*, v. 38).

in strange way: 'on an unfamiliar road'.

l. 78. Cf. 'a man may stand upon the way, and inquire, and then proceed in the way, if he be right, or to the way, if he be wrong; But when he is fallen, and lies still, he proceeds no farther, inquires no farther' (*Sermons*, vi. 69).

ll. 79–81. For the ancestry of this passage, on which Donne bestowed so much care in revision, see Appendix C.

l. 80. *Cragged*. The 'ragged' of earlier versions (of which 'rugged' in *Q* is probably a mis-reading) seems authentic. Donne writes, 'He shall . . . rectifie thee in all ragged wayes' (*Sermons*, v. 373); Shakespeare uses the word several times, e.g. *The Two Gentlemen of Verona*, I. ii. 121 ('a ragged, fearful, hanging rock'); and in *The French Academy*, 1594 (i, p. 12) we have, 'the ragged and uneven waie'.

l. 81. *about must, and about must goe*. The omission of the second 'must' from all manuscripts but *JC* (and *D 17*) and *Lut*, though explicable, is rather surprising. Both the Group I and the Group II manuscripts used by the editor of *1633* were probably defective, and he appears to have made here an obvious emendation.

l. 82. 'And by this means gain what the unexpected abruptness of the hill prevents (you from obtaining).' The sense is clear—when the climber comes to a sudden towering crag, he must contour it—but the expression is elliptical.

l. 84. Cf. John ix. 4: 'the night cometh, when no man can work'. The change of 'mind' to 'Soule' in revision was made in the light of a distinction which Donne draws in a letter of the Mitcham period: 'though our souls would goe to one end, Heaven, and all our bodies must go to one end, the earth: yet our third part, the minde, which is our naturall guide here, chooses to every man a severall way' (*Letters*, p. 72).

ll. 86–87. Grierson paraphrases: 'Act *now*, for the night cometh. Hard deeds are achieved by the body's pains (i.e. toil, effort), and hard knowledge is attained by the mind's efforts.' The spelling 'too' (for the 'to' in *1633*) in l. 86 is found in *Dob*, *H 51*, *JC* (*D 17*), *P*, and *S*.

ll. 87–88. 'No endeavours of the mind will enable us to *comprehend* mysteries, but all eyes can *apprehend* them, dazzle as they may' (Grierson).

In all Philosophy there is not so darke a thing as *light*; As the sunne, which is *fons lucis naturalis*, the beginning of naturall light, is the most evident thing to bee seen, and yet the hardest to be looked upon, so is naturall light to our reason and understanding. Nothing clearer, for it is *clearnesse* it selfe, nothing darker, it is enwrapped in so many scruples. Nothing nearer, for it is round about us, nothing more remote, for wee know neither entrance, nor limits of it. Nothing more *easie*, for a child discerns it, nothing more *hard*, for no man understands it. It is apprehensible by *sense*, and not comprehensible by *reason*. If wee winke, wee cannot chuse but see it, if we stare, wee know it never the better (*Sermons*, iii. 356).

l. 89. *Keepe the truth*, etc. Cf. 2 Tim. i. 14: 'That good thing which was committed unto thee, keep by the Holy Ghost which dwelleth in us'; on which Donne says: 'Depart not from thy *old gold*; leave not thy *Catechism-divinity*, for all the *School-divinity* in the world; when we have all, what would we have more?' (*Sermons*, v. 124).

l. 90. *so'ill case*: such evil circumstances.

here: 'on earth', or (as Professor J. C. Maxwell has suggested to me) 'in religion', or 'in matters of the soul'. The omission of 'here' in *C 57*, *Lec*, and *TCD* seems to be an error, which the scribe of *L 74* also made, but corrected as he was copying.

l. 91. *blanck-charters*. These were originally papers which the wealthy were forced to sign as promises to pay, a space being left blank for the amount, which was filled in at the pleasure of the King's (Richard II's) officers. Cf. *Richard II*, I. iv. 48, II. i. 250. God has not given earthly kings a signed warrant to kill, the names of victims being filled in at the king's will.

l. 92. Kings who do kill 'whom they hate' for differing from them are not the responsible agents of Fate, but her hangmen. D. C. Allen (*M.L.N.* lxv, 1950) points out a resemblance in Luther's *Von weltlicher Oberkeit*, 1523 (Latin version, 1525). I quote the words as translated by W. I. Brandt, Luther's *Works*, xlv (*The Christian in Society*), 1962: 'where the temporal authority presumes to prescribe laws for the soul, it encroaches upon God's government, and only misleads souls and destroys them' (p. 105); bad princes 'are God's executioners and hangmen', but we should be subject humbly to them as long as they do not try 'to become shepherds instead of hangmen' (p. 113).

ll. 93–95. *wilt thou let thy Soule be ty'd*, etc. St. Augustine says: 'Ad fidem quidem nullus est cogendus invitus' (Migne, *P.L.* xliii. 315). Compare Christopher Goodman, *How Superior Powers ought to be Obeyed*, 1558: 'God will not regarde by what means, or by whose commaundement we transgresse his lawes.

For that can be no excuse for us, thoghe he be Kinge, Quene, or Emperour that commandeth or threatneth us. . . . Is the punishement of earthe, ashes, of vile man . . . more to be feared then the plages of God, who hath power both of body and soule to destroy them everlastingly?' (Facsimile Text Society, 1931, p. 46; see C. H. McIlwain's Introduction).

ll. 96–97. *Philip . . . Gregory . . . Harry . . . Martin*: Philip II of Spain, Pope Gregory XIII (d. 1585) or Gregory XIV, Henry VIII, and Martin Luther. A Roman Catholic King (defender of the faith) and religious leader are balanced against a Protestant King (defender of the faith) and Protestant religious leader.

l. 98. *mere*: absolute, complete.

Satyre IV (p. 14)

MSS.: Also in *HN* and the miscellany *Ash*; *A 23* contains ll. 203–44 (with a text like *C 57, Lec*); *Bur* also contained a copy.

Two and a half lines (ll. 134–6), omitted from *1633* (but present in all manuscripts), were printed in *1635*, whence I take the accidents of their text. I depart from *1633* fifteen times. A word was accidentally dropped from the edition in l. 230; in ll. 83, 106 only *L 74* supports it (and the scribe corrected the first of these errors in the manuscript); in l. 111 only *Lut, O'F* agree with *1633*; and in ll. 4 and 69 I reject a reading despite the overwhelming support given by the manuscripts. In the other nine places the edition follows its Group I manuscript: in l. 16 only *C 57, Lec* read with it, and in ll. 9, 164, 238 these manuscripts and *1633* have only random support; elsewhere (ll. 62, 67, 68, 113, 154, and in a spelling in l. 59) the error seems to derive from the archetype of manuscripts with the final version of the satire. I disagree with Grierson's text on eight occasions.

Drummond of Hawthornden wrote 'anno 1594' beside this poem in *HN*; and it was in 1594 that Guiana (l. 22) first came prominently to the attention of most Englishmen. This date, however, is too early; for l. 114 refers to the fall of Amiens, which was 'lost' to the Spaniards in March 1597, and 'lost' by the Spaniards to Henry IV in September of the same year. There is no indication that this reference was a later insertion, and there is no manuscript copy of the poem without it. It is very probable, therefore, that Donne composed the Satire between March and September 1597, and indeed in the earlier part of that period, before he set off on the Islands Expedition in July. The poem might be the fruit of personal observation of behaviour at Court, since it is likely that Donne's first appearance there was made between the Cadiz and Islands Expeditions.

That 'Satire IV' is to some extent imitative of Horace, *Sat.* i. ix ('Ibam forte via Sacra'), was recognized by contemporary readers, e.g. by Clement Paman, who imitates Donne in his turn in 'The Taverne', and writes:

Oh happy Donne & Horace, you h'd but one
Devill haunted you, but me a legion.

(See J. Carey, 'Clement Paman', *T.L.S.*, 27 March 1959.) The theme and the
main character of Donne's satire are, however, different from those of
Horace's. Donne's bore is a composite figure, with traits of several stock
characters in the comedy and satire of the day: of malcontent, traveller, politician, intelligencer (informer), and even of the Jesuit in disguise (see J.
Bamborough, *The Little World of Man*, 1952, p. 170). The choice of such a
complex character enables Donne to satirize a great variety of foibles and
evils; and since many of the topics of satire are connected with the Court, and
the bore is a hanger-on there, the transition to a more general picture of
Court life (l. 171) is reasonably smooth. Though the subject-matter is topical
and thoroughly English, some hints have been taken from Horace and other
classical writers. See Niall Rudd, 'Donne and Horace', *T.L.S.*, 22 March 1963.

In *A 25* the poem is called 'Mr Dunns first Satire', in *Cy* 'Another Satyre by
the same J: D.', in *S 962* 'Satyre 4. Of the Courte', and in *Ash* 'A Satire against
the Court wrighten by Doctor Dunn, In Queene Elizabeths Raigne'.

ll. 1–4. Grierson notes a resemblance to the three lines which open Régnier's
imitation of the same Satire of Horace:

Charles, de mes pechez, j'ay bien faict penitence,
Or toy qui te cognois auz cas de conscience,
Juge si j'ay raison de penser estre absous.

(*Les Satyres et autres oeuvres Folastres du S^r. Regnier*, 1616, f. 32^r). The similarity
(confined to these lines) is almost certainly accidental, since Régnier's work
was not printed until 1608 and 1613.

l. 1. *receive*: i.e. Holy Communion (*O.E.D.*, 'receive', vb. IV. 23).

l. 4. *recreation to*. Only *Q* and *D 16* have the 'to'; the sense, however, requires
it, since Donne's point is not that Hell is a duplicate of his trials at the hands
of the bore but that Hell affords the less punishment (an idea conveyed also
by 'map'). Hell does not 're-create' the anguish, but is by comparison 'a di-
version, an enjoyment'. The dropping of 'to' is the kind of error that could
be made frequently and independently in manuscript copies.

l. 6. *love to see, or to bee seene*. So Ovid, of ladies at the play, *Ars Amatoria*, i. 99:

Spectatum veniunt, veniunt spectentur ut ipsae.

Cf. the elegy 'Tutelage', l. 22: 'neither to be seene, nor see'.

l. 7. *suit . . . suite*. The pun equates in importance (as courtiers do) a petition
to the Queen and the clothes worn by the petitioner.

l. 10. *the Statutes curse*. A Statute (23° Eliz. c. 1, sect. iii) was passed in 1580
prescribing a fine of 100 marks for attending, 200 marks for presiding at,
Mass, with a year in prison. A 'mark' was originally a weight of 8 oz.; then

the value of this weight of silver, fixed at 20 pennies to the ounce; and hence equivalent to 13*s*. 4*d* (but there was no separate coin of this value).

l. 16. *dwell*: are continually in attendance at. The satirist suffers the same penalty as regular *habitués*, though (like Glaze) he erred by making only one feckless visit.

l. 17. *Towards . . . did runne*. Horace's 'accurrit', *Sat*. I. ix. 3 (Rudd).

ll. 18–19. This commonplace of 'natural history' derives from Pliny, *Nat. Hist*. ix. 84. Cf. 'To E. of D. with six holy Sonnets', ll. 1–2:

> See Sir, how as the Suns hot Masculine flame
> Begets strange creatures on Niles durty slime.

l. 19. *all which into Noahs Arke came*. In addition to ordinary creatures, the occupants of the Ark (Gen. vi. 19–20, vii. 8–9) must, it was thought, have included the more exotic denizens of the world of 'natural history': basilisk, amphisboena, leocrocuta, etc. For a long list, see Benedict Pererius Valentinus, *Comment. et Disput. in Genesim*, 1601, ii. sects. 187–205, pp. 457 ff.; and cf. Drayton, *Noah's Flood*, ll. 456 ff.

l. 20. *would have pos'd Adam to name*. Adam named every living creature (Gen. ii. 19–20), his ability to do this, according to the commentators on *Genesis*, being due to a perception of their true natures.

l. 21. *seaven*. Like 'ten', l. 97, this means simply, 'several'.

l. 22. *Africks Monsters*. These were thought to be as prodigious in number as in their natures: lyonsbane, crocute, cerast, anthropophages, blemmyes, and many more. Of many lists, the most entrancing is that (mostly from Pliny) given by C. I. Solinus Polyhistor (*The excellent and pleasant work of J. Solinus*, tr. A. Golding, 1587, Scholars' Facsimiles and Reprints, 1955, introd. by G. Kish, Ch. 39 ff.). Cf. Jonson, *Every Man out of His Humour*, III. vi. 176–8: 'When any stranger comes in among'st 'hem, they all stand up and stare at him, as he were some unknowne beast, brought out of *Affrick*.'

Guianaes rarities. Raleigh sent Capt. Jacob Whiddon on the earliest English expedition to Guiana in 1594, but for an account of the 'rarities' Englishmen had to await Raleigh's story of his own voyage (1595) in *The discovery of Guiana*, 1596. Apart from the armadillo, the chief curiosities were Amazons, Anthropophagi, and (pp. 69–70) 'a nation of people, whose heades appeare not above their shoulders . . . called *Ewaipanoma*: they are reported to have their eyes in their shoulders, and their mouths in the middle of their breasts, & that a long train of haire groweth backward betwen their shoulders.' Joseph Wybarne quotes ll. 18–23, attributing them to 'Dunne in his Satyres', in *The New Age of Old Names*, 1609, p. 113 (Keynes, p. 224).

l. 23. *strangers*: foreigners.

l. 24. *the Danes Massacre*. King Ethelred (the Unready), wearying of buying them off, ordered a massacre of the Danes throughout England on St. Brice's

Day (13 November) 1012. The chroniclers kept the memory of the incident alive, as did also, perhaps, the name of the London church, St. Clement Danes (cf. Stow, *Survey of London*, ed. C. L. Kingsford, ii. 96, 372–3). During the Queen's progress to Kenilworth (1575) the men of Coventry asked that they might revive their old 'storiall sheaw', the massacre of the Danes, which, they said, 'iz grounded on story, and for pastime woont too bee plaid in oour Citee yeerely' (*Captain Cox, his Ballads and Books; or, Robert Laneham's Letter*, 1575, ed. F. J. Furnivall, 1871, pp. 26–27).

l. 26. Riots against foreigners, in which apprentices took a leading part, had occurred on May Day 1517 (Stow, *Annals*, 1601, pp. 848–51); but English merchants and retailers continued to be resentful against foreign traders who set up competitive businesses until and beyond the date of this Satire. Most recently threats and libels had been published against 'strangers' in 1593. In one of these, quoted by Grierson, after much abuse of foreigners, the writer says: 'Be it known to all Flemings and Frenchmen, that it is best for them to depart out of the realm of England between this and the 9th of July next. If not, then to take that which follows: for that there shall be many a sore stripe. Apprentices will rise to the number of 2336. And all the apprentices and journeymen will down with Flemings and strangers.' The projected rising was prevented by vigorous action. See Strype, *Annals of the Reformation*, edition of 1824, iv. 234–6, 296–301.

l. 27. *at noone*: even in full daylight.

ll. 28–29. A series of proclamations (especially those of 1581, 1585, and 1591) branded Jesuits and seminary priests as traitors, under penalty of death if they entered the Queen's dominions. Some did enter, in disguise, and some of these were detected and executed. See Strype, *Annals*, 1824, iv. 83–84, and Fynes Moryson, *Itinerary*, edition of 1907, i. 422, ii. 115.

l. 30. *bare*: bare of ornament, or threadbare.

l. 31. *jerkin*: 'a short coat with a collar, sometimes sleeveless, but usually sleeved' (Linthicum, p. 202, where from a will of 1558 is quoted: 'old tuftafita jerkin w^{th}out sleves').

l. 33. *Tufftaffatie*: tufted taffeta. Taffeta was a thin, fine silk cloth, which could be woven with stripes or spots raised above the 'ground' (cf. Linthicum, p. 124).

l. 34. *Rashe*: a twilled fabric of silk, as here, or of wool (Linthicum, pp. 85–86).

l. 35. *saith*: so he says.

l. 38. *speakes one language*: as men did before the confusion of tongues (Gen. xi. 1–9; cf. l. 65). Grierson adopts the reading of *Q*, *D 16*, *A 25* (possibly that of Donne's first version), citing Jonson's remark that Spenser 'in affecting the ancients writ no language'. But the reading of *1633* and all other manuscripts, 'one', seems more pointed than Grierson allows: the bore undoes the confusion of tongues. For a 'no language', moreover, the bore's mode of speech seems quite efficacious (ll. 45–48).

l. 39. *Art*: the cook's skill.

l. 40. *Pedants motley tongue*: learned jargon that mixes together English, Latin, and Greek terms.

souldiers bumbast: the bragging jargon of soldiers, stuffed with camp slang and scraps of foreign tongues picked up on campaigns. 'Bumbast' was mixed scraps of cotton or other material used to pad out clothing, particularly 'slops' or breeches.

l. 41. *Mountebankes drugtongue*: the jargon of quacksalvers. 'Drug-tongue' is not in *O.E.D.* Professor Legouis suggested that it meant that the jargon was stupefying like drugs; but the coinage is paralleled in *Volpone*, II. v. 2–5: 'A juggling, tooth-drawing, prating mountebanke. . . . / To his drug-lecture drawes your itching eares.' In a previous scene Volpone's speech when disguised as a mountebank is plentifully interlarded with Italian terms.

termes of law: a jargon of Law-French and Latin and formal English phrasing often satirized; e.g. in the person of Tangle in Middleton's *The Phoenix*.

l. 42. *preparatives*: medically, the means by which the system is prepared to endure a course of treatment; also used of drinks before a meal, appetizers.

l. 44. *complement*: accomplishment; that is, fine conversation and polished behaviour.

l. 45. *win widdowes*. Cf. 'It was the naturallest courtesy that ever was ordained; a young gentleman being spent, to have a rich widow set him up again' (Middleton, *The Widow*, I. ii. 1–4). This way of improving one's fortunes was common, and references to it are numerous and frank; see, for example, Chamberlain, *Letters*, i. 31–32, 476.

l. 46. *cosen subtlest whores*. Readers of Greene's 'coney-catching' pamphlets learn that whores often used their charms with cunning ('subtly') to cheat and rob, usually in collusion with other criminals. The bore's 'complement' enables him to cheat even these practised cheaters.

l. 47. *out-flatter . . . outlie*. Cf. 'Satire II', ll. 32–33, and note, p. 132.

l. 48. *Jovius*. Paulus Jovius, an Italian (1483–1552), Bishop of Nocera, published (among other works) *Historiarum sui temporis Libri XLV*, 1550–2. The work was condemned by many for its lack of veracity, e.g. by Jean Bodin (cf. W. F. Staton, 'Roger Ascham's Theory of History Writing', *Studies in Philology*, lvi, 1959).

Surius. Laurentius Surius, born at Lubeck in 1522, became a Carthusian monk, and died in 1578. He wrote *Commentarius brevis rerum in orbe gestarum ab anno 1550* (1568), four volumes on Councils, and *Vitae Sanctorum* (6 vols., 1570–5). Protestant writers accused him, it seems unfairly, of inventing legends and of inaccuracy.

The reading 'Sleydan', in *Q*, *D 16*, *A 25* ('Snodons'), *Lut*, *O'F* and (written in as a correction) in *Dob*, refers to John Sleidan, a Protestant writer (1506–56), the first lay author to treat extensively of the religious conflicts of the time. Among his works are *De quattuor Summis Imperiis, Babylonico, Persico, Graeco, et Romano*, 1556, and *De Statu Religionis et Reipublicae*, 1555; to the latter Surius's Commentary is a reply. Donne's first idea seems to have been to bracket a Protestant with a Roman Catholic historian to emphasize the versatility of the bore (and of historians) in lying. In revising the Satire (perhaps in the first place, as I have suggested, for Egerton) he would have thought it more prudent to substitute the name of another Roman Catholic historian.

l. 49. Grierson cites Nashe (*Works*, i. 163): 'I was encountred by a neat pedantical fellow, in forme of a Cittizen; who thrusting himselfe abruptly into my companie, like an Intelligencer, began very earnestly to question with me.'

l. 50. *rod*: 'this fellow', who is, as it were, the scourge of God.

l. 51. *saith*. Two syllables.

l. 53. *seelily*: naïvely.

l. 54. *Calepines Dictionarie*. The Italian friar, Ambrosius Calepine (1455–1511), published a Latin Dictionary in 1502, which, after being superseded by *Thesaurus Linguae Latinae* of Robert Stephanus (1531, 1543), developed into a polyglot dictionary, and eventually to a *Dictionarium undecim Linguarum* (Basle, 1590; in Latin, Hebrew, Greek, French, Italian, German, Belgian, Spanish, Polish, Hungarian, and English).

ll. 55–56. *Beza then, Some Jesuites*. Theodore Beza (1519–1605) was a distinguished Calvinist theologian, who translated the Greek New Testament into Latin. Copies of two of his tracts were at some time in Donne's library (Keynes, p. 210). The reading 'Some other Jesuites' found in *HN* (and only there) seems to be due to ignorance.

For the omission of a medial syllable at a pause cf. the note to 'Satire III', l. 17.

ll. 56–57. *two reverend men Of our two Academies*. These were identified (in the mind, at least, of one contemporary reader) in a marginal note in *Dob*, as 'Dr Reinolds and Dr Andrewes' (see E. M. Simpson, 'Notes on Donne', *R.E.S.* xx, 1944). John Reynolds (1549–1607) was Reader in Greek at Corpus Christi College, Oxford, 1573–8; he supervised the translation of the Prophets for the *A.V.*; Donne calls him 'our learnedst Doctor' in Simpson, *Essays*, p. 25. Lancelot Andrewes (1555–1626) was Master of Pembroke Hall, Cambridge, 1589–1605. He was said to have mastered eleven languages; he worked with the Westminster committee on the translation of parts of the *A.V.* Both were distinguished churchmen.

The main accent in 'Academies' falls on the third syllable: cf. 'A Litany',
l. 109, 'Thy sacred Academe above'.

l. 58. *Apostles.* A reference to the Gift of Tongues at Pentecost, Acts ii. 4, 6
('every man heard them speak in his own language').

l. 59. *Panurge.* His skill in a dozen languages is manifested in Rabelais,
Gargantua and Pantagruel, Bk. ii, Ch. 9.

l. 60. *passe*: surpass.

l. 61. *By travaile*: by travel and by toil.

ll. 61–62. *as if he would have sold . . . he prais'd.* Proverbial; Tilley, P546: 'He
praises who wishes to sell' (from Horace, *Epist.* II. ii. 11, 'Laudat venalis qui
volt extrudere merces').

l. 62. *wonders.* The reading 'words' in *1633* derives from a primitive error in
the text of the final version, probably due to a misreading of 'wõders'.

l. 65. *Tower*: of Babel. See l. 38, and note.

l. 67. *leave lonenesse*: 'stop keeping to yourself'. Since the satirist goes on to say
that this alone-ness is not loneliness, I attribute the reading of *1633* and manuscripts with the same version to an easily made error.

ll. 67–68. *Not alone My lonenesse is.* The allusion is made clear in Pope's version:
'But *Tully* has it, *Nunquam minus solus*' (l. 91). 'Publium Scipionem . . . , dicere
solitum scripsit Cato, . . . nunquam se minus otiosum esse, quam cum otiosus,
nec minus solum, quam cum solus esset' (Cicero, *De Officiis*, III. i. 1; similarly
De Repub. I. xvii. 27). This is the 'wholesome solitarinesse' of l. 155 below.

l. 68. *. . . is. But Spartanes fashion.* I have strengthened the punctuation of *1633*
by altering the comma after 'is' to a full stop, to make clear that 'Spartanes
fashion' refers to teaching by painting drunkards and not to a virtuous solitude. Editions from 1635 to 1669 preserved the comma after 'is' and altered
the comma after 'fashion' to a full stop, thus attaching 'Spartanes fashion' to
the Ciceronian quotation. The error was corrected in the edition of 1719
from which Pope worked, and he rightly paraphrased 'No Lessons now are
taught the *Spartan* way'.

According to Plutarch (*Lycurgus*, 28. 4) the Spartans would make helots
drunk and bring them into their messes to disgust the young men with
drunkenness. Donne describes as 'Spartanes fashion' a similar attempt to
inculcate sobriety by pictures of drunken men.

l. 69. *tast*: 'keep its relish'; 'go down' (Grierson). 'This method of teaching is
no longer relished, or acceptable', and so is ineffective. 'Tast' is the better
reading, and the word could very easily be misread as the more obvious
'last'.

l. 70. *Aretines pictures.* More properly, sixteen designs illustrating love-making,
by **Giulio Romano** (Jules Romain), engraved by Raimondi, for which Pietro

Aretino (1492–1557) wrote sixteen equally obscene *Sonnetti lussuriosi* in 1524.

l. 73. Rudd suggests a reminiscence here of Horace, *Sat*. I. iii. 7–8:

> citaret Io Bacche! modo summa
> Voce, modo hac, resonat quae chordis quattuor ima.

l. 74. *talke of Kings*. Cf. Horace, *Sat*. I. iii. 12, where Tigellius prates of 'reges atque tetrarchas'; and the play on 'Rex' in Horace, *Sat*. I. vii (Rudd).

l. 75. *The man that keepes the Abbey tombes*. He was apparently something of a 'character' in London at the time; cf. Sir John Davies, Epigram 30, 'On Dacus', ll. 9–10: 'taught him that keepes the monuments / At Westminster, his formall Tale to say'.

l. 80. *Kingstreet*. This street led from Charing Cross to the King's palace at Westminster (Stow, *Survey of London*, ed. C. L. Kingsford, ii. 102). 'Till long after Stow's time it was the only way to Westminster from the north' (Kingsford's note, p. 374).

l. 81. *smack'd*: sc. his lips.

Mechanique: vulgar, low (like one 'engaging in a manual occupation').

l. 83. *neate*: nice, exact, spotless (= 'neatly cloth'd', l. 85).

your ... Mine. The bore uses the indefinite 'your' (meaning roughly, 'which is within your knowledge'); the satirist pretends to misunderstand, and refers it to himself ('Mine?').

l. 84. *hee followes mee*. Donne had a French servant later (if not in 1597); he speaks of 'my promise to distribute your other Letters, according to your addresses, as fast as my Monsieur can doe it' (*Letters*, p. 201).

l. 86. *Grogaram*: 'the name of a taffeta weave with "gros grains" or cords in the warp', the cloth being of silk, worsted, or hair (Linthicum, pp. 77–78). The bore is referring to French grosgrain, which was of silk.

l. 87. *I have more*. The bore has said, 'Grogaram is the only fabric one can really wear'. The satirist again pretends to misunderstand, and replies, 'You are wrong in thinking one grogaram suit is all I have to wear'.

ll. 87–88. *Under this pitch He would not flie*. The 'pitch' was the height to which a trained hawk soars. The satirist's quarry will not fly under the pitch, i.e. the bore will not place himself in a position to be swooped upon with further ridicule.

l. 88. *chaff'd*: teased, provoked. But the satirist finds that this 'crossing' of his companion is more irritating to himself (l. 91).

l. 94. *takes my hand*. Cf. Horace, *Sat*. I. ix. 4, 'Arreptaque manu' (Rudd).

ll. 94–95. *as a Still*, etc. The simile attracted Pope; cf. the verse letter to Cromwell, *Minor Poems*, ed. N. Ault and J. Butt, 1954, pp. 24–25:

> Who slow, and leisurely rehearse,
> As loath t'enrich you with their Verse;

> Just as a Still, with Simples in it,
> Betwixt each Drop stays half a Minute.
> (That simile is not my own,
> But lawfully belongs to *Donne*).

He uses it again in the *Guardian*, 92 (*Prose Works*, ed. N. Ault, 1936, i. 126–7).

staies A Sembriefe: pauses for the duration of a semibreve, or 'whole note' in music.

l. 97. Raphael Holinshed, Edward Hall, and John Stow published *Chronicles* of England in 1577, 1542, 1565 (and 1580), respectively.

l. 98. *triviall houshold trash*. Nashe also writes contemptuously of trifling and homely details mixed with the accounts of important events of state in the Chronicles: 'your lay Chronigraphers, that write of nothing but of Mayors and Sheriefs, and the deare yeere, and the great Frost' (*Works*, i. 194).

l. 100. *subtle States-man*. Donne writes in a letter (Gosse, ii. 46) of 'Statesmen who can find matter of state in any wrinkle in the King's socks'.

ll. 101 ff. Cf. Juvenal, *Sat*. vi. 402–12 (Alden):

> Haec eadem novit, quid toto fiet in orbe:
> Quid Seres, quid Thraces agant: secreta novercae,
> Et pueri: quis amet: quis decipiatur adulter etc.

Also Juvenal, x. 220–4, and Martial, *Epig*. III. lxiii. 3–12:

> Bellus homo est . . .
> Qui scit quam quis amet, qui per convivia currit,
> Hirpini veteres qui bene novit avos.

l. 102. *reversion*: the right of succession, usually on the death of the original grantee, to an office or estate. Here it is the date of succession that is 'hastened'.

l. 103. *sold his land*. Cf. ll. 180–1 below, and 'Satire II', ll. 103–4.

l. 104. *licence*. The granting of licences, patents, and monopolies to those trading in various kinds of merchandise was common practice in Elizabeth's reign (and even more in James I's); it was a lucrative source of income to the courtiers responsible for granting such privileges (some of whom received 'toll', l. 107, from the successful applicant).

l. 105. *transport*: both 'import' (as in l. 170 below) and 'export'. The *O.E.D.* quotes Hall, *Chronicles*: 'imported and transported, into and out of this realme'.

l. 106. *span-counter*. Using counters instead of marbles, this is the same game as that described in J. Strutt, *Sports and Pastimes of the People of England*, 1801, revised J. C. Cox, 1903, p. 304:

Boss out, or boss and span, also called hit or span, wherein one bowls a marble to any distance that he pleases, which serves as a mark for his antagonist to bowl at, whose business it is to hit the marble first bowled, or lay his own near enough to it for him to span the space between them and touch both the marbles; in either case he wins, if not, his marble remains where it lay and becomes a mark for the first player, and so alternately until the game is won.

blow-point. Grosart was right, I believe, in supposing that this game was the same as 'dust-point'. The 'points' here (as in 'pick-point' and 'venter-point') were the tags or laces by which hose was fastened to the doublet. J. B. Leishman (*The Three Parnassus Plays*, 1949, p. 289) cites Cotgrave's description of 'Darde' in his *Dictionary*, 1611: 'A play, wherein boyes having layed a heape of points under a stone, and made a circle about them, dart at them with a rod, and win as many as they drive out of that circle; (Our boyes laying their points in a heape of dust, and throwing at them with a stone, call that play of theirs, Dust-point.).'

l. 109. *home-meats*: trivial gossip 'relating to one's country or nation' (*O.E.D.*, 'home', B. 3). The meaning 'homely' gives way to 'at home', and this provides the transition to 'foreign news', ll. 113 ff. (P. Legouis, *S.N.* xiv. 190–1).

belch. The metaphor of not being able to 'stomach' the bore's talk is carried on from l. 38.

l. 112. *Gallo-Belgicus*. *Mercurius Gallo-Belgicus* was an annual register of news begun in 1588 by Michael von Isselt. It was very popular and for some years it appeared half-yearly; the last volume, called xxix, was dated 1654. Its information (often mere gossip) was not always reliable, and its Latin was far from elegant (Jonson speaks of a '*Gallo-Belgick* phrase', in *Poetaster*, v. iii. 553).

l. 114. *The Spaniards came*: with their Armada in 1588. The bore's information begins at the same time as the *Mercurius*, and it seems as if he had learnt that periodical off by heart ('without booke').

the losse of Amyens. The Spaniards surprised and took Amiens on 11 March 1597; the French re-took the town on 25 September that year.

ll. 115–16. Like a pregnant woman shocked into labour by the sight of food of a kind that she (in that condition) hates.

l. 116. *sweat*. Like Horace, *Sat.* i. ix. 10–11: 'quum sudor ad imos Manaret talos' (Rudd).

l. 117. *Makeron*. Florio (*Queen Anna's New World of Words*, 1611) gives 'Maccarone, a gull, a lubby [looby], a loggar-head that can doe nothing but eat Maccaroni'; hence *O.E.D.*, 'macaroon', 3: 'buffoon, dolt, blockhead' (Donne's use here being the first recorded). In another sense the word could mean 'fop, dandy', especially one whose manner or speech showed foreign affectations.

l. 119. *priviledg'd spie*. An informer can say anything without danger, in attempting to trap others into indiscretions.

l. 120. *Libells*. For Donne's hatred of libels and calumny see, e.g., *Sermons*, iv. 54, *Letters*, pp. 89–91, and *The Second Anniversary*, ll. 331–4.

l. 123. *entail'd*. An entail was, strictly, a settlement of an estate so that it could not be bequeathed at pleasure. Here the idea is that succession to offices has been secured into the distant future.

l. 124. *Perpetuities*: inalienable rights in perpetuity. Cf. 'all your Entayles, and all your perpetuities doe not so nayle, so hoope in, so rivet an estate in your posteritie, as to make the *Sonne of God your Sonne too*' (Sermons, iv. 189).

l. 126. *Dunkirkers*. Dunkirk was for more than a century the headquarters of pirates who preyed indiscriminately on honest ships of all nations. They raided English coastal ports, like Yarmouth (cf. Nashe, *Works*, iii. 171), and in the first Parliament in which Donne sat (1601) they were said to have nearly twenty ships (the Burgess from Yarmouth spoke feelingly on the subject); see *The Journals of all the Parliaments, During the Reign of Queen Elizabeth*, by S. D'Ewes, revised P. Bowes, 1682, pp. 665–6. I know of no evidence that officers of state were in league with them.

l. 128. Cf. Marston, *Scourge of Villainy*, iii. 29–50.

ll. 129–30. *Circes prisoners . . . beasts. Odyssey*, x. 203 ff.

l. 131. *Becomming Traytor*. The satirist feels himself falling under the sway of 'complement' (cf. l. 46 above), and fears that he might be led on to say things that make him liable to punishment, under provisions of one of the many statutes dealing with treason; he might then (ll. 135–6) become guilty, and the man who infected him might remain free.

ll. 134–5. The superstition that a person afflicted with venereal disease ('burnt') could free himself of it by infecting someone else seems to have been an old wives' tale, unsupported (so far as I can determine) by medical opinion. Cf. *Timon of Athens*, IV. iii. 63–64, 84, and Beaumont and Fletcher, *The Custom of the Country*, III. ii. 182.

l. 134. *venom'd*: infected. HN and S 962 agree with 1635 in reading 'venome' (venomous), an error for 'venomd'.

l. 136. *free*: guiltless.

l. 137. *in*: involved.

l. 138. *my forefathers sinne*. His own sins can hardly have deserved so much punishment; he must be paying for his forefathers' sins as well.

l. 139. *to my power*: to the limits of my endurance.

l. 143. *spare me*. The satirist takes 'spare me' (as in 'Satire II', l. 53) to mean 'excuse me', 'allow me to leave'.

l. 150. *prerogative*: the special right of the sovereign (i.e. of the Crown); but the bore has gone off with the special privilege of having the satirist's crown piece.

Scant: scarcely.

l. 154. *make*. The construction is 'doth make haste': 'with such haste as, or more haste than, a man makes' to get away from prison. There is a primitive error (the repetition of 'hast' from l. 153) in the text of the final version.

l. 156. *precious*. The reading of the final version might be due to a misreading of 'piteous' as 'pretious'. It is more likely that Donne himself, seeing that the idea of 'pity' is already expressed in 'mourn', changed the word.

l. 158. *who dreamt he saw hell*. Dante (see *Inferno*, Canto I, ll. 11, 25). Donne's references to Dante are amongst the earliest in England; his copy of *L'Amoroso Convivio* is in the Bodleian Library (Keynes, p. 213).

l. 162. *high borne, or rais'd*: born to, or elevated to, noble rank.

l. 164. *th'huffing braggart, puft Nobility*. Compare Burton's tirade, *Anatomy*, part. 2, sect. 3, memb. 2, ending: 'This is it belike which makes the Turks at this day scorn nobility, and all those huffing bombast titles.' Grierson cites Sylvester's translation of Du Bartas (Second day, First week, 1605, p. 63): 'The huft, puft, painted, curld, purld, Wanton Pride'. 'Huffing' has the suggestion of bullying arrogance. *L 74* shows, I believe, that 'th'huffing' stood in the last, as well as in each earlier, version, and that 'th'' was dropped in error from other manuscripts with this text, and from *1633*.

'Braggart' is more usually a noun than an adjective at this period.

l. 168. *swells the bladder of*: puffs up, like a balloon (l. 176).

l. 169. *your waxen garden*. The only other reference to this Italian waxwork, exhibited in London, seems to be that in Drayton's *Heroical Epistles* ('Edward the Fourth to Mistress Shore', ll. 53–56), *Poems*, ed. J. W. Hebel, 1932, ii. 248:

> I smile to thinke, how fond th'*Italians* are,
> To judge their artificiall Gardens rare; etc.

your. The manuscripts show some confusion of 'yoͬ' with 'yon' and 'yͤ' (the); but, despite ll. 82–83, 86 above, 'your' seems to be right here.

l. 170. *Transported*: imported (cf. l. 105 above, and note). Donne may have written 'transplanted' in one version, but some manuscripts seem to have hit upon it (as appropriate to 'garden') independently.

l. 171. *flouts*: insults, defies, mocks (by being too close a resemblance).

Presence. This, the reading of the final version, makes (by a pun) the point that the Court is, like the Italian gardens, all show.

Paul Hentzner, describing the Court at Greenwich in 1598 (*Itinerary*, 'Travels in England', trans. R. Bentley, 1889, pp. 46–49), mentions 'the presence chamber, hung with rich tapestry, and the floor, after the English fashion, strewed with hay, through which the Queen commonly passes on her way to chapel'. Those who spoke to the Queen, or came under her gaze, 'fell down on their knees'. 'The Presence' can mean the chamber itself whether the monarch is present or not, as in ll. 179 and 199 below, or, as here, the assemblage of courtiers before the Queen in state or waiting for her arrival.

l. 174. *stocks*. Some courtiers are of noble 'stock', others are not 'naturally' noble but are, as it were, grafted on to the 'stock' of nobility (cf. l. 162 above, 'high borne, or rais'd men'); all are, however, illegitimate, impure, nondescript when it comes to a question of moral worth.

fruits. 'By their fruits ye shall know them'; 'the tree is known by his fruit' (Matt. vii. 20, xii. 33).

l. 175. *ten a clock.* Cf. *The Courtier's Library,* ed. E. M. Simpson, p. 41: 'sleep, which you must not shake off, as a rule, till after ten o'clock', etc.; and *The Overburian Characters,* ed. W. J. Paylor, p. 7 ('A Courtier'): 'His wit, like the *Marigold,* openeth with the *Sunne,* and therefore hee riseth not before ten of the clocke.'

For the idea of the fashionable round, cf. Juvenal, *Sat.* i. 127 ff.: 'Ipse dies pulchro distinguitur ordine rerum', etc.

Mues: mews, a set of stables. Inquiring why courtiers should be there in the morning, Professor Legouis (*S.N.* xiv. 191) points to a quotation *s.v.* in *O.E.D.* from T. de Gray's *The Complete Horseman . . . ,* 1639: 'Others . . . by sometimes frequenting the Muze, and other places, where Riders use to menage' (p. 26). Thus the Mews seem also to have been riding-schools (Fr. 'manèges').

l. 176. *Baloune:* wind-ball, leather ball filled with air. The reference is to the game in which the ball was struck with hand or fist, the arm of the player being sometimes strengthened by a wooden brace. See Strutt, *Sports and Pastimes,* ed. Cox, 1903, pp. 90–91; and for tennis ('royal' tennis), see p. 87.

Dyet. The 'bloods' made preparations for their sexual pleasures by eating aphrodisiac foods, to which there are many references (e.g. Middleton, *A Trick to Catch the Old One,* III. i. 93–94: 'I would forswear brothel at noonday, and muscadine and eggs at midnight'). While it is possible that Donne is referring to dieting before a visit to the stews, it is much more likely that the 'Dyet' in question was intended as a cure for disease contracted in the stews ('the restrictions in diet consequent on visiting the place of resort next mentioned'—Grosart). Cf. A. Schmidt, *Shakespeare Lexicon,* 'diet' 2, 'a regimen prescribed (especially for persons suffering from the French disease)'; as in *Timon of Athens,* IV. iii. 87.

stewes. Cf. Hall, *Virgidemiarum,* IV. i. 94–95:

> Not, if hee were as neere, as by report,
> The stewes had wont to be to the Tenis-court.

l. 178. *made ready:* dressed.

l. 179. *and I:* I was there too.

l. 181. *The fields they sold.* A variation of the idea of wearing manors, or lands, upon one's back. See Tilley, L452, W61, and cf., for instance, Burton, *Anatomy,* part. 3, sect. 2, memb. 2, subsect. 3.

l. 184. *Wants reach all states:* men of every rank or condition can feel the pinch.

l. 186. *dare not goe:* because of the debts they owe in the clothiers' shops that lined Cheapside.

l. 189. *Cutchannel:* cochineal, dried bodies of the female of the *coccus cacti* insect (found in Mexico and Peru) used for making scarlet dye. It was of great value; in *The Devil's Law-Case*, IV. ii. 154 (Webster, *Works*, ed. F. L. Lucas, ii. 293), it is classed with gold and spices. Hence it was of great interest to 'Pirats'.

l. 190. *board*: accost. Donne brings out (by the words 'As Pirats') the metaphor latent in this common expression.

ll. 192–4. The reason why clever men do not wear scarlet gowns is that the lords buy their brains to provide them with speeches (for which the true authors get no credit), and the ladies buy up for cosmetics all the red dyes which are needed for dying scarlet.

scarlet gownes: ceremonial robes, worn by doctors of the university, by the Lord Mayor and Aldermen of London, and by judges.

l. 195. *her beauty limetwigs, her haire net*. The compliments are very trite; both refer to methods of trapping small birds.

l. 196. *drugs ill laid*: cosmetics badly applied.

l. 197. *Heraclitus*: called the 'weeping philosopher', because of his gravity. But even he would laugh.

Macrine. Perhaps from Persius, *Sat.* II. i, which is addressed (respectfully) to Plotius Macrinus.

l. 198. *refine*: make fine again.

l. 199. *Moschite*: mosque (*O.E.D.*, quoting this passage). Macrine's tidying of his attire is like the removal of one's shoes before entering a mosque.

ll. 199–200. He lifts the skirt of his cloak to examine his hose; then he pulls up his hose to remove wrinkles.

l. 200. *call . . . to shrift*: summon to confession.

ll. 201–2: *mortall . . . veniall*: the theological distinction between 'deadly' sins (cf. l. 232 below) and excusable or pardonable sins. The holes and stains are 'mortal' because irreparable; the feathers and dust can be removed without damage to the fabric, and are only minor faults.

l. 203. *wherewith they fornicate*: i.e. the feathers and dust cling close to the fabric.

l. 204. Durers *rules*. Albrecht Dürer, the great engraver, wrote *Vier bücher von menschlicher Proportion*, published in 1528, a few months after his death (Latin translation by J. Camerarius, 1532). Half the book consists of diagrams of male and female figures with elaborate proportions of parts of the body to other parts and to the whole, repeated endlessly. These are the proportions ('odds') Macrine tests ('tries'), with pieces of string as means of measurement.

l. 208. *Perfect as circles*. The circle was universally regarded as a symbol of eternity, of God, of perfection.

l. 212. *protests*. The absence of punctuation suggests the compulsive bore in action. 'Protests' is used in its original sense of 'makes protestation', with a pun on its religious sense of being a 'Protestant'. Cf. Herrick's promise to be Anthea's 'Protestant'.

l. 214. *Ten Cardinalls*. For 'ten', cf. l. 21 and note. Even Cardinals, if they 'protested' as much as Macrine would be condemned as heretics.

The scansion seems to be:

$$\text{/ / × × × / × / × ×}$$
Ten Card | 'nalls in | to th'In | quisit | ion.

ll. 215–17. *And whisperd 'by Jesu'*, etc. If Macrine's protestations would bring him into danger in Rome, the oath by which he frequently supports them would make him suspected, in England, of being a Roman Catholic.

'Our Ladies Psalter' is the Rosary, or 'The Rosary of Our Lady', called 'Psalter' because in the chain of prayers the number of Aves was the same as the number of the Psalms (150) (*O.E.D.*, 'psalter', 3; see Rosemary Freeman, *English Emblem Books*, 1948, pp. 179–81). As Legouis points out (*S.N.* xiv. 192–3), Macrine would not use the name of Jesus so very much, for in telling his beads a Roman Catholic would use it once in each Ave. Hence the interest of the reading in *Lut, O'F*, 'Jesus Psalter': this was a form of devotion consisting of fifteen petitions, each beginning with a tenfold repetition of the name of Jesus (which was thus said 150 times). See *O.E.D., s.v.*, and A. F. Allison and D. M. Rogers, *The Library*, 5th Ser., vi, 1951, p. 56. It would be rash to suppose, with Legouis, that Donne has mistaken the Lady's Psalter for the Jesus Psalter. In Protestant England the Rosary would have contained enough 'vain repetitions' of the name of Jesus to make the point here. The reading 'Jesus Psalter' is, I believe, an 'improvement' in *Lut*, without authority.

l. 216. *Pursevant*: a public officer employed in search and inquiry, most often in this period (as here) employed in ferreting out Roman Catholics and disguised priests and Jesuits. Cf. 'Satire V', l. 65, and notes.

The earliest version read 'Topcliffe', i.e. Richard Topcliffe (1532–1604), one of the most cruel and most hated of the informers against Roman Catholics. He tortured Southwell and investigated Nashe. Donne mentions him in the second item in *The Courtier's Library*. Though he was hated by many Protestants as much as by Catholics, disrespectful references to him might have been risky; and in revising his Satires, probably as a new servant of a high officer of state, Donne changed his text to give a more general satiric reference.

l. 219. *Glorius*. For the type, cf. Nashe, *Works*, i. 361: 'Filthie Italionat complement-mungers they are, who would faine be counted the Courts *Gloriosos*'; and ii. 108: 'Hee that (to be counted a Cavaleir, and a resolute brave man) cares not what mischiefe he doe, whom hee quarrels with, kils, or stabbes'.

l. 220. *in the other extreme*: as a complete contrast (to Macrine).

ll. 220–1. Perhaps suggested by Horace, *Epist.* I. xviii, 5–6 (Rudd):

Est huic diversum vitio vitium prope maius
Asperitas agrestis et inconcinna gravisque.

l. 222. *Whose cloak his spurres teare.* Cloaks long enough to be torn by spurs were
an affectation of returned travellers and their apes (cf. Nashe, *Works*, ii. 300).
The wearing of cloaks and spurs at Court would have been an indecorum;
even at the Middle Temple (*Calendar of Records*, i, p. xxxvii) the wearing of
cloaks was forbidden in church, buttery, and hall, and spurs might not be
worn in the City unless the wearer was riding out of town.

l. 226. *which in old hangings whip Christ*: who in old tapestries are shown scourg-
ing Christ (before the Crucifixion). This is one of several passages in this
Satire imitated by William Fennor, in *The Compter's Commonwealth*, 1617
(Keynes, p. 225).

l. 231. *the great chamber.* Those leaving Court passed from the Presence
Chamber into the Great Chamber (chiefly a place of assembly) and thence
through the Guard Chamber (past 'Those Askaparts', l. 233).

ll. 231–2. (*why is it hung With the seaven deadly sinnes?*). Wolsey bought seven
early Flemish tapestries representing the deadly sins for the Legate's Chamber at Hampton Court in 1522. These 'now hang in the Great Watching
Chamber there. It seems possible that these tapestries hung in the same
position in late Elizabethan and Georgian days, for this room was used as the
guard chamber of the Tudor Presence Chamber, which survived until Kent's
alterations to the Palace in 1732' (J. Butt, in a note to Pope's version of this
line, *Imitations of Horace*, Pope's *Poems*, iv. 48). In Cromwell's time, 1659, an
inventory mentions 'In Paradice Roome. Seaven peices of rich hangings of
Arras, of the Tryumphs of the Capitall Sinns' (E. Law, *History of Hampton
Court Palace*, ii, 1888, p. 281).

The satirist's question is answered by Corbett (*Poems*, ed. J. A. W. Bennett
and H. R. Trevor-Roper, p. 27, ll. 107–8):

> And look't soe like the Hangings they stood nere,
> None could discerne which the true *Pictures* were.

l. 233. *Askaparts.* Ascapart, a giant thirty feet high, was vanquished by Sir
Bevis of Hampton in the old romance (cf. Drayton, *Poly-olbion*, Song ii, ll. 260
ff.; the story was, as far as we know, first printed in 1500). The reference is to
'the big bodied Holberders that guarde her Majestie' (Nashe, *Works*, i. 78).

ll. 233–4. *throw Charing Crosse for a barre.* Throwing the wooden or iron bar
was regarded as one of the most vigorous forms of exercise (see Strutt, *Sports
and Pastimes*, ed. J. C. Cox, 1903, p. 62).

Charing Cross, the last of the Gothic crosses set up by Edward I to mark
the places where the coffin of Queen Eleanor was set down on its way to
Westminster, was apparently of imposing size; it was removed in 1647 by
order of Parliament.

l. 235. *no token of worth*: no sign of merit (but to be called 'Queen's men', to enjoy fine living, etc.).

Queenes man. Not in *O.E.D.*, but analogous to 'King's man': one in the Queen's service.

l. 236. *barrells.* The barrel is made up of the trunk (belly and loins) (*O.E.D.* 8); but 'barrells' also suggests vast quantities.

beefe. The name 'beefeater' was given to the Yeomen of the Guard, who (since 1485) guarded the Royal houses and the Tower of London. References to their appetites are frequent; Corbett, for instance (cf. note to ll. 231–2 above), says (p. 28, ll. 129–31):

> the *Guard*, those Men of warre,
> Who but two weapons use, *Beife*, and the *Barre*,
> Began to gripe mee.

l. 237. *spyed*: detected.

l. 238. *you can, then dare*: you have the ability and skill, then dare to use them.

l. 240. *scarce*: scanty.

l. 241. *the.* There is a choice between 'the' and 'these' for the reading of the last version. The meaning seems to be 'the stains of these sins'; preachers have the power to sweep sins away like the sea, but a mere satirist can only cleanse the effect ('the staines') upon himself of viewing these sins. The initial 's' in the following word might have caused copyists (cf. *L 74, TCD*) to 'see' 'these'.

l. 242. Macchabees *modestie.* Cf. 2 Macc. xv. 38: 'And if I have done well, and as is fitting the story, it is that which I desired: but if slenderly and meanly, it is that which I could attain unto.' The books of *Maccabees* are believed by Protestants to be apocryphal, i.e. not 'canonical' or fully authoritative. Although the satirist (knowing that his work has merit) affects the modesty of the writer of *Maccabees*, he hopes that someone with the necessary wisdom will recognize that his work (because it tells the truth) can be fully believed.

Satyre V (p. 22)

MSS.: Also in *A 23* (with a text like that of *C 57, Lec*), but missing from *H 49* and *Cy*. The text in *D (SP)* in this Satire is that of *C 57, TCD*, not (as in Satires I–IV) that of *W*.

I have departed from the wording of *1633* in five places: in l. 76 the edition is alone in error; in l. 68 the editor's Group I manuscript (like *C 57, Lec, A 23*, which alone share this reading) was wrong; in ll. 61 and 80 I believe that *L 74* best represents the true reading of this tradition of the text, while *1633* (agreeing with *C 57, Lec, A 23, TCD, D*) is inferior; and in l. 72 *1633* shares what I think to be a primitive error copied into all these texts. I reject one of Grierson's readings, in the last line.

There seems to have been only one version of this Satire, but surviving copies show that there were two traditions of the text, each in some ways imperfect.

The poem was obviously written before the Queen's death in 1603 (l. 28) and after the capture of the Great Carrack in 1592 (l. 85). It is doubtless addressed to Egerton (ll. 31–32), who became Lord Keeper in 1596, and whom Donne had 'leave to serve' probably towards the end of 1597. The poem presumably follows 'Satire IV' in date (i.e. after March 1597). Since Donne says that Egerton was 'authoriz'd' (by the Queen's favour) to weed out a 'sinne' (ll. 33–34), the Satire pretty certainly refers to some specific reforming activities of Egerton at the time; and these have been convincingly identified as his attempts to restrict the fees charged by the Clerk of the Star Chamber. Egerton gave his attention to these abuses from 1597 until 1605. 'Satire V' is like the eager attempt of a new assistant to employ his talents in support of a crusade (of which he approved) just launched by his employer. The date of composition was most probably the early part of 1598.

This is the weakest of the five Satires, and has the air of a rather hastily-put-together occasional piece. Donne repeats imagery which he had used with greater power and freshness elsewhere: the river as symbolizing Power (from 'Satire III', ll. 103 ff.) in ll. 29–30, and the seas and the brook (cf. 'Satire IV', ll. 238–40) in ll. 13–16. The gnomic lines are rather trite (e.g. ll. 9–13, 19, 56), and seldom approach the power and originality achieved in other Satires. The generalizations about the Law occasionally resemble those in the long speech of the hero of Middleton's *The Phoenix*, I. iv. 197 ff. The tones of homily and complaint are too often heard to permit the achievement of a forceful and cumulative satiric effect.

Only *S 962* elaborates the title: 'Satyre 5. Of the miserie of the poore suitors at Court'.

ll. 1–2. *laugh . . . pitty.* Compare 'Satire III', ll. 1–3, and note.

ll. 2–6. *He which did lay Rules,* etc. Castiglione, in *The Courtier*, says (p. 138) that 'it provoketh no laughter to mocke and scorne a sillie soule in miserie and calamitie, nor yet a naughtie knave and common ribauld', etc.; see also pp. 168–9.

l. 2. *lay:* lay down.

l. 6. *wrech'd or wicked.* The wretched are those involved in law-suits ('Suiters misery', l. 8), the wicked the unscrupulous 'Officers' of the courts.

l. 8. *rage:* violent or savage behaviour (as 'leaders rage', 'Satire III', l. 19).

l. 9. *If all things be in all.* Grierson quotes Paracelsus: 'All things are concealed in all' (*Hermetic and Alchemical Writings*, trans. A. E. Waite, 1894, i, p. 5). 'Of this first matter which contained all the elements, and which God made the mother of all things, and capable of all formes, every bodie is compounded' (*The French Academy*, 1594, ii. 18–19).

l. 11. *the same elements*. 'Nature hath given us certain Elements, and all Bodies are compos'd of them' (*Sermons*, ix. 173). 'Nature hath made all bodies alike, by mingling and kneading up the same elements in every one' (*Letters*, p. 96).

ll. 13–19. There are equivoques on both 'man' and 'world'. 'Man' is first 'mankind' (human beings collectively), compared to the natural world (in which Officers are seas, etc.); and then 'individual man', whose body is compared to the 'world of men' or body-politic (in which Officers are stomachs, etc.). There is therefore a double logical fallacy in Donne's 'proof' that 'man is the world' and that, consequently, 'the world is man'.

l. 16. *selfe*: same.

l. 19. *excrements*: because all the substance has been taken from them by rapacious officials.

l. 20. *lust*: greed.

l. 21. *wormes meat*. Cf. Tilley, M253: 'A man is nothing but worms' meat' (from St. Bernard).

l. 26. *Adulterate*: falsify by admixture of baser ingredients (greed, cruelty, lack of scruple).

l. 27. *wittals*. A wittol is a man who winks at, or acquiesces in, his wife's adultery.

   issue: result (with a play on 'children', i.e. of the adulterous relationship in which the wittol acquiesces).

l. 29. *calme head*. Queen Elizabeth is the 'serene source' of power; she is unaware of, and not responsible for, the abuses of those far from the source of power (whose activities are symbolized by flood or turbulence in the lower reaches of the river). Jonson borrows the image in the Prologue to *The Sad Shepherd*, ll. 24–25.

l. 31. *You Sir, whose righteousnes*, etc. Sir Thomas Egerton (1540?–1617), in James I's reign made Baron Ellesmere and Lord Chancellor. He had a well-earned reputation for integrity; Jonson's phrase is 'justest Lord' (*Underwood*, xxxi).

l. 33. *authoriz'd*. The accent is on the second syllable.

l. 35. *Age of rusty iron*. Cf. *The First Anniversary*, ll. 425–6:

> and much more could doe,
> But that our age was Iron, and rustie too.

Cf. Juvenal, *Sat.* xiii. 28 ('Nunc . . . pejora saecula ferri'; Alden), and vi. 23 ('Omne aliud crimen mox ferrea protulit aetas'). The next step was usually rather the Leaden Age than the age of 'rusty iron' (as in Stubbes, *Anatomy of Abuses*, Part II, 1583, B2ᵛ).

l. 36. *if ought equall it*: if another suitable metaphor or phrase could be found to which it is equivalent.

ll. 37–41. Grierson's punctuation, which I adopt, makes the sense clearer: '*That* was the iron age when justice was sold. Now, injustice is sold dearer. Once you have allowed all the demands made on you, you find, suitors (and suitors are gamblers), that the money you toiled for has passed into other hands, the land for which you urged your rival claims has escaped you, as Angelica escaped while the knights fought for her.'

l. 39. *demands, fees.* Grierson (rightly, I think) identified the occasion of this Satire as the campaign of Egerton against abuses in the administration of the Clerkship of the Star Chamber. This Court (on which sat the high judicial officers of the State) was supposed to be the 'poor man's' Court, enabling ordinary people to obtain redress against the great lords. This purpose was being defeated by the charging of exorbitant fees by the Clerk. See Spedding, *Letters and Life of Francis Bacon*, ii. 56; Bacon, who held the reversion of the Clerkship, wrote at length to Egerton about what he called the 'claim'd fees'.

The alternative text of the Satire reads 'claim'd fees', but in many scripts 'claimed' and 'demands' are easily mistaken for each other. 'Demands', meaning 'legal claims', seems rather more in Donne's manner.

gamsters: gamblers. Cf. Burton, *Anatomy*, part. 2, sect. 3, memb. 7: 'for as it is with ordinary gamesters, the gains go to the box, so falls it out to such as contend; the lawyers get all'.

l. 40. *sweare for*: about which you take oaths in the law-courts.

l. 41. *controverted*: disputed, of which the title is in dispute.

l. 42. *Angelica.* Angelica, in Canto i (stanzas 14–23) of Ariosto's *Orlando Furioso*, escapes from Rinaldo and Ferrau while they are fighting for her; in Canto ii (stanzas 2–12) she similarly escapes from Rinaldo and Sacripante.

l. 44. *letter, or fee*: a letter from a person of influence, or a bribe, which might corrupt the judge.

l. 46. *Flow.* The plural form is normal usage (only *Lut, O'F* 'correct' it). Cf. *King Lear*, III. vi. 4–5: 'All the power of his wits have given way to his impatience.'

first maine head: the Queen. The imagery is resumed from l. 29.
these: 'the Courts below' the Queen.

l. 50. *when upwards*: when you try to appeal to higher authority. Power flows down from above through the courts; to attempt to appeal against them is to swim against the stream, which is particularly difficult when you are heavy ('sad') and faint ('exhausted by previous efforts').

ll. 54–55. As a bridge enables you to pass beyond the water it crosses, money will persuade the Court officers to get your complaint beyond them and have it heard; but all you will discover is that these same officers ('seas') have appropriated ('drown'd') all the money you have already spent in fees; you have nothing left to pay (?bribe) them with.

l. 56. *only who have may'have more.* A perversion of Matt. xxv. 29: 'Unto every one that hath shall be given.'

The line is an alexandrine. For other examples, cf. 'The Progress of the Soul', ll. 383, 398; the epigrams 'A Burnt Ship', l. 6, 'A Self Accuser', l. 1, and 'Manliness'; 'To Mr R. W.' ('Kindly'I envy'), ll. 13–14; 'To Mr I. L.' ('Of that short Roll'), l. 14; letters to Wotton—'Sir, more then kisses', ll. 24, 59, 'Here's no more newes', l. 2, and 'H. W. in Hibernia Belligeranti', l. 16; the 'Epitaph', l. 5; and possibly also 'Satire IV', l. 217.

l. 57. *Judges are Gods.* Cf. Ps. lxxxii. 2, 6: 'How long will ye judge unjustly . . . ? I have said, Ye are Gods'; and *Sermons*, i. 233: 'those of whom God said, *Ye are Gods*, that is, all those who have Authority over others' (also, vi. 297).

l. 59. *Angels*: bribery. The angel (or angel-noble), worth about 10s., was a gold coin, so called from the device of the archangel Michael killing the dragon which it bore.

ll. 60–61. *Dominations, Powers, Cherubins.* The pun on 'angels' was irresistible (cf. *Sermons*, v. 258).

The orders of angels are: Seraphim, Cherubim, Thrones; Dominations, Principalities, Powers; Virtues, Archangels, Angels. Donne's choice of the three named here is due rather to convenience of rhyme and metre than to the sharper wit of 'The Bracelet', l. 78.

l. 61. *Courts.* The manuscripts show confusion here, but 'Courts' seems to be right. Cf. 'so the *Roman* profession seems to exhale, and refine our wills from earthly Drugs, and Lees, more then the Reformed, and so seems to bring us nearer heaven; but then that carries heaven farther from us, by making us pass so many Courts, and Offices of Saints in this life, in all our petitions', etc. (*Letters*, p. 102).

l. 62. *pay fees.* If we had to pay fees for petitions in our prayers as we have in petitioning earthly courts, even kings would lack the 'daily bread' they pray for in repeating the Lord's Prayer.

l. 63. *so 'tis*: so things are.

l. 64. *A Stoicke, a coward, yea a Martyr.* These three would be the least likely to feel anger, the Stoic because he believed that one should be unmoved by circumstance or by passion, the coward because of his timidity, and the martyr because of his willingness (and power) to suffer without complaint for his beliefs.

l. 65. *Pursivant.* Cf. 'Satire IV', l. 216, note (p. 162).

ll. 65–66. *call All his cloathes, Copes,* etc. The finding of missals and of vestments and utensils required for Mass was crucial evidence in the conviction of Roman Catholics under the statutes dealing with recusancy and the banishment of priests. Robert Southwell (*An Humble Supplication*, ed. R. C. Bald, 1953, pp. 43–44) tells of 'the continuall hell we suffer by the merciles searching and storming of Pursevants and such needy Officers', and says that even thieves, with false badges and warrants, 'have under the pretence of Pursevants, spoiled us in our howses, having th'officers to assist them in the Robberies'. The Jesuit, Robert Parsons, tells how these abuses were intensified after the Gunpowder Plot, when nearly every night houses were broken into and 'Bookes, Cuppes, Chalices, or other furniture, that might any wayes seeme, or be pretended to belong to Religion, was taken for a prey, and seazed on' (*The Judgement of a Catholic Englishman*, 1608, p. 43, etc.). William Barlow, in his *Answer* to Parsons's book, 1609, admits that there was truth in these charges (pp. 351-2).

l. 66. *Primers.* The Roman Catholic Primer was a prayer-book for the use of the laity, at first mainly a translation or copy of parts of the Breviary and Manual.

l. 67. *mistake*: 'mis-take', take wrongly, misappropriate; as in Simpson, *Essays*, p. 31: 'the mistakings, and furies, and sloth of Princes'.

l. 68. *aske a fee.* Cf. 'If a Pursevant, if a Serjeant come to thee from the King, in any Court of Justice, though hee come to put thee in trouble, to call thee to an account, yet thou receivest him, thou entertainest him, thou paiest him fees' (*Sermons*, v. 370).

l. 69. *white*: pure, innocent of wrong.

ll. 71-73. Although I know no parallel for this view of the Law as Recorder of Fate, the conception is not inappropriate if we take Fate, or Destiny, as 'the Commissary of God' ('The Progress of the Soul', l. 31). In the same way as 'positive', that is man-made, law should be in accord with 'natural law', so the judgements of the law should record the decrees of Fate.

l. 73. *chaires*: chairs of State, or high offices.

ll. 74 ff. The 'foule long nailes', the only blemish on the Law's beauty, are only the 'extremities' of the body and can be pared.

l. 79. *bar'st*: *sc.* thy head in respect. This intransitive use is not recorded in the O.E.D.

l. 81. *bought wrong*: bought injustice.

l. 82. *right*: justice.
  dole: either, 'portion or lot in life, destiny' (*O.E.D.*, sb. 3, 4), or 'distribution of gifts' (*O.E.D.* 5), boon.
  these: law-officers.

ll. 83-84. You had much (but have lost it); you would test the Urim and Thummim of the Law in the hope of gaining (or re-gaining) more (than you now have; or, than you had at first, before legal redress was made).

l. 83. *Urim and Thummim.* Intensive plurals of Hebrew *ur* = 'light', and *tom* = 'perfection'; hence the 'clarity and integrity' of the Law (cf. Deut. xxxiii. 8).

The nature of the gems Urim and Thummim (e.g. in Num. xxvii. 21, I Sam. xiv. 41 ff.) is not known (see R. J. Beck, 'Urim and Thummim', *N. and Q.*, January 1957); they were used, however, for divination. The suggestion here might be that Law is a kind of oracle, revealing the decrees of Fate. Donne's usage is that of *O.E.D.* I. b.

l. 84. *paper*: in legal documents (cf. 'Satire II', ll. 87–90)—enough to wrap a whole cargo of pepper (cf. 'Upon Mr Thomas Coryate's *Crudities*', ll. 33–34). The line scans with a defective medial foot after a pause (see note on 'Satire III', l. 17):

$$\times \quad / \qquad \times \quad / \qquad \times \quad \times / \qquad \times \quad / (\times)$$
Thou wouldst | for more; || and | for all | hast paper

l. 85. *cloath*. The wrapping of pepper and other spices in paper (cones) was an ancient practice also. Cf. Horace, *Epist.* II. i. 269–70:

> Deferar in vicum vendentum tus et odores
> Et piper et quicquid chartis amicitur ineptis.

Also Martial, III. ii. 4; Catullus, xcv. 7; etc.

all the great Carricks Pepper. A carrack was a large merchant-vessel, fitted out for fighting as well as for cargo. The ship generally known as 'The Great Carrack' was the *Madre de Dios*, a seven-decker of 1,600 tons, carrying 600–700 persons. She was taken on 3 August 1592 and was reckoned the greatest prize ever brought to England. (For the best of the many accounts see W. R. Drake, *Archaeologia*, xxxiii, 1849.) Pepper formed the greatest part of her cargo. Members of the Portuguese crew said that there were on board 8,500 quintals (cwt.), i.e. 952,000 lb.; but there was much pilfering, and by the time the ship reached London from Dartmouth, as a detailed estimate taken at Leadenhall shows (Lansdowne MS. 70, item 89), there were 648,744 lb., worth (at 2s. 2d. a lb.) £70,280. 12s. 0d.

ll. 86–87. 'Sell your paper and you will lose more than Haman did when he sold his old rubbish.' I assume that Haman got much less than he had paid for his 'treasures'; the wretched suitor will do even worse when for all he has paid out he gets only the price of the paper.

l. 87. *Haman, when he sold his Antiquities*. The manuscripts spell 'Haman', 'Hammon', 'Hammond'. In the epigram 'Antiquary' (p. 52), the spelling is 'Hammon'. There is no one with a name resembling these among the members of the Elizabethan society of antiquaries listed in *Archaeologia*, i, 1770, Introduction, or by William Oldys in his account, *Life of Raleigh*, prefixed to Raleigh's *Works*, 1829, i. 317.

l. 88. *that*: in that. You are wretched in that your experiences provide an illustration, or a moral, of one of Aesop's fables, and turn his tale into a prophecy of your own fate.

l. 90. *the swimming dog*. This form of the fable is found in the Latin version of Phaedrus (I. iv, in *Der Lateinische Äsop des Romulus*, ed. G. Thiele, 1910, p. 23):

'canis per flumen carnem dum ferret natans, / lympharum in speculo vidit simulacrum suum', etc. In snapping at the meat held in the mouth of its reflected image the dog loses the real meat. The moral of the fable is 'amittit merito proprium qui alienum adpetit'; the victims of legal officers in Donne's poem, however, lose their substance, not in grabbing at someone else's property, but in pursuing a chimera (justice).

l. 91. *what vanished.* I have restored the *1633* reading. Grierson reads 'what's' on the authority of *N* (but not, as he claims, of *TCD* also). *N* is, however, a direct copy of *TCD*, which here reads (as Grierson's apparatus correctly shows) 'what'; 'whats' in *N* has therefore no authority.

THE PROGRESSE OF THE SOULE (p. 25)

MSS.: Group I (*C 57*); Group II (*A 18, N, TCC, TCD*); Group III (*O'F*); *G*; *H*.

In *1633*, which I take as my copy-text, the printer used a manuscript very like *C 57*, in which, as in *1633*, the poem appeared at the beginning. The editor was not as certain of his procedures here as he became later in the book. Nearly twice as many marks of elision or contraction have to be inserted as in the lyrics and verse letters. A considerable number of misreadings of the manuscript appear in uncorrected sheets of the book, but all but six of these were put right as printing proceeded. The printer's manuscript was itself defective in a good many places, and in five of these the editor invented readings to improve the text. These errors and sophistications I have rejected.

I depart from the reading of *1633* in thirty other places, eleven of its readings being errors in the printer's manuscript shared by *C 57* (only two of which were made independently in one other manuscript), and nineteen being errors shared also by Group II (and often by *O'F*). In two places (ll. 83, 383) the editor of *1633* has gone beyond his primary manuscript, and the Group II manuscript used elsewhere in the book, to a superior source for the correct reading. I differ from Grierson in twenty-one readings.

The theme and purpose of this poem are discussed in the General Introduction. Donne has so far honoured his determination not 'to come into any mans debt' ('Epistle,' ll. 13–14) that it is impossible to point very precisely to sources. The theory of metempsychosis on which the poem is based was accessible to him in many forms (see D. C. Allen, in *A Tribute to George Coffin Taylor*, ed. A. Williams, 1952). Accounts of Pythagoras's doctrine were available in Aulus Gellius, *Noctes Atticae* (mentioned by Donne in *Pseudo-Martyr*), IV. xi, and possibly also in Diogenes Laertius, viii. 4–6. The Platonic version could be found in the *Timaeus* 42 b–d, the *Phaedo* 810, and the *Phaedrus* 249, and of course in the commentaries of the neo-Platonists, who were beginning to attract Donne's attention. Many Church Fathers refer to the theory, and Tertullian has a full-scale discussion in *De Anima*, xxviii–xxxv (Migne, *P.L.*

ii. 697–712). *The French Academy*, translated by T. B. from Primaudaye, 1594, has a good summary of popular information on the subject.

For any expression of approval the poem had to await Coleridge, Charles Lamb (who calls it 'this admirable poem', *Letters*, ed. E. V. Lucas, 1935, ii. 421), and De Quincey (see Introduction, p. xxxi). Oliver Elton thought it 'a Caliban of a poem . . . ; but, as in Caliban, there is music' (*The English Muse*, 1933, p. 211); and W. P. Ker probably had it in mind when he wrote that 'Donne is besides a comic or humorous poet, fond of grotesque work, not generally for its own sake, but as the expression of a deep and ironical mind, not always in pleasant mood and working through contradictions' (*Form and Style in Poetry*, 1928, p. 260).

Epistle

l. 3. *through light*: translucent, as in 'A Funeral Elegy', l. 61.

l. 4. *sticke*: hesitate.

l. 8. *to do it* sine talione: without punishment in kind, by the *lex talionis* (an eye for an eye, etc.). *Sine talione* is from Martial, XII. lxiii. 10.

l. 10. *like the Trent Councell*. This is a malicious deduction from the decisions of the Council that no book was to be published on sacred matters without the author's name, and that an Index of prohibited books was to be prepared (*Council of Trent, Canons and Decrees*, translated by J. Waterworth, 1848).

ll. 24–25. *the same soule in an Emperour . . . Mucheron*. A 'mucheron' is a mushroom (the seventh of the spellings given in *O.E.D.*). In pointing this out C. S. Harris (*N. and Q.* IX. ix, 1902, p. 284) cites Burton, *Anatomy*, part. I, sect. I, memb. 2, subsect. 9:

> The Pythagoreans defend metempsychosis and *palingenesia*, that souls go from one body to another . . . as men into wolves, bears, dogs, hogs, as they were inclined in their lives, or participated in conditions:
>
> > Inque ferinas
> > Possumus ire domus, pecudumque in corpora condi.
> >
> >   [Ovid, *Metam.* xv. 457–8]
>
> Lucian's cock was first Euphorbus, a captain:
>
> > Ille ego (nam memini) Trojani tempore belli,
> > Panthoides Euphorbus eram,
> >
> >   [Ibid., ll. 160–1]
>
> a horse, a man, a sponge.

To Burton a 'sponge' meant any fungus. As often elsewhere, Donne is thinking of the three faculties of the soul and the three levels of living creatures— 'vegetal plants, sensible beasts, rational men' (Burton, *Anatomy*, part. I, sect. I, memb. 2, subsect. 5); Donne's order is in reverse, 'Emperour, Post-horse, Mucheron'.

The scribe of *O'F*, misunderstanding the last word, wrote 'Macaron' (cf. 'Satire IV', l. 117), copied in *1635* and later editions.

ll. 25-26. *no unreadinesse in the soule*, etc. The soul is ready to occupy the body of a man and to use all three of its faculties, but the organs of the available body (human, animal, plant) determine ('workes') the kind of life it will lead.

l. 33. *apple*. Others thought that the fruit of the Tree of Knowledge (Gen. ii. 17, iii. 3) was the fig or pomegranate. Most commentators agree with Browne (*Vulgar Errors*, vii. 1): 'curiosity fruitlesly enquireth'.

l. 34. *eate*: ate.

shee is hee. The reading 'shee is Shee' has no authority, originating as a sophistication in *O'F*.

The Progresse of the Soule

First Song: 'Canto I'.

l. 1. *I sing*: the regular epic (or mock-epic) opening.

l. 2. *Fate, which God made, but doth not controule*. This seems inconsistent with l. 31 (on which see note), where Destiny is God's 'Commissary'.

l. 3. *law*. The Law given to Moses in the Commandments and by him to the Israelites.

l. 5. *his aged evening*. 'The world is now growne into his last age, wherein sects, schismes, and errors doo spread, and sinne and iniquitie aboundeth' (Charles Gibbon, *The Remedy of Reason*, 1589, A2ᵛ). Cf. 'Satire III', ll. 36-38 and notes.

ll. 7-8. *gold Chaldee . . . silver Persian . . . Greeke brasse . . . Roman iron*: the Four Monarchies (Babylon, Persia, Greece, Rome) of l. 22 below, 'Elegy on Mistress Boulstred', l. 24, and *Sermons*, vii. 139. Each is associated here with a stage in the general deterioration of the world from the Golden to the Iron ages (cf. 'Satire V', l. 35 and note). See Daniel ii. 31-40.

l. 9. Seths *pillars, bricke and stone*. In a passage much cited in Donne's day Josephus tells how Seth, the son of Adam, left children who imitated his virtues (*Jewish Antiquities*, i. 68-71, translated by H. St. J. Thackeray and R. Marcus, Loeb ed., 1930-41, iv. 33):

They also discovered the science of the heavenly bodies, and their orderly array. Moreover, to prevent their discoveries from being lost to mankind and perishing before they became known . . . they erected two pillars, one of brick and the other of stone, and inscribed these discoveries on both; so that, if the pillar of brick disappeared in the deluge, that of stone would remain to teach men what was graven thereon, and to inform them that they had also erected one of brick. It exists to this day in the land of Seiris.

ll. 11-20. This stanza and stanza IV, quoted in Ch. xviii of *Biographia Literaria*, Coleridge describes as 'excellent, and the legitimate language of poetic fervour self-impassioned'.

l. 12. *male force*: power of engendering. Cf. 'the Suns hot masculine flame', etc., 'To E. of D. with six holy Sonnets', ll. 1-2.

l. 16. *Danow*. From Lat. 'Danuvius', collateral with 'Danubius', the (upper) Danube river.

l. 17. *Westerne land of Myne*: America and the West Indies, usually coupled with the Eastern land of spices, as in 'Upon Mr Thomas Coryate's *Crudities*', l. 29, and 'The Sun Rising', l. 17.

l. 19. *before thee, one day beganne to bee*. The creation of the plants (Gen. i. 11–13), and hence of the vegetal souls (as Pico della Mirandola says, *Heptaplus*, I. iv), took place on the third day; the sun was made on the fourth (Gen. i. 14–19).

l. 21. *holy* Janus. 'We call *Noah*, *Janus*, because hee had two faces, in this respect, That hee looked into the former, and onto the later world, he saw the times before, and after the flood' (*Sermons*, viii. 112). Lactantius mentions the identification (Migne, *P.L.* vi. 188), but it was given wider currency by Annius of Viterbo, who published in 1498 *Antiquitatum volumina XVIII*. Apart from the first book, these purport to be digests of works of ancient history; Book xv is said (falsely) to summarize one by Berosus, a Chaldean writer mentioned by Josephus, and the third section of this is entitled *Berosi de antiquitate Jani patris quem Noam nominat*. See D. C. Allen, *The Legend of Noah* (Illinois Studies in Lang. and Lit. xxxiii, 3–4, 1949).

Noah is 'holy' because he 'found grace in the eyes of the Lord' (Gen. vi. 8); because, according to Annius of Viterbo's book, vii, fº. lvii, he was the first to exercise the priestly function (offering 'sacrificia et holocausta'); and because he was the type of the clergy (e.g. St. Augustine, Migne, *P.L.* xxxvii. 1731: 'Noe significat rectores Ecclesiae').

l. 22. *The Church, and all the Monarchies*: because all living men were on the Ark, and hence (prospectively) all their descendants. The Ark was a type of the Church (e.g. St. Augustine, Migne, *P.L.* xxxiii. 847).

l. 23. *Colledge*. In another work by Annius of Viterbo, *Berosi . . . Antiquitatum Italiae ac Totius Orbis Libri quinque* (Antwerp, 1552) we read (pp. 77–78) that Noah taught religion, astronomy, etc.: 'Noa, iam antea edoctos Theologiam et sacros ritus, coepit eos erudire humanam sapientiam', etc.

Hospitall: refuge, place of lodging (*O.E.D.* 5).

l. 24. *vivarie*: vivarium, a place artificially prepared for keeping animals and birds.

l. 26. *latest nephewes*: remotest posterity (*O.E.D.*, 'nephew', 4: 'descendant').

l. 27. *thence*: the Ark, and those in it.
this All: the world (*orbis totus*).

l. 29. *parke*. Cf. the Palatine 'Epithalamion', ll. 20–21: 'the Arke / (Which was of foules, and beasts, the cage, and park . . .)'.

l. 30. *heavenly sparke*: the soul whose adventures are described in the poem. It was to enter more types of body than the Ark itself contained (cf. 'most shapes', l. 3).

l. 31. *Great Destiny the Commissary of God.* Cf. the letter to Wotton ('Here's no more newes'), ll. 10–11, 'rugged Fate, / (Gods Commissary,)', and 'A Funeral Elegy', ll. 95–96 (Grierson, i. 248):

> Her modestie not suffering her to bee
> Fellow-Commissioner with Destinie.

A 'commissary' is a delegate or deputy; a bishop's commissary, for example, carries his jurisdiction to remote parts of a large see. Ultimately the action of Fate or Destiny lies in the will of God and his Providence; but seen 'in the world of change and becoming, accidents and events are ascribed to Destiny'. So Grierson (annotating the lines from the letter to Wotton just quoted), citing Boethius, *De Consolatione Philosophiae*, IV, Prose vi (Migne, *P.L.* lxiii. 817): 'Uti est ad intellectum ratiocinatio; ad id quod est, id quod gignitur, ad aeternitatem tempus, ad puncti medium circulus; ita est fati series mobilis ad Providentiae stabilem simplicitatem.' In saying that God does not 'control' Fate (l. 2), Donne seems to be referring to the visible world of change in which the action of Providence is not obvious, but can only be inferred. 'God is not Destiny; Then there could be no reward, nor punishment: but God is not Fortune neither, for then there were no Providence' (*Sermons*, ix. 303).

l. 41. *sixe lustres*: thirty years (of age), a 'lustre' being a 'period of five years'. Donne was born between 24 January and 19 June 1572, and would have been twenty-nine years and some (at most, seven) months old in August 1601. See I. A. Shapiro, 'Donne's Birthdate', *N. and Q.* cxcvii, 1952, 310–13.

l. 43. *letts*: hindrances.

l. 45. *Spirit-quenching*. The 'spirit' destroyed by sickness is (as in l. 49) the refined and vitalizing part of the blood, by means of which the soul is able to act upon and through the organs of the body. Cf. 'The Ecstasy', ll. 61-62, and notes in Gardner, *Elegies etc.*, 'Spirit' is here a monosyllable (as shown by the spelling in *G*, 'Sprighte-quenching').

l. 47. *other*: any other pursuit.

l. 52. *this sea*: the labour of writing this poem, on which he has 'embarked'.

l. 55. *light, and light*. 'The two senses of *Light* are opposed to different opposites' (Lamb, *Letters*, ed. E. V. Lucas, ii. 421); i.e. to 'darke' and to 'heavy'.

l. 56. *streights*: (*a*) narrow sea-passages, the geographical extent of the soul's wanderings, and (*b*) difficulties (in composing the poem).

l. 57. 'I begin my poem in Eden and bring its story to England at the end' (cf. l. 60).

l. 59. *hoised*: set. Cf.: 'as soone as they hoysed their sailes'; 'from his hoysing sayle here, to his striking sayle there' (*Sermons*, vi. 305, ix. 68).

l. 60. *at Tigrys, and Euphrates*. Donne follows the accepted belief that Paradise was in Mesopotamia.

l. 61. *this great soule*. For a discussion of the identity of this person, see the General Introduction, pp. xxv–xxvi.

l. 66. *Mahomet*. The word is a dissyllable here and in 'To his Mistress Going to Bed', l. 21.

l. 67. *Prisons of flesh*. For the idea of the soul as being imprisoned in the body, cf. Plato, *Phaedo* 82, and 'The Ecstasy', l. 68.

l. 68. *th'Empire, and late Rome*: the Roman Empire (or possibly the Holy Roman Empire, or both) and Rome in recent times. The latter phrase might refer to the turbulent history of the Papal States in the century or two just passed, or, more probably, to the 'ruins' wrought by the Reformation.

l. 70. *a low, but fatall roome*. The place ('roome') occupied by the soul in Eden was 'low' because only on the vegetable plane of being; it was 'fatall' because the apple was doomed to be plucked, because the plucking brought death into the world, and hence because it was 'fateful' to mankind.

ll. 71–78. *Yet no low roome*, etc. The position of the soul was, however, far from being 'low' if it is true that the Cross on Calvary stood in the same place as the Tree of Knowledge. For the idea, cf. 'Hymn to God my God, in my sickness', ll. 21–22:

> We thinke that *Paradise*, and *Calvarie*,
> *Christs* Crosse, and *Adams* tree, stood in one place.

The soul in the apple on the Tree of Knowledge occupied a 'roome' not less than the 'greatest' because the tree stood by the Tree of Life 'in the midst of the garden', in the place of honour. I know of no statement that the Cross stood on this exact spot. Miss Gardner argues (*Divine Poems*, p. 137) that 'roome' refers to 'relative position'; Calvary was thought by many to be in the centre of the habitable world, as the Tree was in the first days of the life of mankind; thus to the many connexions already made between the *lignum perditionis* and the *lignum salvationis* Donne adds this of his own—both stood in the same position because both were *in medio*.

ll. 74–76. Used with only a change of tense in *La Corona* 2 ('Annunciation'), ll. 2–3.

l. 76. *could not chuse but die*. 'Lord of life, life it selfe, and yet prisoner to *Death*' (*Sermons*, vi. 155).

l. 78. *forbidden learned tree*: the Tree of Knowledge (learning) of Good and Evil; eating its fruit was 'forbidden' to Adam (Gen. ii. 17).

l. 79. *security*: perfect safety, one would have thought, since God had willed that it should not be plucked (and hence it was 'fenc'd with the law', l. 82).

l. 82. *ripe as soone as borne*. The plants in Eden bore ripe fruits since they were edible by man and woman three days after the plants were created. 'In para-dise, the fruits were ripe, the first minute' (*Sermons*, vi. 172); 'not unripe but at their prime, to be perfectly ready for the immediate use and enjoyment of the animals' (Philo Judaeus, *De Plantatione*, xiii; *Works*, translated by F. H. Colson and G. H. Whitaker, Loeb ed., i. 33).

ll. 84–85. *the then climing serpent*, etc. The curse upon Satan, the serpent of Gen. iii. 14, for having tempted Eve was 'upon thy belly shalt thou go'. This suggested that before the Fall the serpent 'went' in another fashion: cf. Basil, *De Paradiso*, iii. 7 (Migne, *P.G.* xxx. 67), 'erectus celsusque in pedes incedens'. Josephus seems to have originated the idea that God bereft the serpent 'of feet and made him crawl and wriggle along the ground' (*Jewish Antiquities*, i. 50, translated by H. St. J. Thackeray and R. Marcus, iv. 25); cf. *Sermons*, x. 184.

l. 90. *treason taints the blood.* To be convicted of treason meant (apart from the penalty of death for the offender) forfeiture of all property and 'corruption of blood', so that the offender's descendants could not be his heirs (*O.E.D.*, 'attainder'). By treason to God's will, Adam and Eve incurred the penalty of death, so corrupting the blood of their descendants and preventing them from inheriting the bliss of Eden.

die: 'because all sinne is deriv'd upon us, by *generation*, and so implyed, and involv'd in *originall sinne*' (*Sermons*, vi. 192), and the wages of sin is death.

sweat. 'In the sweat of thy face shalt thou eat bread' (Gen. iii. 19).

ll. 91–93. *by woman slaine*, etc. Cf. *The First Anniversary*, ll. 105–7, 180:

> For that first marriage was our funerall:
> One woman at one blow, then kill'd us all,
> And singly, one by one, they kill us now.
>
> The poysonous tincture, and the staine of *Eve*.

Women now 'kill' men, or hasten their death, by provoking coition; see ll. 206–10, and note.

The orthodox view was that it was the man's sin that brought about the Fall (1 Cor. xv. 21–22); but Ecclus. xxv. 24 says: 'Of the woman came the beginning of sin, and through her we all die.'

l. 93. *poison'd the well-head.* 'The devill . . . so surprized us all, as to take man-kinde all in one lump, in a corner, in *Adams* loynes, and poysoned us all there in the fountain' (*Sermons*, ix. 247).

l. 94. *Rivulets.* The rivulets flowing from the spring, or well-head, of humanity —Adam—are 'us' men, his descendants.

l. 97. *turning*: returning (to paradise).

ll. 98–99. *Were prisoners Judges*, etc. If the situation were reversed, and we prisoners of God's justice could ourselves pass judgement, we should deem it harsh that we should bear the penalty of Eve's sin. This is a cautious state-ment, tending to 'atheism'. Estienne, speaking of atheists, tells of an Italian lord who, among his 'fearfull blasphemies' 'was not ashamed to say, that God dealt unjustly when he condemned mankind for a peece of an apple' (translated in *A World of Wonders*, 1607, by R. Carew, p. 73).

l. 99. *paine.* TCC and *A 18* paraphrase as 'sinn'. The 'paine' is *poena*, the penalty for sin.

ll. 101–10. These speculations about the justice of God in relation to Adam, Eve, the Serpent, and to mankind in general are traditional, descending mostly from rabbinical sources. They are set out in full, for example, in Pererius's *Comment. et Disput. in Genesim*, 1601, vi. 283–96. The 'curious' (ingeniously argumentative) rebel who entertained them would not be very daring; even so, Donne says that these questionings are due to the 'corruption' of man, and are characteristic of 'heretiques' (l. 118).

l. 106. *For one*: for the offence of one.

ll. 107–9. *'twas not forbidden,* etc. In Gen. ii God's command not to eat of the Tree is given to Adam alone, apparently before the creation of Eve; yet the beginning of Ch. iii shows that Eve and the Serpent were well aware of the prohibition. Again, the Bible does not say that Adam actually picked the apple (Gen. iii. 6), or that he knew which tree it came from.

ll. 111–12. *vaine Reckoning*: fruitless enumeration of.

ll. 112–14. *lesse is the gaine,* etc. To think about evil, though with good intentions, always involves a danger greater than the possible benefits produced by such speculations.

l. 115. *bubbles.* For the image cf. *Sermons*, vii. 294.

l. 117. The line has only nine syllables:

$$\overset{\times}{\text{That}} \; \overset{/}{\text{they}} \mid \overset{\times}{\text{them}} \; \overset{/}{\text{selves}} \mid \overset{/}{\text{breake}}, \parallel \overset{\times}{\text{doe}} \; \overset{/}{\text{them}} \mid \overset{/}{\text{selves}} \; \overset{/}{\text{spill}}.$$

See note on 'Satire III', l. 38.

l. 119. *As wrastlers*: as in the case of wrestlers.
perfects them: sc. in their heresy.

l. 121. *the serpents gripe.* Cf. ll. 84–86. Eve, according to Scripture, 'took of the fruit' (*V*. 'tulit de fructu'). Some authorities thought that she did not, as in *Paradise Lost*, herself pluck the fruit, but that she took it from the serpent, the actual plucker.

l. 124. *Life, and growth*: the qualities of the 'vegetal' faculty of the soul.

l. 125. *old, one and another day*: two days old, but fully mature (cf. l. 82).

ll. 127–8. *better proofe,* etc. Faith, by its nature, accepts without 'scientific' proof, or proof to the senses; but the senses themselves are easily deceived, and we require proof that our perceptions are accurate.

l. 129. *a darke and foggie Plot.* 'Foggy' = 'boggy, marshy' (*O.E.D.* 2). 'Mandrage groweth willingly in darke and shadowie places' (Dodoens, *Herbal*, 1578, pp. 437–8).

l. 130: *th'earths pores*. The earth was supposed to have pores like those in the human skin. 'And when the pores of the earth open, then by heate of the Sunne, this serpent *Vipera* awaketh and commeth out of his den' (*Batman upon Bartholome*, 1582, f. 386ʳ).

l. 131. *thus abled*. The soul 'is made a slave to this body, by comming to it; It must act, but what this body will give it leave to act, according to the Organs, which this body affords it' (*Sermons*, vi. 75); but without the body the soul 'could nothing doe' ('Air and Angels', ll. 7–8).

l. 134. *throng'd*: squeezed. The plant pressed the thinner water out of the boggy soil.

l. 137. The copy of the poem in *C 57–TCD–O'F* and in the manuscript used for *1633* was defective, 'have' being omitted. In some copies of *1633* a 'corrected' reading is found, 'Princesse' for 'Prince', the corrector being aware that the poem dated from the reign of Elizabeth.

'Prince' is regularly used to refer to a Queen. The *O.E.D.* quotes, among other examples, *Willobie his Avisa*, 1594, 'Cleopatra, prince of Nile'. Cf. 'To the Countesse of Huntingdon' ('Man to Gods image'), l. 44, and 'To Mrs M. H.', l. 12.

l. 142. *digest*: divide.

l. 147. *his middle parts*. Donne is fancifully developing the supposed resemblance of the mandrake to a man, consisting in 'a bifurcation or division of the Root into two parts, which some are content to call Thighs' (Browne, *Vulgar Errors*, ii. 6).

l. 148. *loves businesse*. By a play on words Donne attributes to the mandrake the capacity for sexual adventures which was, in fact, possessed by those who used the mandrake as aphrodisiac or to procure abortions (l. 150).

l. 150. *His apples kindle*, etc. The aphrodisiac qualities of the fruit of the plant are frequently mentioned, e.g. by Burton, *Anatomy*, part. 3, sect. 2, memb. 2, subsect. 5. The lore of the mandrake is collected by D. C. Allen, *M.L.N.* lxxiv, 1959, but there is no mention of the power of the plant to 'kill' the power of conception. Browne relates from Dioscorides (cf. *Matthiolus in Dioscoridem*, 1558, p. 535) the belief that 'the grains of the apples of Mandrakes mundifie the Matrix, and applied with Sulphur, stop the fluxes of women', adding 'that the juice . . . procures abortion' (*Vulgar Errors*, vii. 7); but not specifically the juice of the leaves.

l. 156. *red*. The fruit of the male mandrake is usually described as bright golden yellow in colour ('luteo colore croci', Dioscorides, *Pedacii*, 1529, p. 514).

l. 159. *guest*: the soul itself, that built its own 'Inne' to sojourn (not dwell) in. In *Ignatius his Conclave*, Hayward, p. 359, Donne translates the poem attributed to the dying Hadrian ('Animula vagula', etc.): 'My little wandring sportful Soule, / Ghest, and Companion of my body'.

l. 165. *moist red eyes*. The child was Cain, whose name was often (wrongly) translated as 'lamentation', 'constant weeping' (as in Rabanus Maurus, *De Universo*, II. i; Migne, *P.L.* cxi. 32).

l. 167. *Poppie . . . mandrakes might*. Poppy and mandragora were well-known soporifics; cf. *Othello*, III. iii. 335-8, Jonson's *Sejanus*, III. 598. They were also good for inflamed eyes. Dodoens says that juice from the roots of a fresh mandrake is good in 'medicines, that do mitigate the paynes of the Eyes', and that opium with vinegar 'is good to be layde to the disease, called *Erysipelas*, or Wild fire, and all other inflammations' (*Herbal*, 1578, pp. 438, 433).

For the tradition that Adam was a *thaumaturgos*, with almost divine wisdom, skilled in the secret properties of all herbs, see H. W. Janson, *Apes and Ape Lore in the Middle Ages and the Renaissance*, 1952, p. 94.

l. 169. *Unvirtuous*: not having medicinal 'virtues'.

ll. 171-3. Cf. *The Second Anniversary*, ll. 185 ff.

l. 176. *firme destiny*. Donne insists throughout that the sub-rational souls are at the command of Fate; cf. ll. 245-7, 301, as earlier, l. 129.

l. 181. *moving*. The new body gives scope to the 'sensible' faculty of the soul, adding the power of motion to those of life and growth (l. 124).

l. 185. *All*: the bird's whole body.

l. 188. *Meat fit for men*. The sparrow's conduct, after being fed, is also 'fit' for men. The innuendo seems to involve a play on I Cor. iii. 1-3: 'I have fed you with milk, and not with meat: . . . are ye not carnal, and walk as men?'

ll. 191-2. Compare Drayton, *Noah's Flood*, ll. 26-30.

ll. 193 ff. The sparrow was proverbially lecherous. Cf. Pliny, *Nat. Hist.* x. 52, and Tilley S715: 'as lustful as Sparrows'.

l. 194. *next*: nearest.

ll. 201-3. For other expressions of this 'naturalism', cf. 'The Relic', l. 30, 'Confined Love', ll. 5-8, and the elegy 'Change', ll. 10 ff. The main ancient source was Ovid, *Metamorphoses*, x. 320 ff., often linked, as here, with the problems of peopling the earth when only the children of Adam were living to accomplish it. Cf. Beza, *Tractatio De Polygamia*, 1568 (a copy of which was in Donne's library), pp. 4-5: 'mundi initio . . . necesse etiam fuerit . . . sorore a fratre duci', etc.; similarly Annius of Viterbo, *Berosi . . . antiquitatum . . . libri quinque*, 1552, p. 44: 'Commiscebantur matribus, filiabus, sororibus, et masculis, brutis.' The same material appears in Lydgate's 'Chaucer's Flower of Courtesy' (*Minor Poems*, ed. H. N. MacCracken, E.E.T.S., o.s. 192, p. 412), ll. 64-70; Gower, *Confessio Amantis*, viii. 68-70 ('it was no

Sinne / The Sostor forto take hire brother, / Whan that ther was of chois non other'); and Drayton, *Noah's Flood*, ll. 99–100.

l. 202. *ingresse*: enter (carnally), *O.E.D.* 2 (this being the only instance quoted).

l. 204. *jolly*: over-confident (as in 'Satire I', l. 7).

l. 205. *kindnesses*. Grosart suggests a pun: 'acts of kind', 'acts of kindness'.

ll. 206–10. *selfe preserving it hath now forgot*, etc. Browne expresses the common belief that 'immoderate salacity, and almost unparallel'd excess of venery . . . is supposed to shorten the lives of Cocks, Partridges, and Sparrowes' (*Vulgar Errors*, iii. 9). It is the 'Sparrow that neglects his life for love' (Palatine 'Epithalamion', l. 7); but this is only a special case of the general rule that 'Wee kill our selves to propagate our kinde' (*The First Anniversary*, l. 110). Cf. 'A Farewell to Love', ll. 24–25, and note in Gardner, *Elegies etc.*, p. 214; and l. 220 below.

l. 207. *knot*: the spirits that tie together the soul and body, and are exhausted by venery. Cf. 'That subtile knot, which makes us man' ('The Ecstasy', l. 64).

l. 208. *streightens*: makes firmer.

l. 209. *spirit*. Cf. note to l. 45.

l. 210. *three yeares*. One year is usually given as the life-span of cock-sparrows (from Pliny, *Nat. Hist.* x. 52), though Riolanus says two (*Physiologia*, v. xxvii, *Opera Omnia*, 1610, p. 310). Donne says three years perhaps because in those days things 'did longer last' (l. 192).

l. 213. *bird-lime*: made of the sticky sap ('gummie blood') of the holly. Cf. 'Satire II', l. 46, and note.

l. 215. *Plyant*: yielding.

l. 217. Certain roots (e.g. of mandrakes, potatoes) and the flesh, eggs, and dung of sparrows, when eaten, were supposed to be aphrodisiac or to aid conception.

l. 218. *these*: bird-lime, feigned calls, nets, snares (ll. 213–14).

l. 219. *streightned*: restricted, confined.

l. 227. *inform'd*: gave form (and hence its special nature) to, imbued with life. *abled*. Cf. l. 131, and note.

l. 228. *she did fit*. The soul works with and through the body to frame it according to its nature; cf. l. 159, 'built by the guest'.

l. 237. *scorn'd*. The swan, according to Rabanus Maurus (Migne, *P.L.* cxii. 894), is an allegory of Pride (*superbia*).

l. 243. *digestive fire*. The digestive process is usually spoken of in terms of heat. Burton speaks of the stomach as 'the kitchen, as it were, of the first concoction' (*Anatomy*, part. 1, sect. 1, memb. 2, subsect. 4).

l. 244. *vapour'd*. A familiar word in Donne's work to describe the soul's leaving the body, as in 'The Expiration', l. 2.

l. 254. *windowes*. Cf. 'The Bait', l. 20: 'strangling snare, or windowie net'.

ll. 254–5. *Need first taught*, etc. Cf. Origen, *Contra Celsum*, iv. 76 (Migne, *P.G.* xi. 1147): 'ea causa hominem creasse indigentem, ut penuria ipsa cogeretur artes invenire'. The proverbial form, 'Necessity is the mother of invention', derives ultimately from Aeschylus, *Prometheus Bound*, l. 514, in its Latin form, 'Artis magistra necessitas'.

l. 256. *curious*: ingenious.

ll. 259–60. The ferocity of the pike (*lupus marinus*) is always emphasized.

l. 261. *two deaths*: being killed by the pike, or by the owner of the net (presumably Adam).

l. 262. *Once*: for once.

ll. 264–8. The controversy over the manner in which a fish breathes began in Plato's *Timaeus*, 92 b, and in Aristotle, *De Respiratione*, ii–iii, x, xix; it was unsettled in Donne's day, and there are many discussions, e.g. in Rondeletius, *De Piscibus Marinis*, 1554, pp. 96–105, and Cardan, *De Rerum Varietate*, vii. 37 (edition of 1557, pp. 216–21).

l. 266. *limbecks*: alembics, stills—vessels in which substances were vaporized (made 'thinne and airelike').

ll. 267–8. *faith Cares not*: because this is a dispute on the level of knowledge and the senses.

l. 270. *makes a boord or two*. A nautical phrase: 'tacks once or twice'; i.e. moves to and fro uncertainly.

l. 274. *sea Pie*: the oyster-catcher, a bird of the sea-shore.

l. 275. *spectacle*: 'a means of seeing' (*O.E.D.* II. 5); window, or mirror.

l. 276. *seely*: foolish, harmless, pitiable.
   disputing: arguing with itself, hesitating.

l. 290. The change in religion in England and the lessening of the number of fasts and fish-days caused a decline in the fishing industry. In a statute of 1564, accordingly (5 Eliz. c. 5, xi–xii; *Statutes of the Realm*, iv, Part i, p. 424), Wednesdays as well as Saturdays were made fish-days throughout the year, on which it would not be lawful to eat flesh under penalty of three pounds or imprisonment for three months. There is a more general reference also to fasts ordained by the Church, including the forty days of Lent.

l. 293. *cares not*: although a shore-bird.

l. 294. *best orator*. A loose phrase, meaning, perhaps, that the bird proclaims gluttony by its indifference to the danger of being blown out to sea.

l. 296. *many*. This word was omitted in *C 57–TCD–O'F* and the printer's copy for *1633*. In the edition the line is patched by the insertion of the tautologous 'o'erpast'.

l. 298. *soules no longer foes*. Enmity is felt in the soul, in its sensible faculty (cf. Burton, *Anatomy*, part. I, sect. I, memb. 2, subsect. 8), but (sect. 2, memb. 3, subsect. I) the real cause of passions lies in the 'bad humours' of the body. Hence, despite ll. 506–8 below, the enmity of these two 'sensible' souls ceased when they entered new bodies. Cf. l. 371.

l. 300. *lives*: i.e. as a creature preying on others 'for game and not for hunger' (l. 274).

l. 302. *throwne out*: as a complete creature. (It had been 'thrown in' as a pure soul.)

l. 304. *that*. This word stands for the repeated conjunction ('if'), like French 'que'; similarly, e.g., in 'The Apparition', l. 2.

l. 305. *loose Morea swome*. Morea was a name for the Peloponnesus, which Donne here imagines as separated across the Isthmus of Corinth and from the sea-bed, 'swimming' like an island. The idea of floating islands was a commonplace (cf. Pliny, *Nat. Hist.* ii. 96). For the comparison of a mighty fish to such an island cf. *Paradise Lost*, i. 200 ff. and vii. 412–15. Bartholomew says that bushes grow on the whale's back 'so that that great Fish seemeth an Ilande' (*Batman upon Bartholome*, 1582, f. 200ᵛ).

l. 307. *hopefull Promontories head*: tip of the Cape of Good Hope; *Caput* (head, cape) *Bonae Spei*. For the use of the adjective, compare 'learned tree', l. 78.

l. 308. *hopes*: of giving an adequate image of the whale; with a play on 'hopefull'.

l. 309. *overset*: capsized.

ll. 309–10. *without saile Hulling*: making the ship like a hull by taking in all, or nearly all, sails in calms or when lying-to in storms. Fynes Moryson writes (*Itinerary*, edition of 1907, ii. 106): 'the windes were so contrary, as wee were forced to strike sayles, and lie at hull (that is, tossed to and fro by the waves)'.

l. 320. *seas above the firmament*. Cf. Gen. i. 7, 9. The location of these waters caused great perplexity among commentators. Aquinas discusses the two possibilities (*S.T.*, Iᵃ pars, q. lxviii, art. 2): either they were situated above the 'firmament' of fixed stars, or (like the 'sphere' of water in the Ptolemaic system) in the upper air. In either case Donne's hyperbole holds.

ll. 321–2. *an officer . . . as his owne net*. The reading of *H* is an accurate paraphrase of the meaning. The officer needs only to stay where he can be found to act as a snare for those who come to seek his favours. Grierson quotes Ps. x. 9 ('he lieth in wait to catch the poor: he doth catch the poor, when he draweth him into his net') and Jeremiah v. 26; cf. *Sermons*, iv. 191, vii. 377.

l. 324. *wantoning*: taking his pleasure, like Leviathan in Ps. civ. 26.

ll. 334–5. *And like a Prince*, etc. 'My soule may be King, that is, reside principally in my heart, or in my braine, but it neglects not the remoter parts of my
body' (*Sermons*, viii. 117). The orthodox belief was that the soul is equally in
all parts of the body: 'Nam singulis sui corporis particulis tota [anima] praesto
est, cum tota sentit in singulis . . . ubique tanta est, quia ubique tota est' (St.
Augustine, Migne, *P.L.* xlii. 185). Cf. Aristotle, *De Anima*, 411^b; Aquinas,
S.T., I^a pars, q. lxxvi, art. 8; Franciscus Georgius, *Problemata*, 1574, f. 78a;
etc.

ll. 336–7. *The Sunne hath twenty times . . . Parched*: twenty years have passed. In
the Zodiac (a belt of the celestial sphere extending eight or nine degrees on
each side of the ecliptic, within which the apparent movements of the heavenly bodies were supposed to take place) the Crab (Cancer) and the Goat
(Capricornus) are chosen here as being two divisions furthest apart; they are
in fact the solstitial positions of the sun, which passes through all divisions
once a year.

ll. 338–40. These lines are quoted by Browning in a tribute to the verse of 'revered and magisterial Donne' in 'The Two Poets of Croisic', cxiv (ll. 904–12).

l. 340. *station*: permanent resting-place (*O.E.D.* I. 1–3). A man can be great for
a time but cannot remain so.

l. 345. *thence*: from the torn flesh.

   outstreat: 'outstretch', used (owing to exigencies of rhyme) loosely for
'exude'.

   Whale oil was still rather a mystery. See Browne's account of the whale cast
up in Norfolk, *Vulgar Errors*, iii. 26.

l. 349. *projects*: plots, schemes.

l. 351. *Thresher*: 'thrasher', the sea-fox or fox-shark, 'so called from the very
long upper division of the tail with which it lashes an enemy' (*O.E.D.*).

ll. 353–9. The essential detail of this battle is given by Bartholomew (*Batman
upon Bartholome*, Book xiii, 1582, f. 200^v), but I give the livelier statement in
'Newes from the Barmudas', 1613 (in *Tracts and Other Papers . . .* , ed. P. Force,
1844, iii. 3. 22):

   Likewise there commeth in two other Fishes with them, but such, as the Whale
   had rather bee without their company; one is called a Sword-fish, the other a
   Threasher: the Sword-fish swimmes under the Whale, and pricketh him upward;
   the Threasher keepeth above him, and with a mightie great thing like unto a flaile,
   hee so bangeth the Whale, that hee will roare as though it thundered, and doth give
   him such blowes, with his weapon, that you would thinke it to be a cracke of great
   shot.

Cf. Spenser, *Visions of the World's Vanity*, ll. 62 ff., and earlier, of a different
exemplum, l. 28: 'So by the small the great is oft diseased.'

l. 360. *dole*: portion, thing distributed; he is himself what he distributes as
dole.

l. 368. *that act.* Their love for the dead king should make them act against his slayers (but he cannot now reward their loyalty).

l. 371. *and passion.* The soul is subject to the effects of passion only while it is imprisoned in the body. Cf. note to l. 298.

l. 375. *streight cloyster*: narrow confines. 'Cloister', *O.E.D.* 1.

mouse. Pouring scorn on the idea of metempsychosis, Antonius Brunus (*Entelechia*, 1597, of which Donne owned a copy) points out the absurdity of the idea that the same soul could be in great and little creatures: 'ut ex homine in elephantum, ex elephanto in culicem, aut formicam immigrare cogamur' (p. 137).

ll. 379–80. An example of the soul's ability to remember what occurred in a previous incarnation, and to 'keep some quality' (ll. 506–7), usually evil, of the life she formerly led.

l. 382. *harmlesse.* So Pliny, *Nat. Hist.* viii. 7, 'nec nisi lacessiti nocent', etc. Topsell, *History of Four-footed Beasts*, 1607, following the traditional lore as found in Gesner, enlarges on the elephant's fidelity, love of flowers and of beautiful women, chastity, modesty, and tractability; 'Their love and concord with all mankind is most notorious' (p. 208).

l. 385. *no knees to bend.* Browne calls this 'an old and gray-headed error, even in the days of Aristotle' (*Vulgar Errors*, iii. 1). Aristotle states the theory only to refute it (*De incessu animalium*, 709ᵃ, 712ᵃ), and Pliny (viii. 1), Bartholomew, and Topsell (p. 196) say the elephant can kneel. The idea was, however, irresistible and turns up with wearisome frequency (as in Rowley, *All's Lost by Lust*, 1633, C3ᵛ: 'Stubborn as an elephant's leg, no bending in her').

l. 386. *Himselfe he up-props.* Topsell says that after they grow old elephants do not lie down or strain their legs 'by reason of their great weight, but take their rest leaning to a tree' (p. 196).

l. 388. *vex't.* The subject of the verb is 'dreames': no horrible dreams troubled his fancy.

l. 390. *remisly*: both 'carelesly' (l. 389), and 'slack'.

ll. 391–5. Though the elephant's fear of rodents was a commonplace (from Pliny, *Nat. Hist.* viii. 10) nothing is heard of the ability of the mouse to kill the elephant by gnawing its brain until Elizabethan times. The source of the idea seems to have been a study of the spices and simples of India by a Portuguese physician, Garçia de Orta, published in Goa (1563). A Latin translation by Charles de l'Escluze (Clusius) published in 1567, *Aromatum, et simplicium aliquot medicamentorum apud indos nascentium Historia*, became very popular; here, in a digression on elephants, we read (p. 70): 'si mures in suis stabulis versari senserint, nunquam nisi contorta in se et convoluta promuscide Elephanti dormient, ne eam mures ingrediantur et mordeant'. The elephant's carelessness (l. 389) lies in its not having knotted its trunk. Cf. *Locrine* (published 1595), v. i. 83–84:

> Have you not seene a mightie elephant
> Slaine by the biting of a silly mouse?

See 'A Difficult Allusion in Donne and Spenser', *N. and Q.*, January 1966.

l. 393. *the soules bedchamber*. It was disputed whether the seat of the soul was the heart, brain, liver, or blood (cf. *Sermons*, i. 192, iv. 294). Donne selects the brain here, as more satisfactorily explaining the destruction of the elephant.

l. 398. *roome*: station, rank (as filling a better 'position').

ll. 405–6. *Who, in that trade . . . type*. As the first shepherd (Gen. iv. 2) Abel is the earliest 'type' of the Church; cf. Peter Lombard, Migne, *P.L.* cxci. 1121 ('Ecclesia . . . cuius primitiae fuit sanctus Abel'), Augustine, *P.L.* xxxvii. 1589, and Ambrose, *P.L.* xiv. 318.

He is also the desirable type of a king: 'refert praeterea imaginem quandam regalis administrationis & gubernationis: talem enim decet esse regem erga sibi subditos, qualiter pastor gregem suum regit' (Pererius, *Comment. et Disput. in Genesim*, 1601, vii, p. 330 b).

l. 406. *still*: continually.

l. 419. *Now much resist*. This reading has the weight of authority, and makes 'resist' a noun, object of 'show'. The *O.E.D.*, 'resist', sb. 1, quotes among the examples Lodge's *Forbonius and Prisceria*, 1584: 'I make no resist in this my loving torment'.

streighten: confine, restrict the movements of, 'coerce'.

l. 420. *were*: even were (she free).

l. 421. *engag'd*: won over, persuaded; or possibly, 'entered into love's combat' (as one engages an enemy).

ll. 428–30. Donne's account of the formation of the embryo here and in ll. 494 ff. is that commonly accepted, and is orthodox in every detail. Cf. *Batman upon Bartholome*, 1582, vi. 4, and Thomas Vicary, *The Anatomy of the Body of Man* (1548, as re-issued 1577, ed. F. J. and P. Furnivall, E.E.T.S., Extra Ser. liii, 1888); D. C. Allen quotes other authorities in 'John Donne's Knowledge of Renaissance Medicine', *J.E.G.P.* xlii, 1943.

ll. 429–30. *that masse Of blood*. As Vicary says, pp. 78–80, the 'sparme' of the parents is 'gathered of the most best and purest drops of blood' in the body, and for some days the embryo remains 'but as a lumpe of blood'. Donne telescopes the process here, since the soul was thought normally to enter the body only when 'al the other members be perfectly shapen' (Vicary).

l. 431. *Some have their wives*, etc. By marrying their daughters in the first case, and having sexual relations with their mothers in the second. Cf. note to ll. 201–3; of the second case Oedipus is the best-known example.

l. 432. *the lives of Emperours.* Presumably a reference to Suetonius, 'Lives of the Caesars', especially Nero and Domitian.

ll. 436-8. *hee is A ridling lust,* etc. The reincarnation of the father's soul in the son makes this creature, as it were, the personification of lust—a lust which is 'puzzling', 'enigmatic', and which is a sin that the Schoolmen could not classify (cf. 'Satire II', ll. 35–38).

l. 438. *both these*: Abel's bitch and the wolf.

l. 439. *Moaba* (l. 457, Siphatecia; l. 487, Tethlemite; l. 509, Themech): Grierson was instrumental in tracing the source of these names, in rabbinical mythology. In the Hebrew *Chronicle of Jerahmeel* (translated by the discoverer, Rabbi M. Gaster, in Publications of the Royal Asiatic Society, Oriental Translation Fund, N.S. iv, 1899, Ch. xxvi) there is a list of Adam's children, including Cain and his twin wife Qualmana, Seth and his twin wife Nōba, and the following daughters: Ḥavah, Giṭsh, Harē, Bikha, Zifath, Hēkhiah, Shaba, and ʿAzin. We also read that ʿCain and his wife Tēmēd dwelt in the land of Nod' and that Enoch was their son (p. 55). The *Chronicle* is a fourteenth-century work, preserving with great accuracy a text which, translated into Greek about a thousand years earlier and then into Latin, appeared in a work falsely attributed to Philo Judaeus; it was abstracted in the compilation of Annius of Viterbo mentioned in the note on l. 21 above, and published in full (among genuine works of Philo) in *Philonis Judaei Alexandrini. Libri Antiquitatum . . . ,* 1527, edited by Budaeus. In the latter (p. 1) Nōba appears as 'Noaba' (for which Donne's 'Moaba' seems to be a slip). The names of two other daughters of Adam, Zifath and Hēkhiah, are telescoped into one, 'Siphatecia', who thus replaces Zifath as 'Adams fift daughter' (l. 457), although in this Latin version the name is fourth. Tēmēd in the Hebrew becomes 'Themech' in the Latin; she should be identical with Qualmana, 'Sister and wife to Caine' (l. 510), but neither document helps us here. The name 'Tethlemite' has not been traced. Donne seems to have supplemented the pseudo-Philo from another source, or to have used a version of the work which had itself been supplemented. It is perhaps too far-fetched a suggestion that in the nearer source the names of two daughters of Enoch as given in the Latin text of 1527, Theth and Lephith, were run together into one, which was taken as a masculine name, 'Tethlemite', and further mistaken as the name of a son of Adam.

l. 443. A syllable is dropped after the medial pause.

l. 446. *cosen'd*: cheated.

l. 451. *a toyfull Ape.* Topsell takes from Gesner a brief account (*The History of four-footed Beasts*, 1607, p. 10) of a kind of 'Munkey' very like a man: 'he loveth women and children dearly, like other of his own kind, and is so venerious, that he will attempt to ravish women'. The description, he says, 'was taken forth of the booke of the description of the holy Land'; more directly, it comes from Cardan, *De Subtilitate*, x (edition of 1560, p. 323). The baboon was said to have similar traits; cf. Aelian, *Nat. Animal.* vii. 19, xv. 14. For other possible sources see H. W. Janson, *Apes and Ape Lore* . . . , 1952, Ch. ix.

l. 455. *laugh, and speake his minde.* Cf. 'Upon Mr Thomas Coryate's *Crudities*', ll. 13–14: 'If man be therefore man, because he can / Reason, and laugh'. Aristotle says that man is 'the only animal that laughs' (*De Partibus Animalium*, 673^a) and that reason distinguishes man from the lower animals (*Magna Moralia*, 1189^a); hence laughter and speech, or laughter and reason, are often coupled as the distinguishing marks of man. The phrase 'He wonders' in l. 456 suggests a power of reasoning in the ape which, strictly speaking, it could not possess.

l. 460. *true lover*: of the conventional sort, adopting the fashionable poses of the 'true lover'.

ll. 461–2. *He was the first that more desir'd*, etc.: by contrast with the more usual practice (cf. ll. 195–203) before the coming of law.

l. 465. *The valters sombersalts*: feats on the vaulting-horse, to impress the lady. Cf. *Henry V*, v. ii. 138 ff.; and Jonson, *Cynthia's Revels*, II. i. 63–65.

l. 466. *hoiting*: rioting, full of noisy mirth.

Bartholomew was apparently the first to say that the ape can be taught 'to leape and play in divers manner wise' (*Batman upon Bartholome*, 1582, f. 380^r; cf. Janson, *Apes and Ape-Lore* . . . , p. 82).

ll. 467–8. *to wreake Her angers on himselfe.* In Jonson's *Cynthia's Revels*, IV. i. 205 ff., Phantaste would see how Love in a man 'could varie outward, by letting this gallant expresse himselfe in dumbe gaze; . . . a fourth, with stabbing himselfe, and drinking healths, or writing languishing letters in his bloud'. Some more striking response to the lady's scorn might, however, be meant, e.g. suicide.

l. 470. *outward beauty.* Despite the surface cynicism of the poem, the central conviction of Donne's mature love-poetry remains firm. Cf. 'The Under-taking', ll. 13–16.

l. 472. *beasts and angels.* Burton's list remains unsurpassed, *Anatomy*, part. 3, sect. 2, membs. 1–2.

l. 473. *through-vaine*: thoroughly vain.

l. 480. *nature hath no gaole*, etc. Donne refers here to the 'libertine' conception of the Law of Nature, interpreted to mean that to live under that Law was to be free of the restraints and punishments ('gaole') imposed by the Laws of God and man. Cf. Lucretius, *De rerum natura*, v. 958–61:

> Nec commune bonum poterant spectare, neque ullis
> Moribus inter se scibant nec legibus uti.

Quod cuique obtulerat praedae fortuna, ferebat
Sponte sua sibi quisque valere et vivere doctus.

The idea is fully discussed by L. I. Bredvold, *J.E.G.P.* xxii, 1923. Donne is not here expressing any opinion for or against the notion; he is characteristically pointing to a paradox—that under this 'Law' (of nature), even violators of this Law (by 'unnatural' conduct, e.g. 'Sinnes against kinde') incur no penalty and suffer no restraint.

l. 481. *silly*: innocent.

l. 483. *Succeeds an itchie warmth*: a nagging desire follows (and overcomes 'that vertue', innocence). For 'itchie', cf. 'Satire I', l. 38 and note.

l. 492. *where*: i.e. from a human body.

l. 493. *mingled bloods*. This is the usual theory of coition; cf. Aristotle, *De Generatione Animalium*, I. xix. 726ᵇ, and note to ll. 429–30 above.

ll. 494–5. *Like Chimiques equall fires*. The analogy between human generation and the preparation of the 'philosophers' stone' by alchemists ('Chimiques') is very common. See E. H. Duncan, 'Donne's Alchemical Figures', *E.L.H.* ix, 1942. A constant temperature ('equall fire') was desirable for both processes. In generation, says *The French Academy*, 1594, ii. Ch. 71, p. 395, 'the heate of the Matrix warmeth all this matter as it were in a little fornace'.

l. 496. *spungie liver*. The liver was thought to be 'spongy' because it controlled most of the moisture of the body, the blood being 'engendered' there.

l. 499. *hardned . . . to a thicker heart*. D. C. Allen (*J.E.G.P.*, 1943) quotes Pareus: 'le coeur, qui est de substance charneuse, solide & espesse, ainsi qu'il appartient au membre le plus chaud de tous les autres'.

l. 500. *spirits*. See note to l. 45 above.

l. 502. *well-arm'd*: being protected by the hair, the skin, the flesh, the skull, the *dura mater* and the *pia mater* (cf. T. Vicary, *Anatomy*, E.E.T.S., 1888, p. 25).

l. 503. *Those sinowie strings*. 'And the braine is chiefe foundation of the sinewes: for it is the well of wilfull moving & feeling. For all sinewes spring and come out of the braine' (*Batman upon Bartholome*, 1582, f. 66ʳ). 'Sinewes' meant both sinews and nerves; hence 'moving and feeling'.

ll. 504–5. *fast there by one end*, etc. Donne says that the soul joins the body when the limbs are completely formed (the orthodox opinion; contrast ll. 429–30, and note). The seat of the soul is here made the brain (consistently with l. 393; see note). Hence the soul is 'fast' at the end of the spinal cord and (apparently) radiates out to all parts of the body with the sinews and nerves.

l. 510. *that first did plow*. 'Cain was a tiller of the ground' (Gen. iv. 2).

l. 511. *sullen*: drab, gloomy, unsociable.

l. 512. *Which just so much courts thee*, etc. The tone of the Epistle returns ('I would have no such Readers as I can teach', etc.): 'you will find my poem just as congenial to you as you are sympathetic to it'. B. C. Clough (*M.L.N.* xxxv, 1920) compares *Hudibras*, I. i. 649–50.

l. 516. *cursed* Cains *race*. Cain, the first murderer, is cursed in Gen. iv. 11–15, made to be 'a fugitive and vagabond in the earth', and marked by God lest anyone should kill him and end his punishment. He is the type of the persecutor of the Church (Augustine, Migne, *P.L.* xli. 456). His 'race' (Gen. iv. 17–22) included Jabal, ruler of tents and raiser of cattle ('ruling', l. 514); Jubal, 'father of all such as handle the harp and organ' ('arts', l. 515); and Tubal-Cain, 'an instructor of every artificer in brass and iron' ('building').

It was a problem why the reprobate Cain's race should have founded and developed the arts and crafts. Cf. A. Williams, *The Common Expositor*, 1948, pp. 145–6, and the references there given (e.g. to Cornelius Agrippa, Calvin, etc.). Pererius, *Comment. et Disput. in Genesim*, 1601, discusses the matter, vii. 345, and concludes that the arts would probably have been discovered anyway, and were as much used among Seth's descendants as among Cain's.

In this line, and at least once in l. 510, the word 'Cain' seems to be dissyllabic, 'Caïn'.

l. 517. *blest* Seth *vext us with Astronomie*. Seth was regarded as 'blest' for several reasons. In Gen. iv. 25–26 Eve looks upon him as successor to the murdered Abel, whose character he shared. He succeeds Abel as the type of Christ: 'Seth quippe, ut quidam putant, interpretatur *resurrectio*, qui est Christus' (Rabanus Maurus, *Comment. in Genesim*, II. ii, Migne, *P.L.* cvii. 509). Cain and his race are the children of the world, but Seth and his children are the children of Light, and the 'sons of God' in Gen. vi. 2, 4 (cf. D. C. Allen, 'Milton and the Sons of God', *M.L.N.* lxi, 1946).

For Seth as the discoverer of 'Astronomie' the usual reference given (in many places) is the passage from Josephus quoted in the note to l. 9 above. Du Bartas shows Adam teaching astronomy to Seth (*Divine Weeks and Works*, Second Week, First Day, trans. Sylvester, 1605, p. 376). Cf. Suidas, *Historica*, edition of 1581, col. 849: 'Deum enim, Sethum illius aetatis homines appellabant, eo quòd et Hebraicis literas, et stellarum appellationes invenisset, ob insignis eius pietatis admirationem', etc.

The terms 'Astronomie' and 'Astrologie' 'both are indifferently taken & used by the learned for one and the selfesame Arte' (Sir Christopher Heydon, *A Defence of Judicial Astrology*, 1603, p. 2; he cites Josephus to 'prove' that Adam and Seth 'did addict themselves unto it', pp. 74, 305). It was astrology, with its predictions and horoscopes that Seth introduced to 'vex' mankind.

l. 518. *simply*. The force of this word is discussed by J. P. Wendell, *M.L.N.* lxiii, 1948. Donne distinguishes 'simples' (containing no 'contrarieties') from compounds; in this sense only God is 'simply' good (cf. Simpson, *Essays*, pp. 29, 62), everything else being by comparison imperfect, and so a mixture of good and evil. He asserts that 'nothing is Essentially good, but God', and

'That this Essentiall goodnesse of God is so diffusive, so spreading, as that there is nothing in the world, that doth not participate of that goodnesse. . . . So that now both these propositions are true, First, That there is nothing in this world good, and then this also, That there is nothing ill' (*Sermons*, vi. 231). This is the mode of Donne's assertion in the poem also, where he uses one of the most familiar examples of the 'mixed' nature of earthly things—the paradoxical nature of the 'benefits' to mankind of Cain and Seth in relation to their respective characters; the illustration is in keeping with the other material in the poem, and might, indeed, have been intended to come more fully into the next Canto, had there been one.

ll. 518–20. 'Comparison is the only means of measuring every quality, opinion the only basis of judging it.'

Donne's thought here is quite in agreement with his mature opinions. Of Opinion he says that it is 'a middle station, betweene ignorance, and knowledge; for knowledge excludes all doubting, all hesitation; opinion does not so; but opinion excludes indifference, and equanimity' (*Sermons*, vi. 317). This world is (in terms of the previous note) relative in its nature, and one cannot 'judge' without doubting and hesitation; it is 'opinion', not 'knowledge', on which judgement must rely. 'Opinion' is, as Mr. Wendell points out, a useful and necessary activity of the mind.

The interpretation of these lines and, indeed, of the whole poem has been too much coloured by some lines (50–55) in the Elegy 'Variety', of which Donne's authorship is unlikely:

> Our liberty's revers'd, our Charter's gone,
> And we made servants to opinion, etc.

If Donne had written the Elegy it would have been in a different mood and at an earlier time. He was not, in 1601, the 'libertine' Jack Donne some writers have conjured up, but a man (by the standards of the time) of middle age, and with heavy responsibilities. His discontent seems to be at once more orthodox and more mature than some have thought.

Compare *Hamlet*, II. ii. 249–50: 'there is nothing either good or bad, but thinking makes it so'; Marston, *What You Will*, I. i, in *Plays*, ed. H. H. Wood, ii. 237: 'all that exsists, / Takes valuation from oppinion'.

Upon Mr Thomas Coryats *Crudities* (p. 46)

These verses, and the 'macaronic' quatrain which follows, are fifteenth and sixteenth among the mass of 'Panegyricke Verses upon the Author and his booke', written by all the recognized 'wits', and prefixed to *Coryat's Crudities Hastily gobbled up in five Months' travels* . . . 1611, by Thomas Coryate. Most of the introductory matter, and all the 'panegyric' verses, including Donne's, were also printed in *The Odcombian Banquet*: *Dished forth by Thomas the Coriat* . . .

1611. The lines, excluding the macaronic quatrain, were first included among Donne's collected poems in 1649. I take the title from this text, since in the *Crudities* the heading is simply *Incipit Joannes Donne*. I base my own text on that printed in the *Crudities* in 1611.

Thomas Coryate was born about 1577, the son of the Rector of Odcombe. After about three years at Oxford he joined the household of Henry, Prince of Wales, where, though a man of ability and erudition, he won a reputation as an eccentric and became (in a manner more pleasant than their verses suggest to the modern reader) the butt of the wits. In May 1608 he set out on the voyage described in the *Crudities*; and in 1616 on a later journey we hear of him in Agra. He died at Surat in the following year. His *Crudities* is so good a book that the wits were hard put to it to be funny; Donne's verses are among the best of the clod-hopping mock-panegyrics written for it. For a full account of Coryate, see M. Strachan, *The Life and Adventures of Thomas Coryate*, 1962. I refer, for the reader's convenience, to the accurate reprint of the *Crudities* (James MacLehose & Sons, 2 vols.), 1905.

John Taylor, the Water Poet, comments on and imitates Donne's verses in *Laugh and Be Fat: or, A Commentary upon the Odcombyan Banket*, 1612 (Keynes, p. 258).

l. 2. *leaven'd*: puffed up (by 'love of greatnesse') as dough by leaven.
Sesqui-superlative: 'a superlative and a half'.

l. 3. *Venice vast lake*: the Venetian Lagoon (*Crudities*, i. 303–4).
than: then.

l. 4. *Cortizan*. Coryate was much impressed by the courtesans of Venice and describes them at length (i. 401–9) 'because the name of a Cortezan of Venice is famoused over all Christendome'. In the first edition of the *Crudities* he included a picture of himself (pp. 262–3) being saluted by 'one of their nobler Cortezans'.

l. 6. *Cellar-gulfe*: the Great Tun of Heidelberg (which held as much liquid, Donne implies, as the Gulf of Venice). Coryate tells how it was shown to him by 'the Gentlemen of the Court' (ii. 218–23); he says that it held over 530 hogsheads (i.e. nearly 28,000 gallons) of wine, and was made of beams 27 feet long held together by iron hoops weighing 11,000 lb. The bung-hole was reached by stairs, and Coryate warns his readers to drink moderately while at the top of them; for otherwise, as he says, 'thou wilt scarce finde the direct way downe from the steepe ladder without a very dangerous precipitation'. Hence Donne says that in this sea of wine one could in a double sense sail to Hell through drunkenness.

l. 10. *to any end*: (1) because it is endless, 'infinite'; (2) 'to any good purpose'.

ll. 13–14. Cf. 'that which is the essence of man, Reason, and discourse, . . . those which are the properties of man onely, which are, To speak, and to laugh' (*Sermons*, i. 226). See also 'The Progress of the Soul', l. 455, and note.

l. 14. *halfe make man*: by merely arousing laughter.

l. 17. *at full, great Lunatique*. 'Lunatic': one whose whims and moods are controlled by the changeable moon (*O.E.D.* 2. a). 'When will you have written at the greatest length of which you are capable?'

l. 19. *wenne*: swelling.

l. 20. *mother-nose*: i.e. the world (which will be smaller than the extent of Coryate's travels, and smaller also than his books).

l. 22. Munster. In his 'Epistle Dedicatory' (i. 4) Coryate says that he is 'sometimes beholding to Munster for some speciall matter which neither by my owne Observations, nor by the discourse of learned men I could attaine unto'. The *Cosmographia Universalis* of Sebastian Munster (1489–1552) appeared in 1541.

Gesner. Konrad von Gesner of Zurich (1516–65) wrote *Historia Animalium* (1551–8), but it was his *Bibliotheca Universalis, sive Catalogus Omnium Scriptorum in Linguis Latina, Graeca, et Hebraica*, 1545, that showed 'Authors' as Munster's book 'did Townes'. Coryate's debt to Gesner is slight.

He pays tribute to the scholarship of Munster (ii. 229) and of Gesner (ii. 98, 111). Donne's jest is very unfair, both to the variety of Coryate's authorities and to his energy and skill in using them. He is no 'wit-pyrat' (l. 65).

l. 23. Gallo-Belgicus. See note on 'Satire IV', l. 112.

l. 24. *deepe*: profound.

States-man. The *Mercurius Gallo-belgicus* will inform him on politics and current affairs. But in his Introductory Essay on travel Coryate emphasizes the importance of travelling in foreign countries in the formation of a statesman's character.

Gazettier: a writer in a gazette, a retailer of news (*O.E.D.* 1, quoting this line). 'The *Gazetta* was a Venetian invention . . . , a compilation of current news, and is said to have been first issued in 1536'; it was circulated in manuscript (Grolier).

l. 26. Prester Jacke. Prester ('Priest') John was the name given in the Middle Ages to a mythical priest-king reigning in the extreme Orient beyond Persia. From the fifteenth century he was often identified as the Emperor of Ethiopia (cf. Munster, *Cosmographia*, edition of 1572, p. 1329); but here his name is used to suggest that the 'news' in Coryate's next work would be imaginary, as William the Conqueror's name suggests that it would be stale.

l. 29. *both Indies*: 'both the'India's of spice and Myne' ('The Sun Rising', l. 17; cf. 'The Progress of the Soul', l. 17, and note).

l. 31. *presse*: in printing so huge a book.

l. 33. *thy leaves must embrace*, etc. For this ancient jest, see note on 'Satire V', l. 85.

l. 35. *magnifies*: dignifies.

l. 41. *a better methode*: i.e. of handling and selling; the barrels and tons of merchandise are broken down into handy packages.

l. 43. *vent*: vend, sell (*O.E.D.*, vb. 3. 1).

l. 44. *thicke*: crowded (*O.E.D.* II. 4).

l. 48. *all kinde of matter*. This jest is the culmination of the long sentence beginning at l. 35. The leaves of the book might be used to wrap rich spices (l. 35), or small quantities of commoner merchandise (ll. 35–42), or (more humbly still) home-made sweets, etc., sold on stalls at village fairs; in the last case, as they lie in the heat, the leaves might be said to engender ('hatch') all the kinds of goods that people buy (hence *'omnipraegnant'*; see 'The Progress of the Soul', ll. 494–5, and note, p. 189). Thus Coryate's book can be said to 'cover' ('comprehend') or include every kind of 'matter': i.e. (1) all subjects, and (2) all sorts of goods or physical material.

l. 50. *Pandect*. The *Pandectae* or *Digesta* are the compendium of Roman common law in fifty books codified from the opinions of eminent jurists by order of the Emperor Justinian (sixth century A.D.), and by him given the force of law.

Universall Booke: like Munster's *Cosmographia Universalis* and Gesner's *Bibliotheca Universalis*, referred to in l. 22.

l. 51. *Heroes*: 'Heroës', with three syllables.

l. 53. *prize*: prey, victims. To murderers men are as ships to pirates or to an enemy, a 'prize' to be robbed and destroyed.

l. 54. *Doe publique good, cut in Anatomies*. An Act of 32 Henry VIII, cap. xlii, 1540, says that the 'misterie' of Barbers and Surgeons of London shall have the right in perpetuity to take four persons put to death for felony 'for anathomyes . . . and to make incision of the same . . . for their further and better knowledge instruction insight lerning and experience, in the said science or facultie of surgery'. The knowledge gained by these dissections was for the 'public good'; but there may also be an allusion to the yearly anatomy lecture given 'publicly' before students (cf. note to 'Love's Exchange', l. 42, in Gardner, *Elegies etc.*, p. 169).

ll. 55–58. *For a Lord*, etc. Grosart, who found these lines baffling, in fact provides the only satisfactory explanation of their meaning. He quotes Harington 'On Play': 'Where lords and great men have been disposed to play deep play, and not having money about them, have cut cards instead of counters, with asseverance (on their honours) to pay for every piece of card so lost a *portegue*'. Instead of pieces of playing-cards, fragments of the *Crudities* will be used as counters; for a large collection of gamblers playing for high stakes enough of the *Crudities* to make whole books (of ordinary size) will have to be cut up; but for a few friends, having a social game to pass the time, one leaf (in pieces) will suffice.

The 'portegue', 'portaque', or 'portuguese' was the great *crusado* of Portugal, a coin worth (according to McKerrow, Nashe, *Works*, iv. 250) about £4. 10s. 0d. 'Portescue' is not among the forms of the name given in *O.E.D.*, but, as Grierson suggests, a false etymology connecting the coin with 'escus' (crowns) might have produced it. The phrase 'casts at' troubled Chambers, who thought it should be 'casts for'; but 'casts at', i.e. casts the dice towards (winning) the coins, though forced, is not perhaps impossible.

ll. 59–60. These two lines are a digression. The words 'keepe companie' call up a picture of good companions drinking heartily to Coryate's health ('carousing him up'). 'Thou' refers to each of the friends, 'thee' to Coryate: 'No, you cannot drink bumpers to Coryate; you must limit the amount ('fit measures') to the capacity of the man you are toasting, and fill the tankards only to the half-pint mark, to match Coryate's wit.'

ll. 63–64. *shalt not ease the Critiques*, etc. The critics of the next generation will not have the convenience of being able to read your book all at once to satisfy their eager curiosity ('hunger'), because the leaves are scattered and the book is in pieces.

ll. 65–66. The metaphor is of pirates attacking a ship ('bottome') laden with wealth; the treasure of the *Crudities* will not be available to the plagiarist in any one library.

ll. 67–70. *Some leaves may paste strings*, etc. Paper was pasted over the strings used to tie the quires of a book together, usually on the spine and at front and back to conceal the strings as they entered the boards (cardboard covers). Leaves of the *Crudities* will be used for this purpose, so that in reading another author a plagiarist might come across a page of Coryate and be able to steal (but, alas, only a little) from his work.

ll. 71–72. *As* Sybils *was*, etc. The Cumaean Sibyl came to the palace of Tarquin II with nine volumes (the 'Sibylline books'), which she offered at a high price. When Tarquin refused, she burnt three, and offered the other six for the same price; when the Roman king again refused, she burnt three more, and Tarquin bought the last three for the price originally asked for the nine. The story is told, e.g., by Aulus Gellius, *Noctes Atticae*, i. 19; Dionysius of Halicarnassus, *Roman Antiquities*, iv. lxii. 1–4; Munster, *Cosmographia*, edition of 1572, p. 208. Coryate's book is as mysterious, each fragment being worth as much as the whole (i.e. nothing).

l. 74. *healths*: complimentary emotions (as expressed in drinking another's health). Donne is powerless to express so great an admiration.

In eundem Macaronicon

This quatrain was first included in a collected edition of Donne's poems (reprinted from Coryate's *Crudities*) by Chambers, ii. 290. A correspondent in *N. and Q.*, 3rd Ser. vii, 18 February 1865, offers the following translation:

As many perfect linguists as these two distichs make,
So many prudent statesmen will this book of yours produce [i.e. none].
To me the honour is sufficient of being understood; for I leave
To you the honour of being believed by no one.

Macaronicon, or 'macaronic' verse, is a form in which, strictly speaking vernacular words are inserted into a Latin context (with Latin inflexions and constructions), and the verse is made to scan. More loosely, as here, it is verse in which two or more languages are mingled.

EPIGRAMS

The twenty Epigrams are printed here in the order of *W*, the only manuscript in which all are found. Other manuscripts contain varying numbers of them, and I list at the beginning of the commentary on each epigram the manuscripts in which I have found it (omitting Harleian MS. 3991, British Museum, which has twelve of the epigrams among 'Donnes quaintest conceits', since the text is copied from an edition). The text in *1633* was taken from the editor's Group II manuscript, which had three more than surviving members of the Group (though two are found in *DC*, which is here very closely related to Group II); the order, allowing for omissions, is the same as that in *W*. I take *1633* as the copy-text for the sixteen Epigrams it contains, rejecting five readings which are editorial emendations, and three in which the edition follows Group II in error. The text of the other four epigrams is based on *W*.

Georg Rodolf Weckherlin translated or adapted six of Donne's Epigrams in his *Gaistliche und Weltliche Gedichte* (Amsterdam); cf. Keynes, p. 259. I have seen only one copy of the 1641 edition, which contains the religious poems; the *Weltliche Gedichte* were published separately in 1648, and here we find 'Leander und Hero' (p. 799), 'Niobe' (p. 799), 'An den Pfarrern Schandflecken' (translating 'A Licentious Person', p. 808), 'An Herrn K. Liebhabern der Antiquitäten' ('Antiquary', pp. 808–9), an adaptation of the word-play on 'lie' (from 'A Lame Beggar') in 'An die Schöne Marina' (p. 829) and of 'Phryne' in 'An die Ros' (pp. 825–6). Weckherlin's poems were written up to thirty-five years before their publication.

William Drummond of Hawthornden said of Donne that 'if he would, he might easily be the best Epigrammatist we have found in *English*' (*Works*, 1711, p. 226, from a manuscript written 1612–16).

Hero and Leander (p. 50)

MSS.: Group II (*A 18, N, TCC, TCD*); Group III (*O'F*); *W*; *HN*.
Miscellanies: *S 962*; Brit. Mus. MS. *Egerton 2230* (copied twice).

The point of the epigram, as J. B. Leishman has said (*The Monarch of Wit,*

5th ed., 1962, p. 54), lies in the introduction of the four elements. Cf. Sidney, *Arcadia*, Third Eclogue (in *Poems*, ed. W. A. Ringler, p. 105, ll. 67–68):

> Man oft is plag'de with aire, is burnt with fire,
> In water dround, in earth his buriall is.

The 'one fire' (l. 2) is that of mutual love.

Pyramus and Thisbe (p. 50)

MSS.: Group II (*A 18*, *N*, *TCC*, *TCD*); Group III (*Cy*, *O'F*, *O*, *P*); *W*; *HN*.
Miscellanies: *S 962*; Bodleian MS. *Malone 19*.

The punctuation of *1633* brings out the wit by which every detail of Ovid's account (*Metamorphoses*, iv. 55 ff.) is referred to in two short lines. Grierson paraphrases: 'These two, slain by themselves, by each other, by fear, and by love, are joined here in one tomb, by the friends whose cruel action in parting them brought them together here.'

Niobe (p. 50)

MSS.: Group II (*A 18*, *N*, *TCC*, *TCD*); Group III (*O'F*); *W*; *HN*.
Miscellany: *S 962*.

The point seems to be that Niobe ('all tears', cf. *Hamlet*, I. ii. 149) by paradox claims to be 'dry'. The birth of her twelve children, their death, and her own death (by being changed into a stone) have left her dry. This contradicts the usual conception of Niobe as herself weeping the trickling waters of a stream or fountain, in sorrow for her children's death.

A Burnt Ship (p. 50)

MSS.: Group II (*A 18*, *N*, *TCC*, *TCD*); Group III (*O'F*); *W*.
Miscellany: *S 962*.

The epigram does not necessarily refer to any particular incident in Donne's own experience, and, like the three preceding, it cannot be precisely dated.

There is a play on 'rescued', 'lost', and 'found' as well as on 'burning' and 'drowning'.

The final line is an alexandrine.

Fall of a Wall (p. 51)

MSS.: Group II (*A 18*, *N*, *TCC*, *TCD*); Group III (*B*, *Dob*, *O'F*); *W*; *HN*.
Miscellany: *S 962*.

Grierson thought it likely that this epigram, among others, might refer to Donne's own observations during the Cadiz expedition in 1596. R. C. Bald, however, pointed out ('Three Metaphysical Epigrams', *P.Q.* xvi, 1937) that

Stow (*Annals*, 1615, pp. 752–3) describes the fall of a wall at Corunna in 1589 that killed some English soldiers, including a Captain Sydenham, during a battle. Sir George Buc wrote an account of this incident (in MS., 1614) and also an account of the Cadiz expedition, of which he was a member; in the latter account (Stow, *Annals*, 1615, pp. 770 ff.), however, he does not mention any incident like that described in this epigram, though he could hardly have failed to remark on the coincidence had he known of it. Donne could have heard of the falling wall at Corunna at any time after the occurrence.

A Lame Begger (p. 51)

MSS.: Group II (*A 18, N, TCC, TCD*); Group III (*Dob, O'F, O, P*); *W*; *HN*.

Miscellanies: *S 962*; Brit. Mus. MS. *Egerton 2421*; Bodleian MSS. *Ashmole 47, Don. d. 58* ('In Claudipedem'), *Douce F 5* ('On a beggar & cripple'), *Sancroft 53*; St. John's Coll. Cambridge MS. *S 32* ('On a Beggar'); Corpus Christi Coll. Oxford MS. *f 328* ('On a Cripple'). On 31 March 1603 John Manningham wrote a version in his diary (Brit. Mus. Harleian MS. 5353, f. 118ʳ), apparently from memory, with the heading 'Of a beggar that lay on the ground / Dun' (ed. J. Bruce, Camden Society, 1868, p. 156).
Drummond's copy (in *HN*) runs:

> I cannot stand, nor sitt, this begger cries.
> How can this bee, if he say true, he lies. JD

It is extraordinary both that nobody seems to have thought of this jest before, and that Donne's responsibility for it should have been so clearly recognized. In matter added, however, to Thomas Deloney's *Strange Histories of Songs and Sonnets*, in the posthumous edition of 1607 (ed. J. P. Collier, Percy Society, 1841, p. 69), the epigram is appropriated and made part of another without acknowledgement. See also *Wit's Recreations*, edition of 1641, epigram no. 273, 'On a Bed-rid man'.

Cales and Guyana (p. 51)

MSS.: Group III (*O'F*); *W*.

This epigram was apparently written after the taking and sack of Cadiz in 1596. The position of the town—west of Gibraltar and near the southern extremity of the peninsula—justifies, without too great a licence, the phrase 'th'old worlds farthest end'. Heartened ('kindled') by the success of this venture, and by the 'spoyle' taken, Raleigh and Essex were eager to sail west and attack the Spanish silver fleet (but Howard, the Lord Admiral, ordered a return to England); doubtless others thought of adventuring even further west. Raleigh's account of his own voyage to Guiana was published in 1596 (cf. 'Satire IV', l. 22, and note).

Sir John Wingefield (p. 51)

MSS.: Group III (*O'F*); *W*.

John Wingfield, who was knighted in 1586, served as quartermaster of the army, attached to Essex, on the Cadiz expedition. He was the only notable Englishman (there were two others) to be killed in the capture of the town, and all accounts mention him. Thus Captain H. Price writes to Cecil (Strype, *Annals*, 1824, iv. 399): 'Sir John Wyngfield was killed with a bullet on the head after we possessed the town.'

l. 1. *th'old Pillers*: the Pillars of Hercules, the two mountains (Gibraltar or Calpe on the north, Abyla on the south) opposite each other at the western entrance of the Mediterranean, regarded as the limits of the old world, and supposed to have been parted by the arm of Hercules.

l. 2. *his throne*: the south, where he reigns in strength.

l. 3. *our Earle*: of Essex, who has given Wingfield to the soil of Cadiz, and made a new Pillar to mark the westward limit of human adventure.

l. 4. *that late Iland*: Cadiz itself; 'the island of Cales', as Capt. Price calls it (Strype, *Annals*, iv. 399). The town was built at the tip of the headland that closes the Bay of Cadiz on the west, and was connected to the mainland by a bridge (the scene of the hottest fighting in 1596).

late: either 'lately visited'; or 'on which the sun sinks last (latest)' since, as in the preceding epigram, Cadiz is, westwards, 'th'old worlds farthest end'; or both.

A Selfe Accuser (p. 52)

MSS.: Group III (*B, Dob, O'F*); *W*; *HN*.
Miscellanies: Bodleian MS. *Sancroft 53*; St. John's Coll. Cambridge MS. *S 32*.

A Licentious Person (p. 52)

MSS.: Group II (*A 18, N, TCC, TCD*); *DC*; Group III (*Dob, O'F*); *W*; *HN*.
Miscellanies: Bodleian MSS. *Don. d. 58* ('In meretricem'), *Rawl. Poet. 31* ('Of an Ould vitious man'), *Sancroft 53*; St. John's Coll. Cambridge MS. *S 32* ('On a whoremaster'); Corpus Christi Coll. Oxford MS. *f 328* ('On a licentious person').

The point of the epigram involves Ps. xl. 12 ('mine iniquities have taken hold upon me . . . : they are more than the hairs of mine head'), and the common joke about 'French crowns', i.e. heads made bald by the *morbus Gallicus*.

Francis Quarles adapts the epigram as part of one of his own (also translated by Weckherlin), in *Divine Fancies . . .* , 1632, p. 97 ('On Sinnes', Bk. ii, no. 66).

Antiquary (p. 52)

MSS.: Group II (*A 18*, *N*, *TCC*, *TCD*); *DC*; Group III (*B*, *Cy*, *Dob*, *O'F*, *O*, *P*, *S 96*); *W*; *HN*.

Miscellanies: *S 962*; *Bur* (cited by Grierson); Bodleian MS. *Malone 19*.

The epigram is based on an old joke. H. Estienne, in *L'Introduction au traité de la conformité des merveilles anciennes avec les modernes*, 1566, p. 11, as translated by R. C[arew], *A World of Wonders*, 1607, p. 22, says: 'And verily the *Savoyard* did feauly and finely, who going about to catch a sottish Antiquary, foolishly fond of such toyes, after that the fantastick had courted him a long time, in the end for a goodly aunctient monument shewed him his wife who was foure score yeares of age.'

For Hammon, or Haman, the antiquarian, see 'Satire V', l. 87 and note; he has not been identified. The antiquary is, however, a fairly obvious butt of the satirist; cf. Martial, VIII. vi, and Guilpin, *Skialetheia*, 1598, near the end of 'Satire I'.

Manliness (p. 52)

MSS.: *W*; *HN*.

The ascription of this epigram to Donne in these two manuscripts is persuasive. The title in *HN*, 'The Jughler', seems pointless, and I have adopted that suggested by R. E. Bennett, who first printed the epigram as Donne's.

Disinherited (p. 52)

MSS.: *DC*; Group III (*B*, *Cy*, *Dob*, *O'F*, *O*, *P*); *W*; *HN*.
Miscellanies: Bodleian MSS. *Malone 19*, *Sancroft 53*.

The epigram has resemblances to two of Martial's, III. x and V. xxxii.

Sir John Harington absorbed Donne's epigram into one of his own, 'Of one that vow'd to dis-inherit his son and give his goods to the poor' (*Letters and Epigrams*, ed. N. E. McClure, pp. 172–3).

The Lier (p. 53)

MSS.: Group III (*B*, *Cy*, *Dob*, *O'F*, *O*, *P*); *W*; *HN*.
Miscellanies: *Bur* (cited by Grierson); Bodleian MS. *Malone 19*.

The epigram was first published among 'Unpublished Poems of Donne', from one of the three commonplace books he used as sources, by Sir John Simeon, in *Miscellanies* of the Philobiblon Society, iii. 3, 1856 (published in 1857).

l. 3. *Nabuchadnezar*. King Nebuchadnezzar 'was driven from men, and did eat grass as oxen' (Daniel iv. 33).

l. 4. The Spanish were commonly supposed by Englishmen to live on a poor diet. Nashe writes that they are 'Good thrifty men, they draw out a dinner with sallets ... and make *Madona* Nature their best Caterer' (*Works*, i. 200). Cf. James Howell, *Familiar Letters*, ed. J. Jacobs, i. 57: 'As I pass'd between some of the *Pyreney-Hills*, I perceiv'd the poor *Labradors*, some of the Country People, live no better than brute Animals, in point of Food; for their ordinary Commons is Grass and Water.'

Mercurius Gallo-Belgicus (p. 53)

MSS.: Group II (*A 18, N, TCC, TCD*); *DC*; Group III (*B, Dob, K, O'F, S*); *W*. Miscellanies: *HK 1, S 962*.

For the *Mercurius* cf. 'Satire IV', l. 112, and note.

ll. 1–3. *Like Esops fellow-slaves*, etc. In the traditional *Life of Aesop* we read how Aesop was purchased by Xanthus. The ugly Aesop was to be sold with two handsome slaves, a musician, Liguris, and a teacher, Philocalus. Of all three Xanthus asked the question, 'What do you know how to do?' Liguris and Philocalus replied, 'Everything'; Aesop, 'Nothing at all'. 'Why', said Xanthus, 'do you say, nothing?' Aesop replied, 'Because the other two boys know everything there is'. Cf. 'Vita Aesopi' 20–25, *Aesopica*, ed. B. E. Perry, 1952, pp. 84–85.

l. 5. *Thy credit lost thy credit*: your credulousness destroys my credulity ('faith', power to believe).

ll. 5–7. *'Tis sinne*, etc. The Golden Rule (Matt. vii. 12) does not apply here; it would be sinful to believe lies.

l. 8. *Mercury*. The god Mercury was patron of thieves. His Greek name was Hermes.

Phryne (p. 53)

MSS.: Group II (*A 18, N, TCC, TCD*); *DC*; Group III (*B, Dob, O'F*); *W*; *HN*. Miscellanies: *S 962*; Corpus Christi Coll. Oxford MS. *f 328*.

In the manuscript recording Ben Jonson's conversations with him in 1619, William Drummond says that Jonson 'had' (i.e. quoted) this epigram 'oft' (Jonson, *Works*, i. 150).

The name 'Phryne' might have been suggested by the famous courtesan of that name (cf. Burton, *Anatomy*, part. 3, sect. 2, memb. 2, subsect. 2).

An Obscure Writer (p. 53)

MSS.: Group II (*A 18, N, TCC, TCD*); *DC*; Group III (*B, Dob, O'F*); *W*.

The name 'Philo' occurs in Martial, V. xlvii; no particular person is necessarily meant here.

Klockius (p. 54)

MSS.: Group II (*A 18, N, TCC, TCD*); *DC*; Group III (*B, Dob, O'F*); *W*; *HN*. Miscellanies: *Bur* (cited by Grierson); Bodleian MS. *Sancroft 53*.

The reading 'Rawlings' reported by Grierson from *Bur* is mentioned for its interest; I doubt whether it is authentic.

Raderus (p. 54)

MSS.: Group II (*A 18, N, TCC, TCD*); *DC*; Group III (*O'F*); *W*. Miscellany: *S 962*.

Matthew Rader (1561–1634), a German Jesuit, published an expurgated edition of Martial in 1602: *M. Valerii Martialis Epigrammaton Libri Omnes.* . . . Since the book was to be used in schools, Rader says (sig. *3): 'Nihil ad haec templa et sacraria sapientiae nisi castum, sanctum, integrumque aspiret; ne iuventus dum scientiam quaerit, perdat innocentiam. . . . Asterisci partem epigrammatis sublatam docent.'

In *Ignatius his Conclave* (Hayward, p. 391), Donne writes:

> He added moreover, that though *Raderus*, and others of his *Order*, did use to gelde *Poets*, and other *Authors:* (and heere I could not choose but wonder, why they have not gelded their *Vulgar Edition*, which in some places hath such obscene words as the *Hebrew* tongue, which is therefore called *Holy*, doth so much abhorre, that no obscene things can be uttered in it) . . . yet (said hee) our men doe not geld them to that purpose that the memory thereof should bee abolished.

The real reason, he says (as implied in l. 2 of the epigram), is that 'they reserve to themselves the divers formes, and the secrets and mysteries in this matter, which they finde in the *Authors* whom they geld' (p. 392).

For a similar reason, Donne says, Katherine suppressed brothels, the phrase 'for the Courts sake' being ambiguous. Preaching to a congregation at Lincoln's Inn, some of whose members probably had this epigram copied in their commonplace books, Donne (with some courage) makes the same point: 'We may have heard of Princes that have put down Stewes, and executed severe Lawes against Licentiousness; but that may have been to bring all the Licentiousness of the City into the Court' (*Sermons*, i. 256).

Grosart thought that these references were to Catherine de Medici, though on what evidence I do not know. Henry VIII prohibited the public stews on Thames-side in Southwark (Camden, *Britannia*, translated by Holland, 1610, p. 434). I can only suggest that Donne is using some old joke connecting Henry's action with one of his three Queens named Catherine.

Ralphius (p. 54)

MSS.: *DC*; Group III (*B, Dob, O'F*); *W*; *HN*.

An expanded and rewritten version of this epigram appears in St. John's Coll. Cambridge MS. *James 548*.

The broker's apparent act of sympathy is due to the shock induced by the prospect of losing, through Ralphius's possibly fatal illness, the sums of money Ralphius owes him; but Ralphius has pawned his bed also, and cannot lie on it, though ill.

VERSE LETTERS

The Storme (p. 55)

MSS.: Group I (*C 57, D, H 49, Lec, SP*); Group II (*N, TCD*); *DC*; *L 74*; Group III (*A 25, B, Cy, Dob, D 16, D 17, HN, JC, K, Lut, O'F, O, P, Q, S*); *W*.
Miscellanies: *HK 2, La, RP 117* (1), *S 962*; Brit. Mus. MS. *Harley 3511* (extracts; cf. G. Tillotson, 'The Commonplace Book of Arthur Capell', *M.L.R.* xxvii, 1932).

The text in *1633* was taken from a Group I manuscript like *C 57*. There are a few minor misprints, three of which are most probably due to misreading of the copy (cf. ll. 11, 47, 68).

In *JC (D 17), K*, and *S* the poem is said to be addressed to 'Sr. Basill Brooke', but this is clearly an error.

Christopher Brooke was one of Donne's closest friends. He was born *c.* 1570, and was admitted to Lincoln's Inn early in 1587. Donne joined him there in May 1592, and shared his chamber; he gave the bride to Donne at his clandestine marriage to Anne More in 1602 (Walton, *Lives*, p. 29), and was consequently imprisoned. Brooke was Bencher (from 1610) and Treasurer (1623–4) of Lincoln's Inn, and was elected to Parliament six times, 1604–26. He died in February 1628. See *D.N.B.*, *Sermons*, ii. 1–8, and I. A. Shapiro, 'The Mermaid Club', *M.L.R.* xlv, 1950.

After the attack on Cadiz in 1596, Philip II began to assemble a second Armada (cf. 'Satire I', l. 58, note). Queen Elizabeth therefore caused a fleet to be got ready 'to set upon the King of Spaines navie whersoever they can finde yt, or to meet with the Indian fleet' (Chamberlain, *Letters*, i. 30). It was hoped also that a foothold could be gained in the Azores (hence, the 'Islands Expedition'). With the Earl of Essex as General, Lord Thomas Howard as Vice-Admiral, and Raleigh as Rear-Admiral, the expedition of over sixty ships set sail on 5 July 1597. After two or three days, however, it was overtaken by the tremendous storm described in this poem. The fleet was much damaged, and put back to Plymouth for refitting. Donne remained with the expedition, and probably sent his poem from Plymouth before improving weather allowed the fleet to sail again on 17 August.

For the literary antecedents of this and the following poem see B. F. Nellist, 'Donne's "Storm" and "Calm" and the Descriptive Tradition', *M.L.R.*, 1964.

l. 1. *which art I*: because in friendship one soul rules two hearts, one heart dwells in two bodies. Cf. Deut. xiii. 6 ('thy friend, which is as thine own

soul'); Plato, *Symposium* 192; and Tilley F696 ('A friend is one's second self').
'Zeno Citiensis interrogatus, *quid revera esset amicus*? Respondit; *Alter ego*' (O
Casmannus, *Biographia*, 1602—a book in Donne's library—p. 210).

l. 2. *these*: these lines.

l. 4. Hilliard: Nicholas Hilliard (1547–1619), painter, jeweller, and goldsmith
to Elizabeth I and James I; he was a disciple of Holbein and won fame as a
miniature painter. Cf. Gardner, *Elegies etc.*, p. 266, and Erna Auerbach,
Nicholas Hilliard, 1961. Donne's reference to him here is quoted in the printer's
Preface in *1633*, and in Edmund Gayton's *Pleasant Notes upon Don Quixote*, 1654,
p. 35.

l. 6. *dignifi'd*. Cf. the letter 'To Mr B. B.', II, ll. 13–14.

ll. 11–12. 'For nobody can predict what Fate and Fortune intend; the path
to honour and the path to wretchedness have the same appearance.' The
sense seems to be that, while the young men think of themselves as setting
out to win honour, England, more pessimistically, sees them as setting out
to their deaths.

l. 13. *her pregnant intrailes*. It was thought that winds were caused by exhalations from the bowels of the earth. Cf. Seneca, *Quaestiones Naturales*, v. 4, and
Batman upon Bartholome, 1582, f. 158ʳ.

l. 14. *th'ayres middle marble roome*. In the old cosmology the middle region of the
air, where hail, snow, and other 'meteors' were engendered, was intensely
cold (cf. *Blundeville his Exercises*, 1594, p. 179): 'the coldest of all' (*Sermons*, vi.
308). Wind, says Donne (*Sermons*, ix. 96) 'is a mixt Meteor, to the making
whereof, diverse occasions concurre with exhalations'. Grierson notes that
Studley, in translating Seneca's tragedies, means sometimes by 'marble', not
'hard', but 'blue' (rendering 'caerulei maris', for example, as 'of marble seas');
this is a possible secondary meaning here.

ll. 15–16. *Such strong resistance*, etc. According to one theory, the exhalations of
air from the earth were thrown back from their rising course by inability to
penetrate the frozen middle region of the air. Cf. Bacon, *The . . . History of
Winds*, translated by R. G., 1653, p. 76, and Sylvester's translation of Du
Bartas, *Divine Weeks and Works*, First Week, Second Day (1605, pp. 50–51).

l. 17. *deare time did leese*: 'was losing precious time'.

l. 18. *prisoners, which lye but for fees*. They have served their time in jail, and
are detained there only because they cannot pay the jailer's fees. Cf. *Sermons*,
x. 233 ('as prisoners discharg'd of actions may lye for fees') and *Letters*,
p. 249. In later life, Walton tells us, Donne 'redeemed many from thence
[*sc.* prison] that lay for their Fees or small Debts' (*Lives*, p. 70).

ll. 19–22. Cf. Sir A. Gorges, 'A larger Relation of the . . . Iland Voyage' (*Purchas his Pilgrims*, edition of 1907, xx. 41): 'We imbarked our Army, and set
sayle about the ninth of July, and for two dayes space were accompanied with
a faire leading North-easterly wind.'

l. 22. Sara. Cf. Gen. xviii. 12, xxi. 6–7.

l. 24. *bring friends one dayes way*. This was an ancient courtesy to a departing guest. Cf. Gen. xviii. 16; 3 John 6; and *Richard II*, I. iii. 304, I. iv. 1–4.

l. 34. *did wake thee*. Cf. Jonah i. 5–6.

l. 38. *I*. The reading 'yea' in *Q* suggests that 'I' here is a spelling of 'Ay'.

l. 39. The line scans with a syllable omitted to make a dramatic pause after 'Night':

East, West, | Day, Night, | and | I could | but say.

O'F and *1633* patch in different ways.

ll. 47–48. *from graves will creepe, At the last day*. Most of the early Fathers of the Church agreed that the souls of the righteous were not admitted to the sight of God until the last day, at the time of the resurrection of their bodies. Miss Gardner suggests (*Divine Poems*, pp. 114–17) that in 1610 Donne adopted the view that the soul was, in fact, in heaven at the moment of death, rejecting the 'error' of many Fathers 'That the soule of man comes not to the presence of God, but remaines in some out-places till the Resurrection of the body' (*Sermons*, vi. 266). The text for this Sermon shows that 'graves' is right (*1633*, *Cy*, 'grave'): 'all that are in the graves shall hear his voice, And shall come forth' (John v. 28–29).

ll. 49–50. *doe heare so, Like jealous husbands*, etc. Cf. Paradox 6 (Keynes, *Paradoxes and Problems*, p. 20): 'that *ridling humour of Jealousie*, which seekes and would not finde, which requires and repents his knowledge'. Grierson quotes Ovid, *Amores*, II. ii. 51–60 (e.g. 'Viderit ipse licet, credet tamen ipse neganti').

l. 52. *feare away*: frighten away.

l. 53. *There*: i.e. from their position on the hatches.

l. 54. *Wast*: amidships. The waist was the part of the ship between forecastle and quarter-deck, where the deck-curve was lowest and the water was slow to flow off (hence 'clog'd', l. 55).

ll. 55–56. For the 'Simpsonian' rhyme, cf. note on 'Satire I', l. 8.

l. 57. *totterd*: tattered (as in Dekker, *A Knight's Conjuring*, 1607, H4ʳ: 'their tottered soules, patcht out with nothing but rags').

l. 58. *one hang'd in chaines*. Nicholas Breton speaks of 'murtherers' who 'hang in iron chaines' (*A Mad World my Masters*, etc., ed. U. Kentish-Wright, 1929, i. 121). Cf. 'The Bracelet', l. 95; Middleton, *The Phoenix*, I. iv. 223–5; and Jonson, *The Masque of Queens*, ll. 179–82.

ll. 59–60. *Even our Ordinance . . . Strive to breake loose*. In his *Relation* of the voyage, Essex writes (*Purchas his Pilgrims*, edition of 1907, xx. 25) that two masts cracked on his ship, and 'her very timbers and maine beames with her labouring did tear like lathes; so as we looked hourely when the Orlope [the lowest deck, above the hold] would fall, and the Ordnance sinke downe to the keele.' See E. M. Tenison, *Elizabethan England*, x (1953), pp. 229, 232–4, 261.

'Strive' is correct; the word 'ordinance' (= ordnance) was used as a plural (*O.E.D.*).

l. 66. *lightsome*: cheerful, without pain or care (*O.E.D.* 2).

Bermuda. Raleigh (*Discovery of Bermuda*, 1596, p. 96) calls 'the *Bermudas* a hellish sea for thunder, lightning, and stormes'. Cf. 'the still-vex'd Bermoothes' of *The Tempest*, I. ii. 229.

l. 67. *Darknesse, lights elder brother*. Cf. Simpson, *Essays*, p. 19: 'We must . . . end with this, *That this Beginning was, and before it, Nothing*. It is elder then darknesse, which is elder then light; And was before Confusion, which is elder then Order, by how much the universall Chaos preceded forms and distinctions.'

l. 69. *none can be*. All things are reduced (in the darkness) to one thing, and that thing cannot be anything (i.e. is 'none', nothing) because a uniform lack of form ('deformity') covers all the forms of things; all is reduced again to the first Chaos, and even light, God's first creation, has been withdrawn 'to heaven' whence it came.

For the use of 'none' to mean 'nothing', cf. 'A Nocturnal upon St. Lucy's Day', l. 37: 'I am None'.

l. 71. *Another* Fiat. The process of Creation, which began with the words *Fiat Lux* (Gen. i. 3), will have to be repeated. John Manningham notes (from memory) in his Diary, 31 March 1603: 'It was soe darke a storme, that a man could never looke for day, unles God would have said againe *Fiat Lux*' (ed. J. Bruce, 1868, p. 154).

Dekker quotes from this passage in *A Knight's Conjuring*, 1607, B2ʳ, as 'the wordes of so rare an *English Spirit*'; and Vaughan uses the lines in 'The Charnel-house', ll. 1–4 (*Works*, ed. L. C. Martin, 2nd ed. 1957, p. 41).

The Calme (p. 57)

MSS.: Group I (*C 57, D, H 49, Lec, SP*); Group II (*N, TCD*); *DC*; *L 74*; Group III (*A 25, B, Cy, Dob, D 16, D 17, JC, K, Lut, O'F, O, P, Q, S*).

Miscellanies: *D 54, HK 2, RP 117* (1), *S 962*; Brit. Mus. MS. *Harley 3511* (extracts).

In *1633* there is a good text, from a manuscript like *C 57*. I change only one of its readings, in l. 21.

After setting out for the second time on the 'Islands Expedition', the English fleet was divided. Essex was delayed in reaching Finisterre, the first rendezvous, and Raleigh went on to the second, Lisbon. Hearing that a Spanish flotilla had sailed from Ferrol to the Azores (the information, as it turned out, being false), Essex set off in pursuit, sending word to Raleigh to follow.

Arriving at Terceira, Essex found no treasure-fleet, and cruised off Corvo awaiting Raleigh's squadron. Essex does not mention being seriously becalmed in his account of the voyage, though his ships experienced some periods of calm lasting a few hours. Gorges, who was with Raleigh's ships, does, however, mention a calm after having 'made the Ile called the Tercera' (*Purchas his Pilgrims*, edition of 1907, xx. 65–66). The ship, or (it may have been) troop-transport ('fly-boat'), on which Donne was sailing was apparently behind Gorges, since he and his comrades were still 'seeking' the Azores (ll. 9–10). He does not seem to have been with Essex, since by this time the General and his squadron knew that there were no Spanish ships about, whereas Donne is with those becalmed, and irked by not being able to make contact with 'sought foes' (l. 21). Any part of the squadrons of the fleet could have been described as 'left' (l. 21), at some stage or other, by any other part during the voyaging to the Azores. Cf. R. C. Bald, 'Donne's Letters', *T.L.S.*, 24 October 1952.

The poem may perhaps have been addressed, as in the Grolier Club edition, to Christopher Brooke, like 'The Storm'; but it is not so headed in any manuscript or previous edition. The only manuscripts to expand the title are *DC* ('The Calme in the same voyage'); *B, RP 117* ('A Calme described'); and *D 54* ('A Calme by M^r. JOHN DVNNE').

l. 2. *stupid*: without consciousness or feeling (*O.E.D.* 2), torpid.

nothing it, doth swage: nothing assuages the miseries of the calm (as the calm itself had assuaged those of the storm).

ll. 3–4. *The fable is inverted*, etc. In one of the fables attributed to Aesop (*Der Lateinische Äsop des Romulus*, ed. G. Thiele, no. xxvii) the frogs ask Zeus for a king, and he throws a log ('blocke') into their pond. Awed at first, they come to despise the motionless log, and importune Zeus for another king. Angry at their insistence, he sends them a water-snake, which quickly devours them. The change (by the thirteenth century) in some forms of the fable from water-snake to stork is discussed by Eric Jacobsen ('The Fable is Inverted . . .', *Classica et Mediaevalia*, xiii. fasc. 1, Copenhagen, 1952; Miss Gardner kindly referred me to this article). The vernacular versions of Donne's youth had the familiar stork (cf. T. W. Baldwin, *William Shakspere's Small Latine and Lesse Greeke*, 1944, i. 511).

Donne's image is only superficially appropriate, and involves a pun on 'blocke': the calm, in which the ship lies like a motionless log ('blocke'), is harder to bear than the storm (which is in the place of the stork), and is also a 'blocke' to the ship's progress.

l. 12. *a fir'd Church*. The roofs of most churches in England (and sometimes their steeples) were covered with lead (see P. Hentzner, *Itinerary*, translated by R. Bentley, 1889, pp. 15–16). The steeple of St. Paul's was 'fiered by Lightning' on 4 June 1561 (Stow, *Survey of London*, ed. Kingsford, i. 331);

accounts mention the melting of lead from the roof (e.g. *The true Report* of the incident, 1561, reprinted in *Archaeologia*, xi, 1794); but the sight was no doubt fairly common.

l. 14. *Like courts removing*. 'When the hangings and the furniture are taken downe, it is a token that the King and the Court are remooving' (G. Goodman, *The Fall of Man*, 1616, p. 383). Jonson borrows Donne's line in *The New Inn*, IV. iv. 252, also l. 247. The juxtaposition of 'Court' and 'playes' has an edge to it; cf. the letters to Wotton, 'Here's no more newes', ll. 19–21, and 'Sir, more then kisses', ll. 23–24.

l. 15. *The fighting place*: not required for fighting, since no enemy could approach in the calm; and so used for drying clothing, etc. The 'fighting-place' was presumably (as Grosart suggests) the 'place' between foremast and mainmast closed off during battle by 'close-fights' or 'close-quarters'. These (*O.E.D.*) were stout wooden gratings put up as a protection against boarding parties; the area was the main centre of hand-to-hand fighting.

l. 16. *frippery*: a second-hand clothes shop.

l. 17. *No use of lanthornes*. The flagship, or 'Admiral', carried at night a lantern high on the stern, by which following ships of the squadron steered. Essex writes that he missed Raleigh 'with thirty sailes that in the night followed his light' (*Purchas his Pilgrims*, edition of 1907, xx. 27). In the calm there was no fear of the ships' losing one another, even in the dark.

l. 18. *Feathers and dust*. William Drummond wrote that Jonson 'esteemeth John Done the first poet in the World in some things his verses of the Lost Chaine, he heth by Heart & that passage of the calme, that dust and feathers doe not stirr, all was so quiet' (Jonson, *Works*, i. 135).

ll. 19–20. Cf. Bacon, *The . . . History of Winds*, translated by R. G., 1653, p. 88: 'many windes are engendred in the lowest Region of the Aire, and breathe out of the earth, besides those which are throwne down and beaten back' from 'the cold of the middle Region'. The 'upper valt of aire' was completely calm because no movement of air could penetrate the 'middle Region'. Cf. 'The Storm', ll. 13–16, and notes (p. 204). Donne means here that all movement of the air of every kind has ceased.

l. 21. *left*. The weight of manuscript evidence favours this reading, for which 'lost' is an easily made error. In some instances the word might have been changed to 'lost' to produce the easy antithesis 'lost'—'sought' which, I think, Donne was at pains to avoid. Cf. *O.E.D.*, 'left', ppl. a. I.

l. 22. *meteorlike*. Cf. 'you hange betweene Heaven and Earth, like *Meteors*' (*Pseudo-Martyr*, p. 128). Wind itself was a meteor, one of the phenomena of the lowest region of the air. Donne means here 'we are poised between friend and foe'.

l. 23. *Calenture*: a frequently mentioned fever suffered by sailors in the Tropics, in which, from desire of seeing land, the delirious victim takes the sea for green fields and tries to jump into it.

l. 28. *walkers in hot Ovens*. Cf. 'Satire III', ll. 23–24, and note (p. 142).

l. 29. *these*: the 'great fishes' of l. 24; sharks.

l. 30. *our brimstone Bath*: perhaps 'Hell'. I suspect, however, that the phrase should be taken literally, and that it refers to hot, stinging sulphur baths, used to prevent or cure venereal disease. For this treatment, cf. Chapman, *The Widow's Tears*, I. ii. 32–34. I cannot find evidence, however, that any of the large quantities of brimstone (e.g. '400 weight', *Acts of the Privy Council*, 23 August 1588) delivered to the fleet was used for this purpose.

l. 32. *parboyl'd*: referring to cooking by 'partly boiling' and then completing the process by baking or broiling over 'coales'.

l. 33. Bajazet *encag'd, the shepheards scoffe*. In Marlowe's *Tamburlaine*, Part I, IV. ii, Tamburlaine, the Scythian shepherd, has the conquered Emperor of the Turks, Bajazeth, locked in a cage and brought before him to be mocked.

l. 34. Sampson, *his haire off*. Cf. Samson's words in Judges xvi. 17: 'If I be shaven, then my strength will go from me, and I shall become weak'. The caged Bajazeth and the shaven Samson, like the becalmed ships, indicate majestic power rendered useless and contemptible.

ll. 35–36. *as a Miriade Of Ants*, etc. Suetonius, *Life of Tiberius*, Ch. 72, tells how the pet snake of Tiberius was eaten by ants; the Emperor saw in this a warning of the power of the people, and turned back from his proposed entry into Rome. Here the point is that galleys rowed by many persons (like ants) might successfully destroy greater things, and royal possessions at that.

l. 37. *crawling Gallies, Sea-gaoles, finny chips*. Galleys, usually confined to the Mediterranean, are thought of as contemptible and un-English. They 'crawl' because propelled by oars; they are 'gaols' because they are rowed by chained prisoners; they are like 'chips' because relatively small; they are 'finny' because the oars protrude and act like fins.

finny. Cf. 'The Progress of the Soul', ll. 227–8 ('to rowe It selfe with finnie oares'), and Herrick, 'His tears to Thamasis', l. 11 ('with Finnie-Ore').

l. 38. *brave*: defy.

Venices. The ships are as motionless as cities rising out of the sea like Venice; and are now also like bed-ridden patients in their helplessness.

In *B*, *Lut*, and *O'F* the reading 'Venices', found in all other manuscripts, is sophisticated to 'Pinnaces', a reading adopted by Grierson. But pinnaces were light small boats used for exploring creeks, etc., and cannot be the type of large vessel obviously meant here.

l. 40. *disuse*: unaccustom, find relief.

ll. 43–46. Compare 'Love's War', ll. 17–28.

l. 44. *A desperate*: a desperado, careless of death.

l. 47. *grudges us all*: begrudges us all we desire.

l. 48. *forget*. This is the Group I reading, superior to the alternatives. Donne is making a general statement about the customary workings of Fate: 'Fate denies us our wishes and cunningly devises miseries too out-of-the-way to enter our minds as possibilities as we pray.' He goes on to give the particular application: who would have remembered to pray for more *wind* after experiencing the storm just passed? 'Forgot' suggests that the calm is just an isolated caprice of fate; it does not fit the sequence of tenses; and it is more likely that a scribe would misread or alter 'forget' than the reverse.

ll. 51 ff. *What are wee then?* etc. The same cluster of ideas is found in *Sermons*, iii. 97, where Donne discusses the question of personal identity ('The *specification* of Creatures'). He mentions the old 'case' of a man eaten by a fish (cf. ll. 23–24 above) which is then eaten by another man; he asks his hearers to go further, and imagine themselves not assimilated, but

annihilated, become nothing, canst thou chuse but thinke God as perfect now, at least as he was at first, and can hee not as easily make thee up againe of nothing, as he made thee of nothing at first? *Recogita quid fueris, antequam esses;* Thinke over thy selfe; what wast thou before thou wast any thing? *Meminisses utique, si fuisses;* If thou hadst been any thing then, surely thou wouldst remember it now. *Qui non eras, factus es; Cum iterum non eris, fies;* Thou that wast once nothing, wast made this that thou art now; and when thou shalt be nothing againe, thou shalt be made better then thou art yet.

Donne refers to Tertullian, and is quoting a passage from *Apol. adv. Gentes* (Migne, *P.L.* i. 591) beginning, 'Considera temet ipsum, o homo'.

l. 54. *it*. The pronoun has no precise antecedent: perhaps, 'what we are' (l. 51), or more exactly, what we might be. Luck, or our own weakness or sin, always spoils the harmony and order of our lives.

l. 55. *will . . . power*. This order is better supported than that in Group I and *1633*, and is perhaps more logical, making an anticlimax—'will', 'power', 'sense'. Cf. 'To Mr B. B.' II, l. 8: 'Not my will only but power doth withhold.'

To Mr T. W. (p. 59)

MSS.: Group II (*A 18*, *N*, *TCC*, *TCD*); *DC*; Group III (*B*, *Cy*, *Dob*, *K*, *Lut*, *O'F*, *O*, *P*, *S*, *S 96*); *W*.

Miscellanies: *D 54*, *E 22* (fragments), *HK 1*; the Farmer-Chetham MS. (Chetham Society Reprint, 1st Ser. lxxxix–xc, ed. A. B. Grosart, 1873, pp. 108–9).

In *1633* the text is taken from a Group II manuscript, which it follows in three errors (ll. 16, 23, 29). The 'I' in the title in *1633* comes from the 'J' in Group II and *DC*; this in turn (like the 'F' in *K*) seems to be a misreading of

'T' (found in *W*, *O*, *P*, *S*, and *HK*). The copies in *B*, *Cy*, and *D 54* are untitled, and in *S 96* the title 'Ad amicum' has been supplied.

The uncertainty about the identity of 'T. W.' felt by the scribes of *Dob*, *Lut*, and *O'F* persists. Grosart suggested that he was a member of the Woodward family, and this is very probable. Rowland Woodward had a brother Thomas, christened on 16 July 1576 (see M. C. Deas, 'A Note on Rowland Woodward, the Friend of Donne', *R.E.S.* vii, 1931). Another Thomas Woodward, possibly a kinsman, was admitted (as a gentleman, from Buckinghamshire) to Lincoln's Inn on 8 October 1597; he had just left Cambridge. I have not been able to identify 'T. W.' positively.

l. 2. *hath or shall enkindle*. Donne frequently couples auxiliaries requiring different dependent parts of the main verb, using only the dependent part required by the second auxiliary; cf. l. 5 below.

l. 3. *what*: all that.

l. 4. *Wit and Art*: frequently coupled in the literature of the time. 'Wit' is part of 'what nature gave', native ability; 'Art' is what is gained by training (technique, skill). Cf. 'Satire IV', l. 238.

ll. 9–10. *Men say*, etc. Cf. Tilley E177: 'Better be envied than pitied.' The proverb derives ultimately from Pindar, *Pythian Odes*, i. 163.

ll. 10–11. *envy'd . . . envie*: usually accented on the second syllable, as in 'To his Mistress going to Bed', l. 11; Shakespeare, Sonnet 128, l. 5; etc.

ll. 13–16. *I, that ever was*, etc. 'In contrast with you, furnished as you are with the artistic graces you have learned in the school of the Muses, I have always been without the gifts of Nature, and a beggar in respect of the gifts of Fortune; now, by receiving these verses from you, I am made a fool ['zanee', l. 30] as well.' He has always been plain and poor; now he is shown up as a fool by his friend's superior poetic gifts.

The syntax is slovenly, and the confusion in the manuscripts and in the mind of the editor of *1633* (who tried emendation) is understandable. Grierson departed from the arrangement of the brackets in *1633*, but returned to the (unemended) *1633* text in his one-volume edition of Donne's poems in 1929.

ll. 14–15. *Natures . . . Fortunes gifts . . . grace*. Donne is playing rather clumsily upon the ancient distinction of the gifts of Nature from the gifts of Fortune and the gifts of Grace (detailed, for example, in Chaucer's *The Parson's Tale*, x. 450). The bodily gifts of Nature (e.g. strength, beauty) a 'monster' lacks; the gifts of Fortune (e.g. wealth, kinsmen, friends) a 'begger' lacks; the gifts of Grace (e.g. knowledge) a 'foole' lacks.

l. 15. *Before*: in front of, juxtaposed to, and hence 'compared with'.

l. 16. The line has eleven syllables. See note on 'Satire I', l. 28.

now. Grierson thought it possible that the reference here is to Donne's marriage and consequent disgrace early in 1602. The evidence of style, how-ever, makes it practically certain that, like others in the sequence (which it begins in the authoritative MS. *W*), it was written about eight years earlier. I take 'now' to mean 'on receipt of your poem'.

l. 18. *easie waxen*: easily impressed, easily influenced.

l. 20. *suspect*: suspicion. Donne elsewhere uses verbal forms as nouns, e.g. 'show . . . resist' ('The Progress of the Soul', ll. 418–19).

  surquedrie: O.E.D., 'surquidry' = arrogance, presumption.

l. 24. *writ by thee*. Cf. Ralph Brideoak's contribution to *Jonsonus Virbius*, l. 60: 'None but *thyselfe* could *write* a *verse* for *thee*' (Jonson, *Works*, xi. 468).

l. 26. *The Painters bad god*, etc. I do not know whether there is a particular allusion here. Cf. Tilley P27: 'A good painter can draw a devil as well as an angel.'

ll. 27–28. If you overlook the rhymes as you read, this song will seem like good prose.

l. 30. *foyle*: setting off your brilliance by contrast.

  zanee: an imitative clown, usually an ineffective or burlesque imitator. Grierson quotes Jonson, *Every Man out of his Humour*, IV. ii. 44–45: 'Hee's like the *Zani*, to a tumbler, / That tries tricks after him, to make men laugh' (*Works*, iii. 532).

  In *W* this letter is followed by one addressed to Donne, presumably by T. W., and part of an exchange of such poems:

> To Mr J. D.
>   Thou sendst me prose & rimes, I send for those
> Lynes, wᶜ beeing nether, seeme or verse or prose.
> They'are lame & harsh, & haue no heat at all
> But what thy liberall beams on them let fall.
> The nimble fyer wᶜ in thy brayne doth dwell
> Is it yᵗ fyre of heaven or yᵗ of hell.
> It doth beget & comfort like hevens ey
> And like hells fyer it burnes eternally.
> And those whom in thy fury & iudgment
> Thy verse shall skourge like hell it will torment.
> Haue mercy on me & my sinfull Muse
> Wᶜ rub'd & tickled wᵗʰ thyne could not chuse
> But spend some of her pithe & yeild to bee
> One in yᵗ chaste & mistique tribadree.
> Bassaes adultery no fruit did leaue,
> Nor theirs wᶜ their swolne thighs did nimbly weaue,
> And wᵗ new armes & mouthes embrace & kis
> Though they had issue was not like to this.
> Thy Muse, Oh strange & holy Lecheree
> Beeing a Mayd still, gott this Song on mee.

Copies of the poem, detached from Donne's, are found in *B*, *Lut*, *O'F*, *O*, *P*, *S 96* and *HK 1* (in *O*, *P* it is copied twice).

To Mr T. W. (p. 60)

MSS.: Group II (*A 18, N, TCC, TCD*); *DC*; Group III (*Lut, O'F*); *W*.

The title and text in *1633* are taken from Group II. I have not followed the edition in indenting alternate lines.

The reference to serious plague in ll. 11–12 suggests a date in or after August 1592, in which month, after about nine years without alarm, plague was reported in London, growing more serious daily; the danger lasted into 1594.

l. 6. Omitted from most copies of the poem because of blasphemy. The poet is the Creator, the poem his son who pleads for him. The analogy, of course, breaks down as soon as it has begun, since God's Son is not God's Saviour and does not plead for his Father with a third party. The passage is interesting, however, as a first (disastrous) attempt at a daring type of compliment perfected later, especially in the verse letters to great ladies.

Saviour. Pronounced here with three syllables.

ll. 7–8. *all questions . . . of the place and paines of hell.* The subject was hotly contested. Cf. *Sermons*, i. 165, v. 265–6, vii. 137; and Burton, *Anatomy*, part. 2, sect. 2, memb. 3.

l. 9. *hell is but privation.* 'Privation of the presence of God, is Hell' (*Sermons*, i. 186; cf. also vii. 366).

l. 13. *Live I or die.* In the one case his verses will be pledges ('pawnes') of his friendship; if he dies, however, as is possible in a plague-ridden city, they will be his last will ('Testament').

To Mr T. W. (p. 61)

MSS.: Group II (*A 18, N, TCC, TCD*); *DC*; Group III (*Lut, O'F*); *A 23, W*.

The text and title in *1633* are taken from a Group II manuscript, from which it varies in two places (ll. 5, 7). I reject both readings of the edition, but Grierson accepts the second.

This and the next poem are couched in the warmly affectionate terms of the religion of friendship. T. W. has not written, and his silence has 'killed' the poet (l. 8). Now he has written protesting his love, and his 'poore starveling' has revived. But (ll. 12–14) T. W.'s protestations of love are like those of gluttons, who declare that they love what in fact they destroy. T. W.'s love is killing Donne.

To Mr T. W. (p. 62)

MSS.: Group I (*D, H 49, SP*); Group II (*A 18, N, TCC, TCD*); *DC*; Group III (*B, Dob, Lut, O'F, O, S 96*); *A 23, W*.

Miscellanies: *HK 1, S 962, TCD* (2); *A 34* (on a separate sheet in folio, containing also the Lincoln's Inn 'Epithalamion'); *RP 116* (Bodleian MS. Rawl. Poet. 116).

The editor of *1633* followed his Group II manuscript even in running on this letter (without title) from the preceding without a break. The Group II manuscripts and *DC* agree in this arrangement.

Only *W* has the address 'To Mr T. W.'; the closely similar fragment, *A 23*, has 'M. T. W.' The copies in *B*, *TCD* (2) and *S 962* are untitled; in *O* and *RP 116* the poem begins 'Madam / At once . . . '. The Group I title is 'An Old Letter'; *A 34*, *HK*, *S 96*, and *O'F* head it simply '(A) Letter', to which *Lut* adds 'Incerto' and *Dob* 'Incog.'

l. 2. *my soft still walks*. 'Most pleasant it is at first, to such as are melancholy given . . . to walk alone in some solitary grove' (Burton, *Anatomy*, part. 1, sect. 2, memb. 2, subsect. 6).

my Heart: my friend T. W., the 'child of Art'.

l. 3. *the Nurse . . . of Art*: i.e. leisure. Grierson quotes in support of this suggestion Aristotle, *Metaphysics* A 981[b] (translated by W. D. Ross): 'Hence when all such inventions were already established, the sciences which do not aim at giving pleasure or at the necessities of life were discovered, and first in the places where men first began to have leisure. This is why the mathematical arts were founded in Egypt; for there the priestly caste was allowed to be at leisure.'

ll. 7–9. The poet's happy verse will see T. W.; for want of that sight he himself languishes and is dying. His 'Melancholy' is that of the neglected lover; cf. L. Babb, *The Elizabethan Malady*, 1951, p. 182. Like the previous poem, this one has the tone of Shakespeare's sonnets to the 'fair friend'.

l. 12. *bare Sacrament*. In legal usage the *sacramentum* was a pledge which each of the parties deposited or became bound for before beginning a suit (*O.E.D.*, 'sacrament', 5); it is 'bare' by contrast with a coloured 'Picture'. 'Take my poem as a portrait of myself or as an unadorned pledge of my love.'

To Mr R. W. (p. 62)

MSS.: *A 23*, *W*.

A correspondent in *N. and Q.*, Ser. III, vii (1865), 439, thought to be Revd. T. R. O'Flaherty, first suggested that 'R. W.' stood for Rowland Woodward. Since *W* (on which my text is based) is in Woodward's handwriting and there is no other early copy save that in the closely related fragment in *A 23*, this identification is convincing.

Rowland Woodward, born in London in 1573, was admitted to Lincoln's Inn in January 1591. He served with Wotton in Venice 1605–7 and was 'placed' with the Bishop of London from 1608. In 1630 he became Deputy to the Master of Ceremonies, and died in 1636–7. In later life he was a protégé of the Earl of Westmorland; the manuscript *W*, and a copy of *Pseudo-Martyr* given by Donne to Woodward, were preserved in the Library of successive Earls. See M. C. Deas, in *R.E.S.* vii, 1931.

l. 4. *Like fyer*: similar poetic inspiration.

Muse: here taking the place of the soul in the trinity of elements that make 'all thee' (l. 1); cf. ll. 8–9 of the following letter.

l. 5. Are you recovering from sickness, or keeping out of the way of infection (perhaps by the plague, 1592–4)?

l. 9. *devout*: devoted to her task.

To Mr R. W. (p. 63)

MSS.: *A 23*, *W*.

See the introductory note to the preceding letter.

l. 2. *distempered*: put out of 'temper', disordered, disturbed.

If R. W.'s mind can affect Donne's mind, he should not be surprised that it can affect his own body (l. 1).

ll. 7–8. *a Lay Mans Genius doth controule Body and mind*. The 'layman' is contrasted with the poet, being excluded from the Muse's mysteries. As the Muse controls the poet, so their Genius controls ordinary men.

The 'Genius' was a tutelary spirit supposed to be allotted to a man at birth, which governed his fortune, determined his character, and conducted him from the world (*O.E.D.*, I).

l. 12. *soveraigne*: like a 'sovereign remedy', of supreme power (to 'charm' and 'cure').

To Mr C. B. (p. 63)

MSS.: Group II (*A 18*, *N*, *TCC*, *TCD*); *DC*; Group III (*Lut*, *O'F*); *A 23*, *W*.

The text in *1633* is taken from the editor's Group II manuscript. It contained one erroneous reading (l. 10) which, like Grierson, I reject.

The letter is almost certainly addressed to Christopher Brooke, on whom see the introductory note to 'The Storm' (p. 203).

The vocabulary of the poem comes from the conventional Petrarchan stock: 'Saint of his affection', 'complaine', 'amorous paine', 'martyr', 'scalding sighes', 'Ice . . . which walls her heart', and the like. Donne here takes the trouble to achieve a genuine sonnet. There is no indication of the date or occasion of its composition.

l. 2. *inexcusable*: from which he cannot be excused.

l. 4. *both wants*: the absence of both of you.

l. 11. *wonne*: dwell.

To Mr E. G. (p. 64)

MS.: *W*.

Gosse, who first printed this letter from *W*, suggested that E. G. was Everard Guilpin (author of *Skialetheia*, mentioned in the introductory note to 'Satire I', pp. 116–17). R. E. Bennett (*R.E.S.* xv, 1939) and P. J. Finkelpearl (*R.E.S.*, N.S. xiv, 1963) have since put the identification beyond reasonable doubt. Guilpin entered Emmanuel College, Cambridge, on 1 June 1588, and Gray's Inn in April 1591. On his father's death, early in 1591, he shared with his mother the inheritance of his father's house in Highgate (whence he could be said to 'oversee' London, l. 5). He was connected with the Guilpins of Suffolk; he found his wife in that county and is last heard of as residing there (in 1608). Guilpin's interest in the theatre is evident in *Skialetheia*.

Donne's poem seems to refer to a time of plague in London, doubtless the serious visitation from August 1592 until 1594; his correspondent has retired to Suffolk. The suggestions of spring and early summer in the last lines would not be appropriate to the period of plague in 1592. The reference to the satirist's 'spleene' in l. 11 might be the self-conscious remark of a newly fledged writer of satire, and this I suppose Donne to have been in 1593. The early summer of 1593 seems a likely date for the composition of this letter.

In the State Papers (James I, vol. cxlv, 17 May 1623) there is a poem written out and signed by Donne's friend Sir Henry Goodyer, sent to Prince Charles through his Secretary, Sir Edward Conway; it versifies a passage from one of Donne's prose letters to Goodyer, and begins:

> As lame things thirst for their perfection, soe
> These raw conceptions towards our Sunn doe goe.

See S. Johnson, 'Sir Henry Goodere and Donne's Letters', *M.L.N.* lxiii, 1948.

l. 2. *slimy rimes*. The reference is to the engendering of creatures from slime by the sun's heat. Cf. 'Satire IV', ll. 18–19, and note, p. 150; and *The Return from Parnassus*, Part II, l. 151: 'Slymy rimes, as thick as flies in the sunne'.

l. 6. *overseene*: 'imprudent, rash'; or perhaps, 'overlooked, disregarded'.

l. 8. *Our Theaters*. For Donne's interest in the theatre see V. Harris, 'John Donne and the Theatre', *P.Q.* xli, 1962. In Bodleian MS. *Tanner 306* there is a single sheet bearing a verse letter by Sir William Cornwallis, the essayist, 'To my ever to be respeckted freand Mr John Done Secretary to my Lorde Keeper'; lines 15–16 read:

> If then for change, of howers you seem careles
> Agree wth me to loose them at the playes.

l. 17. *Russian Marchants*: members of the Muscovy Company, who accumulate stocks imported from Russia while the sea is navigable, and spend the winter retailing them in England when the seas are frozen. Cf. T. S. Willan, *The Early History of the Russia Company, 1553–1603*, 1956, pp. 49–56, etc.

l. 18. *retaile it here abroad*: distribute it from the central store for sale.

To Mr R. W. (p. 64)

MSS.: Group II (*A 18, N, TCC, TCD*); *DC*; Group III (*Lut, O'F*); *W*. Miscellanies: Brit. Mus. MSS. *Add. 25303* and (its copy) *21433*.

   The text in *1633* avoids two errors made in surviving Group II manuscripts, and the Group II manuscript used by the editor might have been in these places superior. The edition has, however, a unique reading in l. 22, which I reject as an error or an editorial 'correction'. I follow *1633* in grouping the lines into two stanzas of 14 lines and a quatrain, but not in the indentation of alternate lines.

   The occasion and date of this letter were, I believe, satisfactorily determined by R. C. Bald (*H.L.Q.* xv, 1952). Donne is away from London, the centre of 'newes' (l. 15). The abrupt reference to 'Havens' seems to have a literal (though it also develops a figurative) meaning, and could best apply in Donne's experience (as far as we know) to Plymouth—the haven to which the battered fleet returned after the great storm had interrupted the Islands Expedition. Guiana (l. 4) attracted much interest after the appearance in 1596 of Raleigh's account of his voyage there in the previous year. In 1596, too, Lawrence Keymis made a second voyage to Guiana, and published a *Relation* of it in October. Raleigh had meantime sent out the pinnace *Wat* to Guiana, and the small vessel returned on 2 July 1597 to Plymouth, amongst the ships assembled to begin the Islands Expedition. When the fleet returned after the storm (cf. the introductory note to 'The Storm', p. 203) to refit, Essex and Raleigh went to London to try to persuade the Queen to let them attack the Spanish colonies across the Atlantic; but Elizabeth refused, causing much disappointment throughout the fleet. The ships might otherwise have been 'Angels' bringing 'sterne threatnings' to the Spaniards and the Gospel to the natives (ll. 16–17). Raleigh, like the Spaniards in respect of their own conquests, brought forward the missionary motive as one justification for colonizing Guiana; Donne's image in ll. 20–21 seems at once to comprise this motive and the Queen's unwillingness to put the adventure in hand. In l. 22 he sounds the same note of urgency as Keymis in his *Relation* and Chapman in the poem (*De Guiana: Carmen Epicum*) prefixed to it. An expedition to Guiana was generally thought to be a proper sequel to the Cadiz Expedition; see the epigram 'Cales and Guyana' and the note upon it (p. 198). The 'businesse' of l. 23 would then be the attacks on Spain and on fleets near it, achieved at Cadiz and projected in the Islands Voyage; when these are finished with, 'hopes' (l. 26) of colonizing Guiana can perhaps again be entertained. The word 'slumber' in the first line would refer to weariness, frustrated hope, and the boring inactivity of waiting for the fleet to sail again.

If this interpretation is correct, the poem belongs to early August 1597. It is doubtless addressed to Rowland Woodward, on whom see the prefatory note to the letter 'Zealously my Muse', pp. 214–15.

l. 3. *brother*. Morpheus, god of sleep, had many brothers, and the 'brethren' of *W* seems to be an emendation to correct an apparent lapse in Donne's mythological lore. But only two of Morpheus's brothers had the power to assume and to give dream-shapes, and of these Phantasus took inanimate forms. Donne must therefore mean Phobetor, or Icelus, who assumed the shapes of other animals as Morpheus assumed those of men. Cf. Ovid, *Metamorphoses*, xi. 635–41.

ll. 7–8. *deed of gift . . . Will*: two methods of freely conveying property, one when the donor is alive, the other after death.

ll. 9–10. *retyrings . . . wise melancholy*. According to one theory (arising mainly from discussions of Aristotle, *Problemata*, xxx. 1), melancholy, wisely controlled, can make men of letters and contemplative people happy and truly blessed; cf. L. Babb, *The Elizabethan Malady*, 1951, pp. 58 ff. This is not the Galenist theory of melancholy, as a humour run to excess (as in the Letter to Lady Carey, ll. 25–27). Woodward's 'retyrings' are the normal rewarding state of a contemplative man, not the morbid symptom of an 'unnatural' or corrupt melancholy.

l. 13. *Patient*: sufferer.

l. 20. *the Jewes guide*: Moses. Cf. Num. xx. 12, Deut. xxxiv. 1–5.

l. 22. *punishment and sinne*. Donne is fond of this phrase, doubtless because (as he says also in other places) 'when we consider *Caines* words in that originall tongue in which God spake, we cannot tell whether the words be, My punishment is greater then can be born; or, My sin is greater then can be forgiven' (*Letters*, p. 9). Cf. Gen. iv. 13.

l. 23. *these . . . businesse*. The use of the singular form of the noun with plural meaning is normal. Cf. 'Idle, and discoursing men, that were not much affected, how businesse went, so they might talke of them' (*Sermons*, iv. 182).

l. 27. *all th' All*: the whole universe. Cf. Sylvester's *Bartas His Divine Weeks and Works*, 1605, p. 2: 'But all this *All* did once (of nought) begin.'
 smoake away: referring to the destruction of the world by fire.

l. 28. *an India*: a source of priceless benefits, usually material (as in 'Satire I', l. 58), but here, spiritual.

ll. 29–31. If the correspondence of the microcosm (Man) to the macrocosm is valid, there must be something to correspond with all material benefits (the world's wealth), and in good men this is virtue.

ll. 31–32. *our formes form and our soules soule*. Donne refers to the Aristotelian theory that the soul is the 'form' of the body—that by which the body has life, activity, and individuality. Cf. *De Anima*, ii, 414ª; and Aquinas, *S.T.*, Iª pars, q. lxxvi, art. I. Paradoxically, says Donne, the soul itself has a 'form' or 'soul' which gives it effective life—virtue. In 'Goodfriday', ll. 1–10, the 'Soules forme' is 'devotion'.

To Mr R. W. (p. 66)

MS.: *W*.

This letter is a sonnet, built on the conceit of the four elements (like the epigram 'Hero and Leander').

l. 1. The scansion seems to be:

/ / × / × / × / × ×
Kindly'I | envy | thy Songs | perfec | tion.

For the pronunciation of 'envy' cf. 'To Mr T. W.' ('All haile sweet Poët'), ll. 10–11, and note, p. 211.

l. 6. *it*: 'Griefe' = tears = the element of water.

l. 12. The line is intentionally 'lame':

/ × × / / × × / × ×
Which as a | lame Ec | cho of | thine doth | rebound.

l. 14. *thy creature*: R. W.'s poem.

To Mr S. B. (p. 66)

MSS.: Group II (*A 18*, *N*, *TCC*, *TCD*); *DC*; Group III (*Lut*, *O'F*); *W*. Miscellany: Harvard Coll. MS. *Eng. 686*.

The text in *1633* is taken from a Group II manuscript. I accept an obvious correction of errors made in all surviving manuscripts in l. 12.

'S. B.' is almost certainly Samuel Brooke, younger brother of Christopher. Born about 1575, he took his M.A. from Cambridge in 1598, was ordained in 1599, and was Chaplain of Trinity College, Cambridge, 1600–15. He performed Donne's marriage to Anne More, and was consequently imprisoned. This entailed no lasting disgrace, and Brooke became a Royal Chaplain; in 1618 he was admitted to Lincoln's Inn, his brother Christopher being a Bencher and Summer Reader, and Donne Divinity Reader. He became Master of Trinity, Cambridge, in 1629, and died in September 1631, four months after becoming Archdeacon of Coventry. For a full biography see J. S. G. Bolton's edition of one of Brooke's three Latin plays, *Melanthe* (Yale Studies in English, lxxix, 1928).

This letter probably belongs to 1592 or 1593. The tone is appropriate to the occasion: the sending of a verse letter to a younger brother of a close friend, a talented undergraduate ('of good hope') recently entered in the Faculty of Arts. R. C. Bald (*H.L.Q.* xv. 285) suggests that the 'Scismatiques' were the Harvey brothers, whose war with Nashe was then at its hottest, and that Donne is warning Brooke not to become a supporter of Gabriel Harvey, or of his theories.

The first eight lines are based on the two meanings of 'travail'—'labour' and 'travel'.

l. 10. *Scismatiques*: pronounced with an accent on the first syllable.

To Mr I. L. (p. 67)

MSS.: Group II (*A 18, N, TCC, TCD*); *DC*; Group III (*Lut, O'F*); *W*.

The text in *1633* is that of Group II.

The identity of I. L. or J. L. is unknown. He was probably an Inns-of-Court man, or a University man, or both; but the registers list nobody identifiable as Donne's correspondent. He was certainly recently married, and had gone to live on a good estate north of the Trent.

l. 4. *Po, Sequan, or Danubie*. This could refer only to Henry Wotton, among Donne's close friends. He was abroad in 1589–94, making fairly lengthy visits to Padua, Paris, Vienna, and Prague; he could thus be said to 'drinke' from the Po, Seine, and Danube rivers. He was obviously still abroad when the poem was written.

l. 6. *Lethe*: the river of forgetfulness in the underworld. The river Trent fulfils this function when I. L. crosses it on his way home. 'It is not a lake of Lethe, that makes us forget our friends, but it is the lack of good messengers' (Sir John Harington, writing from Kelston, Somerset, in 1600; *Letters and Epigrams*, ed. N. E. McClure, 1930, p. 79).

To Mr B. B. (p. 67)

MSS.: Group II (*A 18, N, TCC, TCD*); *DC*; Group III (*Lut, O'F*); *W*. Miscellany: *HK 1*.

In *1633* these sonnets are printed as one poem from a Group II manuscript; an error was made in II. 5 in setting up the type.

'B. B.' is not certainly known. R. C. Bald (*H.L.Q.* xv. 284) suggested a very likely identification with Beaupré Bell, son of Sir Robert Bell. He was admitted to Emmanuel College, Cambridge, in 1587, graduated B.A. in 1591, and M.A. (from Queens' College) in 1594; he went straight on to Lincoln's Inn, joining Donne there in May 1594. He was buried at Outwell, Norfolk, on 27 August 1638. We know of no definite connexion of Bell with Donne, but nobody else of whom we know anything at all in this period fits the circumstances, and Bell fits them perfectly. He is very probably the man who stayed on at the University to take a higher degree after his contemporaries left for the Inns of Court.

I regard this 'letter' as two separate sonnets, which were lent by the recipient to be copied together, and have stayed together ever since. If it is to

Bell, the first poem must have been written before May 1594, but probably not long before, since it seems that the poet expected his friend to 'begin soone' the study of the law. The second poem is possibly only a little later in date.

I

l. 4. *spirits and their Quintessence*. The 'spirits' of metals are their essence, extracted by the alchemist by distillation, etc. The 'quintessence' (*O.E.D.* 1) is matter purged of all impurities and mortality which could be extracted from all substances. B. B. derives from the subjects of his Arts course the essential and lasting matter.

l. 6. *the rest*: your friends.

l. 8. *immense vast volumes*. Cf. 'Satire II', ll. 88, 112.

l. 12. *Giddy*: foolish (*O.E.D.* 1).

II

l. 4. *widowhed*. For the spelling cf. 'A Litany', l. 108: 'call chast widowhead Virginitie'.

ll. 5–8. The colon after 'selfe' (l. 6) is from *W*. To take 'the cause being in me' with 'divorc'd' is to make the phrase merely repeat 'because I'am cold', and to leave the meaning of ll. 7–8 vague. What Donne says is rather: 'My Muse divorced me because I am cold (lack interest in writing); since the cause of the divorce was, and remains, in myself, I am unwilling, and therefore unable, to marry a second Muse (which would, in any case, in the eyes of the Church, be bigamy).' 'The cause being in me' is an absolute construction; the clause 'That I . . . Bigamye' is the object of 'withhold'.

ll. 10–11. *Mother . . . matter, . . . forme . . . Father*. In Plato's *Timaeus* (50 d–51 a) the 'mother' is the invisible formless stuff of creation which receives all 'forms', that are imposed by the 'father' (or creator, 37 c). The 'mother' was identified with the Aristotelian 'matter'; cf. Ficino, *Comment. in Convivio Platonis*, II. vii (*Opera*, 1576, ii. 1326), 'quoniam mater apud Physicos materia est'.

l. 14. *Bishoped*: confirmed by a Bishop.

To Mr I. L. (p. 68)

MSS.: Group II (*A 18, N, TCC, TCD*); *DC*; Group III (*Lut, O'F*); *W*.

The text of *1633* comes from a Group II manuscript, which, like all surviving manuscripts except *W*, omitted ll. 11–12. The address to 'M. I. P.' might have been found in the manuscript used by the printer, since *DC* (closely similar here to Group II) has 'To Mr J. P.' The rest of the Group II manuscripts and *W*, however, have 'To M. J. L.' (in *Lut, O'F* misread as 'Mr

T. L.'); there is no doubt that it is the same I. L. or J. L. to whom a previous letter was addressed.

This letter to him seems later than the other, in which contact is being made after a long silence; here the friends are so much in touch with each other that Donne's mistress has gone to I. L.'s estate for a visit. R. C. Bald (*H.L.Q.* xv. 286) has shown that this poem belongs almost certainly to August 1594. Stow (*Annals*, 1601, p. 1278), writing of 1594, says:

> This yeere in the month of May, fell many great showres of raine, but in the moneths of June and July, much more: for it commonly rained everie day, or night, till S. James day, and two daies after togither most extreamly, all which, notwithstanding in the moneth of August there followed a faire harvest, but in the moneth of September fel great raines, which raised high waters . . .

This is the only year of those in which Donne might plausibly have written this letter which was marked by prolonged absence of the sun (l. 3), followed by a spell of hot weather in which it was feared that the plague might revive (l. 6); this 'threat' passed in September, when the sun ceased to 'rage'.

l. 2. *My Sun*: my mistress.

ll. 11–12. These lines appear only in *W*. They were perhaps suppressed elsewhere because of the suggestion of blasphemy. The 'Paradise' where joy is complete is Heaven; 'save' has therefore a religious connotation.

l. 16. *when thee list*: when it pleases you (to cut or lop them).

l. 20. *Thy Sonne ne'r Ward*: because then I. L. would be dead and his son a minor. Grierson quotes the will (ii, p. cxxxiii), 1595–6, of William Roe; he leaves a large sum for the purchase of the wardship of his eldest son 'that his utter spoyle (as muche as in them is) maie be prevented' (Somerset House, P. C. C., Drake 62). For a solemn warning as to the perils of wardship, see *Advice to his Son*, by Henry Percy, 9th Earl of Northumberland, ed. G. B. Harrison, 1930, pp. 51–52.

l. 22. *As*: according as, in the degree that.

To Mr Rowland Woodward (p. 69)

MSS.: Group I (*C 57, D, H 49, Lec, SP*); Group II (*A 18, N, TCC, TCD*); DC *L 74*; Group III (*B, Cy, Dob, D 17, JC, K, Lut, O'F, O, P, S, S 96*); *W*. Miscellany: *H 40*.

The editor of *1633* returned to his Group I manuscript for the text of this poem. I reject only two of his readings (ll. 26, 31), which have no manuscript support. In essentials this is the text of Group II and *W* also. The Group III manuscripts (except *B*, and *H 40*) derive from a different copy, the main variants in which (ll. 3, 14, 33) are scribal 'corrections', or glosses absorbed into the text.

All copies of the letter are addressed to Woodward or 'To Mr R. W.', except those in the four Group II manuscripts, in *O*, *P*, *K* (untitled, but in *K* there is a running title 'Dalla Corte'), and in *JC*, *D 17*, and *H 40* ('A Letter'). The title in *B* is 'A Letter of Doctor Dunne to one that desired some of his papers'.

The poem was apparently written in response to a request for copies of other poems by Donne from his friend Rowland Woodward (on whom see the introductory note to the letter 'To Mr R. W.', p. 214). It is found in so many manuscripts of all groups together with 'The Storm', 'The Calm', and the two letters to Wotton that immediately follow here, or with one or more of these poems, that its date is probably close to theirs. From l. 10 to the end the style resembles that in these letters to Wotton; but the early part of the poem is rather in the style of the short letters of 1592–5, and hence this letter might in date also be preliminary to those written to Wotton. The scribe of *K* is, however, probably right in associating it with others written 'from Court'. I think 1597 a likely date.

l. 2. *to*. The Group II manuscripts (with *DC* and *L 74*) and *W* read 'to a'; the evidence of the manuscripts is thus evenly balanced. It is true that the 'a' could easily have been dropped (as in 'Crucifying', l. 8, in *La Corona*), and that Donne is fond of using the article in this way before an abstract noun (e.g. 'a . . . fallownesse' in l. 3, and 'out of a retirednesse', *Sermons*, ii. 228). Nevertheless the reading of *1633* (and Groups I and III) makes a distinction between the permanence and genuineness of the nun's commitment, and the affectation of a similar state by the poet's Muse, whose 'fallownesse' is a phase (as in all farming, l. 31).

l. 3. *a . . . fallownesse*: a period of fallowness (unproductiveness).

ll. 5–6. The farming metaphors continue. The 'love-song weeds' were, for the most part, the Elegies, Donne's 'book' of which was by now completed. There is a suggestion that he had finished with the 'thorns' of satire, and proposed a period of fallowness here also; perhaps he had completed 'Satire IV' and intended it to be his last (the fifth being called forth by a special occasion later).

l. 9. *Omissions of good, ill*, etc. Cf. 'the devill doth not only suffer but provoke us to some things naturally good, upon condition that we shall omit some other more necessary and more obligatory. And this is his greatest subtilty; because herein we have the deceitfull comfort of having done well, and can very hardly spie our errour because it is but an insensible omission, and no accusing act' (*Letters*, pp. 49–50).

l. 11. *faithfull*: accurate.

l. 12. *vanity*: the pursuit of vain or trivial things.

l. 14. *deare*: dearly bought, precious.
honestie: righteousness.

l. 15. *as native puritie*: as if we were born without (Original) sin. Faith and righteousness are imputed to us by God as cancellation of the sin of Adam that stains our soul's 'first white'. Cf. Rom. iv. 22–25, v. 12–21, etc.

ll. 16–19. The only true virtue is Religion. Wisdom, courage, temperance, and justice, the pagan virtues, are mere names which anyone can have who does not lack the discretion to cover up his vices. Let us then seek to know ourselves as we truly are, and not as we appear.

l. 16. *no Vertue, but Religion*. Grierson cites St. Augustine, *De Civ. Dei*, xix. 25: 'Quod non possint ibi verae esse virtutes, ubi non est vera religio' (Migne, *P.L.* xli. 656).

l. 17. *Wise, valiant, sober, just. Prudentia, fortitudo, temperantia, justitia*: the cardinal virtues propounded by Plato, *Phaedo* 68, by Aristotle and the Schoolmen.

l. 19. *Seeke wee then our selves in our selves*. 'I had rather understand my selfe well in my selfe, then in Cicero' (Montaigne, *Essays*, translated by Florio; Tudor Translations, 1893, iii. 338–9). 'No study is so necessary as to know our selves' (*Sermons*, ix. 257).

l. 22. *if wee into our selves will turne*. Cf. St. Augustine, *De Vera Religione*, xxxix. 72: 'Noli foras ire, in teipsum redi; in interiore homine habitat veritas' (Migne, *P.L.* xxxiv. 154).

l. 23. *outburne*: burn out, burn away. (The *O.E.D.* records only intransitive uses.)

l. 26. *oyle*: the liquid form of a metal or other substance made by an alchemist.
  Soule: the spiritual, pure, lively, or 'virtuous' part of any substance.
  Simples: substances composed of one constituent throughout.

l. 27. Constant heat is recommended for the processes of extraction, separation, and infusion involved in alchemical experiments, horse-dung being a frequent means of providing it. Paracelsus writes (*Hermetic and Alchemical Writings*, translated by A. E. Waite, 1894, ii. 15) that when the metal has been reduced to liquid the 'chymist' must 'add to one part of this oil two parts of fresh *aqua forti*, and when it is enclosed in glass of the best quality, set it in horse-dung for a month'.

l. 28. *So workes retirednesse in us*. In retirement virtue can be infused into our lives as the 'virtue' of medicinal simples into harder substances. Cf. 'To Mr R. W.' ('If, as mine is'), ll. 9–10, and note, p. 218; and *Letters*, p. 48: 'The primitive Monkes were excusable in their retirings and enclosures of themselves: for even of them every one cultivated his own garden and orchard, that is, his soul and body, by meditation, and manufactures.'

l. 31. *farmers of our selves*. 'Farmer' is used in the sense 'a cultivator of land which he does not own'; for we are not our own, but God's. The reading 'termers' in *1633*, though possible, seems to be a mistake. 'Termer' means 'one who holds for a term', but the phrase 'termer of oneself' is clumsy. What is needed is a word that carries on the metaphor of cultivation, farmers' work (as in 'stocke', 'uplay', 'manure'). See Philo Judaeus on 'soul-gardening', *De Agricultura*, Chs. v ff.

ll. 32–33. *uplay . . . treasure*. 'Lay up for yourselves treasures in heaven' (Matt. vi. 20).

l. 33. *the great rent day*: the Day of Judgement, when we render account of the stewardship of our talents (Matt. xxv. 19–31, etc.). Grierson quotes Benlowes, who writes of the soul (*Theophila's Love-Sacrifice*, II. lxxiii; *The Caroline Poets*, ed. Saintsbury, i. 351):

> She, her own farmer, stock'd from Heav'n, is bent
> To thrive; care 'bout the pay-day's spent.
> Strange! She alone is farmer, farm, and stock, and rent.

. 34. *to thy selfe be' approv'd*. Grierson quotes Epictetus, *Discourses* (Arrian), ii. 18, 19 (*The Golden Sayings*, translated by H. Crossley, 1903, p. 67): 'Resolve, now if never before, to approve thyself to thyself; resolve to show thyself fair in God's sight; long to be pure with thine own pure self and God.'

l. 35. *vaine outward things*. Cf. l. 12, and note.

To Sir Henry Wotton (p. 71)

MSS.: Group I (*C 57, D, H 49, Lec, SP*); Group II (*A 18, N, TCC, TCD*); *DC*;
Group III (*A 25, B, Cy, D 17, HN, JC, K, Lut, O'F, O, P, S, S 96*); *W*.
Miscellanies: *D 54, HK 2* (ll. 1–48), *La, S 962*.

The text in *1633* follows the editor's Group I manuscript. I reject (though Grierson accepted) a reading in which this manuscript was in error (l. 47), two readings in which the edition has only accidental support (ll. 12, 18), and three in which it has no manuscript support (ll. 11, 22, 44).

Henry Wotton (1568–1639) went up to New College, Oxford, from Winchester College, in 1584. He had transferred to Hart Hall by the time Donne arrived there in October 1584, and became his friend (Walton, *Lives*, pp. 15, 106). We do not know whether they were associated at any time during Wotton's first trip abroad, 1589–94, referred to in ll. 65–68, and presumably in 'To Mr I. L.' ('Of that short Roll'), l. 4; but Wotton, who entered the Middle Temple in 1595, and became a secretary of Essex, went (like Donne) with the Earl on the Cadiz and Islands expeditions.

The poem seems to belong to 1597 or early 1598, when Wotton and Donne were securing positions at Court. Grierson adduces evidence of its approximate date in 'Bacon's Poem *The World* . . . ', *M.L.R.* vi, 1911 (reprinted in *Essays and Addresses*, 1940). It is part of a literary debate among some of the wits associated with Essex: 'Which kind of life is best, that at Court, that in the City, or that in the Country'. There was a copy of Bacon's contribution, 'The World' ('The world's a bubble', etc.), among Wotton's papers, signed 'Fra. Lord Bacon' (printed in *Reliquiae Wottonianae*, 1651); and Donne certainly had a copy, since he echoes Bacon's lines (notably in ll. 19–20). Wotton's contribution (found, e.g., in *O*, *P* and *B*, and headed in *B*: 'To J: D: from M^r H: W:') begins: 'Worthie Sir: / Tis not a coate of gray or Shepheards life'. Another contributor was Thomas Bastard, who has in his book *Chrestoleros* an epigram (Bk. ii. 4, p. 29) 'Ad Henricum Wottonum' referring to the debate. It is this last poem that gives us a relevant date, since Bastard's book was entered in the Stationers' Register in April 1598.

The debate derives ultimately from two epigrams in the *Greek Anthology* which were paraphrased by Nicholas Grimald in *Tottel's Miscellany*, 1557, and again in Puttenham's *Art of English Poesy*, 1589 (ed. G. D. Willcock and A. Walker, 1936, pp. 205–6). The topic was much discussed in the Renaissance; it appears in *As You Like It*, in Guevara's *The Praise and Happiness of the Country-Life* (as Henry Vaughan called his translation, *Works*, ed. L. C. Martin, 1957, pp. 121 ff.), etc. Donne refers to it in 'Love's Usury', ll. 14–15, and in 'The Canonization', ll. 43–44.

The manuscripts have the *1633* title (*S* adding 'Knight'), with the following exceptions: *B*, *HN*, *W* ('To Mr H. W.'), *DC* ('To Sr H. W. many yeares since'), *A 25* ('Letters'), *S 962* ('A Letter'); *O*, *P*, *D 54* and *HK* have no title.

l. 1. *kisses . . . mingle Soules*. For this idea, descending from an epigram in the *Greek Anthology* ascribed to Plato, see the note on 'The Expiration', ll. 1–2, in Gardner, *Elegies etc.*, p. 159, and cf. Castiglione, p. 315: 'Chaste lovers covet a kisse, as a coupling of soules together. And therefore Plato the devine lover saith, that in kissing, his soule came as farre as his lippes to depart out of the bodie.'

letters mingle Soules. Cf. St. Ambrose, *Epistolae* (Migne, *P.L.* xvi. 1151), speaking of letters, 'in quibus etiam cum amico miscemus animum, et mentem ei nostram infundimus'. James Howell refers to this idea, *Familiar Letters*, ed. J. Jacobs, 1892, i. 13, 28.

l. 2. *ease controules*: 'easing' or 'relief' (of loneliness, or strain) 'modifies' (my boredom).

l. 4. *ideate*: form an idea of. Cf. 'that forme of a State which *Plato* Ideated' (*Pseudo-Martyr*, p. 4); 'the Ideating of this world, which was from everlasting' (Simpson, *Essays*, p. 63).

l. 5. *wither in one day*. Cf. Ps. xxxvii. 2, ciii. 15. The Vulgate in the latter place (= Ps. cii. 15) has 'foenum' ('hay') for the *A.V.* 'grass'.

l. 6. *bottle*: bundle (Old Fr., 'botteau'). Cf. Bottom's desire for 'a bottle of hay' (*A Midsummer Night's Dream*, iv. i. 30).

locke: tuft (as in 'lock of hair').

l. 8. *Remoraes*. The Remora was a small sucking-fish which, fastening on to the rudder or keel, was supposed to be able to stop a ship. Cf. Pliny, *Nat. Hist.* ix. 79, xxxii. 1; many references are collected by C. Camden, 'Spenser's "Little Fish that men call Remora" ', *Rice Institute Pamphlets*, xliv. 1, 1957.

l. 10. Cf. Tilley, P358: 'He that touches pitch shall be defiled' (Ecclus. xiii. 1).

l. 11. *even line*: Equator. It is 'even' because it is 'the *Aequinoctiall line*, / Whiche doth declare the dayes and nightes, of equal length and time' (Palingenius, *Zodiac of Life*, translated by Googe, ed. R. Tuve, p. 205); but also because it is midway between the Poles (*O.E.D.* 11, 'a just mean between two extremes'). In *1633* 'even' is replaced by 'raging'; the appropriate meanings of 'even' were obsolescent, and the word was perhaps not understood (or approved of) by the editor.

l. 12. *adverse*: opposite to each other; also, perhaps, 'hostile' (to one pining under them).

Poles. The plural is needed if there are to be two temperate regions (l. 13). It is, of course, impossible to be under two poles at once, but (as in 'The Calm', l. 50) the meaning 'under either of the poles' emerges without strain.

The phrase is 'under the Poles' because in the old cosmology they are the termini, not of the earth's axis, but of the heavens'; 'For the North and Southern Pole, are the invariable terms of that Axis whereon the heavens do move' (Browne, *Vulgar Errors*, vi. 7). Grierson quotes Ovid, *Epist. ex Ponto*, 11. vii. 64: 'Tristior ista / Terra sub ambobus non iacet ulla polis.'

l. 15. Donne handles the same ideas in a long passage in *Letters*, pp. 62–64. Cf. note to ll. 60–61 below.

l. 17. *Can dung and garlike be'a perfume?* 'Can we make a sweet scent from two unpleasant ones (and isn't it just as useless trying to blend into a pleasant combination the blaze of the Court and the chillness of the Country to make a City life)?' We might have a better chance with dung alone: 'if, as Paracelsus encourageth, Ordure makes the best Musk, and from the most fetid substances may be drawn the most odoriferous Essences' (Browne, *Vulgar Errors*, iii. 26).

l. 18. *Scorpion and Torpedo*. The point, as in l. 17, is the impossibility of mingling two harmful things to produce a beneficial thing. Hence 'and' is right here, as in l. 17, and *1633* and *C 57* have joined Group III in error. By itself, in fact, the scorpion, at least, *could* cure a man; it was a commonplace that 'To a man smitten of ye scorpion, ashes of scorpions burnt, dronke in wine, is remedy' (*Batman upon Bartholome*, 1582, f. 381^r).

The torpedo, numb-fish, or cramp-fish caused numbness or cramp on contact with a man. Cf. the 'Elegy upon Prince Henry', l. 30.

ll. 19–20. *Cities are worst*, etc. The 'knottie riddle' is that Court and Country could each also be called the 'worst'. Cf. Bacon's 'The World', ll. 15–16 (N. Ault, *Elizabethan Lyrics*, 3rd ed., 1949, p. 248):

> And where's a city from all vice so free,
> But may be termed the worst of all the three?

l. 22. *no such*: no such people (they are like walking dead).

l. 23. *Courts are Theaters.* Cf. the following letter to Wotton, ll. 20–21.

ll. 25–26.   *The Country is a desert, where no good,*
                    Gain'd (as habits, not borne,) is understood.

The crabbed and ambiguous syntax in these lines has given trouble to
copyists and editors from the first. Donne is using the terms of Aquinas, who
says that virtue is a good habit, attributed to reason (hence to 'understanding') (*S.T.*, Iª pars, II, q. lv, art. 3); it is not inborn. On the other hand,
original sin is a habit inborn because of our corrupt origin (Iª pars, II, q.
lxxxii, art. 1).

   In the country the good which men achieve (for it is not inborn, and they
must achieve it by the use of reason) is not recognized for what it is, so much
does living in the country dull the understanding. Hence men there become
as beasts, but are liable to sin even more than they (l. 27), because, though
beasts lack the understanding needed to develop virtue, they also lack the inborn habit of original sin (and so 'sinne not', and have a 'white integritie'
which men lack, ll. 41–42).

   I have adopted from Grierson the parenthesis which brings out the meaning
of the better authenticated text. In some Group III manuscripts attempts
(due to misunderstanding) have been made to 'improve' the lines, to account
for (supposedly) two sorts of 'good', that acquired as habits, and that
inborn; the emendations were adopted in *1635*, and still have their defenders
(see J. V. Hagopian, 'Some Cruxes in Donne's Poetry', *N. and Q.* ccii, 1957,
p. 501).

l. 28. *blockes*: logs, dullards.

ll. 29–33. *As in the first Chaos,* etc. Before the Creation matter was without
form and the four elements were mixed and confused; the Gloss on Gen. i. 2
says that they did not have their proper accidental qualities till they were
made distinct elements on the third day. The idea that the elements 'originate
from one another, and each of them exists potentially in each' derives from
Aristotle, *Meteorologica*, I. 3 (339ª⁻ᵇ).

   In the moral sphere pride, lust, and covetousness are 'elemental' (being
three of the deadly sins); they are typical, respectively, of Country, Court,
and City, yet, in the chaotic moral state of modern life, each is equally in all
three places (cf. l. 20). The more complex sins that issue from the mixture of
these three are monstrous, resulting from an 'incestuous' union between
closely related beings.

l. 34. *denizon'd*: naturalized. A 'denizen' was a person not native to a country,
but allowed to enter and reside, with the rights of a citizen. Falsehood was not
originally part of life at any of the 'three places' (l. 32).

ll. 39–40. *For in best understandings,* etc. Cf. 'God made this whole world in such
an uniformity, . . . as that it was an Instrument, perfectly in tune: we may say,

the trebles, the highest strings were disordered first; the best understandings, Angels and Men, put this instrument out of tune' (*Sermons*, ii. 170).

ll. 41–42. *wretched wee Are beasts*. Man, having reason and moral understanding,
is worse than the beasts if by the uncontrolled activity of the irrational part
of his nature, which he has in common with the beasts, he sins and debases
himself. Cf.

> when the purest Understandings of all, The Angels, fell . . . ; when *Lucifer* was
> tumbled downe . . . then he tried upon them, who were next to him in Dignity, upon
> Man. . . . So he overthrew man. . . . Ever since this fall, man is so far from affecting
> higher places, then his nature is capable of, that he is still groveling upon the
> ground, and participates, and imitates, and expresses more of the nature of the Beast
> then of his owne. There is no creature but man that degenerates willingly from his
> naturall Dignity; Those degrees of goodnesse, which God imprinted in them at first,
> they preserve still . . . ; we are not onely inferior to the Beasts, and under their
> annoyance, but we are our selves become Beasts . . . (*Sermons*, ix. 372–6).

l. 44. *looke for themselves*: seek their true natures as men. Donne's thought
turns to the Stoic belief that only through self-knowledge could the irrational
parts of man's nature, the passions, etc., be subdued and virtue attained. Cf.
'To Mr Rowland Woodward', l. 19, and note, p. 224.

l. 45. *strangers*: including the meaning 'foreigners' ('Italian', l. 46).

l. 46. *Utopian*. Donne's use of the adjective (referring to his ancestor's *Utopia*)
is quite modern: 'ideally nurtured and trained'.

old. There is a pun on two senses: (1) 'when older', (2) 'completely', 'plentifully'.

Italian: degenerate in morals and manners; after the proverb, 'Inglese
italianato è un diavolo incarnato'.

l. 47. *in thy selfe dwell*. 'For as every Man is a little World, so every man is his
owne House, and dwels in himselfe; And in this *House God* dwells too' (*Sermons*,
vi. 251). 'Respue quod non es . . . tecum habita' (Persius, *Sat*. iv. 52).

l. 48. *Inne*: lodge, sojourn, as at an inn; opposed to dwelling in one's home.
Thus Donne says that vices 'Inne not, but dwell in me' (*Letters*, p. 80).

continuance maketh hell. To 'continue' in any one place (Country, City,
Court) is to be restricted by its values, hence by its vices—the reward for
sharing which is Hell.

l. 49. *the snaile*: 'a Stoicke, because he carries all whatsoever hee hath on his
backe' (*A Strange Metamorphosis of Man*, 1634, ed. D. C. Allen, 1949, p. 45).

l. 50. *still*: always. Cf. 'Eclogue' before the Somerset 'Epithalamion', ll. 71–
72: 'so is hee still at home / That doth, abroad, to honest actions come'.

ll. 59–62. *Galenist . . . chymiques*. The followers of Claudius Galenus (second
century A.D.) believed that illness was caused by disturbance in the correct
proportions of 'humours' (hot, cold, moist, dry); they therefore used remedies
that had qualities contrary to the humour that was excessive, so that they

would be 'correctives' of the balance of humours. The 'chymiques' or 'chemists' (especially Paracelsus, 1493–1541) acted on a theory like that held in relation to the purifying of metals, etc.: each illness had an essence or 'spiritual seed', which could be 'purged' from the body by an antagonistic remedy prepared by 'extraction'. There is a long discussion of the two schools of medicine in *Letters*, pp. 97–98. Cf. 'The Cross', l. 27, and Burton, *Anatomy*, part. 2, sect. 5, memb. 1, subsect. 3.

Wotton is advised here not to try to compound a balanced life by mingling the (evil) qualities of Court and Country, but rather to live a life purged of all evil.

l. 59. An alexandrine, as l. 24 above. See note (p. 168) to 'Satire V', l. 56.

l. 60. *Courts hot ambitions*. Cf. 'Obsequies to the Lord Harrington', ll. 24–25.

l. 61. *Countries dulnesse*: 'the barbarousnesse and insipid dulnesse of the Country' (*Letters*, p. 63).

ll. 65–66. These 'national characteristics' were commonplaces. Cf. Francis Osborn, *Advice to a Son*, 1656, p. 68: 'the externall *Levity* of France, *Pride* of Spaine, and *Treachery* of Italy'.

l. 70. DONNE. Apparently nobody could resist the pun. The Benchers of Lincoln's Inn (11 February 1622) solemnly recorded in the Black Books (ed. 1898, p. 229) that Donne had been made Dean of St. Paul's, 'by reason whereof he cannot conveniently supply the place of publick Preacher of God's Word in this House, as formerly he hath Donne'.

To Sir Henry Wotton (p. 73)

MSS.: Group I (*C 57, D, H 49, Lec, SP*); Group II (*A 18, N, TCC, TCD*); *DC*; *L 74*; Group III (*B, Cy, Dob, D 17, HN, JC, K, Lut, O'F, O, P, S, S 96; W*). Miscellanies: *D 54, HK 1, S 962*.

The editor of *1633* used the good text of this letter in his Group I manuscript.

L 74, Lut, and *O'F* have the Group I title; *S* adds 'from yᵉ Court' and *HK* 'from Court'; *B* has 'A Letter to Sʳ Henry Wooton' and *Cy* prefixes to these words 'From Courte'. The normal Group II title is 'J.' (or 'Jo') 'D: to Mʳ H: W.'; *DC* has only 'To Mʳ. H. W.' In *K, O, P*, and *S 962* the title is merely 'From' (or 'From the') 'Court'; *JC* (*D 17*) has 'Another Letter'; and *D 54*, where it is without title, has 'By Mr. John Dunne'.

A more informative heading is found in *W* and *HN*: 'To Mʳ H. W. 20 July (Jul. *HN*) 1598 (15098 *W*) At Court'. There is no reason to doubt the correctness of this date.

l. 1. 'There is no more news here than there is virtue.'

l. 2. *Cales, or St Michaels tale*: the story of the Cadiz expedition or that of the Islands expedition (stale news, about two years, and one year, old respectively). The 'Calis' of *1633* is a slip; this was one of the usual forms of 'Calais' ('Callis', 'Callice', etc.). 'Cales', 'Cals', 'Gades', etc., were forms of 'Cadiz'. In *Monsieur d'Olive* (1606, F4ᵛ) Chapman writes, 'the losse of Calice & the winning of Cales'. Browne speaks of 'the Azores, or Islands of Saint Michael' (*Vulgar Errors*, ii. 2). Wotton and Donne had been together on the two voyages referred to.

l. 3. *vice*. In a letter, to Mrs. Herbert, Donne writes of 'plaguy *London*; a place full of danger, and vanity, and vice, though the Court be gone' (Walton, *Lives*, p. 336).

l. 9. *still*. This word is so placed to bring out both meanings: (1) 'is even worse', (2) 'is invariably worse'.

l. 10. *this worlds warfare*. For the commonplace, of life as soldiering, cf. Seneca, *Epist.* li. 6, and Epictetus, *Discourses*, III. xxiv. 31–36. Cf. 'Satire III', l. 31, and note, p. 142.

ll. 10–11. *Fate*, (*Gods Commissary*). Cf. 'The Progress of the Soul', l. 31, and note, p. 175.

l. 13. *seely*: simple, innocent, naïve.

l. 14. *wishing prayers*: petitions. There may be an analogy with 'bidding prayers' in its original sense, 'praying of prayers' (*O.E.D.*, 'bidding', 6).

l. 16. *Suspitious boldnesse*: 'boldness to suspect', i.e. a readiness to believe the worst.

l. 21. *like playes*: because 'in the Princes hall, / There, things that seeme, exceed substantiall' ('The Perfume', ll. 63–64).

ll. 22–24. *jeast . . . gests . . . Chests*. The rhyme was thought tolerable, perhaps, in the familiar style of the verse letter.

l. 22. *mimicke antiques*: posturing eccentrics ('antics').

l. 23. *projects*: plots.
  gests: doings (Latin, *gesta*).

l. 24. *dull Moralls of a game at Chests*: dull representations of moral situations illustrated by analogy in a game of chess. Chess as a moralization or allegory of human life was a familiar subject in England after Caxton's translation, *The Game of Chess*, 1474. The most recent 'morals' were those in *Ludus Scacchiae: Chess-play . . . , Translated . . . by G. B.*, 1597. The address 'To the Reader' says that the game 'breedeth in the players, a certaine study, wit, pollicie, forecast and memorie, not onely in the play thereof, but also in actions of publike governement, both in peace and warre: wherein both Counsellers at home, and Captaines abroad may picke out of these wodden peeces some pretty pollicy, both how to governe their subjects in peace, and howe to leade or conduct lively men in the field in warre'.
  Chests: a regular form of 'chess' (*O.E.D.* 1).

l. 27. 'I subscribe my letter "At Court" (I am writing from there), but it would be better if I were able to put instead, "(away) From Court".'

H. W. in Hiber. Belligeranti (p. 74)

The manuscript *Bur*, Wotton's commonplace book, which contained the only early copy of this poem, was destroyed. I use Grierson's version of it as a basic text, but rely also on a transcript made by Logan Pearsall Smith. Grierson expanded contracted forms and supplied some punctuation; I have followed his example, but have returned in places to the spelling of *Bur*, as Pearsall Smith copied it, where it seems closer to Donne's autograph, from which, presumably, Wotton's secretary copied the poem.

Henry Wotton was 'fighting in Ireland' with his patron, the Earl of Essex, from mid April until late September 1599. The poem seems to have been written some weeks after Wotton reached Ireland.

The ascription of this letter to Donne is based on its being initialed 'J. D.' in *Bur*, on internal evidence of style (especially ll. 13–15), and on its probable connexion with a transcript of a letter in *Bur* almost certainly sent by Wotton from Ireland to Donne. This letter, printed by Pearsall Smith in *The Life and Letters of Sir Henry Wotton*, i. 308, reads in part:

> Sir, It is worth my wondering that you can complain of my seldom writing, when your own letters come so fearfully, as if they tread all the way upon a bog. . . . It is true that this kingdom hath ill affections and ill corruptions; but they where you are have a stronger disease, you diminish all that is here done. . . . These be the wise rules of policy, and of Courts, which are upon earth the vainest places. . . . God keep you and us in those ways and rules and kinds of wisdom that bring mortal men unto Himself.

This accords well with the subjects and spirit of the preceding few letters of Donne to Wotton and to other friends.

l. 3. *Respective*: considerate, courteous (as in *King John*, I. i. 188, 'too respective and too sociable').

ll. 4–5. To win Ireland as an Englishman is not as important as losing Wotton's friendship as a man.

ll. 5–9. *better cheap I pardon death*, etc. 'I could forgive your death in battle as a cheaper loss than that of your energy and liveliness of mind.' 'Better cheap' is adverbial (*O.E.D.*, 'cheap', 9).

l. 9. *skeines*: Gaelic daggers (Gaelic, *sgian*, 'knife'). Cf. *Soliman and Perseda*, I. iii. 21–22 (*The Works of Thomas Kyd*, ed. F. S. Boas, p. 169):

> Against the light foote Irish have I served,
> And in my skinne bare tokens of their skenes.

l. 10. *or*. So Pearsall Smith; Grierson reads 'and'.

l. 11. *yong*: while young, early. For the thought cf. 'The Progress of the Soul', ll. 49–50.

l. 12. *Who payes before his death*, etc. A difficult line. 'A man who fulfils all his obligations before his death is never arrested for not doing so'; hence, I suppose, a man who dies in full discharge of his powers and talents cannot be 'arrested' by sicknesses of the soul—e.g. (l. 16) neglectfulness and sloth.

ll. 13–15. Wotton's soul is likened to the 'soul' of a substance (cf. 'To Mr Rowland Woodward', ll. 25–27, and note, p. 224), which is the highest part of the substance, but can be refined and purified by being distilled ('still'd'). 'Lymbecks' or alembics, which had a curved neck (though Courts and other 'schools' are morally 'crooked') were used for this purpose. In Wotton's life the instruments of purification have been the centres of learning and of state. Cf. 'To Sir Henry Goodyer', ll. 17–18.

l. 19. *a seers Art*: the divining of their contents by powers of 'vision'. There is a pun on 'seer'; the reference is to the common practice of reading some one else's correspondence before re-sealing it and sending on the messenger. Donne is asking, not for secret or dangerous news, but for a letter conveying friendly feelings.

To Sir Henry Wotton, at his going Ambassador to Venice (p. 75)

MSS.: Group II (*A 18, N, TCC, TCD*); *DC*; Group III (*Lut, O'F*).
Miscellanies: *HK 2, La.*

There was a copy of this poem in *Bur*, not transcribed before the manuscript was destroyed; I rely on Grierson's report. The poem appears in *Reliquiae Wottonianae*, 1672. Walton printed it in his *Life of Wotton*, 1670, but the variants in his text seem to have no authority, and I do not quote them.

The text in *1633* is taken from a Group II manuscript, which contained a minor error in l. 10, but was superior to any surviving manuscript of the Group (and to *DC*), or was corrected by the editor, in a reading in l. 24.

Walton introduces the poem as follows: 'And though his dear friend Dr. *Donne* (then a private Gentleman) was not one of that number that did personally accompany him in this Voyage, yet the reading of this following Letter sent by him to Sir *Henry Wotton*, the morning before he left *England*, may testifie he wanted not his friends best wishes to attend him' (*Lives*, p. 114). Wotton was knighted by the King on 8 July (O.S.), set out from London about 13 July, and left Dover for Venice on 19 July 1604. Walton's account, though generally correct, needs modification in the light of a postscript that followed the copy in *Bur* (Simpson, *Prose Works*, pp. 319–20):

S^r though *perchaunce* it were never tryed except in Rabelais his land of tapistry it may bee true *tha*t a pygmey upon a Giant may see further then *th*e giant so after a long letter this postscript may see further into yo*u* then *tha*t if yo*u* will answere to 2 questions whether yo*u* have yo*u*r last despatches at court or whether yo*u* make many dayes stay there or at London. such a one as I may yett kisse yo*u*r hand.

l. 2. *Kings*: James I's. Wotton had known him as James VI of Scotland.

l. 3. *derives*. *O.E.D.*, 'derive', 4: convey, impart, pass on.

his: i.e. his 'soule' (l. 1) or essential quality.

l. 4. *how he may*: as far as is permitted him to give of his rank and authority.

l. 5. *A Taper of his Torch*. Cf. 'The Kings of the earth are faire and glorious resemblances of the King of heaven; they are beames of that Sun, Tapers of that Torch' (*Sermons*, v. 85).

Middleton writes (*The Witch*, IV. ii. 18–20):

> As an ambassador sent from a king
> Has honour by th'employment, yet there's greater
> Dwells in the king that sent him.

ll. 17–20. *allow It such an audience*, etc. 'Give this letter the kind of warm reception which you would yourself like to receive as ambassador. It really means, by its very nature, what you will have to say at Venice only because it is your duty to say it: an avowal of friendship.'

ll. 21–22. *not to be chang'd*, etc. 'My love will not be changed until your inevitable rise to great eminence makes it fitting only to honour you.'

l. 23. *then*: when you have reached your greatest eminence (highest 'fortune').

ll. 23–24. *honour your fortune, more*, etc.: 'hold your eminent position in higher respect than I hold your honourable nature now, while you yet lack that eminence'. Donne plays on the meanings of 'honour': (1) respect given; (2) nobility, high character—compelling respect; (3) 'your honour', as in addressing a judge—'your worthy self'.

The Group II reading, 'noble wanting it', looks like an inexpert gloss, and gives a clumsy phrasing of the idea, 'your noble lack of eminence'. In *Lut*, *O'F* the Group II reading is sophisticated to produce the almost meaningless 'noble-wanting-wit' (adopted in *1635*). Donne is not, of course, speaking of 'wit' but of character.

Grierson quotes the dialogue upon love and honour in Lyly's *Endimion*, v. iii. 150 ff., and especially II. iii. 12–14: 'Nay, *Endimion*, she was wise, but what availeth wisdome without honour? Shee was honourable *Endimion*, belie her not, I but howe obscure is honor without fortune?'

ll. 29–32. In this alchemical metaphor the 'spirits' are the 'spiritual' or essential parts of substances (i.e. Wotton's honourable qualities); they are refined by distillation over heat ('Furnace') to make an elixir or touchstone. The thought is the same as that in the previous letter, ll. 13–15. 'Warres' have now been added to the 'alembics' in which Wotton's character has been refined; he is now entering the last of these—responsible action and endeavour. By this final process his character will be refined into a touchstone to test others' characters to any, even the highest, degree of worth, and by contact with which the virtues of others will be enhanced.

l. 34. *Fortune (if there be such a thing as shee)*. Donne probably has in mind St.

Augustine's regret at having used the word 'Fortune', when in fact God's Providence controls events (*Retractationes*, I. I; Migne, *P.L.* xxxii. 585–7).

l. 36. *nothing else so fit*. There is a tinge of disappointment here as Donne contemplates his lack of preferment after his injudicious marriage. There is, however, no hint of envy; the thought in the last stanza rises with real warmth from this rueful reflection.

ll. 38–40. *God is as neere*, etc. Cf. Epictetus, *Discourses*, IV. iv. 48: 'Are not men everywhere equally distant from God?' The idea became proverbial. 'Staires' in l. 39 is suggested by Jacob's ladder, Gen. xxviii. 12.

A Letter written by Sir H. G. and J. D. *alternis vicibus* (p. 76)

MS.: *A 25*.

There is no reason to doubt that in the only surviving manuscript copy the poem is correctly headed, or that the initials are those of Goodyer and Donne. The second and alternate stanzas (in roman type) are Donne's; as Grierson says (ii. 267), there is a characteristic touch in each. Thomas Pestell had heard of some such poem (though its precise character was not clear to him), and wrote an epigram upon it (MS. *Malone 14*, Bodleian Library, p. 28; cf. Pestell's *Poems*, ed. Hannah Buchan, 1940, p. 28):

> On the Interlinearie poëme begott twixt Sʳ H. Goo. & Dʳ Donne.
> Here two rich ravisht spirrits kisse & twyne;
> Advanc'd, & weddlockt in each others lyne.
> Gooderes rare match with only him was blest,
> Who haes out donne, & quite undonne the rest.

Henry Goodyer (1571–1628) was Donne's great friend, and chief correspondent in his middle and later years. By marriage with his first cousin Frances Goodyer, Henry came into possession of an estate at Polesworth (in the Forest of Arden, Warwickshire); it was apparently failing, and Goodyer himself was of generous and feckless disposition; throughout his life he was perpetually petitioning the Court for a place. He was knighted by Essex in 1599, and in 1605 became one of the Gentlemen of the Privy Chamber; but his decaying fortunes needed a better place. Donne preached at the marriage of his eldest daughter (cf. *Sermons*, ii. 43) in 1620; he was probably the gentleman to whom Donne, when his own position improved, gave £100 (Walton, *Lives*, pp. 70–71). His sister-in-law, Anne Goodyer (Lady Rainsford), became the patroness of Drayton (the 'Idea' of his sonnets), and he himself is celebrated by Jonson. Goodyer wrote occasional verses, sometimes with large assistance from Donne (cf. 'To Mr E. G.', introductory note, p. 216).

The letter seems to be written to two ladies, friends who are staying in the same place (friends like, for example, the Countess of Bedford and Lady Markham); there is no indication, however, of their identity.

l. 6. *digest*: 'divide', scatter as beams.

l. 9. twin'd: 'twinned' rather than 'twined'.

l. 25. Ancors. The Ancor (now 'Anker') is a stream flowing through Poles-worth. Cf. Drayton, *Poly-Olbion*, Song xiii, ll. 10, 281–310.

l. 28. *St. Edith Nunns*. Before the Reformation there was a Benedictine convent at Polesworth, founded by the Saxon saint, Edith (Dugdale, *Warwickshire*, 1656, pp. 216, 797 ff.). It was suppressed in 1538, and in 1544 was sold, with the lordship of the estate, to Goodyer's grandfather, Francis Goodyer.

To Sir Henry Goodyere (p. 78)

MSS.: Group I (*C 57, D, H 49, Lec, SP*); Group II (*A 18, N, TCC, TCD*); *DC*; Group III (*A 25, B, C, Cy, Dob, Lut, O'F*).
Miscellany: *HK 1*.

The text in *1633* is taken from a Group I manuscript, which had a text superior to that in Groups II and III. I disagree with Grierson in making two alterations, ll. 37, 44.

This letter was written between 1605 and 1610 while Donne was living at Mitcham (l. 48). It probably antedates a trip abroad Goodyer apparently made in 1609 (see I. A. Shapiro, *M.L.R.* xlv. 7, n. 3). The first line suggests that it was written to celebrate New Year's Day or Goodyer's birthday.

l. 4. *paire*: a set or 'string' (of beads); *O.E.D.* II. 6.

l. 9. *body*: the soul's 'Palace'.

ll. 9–10. *morning . . . noone . . . night*. Similarly Shakespeare, Sonnet vii.

l. 11. *guest*: the soul. Cf. 'The Progress of the Soul', l. 159, and note (p. 179).

ll. 13–14. Cf. Davies, *Nosce Teipsum*, 1599 (*Works*, ed. Grosart, 1876, i. 99):

> But to the *Soule* Time doth perfections give,
>   And adds fresh lustre to her beauty still;
> And makes her in eternall youth to live,
>   Like her which nectar to the gods doth fill.
>
> The more she lives, the more she feeds on *Truth*;
>   The more she feeds, her *strength* doth more increase:
> And what is *strength*, but an effect of *youth*?
>   What if *Time* nurse, how can it ever cease?

ll. 15–17. *to pamper her With womens milke*, etc. The allusion is to St. Paul's antithesis of milk for babes and meat for men. Cf. note (p. 180) on l. 188 of 'The Progress of the Soul', and Heb. v. 12–14, the last verse of which reads: 'But strong meat belongeth to them that are of full age, even those who by reason of use have their senses exercised to discern both good and evil.'

l. 16. *the end*. The reading of Groups II and III, 'her end', is wrong, since the soul does not have an 'end', being immortal. 'The end' means 'the end of our earthly life'.

l. 20. *In harvests*, etc.: His garners are not as full as they should be, because he has neglected harvesting for play. Goodyer's extravagance and perpetual lack of money were notorious.

l. 21. *it*: your general situation.

l. 22. *outlandish*: foreign.

ll. 25–26. *To be a stranger*, etc. To be a foreigner in another country has the advantage that, being confronted with strange customs, we can abandon them after sampling them ('beginnings'); we cannot abandon the old habits ingrained in us at home.

l. 27. 'Goe' is Donne's urging; 'whither' is Goodyer's imagined question: to which Donne replies, in effect, 'Anywhere, as long as you travel hence, away from temptation; if you *can* forget your present ways, it will be all to your profit.'

l. 28. *prescribe*: generally, 'dictate', 'direct', 'take charge' (*O.E.D.* I. 2. c). Donne is, however, using the word in a precise legal sense (*O.E.D.* II. 6), 'make a claim by prescription', i.e. because of use or possession from time immemorial (as here), sometimes for a fixed period. The right of sins to assert a claim over us has existed, as it were, from the time of Adam's fall.

ll. 33–36. The money Goodyer spends on travel is worth the cost if it teaches him thrift and to be ashamed of being praised for what he praises in his hawks. When a hawk diminishes itself in the air we praise it for soaring to the right place (but this is not praiseworthy in men; and Goodyer has diminished himself, 'lessened' his estate, by extravagance—soaring too high).

   The comparison is forced, but appropriate to Goodyer. Donne refers to his love of hawking in an undated letter: 'God send you Hawks and fortunes of a high pitch' (*Letters*, p. 204). Jonson was a 'witnesse of thy few dayes sport' as a member of a hawking-party at Polesworth (Epigram lxxxv; *Works*, viii. 55).

   toures: the technical term for the circular flight of the hawk to the 'place' from which it 'stoops'.

l. 37. *Howsoever*: the more 'difficult' reading, pronounced (as the spelling in *Dob* suggests) 'hows'ever'.

l. 42. *Else be not froward*: 'let nothing else (but falsehood) make you belligerent'.

   touch: touch upon.

l. 44. *Fables*. Donne refers to morals drawn from fables in 'Satire V', ll. 88–89, and 'The Calm', ll. 3–4. 'Tables' was an error in the Group I manuscript used in setting up the text of *1633*. It is, of course, a possible reading, the 'tables' being pictures or moralized emblems. The two words are easily mistaken for one another, however, and the manuscript evidence is heavily in favour of 'Fables'.

fruit-trenchers: also called 'roundells'. These, and trenchers for other use, were usually ornamented with moral maxims or with texts ('Give us this day our daily bread', etc.). For a discussion, and illustration of some examples, see J. Y. Akerman, *Archaeologia*, xxxiv, 1852. Puttenham, discussing short epigrams (*The Art of English Poesy*, ed. Willcock and Walker, p. 58), says: 'we call them Posies, and do paint them now a dayes upon the backe sides of our fruite trenchers of wood.'

l. 48. *You came with mee*, etc. Cf. 'An Epistle is *collocutio scripta*, saies Saint *Ambrose* [Migne, *P.L.* xvi. 1151; also 1285], Though it be written far off, and sent, yet it is a Conference, and *seperatos copulat*, sayes hee; by this meanes wee overcome distances, we deceive absences, and wee are together even then when wee are asunder' (*Sermons*, i. 285).

Micham. Mitcham, a village in Surrey, where Donne spent about six years in considerable misery, ill health, and frustration of hopes of employment. This letter might have accompanied or replaced one of the prose letters he sent regularly each Tuesday to Goodyer (see *Letters*, pp. 66, 85, etc.).

To Sir Edward Herbert, at Julyers (p. 80)

MSS.: Group I (*C 57, D, H 49, Lec, SP*); Group II (*A 18, N, TCC, TCD*); DC; Group III (*B, Cy, Dob, K, Lut, O'F, O, P, S, S 96*).
Miscellanies: *HK 1, HK 2* (where ll. 43–44 are transcribed again as a separate couplet).

The editor of *1633* used the very good text in his Group I manuscript. I have made only one minor change from his (and Grierson's) readings, in l. 48.

Edward Herbert (1583–1648) was the eldest son of Donne's friend, Mrs. Magdalen Herbert, and brother of George Herbert. He was at Oxford 1595–1600, was knighted by James I in 1603, was traveller, soldier, Ambassador to France 1619–24, poet and philosophical writer. He was made an Irish peer in 1624, and Lord Herbert of Cherbury in 1629. For his life-story see *D.N.B.*, G. C. Moore-Smith's edition of his *Poems* (1923), and his *Autobiography* (ed. S. Lee, revised 1906); his literary relations with Donne are discussed in Gardner, *Elegies etc.*, pp. 254 ff.

Herbert's satire 'The State progress of Ill' draws fairly heavily on Donne's own *Satires*, and this verse letter is obviously connected with Herbert's poem, which ends:

> The World, as in the Ark of *Noah*, rests,
> Compos'd as then, few Men, and many Beasts.

D. A. Keister, who drew attention to the relationship ('Donne and Herbert of Cherbury: an Exchange of Verses', *M.L.Q.* viii, 1947), shows that Donne's letter is not an answer to Herbert's poem at every point, but that Donne has developed some ideas in it that interested him: 'that one poison might free The other' (ll. 10–11 of Herbert's poem); that sins multiply in 'monstrous birth' (l. 51); that an 'honest man' can 'dispose Those beasts' within himself (ll. 62–64); and that the 'great'st rule here Is for to rule our selves' (ll. 106–7). Herbert's satire is dated August 1608.

The date of Donne's letter is fairly precisely fixed by the reference to Juliers. In 1610 Herbert went to join Sir Edward Cecil, who, with an English army of 4,000 men, was assisting the Prince of Orange in the siege of Juliers, begun on 17 July. The town was held by Archduke Leopold for the Emperor; the Dutch, French, and English were fighting in the interests of the Protestant Princes. Herbert claimed to have been the first to enter the town.

Donne's letter pays compliment to his friend, not only in the concluding lines, but also in respecting his tastes for philosophy and for congested meaning in poetry.

l. 1. *Man is a lumpe, where all beasts kneaded bee*. The 'lumpe' is that of clay worked by the potter, as in Rom. ix. 21 (of God as the Maker of man): 'Hath not the potter power over the clay, of the same lump to make one vessel unto honour and another unto dishonour?' 'Dishonour' comes to man by submission to the bestial parts of his nature. The biblical idea is combined with the legend that Prometheus moulded man out of clay, giving him the qualities of different animals (Horace, *Odes*, I. xvi. 13 ff.; cf. Plato, *Protagoras*, 320 d, etc.). This was further linked with the theory that, just as the rational soul absorbs the inferior souls of sense and growth and retains their qualities, so in the Chain of Being each stage possesses the qualities of beings at a lower stage. Hence, 'Man is every creature, sayes *Origen*, because in him, *Tanquam in officina, omnes Creaturae conflantur*, Because all creatures were as it were melted in one forge, and poured into one mold, when man was made', etc. (*Sermons*, v. 253–4). The idea is further connected with that of man as the microcosm (ll. 37–39 below); cf. 'Eclogue' prefixed to the Somerset 'Epithalamion', ll. 50–52.

These theories account for the *fact* of man's animal qualities. The allegory of the beasts in man (his animal passions, etc.) begins with Plato's *Republic*, ix. 588–90, and becomes a commonplace in the Fathers. Donne seems to be closest to St. Augustine, commenting on Gen. 1. 28, where God gives man dominion over the creatures, Migne, *P.L.* xxxiv. 187–8. Cf. also Pico della Mirandola, *Heptaplus*, iv. 5 (*Commentationes*, 1495–6, Cii^v): 'Hactenus de viribus animi cognoscentibus. Nunc ad eas se transfert quorum opus appetere, irae videlicet et libidinis, id est, concupiscentiae sedes, has per bestias designat et irrationale genus viventium quae sunt nobis cum bestiis communes, et quod est infelicius ad brutalem saepe nos vitam impellunt.'

l. 2. *Wisdome makes him an Arke where all agree*. That the animals in the Ark should have been kept at peace is a matter of frequent comment. It was commonly regarded as an allegory of the human soul in which the 'beasts' (passions, instincts, etc.) were properly kept in control by reason or wisdom (often said to be symbolized in Noah). Cf. *The First Anniversary*, ll. 318–21; St. Ambrose, *De Noe et Arca*, ix (Migne, *P.L.* xiv. 374); Pererius, *Comment. et Disput. in Genesim*, 1601, p. 448; etc.

l. 3. *at jarre*: in dissension or discord. Cf. Rom. vii. 23.

l. 4. *Theater*: a place where the spectacle of conflict gives 'sport' to the onlookers (with perhaps a glance at the Roman use of beasts in the arena).

l. 5. Compare: 'in some people the element of the best is naturally weak, unable to rule the monsters (θρεμμάτων) within them, and only capable of learning how to pamper them' (Plato, *Republic*, ix. 590, translated by A. D. Lindsay).

l. 9. *due place*: 'so must we, not cut off, but cure these affections, which are the bestiall part' (*Letters*, pp. 47–48; cf. *Sermons*, ii. 100). 'Make the quarrelling Lapithytes sleep, and Centaurs within lye quiet. Chain up the unruly Legion [cf. ll. 15–17] of thy breast; lead thine own captivity captive, and be Caesar within thyself' (Browne, *Christian Morals*, i. 2).

l. 10. *disaforested*: a legal term, describing land reduced from the status of a forest (in which common law did not apply) and so available for cultivation. Cf. the note on 'Love's Deity', l. 18, in Gardner, *Elegies etc.*, p. 170, and for 'soul-cultivation' the letter 'To Mr Rowland Woodward', ll. 31–36.

l. 11. *Empail'd*: fenced.

l. 13. *his horse, goate*, etc. Cf. Burton, *Anatomy*, i. 75: how, says Chrysostom, 'shall I know thee to be a man, when thou kickest like an ass, neighest like a horse after women, ravest in lust like a bull', etc.

ll. 15–17. *the heard of swine*, etc. Cf. Matt. viii. 30–34, Mark v. 2–14, Luke viii. 27–33.

l. 19. *by our first touch*: 'the purest Soule becomes stain'd and corrupted with sinne, as soone as it touches the body' (*Pseudo-Martyr*, p. 31). Cf. *Sermons*, i. 177, v. 349, etc. The orthodox view was that 'if the soule were not infected, the body shoulde not bee stained therewith' (*The French Academy*, II, Ch. lxxxi, p. 492; also lxxxvi, p. 519).

l. 20. *The poysonous tincture of Originall sinne*. In alchemy the 'tincture' was the spiritual principle or immaterial substance that can be fused into material things, the quintessence. The 'universal tincture' was the 'elixir', which at a touch could purify other substances. Donne's use of the term here is paradoxical. The tincture was entirely beneficial as medicine or as the purifying principle in a substance: the very reverse of poison.

l. 22. *Our apprehension*: our way of accepting, or understanding, them.

ll. 23–24. *To us, as to his chickins*, etc. 'Chickens' refers generally to small birds (but particularly to Matt. xxiii. 37). Galen writes of hemlock: 'cicuta quae sturnos alit, nec in eis mortiferam vim exercet, in nobis autem vitae calorem extinguit' (*De Theriaca* iv; *Opera*, Venice 1586, iii. f. 91^r); there are many variations of the idea. But in *De Temperamentis* iii (*Opera*, i. f. 24^v) Galen says: 'cicuta sturno nutrimentum est, homini medicamentum'; hence l. 30 below, 'At lest for physicke, if not for our food'. Hemlock was 'cold' (l. 26): 'gelidas . . . cicutas' (Juvenal, *Sat.* vii. 206; Ovid, *Amores*, iii. 7. 13).

ll. 26–27. *Corrosivenesse ... intense cold or heat ... specifique poyson.* Donne had been reading the *De Venenis*, 1606, of Forestus (the great Dutch doctor, Pieter van Forest), and in *Pseudo-Martyr* (belonging to the same year as this letter) he cites van Forest's book as a source of the following passage (Preface, C3):

> those poysons, which destroy not by heat nor cold, nor corrosion, nor any other discerneable quality, but (as physitians say) out of the specifique forme, and secret malignity, and out of the whole substance ... no Artist can finde out, how this malignant strength growes in that poyson, nor how it workes ... these specifique poysons, or of the cause and origen thereof, which is, *Antipathie*.

Forestus says, for example, that the first main type of poisons 'humanae naturae contrarium est ex tota sua substantia, quam medici proprietatem seu formam specificam appellant' (p. 8); the other type 'humanam naturam corrumpit ex sua qualitate vel temperie', either 'per caliditatem extremam incidendo, et corrodendo membrorum nobilium substantiam' or 'per frigiditatem extremam' (p. 9). There are many suggestions as to how the first type kills (pp. 15–16), but 'we know not how' ('ab occulta quadam agat proprietate', p. 19). This 'specific' type is 'humana natura et complexioni extreme repugnante'; Donne appropriates this last idea in his own word, 'antipathy'.

As usual Donne's method is to use this knowledge to image out a relationship of man to man or of man to God. The harmful quality of God's punishments (like corrosiveness, cold, or heat in poisons) is imported by man's sinful nature. Even God's severest chastening is not essentially harmful (is not like the unknown special quality of poisons and the antipathy that causes it); there is no secret malignancy in His dealings with us—the harmful qualities are plain to view, and man himself is responsible for them.

l. 27. *specifique.* The *O.E.D.* quotes this passage for 'specific', 1: having a special determining quality.

l. 30. *physicke.* 'Call not his Phisicke, poyson, nor his Fish, Scorpions, nor his Bread, Stone: Accuse not *God*' (*Sermons*, vi. 260).

ll. 31–32. *Thus man, that might be'his pleasure,* etc. 'His' means 'his own'. Man, who has the capacity to enjoy the highest pleasure (of living virtuously) makes a spiritual rod for his own back, and acts like a devil in ruining his life when he might be so like God as to work for his salvation. 'Nor is this affliction appertaining to man, because man himselfe inflicts it upon himselfe, our owne inherent corruption being become *Spontaneus Daemon*, a Devill in our owne bosome' (*Sermons*, vii. 187; also p. 217).

l. 34. *what she was*: before the Fall (by realizing his best powers and making use of God's redemptive plan).

ll. 34–37. *wee'are led awry ... bestow On him.* People who talk of man as a microcosm lead us astray; we can in fact speak of man in no terms that do justice to his greatness. 'It is too little to call *Man* a *little World*; Except God, Man is *diminutive* to nothing', etc. (Sparrow, *Devotions*, p. 15).

The properties, the qualities of every Creature, are in man; the Essence, the Existence of every Creature is for man; so man is every Creature. And therefore the Philosopher draws man into too narrow a table, when he says he is *Microcosmos*, an Abridgement of the world in little: *Nazianzen* gives him but his due, when he calls him *Mundum Magnum*, a world to which all the rest of the world is but subordinate: For all the world besides, is but Gods Foot-stool; Man sits down upon his right hand (*Sermons*, iv. 104).

l. 43. *Calentures*: fevers. Cf. 'The Calm', l. 23, and note, pp. 208–9.

Opium. 'Al the Poppies be colde and drie', opium also (Dodoens, *Herbal*, 1578, p. 432).

Knowledge stimulates some people to feverish speculation, hot temper, rashness; others it benumbs.

l. 47. The semi-colon after 'credible' brings out the meaning. 'It is because . . . Herbert has dwelt upon all worthy books that it is credible that he knows man' (Grierson).

l. 49. *Actions are authors*. 'Our actions, if they be good, speak louder then our Sermons; Our preaching is our speech, our good life is our eloquence' (*Sermons*, ix. 156).

l. 50. *mart*: a large stock, as in a market, daily renewed.

To the Countesse of Huntington (p. 81)

MSS.: *O*, *P*, *TCD*(*2*).

My text, like Grierson's, is based on *1635*, where the poem first appeared in print. The editor's copy was superior to that in the surviving manuscripts, but needs correction from the manuscripts in ll. 69, 74, 121, 123, 125; a line (128) left incomplete in the edition can be correctly filled out from *O*, *P*.

In the manuscripts the poem is headed 'Sʳ Walter (Wal:) Ashton to the Countesse of Huntington'. For a discussion of its authorship see Appendix D.

Lady Elizabeth Stanley was the youngest of the three daughters of Ferdinando and Alice, Earl and Countess of Derby. On the death of the Earl (1594) and after six years of widowhood, the Countess married Egerton, as his second wife (1600). Donne, then Egerton's secretary, would have come to know fairly well the four ladies thus added to the Lord Keeper's household. Elizabeth Stanley married Henry Hastings in June 1603, and became Countess of Huntington on her husband's succession as fifth Earl in 1605. Donne mentions her with respect and affection at various periods later (e.g. *Letters*, pp. 169, 200, 236). She died in 1633. See J. Yoklavich, 'Donne and the Countess of Huntingdon', *P.Q.*, 1964.

The date of this poem cannot be fixed with any precision. The titles of people addressed in poems of the day were often brought up to date as they were copied, but there is no reason why the letter could not have been written after (probably soon after) the Lady Elizabeth became a Countess (1605) and a potential patroness as well as an established friend. The address 'Madame' implies that she was married; indeed to send such a poem to an unmarried noblewoman would have been an indecorum. The poem is, in great part, an essay on various types of love, conducted with such liveliness that H. M. Belden (*J.E.G.P.* xiv. 139–40) thought that behind it he glimpsed 'the possibility of some early amour' with the lady (not the Countess) to whom the letter was written. In fact, Donne is careful to dissociate from her person his account of kinds of love inappropriate to his position in respect of the Countess (ll. 21 ff., 77). Only the second half deals with the kind of 'love' the poet can feel for his patroness. Donne had satirized the 'Petrarchan' lover (cf. ll. 21–36, 57–76 of this poem) in 1601 in 'The Progress of the Soul', ll. 451 ff. In the few years after this, as Miss Gardner has persuasively suggested, Donne was writing lyrics which examined, as they dramatized, more profound and complex aspects of the love of man and woman. Here he seems to be further examining the sort of love that can be supposed to exist between a man and a woman of higher station—a difficult complex of friendship, admiration (in some ways mutual), dependence, flattery, and self-respect. The poem has the air of an exercise in modes of address used more confidently in the other letters to great ladies, which I think it precedes.

Writing to Goodyer about a verse letter on the Countess's 'picture', which has not survived among his poems, Donne shows amid what tremors and complexities of decorous conduct this and the following verse letters were written: he speaks of

my integrity to the other Countesse, of whose worthinesse though I swallowed your opinion at first upon your words, yet I have had since an explicit faith, and now a knowledge: and for her delight (since she descends to them) I had reserved not only all the verses, which I should make, but all the thoughts of womens worthinesse. But because I hope she will not disdain, that I should write well of her Picture, I have obeyed you thus far, as to write: but intreat you by your friendship, that by this occasion of versifying, I be not traduced, nor esteemed light in that Tribe, and that house where I have lived. If those reasons which moved you to bid me write be not constant in you still, or if you meant not that I should write verses; or if these verses be too bad, or too good, over or under her understanding, and not fit; I pray receive them, as a companion and supplement of this Letter to you (*Letters*, pp. 104–5).

I have supplemented the inadequate paragraphing in *1635* in order to show better the drift of the poem. The opening sentence is defective at the beginning, presumably because of the loss of some lines before the Countess allowed any copy to be taken. I conjecture that the poem began with the thought that people who do not know the Countess and who live outside the range of her 'influence' are like those remote, uncivilized men who live in the uncultivated ('unripe') half of the earth only now coming into our knowledge.

l. 1. *heavy*: humid, tropical.

l. 2. *like* Adams *time*. In *A Treatise of Brazil* we read of the Indians that 'All of them goe naked as well men as women, and have no kind of apparrell, and are nothing ashamed', etc. (*Purchas his Pilgrims*, edition of 1906, xvi. 422). Cf. Gen. ii. 25.

l. 3. *Before he ate*: i.e. of the fruit of the Forbidden Tree.

ll. 3–6. *mans shape*, etc. 'Creatures in the shape of man, who would still be (if they did not know their nakedness and shun the company of animals) as naked to this day as though they were so far from Paradise', etc.

The aborigines are distinguished from Paradisal Man by knowing they are naked and by being afraid of the animals; whereas it was only after the Fall that Adam knew that he was naked (Gen. iii. 7) and felt fear of the beasts, which had hitherto been friendly to man.

l. 6. *Paradise*: Eden.

l. 9. If there could have been those in 'mans shape' who had not heard of the Fall, their state of apparent freedom from sin would be illusory, since in Adam they 'beare the sinne'.

l. 10. *wanting the reward*. Not having heard of Christ, they lack redemption ('the reward'), and know nothing of it. 'This people hath not any knowledge of their Creator, nor of any thing of heaven . . . but they know that they have soules, and that they dye not' (*A Treatise of Brazil*, in *Purchas his Pilgrims*, 1906, xvi. 419).

l. 12. *at*: as, as occupying the position or status of.

l. 13. *younger*: smaller (before they have 'grown' older and hence bigger, whether children or brooks).

ll. 14–18. People unacquainted with the Countess are in their ordinary lives ('at home') mere atoms in size, measured by their 'wit' or abilities; so that when she sees them from *her* elevation they look like mist or nothing at all. The poet, having risen half-way to the Countess's level by her friendship and patronage, is still able to see these lesser folk as discrete tiny beings in motion or at rest ('move and stay').

l. 16. Atomi: the usual plural, from *atomus* or *atomos*.

l. 20. *sick*: hence 'wasted', 'diminished'.

must I to you. A transition is made to the idea of the love-'sick' swain suing for the pity of a remote ('distant') mistress.

l. 22. *crosse-arm'd*. Folded arms were the conventional sign of the sorrow of a lover or mourner, of discontent and melancholy: see L. Babb, *The Eliza-bethan Malady*, 1951, pp. 76 ff., 156 ff. The Lothian portrait shows Donne in this posture of the pining lover; cf. Gardner, *Elegies etc.*, pp. 267–8.

l. 24. *white-liver'd*. The four humours tended to dominate in the body each at a different stage: blood in youth, then choler, then melancholy, and, in old age, phlegm (hence white hair, watery eyes, and a liver lacking a proper degree of blood).

l. 26. *faithfully*: still the faithful lover.

l. 27. *tempest of a frowne.* Anger in the microcosm corresponded to a storm in the macrocosm. Cf. *Zepheria*, 1594, Canzon. 27:

> Neare from the deepe, when winds declare a tempest,
> Posts with more haste the little *Halcion*,
> Nor faster hyes him to some safer rest,
> Then I have fled from thy death-threatening frown.

l. 38. *heape*: Chaos.

ll. 40–42. *Water declin'd with earth*, etc. This is the conventional account of the Creation. For ancient sources cf. W. C. Curry, 'The Genesis of Milton's World', *Anglia* (*Zeitschrift*, etc.), lxx, 1951. Paracelsus (*Hermetic and Alchemical Writings*, translated by A. E. Waite, ii. 256) writes that 'the four elements of things were in the beginning severally separated from one single matter, in which, however, their complexion and essence were not present—those complexions and natures emerged by that process of separation. The warm and dry withdrew to the heavens and the firmament. . . . The warm and moist withdrew to the air' . . . etc. (also p. 253). Cf. Sylvester, *Bartas his Divine Weeks and Works*, the Second day of the first Week (1605, p. 41):

> Earth, as the Lees, and heavie drosse of All,
> After his kind did to the bottome fall:
> Contrariwise, the Light and nimble Fire
> Did through the crannies of th'old Heape aspire
> Unto the top . . .

l. 55. *about*: too circuitous a way.

l. 57. *sueth, or doth contend.* The metaphors are of 'love's war'.

l. 59. *better part*: i.e. than passion; 'reason'.

l. 62. *summer-way*: free passage, as for a ship with the thawing of ice in northern seas.

l. 63. *weather-beaten.* Continuing the image of a voyage of discovery, Donne refers to the conventional lover as 'buffeted' by the lady's disdain ('scornes', l. 65).

l. 76. *porter*: at the gate of a mansion (as the lover pining for entry to his mistress's favour).

ll. 78–80. When we are at our highest point of brilliance you are merely just appearing above the horizon; we are only the clouds you rise from; our noon-beams are like a foul shadow, not even equivalent to your dawn.

l. 83. *so curious hit*: so exquisitely and accurately attained.

l. 84. Even small and delicate flatteries are so inadequate to express your perfection as to be like a scandal or blot on your character.

ll. 85–86. 'What is beyond the truth concerning you, no less than what falls short of it, misses and limits what you are, and in going beyond, instead of staying at the summit of truth, goes down, as it were, on the other side' (Grolier).

l. 87. 'There is no direct, short way to you; we have to go cross country.'

l. 88. *straight line, thing prais'd, attribute*. The thing praised is virtue; but she *is* virtue (the 'attribute' in question); its symbol is a straight line (rectitude), and she is that too.

ll. 89–92. Each good quality in the Countess throws a light, and as she lives and moves in these lights each throws a shadow which accurately delineates her; there are many such 'shadows' or pictures of her, for each virtue shows up a new facet of her character. Her distant admirers see her moving in the light of these virtues and imitate her.

l. 92. *Zani's*: clownish imitators. Cf. note (p. 212) to 'To Mr. T. W.' ('All haile sweet Poët'), l. 30.

l. 94. *shew*: appear.

l. 96. Love is the 'shade' (l. 89) corresponding to the purest light in which she walks; it exemplifies her highest virtue.

ll. 97–98. A familiar part of the theory of man as microcosm. The soul is, however, more intimately associated with the body (for man's greater convenience and welfare) than the heaven with the earth.

ll. 99–100. 'If nevertheless we understand the thoughts in our souls to be like stars in the heavens, then, as with the stars, we do not comprehend their full meaning, their entire nature, but we recognize and admit their authority.' As the stars influence ('command') us, so do our thoughts, though we do not fully understand the concepts, such as 'virtue', by which we live. So with 'love' (l. 101), as it streams inexhaustibly from the Countess.

ll. 101–6. Love in the Countess is like the sun, that bountiful source of light, shining on all, but inexhaustible. As the sun causes vapour to rise towards it so the Countess's love attracts our souls, which we find, however, to be too clogged with earthly dross to rise to that height, till slow approach to this perfection of love gradually purifies the soul completely, and makes it able to endure the sight of the deathless purity of her love.

l. 109. *retaine*: keep himself.

l. 111. *unforc'd*: 'unrefined'; a technical term in alchemy. Cf. 'To the Lady Bedford', l. 37.

l. 112. *converse*: keep company with (*O.E.D.* 2); 'mingle'.

l. 119. *ayre takes the Sunne-beames equall bright*. Cf. Kepler, *Ad Vitellionem Paralipomena*, 1604, p. 22: 'Cum Sol aerem undique aequaliter collustret'.

l. 127. *Love that imparts*: i.e. 'Love which, when it is genuine, imparts'.

l. 129. *the vertues*: the cardinal virtues of the pagan philosophers (cf. 'To Mr Rowland Woodward', ll. 16–17, and notes, p. 224). In l. 130, however, the thought reverts to the Christian virtues, all subsumed in love.

To the Countesse of Huntingdon (p. 85)

MSS.: Group II (*N, TCD*); *DC*; Group III (*Lut, O'F*).

In *1633* the text is based on a Group II manuscript. I ignore the editorial changes or errors in ll. 13, 47, 66 and (the form of the pronoun) l. 43; in the last two places I disagree with Grierson.

The date of this letter cannot be exactly determined. The Countess could hardly have been 'wife' and 'mother' before 1604 or 1605; in the latter year she received her title (cf. introductory note to the preceding letter). The 'new starre' (l. 6) in itself does not suggest a date, since new stars had been noticed in 1572, 1600, and 1604; but the suggestion that this would be a 'miracle' points to a date before the publication of Galileo's work in 1610 (of which Donne learned quickly); for Galileo revealed countless multitudes of stars never known before, and people ceased to think of new stars as isolated miracles. In l. 58 Donne speaks of having prophesied the Countess's future virtue 'long agoe', that is, presumably, in 1600 when he first met her in Egerton's household. Grierson suggested that the letter was written just before Donne's ordination in 1614, an idea probably due to his statement that he is now her 'Chaplaine'. I take this to be no more literal a remark than that Donne was once her 'Prophet'. I think 1608–9 a more likely date.

l. 1. *to Gods image*. Cf. Gen. i. 26, 27.

Eve, *to mans*. This is a fiction. Gen. i. 27 states that 'in the image of God created he him; male and female created he them'.

That one thing alone hath been enough to create a doubt, (almost an assurance in the negative) whether S. *Ambroses* Commentaries upon the Epistles of S. *Paul*, be truly his or no, that in that book there is a doubt made, whether the woman were created according to Gods Image. . . . No author of gravity, of piety, of conversation in the Scriptures could admit that doubt, whether woman were created in the Image of God, that is, in possession of a reasonable and an immortall soul (*Sermons*, ix. 190).

The pseudo-Ambrose was commenting on 1 Cor. xi. 7 ff., xiv. 34.

l. 2. *Nor finde wee that God breath'd a soule in her*. In the Sermon just quoted Donne says that some men 'out of the extravagancy of Paradoxes . . . have called the faculties, and abilities of women in question, even in the root thereof, in the reasonable and immortall soul'. He himself had been one: cf. his Problem, 'Why hath the common Opinion afforded Women Soules?' (Keynes, *Paradoxes and Problems*, pp. 47–48). Later, however, he writes: 'Wee are sure *Women* have Soules as well as *Men*, but yet it is not so expressed, *that God breathed a Soule into Woman*, as hee did into Man' (*Sermons*, iv. 241). Jonson rejects the opinion that women have no souls, appending a note: 'There hath beene such a profane *paradoxe* published' (*The Masque of Beauty*, ll. 369–70; see the editor's notes, *Works*, x. 464, and *Sermons*, ix. 20–21).

l. 3. 'The canons of the church will not let you (as a woman) invade (assume) any function in the church'; this would be an invasion of men's functions. An unusually violent ellipsis.

l. 4. Civil laws prevent women from assuming office in the state, as canon laws do in the church.

ll. 5–6. *Who vagrant transitory Comets sees*, etc. The comets 'wander and cross the sky', causing wonder by their rarity, but not (nowadays) as portents of evil. Donne shows an awareness of the new astronomy as much by his attitude as by his information. Tycho Brahe had proved the great distance of comets from the earth, and suggested that they were 'transitory' in oval courses.

ll. 6–8. *But a new starre*, etc. In the old cosmology the 'fixed stars', 1022 in number, were placed in the eighth sphere or 'unchangeable firmament' ('A Fever', l. 24), with which their motion agreed (since they were 'fixed' in it). In the regions above the moon there was thought to be no change; 'there no new things are'. Donne's language here is precise; many people, however, confused the new stars with comets (whereas Tycho Brahe and Kepler went to great pains to distinguish them from one another). To accommodate the undoubted reality of the new stars to the theory of the immutability of the heavens, it was usual to ascribe them to miraculous acts of God.

l. 9. *innocence*: passive goodness (opposed to the miraculous 'active good', l. 10).

l. 12. By nature (being without a soul, and hence without reason) and training they are prevented from achieving active goodness. 'A miracle is a thing done against nature' (*Sermons*, vii. 300).

l. 13. *such a starre*. Of new stars the most miraculous of all was that which led the Magi to Bethlehem (Matt. ii. 2, 9). Beza, indeed, thought the star of 1572 to be the same one; Tycho denied it. But if anything could be more miraculous than a new star whose motion agreed with the firmament, it would be a star like that in Matt. ii. 9 whose motion did not agree; its special miraculousness matched the miracle to which it pointed—the perfect Virtue to which it led. The Magi's star is like the Countess's reputation for virtue (l. 15).

Cf. the Palatine 'Epithalamion', ll. 39–40:

> Bee thou a new starre, that to us portends
> Ends of much wonder.

l. 17. *the worlds age, and death*. The age of the world was pretty accurately known: 'From the beginning of the *world* to the Birth of *Christ*, in the accompt of *Beroaldus*, are 3928. yeers; 3945. in the computation of the *Genevians*; 3960. in the esteem of *Luther*, and 3963. in the calculation of *Melanchthon*'

(P. Heylin, *Cosmography*, 1652, p. 3). A familiar idea was that 2,000 years elapsed in which Nature ruled after the Creation, 2,000 years under the Law of Moses, and 2,000 more would elapse under Grace before the world then ended; hence the world was already in its 'aged evening' ('The Progress of the Soul', l. 5).

l. 18. *the Sunnes fall*. Here, and in *The First Anniversary*, ll. 268–74, the reference is to the variations in the obliquity of the ecliptic. Bodin and Melanchthon also held that the sun was nearer the earth than in the past. Both this idea and the declination of the sun were adduced as arguments of the impending 'death' of the world. See C. M. Coffin, *John Donne and the New Philosophy*, 1937, pp. 135–6, 272.

l. 21. This marks the beginning of Donne's extrication of himself from an apparently impossible position; an almost insulting opening of the letter is turned into a triumph of flattery.

ll. 25–28. Virtue merely spread over all men like a thin veneer (l. 23), making us appear virtuous but not really affecting our deeper nature; in the Countess, however, virtue has changed the whole substance so that through and through she is transmuted to virtue itself ('Shee', l. 25).

E. H. Duncan (*E.L.H.* ix, 1942, pp. 272–5) explains the metaphor. In alchemy the elixir (l. 28) is gold 'digested' to the highest degree; it 'corrects and purifies everything that is not pure', says Paracelsus (*Hermetic and Alchemical Writings*, translated by A. E. Waite, ii. 333), and has the power of transmuting all baser substances into its own substance—gold; hence it not only makes 'cleane', but even makes 'new' substances. This is distinguished from 'gilding' or 'colouring', in which only the appearance of gold is achieved.

The 'form', in scholastic philosophy, was that which, added to the substance, made it what it was to us, or appeared to be. In the Mass the 'form' made the bread bread and the wine wine; but the process of transubstantiation changed the whole substance of both bread and wine. Similarly virtue has 'inform'd' us, and made us appear good men; but it 'transubstantiates' the Countess into Virtue itself.

According to alchemical theorists, when the inferior substance has been changed into the stuff of the elixir itself, it retains its same outward form and appearance (like the elements in the Mass). Hence the Countess is still able to appear as woman, wife, and mother (ll. 29–30), though made of the stuff of Virtue itself.

ll. 29–36. These difficult stanzas have been elucidated by Helen Gardner, 'Notes on Donne's Verse Letters', *M.L.R.* xli, 1946. The Countess is known as wife and mother, but this is not in virtue of her womanhood, since not all women are wives and mothers (and our problem is to account for virtue in women). But Virtue, having transmuted the Countess into her own substance, has to find a way of showing the Countess and herself ('her and you to show') to the world; for both are too 'pure' for us to see (l. 33). Just as when water evaporates into air neither water nor air is visible until the aqueous vapour is condensed into cloud (which is less pure, lower), so to become visible to the inadequate and sullied people about her ('for our sakes') the Countess shows virtue in the forms, with the 'low names', of woman, wife, and mother (ll. 29–30); in these Virtue must 'adhere' to be shown at all (l. 32).

l. 34. *water being into ayre rarify'd.* Cf. Plato, *Timaeus*, 49 c, and *Batman upon Bartholome*, 1582, f. 165^{r}a: 'Neither is there any of the sensible Elementes pure, but according to more or lesse they are mixed together, and apt to bee transmuted one into another: Even as durtye and loosed earth is made water, & that beeing ingrosed & thickened, becommeth earth, and beeing evapored by heate tourneth into Ayre, and that waxing hot, turneth into Fire', etc.

l. 41. *one*: her husband.

l. 42. *others*: her kinsmen.

l. 46. *'tis not none*: there is some degree (of virtue).

l. 48. *that*: the privilege of contemplating you.

ll. 49–52. 'If you think I flatter you, then you have not a true perception of your virtues; in that case, since you have not the power (discretion) to judge properly of virtue, I have been flattering you after all. In any case, if what I say is flattery, it can serve as advice and give you a standard to aim at.'

l. 53. *ill reaching you*: clumsy attempt to portray you.
  there grow good: in that way produce a benefit.

l. 56. *my will*: my intention in writing of you.

ll. 63–64. To give God due honour, the Countess would have to confess the extent of His gifts to her; Donne is merely doing this in her stead.

l. 66. *universe*: the Countess, being 'heaven' (l. 22), Virtue, a queen (l. 44), is a universe in herself, or a demonstration of the main forces acting in the universe.

l. 68. *you and fame.* The Countess and her reputation say what the poem says. Donne is merely a notary, copying it down.

l. 69. *your yonger dayes.* In a letter to Goodyer in 1622 (*Letters*, pp. 184–5) Donne writes of 'my Lady *Huntington*' and of his gratitude 'that her Ladiship retains my name in her memory . . . though I had a little preparation to her knowledge in the house where I served at first, yet, I think, she took her characters of me, from you'.

ll. 69–70. He foretold God's gifts to her, and did the office of a prophet; now he praises God's gifts in her, and does the office of a chaplain.

To Mrs M. H. (p. 88)

MSS.: Group II (*A 18*, *N*, *TCC*, *TCD*); *DC*; Group III (*A 25*, *B*, *C*, *Dob*, *Lut*, *O'F*, *O*, *P*, *S 96*).
Miscellany: *HK 1*.

The editor of *1633* used the very good text in his Group II manuscript; I reject only one of his (and Grierson's) readings, in l. 27.

It can hardly be doubted that this letter was addressed to Magdalen Herbert, mother of Sir Edward Herbert and of George Herbert. For an account of her relationship with Donne, cf. Gardner, *Elegies etc.*, pp. 251 ff. He met her probably in Oxford about 1600, but their close friendship seems to date from 1607. Donne took shelter in her house for several months during the dreadful plague of 1625; he lent money to her second husband, Sir John Danvers; and he preached a sermon in her honour on her death in 1627 (*Sermons*, viii. 3–9, 61 ff.).

H. W. Garrod (*R.E.S.* xxi, 1945) plausibly suggests that the last five stanzas of this letter refer to her imminent marriage to Danvers, which took place in 1608.

Apart from Group II (with *DC*), *Lut*, and *O'F*, only *S 96* has a title ('Elegie').

l. 1. *Mad paper stay*, etc. In this pleasant fancy, in which, by seeming to address the paper (or the written poem), the poet can say things perhaps a little more intimate than he would venture to say to the lady outright, Donne is using another convention of earlier love poetry. Cf. Dorus's letter in *Arcadia*, ii, Ch. 5 (ed. Feuillerat, i. 181) beginning: 'Most blessed paper, which shalt kisse that hand, where to al blessednes is in nature a servant, do not yet disdain to cary with thee the woful words of a miser now despairing: neither be afraid to appear before her, bearing the base title of the sender. For no sooner shal that divine hande touch thee, but that thy basenesse shall be turned to most hie preferment.'

l. 2. *sonnes*. For the pun, cf. the Holy Sonnet, 'As due by many titles', l. 5: 'I am thy sonne, made with thy selfe to shine'.

ll. 7–8. Unworthiness takes you a long way on the road to high office, admittedly; it gives you courage to struggle forward and thrust others out of the way; but for complete success you need to be thoroughly wicked (and this I cannot teach you, l. 9).

l. 13. *perplexing*: either 'puzzling over you'; or 'so searching as to cause you perplexity', challenging.

l. 14. love *and* reverence. For the theological overtones of this phrase, cf. Puente's *Meditations*, quoted by L. L. Martz, *The Poetry of Meditation*, 1954, p. 80: 'for with these two armes God desireth to bee embraced: with charity, and humility: with love, and reverence'.

l. 15. *dispute it*: argue my case (to win her favour).

l. 19. *saples leafe*: the dry leaf of paper. It is a sort of little Chaos out of which Mrs. Herbert will make a new and glorious creation ('creature').

ll. 21–22. Cf. 'From these overtures of repentance, which are as those unperfect sounds of words, which Parents delight in, in their Children, before they speake plaine, a penitent sinner comes to a verball, and a more expresse prayer' (*Sermons*, vi. 49).

l. 22. *early*: young.

l. 27. *ill, and her*: evil and goodness (for, l. 28, she *is* goodness).

l. 31. *they*: *sc.* her 'shape and beauty and grace' (l. 32), as in 'The Undertaking', ll. 15–16: 'he who colour loves, and skinne, Loves but their oldest clothes'.

l. 36. The letters from noble and intelligent friends, or from poets 'ambitious' for a patroness, together make up a bonanza of virtue almost as rich as Mrs. Herbert's own character.

l. 37. *any*: anyone; probably Mrs. Herbert's prospective second husband, John Danvers.

l. 38. *sav'd*: (1) preserved, not thrown away; (2) redeemed, to partake of heaven.

l. 43. 'Protest' seems best taken in its legal sense (*O.E.D.* 5), 'demand', 'stipulate', though the construction is rather unusual: 'Mark if she does what they stipulate.'

l. 44. 'Mark whether she is aware of her woman's entering the room.' Is she so absorbed in reading her lover's letters as not to notice her maid's presence?

l. 45. 'Note whether (in the way of people in love) she makes difficulties of trifles, only to brush them aside.'

ll. 46–47. *if her oathes . . . Reserv'd*: 'if her vows to reject suitors be not reserved in his case, whether she makes an exception of him' (and hence is 'not her owne' mistress).

l. 47. *and that*: and if ('that' replacing a repeated conjunction, as in 'The Progress of the Soul', l. 304).

l. 50. *familiar*: familiar friend, close companion.

To the Countesse of Bedford (p. 90)

MSS.: Group I (*C 57, D, H 49, Lec, SP*); Group II (*N, TCD*); *DC*; *L 74*; Group III (*B, Cy, Dob, Lut, O'F, S, S 96*).

Miscellanies: *HK 1, La, RP 31*; Grierson reported a copy in *M* (a manuscript once owned by the Marquis of Crewe).

The editor of *1633* seems to have taken his text of this letter from his Group I manuscript; but he corrected l. 19 from his Group II manuscript, and attempted emendations (which I reject) in ll. 16 and 36. Group II may also have supplied a reading in l. 4 (but this may be due to independent error). In l. 3 I depart from the edition in two readings (adopted by Grierson), one an error in Group I, the other a misreading of the copy by the printer.

Lucy Harington, who married Edward Russell, third Earl of Bedford, in 1594, was one of the most interesting members of the Court of James I, and was a favourite of the Queen. Henry, Earl of Huntingdon, husband of Elizabeth Stanley, to whom Donne's verse letters are addressed, was the Countess of Bedford's nephew. Sir Henry Goodyer was in her husband's service, and (in 1607) with Edward Woodward handled the reversion of Twickenham Park, which soon afterwards became the Countess's residence. She received the homage of dedications or other tributes from Florio, Jonson, Daniel, Davies of Hereford, Drayton, Chapman, and Dowland. With Donne she exchanged verses (cf. Gardner, *Elegies etc.*, pp. 250-1); she stood god-mother to his second daughter, Lucy, in August 1608; on the deaths of her kinswomen Cecilia Bulstrode and Lady Markham, and of her brother John (second Lord Harington) he wrote elegies; it was to her he applied for help in settling his debts before his ordination. The references to her in Donne's prose letters show a genuine warmth of friendship, though this became less close after her illness in the winter of 1612-13 (see P. Thomson, 'John Donne and the Countess of Bedford', *M.L.R.* xliv, 1949). Donne preached before her in 1621 (*Sermons*, iii. 13-15, 187 ff.). She died in retirement in 1627.

Goodyer probably introduced Donne to the Twickenham circle, with the help of Ben Jonson, who sent, with a covering epigram, a copy of the *Satires* to the Countess. Her close acquaintanceship with Donne dates very probably from 1608, and his verse letters to her seem to belong to the years 1608-12. This one, which has been elucidated by Helen Gardner (*M.L.R.* xli, 1946), is probably the first he wrote to the Countess; it is less intimate and occasional than the others, and has the tone of an introductory address.

The only variants in the title not noted in the apparatus occur in *S*, which prefixes 'Elegia Septima' to the *1633* title, and in *HK*, which adds 'Elegy 17th'.

l. 1. *Reason is our Soules left hand, Faith her right.* The relative places of these two faculties in 'reaching divinity' constituted an important problem in Mediaeval and Renaissance philosophy; for an account of the main traditions of thought, see D. C. Allen, *The Legend of Noah* (Illinois Studies in Lang. and Lit., xxxiii. 3-4, 1949), Ch. 1. Donne frequently takes up the subject: 'Mercy is Gods right hand, with that God gives all; Faith is mans right hand, with that man takes all'; 'A Regenerate man is not made of Faith alone, but of Faith and Reason'; 'Mysteries of Religion are not the less believ'd and embrac'd by Faith, because they are presented, and induc'd, and apprehended by Reason' (*Sermons*, vii. 370; vi. 175; i. 169; etc.).

l. 3. *your sight*: seeing you. Cf. John xx. 29: 'because thou hast seen me, thou hast believed: blessed are they that have not seen, and yet have believed'.

l. 4. *far faith*: faith that grasps the truth at a distance. Cf. Heb. xi. 1: 'faith is
. . . the evidence of things not seen'; and xi. 13: 'These all died in faith, not
having received the promises, but having seen them afar off.' In Group II,
I think, 'far' has been misread as 'fair'; the compiler of *1633* was attracted by
this reading, or himself misread his copy.

ll. 5–8. In writing his poem Donne uses Reason as men do in religion, not to
increase their Faith, but to clarify ('expresse') it in their understanding.

l. 10. *your election glorifies*: like those whom God 'chooses' to be saved. Cf. 2
Pet. i. 10–11.

l. 11. *accesses, and restraints*: the granting of access, or refusing it, i.e. the giving
or withholding of her favour.

l. 12. *what your selfe devize*: what the Countess herself writes (and also, perhaps,
how she plans her life generally).

l. 15. *implicite faith*. Cf. Brown, *Religio Medici*, i. 5, 6, 10:

where the Scripture is silent, the Church is my Text . . . , where there is a joynt
silence of both, I borrow not the rules of my Religion from Rome or Geneva, but the
dictates of my owne reason . . . in Divinity I love to keep the Road; and, though not
in an implicite, yet an humble faith, follow the great wheel of the Church, by which
I move, not reserving any proper Poles or motion from the Epicycle of my own brain
. . . by acquainting our Reason how unable it is to display the visible and obvious
effects of Nature, it becomes more humble and submissive unto the subtleties of
Faith; and thus I teach my haggard and unreclaimed Reason to stoop unto the lure
of Faith.

l. 16. *Catholique voice*: the general consensus, to be accepted as faith. The reading 'faith' for 'voice' is found only in *S* and *RP 31* among the manuscripts;
here and in *1633* 'voice' has been independently altered, I think, either by repeating 'faith' from l. 15, or by thoughtless substitution of the more obvious
phrase.

l. 20. *wash*: wash harmlessly over. The Countess's goodness resists all deni-
gration.

l. 22. *A* Balsamum. Paracelsus taught that every living body contained a sweet
balsam or 'balm', a healing fluid which preserved the body and counteracted
poisons (*Hermetic and Alchemical Writings*, translated A. E. Waite, ii. 69–74,
etc.). The balsam was exhausted by age, and the man, animal or plant then
died; or it could be cut off from parts of the body by 'blows' from outside (e.g.
a tight ligature round the finger eventually causes gangrene, since the balsam
cannot reach the finger; cf. *Sermons*, ii. 81). 'Every thing hath in it, as Physitians
use to call it, *Naturale Balsamum*, A naturall Balsamum, which, if any wound or
hurt which that creature hath received, be kept clean from extrinsique putrefaction, will heale of it self' (*Sermons*, vi. 116). In a letter to Goodyer written
about the same time as this poem (*Letters*, pp. 97–99), Donne says:

For vertue is even, and continuall, and the same, and can therefore break no where,
nor admit ends, nor beginnings. . . . He is not vertuous, out of whose actions you can

pick an excellent one. Vice and her fruits may be seen, because they are thick bodies, but not virtue, which is all light. . . . The later Physitians say, that when our naturall inborn preservative is corrupted or wasted, and must be restored by a like [i.e. balsam] extracted from other bodies; the chief care is that the Mummy have in it no excelling quality, but an equally digested temper: And such is true vertue . . . we have Christianity, which is the use and application of all vertue.

The idea that virtue is an indivisible whole comes from the opening and closing sections of Plato's *Protagoras*; cf. a later letter to the Countess, 'T'have written then', ll. 77–78, and 'Obsequies to the Lord Harington', ll. 50–51. Plato uses the uniform substance of gold as an image of the idea, as Donne does in his own way, in the letter to the Countess of Huntingdon, 'Man to Gods image', ll. 25–26. The alchemical processes gave him a number of other images of virtue as an animating force—balsam, mummy, tincture, the 'virtue' of a substance; see L. Stapleton, *S.P.* lv, 1958. An appreciation of Donne's usual thoughts and images enhances our sense of the 'wit' and resource with which here he achieves a rather different conceit; the Countess's birth and beauty are the balsam, her virtue is described in another way.

l. 27. *methridate*: a composite antidote against poisons supposed to have been used by King Mithridates VI of Pontus (120?–63? B.C.). Several different recipes are given (e.g. by Galen, *De Antidotis*, II. viii, ix; *Opera*, 1586, iii, f. 115).

Donne distinguishes the qualities of the Countess given by nature (birth and beauty) from those acquired by education, 'learning', 'religion', 'vertue' (which are like mithridate, added to what is naturally in the body).

l. 28. *what*: whatever (intended to harm you).

l. 29. This mixture of learning, religion, and virtue is not a medicine, like mithridate, but the Countess's food. At the back of Donne's mind might have been the further story of Mithridates, that he tried to commit suicide by poisoning himself, but had so built up protection by taking mithridate in the past (almost as 'food') that the poison could not take effect; so, e.g., Forestus, *De Venenis*, 1606, pp. 30–32, 41.

ll. 31–32. *The first good Angell*, etc. Cf. *Sermons*, ix. 190: 'to recompence that observation, that never good Angel appeared in the likenesse of woman, here are good women made Angels', etc.

l. 34. *His Factor for our loves*: God's agent ('Factor') winning our love for Him by illuminating (as angels do) the minds and consciences of men. She is a sort of tutelary angel to those about her.

do as you doe: continue in this angelic function. Cf. another letter to the Countess, 'Honour is so sublime', ll. 52–54: 'Goe thither still', etc.

l. 35. *home*: to heaven (whence angels are sent).

gracious: happy, fortunate, prosperous (cf. *The Winter's Tale*, III. i. 22: 'gracious be the issue'; *Measure for Measure*, V. i. 76: 'her gracious fortune', etc.). Her return to her native heaven will be blessed, for she will be accompanied by the souls she had helped to save.

ll. 35–36. *bestow This life on that*: devote this life on earth to the life of heaven, live your life here as part of eternal life, and so make one life of two: for 'this, and the next, are not *two Worlds*' (*Sermons*, iv. 240).

l. 36. *make one life of two.* The Countess's angelic work in this life will make one life of two also in another way—when she (already an angel) and Donne (who by her influence will become one) meet as redeemed spirits in heaven. Faithful souls are 'alike glorifi'd As Angels' (the Holy Sonnet, 'If faithfull soules', ll. 1–2), and in this state she and Donne will be united. In the 'Obsequies' on the Countess's brother, Lord Harington, Donne complains that he did not 'stay, t'enlarge' God's kingdom, 'By making others what thou didst, to doe' (ll. 213–14), even though (like the Countess here) 'he was joyned in commission With Tutelar Angels' (ll. 227–8). This commission, however, the Countess discharges.

l. 38. Compare: 'Truely I would not change that joy and consolation, which I proposed to my hopes, upon my *Death-bed*, at my passage out of this world, for all the joy that I have had in this world over again' (*Sermons*, vii. 360). All the good that might accrue to Donne from contemplating the Countess in this life would not compensate for his not being able to join her in heaven.

To the Countesse of Bedford (p. 91)

MSS.: Group I (*C 57, D, H 49, Lec, SP*); Group II (*N, TCD*); *DC*; Group III (*B, Cy, Dob, Lut, O'F*).
Miscellanies: *H 40, HK 1.*

In *1633* the text of a Group I manuscript was used, though in one place (l. 21) it was emended from the editor's Group II manuscript (or on his own initiative); this emendation I accept. The Group I text was a good one, and passed on only one small error to *1633* (l. 60). Otherwise there is only one reading which (unlike Grierson) I reject—an error peculiar to the edition in l. 52.

The opening lines of this letter suggest a further stage in Donne's relations with the Countess. He is now at Twickenham on a visit (as in *Letters*, p. 59), or else is sufficiently close to the Countess for it not to be improper that he should imagine himself there. The usual position of the poem immediately after the previous letter, in manuscripts where both appear, suggests that this one is later in date (but probably not very much later).

ll. 1–4. *You have refin'd mee*, etc. 'Refin'd' is an alchemical metaphor. Contact with the Countess has transmuted the poet, and in his new state of virtue his perceptions have been sharpened. Grierson paraphrases: 'You have refined and sharpened my judgement, and now I see that the worthiest things owe their value to rareness or use. Value is nothing intrinsic, but depends on circumstances.' Hence, as the next two stanzas show, at Court it is the Countess's virtue that is transcendent, in the country it is her beauty. The brackets added by Grierson are helpful in bringing out the sense. The 'worthyest things' are those enumerated in the preceding letter, ll. 24–26.

l. 3. This seems to be a witty variation of the familiar idea that three things are needed for obtaining virtue, 'Nature, Reason, and Use' (*The French Academy*, 1594, i. 59, 165).

ll. 5–6. *Two ills*, etc. 'God never puts his children to a perplexity; to a necessity of doing any sin, how little soever, though for the avoiding of a sin, as manifold as *Adams*' (*Sermons*, i. 197; also i. 170, ii. 106). Donne may have reached this conclusion at about the date of this letter; for writing to Goodyer (*c.* 1608; *Letters*, p. 49), he says that 'God doth thus occasion, and positively concurre to evill, that when a man is purposed to do a great sin, God infuses some good thoughts which make him choose a lesse sin'. In *Pseudo-Martyr* (1610), however, he says that Gratian deceives us 'As when he allowes *that there may be perplexities in evill*, and so in some cases a necessitie of sinning, and then, sayes he, *the remedie is to choose the lesse evill*' (p. 270). Cf. Gratian, *Decreti*, pars Iᵃ, dist. xiii: 'Minus malorum de duobus eligendum est' (Migne, *P.L.* clxxxvii. 67); here Gratian ratifies the proverbial solution (from Plato, *Protagoras*, 358 d; cf. Tilley, E207). Aquinas, of course, states that God does not cause anyone to sin, and cannot will evil (*Summa contra Gentiles*, clxii, xcv).

ll. 8–9. For double brackets cf. *Letters*, p. 43; *Sermons*, vii. 304; etc.

l. 9. *not be, or not show*. Virtue is too ineffable a quality to be or to be seen at Court; Donne is too 'low' to be or to be noticed there.

ll. 9–10. *all my rime Your vertues challenge*. An inversion: 'your virtues challenge all my poetic powers' because at Court rareness (l. 3) gives them transcendent value.

l. 11. *darke*: difficult to understand.

l. 12. *usher*: act as an usher for. At Court, where no one understands or recognizes virtue, someone must announce and identify her.

l. 13. *this place*: Twickenham Park (l. 70).

l. 16. *Exhale*: cause to exhale (*O.E.D.* I. 4).
   thick close bud display: cause the buds to open (as the sun does), releasing the scent.

l. 17. *enshrines*: shuts up (like precious things in a shrine).

ll. 19–24. The comparison of the Countess to the sun continues. When she arrives at Twickenham in her coach (like the sun in his chariot) it is morning, even if, in common parlance, it is 'night-time'. I follow *1633* in reading 'light' in l. 23, because it is the sun's light that brings morning, even if the sun cannot be actually seen; 'sight' seems to be a misreading, the two words being easily confused in some scripts (cf. l. 3 of the preceding letter).
   The stanza turns, as Miss Gardner showed (*M.L.R.* xli) on two 'computations' of the length of the day; the 'natural day' (i.e. twenty-four hours) is

distinguished from the 'artificial day' (i.e. the time between sunrise and sun-set). The latter is a common phrase; Chaucer uses it in l. 2 of the Introduction to *The Man of Law's Tale*, and explains the calculation in his *Treatise on the Astrolabe*, ii. 7. The two 'computations' are discussed in relation to Gen. i. 5, 15–16, in the Gloss and in many commentaries (e.g. that of Pererius) until at least 1657 (in *Annotations upon all the Books of the Old and New Testaments*); cf. *Sermons*, ii. 147. The Countess's arrival falsifies both methods of calculating the length of the day, and she creates a new sort of world (l. 21) in which the 'light' (for there is but one in this creation) in the firmament obeys different laws. As it is day wherever she goes, the Countess cannot be associated with an 'artificial day', and her daylight fills the whole 'natural day'. Hence with witty absurdity Donne shows that the Countess's behaviour in arriving at night is in accordance with 'nature' (l. 23).

l. 30. *sound ... say*: sound as Organs, say (reading the Countess's sacred words) as Priests.

l. 38. *Esteeme*: estimate, weigh the respective merits of.

l. 39. *serve*: minister to, satisfy.

l. 40. With the trappings of religion.

l. 41. *Schooles*: theological controversialists.

ll. 44–48. *You as you'are vertues temple*, etc. Donne probably has in mind here the temple made by Nero of 'specular stone', described by Guido Panciroli; see the note, pp. 269–70, to the letter to the Countess, 'Honour is so sublime per-fection', ll. 28–31. As Mr. R. N. Ringler points out (*M.L.R.* lx, 1965, pp. 335–6), Pliny (but not Panciroli) describes one kind of specular stone as 'mollitia nota', notoriously soft (*Nat. Hist.* xxxvi. 45. 162) as well as trans-parent; hence 'tender christall', l. 45. Since Nero's temple was dedicated to Fortune, the phrase 'vertues temple' has a touch of witty paradox (Fortune and Virtue being opposed); and since Panciroli speaks of 'sacellum [chapel] sive templum Fortunae', he himself is a 'Babler' of chapels (l. 48).

Even so the analogy requires a certain sleight of hand since the 'Altars' (l. 46) should really be inside a temple; but it would be unfair to press too hard this pleasant froth of complimentary imagery.

l. 48. *Escuriall*. Philip II of Spain completed his magnificent palace and mauso-leum in 1584. Beside it all other churches are 'Chappels', those who praise them mere 'Bablers'.

l. 50. *these*: the 'Altars' of l. 46 (eyes, hands, bosom), which are not conse-crated (because only her virtuous soul would be sacred), but beautiful; as such he admires them as a layman (not dealing in sacred things) and a country-man (not educated to subtle mysteries).

l. 51. *past and future stories*. The transition of thought might be due to Donne's recollection of friezes on ancient altars depicting 'stories' (history or legend);

or to the fact that the Escurial was also a library, a university, and a monastery; or to a more theological connexion of ideas—'all *promise*, all *performance*, all *prophecy*, all *history* concern us, in and by *him* [Christ]' (*Sermons*, v. 169).

l. 57. The analogy is with the birth of a human being, who is a 'little world made cunningly Of Elements, and an Angelike spright' (Holy Sonnet, 'I am a little world', ll. 1–2). 'Growth' suggests one faculty of the soul, which (like goodness and loveliness) is in 'every peece' of the body; see note (p. 184) to 'The Progress of the Soul', ll. 334–5.

l. 60. *thing*. The 'things' of *1633* is a misreading of 'thinge', or a misunderstanding of the sense, taken from the Group I manuscript used as copy. The singular is required, in opposition to 'two'.

l. 61. *these*: these lines.

l. 66. *aliens*: makes aliens of; makes unrecognizable.

l. 68. *higher Courts*: i.e. in the mind's Judgement. He will discard Reason, Memory, etc. and submit to the evidence of Sense.

senses decree is true. It is paradoxical that the fallible senses should declare essential truth.

l. 69. *Magazine*: storehouse.

l. 71. *Who hath seene one, would both*: whoever had seen Twickenham would inevitably wish to see the Countess.

l. 72. *Cherubin*. The cherubim were traditionally the beautiful angels; *O.E.D.* refers to Bacon, *New Atlantis*, 1658: 'The Spirit of Chastity . . . in the likenesse of a faire beautifull Cherubine'. 'For the beame of the lyght of God, shineth principally in the Angells of this order' (*Batman upon Bartholome, s.v.* 'Cherubin', 1582, Bk. ii, Ch. 9, f. 7ʳ).

To the Lady Bedford (p. 94)

MSS.: Group II (*N*, *TCD*); *L 74*; Group III (*Cy*, *Lut*, *O'F*, *O*, *P*, *S*). Pages lost from *DC* almost certainly contained this poem.
Miscellanies: *A 30*, *H 39*, *HK 1*, *RP 31*, *Wy*.

In *1633* a good text was taken from a Group II manuscript. I follow the edition against an unnecessary emendation adopted by Grierson in l. 20, and reject unique *1633* readings (which Grierson accepted) in ll. 22, 28; I correct a misprint in l. 42.

In *1633*, *Cy*, *H 40*, *N*, *RP 31*, and *TCD* this poem follows, in *O*, *P* it precedes, the funeral elegy beginning 'Language thou art too narrow, and too weake' (called 'Death' in *1635*); in *L 74* it follows the funeral elegy on Lady Markham, and is itself followed by the letter 'Reason is our Soules left hand', the Elegy on Mistress Bulstrode and 'Language thou art too narrow'; in *A 30* it precedes the elegy on Lady Markham and that on Mistress Bulstrode. All manuscripts (except *Lut*, *O'F* and *A 30*) have the word 'elegy' in the title. Only in *Lut*, *O'F* is it classified as a verse letter.

These facts suggest that it was a covering letter (under the general title 'Elegy') accompanying a funeral elegy on Cecilia Bulstrode (who died in the Countess of Bedford's house at Twickenham on 4 August 1609) or one on Lady Markham (the Countess's first cousin, who died, also at Twickenham, on 4 May 1609). I think the latter more likely, since, like Judith (l. 44), Lady Markham was a widow (Sir Anthony Markham having died in December 1604). In any case the poem seems to belong to 1609.

ll. 1–4. In the mystical mathematics of love and friendship two souls are one and each is two. Love 'makes both one, each this and that' ('The Ecstasy', l. 36). 'You that are she and you, which is (since she is you and she) double she, will see in her dead face half of yourself (since she and you are one).'

l. 4. *one of two*. Friends become one soul; cf. 'The Storm', l. 1, and note (p. 203).

ll. 5–6. Such a two as no third could equal, who were destined to be so perfectly matched before they were born.

ll. 7–8. Cuzco in Peru and Moscow in Russia stand for 'the two ends of the earth'. Twin souls (destined for each other), however far apart they are born, make up, like different stars, one constellation, 'Gemini'.

Donne would normally have made a precise analogy with the natural world , like the following comparison of the ladies to a pair of eyes, to explain their perfect equality and unity. I cannot, however, discover anything in the astronomers or in the myth of Castor and Pollux, the 'heavenly twins', that would give a more precise point to l. 8.

l. 14. *th'other halfe*: here 'the body' (not the twin soul).

ll. 15–16. *here Lies such a Prince*, etc. The heart of Richard I, for example, was buried in Rouen, the rest of his body at the Abbey of Fontevrault (*D.N.B.*).

l. 20. *both was*. The singular is correct: 'you are all (that one being) that was, before, both of you'.

Leone Ebreo says that friendship mixes souls 'exactly as if this love governed but a single soul and being . . . noble friendships make of one person—two; of two persons—one' (*The Philosophy of Love*, translated by F. Friedeberg-Seely and J. H. Barnes, 1937, p. 31).

l. 21. *by this*: by her friend's death.

ll. 23–26. *As of this all*, etc. The 'all' is still the 'third' creature constituted by the friendship of the two ladies. In one image (l. 22) it is 'contracted' into the Countess, as if the essence of the friendship were now in one person. Then Donne proposes that the friendship has been reconstituted in the Countess as are the beings of men at the general resurrection. Then 'God shall work upon this dispersion of our scattered dust. . . . God that knowes in which Boxe of his

Cabinet all this seed Pearle lies, in what corner of the world every atome, every graine of every mans dust sleeps, shall recollect that dust, and then recompact that body, and then re-inanimate that man, and that is the accomplishment of all' (*Sermons*, vii. 115). Though we say that 'many parts' of this whole decay, the pure elements of which they are composed are not destroyed.

ll. 31–32. The exigencies of rhyme and versification have defeated Donne here to some degree. The image seems to be that of the cycle of streams-ocean-rain-streams. The Countess is the source (ocean) of virtues and supplies less worthy people (streams) by her example and influence; now the virtues of the dead friend have returned to their source, also the Countess.

Circular motion, that of the heavens, was regarded as symbolizing eternity (being endless), and hence God; thus it was 'perfect'. Cf. Chapman, *Monsieur d'Olive*, I. i: 'might disproportion her, / Or make her graces less then circular'.

l. 34. *both rich Indies*. For the commonplace, cf. 'The Progress of the Soul', l. 17, and note, p. 174; and William Browne, *Britannia's Pastorals*, 1616, II. iv: 'one Indy gems of price / The other gives you of her choicest spice'.

ll. 35–38. These qualities of gold are frequently mentioned; cf. *Batman upon Bartholome*, 1582, f. 254^{r}a, and E. H. Duncan in *E.L.H.* ix, 1942, pp. 263–5.

l. 36. *last*: endure.

l. 41. *new*: a new friend.

l. 42. *be without*: feel her loss.

l. 44. Judith. *The Book of Judith* displays the virtues of the dead lady as those of Judith herself (viii. 7–8, xi. 21, 23): 'She was also of a goodly countenance, and very beautiful to behold... and there was none that gave her an ill word; for she feared God greatly. . . . There is not such a woman from one end of the earth to the other, both for beauty of face, and wisdom of words.'

To the Countesse of Bedford (p. 95)

MSS.: Group II (*N*, *TCD*); *DC*; Group III (*Lut*, *O'F*).

The text in *1633* was rather carelessly set up from a Group II manuscript. Though a good many minor slips were corrected as the book went through the press, readings remain without manuscript support; I reject those in ll. 5, 14, 20, 30, 32, 75, and 88, in all but the last case following Grierson; but I accept a reading found only in the edition in l. 59. The editor followed his Group II text in errors in ll. 7, 60.

Donne wrote letters in prose to the Countess (e.g. *Letters*, pp. 22 ff.) and received some from her. This poem begins with an apology for not answering one of hers. Donne mentions his verse letters to Goodyer: 'Therefore in stead of a Letter to you, I send you one to another, to the best Lady, who did me the honour to acknowledge the receit of one of mine, by one of hers; and who only hath power to cast the fetters of verse upon my free meditations' (*Letters*, p. 117).

This poem was very probably written in the latter part of 1609; cf. the note on ll. 67–68.

l. 1. *then, when*: immediately after, 'at once in reply'.

l. 2. It would have seemed like buying something sacred to reply at once, as in payment for her letter.

l. 4. Cf. Seneca, *Moral Essays* (Loeb ed., translation by J. W. Basore, iii. 3, 127): 'among all our many and great vices, none is so common as ingratitude'; 'Not to return gratitude for benefits is a disgrace'. 'In all *Solomons* bookes, you shall not finde halfe so much of the duty of thankfulnesse, as you shall in *Seneca* and in *Plutarch*. No book of Ethicks, of morall doctrine, is come to us, wherein there is not, almost in every leafe, some detestation, some Anathema against ingratitude' (*Sermons*, vi. 42).

ll. 5–6. *this . . . that*: 'not t'have written'. . . . 'T'have written'.

l. 13. *Temples were not demolish'd*. Bede quotes Gregory the Great's letter to Mellitus in Britain (A.D. 601) advising him not to destroy heathen temples: 'in obsequio veri Dei debeant commutari'; he also tells how Boniface transformed the Pantheon at Rome, 'in quo ipse, eliminata omni spurcitia, fecit ecclesiam sanctae Dei genetricis atque omnium martyrum Christi' (*Eccl. Hist.*, i. 30, ii. 4; Migne, *P.L.* xcv, 70–71, 88).

l. 14. St. Peter's Basilica in Rome was said to be on the site of a temple of Jupiter Capitolinus (Chambers); I have not traced the source of this information. St. Paul's Cathedral in London was supposed to have been founded by King Ethelbert on the site of a temple and grove sacred to Diana (Camden, *Britannia*, 1594, p. 319).

l. 17. *denizend*. Cf. the letter to Wotton, 'Sir, more then kisses', l. 34, and note, p. 228.

l. 18. *blamers of the times they mard*. Cf. *Sermons*, vii. 408: 'We make *Satyrs*; and we looke that the world should call that *wit*; when God knowes, that that is in a great part, self-guiltinesse, and we doe but reprehend those things, which we our selves have done, we cry out upon the illnesse of the times, and we make the times ill.'

l. 20. *all It; You*. The error in *1633* has thus been well repaired in *1635*. The Countess is the best part of the world—nay, the world itself.

l. 22. *Ostracisme*. The word retains much of its original meaning—a vote by which a dangerously powerful or unpopular citizen could be banished: so virtue from the Court.

l. 23. *fitnesse*: preoccupation with points of procedure, formalities.

l. 24. *only*: 'just by'.

l. 26. *one Court preserves*. The English Court is preserved from corruption while the Countess is in attendance.

ll. 37-40. 'I need not call in new Philosophy, that denies a settlednesse, an acquiescence in the very body of the Earth, but makes the Earth to move in that place, where we thought the Sunne had moved' (*Sermons*, vii. 271; also vi. 265). In the *Sermons* the older view is usually assumed: 'the Earth, that never mov'd' (x. 214; i. 227; ii. 232); 'earth is the center' (viii. 140-1); 'That the *Sun* could *stand still*, . . . is strange, *miraculously strange*' (x. 243).

The thought develops in ll. 39-40 to equate the sun, now stationary ('dull'd', without a purpose or 'end' to which it moves), with the mind, the light of reason; the body, man's lower part, is the more active—the earth that moves and is 'busie'.

l. 40. *pretends*: with the root meaning, 'stretching forward': 'presumes'.

l. 46. *this*: labour. The antecedent is not present, but is suggested by the verb 'labours'. For the thought in this line, cf. 'we are bound to suck at those breasts which God puts out to us, and to draw at those springs, which flow from him to us; and *prayer*, and *industry*, are these *breasts*, and these *springs*' (*Sermons*, iii. 196).

ll. 47-48. *He which said*, etc. 'And Jesus said unto him, No man, having put his hand to the plough, and looking back, is fit for the kingdom of God' (Luke ix. 62).

l. 50. *into cockle strayes*. Donne refers to the belief that poor husbandry caused useful grains to change their nature and degenerate into weeds. In *The Names of Herbs*, 1548 (reprinted by J. Britten, English Dialect Society, 1881, p. 49), William Turner says that *lolium* (darnel), often mistaken for cockle, 'groweth amonge the corne and the corne goeth out of kynde into Darnel'. Browne is more scientific:

But in Plants, wherein there is no distinction of sex, these transplantations are conceived more obvious then any; as that of Barley into Oats, of Wheat into Darnel; and those grains which generally arise among Corn, as Cockle, *Aracus*, *Aegilops*, and other degenerations; which come up in unexpected shapes, when they want the support and maintenance of the primary and master-forms (*Vulgar Errors*, iii. 17).

l. 53. Love (one of the 'minds thoughts') transplanted into the body becomes lust, the exercise of which harms our bodies more than any physical action prompted by hatred.

ll. 54-56. By corrupting influences in ourselves (which could not be exerted by any forces outside us, 'foreign' to us) we ruin the native dignity of the body in its capacity as the container of the soul—or rather, as the temple and palace of the soul (for the soul is both priest and king in our lives).

l. 55. *ingrav'd*: i.e. imposed from without.

ll. 57-58. The body will be redeemed from death at the resurrection; its nobler partner, the soul, is only preserved, not free from death by its own nature. Donne has been speaking of the importance and dignity of the body, which can impede the soul (ll. 40–42) yet should be an instrument of the soul in prayer and work (ll. 43–48). In being united with the body, the soul suffers (ll. 49–52), but so also does the body (l. 53), losing its proper dignity as the temple and palace of the soul (ll. 54–56). Nevertheless, the body will be redeemed; it is not so inferior to the soul as the pagans thought (believing the soul immortal by nature); for like the body the soul is only preserved by the will of God.

l. 58. Donne regarded it as now clear to the Church (though earlier it was not clear, cf. *Sermons*, v. 385) that the soul is not free from death by nature. 'And for the Immortality of the Soule, It is safelier said to be immortall, by preservation, then immortall by nature; That God keepes it from dying, then, that it cannot dye' (*Sermons*, ii. 201). Cf. Sparrow, *Devotions*, pp. 54–55; Simpson, *Essays*, p. 76.

ll. 59–60. The orthodox Christian view was that it was not the body that made the soul sinful, but that the sinful soul corrupted the flesh. Grierson quotes St. Augustine, *De Civ. Dei*, xiv. 3 (Migne, *P.L.* xli. 406): 'Nam corruptio corporis . . . non peccati primi est causa, sed poena; nec caro corruptibilis animam peccatricem, sed anima peccatrix fecit esse corruptibilem carnem.' It may have been his reading in the neo-Platonists that provided Donne with the thought here. It is paralleled elsewhere in his work only in *Pseudo-Martyr*, p. 31, and p. 247: 'the bodie by inhaerent corruption vitiates the pure and innocent soule.' Cf. the letter to Sir Edward Herbert, l. 19, and note (p. 240).

ll. 61–64. The 'first seeds' are not merely the four basic elements out of which all creation is made, but also some part of the quality of other creatures; cf. 'To Sir Edward Herbert', l. 1, and note, p. 239. Hence man's body can produce all kinds of things, whether bad or precious; in fact, however, it has produced only the bad—not pearl, gold, or corn, but lifeless or vile things. Medical men had certain evidence of this; Pareus (quoted by D. C. Allen, *J.E.G.P.* xlii, 1943) says that stones are found in the bladder and elsewhere; bugs, etc., are examples of 'animaux qui se procréent en nos cors'; Houlier, he says, extracted a scorpion from the brain of an Italian, Fernel took from a soldier two hairy worms with horns, Guillemeau extracted a serpent and brought it to Pareus in a glass vial. Other surgeons had extracted frogs, toads, lizards, etc. Grosart mentions the pamphlet published in England by Edward May in 1639: 'A most certain and true relation of a strange monster or serpent, found in the left ventricle of the heart of John Pennant, Gentleman . . . '.

l. 67. *We'have added to the world Virginia*. Expeditions to effect the re-colonization of Virginia were dispatched by the Virginia Company in 1607 and 1609. Early in the latter year, as a new charter was being prepared for the Company, there was a rumour that Donne wished to become its Secretary (Chamberlain, *Letters*, i. 284). Though he failed in this endeavour, Donne was obviously very interested in matters concerning Virginia, as were many of his friends, in 1609. See S. Johnson, 'John Donne and the Virginia Company', *E.L.H.* xiv, 1947.

l. 68. *Two new starres*. Donne's reduction of the three new stars (cf. note, p. 247, on 'To the Countess of Huntingdon', 'Man to Gods image') to two is due to his having in mind two people recently dead, whose souls, according to the ancient fancy, have become stars in the heavens. Cf. Chapman, *Monsieur d'Olive* (1606), I. i:

> Your worthy sister, worthier farre of heaven
> Then this unworthy hell of passionate Earth,
> Is taken up amongst her fellow Starres.

The reference here must be, I think, to Cecilia Bulstrode and Lady Markham (as Chambers suggested); see the introductory note to the preceding letter. If so, this poem would date from the latter part of 1609 (after 4 August, the date of the later of the two deaths, that of Miss Bulstrode); this would accord with the interest being shown by Donne and his friends in Virginia (cf. preceding note).

ll. 69-70. Why are we reluctant to add our souls to those two we have sent before us, and so increase, not heaven's dignity, but our own?

l. 72. *two truths*: the vice of the world ('others ill', l. 74), and her own virtue: she will believe neither.

l. 74. *her*: herself.

l. 77. Cf. note (pp. 254-5) to l. 22 of 'To the Countess of Bedford', 'Reason is our Soules left hand'.
  too much of one: too much humility.

l. 78. *suspition*: i.e. of her own virtue. Too many virtues, or too much humility, makes her suspect her own virtue.

ll. 79-80. If one is ignorant of the existence of vice, one cannot pity the vicious; to this extent one does not (because one cannot) show charitable compassion, and one's virtue is thus made 'lesse'.

l. 81. *aspersion*: sprinkling, admixture, attribution (of what stains or defiles).

l. 82. *complexion*: temperament, habit of mind (ascribed in the next lines by 'correspondence' to the 'body' politic).

ll. 83-84. *Statesmen purge vice with vice*, etc. Wise rulers must be prepared to use guile, cruelty, deceit, etc. to put down corruption and treachery.
  The toad was 'ugly and venomous' (*As You Like It*, II. i. 13), the spider full of poison (cf. *Cymbeline*, IV. ii. 91, etc.).

l. 90. *cordiall*: restorative.

To the Countesse of Bedford at New-yeares Tide (p. 98)

MSS.: Group II (*N, TCD*); *DC*; Group III (*Lut, O'F*).

There is a good text in *1633*, taken from a Group II manuscript, in which there was only one error (l. 35); the edition misprints the copy in ll. 10, 18, 47.

In all surviving manuscript copies this letter follows immediately upon the preceding; this perhaps indicates a fairly close proximity in date. Possibly it was sent to the Countess on New Year's Day (i.e. Lady Day, 25 March) 1610. Donne's friendship with the Countess is now close enough to allow him to offer some advice (ll. 36 ff.), with implied gentle criticism of her indulgence in Court frivolities (she took part in five Court Masques 1604–10). This one might not have been the only New Year letter in verse that Donne sent to the Countess. It is not clear whether it is this one, another, or a letter in prose, to which Donne refers in a note to Goodyer on 'the last of 1607' (*Letters*, p. 204): 'I have bespoke you a New-years-gift, that is, a good New year. . . . If for custome you will doe a particular office in recompense, deliver this Letter to your Lady, now, or when the rage of the Mask is past. If you make any haste into the Country, I pray let me know it.'

ll. 3–4. Meteors were atmospheric phenomena of the lower regions of the air (wind, rain, snow, hail, lightning, rainbows, dew, and prodigies like those touched on by Burton, *Anatomy*, part. 2, sect. 2, memb. 3). See Seneca, *Quaestiones Naturales*, I. i, etc., for discussion of their causes and exact location, which were matters in dispute. 'Perplext' means 'tangled, intricately intertwined', as in Bacon, *Advancement of Learning*, II. vii. 5: 'the forms of substances I say (as they are now by compounding and transplanting multiplied) are so perplexed, as they are not to be inquired'; hence they are 'perplexing', baffling, like the relationship of 'forme' to matter in meteors. Donne usually employs meteors as an image of hovering between two states; here of the uncertainty of his position in life, and perhaps of his lack of occupation ('forme', that would make him something).

l. 5. *misse*: miss my aim, make an error.

l. 10. *bravery*: bravado, swagger.

l. 12. *to'urge towards such*: to strive to equal the virtues Donne shows them, as a model, in the Countess.

l. 15. *corrupt*: corrupting.

l. 16. *Mine*: my verses.

tincture: universal tincture or elixir (cf. 'To Sir Edward Herbert', l. 20 and note, p. 240). The Countess's name is like the tincture made by refining gold to the highest degree, so that it has power to transform other substances to itself. It does this by changing the 'spirits' of those substances into 'new spirits'.

ll. 17–20. For all alchemical processes a controlled and constant heat was thought necessary (cf. 'To Mr. Rowland Woodward', l. 27, and note, p. 224). 'Strong extracts' like aqua fortis, vitriol, etc., keep bodies warm, but are too severe, and destroy ('wast') eventually the new substances they have created. The Countess's name is too powerful an agent, for, after shining a while in Donne's lines, it will be the cause of their destruction. In ll. 21–25 he adroitly extricates himself from this somewhat dangerous position.

l. 25. *it*: my verse. She has such miraculous grace of character that, in recording it, Donne's poem will be regarded as false (too good to be true), and hence both it and the Countess will be brought to shame.

l. 28. *corne*: grain (of dust, etc.); *O.E.D.* I.

l. 32. *leave*: stop trying.

l. 35. *such a prayser prayes*. Faltering or inappropriate praise of God is regarded by Him as a prayer for forgiveness for this inadequacy and for grace to praise Him better.

l. 37. favour: charm.

ll. 38–40. *He will perplex security*, etc. He will intermingle freedom from care with anxieties and then dispel those anxieties, withdraw and then show you favour, and thus increase your desire for Him and satisfy it.

security: freedom from care and anxiety (*O.E.D.* I. 3), as in *Macbeth*, III. v. 32.

ll. 41–42. *have not One latitude*: do not occupy the same respective positions.

l. 43. In the cloister things are either good or bad. In Courts there are many things that are neither good nor bad, but indifferent.

l. 44. *pitty*: tolerance aroused by pity for the sinful. A virtue elsewhere, it is too soft an emotion to feel for vices that deserve anger or contempt.

ll. 44–45. *some vaine disport*, etc. A certain amount of idle entertainment, considered unworthy elsewhere, may be thought tolerable in Court life, so long as it stops short of actual sin.

l. 47. *ingresse*: invade, intrude upon.

l. 48. *what none else lost*: complete virtue. Others never had it to lose.

ll. 49–50. God will give you ways to exercise and increase your virtue, even beyond what you now possess, in your dealings with the weaknesses of others.

l. 57. *discreet warinesse*. One of the four 'elements' of the Christian life, says Donne, 'is a good conscience in my selfe, That either a holy warinesse before, or a holy repentance after, settle me so in God, as that I care not though all the world knew all my faults' (*Sermons*, ix. 230); but this must be tempered with discretion, on which see General Introduction, pp. xxxv–xxxviii.

ll. 58–59. 'Though it be better to avoid than to revenge an offence, God will show you how to do both.' Presumably He will teach her how to 'turn the other cheek' when offended.

l. 60. *state*: chiefly, her financial position (it was no secret that it was more often 'lesse' than not).

l. 61. *teares*: of repentance (for she will not sin).

l. 63. *dis-inroule*: remove from the roll of the redeemed, from the Book of Life. Baptism and repentance are ways of being enrolled there.

l. 65. *This private Ghospell*. The thought occurs in Donne's New Year sermons, especially that opening the year 1625: '*God* presents him [Abraham] thus many *New-years-gifts:* First, he gives him a *new Name;* . . . God shall give us *new Names* (new Demonstrations, that our names are written in the Booke of life) . . . If you wil heare his voice this day, *Hodie eritis, This day you shall be with him in Paradise,* and dwell in it all the yeare, and all the yeares of an Everlasting life' (*Sermons,* vi. 194 ff.).

To the Countesse of Bedford (p. 100)

MSS.: Group II (*N, TCD*); *DC*; Group III (*B, Dob, Lut, O'F, S 96*). Miscellany: *HK 1*.

The editor of *1633* found a good text in his Group II manuscript, and I reject his emendations of it in l. 10 (accepted by Grierson) and in ll. 13, 27, 31. I adopt a spelling from *Dob* in l. 48 to remove a source of possible confusion.

There is no indication of the date or occasion of this poem.

ll. 1–2. *sublime, refinde*. This refers to alchemical purification; Donne intends an image for extreme purity. 'Sublime' = 'refined' is not, however, exemplified in *O.E.D.* (8. c) before 1694.

ll. 2–3. *when God was alone*, etc. Cf. Browne, *Religio Medici,* i. 35:

before the Creation of the World God was really all things. . . . God made all things for himself, and it is impossible he should make them for any other end than his own Glory; it is all he can receive, and all that is without himself. For, honour being an external adjunct, and in the honourer rather than in the person honoured, it was necessary to make a Creature, from whom he might receive this homage; and that is, in the other world, Angels, in this, Man.

Similarly Donne, *Sermons,* i. 272 ff., ix. 99, x. 100, etc.; Simpson, *Essays,* p. 54 and *The Second Anniversary,* ll. 401–5.

l. 4. *those which wee tread*: earth and water, lower than our feet.

l. 6. *barren both*: air and fire. Aristotle says that 'It is because earth and water are the material elements of all bodies that animals live in them alone and not in air and fire' (*Meteor.* iv. 4, 382ᵃ), elsewhere adding that birds live in the air (*De Gen. Animalium,* III. ii. 761ᵇ), but nothing in fire. This last point was one of the chief arguments against the very existence of fire as an element; thus Cardan (*De Subtilitate,* 1560, Bk. ii, pp. 30, 64) says that unlike the other three elements fire does not provide food and assist generation. So Donne, *Sermons*, vii. 184 ('onely the Fire produces nothing'), ix. 231. In the poem Donne uses the passage from Aristotle that suits him for the moment.

ll. 7–9. Cf. *The Second Anniversary*, ll. 407–9:

> But since all Honours from inferiours flow,
> (For they doe give it; Princes doe but shew
> Whom they would have so honor'd) . . .

In the matter of honour, inferior persons, like inferior elements, are productive; their superiors are not—they are in this respect 'barren'.

ll. 11–12. For the use of dung to provide an even warmth suitable for the distillation of the pure parts of substances from the impure or 'grosse' parts, cf. 'To Mr Rowland Woodward', ll. 25–27, and note, p. 224. The use of fire, or of the sun's heat, was also common; but the 'lower' substance, Donne says, was more effective than either.

l. 18. *th'earths low vaults in* Sicil *Isle*: the subterranean caverns under Mt. Etna, the volcano in Sicily (cf. Munster, *Cosmographia*, 1572, pp. 344, 345), the rumbles and explosions from which send their sound further than cannon, even when raised on towers. Again the 'low' is exalted.

l. 21. *but one*: save God.

l. 23. *Soules stuffe*. Donne is thinking of some attenuated form of matter, which would need little change into a 'spiritual body' at the general resurrection. The question of decay arises only because it is the Countess's 'body' for which God is using the 'stuffe' usually reserved for the creation of souls; immortal when made into souls, this 'stuffe' made into a body will not decay for a long time (unless 'late' implies 'never', because the general resurrection will intervene). St. Augustine discusses the nature of 'Soules stuffe', *De Genesi*, vii. 5. The orthodox view was that, souls being immaterial, they could not be made of anything; the soul 'is made of nothing, proceeds of nothing. All other creatures are made of that pre-existent matter, which God had made before, so were our bodies too; But our soules of nothing' (*Sermons*, ix. 82; also Simpson, *Essays*, p. 30).

l. 26. *discovers*: uncovers, reveals.

l. 27. *through-shine front*: transparent countenance.

ll. 28–31. Donne's information about 'specular stone', a stone which, correctly cut, had a transparency like that of glass, comes from Guido Panciroli's *Rerum memorabilium iam olim deperditarum*, written in Italian, but first published in an annotated Latin translation by Heinrich Salmuth in 1599. A second volume on modern marvels appeared in 1602. Donne refers to Panciroli by name in *The Courtier's Library* and in *Ignatius his Conclave*. Panciroli's earlier volume deals with arts once practised but now lost, 'unknowne To our late times'. In the chapter 'De Specularibus' we read that Nero built a Temple of

Fortune with specular stone, and that anyone inside could be seen by those outside ('in quo qui erat, extrinsecus absque ullo obstaculo conspiciebatur'). See Miss Gardner's note to ll. 5–12 of 'The Undertaking', *Elegies etc.*, pp. 179–80, and R. N. Ringler, 'Donne's Specular Stone', *M.L.R.* lx, 1965.

l. 32. This is the secret of 'discretion', ll. 37 ff.; she is concerned that her outward behaviour proclaims what she really is.

l. 33. know *and* dare. For this Renaissance commonplace cf. Sidney, *Arcadia*, I, Ch. xv (*Works*, ed. A. Feuillerat, i. 97), where of Phalantus, the pattern of 'The faire man of armes', it is said that he had got the reputation 'of one, that both durst & knew'. See F. P. Wilson, *Elizabethan and Jacobean*, Oxford, 1945, pp. 51–52 and notes.

ll. 34–36. In Aristotle's theory (*De Anima*) of the threefold soul of man (adopted by Aquinas, *S.T.* Iᵃ pars, q. lxxvi, art. 3), the vegetative and sensible souls were supposed to have existence in man (and had 'birthright' because slightly older) before the rational soul was breathed into him; only the last was immortal, and it transcended and included the powers of the other two (which did not therefore have 'precedence'). Cf. *Sermons*, iii. 85, viii. 221, and Sparrow, *Devotions*, p. 105.

ll. 37–39. Cf. Donne's remark that the deacons in Acts vi. 3 were 'full of Religion towards God, and full of such wisedome as might advance it towards men; full of zeale, and full of knowledge; full of truth, and full of discretion too' (*Sermons*, iv. 287; similarly ix. 199, v. 371–2, vi. 361). Contrast Rom. x. 2.

l. 42. *her yea, is not her no*: discretion and religion say the same things—are not contradictory.

ll. 44–45. *nor must wit Be colleague*, etc. The powers of the mind are not to be brought in to help religion; they must be permeated with, inspired by, indeed identical with, religion. Cf. Donne's reference to divines who 'write for Religion, without it' (*Letters*, p. 160).

l. 46. *types of God*. Cf. the definition (of unknown origin) of God as an infinite circle of which the centre is everywhere and the circumference nowhere. The saying first appears in the 12th century ascribed to Hermes Trismegistus; it was quoted by Aquinas, Bonaventura, Bartolomaeus Anglicus, etc., and became a commonplace (see F. L. Huntley, *Sir Thomas Browne*, 1962, pp. 108–9, 139). Cf. *Sermons*, iv. 51–52, vii. 247, and Sparrow, *Devotions*, p. 4.

The centre of a circle is 'pieceless', an indivisible point; religion is similarly entire. As the centre 'flows' into each radius, so religion should flow into all the ways of our lives. Cf. 'Sir, not onely a Mathematique point, which is the most indivisible and unique thing which art can present, flowes into every line which is derived from the Center . . .' (*Letters*, p. 163; see also *Sermons*, ix. 406). But if religion and discretion are to be divided, then in the Countess religion has determined aims and discretion conduct.

l. 52. *thither*: 'the same way' you have always gone, to the same destination—to God.

l. 53. 'Whoever wishes to change either wants something he does not possess or repents of something he has done.' Neither consideration can affect the Countess.

Epitaph on Himselfe (p. 103)

MSS.: Group I (*D*, *H 49*, *SP*); Group III (*A 25*, *B*, *C*, *Dob*, *Lut*, *O'F*, *O*, *P*, *S 96*).

Miscellanies: *H 40*, *HK 1*, *RP 31*, *S 962*; Brit. Mus. MS. *Harleian 3511*; St. John's Coll. Cambridge MS. *James 548*.

A 25 and its copy *C*, and *S 962* contain the six-line epistle only; in *B* it is separated from the Epitaph by other poems; *A 25* and *C* have no title; *S 962* has 'Epitaph'; *B* has 'Epitath' [*sic*] as title for the epistle, but no title for the Epitaph itself. *O* and *P* have the Epitaph, but not the epistle. The epistle and the complete Epitaph are found in the other manuscripts (except Harleian MS. 3511). In Group I the poem is headed 'Epitaph', and the Epitaph itself is headed 'Omnibus'; *H 40* and *RP 31* are like Group I, except that 'Omnibus' is changed to 'To all'. In *Dob*, *Lut*, *O'F*, *S 96*, and *HK* the poem is addressed 'To the Countesse of Bedford', and the Epitaph has no separate title. In the St. John's manuscript, the commonplace book of John Cruso (d. 1681), once owned by Wordsworth, the Epitaph is also without title, and the whole is headed 'Madame: Epitaph'.

There seem to have been two main copies of the poem: (1) that in Group I, *H 40*, *RP 31*, and *B*, and (2) that in *A 25*, *C* (epistle only); *Dob*; *S 96*; *O*, *P* (Epitaph only); *Lut*, *O'F* (somewhat sophisticated); *S 962* (epistle only). The dropping of one or other part of the poem in the copying of some manuscripts was probably accidental (in *B*, where the parts appear separately, we can see how such an accident could occur).

In *1635*, where the poem was first printed, the epistle and ten lines of the Epitaph, the whole headed 'Elegie', appear among the funeral Elegies; the text is that of the copy (2, above) found in *O'F*, one of the sophistications in which was adopted into the text of the edition. The complete Epitaph (without the epistle), headed 'On himselfe', was printed among the Divine Poems (the first ten lines of the Epitaph thus appearing twice in the edition); the text here is that of the copy (1, above) found in Group I. (Curiously enough, the last 8 lines of the Epitaph in *Lut*, *O'F*, seem to come from a copy of the same type.)

The textual variants in the two traditions of the poem are not sufficiently numerous to allow much speculation on their relations to each other. I deduce that the original form of the poem was an 'Epitaph on Himselfe', with a brief preliminary epistle addressed to the Countess of Bedford, and the Epitaph proper, meant to be (if not actually) addressed 'Omnibus', 'to everybody'.

I make use, accordingly, of all these titles. As copy-text I use *1635*: for the epistle, the text as given under the title 'Elegie' (which is obviously not an authentic title); for the Epitaph the text (of Group I, etc.) given in full (18 lines) under the title 'On himselfe' among the Divine Poems. This seems to give a text of the poem as close as can now be achieved to what Donne wrote.

The occasion of the poem is unknown. It may be a mock-heroic gesture of apology when he has been 'killed' by the Countess's slight displeasure; it may be a valedictory gesture before leaving for France (see the next letter). It has the air of having been written when Donne and the Countess had been friends for some time; hence I print it late in the series of letters to her.

A version of the epistle, worked up into a love-poem, appears in *A 10*.

l. 1. *my tombe*. Donne and his letter are fused into one suppliant voice, as in 'To Mrs M. H.', ll. 34 ff.

l. 2. *fame . . . soule*. The distinction touched on is that between discretion (care for outward conduct and reputation) and religion (the life of the soul). Cf. ll. 37 ff. of the preceding letter.

l. 3. *my soule*. The Countess already has his soul.

l. 5. *Testament*. The reading 'wills' occurs only in *Lut* and as a correction in *O'F*; *1635* obviously took it from this source. The alexandrine is unusual, but 'Testament' is hard to account for unless it is, in fact, Donne's own word.

l. 7. *Fortune . . . choice*: luck and will, chance and choice; the usual distinction between factors of a man's career or condition.

ll. 9–10. Usually a tombstone 'speaks' to the living, by the inscription upon it, of what the person 'was' who lies beneath it. The poet is breaking with this custom; he is revealing what he now is, in the grave, and what we are also (clay). (But, he continues, we are not, being alive, as good as he in our substance, for he has already advanced some way towards the glorification of the body's clay.)

ll. 13–14.   *Parents make us earth, and soules dignifie*
              Us to be glasse;

Our parents give us our physical body of earth; but we are ennobled by the soul (infused by God), which makes of us a glass vessel holding the breath of life. Cf. 'A Litany', l. 26 ('this glasse lanthorne, flesh'), and the note in Gardner, *Divine Poems*, p. 82.

l. 14. *here to grow gold we lie*. According to the alchemists, nature strives towards the perfection of gold (in which the elements are perfectly balanced); base metals were thought to change gradually, owing to the condensation of mercury and sulphur vapours among the stones, into gold over long periods of time (see E. H. Duncan, *E.L.H.* ix, 1942, p. 267). There is perhaps a further suggestion that the decay of the body is like the 'putrefaction' or 'mortification' of base metals to their first elements by alchemical processes, to assist transmutation.

Like base metals, our bodies become transformed in the grave so that at the general resurrection they will arise glorified, at the last Trump (l. 20), and 'scale Heaven' (ll. 19–20).

ll. 15–20. We willingly entertain sin and destroy our true selves by killing our souls (for the wages of sin is death); to kill something immortal is a miracle. God achieves a less miracle when he glorifies the body (usually called a worm-eaten carcass) and allows it to enter heaven re-created at the last day.

l. 21. *mendst me*: dost contribute to my salvation.

l. 23. *compos'd*. The poet is well 'composed' for death, for his poem has been well 'composed' even in the last minutes of mortal sickness.

To the Countesse of Bedford *Begun in France*, etc. (p. 104)

MSS.: *DC*; *O'F*.

The manuscripts and *1633* have the same title and virtually the same text.

Donne was in France with Sir Robert Drury from late November 1611 until April 1612. He had published, as a commemoration of Elizabeth Drury, Sir Robert's daughter, 'A Funeral Elegy' preceded by *An Anatomy of the World* in a small volume in 1611. Lines 511–13 of *The Second Anniversary* show that Donne was still in France when he was completing it, and it was published, with the two other poems on Elizabeth Drury, by early April 1612. The two earlier poems had aroused great interest, and soon after reaching France Donne apparently heard that the great ladies, his patronesses, were indignant at the extravagance of compliment with which he had celebrated the dead girl. This unfinished letter, and that following, to Lady Carey and her sister, were attempts to mend the situation. Donne's embarrassment is obvious in passages in his correspondence from France:

I hear from *England* of many censures of my book, of M^ris. *Drury*; if any of those censures do but pardon me my descent in Printing any thing in verse.... I doubt not but they will soon give over that other part of that indictment, which is that I have said so much; for no body can imagine, that I who never saw her, could have any other purpose in that, then that when I had received so very good testimony of her worthinesse, and was gone down to print verses, it became me to say, not what I was sure was just truth, but the best that I could conceive . . . (*Letters*, pp. 74–75).

In a similar passage, of which versions appear in duplicated letters (pp. 238–9, 255), one dated 14 April 1612 (Continental style), Donne tells George Garrard that he took as his subject 'such a person, as might be capable of all that I could say. If any of those Ladies think that Mistris *Drewry* was not so, let that Lady make her self fit for all those praises in the book, and they shall be hers.'

Donne was, besides, in ill health, and worried by lack of news about his wife's welfare in child-birth. He might have already used up most of the poetic energy he felt worth expending in writing the letter to Lady Carey which follows. For whatever reason, it is easy to discern his lack of real interest in this perfunctory fragment.

l. 2. *Court*: attendance at Court, i.e. the Countess's 'court' at Twickenham (or wherever her 'presence' is).

l. 8. *to growth and to confession*: to natural growth, because it is spring; to Easter duties of taking Communion, preceded by confession.

l. 16. *Mine*. This is, presumably, Elizabeth Drury. Donne will not yield every point: at least Elizabeth Drury *was* a mine of virtue and beauty.

ll. 24–25. *lesse lessons. . . . By studying copies*. Mistress Drury can supply to the world only smaller examples of beauty and virtue than the Countess; but these might be all that people far from the Countess's 'influence' (l. 9), with their puny capacity of moral comprehension, could grasp. It will be enough for them to study Mistress Drury, who is (like any other virtuous person) only a copy of the Countess.

A Letter to the Lady Carey, and Mrs Essex Riche, From *Amyens* (p. 105)

MSS.: Group I (*C 57, D, H 49, Lec, SP*); Group II (*N, TCD*); *DC*; Group III (*B, Cy, Dob, Lut, O'F, O, P, S 96*).

Miscellanies: *HK 1*; *M* (reported by Grierson).

The text in *1633* was taken from a Group I manuscript, which passed on errors in l. 26 (adopted by Grierson) and l. 30; the edition has one error (l. 13) of its own. In l. 57 I agree with *1633* in adopting a Group II reading, although the textual evidence is very evenly balanced.

The sisters to whom this letter is addressed were daughters of Robert, third Lord Rich, and his first wife, Penelope Devereux (Sidney's 'Stella'). Lettice, the elder of the two, married as her first husband Sir George Carey, of Cockington, Devon. Essex, the third child of this unhappy family, was un-married at the date of this letter; she later married Sir Thomas Cheke, of Pirgo, Essex (*D.N.B.*). There is some evidence in Donne's prose letters that he knew Rich's son fairly well. About his connexion with these two offended young ladies we know nothing beyond what this letter suggests. It was apparently written between the end of November 1611 and the beginning of March 1612, while Donne was in Amiens with Sir Robert Drury.

Of manuscripts not mentioned in the apparatus, *O, P, HK* have no title; *DC* has 'To the La: C. of C. / from France'; and Group III generally have 'To (*Cy*: A Letter to) the Lady Carey'.

l. 1. Cf. *The Second Anniversary* (being written about the same time as this letter), ll. 511–13:

> Here in a place, where mis-devotion frames
> A thousand Prayers to Saints, whose very names
> The ancient Church knew not, Heaven knows not yet.

l. 5. *other Sainct then you*. For the common conceit of the adored lady as saint, cf. Hall, *Virgidemiarum*, I. vii. 26 ('Sure will he Saint her in his Calendere') and the note in *Poems*, ed. A. Davenport, p. 170.

l. 7. *a Convertite*: a convert.

l. 8. *tell it*: admit my heresy (since in the milieu of Continental Catholicism, pardons, indulgences, etc., are cheaply obtainable).

l. 10. *Faith is in too low degree*. The Roman Catholic position is that good works are necessary to salvation, the Protestant that justification is by faith alone. Cf. 'Satire II', l. 110, and note, p. 138; and 'The Will', ll. 19–21.

l. 12. *by faith alone I see*. For the blessedness of those who, not having seen, yet believe, cf. 'To the Countess of Bedford' ('Reason is our Soules left hand'), ll. 3–4, and notes, pp. 253–4.

ll. 13–14. *a firmament ... where no one is growne, or spent*. Cf. 'To the Countess of Huntingdon' ('Man to Gods image'), ll. 6–8, and note, p. 248.

l. 17. *In their whole substance*. See the note on l. 22 of the letter to the Countess of Bedford ('Reason is our Soules left hand'), pp. 254–5.

l. 18. *in their humours*: fitfully, as the balance of humours is in various ways disturbed. Donne runs through the resulting 'complexions' in turn, with the corresponding humour: *'flegme'* (phlegmatic), 'Blood' (*'sanguine'*), bile (*'Melancholy'*), choler (*'Cholerique'*). His characterization of each is orthodox, even commonplace; see L. Babb, *The Elizabethan Malady*, 1951, pp. 6–7, 9 ff.

l. 20. *dow bak'd*: doughy, not baked enough; soft, 'spiritless'.

l. 25. *cloysterall*: retiring. 'I cannot praise a fugitive and cloistered virtue, un-exercised and unbreathed, that never sallies out and sees her adversary', etc. (Milton, *Areopagitica*). For one of several similar passages, cf. 'It is not enough to shut our selves in a cloister, in a Monastery, to sleep out the tentations of the world, but since ... God, and the Angels are awake in this businesse, in advancing the Church, we also must labour, in our severall vocations, and not content our selves with our own spirituall sleep; the peace of conscience in our selves; for we cannot have that long, if we doe not some good to others' (*Sermons*, ii. 227).

l. 28. *Spirituall*: dealing with spiritual matters.

ll. 31–32. 'Parcel guilt' means partly gilded, as in 'Satire I', l. 18. The contrast between a superficial appearance of virtue and a complete transformation into a virtuous person, in terms of the same alchemical imagery, is made in 'To the Countess of Huntingdon' ('Man to Gods image'), ll. 25–28; see the note on the passage, p. 249.

ll. 32–36. For Donne's idea of virtue as 'even' and balanced, cf. note on l. 22 of 'To the Countess of Bedford' ('Reason is our Soules left hand'), pp. 254–5; see also another letter to her, 'T'have written then', ll. 77–78, and ll. 29–30 ('To admit / No knowledge of your worth is some of it'). Virtue is unselfconscious, for pride destroys virtue.

The excellence of gold is due to its even 'temperament' or 'complexion', the elements in it being perfectly balanced; virtue is ideal when it is everywhere in proportion and not fitful ('aguish').

True virtue is wholly in every action, in every part of our lives, just as the soul is equally and fully in every part of our body. See the note (p. 184) on 'The Progress of the Soul', ll. 334–5.

l. 50. *sympathie and matter too*. Donne refers to the theory that between higher and lower bodies in the macrocosm (e.g. stars and metals) there was an agreement or 'sympathy', shown in 'signatures' (operation, motion, figure, colour, etc.). There was an 'influence' (l. 45) of the seven planets, by sympathy, on plants, animals, and on man. 'Sympathies' could also exist between parts of the inferior world. Cf. J.-H. Alsted, *Physica Harmonica*, 1616, Part iv, Chs. 17–18, pp. 258 ff., and Paracelsus, *Hermetic and Alchemical Writings*, trans. A. E. Waite, ii. 284 ff.

One of the sisters, her soul born all virtue (ll. 38–39), her beauty made all virtue (ll. 40–45), imparts her virtues to her friends by influencing their substance; but they are not 'sympathetic' to this influence, being ordinary sinful mortals. What then would her influence achieve if it worked upon matter entirely sympathetic, having the same excellent qualities as the lady from whom the influence streams? This matter and this sympathy are found in the other sister.

ll. 53–54. *Extasie And revelation*. 'Ecstasy' is the visionary condition in which the soul 'stands apart', or issues, from the body, and so arrives at the sight of God. The beatific vision of the two sisters is brought to Donne in much the same way as that of Heaven was brought to St. John the Divine in Revelation.

l. 56. *Master*: master-architect.
glasses: mirrors.

ll. 59–60. In description, as in conduct, one moves away from one sister at one's peril, unless it is to describe, or imitate, the other; otherwise one errs both in writing and in living.

l. 62. *devotion*: to his Saints (l. 6).

l. 63. Cf. a letter to Buckingham (Gosse, ii. 176), where Donne says that Spanish authors 'in Divinity, though they do not show us the best way to heaven, yet they think they do. And so, though they say not true, yet they do not lie, because they speak their conscience.'

To the Countesse of Salisbury (p. 107)

MSS.: Group I (*C 57*, *D*, *H 49*, *Lec*, *SP*); Group II (*N*, *TCD*); *DC*; Group III (*Lut*, *O'F*).

The editor of *1633* worked primarily with a Group I manuscript, but repaired omissions, in the Group I text ll. 77–78, and in the nearer source (a manuscript like *C 57*) ll. 43–46. The printed text is very sound; I depart from it only once, in l. 10.

Lady Catherine Howard, youngest daughter of Thomas, first Earl of Suffolk and of his second wife, married in 1608 William Cecil, second Earl of Salisbury (grandson of Lord Burleigh). The notorious Frances Howard, Countess of Essex and then, by a marriage for which Donne wrote his Epithalamion (1613), Countess of Somerset, was the sister of Lady Catherine. We know very little about Donne's connexion with the Earl and Countess of Salisbury. His friend George Garrard was, however, in their service by 1614, and suggested that some complimentary verses would be well received; one of Donne's letters to him (*Letters*, pp. 259–61) clearly refers to this poem.

Grierson justly comments on the mastery of sentence-structure and of the verse-paragraph shown in this poem. The opening sentence continues until l. 36.

l. 6. *Tyres*: apparel. There was, however, a restricted sense of 'tire' (*O.E.D.* 3), a head-dress.

l. 11. Cf. 'for every thing in this world is fluid, and transitory, and sandy, and all dependance, all assurance built upon this world, is but a building upon sand; all will change' (*Sermons*, viii. 323). 'As the world is the whole frame of the world, God hath put into it a reproofe, a rebuke, lest it should seem eternall, which is, a sensible decay and age in the whole frame of the world, and every piece thereof. The seasons of the yeare irregular and distempered; the Sun fainter, and languishing; men lesse in stature, and shorter-lived', etc. (*Sermons*, vi. 323).

l. 15. *shares*: portions. Men are satisfied with pettiness in every department of their lives.

l. 21. *nothing*. Cf. 'The Calm', ll. 51–53, and note, p. 210.

ll. 25–28. Cf. 'To the Countess of Bedford' ('T'have written then'), ll. 17–18, and note, p. 262.

l. 34. *understood*: depending on 'may be', l. 33: 'there may be understood degrees of faire', etc.

l. 35. *sacrifice*: offering (as to a goddess).

l. 37. *things like these*: in previous letters to great ladies.

l. 48. *that you*: that you also are the worthiest.

ll. 52–55. Cf. 'To the Countess of Bedford' ('Honour is so sublime'), ll. 34–36, and note, p. 270. 'For . . . our immortall soule when it comes, swallowes up the other soules of vegetation, and of sense, which were in us before' (*Sermons*, ii. 358).

l. 70. *not reading others, first.* The Countess's virtues are too ineffable to be grasped by a beginner; he must have had some preparative study of the characters of other worthy (though much less worthy) ladies.

l. 72. *Cave.* A general reminiscence of the myth of the cave in Plato's *Republic*, at the beginning of Book vii. The men who 'lie' chained in the cave see but the shadows of reality; one of them is pictured as being released and, after being able to see the lesser light, he can eventually see 'the very sun itself in its own place'.

l. 74. *Illustrate*: illuminate; (1) give light, (2) enlighten, with knowledge.

ll. 75–76. The reference is presumably to Homer, although he is not generally said to have been actually 'borne' blind. '*Homer* . . . as it were in one summe comprehended all knowledge, wisedome, learning, and policie that was incident to the capacity of man' (W. Webbe, *A Discourse of English Poetry*, 1586, in *Elizabethan Critical Essays*, ed. G. Gregory Smith, i. 234).

LATIN POEMS, AND A TRANSLATION

Ad Autorem (p. 111)

This epigram was written by Donne in his copy of William Covell's *A Just and Temperate Defence of the five books of Ecclesiastical Policy: written by Mr. Richard Hooker*, 1603. Cf. Keynes, L 53.

Ad Autorem (p. 111)

These four lines, the longest extant piece of Donne's verse in his own handwriting, are found on the fly-leaf of his copy (Keynes, L 161) of *Opus novum de emendatione temporum in octo libros tributum*, 1583, by Joseph Scaliger. Sir Geoffrey Keynes published a full account of his discovery in *T.L.S.*, 21 February 1958.

Amicissimo et meritissimo Ben. Jonson In Vulponem (p. 111)

This poem appeared in the quarto edition of *Volpone*, 1607. I adopt two emendations suggested by Professor P. Maas (see Jonson, *Works*, xi. 318), the deletion of 'veteres' in l. 3 (as an interpolation from l. 5 which destroys both sense and metre), and the change of 'quod' to 'quos' in l. 7.

l. 3. There is authority for the hiatus after 'sequĭ' in Catullus, lxii, l. 7, 'uno in lectulŏ, eruditi'.

l. 6. sequutor: *secutor*, 'champion', or perhaps 'follower'.

De Libro cum Mutuaretur Impresso, etc. (p. 112)

This letter first appeared in *1635*; no manuscript copy survives. H. W. Garrod wrote a study (with a translation), 'The Latin Poem addressed by Donne to Dr. Andrews', *R.E.S.* xxi, 1945, to which I am indebted. Verse translations were offered by Grosart (ii. 101–2) and Edmund Blunden, *University of Toronto Q y.* xxv, 1955, p. 11.

We are not certain of the identity of Dr. Andrews, but the only man with this surname who was a Doctor of Physic of either Oxford or Cambridge was Richard Andrews (d. 1634), of St. John's College, Oxford, who took his doctorate in 1608; 'he had improved himself much in his faculty in his travels beyond the seas' (Anthony à Wood, *Fasti Oxonienses*, ed. Bliss, Part i, 1815, p. 326). He acted as deputy for William Harvey in 1633; see G. Keynes, *The Life of William Harvey*, 1966, pp. 69, 196–7, 202. Of the occasion of this poem we know only what the heading of the letter tells us: 'To the very learned and friendly gentleman, master Dr. (*Domino Doctori*) Andrews: about a book which, when he borrowed it, was a printed book, but which was torn in pieces at home by his children, and was later returned written out by hand.'

In the title, '*frustatim*' is a rare word, meaning 'in pieces'.

ll. 3–4. This couplet was detached in the Grolier edition and by Grierson as a separate epigram. Garrod argued convincingly against this procedure and showed that the lines make good sense in their context: 'The Maine has become a tributary of the Seine, and (even) Frankfurt moves, brought back as your captive, into the house of the conqueror.' The towns of Frankfurt and Mainz on the R. Maine were the homes of the great printing-houses and book-markets. Manuscript books are, however, more precious than printed books, and in replacing a book printed, perhaps, in Frankfurt, by the same book in manuscript, Andrews has won a victory over the printers. 'Victoris aedes' is Andrews' house in Paris on the Seine, to which, in an amusing conceit, Donne says that the Maine is now a tributary.

l. 3. Sequanam. The short first syllable is allowable within the customary liberties taken with proper names.

l. 15. senibus. The feeling that one was growing old came sooner in Donne's day. If Donne had met Andrews and lent him the book while he was himself in Paris with Sir Robert Drury (1612), he would have been about forty.

Translated out of Gazaeus, *Vota Amico facta* (p. 113)

This poem (like the lines on Jonson's *Volpone*) was among the material added by the younger John Donne to the collected poems of his father in the edition of 1650.

In one of his letters to Goodyer (*Letters*, pp. 207–8) Donne mentions a translation (of which he seemed rather proud) that he thinks the Countess of Bedford might like to see; there is no evidence, however, that it was this one.

The original poem is found in a work by the Belgian Jesuit, Angelinus Gazaeus, *Pia Hilaria Variaque Carmina*. Neither in an edition of 1623 (used by Grierson) nor in a revised edition ('longè auctior & correctior') of 1629 does the poem appear on the leaf ('fol. 160') designated in the title of the translation as given in *1650*. The identification of the exact edition used by Donne is, however, of little moment, since in the two editions mentioned the text is identical.

Vota Amico facta

Tibi quod optas et quod opto, dent Divi,
(Sol optimorum in optimis Amicorum)
Ut anima semper laeta nesciat curas,
Ut vita semper viva nesciat canos,
Ut dextra semper larga nesciat sordes,
Ut bursa semper plena nesciat rugas,
Ut lingua semper vera nesciat lapsum,
Ut verba semper blanda nesciant rixas,
Ut facta semper aequa nesciant fucum,
Ut fama semper pura nesciat probrum,
Ut vota semper alta nesciant terras,
Tibi quod optas et quod opto, dent Divi.

Verbal Alterations in the *Satires, Epigrams,* and *Verse Letters* in the edition of 1635

THE edition of Donne's poems issued in 1635 has a text which often differs from that in *1633* in the poems which they have in common. Miss Gardner showed (*Divine Poems*, pp. lxxxix–xc) that the printer's copy in 1635 was, for these poems, a conflation of *1633* and *O'F*, and that *O'F* itself had previously had some of its Group III readings changed to those in *1633*. The resulting text in *1635* is thus a rather haphazard mixture of Group I readings, or elsewhere of Group II readings, with readings from Group III. Apart from its punctuation, therefore, *1635* has little importance for the modern editor. It was, however, the basis of all later editions of the poems until the Grolier editors and Grierson returned to *1633*; and its readings are of interest to students of the poet.

This list continues Miss Gardner's in *Divine Poems*, Appendix B, and in *Elegies etc.*, Appendix A, and will both illustrate her findings and show the consistency with which the editor of *1635* did his work. It will be seen that, apart from misprints, slips, and obvious corrections, all these readings are found in *O'F*; most are Group III readings, but some are found only in *Lut* and *O'F*, and a few only in *O'F*.[1]

SATIRES

1633	1635	MSS. agreeing with 1635
'Satyre I'		
1 fondling	changeling	*Σ—C 57, Lec, L 74, TCD; S*
7 jolly	wily	*Lut, O'F, S 962*
13 sweare by thy best love	sweare by thy best love, here	None (*but Lut, O'F:* sweare heere by thy best love)
40 or	*omitted*	*Lut, O'F, O, P, S 96, S 962*
46 yet	*omitted*	*Cy, D 16, Dob, Lut, O'F, O, P, S 96, S 962*
60 Sceanes	Scheme	*D, H 49, W; A 25, B, D 16, H 51, JC, Lut, O'F, Q, S 96, S 962*
70 high	his	All *MSS.*
73 then	them	*Σ—Cy, S 96, S 962*
78 stoopt	stoops	*Σ—C 57, Lec, L 74, TCD; S*

[1] I list the manuscripts alphabetically in their groups, omitting *SP, N,* and *D 17* since they are direct copies of *D, TCD,* and *JC,* and ignoring *K* as valueless. The sign '*Σ—*' means 'all *MSS.* containing the poem, except . . .'.

	1633	*1635*	*MSS.* agreeing with *1635*
		1633 alone omits ll. 81–82	
95	s'all	all	Σ—C 57, Lec, L 74
100	stoop'st	stop'st	D 16, Lut, O'F
108	liberty	lechery	All MSS.

'Satyre II'

4	towards	toward	D, H 49; Dob, H 51
32	*omitted*	Dildoes	Σ—Dob
34	of all	all	Σ—C 57, Lec; Cy, O, P, S 96
42	an	an an	
43	was	*omitted*	Lut, O'F, S 962
54	Returne	Return'd	Σ—C 57, Lec, L 74, TCD; Cy

1633 alone omits ll. 69–70 and ll. 74–75

93	When	Where	
105	Where's	Where	Σ—C 57, Lec, L 74, TCD; JC (b.c.), S
	great hals?	In hals	L 74; Lut, O'F, S 96, S 962
107	meanes blesse	Meane's blest	Cy, S, S 96, S 962

'Satyre III'

1	chokes	checks	O, P
7	in	to	Σ—C 57, Lec, TCD; Dob
32	forbidden	forbid	A 25, B, Cy, Dob, H 51, JC, Lut, O'F, S; W
33	h'is	he	Lut, O'F
40	selfe	selfes	Σ—D; Cy, S
44	her	here	All MSS.
47	He	And	Lut, O'F, S, S 962
84	that	the	D, H 49; A 25, Cy, D 16, Lut, O'F, ℺, S
94	shall not	shall	
95	Will	Or will	Lut, O'F, S 962
107	& rockes	rocks	Σ—C 57, Lec, L 74, TCD; Dob, JC, O, P

'Satyre IV'

2	but I	but yet I	Ash, Cy, Lut, O'F (corrected)
8	Glaze	Glare	Σ—Group I
12	of	in	A 25, D 16, Lut, O'F, S 96, S 962
14	as lustfull	lustfull	Σ—C 57, Lec, TCD; B, Cy, Dob, D 16, ℺
35	This	The	Lut, O'F, S 962
57	There	here	
62	words	wonders	Σ—C 57, Lec, L 74 (b.c.), TCD
67, 68	lonelinesse	lonenesse	Σ—C 57, Lec, L 74, TCD
69	last	tast	A 25, Lut, O'F, ℺, S, S 96, S 962
83	Fine	Mine	Σ—L 74 (b.c.)
84	frenchman	Sir	D 16, Lut, O'F, ℺

92	addresse	dresse	Σ—C *57*, Lec, L *74*, TCD
109	tries	cloyes	*Lut, O'F, S, S 96, S 962*
111	as if he'undertooke	as he'had undertooke	B(*b.c.*), *Lut, O'F, S 96, S 962*
113	hath	have	Σ—C *57*, Lec, L *74*, TCD
123	and that	and	

1633 alone omits That . . . free, *ll. 134–6*

146	Though	Thou	
156	precious	piteous	Σ—C *57*, Lec, L *74*, TCD
159	on	o'r	Σ—C *57*, Lec, L *74*, TCD; Cy, O, P, S
171	Presence	Courtiers	*Lut, O'F*
173	have	have have	
178	are	were	
182	the	his	Σ—C *57*, Lec, L *74*, TCD; Dob, S, S 962
215	whisperd	whispers	A *25*, Cy, *Lut, O'F, S 96, S 962*
222	whom	or whom	*Lut, O'F*
223	not	not hee	*Lut, O'F*
226	yet still	still	Σ—A *23*, C *57*, Lec, L *74*, TCD
240	scarce	scant	Ash, A *25*, B, D *16*, Dob, HN, JC, Lut, O'F, O, P, 𝒬, S 962; W
241	though	Although	*Lut, O'F, O, P, S 96, S 962*

'Satyre V'

26	their	the	A *25*, B, D *16*, Lut, O'F, O, P, 𝒬
38	deerer farre	dearer (did	*Lut, O'F*
39	demands	claim'd	A *25*, B, D *16*, Dob, JC, Lut, O'F, 𝒬, S, S 962; W
52	the	thy	A *25*, B, D *16*, Dob, JC, Lut, O'F, 𝒬, S, S 962; W
59	supplications	supplication	
61	Court	Courts	A *25*, B, D *16*, JC, Lut, O'F, O, P, 𝒬
80	men	erst men	D *16*, Dob, JC, Lut, O'F, 𝒬, S, S 962; W
87	when	if	A *25*, B, D *16*, Dob, JC, Lut, O'F, 𝒬, S, S 962; W
91	And	Which	*Lut, O'F*

The Progresse of the Soule

Infinitati Sacrum, etc.

| 25 | Mucheron | Maceron | O'F (Macaron) |
| 34 | hee | shee | O'F |

'The Progresse of the Soule'

7	gold	cold	A *18*, TCC
10	writs	writt	O'F; G
13	begins	beginst	Σ—C *57*

1633	1635	MSS. agreeing with 1635
54 shall	hold	*O'F (b.c.)*
love	lone	*O'F; H*
94 *omitted*	Rivolets	*O'F (corrected); G; H*
99 here	beare	*O'F; G; H*
117 doe	and doe	*O'F*
137 fill'd	fill up	None (*O'F:* filld up)
147 parts	part	
150 kinde	kindle	*G; H*
180 uncloath'd	inclos'd	*O'F (corrected); G; H*
185 downy a new	a new downy	All *MSS.*
220 encrease	encrease his race	*Σ—C 57*
225 intertouched	had intertouch'd	*G; H*
267 wether	water	*O'F; G; H*
273 doubtfull	her doubtfull	
337 this	his	
358 were	well	Group II; *O'F*
383 no more had gone	none had	*O'F*
one	him	*O'F*
443 made	thus made	*O'F*
484 now	nor	*H*
485 Tooth	wroth	*O'F*

EPIGRAMS

'Fall of a Wall'

4 towne	towre	

VERSE LETTERS

'The Storme'

1633	1635	MSS. agreeing with 1635
Title: The Storme. To Mr Christopher Brooke.	*1635 adds:* from the Island voyage with the Earle of Essex	*O'F* (The Storme *after* Essex)
2 these	this	*DC; B, La, Lut, O'F, RP 117, S, S 962*
4 an	a	*Σ*—Group I; *DC, L 74, TCD; A 25, HN, Q*
12 and way	one way	*DC; B, Dob, La, Lut, O'F, RP 117, S*
40 now	yet	*Lut, O'F*
49 tremblingly	trembling	*Σ*—Group I; *DC, L 74, TCD; HN; W*
50 Like	As	*A 25, B, Cy, D 16, Lut, O'F, O, P, Q, RP 117*
54 this	an	*Cy, Dob, Lut, O'F, O, P*
56 too-high-stretched	too-too-high-stretch'd	*B, Lut, O'F* (to too high stretch'd)
59 Even	Yea even	*B, Dob, Lut, O'F, RP 117*
60 Strive	Strives	*Lut, O'F*
66 and the'Bermuda	the Bermudas	*Lut, O'F*
68 Claim'd	Clames	All *MSS.*
this	the	*Σ*—Group I; *DC, L 74, TCD; HN, La; W*

'The Calme'

7 can wish that	could wish	B, Dob, Lut, O'F, RP 117
24 jawes	mawes	Lut, O'F, O, P
30 our	a	A 25, Cy, Dob, Lut, O'F, Q
37 Sea-goales	Sea-gulls	Lut, O'F
38 venices	Pinnaces	B, Lut, O'F
44 a coward	coward	Cy, Lut, O'F

'To Mr T. W.' ('All haile')

2 any	my dull	B, Dob, E 22, Lut, O'F, S, S 96
3 this	thy	B, Lut, O'F, S 96
15 Before|Before by	But for	O'F (corrected)

'To Mr T. W.' ('Hast thee')

14 And you	You	Lut, O'F

'To Mr T. W.' ('At once, from hence')

Title: omitted	Incerto	Lut (Łre Incerto)

'To Mr C. B.' ('Thy friend')

10 earths thrice-faire	the thrice faire	None (but Lut, O'F: the Earthes thrice faire)
11 sterne	sterv'd	Lut, O'F

'To Mr R. W.' ('If, as mine is')

23 businesse	businesses	O'F; W

'To Mr I. L.' ('Of that short Roll')

5 sometimes	sometime	

'To Mr I. L.' ('Blest are')

16 thee	she	Lut, O'F

'To Mr Rowland Woodward'

4 showne	flowne	Lut, O'F (b.c.), O, P
5 love-song	long loves	Lut, O'F
10 and be	but	Cy, Lut, O'F, O, P
31 termers	farmers	All MSS.
33 deare	good	Cy, Dob, Lut, O'F, O, P, S 96

'To Sir Henry Wotton' ('Sir, more then kisses')

7 lifes	lives	B, D 54, La, Lut, O'F, O, P, S 96, S 962
17 and	or	A 25, Cy, Dob, D 54, HN, Lut, O'F, O, P, S, S 96, S 962
be'a	be	Lut, O'F, S 96
22 no	none	Cy, Dob, Lut, O'F, O, P, S 96, S 962
they	there	Σ—Lec
24 and of	of	Lut, O'F
25 no good	the good	Dob, Lut, O'F, O, P, S, S 96, S 962
26 as habits, not borne, is	inhabits not, borne, is not	Lut, O'F, O, P, S, S 962

1633	1635	MSS. agreeing with 1635
27 more	all	Dob, Lut, O'F, O, P, S, S 962
33 issue	issue is	A 25, Cy, Dob, Lut, O'F, O, P, S, S 96, S 962
47 thou	then	Σ—C 57, Lec; B, La
59 this one thing	this	Σ—Group I; Group II; B, HN, JC; W
65 German	Germanies	Lut, O'F (corrected to Germanes)

'To Sir Henry Wotton' ('Here's no more newes')

2 tale for newes	tales	Lut, O'F
14 wishing prayers	wishes, prayers	B, Cy, Lut, O'F, O, P, S 962
21 are like	like	B, Cy, JC, Lut, O'F, O, P, S 962

'To Sir H. W. at his going Ambassador to Venice'

10 pleasures	pleasure	A 18, TCC; La, Lut, O'F
13 where	which	La, Lut, O'F
24 honour wanting it	noble-wanting-wit	Lut, O'F

'To Sir Henry Goodyere'

28 in	to	B, Dob, Lut, O'F

'To Sir Edward Herbert, at Julyers'

Title: To . . . Iulyers	To . . . Herbert, now Lord Herbert of Cherbury, being at the siege of Iulyers	
17 a	an	
28 we	men	B, Dob, Lut, O'F, S 96

'To the Countesse of Huntingdon' ('Man to Gods image')

13 which	the	Lut, O'F
24 amass'd	a masse	TCD; Lut, O'F (b.c.)
26 Us she inform'd	Informed us	Lut, O'F
43 ye	you	All MSS.
47 to you	doe so	Lut, O'F (DC, TCD: doe followed by a blank)
55 But	And	
66 or	and	All MSS.

'To Mrs M. H.'

2 my	thy	
27 For	From	All MSS.
47 grieves	grieve	

'To the Countesse of Bedford' ('Reason is')

3 blessings	blessing	Σ—Group I; RP 31
16 faith	voyce	Σ—RP 31, S
19 top'd and deep rooted	to sense deepe-rooted	Lut, O'F
36 Thy	This	All MSS.

'To the Countesse of Bedford' ('You have refin'd')

58 both	worth	Lut, O'F
66 aliens	alters	Dob, Lut, O'F

'To the Lady Bedford'

Title: Elegie to the Lady Bedford	To . . . Bedford	*Lut, O'F*
20 was	were	*H 39, H 40, Lut, O'F, O, P, RP 31*
42 can can	can	All *MSS.*

'To the Countesse of Bedford' ('T'have written')

7 *nothing*	*nothings*	*Lut, O'F*
11 grounds	ground	
14 have	hath	*Lut, O'F*
20 inyou	It; You	All *MSS.*
30 it some	is some	All *MSS.*
32 Stop	Stoop	All *MSS.*
58 not	borne	*Lut, O'F*
59 new	now	All *MSS.*
60 it	vice	*Lut, O'F*
75 your	you	All *MSS.*
79 makes	make	

'To the Countesse of Bedford At New-Yeares Tide'

10 time	times	All *MSS.*
18 spirit	spirits	All *MSS.*
35 prayer	praiser	*Lut, O'F*
47 With	Which	All *MSS.*

'To the Countesse of Bedford' ('Honour is')

12 or	of	

In 1633 alone ll. 34–39 precede ll. 40–42

'A Letter to the Lady Carey . . . '

13 who is	who are	*Σ—Cy*
30 their	this	*Σ—C 57, Lec*

'To the Countesse of Salisbury'

2 doe, and	doe	*TCD; Lut, O'F*
57 I adore	if I adore	*Lut, O'F*

APPENDIX B

The Crux in 'Satire II', ll. 71-72

Like a wedge in a blocke, wring to the barre,
Bearing like Asses,

IN dealing with the difficulty in these lines Grierson, following a suggestion of Grosart in a note (though he does not insert the reading into his text), joined 'Bearing' and 'like' by a hyphen to make a compound adjective (describing the lawyer's clients). For this reading there is no manuscript support, and it was rightly stigmatized by H. M. Belden (*J.E.G.P.* xiv, 1915, p. 142) as 'a preposterously un-English and so far as I know un-Donnian coinage'. Professor C. J. Sisson suggested (*T.L.S.*, 1930, pp. 142, 214) that a word that looked like 'bearing' had been misread, and proposed an emendation, 'braie-ing' (cf. Grierson's reply, p. 190; and *M.L.R.* xxv, 1930, pp. 246-7). The objection to both emendations is that no scribe shows the slight-est distress in the manuscript copies; to even the most persistent sophisticators among them, the words made sense as they stand. Indeed, the more obvious an emendation seems to be, the more puzzling is it that it was not made by a copyist.

The fact that scribes and owners of manuscripts seemed to under-stand what Donne was saying, and the characteristic virtue of Donne's diction—that, however subtle or recondite the thought, the language is central, idiomatic, and precise in meaning—seem to me to rule out some other interpretations of the passage. Thus Mrs. Lucille S. Cobb (*Explicator*, xiv. 6, March 1956, item 40), in the light of Donne's known interest in coins and medals, interprets 'wedge' as 'ingot', which must be shaped to the mould ('blocke'), and 'asses' as a Norman-French legal term meaning 'concurrence', 'acquiescence'; the mean-ing is that just as the ingot must shape itself to the mould so the dishonest lawyer must strain the purport of his words ('wring') to make his case acceptable to the court. I know of no evidence that 'barre' was used in this way (as equivalent to 'Bench'), and that 'wring' should mean 'wring the purport of his words' seems mere fancy. We are left only with the image of 'straining', which seems to be quite adequately conveyed in any case by the more usual senses of the words. Similar objections can be made to interpretations based on the making of coins by V. Hall and T. O. Mabbott (*Explicator*, xv. 24, xvi. 19, 1957). Others who have discussed the crux have pointed out that 'like' can be the conjunction 'as' or the adjective 'similar'. If it is the latter, however, there seems no clear indication of what the 'Asses' are similar *to*, or whether they are clients or other lawyers; it is perhaps symptomatic that J. V. Hagopian ('A Difficult Crux in Donne's *Satyre II*', *M.L.N.* lxxiii, 1958) is reduced to the suggestion that 'like Asses' means 'similar posteriors'.

Professor G. Williamson ('Textual Difficulties in the Interpretation of Donne's Poetry', *M.P.* xxxviii, 1940, reprinted in *Seventeenth-Century Contexts*, 1960) gives, I think, a sound explanation of the lines, which accords with the logical progress of the syntax. Coscus must 'walke' (l. 65)..., 'talke' (l. 66)..., 'lye' (l. 69)..., 'wring' (l. 71)..., 'lye' (l. 73); he is 'like' a 'watchman' (l. 65), 'like prisoners' (l. 67), like a 'favorite' (l. 70), like a 'wedge' (l. 71), 'like Asses' (l. 72), and like whores (but more shameless than they). 'Bearing' I take to be the participle of an intransitive verb describing Coscus's motion; the two lines seem to give a striking picture of his insensitive, arrogant, and unprincipled behaviour when it comes to the straightforward, as distinct from the more secret and shady, practice of the law.

APPENDIX C

'Satire III', ll. 79-82

On a huge hill,
Cragged, and steep, Truth stands, and hee that will
Reach her, about must, and about must goe;
And what th'hills suddennes resists, winne so;

DONNE seems to have been conscious of the tradition in which he was working in this passage; his revision of it for the final version of the Satire suggests an attempt, in the spirit of Pope, to present 'what oft was thought, but ne'er so well expressed'.

The remote origins of the image are found in Hesiod, *Works and Days*, ll. 286-92: 'But in front of virtue the gods immortal have put sweat; long and steep is the path to her and rough at first; but when you reach the top, then at length the road is easy, hard though it was.'

The idea is imitated in Xenophon, *Memorabilia* (Loeb ed., p. 95). It was adapted by Kebes in his *Tabula*, a book used as a Greek text in the highest form of grammar schools in the sixteenth century ('The *Tablet* of Kebes', in *Theophrastos, Herodas and Kebes*, trans. R. T. Clark, 1909, xv–xviii, pp. 131-3):

'And do you see a tiny door and a road in front of it which has few folk on it—for few ever tread it, because it seems impassable with its stones and roughness?' 'Yes, I do.' 'And there is a hill, too, high and with a steep ascent and deep precipices here and there?' 'Yes.' 'That is the road that leads to True Education.' 'How difficult it seems!' 'Do you see high up the hill a crag which is great and high and sheer all round?' 'I do.'

Two women stand there, the sisters Continence and Endurance, who encourage the traveller to persevere; he will then reach a meadow, where stands Education, and on either side are her daughters, Truth and Persuasion. Kebes seems to have been the first to put Truth on a hill.

With this image was associated the idea, also deriving from Hesiod, of the choice between the arduous pursuit of Virtue and the pursuit of Vice (which was much more easily accessible). The choice was expressed in two ways deriving from ancient sources. One was '*Pythagoras* his Symbolical Letter', as Donne called it (*Sermons*, ix. 181), the letter '५', of which the right-hand stroke represented the difficult and straight line of virtue, the left-hand stroke the twisted path of vice (cf. Persius, *Sat.* iii. 56–57, v. 34–35). The other was the myth of the choice of Hercules (as between Virtue and pleasant Vice); of this see the account in Hallett Smith, *Elizabethan Poetry*, 1952, pp. 293 ff.

By Donne's time, these images and ideas, often intertwined, had become commonplaces, and it is impossible to point to a precise source of the lines in the Satire. It may be of interest, however, to record some of the analogues, and to suggest the context in which Donne was writing. H. Estienne, in *L'Introduction au traité de la conformité des merveilles anciennes avec les modernes*, 1566, as translated by R. C(arew), *A World of Wonders*, 1607, p. 58, writes: 'Hesiod . . . saith, that Dame Wickednesse is easie to be found, as dwelling near unto us; whereas Lady Vertue is inaccessible, and not to be spoken with, without great labour and paine, in that the way unto her house and honour is not onely long and tedious, but also steepe and cragged.'

In Palingenius' *Zodiac of Life* (c. 1535–6, trans. Googe, 1560–5, ed. of 1576, Scholars' Facs. and Repr., 1947, introd. R. Tuve, p. 5) we read of

> the pricking thorny wayes, the clyffes both sharp and sowre,
> By which we do assay to clime, to Lady learnings towre

and again (p. 78) of a pleasant place

> That ryseth up with craggy rocke amid the steamy skies,
> Full of delight . . . here nighe the Pole and nigh *the* starres that shine,
> Dame *Vertue* dwels, and there enjoyes a thousande pleasures fine.
> But vengeance crabbed is the pathes, both narrow and unplaine
> And so be grown wyth thickes of thorne, that never can attaine,
> The vile and slouthfull minde . . .

Introducing *Horace His Art of Poetry*, etc., 1567, Thomas Drant writes:

> He that woulde come to the upmoste top of an highe hill, not beinge able directly to go foreward for the steapnes thereof, if he step a foot or twayne, or more oute of the way, it is not tho out of the waye for that it is a more conveyghable waye to the top of the hill: so to cum to be able utterers of the gospell, whiche is the top, and tip of our climing, we must learne out of men to speake accordyng to the man, (which is a bystep from the pathe of divinitye,) . . . Thus therfore for me to step asyde of meltyng with humanitye, is not to treade out of my way, or lose my way, but to fynde my waye more apparaunte reddie before me.

(Cf. H. Brooks, 'Donne and Drant', *T.L.S.*, 1934, p. 565.)

Of older possible sources two might have been found suggestive: the opening lines of Lucretius, *De Rerum Natura*, ii (paraphrased by Bacon in the essay 'Of Truth' and in *Device on the Queen's Day*, 1595, in Spedding's *Life*, i. 378–80), and a passage in St. Augustine's *Confessions*, x (xxvi), 37, translated by Pusey as follows (cf. J. Lindsay in *T.L.S.*, 1934, p. 577): 'Place there is none but to find Thee in Thee above me; we go backward and forward, and there is no place. Everywhere, O Truth, dost thou give audience to all who ask.'

Only two passages definitely written later than Donne's Satire, in which similar material is used, might have been influenced by his lines. In Emblem 28 (p. 55) in *The Mirror of Majesty*, 1618, there is a resemblance (pointed out by J. Lederer, *R.E.S.* xxii, 1946):

> Th'ascending Path that up to wisedome leads
> Is rough, uneven, steepe: and he that treades
> Therein, must many a tedious *Danger* meet....

A possible echo (noted by S. Johnson, *T.L.S.*, 1941, p. 347) of part of l. 79 is found in Jonson, *Forest*, xiii. 27–30 (*Works*, viii. 121): 'Since he doth lacke / Of going backe / Little, whose will / Doth urge him to runne wrong, or to stand still'.

Donne's image is of a type so congenial to the tradition of the emblem that it is surprising that more examples have not been found. Mr. V. Scholderer (*T.L.S.*, 1934, p. 589) drew attention to an Italian medal of 1504, on the reverse of which was shown 'a huge hill' with a man bearing a burden going about 'and about' up a spiral road; at the top was the welcoming figure of Fame.

Later, in the *Sermons*, the hill of Truth becomes the hill of Zion, or of the Church of God (cf. iv. 148, v. 251). It is not now a question of doubting wisely; for 'to possesse us of the hill it selfe, and to come to such a knowledge of the mysteries of Religion, as must save us, we must leave our naturall reason, and humane Arts at the bottome of the hill, and climb up only by the light, and strength of faith' (*Sermons*, viii. 54).

APPENDIX D

The Authorship of
'To the Countess of Huntington'

SINCE the poem beginning 'That unripe side of earth' does not occur in any of the most reliable manuscript collections of Donne's work, or in *1633*, and since in the only surviving manuscript copies it is apparently ascribed to Sir Walter Aston, it is necessary to offer some justification for its inclusion in this edition.

Sir Walter Aston, born about 1580, was knighted in 1603 and was made a baronet in 1611; he was 'Sir Walter' until he was created Baron Forfar in 1627 (*D.N.B.*). There is nothing, I think, to connect this Roman Catholic gentleman with the Countess of Huntingdon. Manuscripts from his seat at Tixall, Staffs., edited by A. Clifford in *Tixall Poetry* (1813) and *Tixall Letters* (1815), offer no evidence that he wrote poetry; there is ample proof, however, that Aston and his family were lovers of literature. Drayton dedicated to Aston both *The Barons' Wars* (1603) and *The Owl* (1604, 1619) and paid him other tributes (printed in *Tixall Poetry*), for example in *Poly-Olbion*, Song xii. Throughout the century the Astons collected poems. Walton presented to Aston's son (also Walter) a copy of the *Lives*, 1670 (*Tixall Letters*, ii. 122); Aston's daughter-in-law, Katherine Thimelby, refers to a poem of Donne (op. cit., i. 147); and Clifford refrained from printing in *Tixall Poetry* (cf. p. xxvi) a short poem 'To Mr Edward Thimelby, dissuading him from translating Dr Donne into Italian'. In a century when any educated gentleman was likely to produce at least one good poem, it would be rash to say that Sir Walter Aston was incapable of writing this verse letter. If a poem, printed in *1635* without his name, and ascribed to a poet whose work was known in his house, had been written by Aston (who died in 1639), we should expect to hear of some protest; but the poem continued to appear among Donne's collected verses 1635–69, that is, through the whole period covered by the documents examined by Clifford, and nothing was said by the Astons in protest or correction. What seems much more likely is that Aston owned a copy of the poem which bore his name, and that this was taken by a copyist as a sign that he composed it. I cannot believe that he did so.

The ascriptions of poems by inference to Donne in *1635* is not always justified, but some care, at least, was taken in *O'F* (on which the compiler of *1635* depended heavily) and the manuscript that lay behind it, *Lut*, to ascertain the authorship of doubtful poems. The younger John Donne, when he supervised the publication of his father's poems in 1650, saw no reason to doubt Donne's authorship of this one. This evidence is, of course, by no means conclusive. Yet no author other than Donne has ever been suggested (Aston apart), and it is difficult to think of anyone else who could have written the poem. There is a great deal in it that can be paralleled in Donne's other letters to great ladies, and in his poems of other kinds. If here and there the movement of the verse seems uncharacteristic, one has only to look again at, say, the 'Obsequies to the Lord Harington' or the 'Eclogue' before the Somerset 'Epithalamion' to settle such doubts. The triple structure in ll. 61, 88 for example (a form of the deca-syllabic line of which I have noted nearly fifty examples in Donne's undoubted poems), is persuasive evidence.

A difficulty has been found in the reference in the opening lines to primitive man; it has been thought, for example by H. M. Belden (reviewing Grierson in *J.E.G.P.*, xiv, pp. 139–40), that this is con-nected with Donne's travels (the poem is 'clearly written from some-where in the outskirts of civilization, among savages'), a suggestion accepted by Grierson in finally admitting the poem to the canon in his one-volume edition of the Poems in 1929. Hence, it is argued, the poem must ante-date Donne's known acquaintance with the Countess, and the poem cannot be addressed to her. Grierson wonders even so, however, what aborigines Donne could ever have seen. These difficulties seem to me to be chimerical. In mid sentence, as the poem opens, Donne is placing mankind in relation to the Countess. Most men are in the Antipodes of her glorious sun (cf. ll. 77–80), and in being 'without her distance' are indeed 'in the outskirts of civilization, among savages'. The poet, more blessed, is 'midway' between the Countess and this remoteness (l. 18). There seems to be no reason to doubt that the letter was addressed, as all the surviving copies indicate, to the Countess of Huntingdon. Its composition seems to fit so well the circumstances of Donne's connexion with her (out-lined in the introductory note to the poem), and to take so logical a place in his own poetic development, that his authorship can hardly be doubted.

INDEX OF FIRST LINES

THE CHRISTIAN ORIGINS
OF SOCIAL REVOLT

by

WILLIAM DALE MORRIS

Fellowship is heaven, and lack of fellowship
is hell: fellowship is life, and lack of fellowship is death: and the deeds that ye do upon
the earth, it is for fellowship's sake that ye
do them, and the life that is in it, that shall
live on and on for ever, and each one of you
part of it, while many a man's life upon
the earth from the earth shall wane.
A Dream of John Ball   WILLIAM MORRIS

LONDON

GEORGE ALLEN & UNWIN LTD

40 MUSEUM STREET

PRINTED IN GREAT BRITAIN
in 11 *point Baskerville Type*
BY WILLMER BROS. & CO. LTD., BIRKENHEAD

CONTENTS

ACKNOWLEDGMENTS

I am indebted to George Allen & Unwin Ltd. and to the following authors for permission to quote from their books:

Social Struggles in the Middle Ages. M. BEER.
History of British Socialism. M. BEER.
Early British Economics. M. BEER.
A Short History of English Rural Life. MONTAGUE FORDHAM, M.A.
Cromwell and Communism. E. BERNSTEIN.
English Radicalism, 1832-1852. S. MACCOBY, Ph.D.
A History of the Fabian Society. E. R. PEASE.
Reflections on the Revolution of Our Time. HAROLD LASKI.

My grateful thanks are also due to the following authors and publishers for permission to quote from their books:

The Town Labourer, 1760-1832. J. L. & B. HAMMOND. Longmans Green & Co., Ltd.
A Century of Co-operation. G. D. H. COLE. Co-operative Union.
British Working Class Politics, 1832-1914. G. D. H. COLE. Geo. Routledge & Sons, Ltd.
The Common People, 1746-1938. G. D. H. COLE & R. POSTGATE. Methuen & Co., Ltd.
Religion and the Rise of Capitalism. R. H. TAWNEY. John Murray.
The Chartist Movement. MARK HOVELL, M.A. Manchester University Press.
The Medieval Village. G. G. COULTON. Cambridge University Press.
The Cambridge Modern History. Cambridge University Press.
The History of Trade Unionism. SIDNEY & BEATRICE WEBB.
Christian Socialism, 1848-1854. CHARLES E. RAVEN, M.A. Macmillan & Co., Ltd.
Keir Hardie. WILLIAM STEWART. Independent Labour Party.
An Outline of Man's History. P. GORDON WALKER. National Council of Labour Colleges.
Workers' History of the Great Strike. POSTGATE, WILKINSON & HORRABIN. National Council of Labour Colleges.
The Communist International. FRANZ BORKENAU.

ACKNOWLEDGMENTS

The Builders' History. RAYMOND POSTGATE. National Federation of Building Trades Operatives.

The 16th and 17th Centuries. P. GORDON WALKER, B. Litt., M.A. Victor Gollancz, Ltd.

Left-Wing Democracy in the English Civil War. DAVID W. PETEGORSKY. Victor Gollancz, Ltd.

Guilds in the Middle Ages. GEORGES RENARD. G. Bell & Sons, Ltd.

WILLIAM DALE MORRIS

CHAPTER I

SOCIAL HERESIES OF THE MIDDLE AGES

> He hath put down the mighty from their seats, and
> exalted them of low degree. He hath filled the hungry
> with good things; and the rich he hath sent empty
> away.
>
> LUKE, I, *52 and 53.*

THE CENOBITES

Like all mass movements Christianity had many sources, and
many currents flowed to make it a social force. In the first
century large numbers of slaves and poor handworkers became
converts to the new faith because it satisfied their thirst for social
justice and freedom from oppression. Others were attracted to
Christianity because it served their spiritual needs. The old
religions and philosophies had largely lost their meaning, and
educated Hellenes, Romans and Jews were seeking some new
belief. Because of their education and superior social status
these converts tended to become the teachers and leaders of the
movement, just as middle-class intellectuals such as Marx and
Lenin have been the main architects of Socialist theory.*

Until the middle of the second century the constitution of
the Christian communities was democratic and equalitarian.
The whole of the members, in so far as they possessed the necessary
qualifications, were eligible for the priestly office. They were
called Elders (*Presbyteroi*, whence priests), and the most prominent members of the Elders were called Overseers (*Episkopoi*,
whence bishop). Moreover, no distinction was made between
clergy and laity; and it was only with the numerical growth of
the Church, and the elaboration of the simple Christian teachings
into a theological system that the clergy became a special class
invested with ever greater powers as the Church won a position
of importance and influence in the state. Then

the primitive Christian presbyters transformed themselves into a
sacred oligarchy with privileges and special attributes: the small
and persecuted community of poor fishermen and handworkers,

---

* "The theory of Socialism . . . grew out of the philosophic, historical and
economic theories that were elaborated by the educated representatives of the
propertied classes, the intellectuals. The founders of modern scientific Socialism,
Marx and Engels, themselves belonged to the bourgeois intelligentsia".

What is to be Done, Lenin.

practising piety and renunciation, became a powerful and affluent State Church. *(Social Struggles in the Middle Ages,* M. Beer, pp. 70-71.)

Christianity (like modern Socialism) became more and more popular and respectable, and by the third century Christians were to be found in every walk of life—in the army and in government positions, at court, and among scholars, students and business men. For a time intermittent persecutions tended to purge the Church of insincere elements,

> but the storms soon passed, and the secularization of Christianity went ahead to the great grief of the old comrades and the pious ones who lived in the traditions of primitive Christianity. *(Social Struggles in the Middle Ages,* M. Beer, p. 74.)

Even in the latter half of the third century, before the Church made its alliance with the Emperor Constantine, there were many Christians who became dissatisfied with the worldliness of the Church, and who withdrew from the world, renouncing all earthly goods in order to pass their lives in solitude and contemplation. Prominent among these anchorites was Saint Anthony, who, about the year 276, gave away his possessions and went to live in the Egyptian desert. Some years later, probably in 320, his disciple, Pachomius, united the anchorites, and founded the first cloistral-communistic colony, or cenoby,* on the Nile island of Tabenna, laying down strict rules for its regulation. These rules included the renunciation of private property.

After Christianity made its peace with the Roman Empire (in the first quarter of the fourth century) it assumed to an ever increasing degree, the character of an organized state religion, and more and more Christians who were disturbed by this development, sought escape in monasticism. Others embraced various heresies.

In some ways these early monastic communities resembled the communist colonies of modern times, for in both cases the members cut themselves off from the rest of society, and tried to create self-contained communities where they would be free to put their social and ethical ideas into practice.

During the first centuries of monastic history, monks and nuns were not counted among the clergy but belonged to the laity. They were at liberty to return to the world, and many of them lived in the married state.

---

*Cenoby from the Greek *Koinobion* (literally "place where people live in common"), from *koinos*—"shared in common," and *bios*—life.

The cloisters were then merely pious, communistic settlements
. . . . Even in the sixth century, married life was not a rare
phenomenon among the cenobites. It was not until later that
celibacy became an absolute rule of monasticism. The high
value which was placed on asceticism, as well as the danger of
cleavage to which communistic institutions would be exposed
by increases in families, eventually led to celibacy being imposed
as a rule. (*Social Struggles in the Middle Ages*, M. Beer, p. 77.)

The cenobite system, or the establishment of cloister-com-
munistic settlements flourished most rapidly in North Africa:
thence it spread to Palestine, Syria, Armenia, Cappadocia, and
throughout the Eastern Empire, and people thronged to the
cloisters in such numbers that the Emperor Valens (375-378)
tried to check the movement, but without success.

Christians of all classes joined the cenobite settlements, but
at the time of Saint Augustine (354-430) it was the working class,
the unfree and manumitted peasants, handworkers and the like,
who furnished the greatest number of recruits.

Later, the monastic system spread to the West, where Benedict
of Nursia (480-543), founded the Benedictine Order. He established
a monastery on Mount Cassino, in the Italian Campania, and
in the year 529 furnished it with a set of rules. These not only
laid it down that the cenoby should endeavour to provide all
the means of life by its own common labour: they also insisted
upon chastity, and prohibited members from leaving the monastery once they had definitely embraced the monastic life.

The discipline and common labour of the monks proved
superior both to the slave economy of the Roman Empire and to
the feudal economy which took its place. The monastic orders
spread rapidly throughout Christendom, and grew wealthy and
powerful. As they did so

Worldliness penetrated into the cloister. . . . The ascetic features
of early monasticism became rarer. . . . The cloisters were no
longer filled with persons from the labouring and oppressed classes,
but filled with scions of the nobility and the higher classes generally. (*Social Struggles in the Middle Ages*, p. 83.)

Attempts at reform were made, but how far short of success
these fell is evidenced by the ordinances of the Paris Synod of
the year 1212, which were directed to the moral improvement of
the cloisters. Among these ordinances we find the declaration
that no monk may have property; the bishops must brick up all
suspicious doors and rooms in the cloisters; no monk may have
his bedroom situated outside the general dormitory; all visits of
female persons are forbidden, as are games, hawking, hunting,

etc.; and no two monks may sleep in one bed, but each in his own bed, and in the prescribed clothing.

HERETICAL-SOCIAL MOVEMENTS OF THE MIDDLE AGES

Long before Luther nailed his ninety-five theses to the church door at Wittenberg in 1517 there had been heretical movements which frequently combined the teaching and practice of communistic ideas with a denunciation of the Church for its laxity of morals and its love of wealth and temporal power. During the Middle Ages these heretical-social movements appeared at one time or another throughout Western and Central Europe. In the main they arose in the towns among poor handworkers—weavers, carpenters, cobblers, masons, and the like—who found themselves oppressed by the rising bourgeoisie, and turned to the traditions of primitive Christianity in their longing for a more just social order. "At the turn of the 12th century", says Max Beer (*Social Struggles in the Middle Ages*, p. 124),

> the towns of Western and Central Europe were honeycombed by heretical sects. The Balkan Peninsula, North and Central Italy, France, Spain, the whole Rhine Valley from Alsace to the Netherlands, a wide tract of Central Germany from Cologne to Goslar, were agitated by sectarian movements, which adopted an antagonistic attitude towards the Church. . . . The sects were known by the general name of Cathari (from the Greek *katharoi*—pure). From the beginning of the 11th century we read of decisions of various ecclesiastical synods and sentences of condemnation against the Cathari, who were then known by numerous other appellations, such as Piphilians, textores (weavers), Paterenians, the Poor of Lombardy, Paulicians, the Poor of Lyons, Leonists, Waldensians, Albigensians, Bogumilians, Bulgarians, Arnoldists, Passengers, the Humble, Communiati. . . . Later their numbers were swelled by the Beguines and the Beghards, who were not heretics originally. These appellations are partly of local, partly of personal origin. The individual heretical movements or organisations were named after the locality where they had their headquarters, or after their most prominent leader, or after their character.

From the time of the episcopal synod of Orleans, in 1022, (where thirteen heretics were accused of "free love", and eleven were condemned to be burned) prosecutions are continuous until at the end of the Middle Ages. In 1025 heretics were summoned before the Synod of Arras because they had asserted that the essence of religion is the performance of good works, and that life should be supported by manual labour, and that whoever puts these principles into practice needs neither church nor sacrament. Again, in 1030, heretics were charged at Montforte, in Turin, with having rejected the ecclesiastical mode of life, and having advocated celibacy, community of earthly possessions, and the prohibition of animal slaughter; and in 1052 heretics were burnt at Goslar because they were opposed to war and the killing of living creatures, including the slaughter of animals.

The Catharian movement was split into sects which were as numerous and as sharply divided as the parties and groups and factions which make up the modern Socialist movement. But two main philosophic tendencies manifested themselves, that of Gnostic-Manichean dualism, and that of Amalrician pantheism. The former was inclined to asceticism and the subjugation of the flesh; the latter went to the other extreme, and those who embraced these tenets claimed to live as supermen, beyond good and evil. In the mass, however, the Catharian sectaries lived austere lives.

But whatever doctrinal differences might separate the various Catharian sects, they had certain basic ideas in common. All were opposed to the worldliness of the Church and the monastic orders, and all of them rejected most of the sacraments, dogmas and authorities of official Christianity. Most of them also advocated evangelical poverty and a communal life.

Many of the sects were divided into two classes, the "Perfect" and the "Faithful". While the former strictly observed the tenets of their faith, and lived ascetic lives in poverty or in communism, the latter were content to separate themselves from the official Church, but otherwise lived normal lives, waiting and hoping for the day when all men would accept and practise their social ethics. In general all the Catharian sectaries were opposed to the use of force, and they even opposed the Crusades for this reason. Only in the last extremity when threatened by literal destruction, would they resort to arms.

Bernard Gui, an experienced inquisitor of the early 14th century, says of the Albigenses (in the *Inquisitor's Guide*), that

> they usually say of themselves that they are good Christians, who do not swear, or lie, or speak evil of others; that they do not kill any man or animal, or anything having the breath of life, and that they hold the faith of the Lord Jesus Christ and his gospel as Christ and his apostles taught. . . . Of baptism, they assert that water is material and corruptible, and is therefore the creation of the evil power and cannot sanctify the soul, but that the churchmen sell this water out of avarice, just as they sell earth for the

burial of the dead, and oil to the sick when they anoint them, and as they sell the confession of sins as made to the priests.

Hence they claim that confession made to the priests of the Roman Church is useless, and that, since the priests may be sinners, they cannot loose nor bind, and, being unclean themselves, they cannot make others clean. They assert, moreover, that the cross of Christ should not be adored or venerated, because, as they urge, no man would venerate or adore the gallows upon which a father, relative, or friend had been hung. . . . Moreover they read from the Gospels and the Epistles in the vulgar tongue, applying and expounding them in their favour and against the condition of the Roman Church.

For our knowledge of the Cathari we have to rely largely upon accounts such as these made by those who opposed and persecuted them. The inquisitors were chiefly concerned with the theological ideas of the heretics, and largely indifferent to their views on economics and their social aspirations. Thus, though the anti-Catharian writings contain detailed information concerning the religious heresies of the Cathari, they provide scanty information about their social-economic theories. Nevertheless, it is clear from a study of this anti-Catharian literature that the Cathari looked on private property as an evil and advocated communal property or evangelical poverty. Thus, the 12th century theologian, Alanus, who wrote a polemic against the Cathari, charged them with saying that the marriage tie is against the laws of nature which ordain that all things be in common: and the same accusation is contained in an indictment drawn up in Strassburg in the years 1210-1213 against about eighty Waldensians. Article 15 of this indictment reads: "So that their heresy might gain wider support, they have put all their goods into a common store"; and Article 16 accused them of "free love". The leader of the accused, Johannes, repudiated the charge of unchastity, and said that the money they collected was for the support of the poor, who were very numerous among them. The Dominican, Stephan of Bourbon (d. 1261) declared that the Waldensians condemned all possessors of earthly goods, and said all things should be in common; and the same charge is made by the English prelate, Walter Map, who officiated as examiner and reporter at the third Lateran Council, held in Rome, in 1179. A deputation of Waldensians appeared before this congress, and were questioned about their teachings. According to Walter Map it was their habit to go barefoot and to clothe themselves in the woollen garments of repentance, and they had no personal property but held all things in common.

Wherever these movements assumed dangerous dimensions they were ruthlessly persecuted by Church and State, for their teachings threatened not merely the authority of the Church but the whole social structure of their day. The Church historian Dollinger says of them:

> Every heretical doctrine which arose in the Middle Ages had explicitly or implicitly a revolutionary character. . . . Those Gnostic sects, the Cathari and the Albigenses, which specially provoked the harsh and ruthless legislation of the Middle Ages, and had to be put down in a series of bloody struggles, were the Socialists and Communists of that time. They attacked marriage, the family, and property.

Partly because of its vast wealth the Church was the main bulwark of the feudal order of society, and as the forces of social change stirred in Europe they came more and more into conflict with it. Temporal rulers were commanded by the Popes to exterminate the Cathari with fire and sword; and in the 13th century the Spiritual Inquisition undertook the systematic extermination of heretics, whom it excommunicated, and delivered over to the secular arm—for theoretically no priest might shed blood.

The Inquisition assumed its most cruel and effective form in France and Spain. In Germany its activities were only sporadic: in England and Bohemia it could obtain no foothold.

But the number of persons who were burned at the stake for heretical opinions was small compared with the multitude who perished in the crusades which the Church launched against whole districts. Thousands of heretics were slaughtered in these religious wars, and thousands more endured torture or lifelong imprisonment. Even death did not save the heretics from the wrath of the Church: in many cases their bones were dug up and burnt, and their property was sequestrated.

By means of such bloody violence the Medieval Church stamped out, time and time again, heresies which threatened its privileged position in society, and, indeed, the very foundations of that society.

THE BOGOMILI

One of the earliest Catharian heresies appeared in Bulgaria, where it took its name from a priest, Bogomil (Beloved of God). The movement spread to Serbia, where it found many ardent supporters, particularly in Bosnia; and by the close of the 10th century the orthodox priests were complaining that the Bogomili preached disobedience to the authorities, denounced the feudal lords and the wealthy, and "stirred up discontent among slaves and prevented them from serving their masters".

The Bogomoli had the usual two orders of the Catharian sects. There were the Perfect, who lived in communal settlements, and the Faithful who gave general support to their doctrines without attempting to practise them fully.

The persecution of the Bogomili began at the end of the 11th century by the orders of the Popes Innocent III and Honorius III, and was continued by means of bloody crusades from Hungary. In 1234 Bosnia was laid waste by these Hungarian crusaders; but the heretics defended themselves with vigour, and survived many defeats. Indeed, about the year 1400 Catharism was proclaimed the State religion in Bosnia, and it required a Hungarian-Polish crusade, in which some 60,000 combatants took part, to break the power of the Bosnian Cathari. When the Turks invaded Bosnia in 1463 the bitterness which the Bogomili felt against official Christendom induced many of them to become Mohammedans.

THE FRANCISCANS AND THE "ZEALOTS"

When St. Francis of Assisi founded his Franciscan Order it was his hope to create a body of missionaries who would reform the world by their zeal and example. He did not demand excessive asceticism from his followers, although they were to live in evangelical poverty, and to earn their living by manual labour, or, when that was impossible, by mendicancy.

The number of his followers grew rapidly, and in the year 1221 the Tertiaries, an accessory order consisting of laymen, was formed. The Tertiaries were mostly workers who lived outside the cloister and devoted themselves to the social work of the Order, and they became a connecting link between the Franciscans and the wider heretical social reform movement.

After the death of St. Francis, in 1226, dissensions arose among his followers, and (to use the modern jargon) a left and a right wing developed. The former were known as the "Zealots", and they desired a strict maintenance of evangelical poverty, manual labour, and mendicancy. The right wing, on the other hand, sought to make the Franciscans an ordinary monastic order. Between these two extremes there was a centre party (the majority, at first) who advocated a monastic order possessing common property, and devoted to the cultivation of theology.

In the year 1247 the Zealots ousted the centre party from control, and their leader, John of Parma, was elected General of the Franciscans. John of Parma supported the "Eternal Gospel" of Joachim of Floris,* and his most intimate supporter was Gerard of San Donnino, author of an Introduction (*Introductorius*) to the doctrines of Joachim.

In 1254 the *Introductorius*, which was critical of the Papacy, was declared heretical, and Gerard of San Donnino was imprisoned. John of Parma was deposed; but the Franciscan "left" continued to hold to the "Eternal Gospel", and to condemn the Church and the Papacy for their love of worldly possessions.

At a later date the struggle against the Papacy was carried on by the "Spirituals"; and in the 14th century over a hundred of them died at the stake for advocating evangelical poverty and for denouncing the rapacity of the Church in defiance of the Bull of Pope John XXII. Another offshoot of the Franciscan "left" was the Apostolic Brethren, who supported the heretical-communist movements in Lombardy and southern France.

THE ARNOLDISTS

In the Middle Ages the towns of northern Italy were the clearing-houses for European trade with the East, and capitalist methods of production developed there, with factories and a proletariat or wage-earning class. This was true of the manufacture of wool as early as the 13th century.

> The manufacture of cloth . . . was the most advanced and the most active industry of the Middle Ages, with its appliances already half mechanical, supplying distant customers scattered all over the world. . . . The wholesale cloth merchants no longer worked with their own hands; they confined themselves to giving orders and superintending everything . . . they often provided the appliances for work; they undertook the sale and distribution of goods. . . . Already they were capitalists, fulfilling all the functions of captains of industry. . . . The washers, beaters and carders of wool, the fullers and the soapboilers, who formed the

---

*Joachim of Floris was born in Southern Italy about the year 1130 (some accounts say 1145), and he died about 1202. He made a pilgrimage to Palestine, and later became an abbot and devoted himself to the study of the Scriptures. At Floris in Calabria, he founded an Order vowed to a life of strict asceticism, which devoted much time to manual labour, and laid great stress on purity. His chief writings were the *Concordia* (a Concordance of the Old and New Testaments), a commentary upon the Revelation of St. John, and a psalter which treated of the Trinity. His guiding idea was that God has divided the world period into three ages, of which the Third Age will be a state of freedom, peace and communism, without classes or social distinctions. The writings of Joachim, or extracts from them, were known as the "Eternal Gospel," and were condemned as heretical. His doctrine of the Third Age was in line with the millennial ideas of primitive Christianity.

lowest grade of the labouring classes (were) a true industrial proletariat—wage-earners already living under the regime of modern manufacture. They were crowded together in large workshops, subjected to rigorous discipline, compelled to come and go at the sound of a bell, paid at the will of the masters—and always in silver or copper, or in small coin which was often debased—supervised by foremen, and placed under the authority of an external official who was a sort of industrial magistrate or policeman . . . empowered to inflict fines, discharges, and punishments, and even imprisonment and torture. In addition, these tools or subjects of the guilds were absolutely forbidden to combine, to act in concert, to assemble together, or even to emigrate. They were the victims of an almost perfect system of slavery. (*Guilds in the Middle Ages,* Georges Renard, pp. 23-26.)

These conditions bred a dangerous discontent, a class struggle which split society into rich and poor, "fat and lean, good and bad", as the chroniclers (who usually belonged to the leisured class) described them; and the latter half of the 14th century in particular witnessed a series of uprisings, notably among the textile workers.

But long before then the misery of these wretched wage-slaves (who were denied all civil rights, and had no hope of worldly improvement) was fertile ground for the breeding of social-heretical movements, critical alike of the social order and the corrupt and wealthy Church which supported it with all the terrors of religion.

The towns and villages of Lombardy became the centres of propagation and the asylums of the Cathari. As early as the year 1130 we hear of episcopal courts to put down heretics, who were also known by the name of Patereni—apparently after the poor quarter of Milan. (*Social Struggles in the Middle Ages,* M. Beer, p. 158.)

Faced by this common danger, the Pope and Emperor patched up their long-standing quarrel, and made common cause against the heretics. A Council was summoned at Verona in 1184, where Pope Lucius III and Frederick I, Barbarossa, promulgated a severe edict against heresy, established the episcopal inquisition, and imposed upon the secular authorities the duty of executing the inquisitorial sentences against heretics.

But Catharism survived this persecution: as it was suppressed in one town, it appeared in another, and at the beginning of the 13th century there appear to have been Paterenian organisations in Florence, Milan, Verona, Prato, Ferrara, Rimini, Piacenza, Viterbo and Treviso.

In 1207 a Papal Bull commanded all believers to institute the death penalty for heresy; but though similar Bulls were issued from time to time they met with little success. Lombardy, and especially Milan, became the centre of Catharism in Europe, and when the Albigenses were persecuted in France many of them found refuge in Lombardy. Something like an international organisation may have existed, for when eighty Waldensian heretics were tried in Strassburg one of the indictments against them was that they had sent money to Pickard, the heretic leader of Milan.

One of these Lombardian sects was the Arnoldists, founded by the priest Arnold of Brescia. He taught that all ownership of goods by the Church was wrong, and his sermons were immensely popular with the people. His teachings were considered by the Lateran Council in 1139, and Arnold was removed from his office, and expelled from Italy. He sought the help of Abelard in Paris; but when the Pope issued orders for their books to be burnt Abelard submitted to the papal discipline. Arnold was made of tougher stuff: he pursued his campaign so vigorously, and won such a following in France that none of the French bishops dared move against him. Eventually the King of France was persuaded to take measures against him; whereupon Arnold left for Germany, and later made his way to Switzerland. Finally he returned to Italy, and attacked the Cardinals, whom he denounced as Scribes and Pharisees, whilst he likened their College to a house of business or a den of thieves. As for the Pope, he "was not an apostolic shepherd of souls but a bloodhound who maintained his rule by murder and fire, coerced the Church, oppressed the innocent, filled his coffers and emptied those of others".

The Pope was helpless, and it was finally Frederick I, Barbarossa, who, coming to Italy in 1155 for his coronation, seized and hanged Arnold. His bones were burnt, and the ashes thrown into the Tiber. The Pope repaid Barbarossa by crowning him Roman Emperor, without the knowledge of the Romans. Arnold left many followers, especially among the workers, who were organised in religious communities and self-help associations.

THE APOSTOLIC BRETHREN

One of the most interesting of the Italian social-heretical sects was the Apostolic Brethren, whose leader was a peasant named Gerard Segarelli. In 1248 he tried to enter the Franciscan Order, but was rejected for being too much of a simpleton. Thereupon he chose the garb of the Apostles, as he had seen it depicted in pictures (white mantle and sandals), let his beard and hair grow long, and sold all his belongings which he gave away to crowds in the market-place.

Gerard quickly won a body of supporters, who lived in poverty, and preached the coming of God's Kingdom, by which they appear to have understood an order based on equality, peace and justice.

Alarmed by the growing influence of the Apostolic Brethren (as they called themselves), the Council of Lyons (1274) ordered them to accept no more novices; but the sect continued to grow; and in 1286 a Papal Bull commanded archbishops and bishops to suppress them. Eventually, about the year 1300, Segarelli was burnt at the stake on a charge of heresy.

But that was not the end of the Apostolic Brethren. Segarelli's place was taken by one of his disciples, Dolcino, who showed considerable ability as a leader, and carried on the struggle against the Church in spite of Council decisions and Papal Bulls. "His struggles against his persecuting enemies", says M. Beer in his *Social Struggles in the Middle Ages,* "are in their way not less worthy of admiration than those of Spartacus against the Romans". For a time he led a roving life in the Trentino, "preaching the community of goods and women", and he seems to have expected the early coming of the millennium and an era of peace and brotherhood.

Later he returned to his native province of Novara, and though his followers were persecuted by the Inquisition, Dolcino never lacked secret supporters who always gave him timely warning of his enemies' plans. In 1305 he withdrew to the mountains with some of his followers, and established a settlement; and when Pope Clement V launched a crusade against him he was warned, as usual, and gave the crusading army the slip. After that the Apostolic Brethren founded a new settlement in the district of Varallo, and heretics flocked to them from Savoy, Lombardy and the south of France. Once again a crusading army marched against the Brethren; and this time Dolcino gave battle and defeated the crusaders with heavy losses. However, the Pope issued fresh appeals to the counts and bishops of Novara to extirpate the heretics, and again and again armies marched against them, always to be repulsed with bloody losses. But they were barren victories, for the Apostolic Brethren remained isolated from the outside world, and suffered badly from lack of food, even though they were able on occasion to ransom some of their prisoners for supplies. In the end they were overwhelmed on the 23rd March, 1307, in a battle on Mount Zebello, which lasted the whole day, and only ended when the majority of the heretics had been slaughtered. One hundred and fifty, all that were left, surrendered when their arms "slipped from their hands, enfeebled by cold and hunger". Dolcino and his wife, Margharita, were among the prisoners, and Church and State vented their vengeance upon them by putting them to death under dreadful tortures.

THE WALDENSES

Catharist influence existed in France as early as the first quarter of the 11th century; but it was a Lyons merchant, Peter Waldus, who, about the year 1170, created a heretical-social movement which secured a mass following. Beginning in the cities of southern France (where, as in Italy, commerce and industry developed earlier than in most parts of western Europe) the Waldenses or Waldensians spread to Italy and Germany. We hear of them in Bohemia, Moravia, Poland, Hungary, Saxony, Pomerania and Swabia. In the year 1315 they are said to have had 80,000 members in Austria, whilst in the diocese of Passau (which comprised eastern Bavaria and northern Austria) there were forty-one schools of Waldensian communes, whose members were almost exclusively peasants or handicraft workers. In Lombardy they combined with the Humiliati (whose support came mainly from poor weavers); and in France, too, they recruited their members mainly from weavers and other artisans.

According to tradition Peter Waldus was a wealthy merchant who distributed his possessions among the poor, and began to preach a primitive Christianity. His followers called themselves "the Poor Men of Lyons" and adopted a distinctive dress. It was not their intention to secede from the Church, but rather to form an order somewhat like that which St. Francis was to establish a generation later. However, their free interpretation of the Gospels, and their calling into doubt some of the dogmas of the Medieval Church resulted in a cruel persecution. About the year 1213 we hear of the charge being made against them of holding goods in common and of practising "free love", and several were condemned to the stake. Others were burned at Strassburg, in 1229; and in 1390 several Waldenses were tortured in the episcopal prison in Mainz to force them to betray the names of their comrades. A couple of years later, in 1392, we hear of thirty-six Waldenses being burned alive at Bingen. Finally the Council of Verona condemned them as heretics, and in 1477 Pope Sixtus IV called for a crusade against them. This persecution continued down to the 18th century: indeed, it was only in 1848 that they attained civil rights and religious freedom in Piedmont and Savoy. Thousands went to the stake or were tortured to death, others rotted away their lives in noisome dungeons.

The Waldenses were divided into the usual two groups, the Perfect, and the Friends or Believers. The former were the teachers and leaders of the movement, and communism and celibacy were obligatory upon them. The Believers, however, were allowed to marry and own property. The Waldenses refused to perform military service or to take an oath, and one inquisitor describes them thus:

> The heretics can be recognised by their morals and their speech, for they are modest and live in well-ordered relationship. They are not ostentatious in their clothing, which is neither costly nor soiled. To avoid lies, oaths, and deceits, they refrain from engaging in trade, but live by the labour of their hands. Shoemakers are their teachers. They do not heap up treasures, but are content to have what is necessary. They are chaste and temperate in eating and drinking. They do not visit inns or balls or other resorts of pleasure. They abstain from anger, labour constantly, teach and learn, consequently they indulge in few prayers. They may be recognized by their modesty and their careful language, as they particularly avoid vulgarities, calumnies, and frivolous speeches.

The Waldenses translated the Bible and studied and learned long passages from it by heart.

> The laborious men and women who belonged to this sect used, after a hard day's work, to meet together in order to devote their evenings to study. And if a number of comrades found it difficult to follow or profit by the instruction, the teachers used to say: 'Learn one word every day, then thou wilt know three hundred and sixty words in a year, and thus shall we triumph'. (*Social Struggles in the Middle Ages*, M. Beer, p. 179.)

THE ALBIGENSES

In the 12th and 13th centuries heresy was rife in Languedoc in southern France, which at that time was one of the most economically advanced and prosperous parts of France. Trade and industry flourished there, together with art and science, and there was religious toleration. Albi was one of the most important centres of the heretical movement, and in Languedoc the Catharist sectaries became known as Albigenses. They preached Apostolic Christianity and were called the "good men". Many of the nobles supported the movement, which seems to have laid little stress upon social and economic questions, and to have been mainly anti-ecclesiastical.

The Albigenses were charged with denying the doctrine of the Trinity and the death and resurrection of Jesus Christ, and in 1119 Pope Calixtus II excommunicated them and summoned the faithful to undertake a crusade against them promising as a reward the absolution of their sins. The first crusade was launched against the Albigenses in 1180, but repulsed by the Counts of Languedoc. In 1195 Count Raymond VI of Toulouse was put under the papal ban, and in 1209 Pope Innocent III organised another crusade, and thus provoked a ferocious religious war which lasted for some twenty years and devastated the south of France. This holy war was waged with utter ruthlessness. Thus, when the crusaders took the city of Béziers they massacred 20,000 of the inhabitants. In the course of the struggle hundreds of thousands of people lost their lives; and when at last peace was concluded in 1229 the once-wealthy south was ruined.

The stubborn resistance of the Albigenses is largely explained by the fact that they were helped in their struggle against the Papacy by many of the feudal lords; but the war broke the practically independent power of the Counts of Languedoc, and in 1232 it was possible to introduce the Inquisition and to extirpate the Albigenses.

THE BEGHARDS AND THE BEGUINS

We have no definite information about the Catharist movements in Flanders much earlier than the 12th century. A measure of religious toleration existed in Flanders, and the inquisitorial processes which might have supplied us with documentary evidence about the movement did not begin till the 11th century.

The social-heretical sects peculiar to Flanders were the Beguins and the Beghards. According to one account they derived their names from Lambert le Bègue (Lambert the Stammerer), a priest of Liège, who, about the year 1180, began to denounce the Church for its corruption and worldliness, and suffered death for these attacks. It is more probable, however, that the names Beguin and Beghard were derived from the old Saxon word *beg*.

The Beguins were a lay sisterhood whose members lived in apostolic poverty and were sworn to chastity. They were required to contribute either by labour or by begging to their common maintenance, and to nurse the sick.

In course of time their example was followed by men, who formed communities, where unmarried men could live and work co-operatively and study the Bible. They became especially popular among the poorer workers in the industrial cities of Flanders, and many of their recruits were weavers. In the main they were encouraged by both Church and lay authorities.

Some Beghards and Beguins, however, became mendicant preachers, and these were soon denounced as heretics and savagely persecuted. It seems that in the course of their wanderings these mendicants came into contact with other Catharist sects and absorbed Amalrician* freethinking ideas, and the millennial notions of the left-wing Franciscans.

The Beghards and the Beguins spread throughout the Rhine valley, and by the middle of the 13th century they were numerous in Mainz, Strassburg, Cologne, and Metz. The movement was also carried to England by Flemish weavers who migrated here, and probably had something to do with making Norfolk (the centre of the woollen industry) a stronghold of Lollardy, another social-heretical movement which had much in common with the Beghards.

---

*Amalrich (died 1204) was born at Bena in France. He and his disciples taught that God is manifest in heathen thinkers and teachers as well as in Jesus Christ. The Amalricians were opposed to ritualism, the adoration of saints, and the praying to relics. They called the Pope the Anti-Christ, and Rome Babylon. They held that those who were partakers of the Holy Spirit were above the law; and marriage and property laws were invalid in their eyes. Their doctrines were borrowed, in some measure, from the Franciscan left wing.

CHAPTER 2

THE LOLLARDS

When Adam delved and Eve span, who was then the
gentleman?

JOHN WIKLIF

One of the most formidable of the heretical movements of the
Middle Ages was Lollardy* or Lollery. The Lollard movement
was made up of divers elements, for

> all the religious and social discontent of the times floated in-
> stinctively to this new centre; the socialist dreams of the peasantry,
> the new and keener spirit of personal morality, the hatred of the
> friars, the jealousy of the great lords towards the prelacy, the
> fanaticism of the Puritan zealot were blended together in a
> common hostility to the Church. . . . Women as well as men
> became the preachers of the new sect. Its numbers increased till
> to the frenzied panic of the Churchmen it seemed as if every
> third man in the street was a Lollard. The movement had its own
> schools, its own books; its pamphlets were passed everywhere
> from hand to hand; scurrilous ballads . . . upon the wealth and
> luxury of the clergy, were sung at every corner. Nobles, like the
> Earl of Salisbury, and at a later time Sir John Oldcastle, placed
> themselves openly at the head of the cause and threw open their
> gates as a refuge for its missionaries. London in its hatred of the
> clergy was fiercely Lollard, and defended a Lollard preacher
> who had ventured to advocate the new doctrines from the pulpit
> of St. Paul's. Its mayor, John of Northampton, showed the
> influence of the new morality in the Puritan spirit with which he
> dealt with the morals of the city. Compelled to act, as he said,
> by the remissness of the clergy, who connived for money at every
> kind of debauchery, he arrested the loose women, cut off their
> hair, and carted them through the streets as an object of public
> scorn. (*A Short History of the English People*, J. R. Green, Every-
> man edition, p. 243).

In a formal petition to Parliament in 1395 the Lollards mingled
denunciations of the wealth and worldliness of the clergy with a
profession of disbelief in confession, transubstantiation, pilgrimages, and image worship, together with a demand " which
illustrates the strange medley of opinion which jostled together in
the new movement" (*A Short History of the English People*, J. R.

---

*"Lollard" may have been derived from *Lollaerd*, one who mumbles prayers or
hymns, and was used as a scornful nickname meaning "idler" or "idle babbler".

Green, Everyman edition, p. 244), that war be declared unchristian and trades such as those of the goldsmith and the armourer which, were contrary to apostolic poverty, be banished from the realm. *

John Wiklif is usually regarded as the founder of Lollardy, although, of course, the religious revolt with which he is associated was part of the much wider heretical movement which manifested itself in varying forms throughout the Middle Ages in almost every part of Christendom.

Born about the year 1320, at a small village in Yorkshire (from which his name is derived), he went to study at Oxford. In 1357 he was a fellow of Merton College, and in 1361 Master of Balliol. As is generally known, he translated the Bible into English. He died on December 31st, 1384, by which time he had a vast following. People came to hear him from all parts of Europe; among them many Bohemians who, carrying his books and tenets back to their native country, contributed largely to the growth of the Hussite movement.

The Lollards had a strong party in the Lower House of the Parliament of 1394 (even though a dozen years before many of Wiklif's opinions had been condemned as heretical by the Earthquake† Council); and Lollardy even found favour at Court, for it was largely through the patronage of Richard II's first queen, Anne of Bohemia, that the tracts and Bible of Wiklif were introduced to her native land. Moreover, the head of the sect was the Earl of Salisbury, who "was of all the English nobles the most favoured by and the most faithful to the king." (*A Short History of the English People*, J. R. Green, Everyman edition, p. 247.)

But, above all, Wiklif's teachings, with their denunciation of the Pope and papal exactions, and their claim that all ecclesiastics should be subject to the civil power, were admirably suited to the economic needs of the city merchants and wealthy burgesses who represented the emergent capitalism of the period. They needed above all a strong and stable central government if they were to develop commerce and industry, and in the circumstances of the times such a government could take only the form of an absolute national monarchy. But that conception of sovereignty clashed with the medieval notion of the unity of Christendom, and the right of the Papacy to meddle in the internal affairs of

---

*The Lollard petition contended that the revenues of the Church would be sufficient to enable the King to maintain fifteen earls, fifteen hundred knights, and six thousand squires, besides endowing hospitals for the relief of the poor.

†So called from a great earthquake shock which did much damage in England while the Lambeth Council was sitting in May, 1382.

the kingdom. Moreover, the economic development of the country was hampered by the drain of papal tribute (which Parliament complained was five times the amount of the taxes paid to the king); and the bourgeoisie could give hearty approval to Wiklif's attack upon the monastic orders for their profligacy and love of luxury, and his advocacy that the monasteries be heavily taxed or their property confiscated outright. That policy, like the claim to make the secular state supreme at the expense of the Church, was also in accord with the needs of the nascent capitalist economy, which badly wanted the vast amounts of capital locked up in the Church.

It was this provision of an ideology suited to the needs of the economically progressive bourgeoisie, together with the support which it found in the rising discontent of the peasants, that gave Lollardy its social significance. It is true that Wiklif's doctrines "preclude all sedition, rebellion, violence, and even party and faction fights " (*A History of British Socialism*, M. Beer, p.25) ; but like many other religious reformers—notably Luther—he helped to loose social forces that went far beyond anything he anticipated or approved.* Some of Wiklif's followers drew from his teachings conclusions which seemed to threaten the whole fabric of medieval society. Lollard propagandists preached to the peasantry and the poor artisans and labourers of the towns that both lay and ecclesiastical possessions should become common property: they urged the poor to pay neither dues nor tithes to the clergy, but they also appealed to servants not to work for their masters. And by their advocacy of a peasant communism they played no inconsiderable part in the great Peasant Revolt of 1381.

Wiklif's attitude towards the Peasants' Revolt was similar to, though less violent than, that of Martin Luther towards the German Bauernkrieg (1525); and John Hus would, in all probability, have taken up the same attitude towards the Taborite wars in Bohemia, had he lived to witness them. The chief leaders of the Reformation brought their reforming zeal to bear upon ecclesiastical and national affairs and left social grievances to be removed by the operation of ethical endeavour . . . however . . . the Reformation movement was in all three countries accompanied by social upheavals. (*A History of British Socialism*, M. Beer, p. 26.)

---

*The Waldensian movement developed the same divergent class tendencies. The poorer peasantry and the poor artisans and labourers of the towns (the forerunners of the modern proletariat) found hope and consolation for the hardships of their lives in communist dreams which they derived from the traditions of primitive Christianity. Where the wealthier peasants and the urban middle class were dominant the movement was mainly concerned with a criticism of the Church.

THE POOR PRIESTS

It was Wiklif's " poor priests " who carried his doctrines to extremes which must have shocked him. To counteract the influence of the begging friars (who were devoted to the Pope), Wiklif created his own order of itinerant preachers, whom he clothed in russet (cloth made of undyed black wool), and sent about the country barefoot to preach his ideas. These poor priests

> were responsible to no authority, and . . . it does not seem that they were to make any place their special residence, nor were they to report themselves to any person, nor to have any restraint put on their utterances . . . It is easy to see how passionate, earnest and sympathetic men could gain influence by these teachings. . . . Wiklif had created an order of ecclesiastics on whom he had imposed no discipline; and these men speedily emancipated themselves from all control. Their violence of language, their contempt of authority, their advocacy of equality, in its coarsest and homeliest form, soon distinguished them, and disgusted those who had at first favoured the movement. (*Six Centuries of Work and Wages*, Thorold Rogers, pp. 250-251.)

One can imagine with what angry dismay, and even downright horror wealthy London Lollards may have listened to the sermon which John Ball preached on Blackheath, on June 13th, 1381, when he declared that

> In the beginning all men were created equal: servitude of man to man was introduced by the unjust dealings of the wicked, and (was) contrary to God's will. For if God had intended some to be serfs and others lords, He would have made a distinction between them at the beginning.
> Englishmen had now an opportunity given them, if they chose to take it, of casting off the yoke they had borne so long, and winning the freedom that they had always desired. Wherefore they should take good courage, and behave like the wise husbandman of scripture, who gathered the wheat into his barn, but uprooted and burned the tares that had half-choked the good grain. The tares of England were her oppressive rulers, and harvest-time had come, in which it was their duty to pluck up and make away with them all—evil lords, unjust judges, lawyers, every man who was dangerous to the common good. Then they would have peace for the present and security for the future; for when the great ones had been cut off, all men would enjoy equal freedom, all would have the same nobility, rank, and power. (*The Great Revolt of 1381*, Sir Charles Oman, pp. 51-52.)*

---

*Professor Oman comments that this "version of his discourse that the chroniclers have preserved for us is no doubt drawn in the most lurid colours, but the main thesis is probably correct".

And so the commonplace of history happened: many who had supported Wiklif's demands for moderate reforms, without perceiving their possible revolutionary implications, were shocked and terrified into renouncing them when the peasantry and the poor craftsmen of the towns pressed Wiklif's teachings into a demand for social equality and freedom, that went far beyond his demand for the partial expropriation of the Church. After the great peasant insurrection of 1381 (which seemed for a time to shake the whole feudal order to its foundations) a general sympathy for Wiklif among the propertied classes changed into hatred. Oxford University condemned his Twelve Articles, and although Wiklif was permitted to die a natural death, a Church Council held at Constance in 1415 (thirty-one years after his death) decided to burn his remains.

One might find many a modern parallel, too, for the way

Some of the most violent of Wiklif's poor priests ultimately deserted the cause they had taken up, conformed to the existing order of things anew, rose to high rank in the Church, and persecuted that which they had aforetime preached. (*Six Centuries of Work and Wages*, Thorold Rogers, p. 251.)

THE GREAT PEASANT REVOLT

The English peasantry had substantial grievances which made them give a ready ear to the teachings of the poor priests. Over a long period of years they had slowly won a measure of social and economic freedom which did not dispose them to submit tamely when the lords of the manors sought to reimpose the cruder forms of serfdom from which considerable numbers had freed themselves.

Long before 1381 many serfs had made bargains with their lords whereby payment in kind or in personal services for their holdings was commuted for a money rent.

During the reign of Edward II the practice became increasingly general to accept money compensations in lieu of labour rents, and by the end of the first quarter of the [14th] century the rule had become almost universal. . . . These commutations would be entered in the manor rental, and would tend to assimilate the tenure of the serf, now increasingly called a tenant by copy or custom, with that of the freeholder. . . . Ultimately the money payments would be deemed fixed and determinate liabilities, the satisfaction of which was a discharge of all the old labour rents, and the proffer of which was a tender which the steward was bound to accept. (*Six Centuries of Work and Wages*, pp. 218-219.)

'At the close of Edward III's reign', says J. R. Green, 'the Lord of the manor had been reduced over a large part of England to the position of a modern landlord, receiving a rental of money from his tenants, and dependent for the cultivation of his own demesne on hired labour; while the wealthier of the tenants themselves often took the demesne on lease as its farmers, and thus created a new class intermediate between the larger proprietors and the customary tenants, (*A Short History of the English People*, J. R. Green, Everyman Edition, p. 233.)

These commutations of labour rent for rent in money or kind suited both the manorial lords and the peasants until the Black Death created a serious shortage of labour. This plague, which is believed to have had its origin in the centre of China about the year 1333, swept across Europe, and devastated one country after another. At length it made its appearance in the seaport towns of Dorsetshire, in August, 1348, whence it soon spread throughout the country.

It is probable that the Black Death killed off between one-third and one-half of the population of England; and the immediate consequence was a serious dearth of labour, and a difficulty in collecting in the harvests of those landowners who depended on hired labour. We are told that crops were often suffered to rot in the fields for want of labour, that land went out of cultivation, and that sheep and cattle roamed at will over the country for lack of herdsmen.

And thus, at

a stroke, the labourer, both peasant and artisan, became the master of the situation in England. The change was as universal as it was sudden. The lord found on all sides a stationary or retrograde market for every kind of produce, in which he dealt as a seller, and a rapidly advancing market for everything he needed as a buyer. . . . Everything he wished to buy . . . had risen by 50 or 100 or even 200 per cent. . . . Besides, he was not the only dealer. A number of industrious and prosperous tenants were settled round his manor house, who tilled their own lands, from which they could not be evicted; on the profits and improvements of which he could not, as long as they paid their dues, lay his clutches, and it was certain that if he strove to force an enhanced price for what his bailiff had to sell, they would undersell him. They were protected against him, as he was against the king, by custom,—a custom which he dared not break if he could, and could not if he dared. . . . The peasant farmer shared the new charges which were put on his calling, but not in the same degree. . . . He found his own labour on his own holding, and hired none. Besides, he could, after his work was over, hire himself and his children out at the enhanced rates;

or, if he had thriven and saved, he could double his own holding, and that on easy terms, for the lord was seeking tenants, not tenants seeking lords. . . . The free labourer, and for the matter of that, the serf, was, in his way, still better off. Everything he needed was as cheap as ever, and his labour was daily rising in value. He had bargained for his labour rent, and was free to seek his market. If the bailiff would give him his price, well; if not, there were plenty of hands wanted in the next village, or a short distance off. If an attempt was made to restrain him . . . the woods were near, and he could soon get into another county. There was no fear in these times that the lord could spare to follow him, or that they who wanted his service would freely give him up. He had slaved and laboured . . . and now his chance was come. (*Six Centuries of Work and Wages*, pp. 240-242.)

In these circumstances it was natural enough that the lords should try to rescind their old agreements and force the peasants back into serfdom. These attempts were the more galling that the peasant had to plead his case in the manor-court* where it was decided by the very person whose interest it was to give judgment in the lord's favour.

Parliament, too, sought by legal enactment to force down wages. Parliament had broken up when the plague was raging, but in 1349 the king issued a proclamation in which he directed that wages no higher than the customary should be paid, under penalty of a fine. This ordinance, however, was everywhere ignored, for landowners were compelled either to pay higher wages or see their crops ungathered. Heavy penalities were laid on abbots, priors, barons and crown tenants if they paid more than the customary wages, and many labourers were thrown into prison for defying the ban, whilst others were fined. But all in vain : labour was scarce, and wages continued to rise.

As soon as Parliament met the royal proclamation was reduced to the form of a statute, which contained eight clauses :

(1) No person under sixty years of age, whether serf or free, shall decline to undertake farm labour at the wages which had been customary in the king's twentieth year (1347), except they

---

*The "halimoot", a court of the manor, came into existence in the 11th or 12th century, and lost much of its power after the 14th. This moot or court assembled usually every three weeks, and holders of land in the manor were bound to attend. Besides dealing with various offences, this court settled questions concerning the rules and customs of the manor, e.g. the introduction of a new tenant on the death of his predecessor, the transfer of land, the rents, services and obligations of the tenants. The lord of the manor or his representative acted as president of the court, but the peasantry were the judges, and decisions were often left to an appointed committee or jury of six or twelve men. However, notwithstanding this fact, the absence of any effective right of appeal against arbitrary action by the lord of the manor gave him a predominant influence.

lived by merchandize, were regularly engaged in some mechanical craft, were possessed of private means, or were occupiers of land. The lord was to have the first claim to the labour of his serfs, and those who declined to work for him or for others were to be sent to the common gaol.

(2) Imprisonment is to be decreed against all persons who may quit service before the time which is fixed in their agreements.

(3) No other than the old wages are to be given, and the remedy against those who seek to get more is to be sought in the lord's court.

(4) Lords of manors paying more than the customary amount are to be liable to treble damages.

(5) Artificers are to be liable to the same conditions, the artificers enumerated being saddlers, tanners, farriers, shoe-makers, tailors, smiths, carpenters, masons, tilers, pargetters, carters, and others.

(6) Food must be sold at reasonable prices.

(7) Alms are strictly forbidden to able-bodied labourers.

(8) Any excess of wages taken or paid can be seized for the king's use towards the payment of a fifteenth and tenth lately granted.

The statue provided for the difference between summer and winter wages, and forbade the emigration of the town population to country places in summer.

THE PEASANTS COMBINE

The attempt to control wages by legal enactment failed. Year after year Parliament complained that the Statute of Labourers was not being kept and re-enacted it with even harsher penalties. But their efforts were in vain : not infrequently the bailiffs themselves connived at breaches of the law.

But though the attempt to restrict wages was largely ineffectual, it nevertheless provoked resentment and strikes among the poorer craftsmen of the towns, and was met by combination by the peasantry. They organised themselves, and subscribed consider-able sums for the defence of serfs who broke the law, and for the payment of fines.

Men like the English peasants of that time, whether farmers or labourers, belonging as they did to a class that had co-operated in their work and their pleasures from the earliest times, would have had little difficulty in organizing themselves for the purposes of this struggle. Nothing definite is known of their organisation, though there are occasional references in contemporary records to a 'Great Society'. Possibly the organisation of the craft gilds may have been utilized; undoubtedly the village artisans or craftsmen, such as the millers, tilers and carters, most of whom would have been gildsmen, took a leading part in the rising of 1381. In any case, in those days it would be easy to find in a village men with special capacity for organisation. Such men would come quickly to the front. It is, indeed, not too much to assume that, in the years that preceded the revolt of 1381, there was some one in most villages in the South and East of England who corresponded to the trade union secretary of the somewhat similar movement which took place under Joseph Arch, five centuries later. (*A Short History of English Rural Life*, Montague Fordham, pp. 57-58.)

Thorold Rogers has suggested that the " poor priests " played the chief part in organising something like a national movement among the English peasantry.

Now a combination such as that which is described by contemporary writers, and which the chroniclers certainly could not have invented, must have needed agents who could be trusted, and who could keep the particulars of their organisation secret, if they could not the fact. But the peasants could not have done this among themselves. Any conferences which they might have held would have been detected, suspected, and punished. The essence of medieval society was that, in every manor, everyone knew everything about his neighbour. The lords, armed with the forces of the law, would never have suffered a conspiracy against the interests of property to have been hatched at their doors. They would have brought their retainers, or some of the discharged soldiers, down on these wretched, isolated helots, and have slain them without mercy, if they had found that they were collecting money, making deposits of arms, and conspiring against the state. (*Six Centuries of Work and Wages*, pp. 252-253.)

Now the poor priests came mainly from the peasantry and felt a natural sympathy with their economic and social ambitions. Wandering the country, as they did, these " Known-men " had every opportunity to organise a widespread resistance among the peasants. They could be trusted with subscriptions, and they could carry messages from one group of conspirators to another.

Wiklif's poor priests had honeycombed the minds of the upland folk (peasants) with what may be called religious socialism. By Wiklif's labours, the Bible men had been introduced to the new world of the Old Testament, to the history of the human race, to the primeval garden and to the young world, where the first parents of all mankind lived by simple toil, and were the ancestors of the proud noble and knight, as well as the down-trodden serf and despised burgher. They read of the brave times when there was no king in Israel, when every man did that which was right in his own eyes, and sat under his own vine and his own fig-tree, none daring make him afraid. . . . The God of Israel had bade

C

his people be husbandmen, and not mounted knights and men-at-arms. . . . We are told that many learnt to read when they were old that they might tell the Bible story. . . . The preacher would discourse . . . of the natural equality of men, of the fact that all, kings, lords, and priests, live by the fruits of the earth and the labour of the husbandman, and that it would be better for them to die with arms in their hands than to be thrust back, without an effort on their part, into the shameful slavery from which they had been delivered. And as their eyes kindled, and they grasped their staves, he could tell them to keep their ears open for the news of their deliverance, that on the password being given, they were at once to hie to the appointed place. . . . This was the way in which the communications were kept up, and the organisation made ready to be called into activity at a moment's notice. The secret was well kept. The storm, which no politician of the time anticipated, burst on June 10th, 1381. The uprising of the upland folk was simultaneous. It extended from the coast of Kent to Scarborough, all through the Eastern towns. Norwich, the richest English town of the fourteenth century after London, full of thriving artisans, who were the disciples of the poor priests, as the county was subsequently their hiding-place, fully shared in the insurrection, for the rioters took Norwich and stormed the castle. On the west it extended from Hampshire to Lancashire. (*Six Centuries of Work and Wages,* pp. 254-256.)

PEASANT COMMUNISM

John Ball was one of the most famous of the poor priests. "A mad priest of Kent," the courtly Froissart calls him. Three times imprisoned by the Archbishop of Canterbury, and once excommunicated, he was hanged, drawn and quartered after the collapse of the Peasants' Revolt. Unlike Wiklif,* John Ball seems to have come from the people, and to have addressed himself in the main to social problems. During the years which intervened between the Black Death and the Peasant Rising he spent much of his time wandering through the south and southeast of England, preaching in churchyards and by roadsides. The pith of his teaching is comprised in the well-known couplet :

"When Adam delved and Eve span,
Who was then the gentleman ? "

The same ideas run through the fragment of his speech which Froissart has preserved for us :

Things cannot go well in England, nor ever will, until all goods are held in common, and until there will be neither serfs nor gentlemen, and we shall all be equal. For what reason have they, whom we call lords, got the best of us ? How did they deserve it ? Why do

---

*According to Sir Charles Oman "John Ball had been preaching his peculiar doctrines many years before Wiklif was known outside Oxford".

(*The Great Revolt of* 1381, p. 19.)

they keep us in bondage ? If we all descended from one father and one mother, Adam and Eve, how can they assert or prove that they are more masters than ourselves ? Except perhaps that they make us work and produce for them to spend! They are clothed in velvets and in coats garnished with ermine and fur, while we wear coarse linen. They have wine, spices, and good bread, while we get rye-bread, offal, straw, and water. They have residences, handsome manors, and we the trouble and the work, and must brave the rain and the wind in the fields. And it is from us and our labour that they get the means to support their pomp; yet we are called serfs and are promptly beaten if we fail to do their bidding.

PERSECUTION OF THE LOLLARDS

It is possible that some of the peasant leaders planned much more than the remedy of grievances and the extinction of serfdom. Thorold Rogers has suggested that they contemplated " the reconstruction of English society."

> It is said, in the confession of some among his companions, that he (Wat Tyler) intended to secure the King's person, to overset the system of feudal dependence, and to establish in its room a government of county districts, over each of which was to be put a person of like principles with himself. The monasteries would provide ample funds for these major-generals of the fourteenth century. It is curious that the scheme was adopted in the seventeenth century by Cromwell. (*Six Centuries of Work and Wages*).

Whatever truth there may be in this, the revolt terrified the ruling class. For three days a peasant army held London and were masters of the situation. In the end they were defeated by trickery and false promises made by the king, and the rising was drowned in blood.

But the memory of *Hurling-time* haunted the ruling class for many a year afterwards, and they shed whatever sympathy they had had for Lollery. The Lollards were driven from Oxford by a royal edict which ordered the instant banishment of all Wiklif's supporters, together with the destruction of all Lollard books on pain of the forfeiture of the University's privileges. The threat produced its effect. Within Oxford—where many of the students had supported the heretical teachings of Wiklif—the suppression of Lollardy was complete. Their preachers were silenced, or, at least, rendered more circumspect. Many fled the country; but some recanted and became bishops or cardinals. And, as is often the way with such renegades, they became persecutors of the cause they had once advocated. But many Lollards still remained in spite of the growing severity with which they were persecuted. You cannot meet five people talking together, said a monkish historian, but three of them are Lollards.

The strength of the movement is shown by the very ferocity of the persecution that was directed against it. In the first Convocation of his reign Henry IV announced himself to be the protector of the Church, and ordered the prelates to take measures for the suppression of heresy and of the wandering friars. An Act of Parliament gave the bishops power to arrest on common rumour, to put the accused to purgation, and to punish with imprisonment. This, however, was but a prelude to the more formidable provisions of the Statute of Heretics (1401), by the provisions of which bishops were not only permitted to arrest and imprison (so long as their heresy should last) all preachers of heresy, all schoolmasters infected with heretical teachings, and all writers or owners of heretical books, but in the event of such heretics refusing to abjure their heresy, or after a relapse following such an abjuration, they were to hand the offender over to the civil officers, and by these he was to be burnt on a high place before the people.

But the new statute was defied, and produced a succession of revolts and conspiracies. The death of the Earl of Salisbury in one of these risings, transferred the leadership of the Lollard movement to Sir John Oldcastle, "one of the foremost warriors of his time". (Green's *Short History of the English People*). He sheltered the Lollard preachers in his castle at Cowling, and defied the bishops and their sentences. Eventually, he was besieged, and taken as a prisoner to the Tower of London.

His escape was a signal for the revolt of his sect. A secret command summoned the Lollards to assemble in St. Giles' Fields. We gather, if not the real aims of the rising, at least the terror that it caused, from Henry's statement that its purpose was 'to destroy himself, his brothers, and several of the spiritual and temporal lords'; but the vigilance of the young King (Henry V) prevented the junction of the Lollards of London with their friends in the country by securing the city gates, and those who appeared at the place of meeting were dispersed by the royal forces. On the failure of the rising, the law was rendered more rigorous . . . and the execution of thirty-nine prominent Lollards was followed after some years by the arrest of Oldcastle himself. In spite of his rank and of old friendship with the King (he) . . . was hung alive in chains and a fire kindled slowly under his feet. (*A Short History of the English People*, J. R. Green.)

Persecution succeeded in destroying much of the vigour which Lollardy had once displayed, but it lived on; and nine years after the accession of King Henry VI we hear of the Duke of Gloucester travelling the country with a troop of men-at-arms for the purpose of repressing its risings and hindering its invectives against the clergy.

Lollardy prepared the way for the Protestant Reformation in this country. Like Calvinism two centuries later, it was in many ways a sour and opinionative creed, and it displayed the same ruthless intolerance. "All Lollards", says one chronicler, "hated images; they even called the image of our Lady at Lincoln the witch of Lincoln". One of the poor priests is said to have lighted the fire at the lepers' chapel at Leicester with an image of St. Catherine. Others cut down the crucifix at Westcheam and threw it into a sewer. Yet these stiff-necked sectaries must command our respect, for they were ready, in many cases, to sacrifice material possessions, and even life, for their beliefs. Many, too, believed passionately in social justice, and devoted their lives to serving the peasants and the poor artisans of the towns and manufacturing districts where they found their most steadfast supporters. Indeed, among the town labourers and poorer peasantry Lollardy took on something of the character of a mass movement for social reform, and may be regarded in some ways as a forerunner of the great working class movements of modern times—Chartism and Socialism.

> I have no doubt (says Thorold Rogers) that the services which the poor priests, Bible-men, and Lollard preachers had done in and about the great crisis of 1381, is the explanation, in some degree at least, of the passionate persistence with which Lollard tenets were secretly cherished during the whole of the fifteenth century . . . the upland folk and the village artisans favoured, protected, and concealed an organisation which was reputed to be hostile to the rights of property. (*Six Centuries of Work and Wages*, p. 272.)

Through the long years of persecution the villagers and craftsmen hid the poor priests and helped them to avoid arrest. William White, for example, one of the most audacious, preached for years in Norfolk, and seemed to bear a charmed life. For years the weavers of Norfolk hid him from his enemies; and it was not until 1427 that he was taken and burnt at Norwich.

Lollardy lingered on among the lower strata of the working people long after 1381, as is proven by pamphlets appearing even at the end of the 14th and the beginning of the 15th centuries, such as "The Ploughman's Prayer" and "The Lanthorne of Light".

CHAPTER 3

THE MEDIEVAL CHURCH AND THE PEASANT

> He who would live for a day in delight, let him cook a
> hen; for two days, a goose; for a whole week, a pig;
> for a whole month, an ox. If he would be happy for a
> whole year, let him take a wife; but if he would live
> in pleasure his whole life long, he must take to the
> priesthood.
>
> *Old Proverb*

THE CHURCH AND FEUDALISM

In the "Age of Faith", when the Church occupied a dominating position in Europe, it was inevitable that popular longings for a juster economic and social order should clothe themselves in theological language and find justification in the Scriptures. Christianity, as interpreted by the "poor priests" and other social heretics, had a revolutionary significance, and provided the theoretical justification for the social aspirations of the poor peasant and artisan. But the Church itself—the wealthiest and most powerful organisation in Europe—was the main bulwark of reaction, and treated its serfs no better than the lay lords did.

This is evidenced by the way many monasteries and religious houses were attacked in the Great Peasant Revolt of 1381. At St. Albans, after a long lawsuit, the millstones had been placed within the abbey cloisters as a witness that no burgess had the right to grind corn within the bounds of the abbot's domain. Headed by William Grindcob, the insurgents burst into the cloisters, and broke the millstones into small pieces "like blessed bread in church", so that each man might carry away something "to show of the day when their freedom was won". At Bury St. Edmunds, where the prior had made himself very unpopular by maintaining the rights of the abbey against the townsfolk, it was his own serfs who condemned him to death and beheaded him: and Archbishop Sudbury suffered a like fate when the peasant army entered London. All over the country similar incidents occurred, for the peasants had smarted for many a long year under the oppression of the ecclesiastical landlords, and saw in them one of the main obstacles to the better world they desired.

Dr. G. G. Coulton, in his carefully documented study of *The Medieval Village*, gives many instances of the age-long struggle between the church and its serfs. In 1229, for instance, the tenants of Dunstable refused to pay tallage to the monks who were their overlords, and "ceased not from their original fury and malice" even when the Church threatened them with excommunication, but declared "they would rather go down to hell than be beaten". In 1280, the tenants of Mickleover had a similar quarrel with the abbot, who impounded the whole livestock of the village, and told the peasants that they were his serfs and therefore possessed nothing but their own bellies. The struggle went on for some time, with the peasants appealing to the king, and following him about from place to place with their wives and children (we are told) until they got a writ for the restoration of the 800 oxen, sheep and pigs which the abbot had confiscated. They got three such writs in all; but despite this royal patronage they were forced eventually to submit to the abbot, who had the strict law on his side.

THE CHURCH AND SERFDOM

Dr. Coulton also adduces an impressive weight of evidence to disprove the claim which is sometimes made that the Church was mainly responsible for the decline of chattel slavery and serfdom. "The great centuries of serfdom" (he writes) "were the great centuries of clerical, and especially of monastic power".

Even before Christianity became the State religion it had conformed to the social system of the day, and accepted endowments in the form not merely of land, money and houses, but also of slaves who went with the land. Thus, from very early times the Church owned many bondmen, and had a vested interest in slavery and serfdom. And so it is not surprising that there should be no reliable evidence to prove that the Church helped to abolish either chattel slavery or serfdom. Gregory the Great is sometimes said to have signed the death warrant of slavery in his preamble to a deed of enfranchisement, when he declared:

> Seeing that the Redeemer and Creator of the world vouchsafed to take on man's flesh in order by grace of freedom to break the chain of our servitude and to restore us to our first liberty, therefore we act well and wholesomely in restoring the blessing of original liberty to men whom nature hath made free, and whom human laws have bowed under the yoke of servitude. Wherefore we declare you, Montanus and Thomas, servants of the Holy Roman Church which we also serve by God's help,

free from henceforth and Roman citizens ; and we leave unto you all your savings.

But, as Dr. Coulton points out

The fact that this single papal announcement is always quoted as a convincing argument speaks volumes for the weakness of the case. . . Gregory in person possessed at least hundreds, and probably thousands, of slaves whom he did not free. Again, as pope, he was trustee for the possession of thousands more, chattels of the Roman Church ; yet he initiated no general papal movement for the liberation of Church serfs. . . . The churchman's general attitude did not . . . differ perceptibly from the layman's . . . and canon law, no less definitely than civil law, treated the bondman as a chattel. (*The Medieval Village*, pp. 151-153).

At a much later date Thomas Aquinas justified slavery as economically and morally defensible (basing himself upon Aristotle rather than the Bible), and other Schoolmen took the same view. The truth is that

in practice, no less than in theory, lay benevolence . . . outstripped that of the ecclesiastic. In Germany the Church was mainly responsible for those reservations which made absolute manumission almost unknown during the Middle Ages proper. . . . . In earlier France it was the same. (*The Medieval Village*, pp. 155-56).

The Church sometimes encouraged wholesale enfranchisements by pious and philanthropic lay lords; but there is no reliable evidence that it ever followed their example. Lay folk were impelled to free their serfs for "the health of their souls", but the clergy felt sufficiently assured of their eternal welfare to grant freedom only for hard cash. And thus

" Monastic manumissions are almost always recorded as definite matters of business ; the serf, like other monastic properties, was sold, exchanged, or embezzled," and " no ecclesiastic had a legal right to free a serf bound to his church, any more than he had a legal right to alienate any other part of his endowment, except at his or its full market value." (*The Medieval Village*, pp. 158-166).

Dr. Coulton sums up his conclusions by saying that

It would, I believe, be quite impossible to produce any instance of the gratuitous emancipation of even half a dozen serfs by any ecclesiastical corporation, except in very early times ; for indeed the thing was strictly forbidden in canon law. Nobody denies that serfdom lingered longest on ecclesiastical, and especially on monastic estates. In 1789, the French Church still possessed very large numbers of bondmen ; 300,000 seems a moderate computation. (*The Medieval Village*, pp. 162-163).

Indeed, far from the Church helping to enfranchise slaves, canon law actually enslaved those whom civil law would have left free. Thus, the Council of Toledo promulgated a decree :

Seeing that the Fathers have hitherto promulgated many decisions concerning the incontinence of the clerical order, and it hath yet been impossible to bring about the correction of their morals, the guilt which they have perpetrated hath so far enlarged the sentence of their judges that vengeance should now strike not only the authors of these iniquities, but also the progeny of those who are condemned. Wherefore from this time forward, whosoever from among these dignitaries, from the bishop down to the subdeacon, shall have begotten children by a detestable marriage with either a bondwoman or a freewoman, those who are proved to be the parents shall be condemned to the canonical penalty ; and the children of this polluted union shall not only be incapable of inheriting from their parents but shall also remain, by an eternal law, as bondfolk of the church of whose priest or minister they are the ignominious offspring.

Again, in 1051, a Council of Rome enacted that the wives of priests should be given to serve the Church as slaves ; and Urban II repeated this decree in 1089. The first Synod of Santa Fe published a similar decree in 1556.

It was also quite common for the Pope to declare a whole community slaves for some rebellion against the Church. Boniface VIII did this in 1303 in his feud with the Colonna family; and Clement V condemned the entire population of Venice to slavery in 1309. A couple of generations later Gregory XI used the same weapon against the Florentines; and similar decrees were issued at various times against Bologna, Venice and Florence. When Henry VIII broke with the Papacy Paul III condemned to servitude all Englishmen who took the kings's side. Later still, Nicholas IV in bulls of 1452 and 1454 granted to the King of Portugal the right of slavery over all the heathen whom he captured; and Alexander VI, in 1493, gave the aborigines of South America over to the Spaniards on terms which were interpreted by theologians to include slavery.

THE CHURCH AS LANDLORD

The Medieval Church was certainly not more liberal than the secular lords in its treatment of tenants. Here again Dr. Coulton has adduced a mass of evidence which leads him to the general conclusion

that it was possibly about 5 per cent. better for the peasant, on an average, to live on a monastic than on a lay estate ; except, that is, on a royal estate, where the conditions were distinctly more favourable than on the monastic.   This is proved most clearly by the constant attempts of peasants to escape from monastic bondage by pleading that they were originally of ' ancient demesne,' that is to say the king's own peasants.   (*The Medieval Village*, p. 178).

He adds that while

it is rash to generalize at this present stage of research . . . my impression is that monastic conservatism and the comparatively strong financial position of the monasteries, enabled them to maintain the earlier and harsher burdens from which the peasant had long bought himself free on other estates.   (*The Medieval Village*, p. 175).

However,

the monastery, in spite of its frequent and sometimes desperate financial shifts, was generally somewhat less indebted and less rapacious than the knight or squire ; the cellarer had generally a little more compassion for his labourers than the lay bailiff ; that conservatism which kept the serf longer in his monastic servitude would sometimes suffer him to jog along at the same old rent, which had now become far lighter with the falling value of money.   (*The Medieval Village*, p. 145).

THE CHURCH AND ENCLOSURES

Finally, in the matter of enclosures there was nothing to distinguish ecclesiastical from lay lords.   Monasteries were among the earliest landlords to enclose common land.   In Germany whole villages were "laid down" by the Cistercians; and in the case of France Guiot de Provins made this accusation, in 1206:

The (Cistercian) priests who used to handle the Lord's Body are now sheepshearers . . . I could tell you of a thousand churches where they have their granges built ; everywhere they have villages and parishes and lands and houses and estates, far more than they had of old.   There are so many sheep and wethers bleating, and oxen and cows lowing, that we have wondrous fear.   In the churchyards, over men's bodies, they have built their pigstyes ; and their asses lie where men were wont to chant Mass . . . much fear do they give to the poor folk whom they cast away from their lands ; for they drive them all forth to seek their bread (elsewhere).

It was the same in this country: monastic enclosures took place long before the practice became so general as to result in governmental attempts to put an end to it.   In the 15th and 16th centuries the chief reason for enclosures lay in the fact that it had become very profitable to rear sheep for their wool*. Arable land

---

*Wool reached its maximum price between 1450 and 1550.

was allowed to go to grass, and whole hamlets were sometimes
destroyed in order to create sheep-walks. Sir Thomas More,
in his *Utopia*, was forced to protest that

sheep, which are naturally mild, and easily kept in order, may
be said now to devour men, and unpeople, not only villages, but
towns.

And he denounced those who

stop the course of agriculture, destroying houses and towns,
reserving only the churches . . . that they may lodge their sheep
in them.

Tenants (he explained) are turned out of their possessions, by
tricks, or by main force, or being wearied out with ill usage, they
are forced to sell them. By which means those miserable people,
both men and women, married and unmarried, old and young,
with their poor but numerous families (since country business
requires many hands), are all forced to change their seats, not
knowing whither to go ; and they must sell almost for nothing
their household stuff, which could not bring them much money,
even though they might stay for a buyer. When that little money
is at an end, for it will soon be spent ; what is left for them
to do, but either to steal and so be hanged (God knows how
justly), or to go about and beg. And if they do this, they are
put in prison as idle vagabonds ; while they would willingly work, but can find none that will hire them ; for there
is no more occasion for country labour, to which they have
been bred, when there is no arable ground left. One shepherd
can look after a flock, which will stock an extent of ground that
would require many hands, if it were to be ploughed and reaped.

The Church was as ruthless in carrying out enclosures as the
most rapacious of lay lords. In Peterborough the abbot enclosed
much arable land for sheep-runs, and in one place he "caused six
cottages to be destroyed and decayed, and 24 persons are thus
lost from the land"; in another instance he

enlarged his park called Meldesworth, and keepeth wild beasts
now in these tenements ; and by what he hath taken one
plough has been put down and 50 persons who were wont to
dwell in the messuage and cottages aforesaid have gone forth and
have been compelled to seek their dwelling elsewhere ; and,
what is sadder still, the aforesaid graveyard wherein the bodies
of the faithful were buried and rest is now made into a pasture
for wild beasts.

In short, the Medieval Church was enormously wealthy, and
despite what individual priests or monks might think or do, it
was governed by the property relations of the times, and its
practice and teachings were utterly remote from those of the poor
carpenter of Nazareth.

CHAPTER 4

THE HUSSITES

He gave them as the dust to his sword, and as driven
stubble to his bow.

Isaiah XLI, 2.

JOHN HUSS

The writings and teachings of John Wiklif found their way to
Bohemia at a time when the Catholic Church was steadily losing
authority among the masses, and when a strong national feeling
was developing, fostered by the growing wealth and power of the
middle class.

The economic development of Bohemia in the 14th century
had been largely helped by its silver mines; but, owing to the
abundance of silver, a price revolution took place which
occasioned much distress among the poor artisans and peasants,
and disposed them to a ready acceptance of radical social ideas.
As in England, there was much popular discontent with the
Church because of the luxury and immorality of its clergy and
its practice of simony; whilst livings and benefices had
multiplied to such an extent in Bohemia and Moravia that even
small churches supported numerous priests in idleness. The
religious and social struggles of the period were further complicated by the fact that whilst the common people were largely
Czechs, the ruling class (both lay and ecclesiastical lords) were
mainly Germans.

Wiklif's ideas were enthusiastically received by the reform
party among the clergy, and when an attempt was made to suppress them John Huss became their most formidable defender.
Born in 1369 of a well-to-do peasant family, Huss had been a
leading figure among the lecturers at the university of Prague
since 1396. As preacher in the Bethlehem chapel at Prague
he enjoyed an unexampled popularity among all classes. He
was excommunicated by the Pope in 1412, but continued his
work with undiminished zeal; and was eventually summoned
before the Council of Constance in November 1414. Despite the
fact that Huss had been guaranteed a safe passage and return, he
was thrown into prison, deprived of his spiritual office by the

Council, and burned at the stake on July 6th, 1415. His ashes were thrown into the Rhine.

Some of his disciples suffered a like fate, but the blood of the martyrs proved to be the seed of the Church, and persecution served only to strengthen the Hussite movement, and to make an armed struggle inevitable.

"A chalice for the layman!" became the slogan of the movement. This was inspired by the fact that the rites of the Catholic Church gave to the layman in communion bread only, but bread and wine to the priest; and the claim for equality in communion became a symbol of the determination of the masses to end the privileges of the Church.

All classes joined in the struggle against the Pope for religious reform, and in the struggle against the Germans for national independence; but each class pursued its own class interests. Thus the nobility seized the opportunity to annex the lands of the Church (which owned about one-quarter of the land); whilst the rich bourgeoisie saw in the Hussite wars a means of spoiling the clergy and gaining possession of the German Catholic cities, of which Kuttenberg, with its famous silver mines, was the most desirable.

TABORITES AND CALIXTINS

The nobility and the rich bourgeoisie who joined the Hussite movement formed the "moderate" party, known as the Calixtins (chalicemen) or Utraquists, from their demand of the Cup for the laity in communion, i.e. "Communion in both kinds," *in utraque specie*. They were also known as Pragers, from the fact that the Prague school was their spiritual centre.

But there were other factions who went far beyond anything that John Huss had taught, just as many English Lollards had carried Wiklif's teachings to an extreme which he had never contemplated. They became known as Taborites, from Mount Tabor, which was their stronghold, and the centre of their propaganda. Tabor was located in the vicinity of gold mines, and trade and industry flourished there.

In the main the Taborites drew their strength from the peasants (who wanted to become free owners of land, just as the English peasants did), and from the lower middle class and proletarian elements of the smaller cities of Bohemia. They preached a primitive Christianity, and their political and social opinions grew steadily more radical. They declared that the

Millennium of Christ was come, and that there "should be no kings, no masters, no subjects on earth, and that taxes and duties should be abolished." They called each other brother and sister, and recognized no difference between "thine" and "mine". Things, they said, should be held in common, and they taught that he who possesses property commits a mortal sin. But their communism was limited to consumption, and did not extend to the sphere of production. Every family worked for itself, and contributed its surplus to the general treasury.

There were among the Taborites (as there always is in revolutionary sects or parties) some extremists who would tolerate no compromise whatsoever with worldliness, and who denounced even the family. These "brothers and sisters of the free spirit" called themselves Adamites; but never won more than a small minority of the Taborites to their extreme views.

Tabor became an international centre—a 15th-century Moscow—where Beghards and Waldenses, and heretics from all parts of Europe found their spiritual home and a refuge from persecution.

Many crusades were launched against the Taborites by the Church and the Empire; but for nearly a generation they more than held their own. The Taborite army was well organised and disciplined, and is said to have been the first to use artillery in battle. Above all the Taborites had that fanatical zeal which two centuries later was to make Cromwell's New Model irresistible. Like the Ironsides, they knew what they fought for, and loved what they knew.

THE HUSSITE WARS

In the summer of 1419, a few days before the death of King Wenzel (the "Good King Wenceslas" of the Christmas carol), public disturbances and street fighting broke out in Prague, beginning when the Catholics insulted a procession. The Hussites, under their leader Ziska, stormed the parliament house in the Neustadt, and threw some of the Catholic councillors out of the windows, after which the wretched men were stabbed and beaten to death by an angry mob. King Wenzel's death is said to have been occasioned by "a fearful access of fury at the outbreak of the revolution".

His heir was his brother, the Emperor Sigismund, king of Hungary.

Knowing that he might expect a bitter opposition so long as he maintained his hostility to the Hussites, Sigismund did not immediately proceed to Bohemia, but entrusted the government of the country to the Dowager-queen Sophie. In December 1419 he appeared in Brünn, where he received an embassy from Bohemia which asked for his recognition of the four articles of belief which had been drawn up by the Hussites a short time previously. They were freedom of preaching, communion in both kinds, the observance of apostolic poverty by the clergy, and the suppression and punishment of deadly sins. Sigismund was evasive, however, and refused to declare his position.

From Brünn the Emperor proceeded to Breslau, making a formal entry into the town on January 5th, 1420. Towards the close of King Wenzel's reign the artisans of Breslau had followed the example of the Hussites of Prague and had raised a revolt against the aristocratic council and the whole system of royal administration. Sigismund executed 23 of the ringleaders in the public square and condemned many other fugitives to death in their absence, besides declaring their rights and property forfeited. In a little while his hostility towards the Hussite movement became abundantly clear, for on March 15th he had a Bohemian Hussite publicly burned as a heretic, and two days later he ordered the bull which Pope Martin V had issued calling for a crusade against the heretics to be read from the pulpits of the Breslau churches.

In face of this threat from their common enemy, the Calixtins and the Taborites achieved an uneasy unity. Sigismund entered Bohemia with an army 80,000 strong, composed chiefly of Germans and Silesians. He laid unsuccessful siege to Prague from May to June, and finally suffered a shattering defeat on November 1st, 1420.

In February, 1421, the Emperor again invaded Bohemia; but once more the Hussites under their formidable general Ziska put him to ignominious flight.

By this time the Taborites had gained the upper hand in the Hussite movement, and they were no longer content to await attack, but took the offensive and conquered a number of towns and fiefs which had remained Catholic.

In September, 1421, Sigismund made yet another invasion of Bohemia at the head of a crusading army said to have numbered 200,000; but as on previous occasions the Hussites inflicted heavy losses upon the crusaders, and soon compelled them to withdraw across the frontier. After that several years passed before any further attack was made upon the Taborites.

On October 11th, 1424, Ziska died of some kind of plague, and the quarrels which had always divided the Hussite factions grew more serious. Ziska's own adherents, who were known as the "Orphans", broke with the Taborites, whose leadership passed to Prokop Rasa (Rasa, the Shorn One). Under his energetic leadership the Hussite Wars spread to Austria, Hungary, Silesia, Saxony, Brandenburg, the Palatinate and Franconia.

The Taborites now began to leave permanent garrisons in the towns and castles which they conquered, and such was the terror which their successes spread among the princes of the Empire they were once more persuaded to undertake a crusade, in the summer of 1427, at a time when the Emperor Sigismund was occupied with the war against the Turks. Once again the crusaders were defeated, and fled panic-stricken before the Taborite army, which it seemed no mortal power could subdue.

In 1431, the Pope, Martin V, summoned a General Council of the Church as Basle, which launched yet another crusade against the Taborites. Like all its predecessors, however, it ended with the overwhelming defeat of the Germans at Taus, on August 14th, 1431.

After this victory at Taus the invincible Hussite armies swept through Austria, Northern Hungary, Silesia, Saxony and Brandenburg, and seemed to threaten all Christendom. But now a split took place between the Calixtins and the Taborites and Orphans. The Bohemian nobles, who supported the more moderate faction, had been quite willing to appropriate the Church lands, but they had no liking for the dangerous social theories of the Taborites, and no desire to wage war against king, pope and the whole of Europe.

The Calixtins started negotiations with the enemy, and Tabor itself was divided. The lower middle-class and the peasantry were largely indifferent to the communist programme: they wanted peace. The truth is that Tabor's communism was unstable. It was communism of consumption, without a foundation in communist production, and the result was that equality of the means of subsistence soon disappeared. There were rich and poor in Tabor.

At the same time the corruption which seems inevitable to all revolutionary movements once they achieve a measure of success, now overtook the Taborites. Their army ceased to consist of honest fanatics prepared to give their lives for the cause: it became crowded by "crooks and riff-raff of all nations".

These mercenaries speedily deserted to the nobility when the latter raised an army for war against Tabor and offered better terms than the Taborites did.

These factors combined to overthrow Tabor. On May 30th, 1434, they suffered a crushing defeat near Lipan in Bohemia, when out of 18,000 Taborite soldiers 13,000 were killed.

In 1437 they were compelled to conclude a treaty with Sigismund, who guaranteed them independence; but in spite of this the communist community of Tabor soon disappeared.

In the circumstances of the time that was bound to have happened sooner or later. The Taborites were many centuries before their time: communism was not possible until capitalism had overthrown the feudal order, and had accumulated the capital which made possible the industrial revolution of the 18th and 19th centuries.

D

CHAPTER 5

THE PROTESTANT REFORMATION

Men, consciously or unconsciously, derive their moral
ideas in the last resort from . . . the economic relations
in which they carry on production and exchange.
Anti-Dühring, Frederick Engels.

THE REFORMATION

Important though Lollardy and the Hussite movement were as
threats to the supremacy of the Catholic Church, it was not until
the coming of Capitalism in the 16th century that economic
conditions made a successful challenge possible.

It has already been pointed out that capitalist methods of
production existed in Northern Italy as early as the 13th century,
but it was not until the 16th century that such methods became
widespread in Europe. Then bricks, beer and glass began to be
manufactured in England in great plants that needed much
capital, and great metal works sprang up, operated by blast-
bellows. At the same time the manufacture of cloth became
highly organised, and coal began to take the place of wood as
fuel, deep mines being sunk (three hundred feet or more), with
timbered underground ways, and expensive pumps to keep them
from being flooded.

There were many reasons why the Medieval Church was not
compatible with this new capitalist economy. Medieval civilization was founded upon agriculture—upon the manor as a largely
self-contained economic and political unit, where serf labour
produced a surplus that went to maintain a hierarchy of lords and
clergy. Feudalism was a traditional, authoritarian society, with
elaborate rules for regulating the social relationships of its
members even to the details of their dress, and there was little
movement of men from one social class to another. Though
there were notable exceptions, most men who were born serfs
died serfs.

And the Church was the great bulwark of this order.

It surrounded feudal institutions with the halo of divine consecration.
It had organised its own hierarchy on the feudal model, and . . .
it was by far the most powerful feudal lord, holding, as it did,
fully one-third of the soil of the Catholic world. Before profane

feudalism could be successfully attacked in each country . . .
its sacred central organisation, had to be destroyed. (*Socialism
Utopian and Scientific*, Frederick Engels).

Even within the towns which had bought the right to govern
themselves or had extorted a charter from some feudal lord by
armed revolt, the old order imposed a multitude of regulations
and restrictions which hampered the growth of a new economy,
for the whole pattern of medieval thought was riddled with ideas
that were alien to capitalist notions of "free" competition and
beggar-my-neighbour individualism. There was the conception
of a "just wage" to be fixed by statute or regulation, and the
belief that no man had the right to profit through his neighbours'
loss. Thus, the guild statutes forbade their members to buy up
raw materials for their own profit.

If the arrival of fresh fish, hay, wine, wheat or leather was
announced, no one might forestall the others and buy cheaply
to sell dearly ; all should profit by the natural course of events
. . . often the maximum amount which an individual might acquire
was strictly laid down. . . . With a view to equalizing matters
between masters, the cornering of the supply of labour was
forbidden, and not only was it forbidden to tempt away a rival's
workmen by the offer of higher wages, but as a rule a man might
not keep more apprentices than others . . . Again it was forbidden
to monopolize customers, to invite into your own shop the
people who had stopped before a neighbour's display of goods,
to call in the passers-by, or to send a piece of cloth on approbation
to a customer's house. All individual advertisement was looked
on as tending to the detriment of others. . . . Equally open to
punishment was the merchant who obtained possession of another
man's shop by offering the landlord a higher rent. . . . Any bonus
offered to a buyer was considered an unlawful and dishonest
bait. (*Guilds in the Middle Ages*, Georges Renard).

In short, the guilds tried to reduce, or, if possible, to do away
with competition.

What was equally an hindrance to the development of the
productive forces, they discouraged innovation.

Invention could not have free play ; it was accused of outraging
healthy tradition ; it was considered dangerous to set out to
create anything new. In Florence in 1286 a cooper complained of
being boycotted by his guild because in making his barrels he
bent his staves by means of water. . . . At Paris it was forbidden
to mould seals with letters engraved on them. . . . Who knows . . .
whether this prohibition did not retard the invention of printing,
to which—when a method of making them movable had been
discovered—these engraved letters gave birth ? (*Guilds in the
Middle Ages*, Georges Renard).

Thus, the guild system, which at one time had fostered the growth of petty industry, now became a fetter on further development: "the material productive forces of society . . . came into opposition with the old conditions of production," in the phrase used by Marx in his *Preface* to *The Critique of Political Economy*.

But the medieval guilds were an essential part of that static, traditional society which the Church sanctified with the tremendous weight of her age-old authority, and their rules often included moral and religious injunctions. To become a member a man had to be respected for his piety and have a good reputation for honesty.

> To be received as a master, it was necessary almost everywhere to make a profession of the Catholic faith and to take the oath, in order that heretics such as the Patarini and Albigenses might be kept out. Punishments were inflicted upon blasphemers. . . . It was obligatory to stop work on Sundays and holidays, and to take part with great pomp and banners unfurled in the feasts of the patron saint of the town and of the guild, not to mention a host of other saints of whom a list was given. The statutes often begin by enumerating the alms it was thought necessary to bestow on certain monasteries and works of mercy and instruction which they promised to support out of their funds. (*Guilds in the Middle Ages*, Georges Renard).

The guild system, along with the medieval notions of trade and industry which were associated with it, had to be destroyed before capitalism was free to develop; but for their destruction it was necessary to discredit and sweep away the whole system of ideas for which the Church stood. It is no accident that when the monasteries were dissolved and plundered of their wealth at the Reformation the guilds also were pillaged. In this country a statute passed in the reign of Edward VI confiscated such part of the property of the guilds as was employed in religious purposes, and many guilds were suppressed.

It cannot be too strongly emphasized that the medieval Church stood for a way of looking at things—for an ideology, to use modern jargon, that was opposed to the whole trend of the new economic order that was struggling to develop. Capitalism, like every other economic system, needs its own code of ethics, its own philosophy, its own set of social values: and that, in the 16th century, meant a new religion. A religion which would not frown upon usury (or the lending of money at interest), or preach (even if the princes of the Church had failed to practise) the virtues of Christian poverty. A religion that would laud the bourgeois virtues of thrift, sobriety, and hard work, and the making of money to the greater glory of the Lord.

To develop its own characteristic morality capitalism had to break the Catholic Church which claimed to be the sole authority in morals, and which, being rooted in an agrarian civilization, looked askance at the rising middle class who sought wealth and power in trade and industry. It had to insist, therefore, that man needed no infallible Church to interpret the Scriptures, or to mediate between himself and his Maker. To break the all-pervading, conservative power of the Church it had to assert that a man's conscience is sufficient guide in matters of faith and ethics. In brief, it had to carry through the Reformation, and shatter the unity and power of the Medieval Church.

It is not suggested, of course, that the Protestant reformers were conscious hypocrites who advocated a new religious outlook because it suited their economic interest to do so; or even that they were conscious that Protestantism could subserve their class interests. No one who knows with what merciless ferocity the religious wars of the 16th and 17th centuries were waged can doubt that the men who hanged, and burned, and tortured one another were in deadly earnest about the doctrinal controversies which divided them.

> As little as we judge an individual by what he thinks he is, just as little can we judge such a revolutionary epoch by its own consciousness. (*The Critique of Political Economy*, Karl Marx).

But Protestantism was a religion eminently suited to the needs of the trading and manufacturing class in their struggle with feudalism, and in general it triumphed wherever they became dominant.

THE GROWTH OF NATIONALISM

On every count Catholicism was incompatible with the new capitalist system. In the first place it was opposed to the rising nationalism which everywhere accompanied the growth of capitalism. Just as the guild system had once fostered the growth of industry, and had then become a fetter on its further development, so the medieval city economy had served at one stage to develop the forces of production, but was now become too narrow and exclusive for their further development. And so the city economy—the production of goods for a very limited local market—had to be replaced by a national economy and (eventually) the world market, since only thus could industry develop.

And that meant the creation of a strong central government in place of a host of petty princelings and feudal lords ; a national government strong enough to suppress the outlaws and the robber-barons who preyed upon the merchants as they moved about the country with their trains of merchandise. One, too, that was able to impose the same language, money, weights and measures over a wide area, and could sweep away the network of local tolls which hindered trade by obstructing the roads and rivers.

But with these economic and political changes there went, inevitably, changes in men's ideas. They began to develop a loyalty wider than to their native village or town: to think of themselves as Englishmen or Frenchmen, as the case might be.

And along with this growth of a strong national sentiment came a weakening of the authority of the universal church. With all its shortcomings and the scandalous abuses which so often discredited it, the Church did give a certain cultural unity to Christendom which transcended local loyalties. As Engels points out in the *Introduction* to his *Socialism Utopian and Scientific*:

> The great international centre of feudalism was the Roman Catholic Church. It united the whole of feudalised Western Europe, in spite of all internal wars, into one grand political system opposed as much to the schismatic Greeks as to the Mohammedan countries.

When it became necessary to transcend the political limitations of feudalism so that capitalism might develop, this "sacred central organisation" had also to be shattered.

There was another way in which the attack on the Catholic Church benefited the rising capitalist economy. The Medieval Church was enormously wealthy. Besides owning about one-third of the arable land in Western Europe, it had vast accumulations of precious metals and stones with which the pious and superstitious in every age had sought its help and blessing. The rising capitalist class were hampered by lack of capital, and, plundering the Church helped to solve that problem. Thus the wealth of the Church was confiscated wherever the Reformation triumphed. When the English monasteries were dissolved and their manors and other property confiscated, Henry VIII announced his intention of disposing of these estates "to the honour of God and the wealth of the nation". He had, however, somewhat curious notions of piety and national wellbeing, for he sold or distributed most of these estates among his courtiers and favourites; and the remainder were sold at derisory prices to speculative farmers and townsmen, who hunted the copy-holders off the land, and threw their separate holdings into huge estates. Some historians estimate that one-fifteenth of the land of England changed hands in this manner in the course of a few years: others have put the proportion even higher.

It was the same in Sweden, where Gustavas Vasa took all the property of the Roman Church in 1527; and in Denmark, where Christian III confiscated Church property in 1536.

Church property was attacked partly to destroy the Church's power of resistance, but chiefly to transfer land and capital from people who were wasting it into the hands of the middle class who were crying out for capital to sink in remunerative ventures like mines and works. (*An Outline of Man's History*, Patrick Gordon Walker).

The Reformation also helped in the more intensive exploitation of labour (which the new capitalist economy required), by abolishing many of the Saints' Days which had been holidays in the Middle Ages.

" Pilgrimages, saints' days and monasteries," says Luther, " are an excuse for idleness and must be suppressed. Vagrants must be either banished or compelled to labour."

The same viewpoint is expressed in a treatise entitles *Policies to Reduce this Realme of Englande to a Prosperous Wealthe and Estate*, written in 1549 by an anonymous author, who demands that the common people must be set to work so that England can export twice as many goods as heretofore. It can be done, the writer argues, considering that in the past

a great nombre of Monkes, Channons, Friars, and Chantrye priestes with their servants were mayntayned in Idleness ; when the Abbeys dyd stande ; and the realme did also bestow them in idleness and idell workes in gooing of pilgrimagis, keeping of Idell holly days : carvings, painting and gilding of images, and yet the artificers and laborers in those days did all the worke . . . for the tilling and manuring and for the victualling and clothing all the people in the holl realme.

The anonymous author wants these superfluous holidays abolished, "for there is yet standing beside the Sundays thirty-five holidays, whereof twenty-five may be well put downe". (Quoted by M. Beer in his *Early British Economics*.)

THE CHURCH AND USURY

But perhaps the greatest service which the Reformation rendered to capitalism was that it ended the medieval notion that usury and money-making is un-Christian, and that the possession of property is a hindrance to salvation. The Church had taught that

> to take usury is contrary to Scripture ; it is contrary to Aristotle ; it is contrary to nature, for it is to live without labour ; it is to sell time, which belongs to God, for the advantage of wicked men ; it is to rob those who use the money lent, and to whom, since they make it profitable, the profits should belong. (*Religion and the Rise of Capitalism*, R. H. Tawney).

> " Some of the Fathers," writes M. Beer (*Early British Economics*), " looked upon commerce as sinful, or as easily conducive to sin and therefore disreputable. Many disputations were argued out on this head, in which the English schoolmen, Alexander of Hales, Ricardus de Media Villa, Duns Scotus, and Ockham took a prominent part. Even as late as in the year 1078 a Roman Council, presided over by Gregory VII, promulgated Canons, the fifth of which declared that whereas soldiers and merchants could not carry on their trade without sin, there was no salvation for them unless they turned to other occupations."

Usury was prohibited in Anglo-Saxon times, King Alfred basing this prohibition upon the Bible (*Exod.* xxii, 25: *If thou lend money to any of my people that is poor by thee, thou shalt not be to him as an usurer, neither shalt thou lay upon him usury*); and the laws of Edward the Confessor declared that no usurer should be permitted to live in England. In Stephen's reign, John of Salisbury could declare that "the love of wealth and possessions is even worse than Epicureanism, since the passion it excites is the more violent. Property chains men to worldly things".

Trade was severely condemned by the Roman Synod of 1078, which was attended by Roman and Gallican bishops, and presided over by Gregory VII. Among the resolutions (or canons) which were adopted, the fifth stated that the business of the soldier and of the merchant could not be carried on without sin, and that no expiation was possible short of giving up these occupations.

In the 11th and 13th centuries Councils of the Church forbid usury to be taken by the clergy or the laity, and

> lay down rules for dealing with offenders. Clergy who lend money to persons in need, take their possessions in pawn, and receive profits beyond the capital sum lent, are to be deprived of their office. Manifest usurers are not to be admitted to communion or Christian burial ; their offerings are not to be accepted; and ecclesiastics who fail to punish them are to be suspended until they make satisfaction to their bishop. The high-water mark of the ecclesiastical attack on usury was probably reached in the legislation of the Councils of Lyons (1274) and of Vienne (1312).

The former re-enacted the measures laid down by the third Lateran Council (1175), and supplemented them by rules which virtually make the money-lender an outlaw. No individual or society, under pain of excommunication or interdict, was to let houses to usurers, but was to expel them (had they been admitted) within three months. They were to be refused confession, absolution, and Christian burial, until they had made restitution, and their wills were to be invalid. The legislation of the Council of Vienne was even more sweeping. Declaring that it had learned with dismay that there are communities which, contrary to human and divine law, sanction usury and compel debtors to observe usurious contracts, it declares that all rulers and magistrates knowingly maintaining such laws are to incur excommunication, and requires the legislation in question to be revoked within three months. . . . Any person obstinately declaring that usury is not a sin is to be punished as a heretic, and inquisitors are to proceed against him. (*Religion and the Rise of Capitalism*, R. H. Tawney).

As time went on the medieval schoolmen distinguished between lawful trading and usury. Thus, Alexander of Hales (d. 1245) declared that usury is prohibited by divine and moral laws, but that if the debtor is unable to repay the loan on the date agreed upon then the creditor is rightfully entitled to be indemnified for the delay, and that such indemnification is not usury. Ricardus de Media Villa, or Richard Middleton (1249-1307) says that

a trade agreement and a loan agreement differ essentially from one another. In trade both parties expect gain, in a loan the intention of gain is prohibited, for the Gospel admonishes the lender to the loan without hope of gain. (*Luke* vi). It is not the money but the man who produces the increase through his labour and industry, and . . . the increase belongs rightfully to him and not to the lender.

However, like Alexander of Hales, Ricardus de Media Villa permits a fine to be paid by the debtor for not fulfilling the provisions of the agreement, and allows the creditor to be indemnified for the loss entailed in lending money which he might have employed for his own purpose.

One of the greatest of the English schoolmen, Duns Scotus (1265-1308), permits trade and commerce so long as they are carried on with a proper regard for the welfare of all. But trade must be carried on without fraud, and at prices freely and justly agreed upon by buyer and seller. Merchants who neither work up, nor transport, nor store goods for regular trade, but who forestall, regrate and engross them in order to make supplies scarce, and thus to raise prices, are to be condemned. Duns

Scotus refers to the Old Testament prohibition of usury, as well as to *Luke* vi. ("*And if ye lend them of whom ye hope to receive, what thanks have ye ? for sinners also lend to sinners, to receive as much again. But love ye your enemies, and do good and lend, hoping for nothing again; and your reward shall be great*"). He argues that a loan is essentially a work of Christian charity to a fellow-man in need, and no material gain should be expected from it. But though every additional payment over the principal is usury, there are a few cases in which such additional payment is lawful, *viz.* a fine for non-payment of the loan on maturity, and indemnification for any loss caused to the creditor owing to delay in repayment, or in the case of risk of losing the principal.

Gratian was another authority who distinguished between lawful and unlawful trading.

> "Whosoever," he said, "buys a thing, not that he may sell it whole unchanged, but that it may be a material for fashioning something, he is no merchant. But the man who buys it in order that he may gain by selling it again unchanged and as he bought it, that man is of the buyers and sellers who are cast forth from God's temple."

Sufficient has been quoted, perhaps, to show the gulf which exists between the ideas which the Medieval Church held regarding trade and money-making, and those which capitalist ethics take for granted. And it must be remembered that in the Age of Faith the Church was able to impose its ideas upon secular governments. Florence was the financial centre of medieval Europe, yet even there the secular authorities fined bankers for usury in the middle of the 14th century, and later, first prohibited credit transactions altogether, then imported Jews to conduct a business forbidden to Christians.

More than that, the Church permeated the whole of Christendom with this hatred and contempt for usury, as is shown by

> innumerable fables of the usurer who was prematurely carried to hell, or whose money turned to withered leaves in his strong box, or who (as the scrupulous recorder remarks) 'about the year 1240', on entering a church to be married, was crushed by a stone falling from the porch, which proved by the grace of God to be a carving of another usurer and his money-bags being carried off by the devil. (*Religion and the Rise of Capitalism*, R. H. Tawney).

Indeed, the medieval usurer (like the modern profiteer) was so unpopular in the Middle Ages

> that most unpopular characters could be called usurers, and by the average practical man almost any form of bargain which he thought oppressive would be classed as usurious . . . Not only the

taking of interest for a loan, but the raising of prices by a monopo-
list, the beating down of prices by a keen bargainer, the rack-
renting of land by a landlord, the sub-letting of land by a tenant
at a rent higher than he himself paid, the cutting of wages and the
paying of wages in truck, the refusal of discount to a tardy debtor,
the insistence on unreasonably good security for a loan, the excessive profits of a middleman—all these had been denounced as
usury in the very practical thirteenth-century manual of St.
Raymond.　　(*Religion and the Rise of Capitalism*, R. H. Tawney).

The Medieval Church, then, barely tolerated commerce,
condemned the taking of undue profits by the cornering of supplies
and similar expedients which are the commonplace of capitalist
ethics, and, above, all, denounced the taking of interest on loans.
True, as Mr. Tawney says:

the Church could not dispense with commercial wickedness in
high places. It was too convenient. . . . No reasonable judgment
of the medieval denunciation of usury is possible, unless it is
remembered that whole ranges of financial business escaped
from it altogether. It was rarely applied to the large-scale transactions of kings, feudal magnates, bishops and abbots. . . . Popes
regularly employed the international banking-houses of the day,
with a singular indifference, as was frequently complained, to
the morality of their business methods, took them under their special protection, and sometimes enforced the payment of debts by
the threat of excommunication. As a rule, in spite of some
qualms the international money-market escaped the ban of usury;
in the fourteenth century Italy was full of banking-houses doing
foreign exchange business in every commercial centre from Con-
stantinople to London, and in the great fairs, such as those of
Champagne, a special period was regularly set aside for the
negotiation of loans and the settlement of debts. It was not that
transactions of this type were expressly excepted; on the contrary,
each of them from time to time evoked the protests of moralists.
Nor was it mere hypocrisy which caused the traditional doctrine
to be repeated by writers who were perfectly aware that neither
commerce nor government could be carried on without credit.
It was that the whole body of intellectual assumptions and practical interests, on which the prohibition of usury was based, had
reference to a quite different order of economic activities from that
represented by loans from great banking-houses to the merchants
and potentates who were their clients. Its object was simple and
direct—to prevent the well-to-do money-lender from exploiting
the necessities of the peasant or the craftsman.

The prohibition of usury by the Church was part of the
morality of an agrarian society, and for capitalism to develop
it became more and more necessary to compromise this old
morality. But that could not be done without discrediting and
finally overthrowing the whole elaborate theological system on

which medieval morality rested. In other words, the economic needs of the new order demanded a new religious and ethical outlook such as could be achieved only by disrupting the Catholic Church, and carrying through a radical reformation.

LUTHER AND CALVIN

We have already noted that capitalism called into being the modern nation-state, with a strong central government, which in this country, for instance, resulted in the Tudor absolutism. Lutheranism was admirably suited to the needs of absolute monarchy.

> "The Lutheran Reformation", says Engels, "produced a new creed indeed, a religion adapted to absolute monarchy. No sooner were the peasants of north-east Germany converted to Lutheranism than they were from freemen reduced to serfs.
>
> (*Socialism, Utopian and Scientific.*)

That is no exaggeration. When the peasants revolted, and Luther had to choose between them and the princes he did not hesitate. "Better the death of all the peasants than of the princes," he said; and urged the nobles to annihilate the rebels, saying:

> He who slays a rioter . . . does what is right. . . Therefore whoever can should smite, strangle or stab, secretly or publicly . . . If you are killed in this struggle, you are indeed to be felicitated, as no nobler death could befall anyone.

Luther strengthened the princes of Germany (even the Catholic ones) by his fierce denunciation of revolution.

> Luther
> created a model religion for the early despotic monarch; and during his lifetime a type of national religion was established in those countries neighbouring Germany where similar conditions prevailed . . . The countries where this happened were England, Denmark and Sweden . . . in all three a national religion similar to Lutheranism was used to help the growth into nationhood.
>
> (*The Sixteenth and Seventeenth Centuries*, P. C. Gordon Walker.)

But it was in Calvinism that the new middle class found the religion best suited to their class interests when they were waging a revolutionary struggle for power.

God, Calvin taught, not only foresaw the fall of the first man, but chose as his Elect certain individuals predestined to salvation from eternity by "his gratuitous mercy, totally irrespective of human merit". None others could be saved by any means whatsoever.

One might have imagined that such a doctrine would have bred a licentious abandon and disregard for all morality, but it had precisely the opposite effect. Above all things the Calvinist wanted to have the assurance that he was numbered among the Elect, and so he tried to live as he supposed a man chosen by God would do. The good life was not a *means* to salvation, but a *sign* of salvation. If a Catholic committed a sin he might still hope for forgiveness; but for the Calvinist there was no forgiveness: the commission of a sin was a sign that he was damned, and nothing, no repentance, no church, not even Almighty God himself, could alter that dread fact. And thus it was that Calvinism laid a much stricter insistence upon morality than the Catholic Church had ever done.

In this way Calvinism sanctified just those qualities and virtues—frugality, sobriety, thrift, and diligence in business—which the new commercial civilization needed if it was to accumulate the capital necessary for its development. It looked with a jaundiced eye on the vanities and fripperies of this world, and taught the worthiness of hard work. The Calvinist with his industrious habits could not help making money, but he had nothing to spend it on save the necessities of a sober life, for all pleasures and luxuries were banned to him. And so the profits which he made went back into his business.

> The Roman Church, it was held, through the example of its rulers, had encouraged luxury and ostentation: the members of the Reformed Church must be economical and modest. It had sanctioned the spurious charity of indiscriminate almsgiving: the true Christian must repress mendicancy and insist upon the virtues of industry and thrift. . . . Such teaching, whatever its theological merits or defects, was admirably designed to liberate economic energies, and to weld into a disciplined social force the rising bourgeoisie, conscious of the contrast between its own standards and those of a laxer world, proud of its vocation as the standard-bearer of the economic virtues, and determined to vindicate an open road for its own way of life by the use of every weapon, including political revolution and war, because the issue which was at stake was not merely convenience or self-interest but the will of God.
>
> (*Religion and the Rise of Capitalism,* R. H. Tawney).

The Calvinist devoted himself to business because (with most other activities barred to him as sinful) that was the best way of occupying his time, and escaping the temptations of the flesh. "To the Puritan", writes R. H. Tawney, "mundane toil becomes itself a kind of sacrament".

In 1525, when he drafted a plan for the reorganisation of poor relief at Zurich, Zwingli wrote that "Labour is a thing so good and godlike". One hears there the authentic note of capitalist morality. Calvin, too, quoted with approval the words of St. Paul: "If a man will not work neither shall he eat", and urged that the ecclesiastical authorities should regularly visit every family to ascertain whether its members were idle or drunken.

> Calvin glorified business as an end in itself demanding the devotion of every moment's leisure; for the worst that could befall a Calvinist was to find that he was not one of the elect; the only way he could make sure was never to slack off for a moment in doing those things that were the marks of one of the elect. . . . A single sin was a sign that he was damned eternally. For fear of finding he was not one of the elect, the Calvinist had to devote himself incessantly to his duty . . . But what, in terms of daily life, was this duty that a Calvinist had to observe so desperately ? In the end it turns out to be nothing less than steady application to business; for Calvinism ruthlessly strips away all other occupations of life. Art, music, all luxury and distraction are artificial props just as ungodly as the sacraments of the Catholic Church. The Calvinist was left with nothing to do in his supreme task of proving to himself that he was one of the elect but to devote himself to his trade, which became the noblest occupation of all, indeed the only occupation for a man of God.
>
> (*The Sixteenth and Seventeenth Centuries*, P. C. Gordon Walker.)

Moreover, just as labour became "a thing so good and godlike", so too did the acquisition of capital.

> " He who has enough to satisfy his wants ", wrote a schoolman of the fourteenth century, "and nevertheless ceaselessly labours to acquire riches, either in order to obtain a higher social position or that subsequently he may have enough to live without labour, or that his sons may become men of wealth and importance— all such are incited by a damnable avarice, sensuality or pride ".

Baxter, the 17th-century Puritan, could write the exact opposite:

> If God shows you a way in which you may lawfully get more than in another way (without wrong to your soul or to any other), if you refuse this and choose the less gainful way, you cross one of the ends of your Calling, and you refuse to be God's steward.

CALVINISM AND THE ANABAPTISTS

Calvinism rendered another great service to the rising capitalist class: it helped to lay the spectre of Anabaptism. Anabaptism was not an organised religion, but rather the closely related beliefs of a number of small sects who were united only in the belief that man's conscience (or the Inner Light, as they termed it) should be the sole guide to his actions. They were called Anabaptists because they denied the validity of infant baptism, arguing that a Christian should not be baptised until he was old enough to choose his own church. By putting forward this claim the Anabaptists struck at all organised churches, whether Protestant or Roman, and

> this, in the sixteenth century was to attack the very organisation of society, for . . . an organised Church was indispensable to society.
> (*The Sixteenth and Seventeenth Centuries*, P. C. Gordon Walker.)

This religion spread wherever the new proletariat was numerous. It had its adherents in urban Switzerland, in south-west Germany, in the towns of south-east England (the old stronghold of Lollardy), and above all in the Netherlands, where the new propertyless working class which capitalism was calling into being was at one and the same time the most miserable and most developed. There, in 1533, Anabaptism broke into open revolt, and for a while won and held political power.

Calvinism was admirably suited to help the capitalist in his struggle with the Anabaptists and to discipline the new proletariat. Its classification of souls into a minority of Elect and a majority of Damned corresponded with the economic division into a few employers and a mass of workers.

> In a theological system which insisted that mankind had already been divided into classes by the arbitrary decree of the Lord, the middle classes found their sanction for a class division that economic development was crystallizing. . . . God, they reasoned, who has already chosen those who are to enjoy the blessing of Heaven, is unlikely to frown on His Chosen while they still tread the earth. And how else could He smile on the elect but by conferring on them the good things of life ? A class consciousness bred of material success was purified by the cleansing waters of theological doctrine to become a conviction of innate superiority. The poverty of the unfortunate became an indication of their moral failure. For if riches were proof of election, poverty was the yellow badge of damnation decreed by God and beyond any human power to revoke. . . . Poverty and suffering, once an eloquent reproach to the luxury of the wealthy and a powerful prick to their conscience, became merely confirmation of their own righteousness. (*Left-Wing Democracy in the English Civil War*, David W. Petegorsky, pp. 23-24.)

> "The rich artificiall theeves doe rob the poore and that under a fained show of justice and seeming holiness," wrote a seventeenth-century pamphleteer. "And when they have done it most impiously they say and affirm that God's providence hath made them rich and those they have robbed poore; for they say that God's providence maketh rich and pore." (*Tyranipocrit discovered with all his wiles wherewith he vanquisheth.* 1649).

Calvinism taught that not only was it the duty of the Elect to discipline themselves, but also that it was their obligation to see that even the Damned honoured God's will.   And so, wherever the Calvinist secured power his conscience drove him to use the full force of government to compel the common people (the Unelect) to the same self-denial and sobriety of behaviour that he (as one of the Elect) practised.   In puritan England, as Macaulay tells us,

> The theatres were closed. The players were flogged. The press was put under the guardianship of austere licensers.

It was the same in Geneva, Scotland, Amsterdam: wherever the Calvinists controlled the government a merciless law was set into action against adultery, gambling, drinking, and all such irregularities.

> The discipline of the masses no less than the self-discipline of the merchant was the key-note of Calvinism. (*The Sixteenth and Seventeenth Centuries*, P. C. Gordon Walker).

Not only did Calvin provide the rising capitalist class with precisely the kind of ideology they needed: he also gave them an organisation for carrying his ideas into effect. His followers were organised into compact, disciplined groups or congregations, each with its minister and elected elders; and these congregations maintained close association one with another, and met from time to time in national synods which put a nation-wide organisation at their disposal. In England these congregations were called presbyteries, which gave the name Presbyterians* to the English Calvinists. The Government was so alarmed by the strength of these organisations that Queen Elizabeth persecuted the Presbyterians more sternly than the Catholics, and admitted Calvinist doctrines into her compromised Anglican religion. In France the Huguenots could raise an army more quickly than the Government itself; and in Scotland and the Netherlands the synods were richer than the Government.

Calvinism was in every respect a creed admirably suited to the revolutionary bourgeoisie: by its grim doctrine of predestination and the Elect of God it gave them just the self-confidence as a class which they needed in their struggles with the feudal aristocracy and the monarchy. Within the shadow of this gloomy creed royal blood or noble lineage dwindled to

---

*The elders (or presbyters) were laymen appointed to watch over the morals of their fellows, and are so conspicuous in Calvin's plans of organisation that they have given their name to the Presbyterian Church.

small account: king or noble might be destined to eternal damnation, whilst the humble merchant or yeoman was of God's elect company. Calvinism gave to the rising middle class a fanatical sense of their own worthiness with which they were able to confront the haughty self-confidence of the born aristocrat. It gave them the certain assurance of ultimate victory; the sense of being an instrument in the hands of Destiny to humble

"The haughty and the strong, who sate in the high places, and slew the saints of God."

Historical analogies can easily be misleading and dangerous; nevertheless one can agree with Mr. Tawney when he says that

It is not wholly fanciful to say that, on a narrower stage but with not less formidable weapons, Calvin did for the bourgeoisie of the sixteenth century what Marx did for the proletariate of the nineteenth, or that the doctrine of predestination satisfied the same hunger for an assurance that the forces of the universe are on the side of the elect as was to be assuaged in a different age by the theory of historical materialism. . . . Like the modern proletarian, who feels that, whatever his personal misery and his present disappointments, the Cause is rolled forward to victory by the irresistible forces of an inevitable evolution, the Puritan bourgeoisie knew that against the chosen people the gates of hell could not prevail. The Lord prospered their doings. (*Religion and the Rise of Capitalism*).

CHAPTER 6

THE PEASANT WAR IN GERMANY

There should be no serfs because Christ has freed us
all! What is that we hear? . . . A worldly realm
cannot stand where there is no inequality; some must
be free, others bond; some rulers, others subject.
Martin Luther on the "Twelve Articles", May 1525.

HANS THE PIPER

About fifty years after the collapse of the Hussite movement a
number of revolutionary conspiracies occurred among the German
peasantry, all of which took to some extent a religious form.

The first of these risings took place in 1476, in the bishopric
of Würzburg, a country impoverished (we are told) "by bad
government, manifold taxes, payments, feuds, enmity, war, fires,
murder, prison, and the like". A young shepherd and musician,
Hans Böheim of Niklashausen, known as Hans the Piper,
or Hans the Drum-Beater, appeared in Taubergrund, and
declared that the Virgin had appeared to him in a vision, and
that she had commanded him to burn his drum and to summon
the people to penance. Everybody (he preached) must purge
themselves of sin and the vain lusts of the world, forsake all
adornments, and undertake a pilgrimage to the Madonna of
Niklashausen to seek forgiveness for their sins.

Hans the Piper's call to repentance evoked a wide response,
and masses of people joined in pilgrimages to Niklashausen.
As his influence extended the young piper expounded a more and
more revolutionary doctrine. The Madonna of Niklashausen,
he said, had announced to him that henceforth there should be
neither king nor princes, nor pope nor any other lay or ecclesiastical authority. All men should be brothers and earn their bread
by the toil of their hands, and none should possess more than his
neighbour. All taxes, ground rents, serf duties, and tolls must be
abolished, and forests, meadows and waters made free to all.

Needless to say, such a gospel was enthusiastically received
by the peasantry, and "the message of our Mother" spread far
and wide. Hosts of pilgrims came from Bavaria, Suabia and the
Rhine. Soon it was reputed that the Piper could perform miracles
and people fell on their knees before him and prayed to him as

o a saint. Others fought, we are told, for small strips from his cap as for amulets or holy relics. The priests denounced his visions as devilish delusions, and his miracles as hellish swindles; but the number of his believers continued to increase, and the Sunday sermons of the young revolutionary attracted gatherings which are said to have numbered 40,000 and more.

Hans the Piper continued to preach for several months. Meanwhile he was in secret communication with the priest of Niklashausen and with two knights, Kunz of Thunfeld and his son Michael, who accepted his teaching, and were to be the military leaders of the insurrection which he planned.

Finally, on the Sunday before St. Kilian's Day, Hans gave the signal to his followers. At the close of his sermon he said;

> And now go home, and weigh in your mind what our Holiest Madonna has announced to you, and on the coming Saturday leave your wives and children and old men at home, but you, you men, come back here to Niklashausen on the day of St. Margaret, which is next Saturday, and bring with you your brothers and friends, as many as they may be. Do not come with pilgrims' staves, but covered with weapons and ammunition, in one hand a candle, in the other a sword and a pike or halberd, and the Holy Virgin will then announce to you what she wishes you to do.

However, before the day appointed for the rebellion the Bishop of Würzburg seized the Piper and carried him off to his castle. 34,000 peasants appeared on the day appointed by Hans, but the majority were disheartened and returned home when they heard of his arrest. Some 16,000 remained, and threatened the castle under the leadership of Kunz of Thunfeld and his son: but the bishop persuaded them to go home by means of ample promises. No sooner did they disperse, however, than he sent his men-at-arms to attack them. Hans the Piper was burned alive, and Kunz of Thunfeld fled, and only made his peace with the bishop by forfeiting all his estates.

THE UNION SHOE

For some years after the death of Hans the Piper the German peasants seem to have made no further attempt to improve their lot by revolutionary action; but towards the turn of the century their conspiracies began afresh, one of the causes of their renewed unrest being the rise in the prices of commodities.

By 1493 there was a secret union in Alsace of peasants and poor townworkers, together with a sprinkling of the middle-class, and even some support, or at least sympathy, from the lower nobility. The conspirators demanded, among other things, the plundering and extermination of the Jews, the introduction of a jubilee year to cancel all debts, the reduction of priests' incomes to a prebend of fifty or sixty guilders, the abolition of auricular confession, the right to ratify taxation, and the abolition of the ecclesiastical and imperial courts and the establishment in the communities of courts elected by themselves.

The conspirators planned to seize the town of Schlettstadt, and to use that as a base from which to rouse the whole of Alsace. They marched under the banner of the *Bundschuh*, or peasant's clog bound with thongs up to the calf (in contra-distinction to the riding-boot or the open shoe of the richer classes) and this symbol of poverty was used in a whole series of peasant risings during the next two decades.

The Union Shoe conspirators held their meetings at night on the lonely Hungerberg, and initiation into membership appears to have been accompanied by mysterious ceremonies and dread threats of punishment against those who turned traitor. (One is reminded of the similar initiation rites of the early trade union movement in this country). However, in spite of these pre-cautions, the authorities got wind of the conspiracy about Easter Week, 1493, which was the time appointed for the rising. Some of the ringleaders were seized and tortured before being executed, and others were crippled by the chopping off of their hands or fingers.

Many, however, escaped into Switzerland, and the Union Shoe maintained a secret organisation. Missionaries spread its ideas through Switzerland and South Germany, where they found the same oppression of the peasantry and the same inclina- to revolt.

> The greatest admiration (says Engels) is due to the tenacity and endurance with which the peasants of upper Germany conspired for thirty years after 1493, with which they overcame the obstacles to a more centralized organisation in spite of the fact that they were scattered over the countryside, and with which, after numberless dispersions, defeats, executions of leaders, they renewed their conspiracies over and over again, until an opportunity came for a mass upheaval. (*The Peasant War in Germany*, pp. 78-79).

In 1502 there was a secret movement among the peasants in the bishopric of Speyer. About 7,000 men joined the Union Shoe organisation, whose articles included the following:

No ground rent, tithe, tax or toll to be paid to the princes, the nobility or the clergy ; serfdom to be abolished; monasteries and other church estates to be confiscated and divided among the people, and no other authority to be recognised apart from the emperor.

These two demands (confiscation of the Church estates in favour of the people, and a unified Germany) figure regularly in the reforms demanded by the more advanced sections of the German peasants and workers until Thomas Münzer carried them a stage further by demanding not the division of Church property among the peasantry but its conversion into common property, and a unified republic in place of a unified German monarchy.

As in the case of the earlier conspiracy, the new Union Shoe movement had its secret meeting place, its initiation ceremony and oath of silence, and its *Bundschuh* banner, with the legend *Nothing but God's Justice*. The course which the conspiracy ran was also very similar. There was a plan to seize the town of Burchsal, where most of the population was sympathetic to the Union, after which a Union army was to be organised and sent to rouse the peasants in the neighbouring principalities.

But once again the conspiracy was betrayed (this time by a priest to whom one of the Union Shoe supporters revealed it in the confessional) and the authorities broke the movement by mass arrests. How widespread the conspiracy had become is evidenced by the terror which seized the governments of the various imperial estates in Alsace and the Union of Suabia; but though here and there peasant armies assembled and offered armed resistance they were speedily overcome by trained troops. Some of the conspirators were executed: others fled into neighbouring countries.

JOSS FRITZ

Another period of apparent pacification followed, although actually the movement continued in secret. During this period Joss Fritz of Untergrombach played a great part in building up the Union. He was (like Wat Tyler) an old soldier, and a fugitive from the 1502 conspiracy, and he showed a remarkable knack in involving the most divergent elements in the Union. "Knights, priests, burghers, plebeians and peasants . . . all serviceable elements were utilized with the greatest circumspection and skill". (*The Peasant War in Germany*, F. Engels, p. 82). Besides the regular emissaries of the Union who travelled the country in various disguises, Joss Fritz made extensive use of the beggars and vagrants, who abounded in such numbers in the first half of the 16th century in Germany, and the "beggar kings" were bribed with 2,000 guilders to take part in the rising with a force of 2,000 men.

Joss Fritz and his chief lieutenant, Stoffel of Freiburg, continually travelled the country, reviewing the rebel armies by night, and the investigations which took place after the suppression of the movement show that it had wide support in the Upper Rhine and Black Forest regions. Most of its adherents were peasants and poor journeymen, but there were in addition a number of innkeepers and unemployed Lansquenets (German mercenaries), and even a few priests and nobles.

The aims of the Union were set forth in Fourteen Articles. There were to be no masters save the emperor (or, according to some accounts, the pope); and the Rottweil imperial court was to be abolished. All interest which had been paid so long that it equalled the capital was to be ended, and 5 per cent. interest on loans was to be the highest permitted. The peasants were to have freedom of hunting, fishing, grazing and wood cutting. Priests were to be limited to one prebend each, and all church estates and monastery gems were to be confiscated in favour of the Union. All inequitable taxes and tolls were to be abolished. There was to be eternal peace within Christendom, but energetic action against all the enemies of the Union.

The conspirators planned to seize the city of Freiburg, to serve as a centre for the Union; and thereafter to open negotiations with the Emperor, or with Switzerland should the Emperor refuse to come to terms with them.

The insurrection was planned to begin in the autumn of 1513, and Joss Fritz went to Heilbrunn to have a Union banner painted. This included, besides various emblems and pictures, the Union Shoe and the words *God help thy divine justice.*

Unfortunately, during Joss Fritz's absence a premature and unsuccessful attempt was made to seize Freiburg, and a number of Union members were arrested, put to the torture, and executed. Once more the movement collapsed.

POOR KONRAD

Simultaneously with the Union Shoe movement in Baden and seemingly in direct connection with it, another conspiracy occurred in Württemberg. It originated in 1503, and when the name Union Shoe became too dangerous after the Untergrombach conspirators were discovered, it adopted the name of *Poor Konrad*. To the discontent caused by the famine years was added the new grievances resulting from newly imposed taxes on wine, meat and bread, together with a capital tax of one penny yearly for every guilder.

As was common with most of these conspiracies, the insurrectionists planned to seize a strong city as a base for their movement. In this case it was Schorndorf. The rebellion broke out in the spring of 1514, when 3,000 (some accounts say 5,000) peasants appeared before the city.

Duke Ulrich contrived to pacify them by promising to abolish the new taxes and to convene a Diet to examine grievances; but the leaders of Poor Konrad were convinced that he was only seeking to gain time while he collected sufficient troops to impose his will by force. They issued a summons to a Union Congress, which was held in Unterürkhein on May 20th, and was attended by representatives from all parts of Württemberg. The Duke was compelled to yield; but even whilst he was calling the promised Diet for June 25th, he was corresponding with the neighbouring princes and free cities, asking for their aid to suppress an uprising which (he said) threatened all princes, nobles and authorities in the empire.

The Diet, which represented the cities and was also attended by delegates from the peasantry, decided to punish the three most hated councillors of the Duke, and to confiscate the property and endowments of the monasteries in favour of the State treasury.

But before these decisions could be operated Duke Ulrich (having gathered troops and been promised military aid by the Elector Palatine and others) felt himself strong enough to strike. On June 21st he appeared in Tübingen with sufficient forces to terrorize the burghers, who deserted their allies the peasants. The Poor Konrad movement collapsed, and offered resistance only in the valley of Rems, where a peasant camp was formed on the mountain of Koppel. The Duke attacked and defeated this peasant army, 1,600 of whom were taken prisoners. Sixteen of them were decapitated, and the rest sentenced to pay heavy fines. Many languished in prison, and a number of penal laws were passed to prevent a rebirth of the organisation, whilst the nobility of Suabia formed a union to suppress all future attempts of an insurrection.

Despite all these setbacks the Union Shoe movement persisted, and developed great activity in 1517 in the Black Forest. Joss

Fritz traversed that district, carrying with him the Union Shoe banner of 1513; but once more the movement was discovered by the authorities, and many of its leaders were seized and executed. Others fled, among them being Joss Fritz, who seems to have died soon afterwards in Switzerland.

CLASS FORCES IN GERMANY

The various Union Shoe conspiracies which occurred in Germany were a prelude to the Great Peasant War of 1525. This took place in two main areas: in the Tyrol and Austria, where it lasted until 1526, and in south-west Germany, where Thomas Münzer's influence was strong, and where communism was preached and sometimes put into practice. Here the rising was suppressed within the year.

The great revolt took place at a time when capitalism was beginning to supplant the medieval economy, and a developing industry in the towns was no longer producing for a local market but for ever more remote markets. The middle class of the cities (who represented the rising capitalist economy) chafed at the limitations of the feudal system, and united in a vague national movement with the lower orders against feudalism.

The old feudal empire was falling to pieces, and the great feudal vassals were becoming practically independent princes who levied taxes, maintained standing armies, and made war of their own accord. With the development of their sovereignty, and a growing taste for luxury came mounting costs of administration. Taxes were oppressive, and (the cities being protected for the most part by privileges) the main weight of this taxation fell upon the peasants.

It was the peasant who carried the burden of all the other strata of society: princes, officialdom, nobility, clergy, patricians and middle-class. Whether the peasant was the subject of a prince, an imperial baron, a bishop, a monastery or a city, he was everywhere treated as a beast of burden, and worse. If he was a serf, he was entirely at the mercy of his master. If he was a bondsman, the legal deliveries stipulated by agreement were sufficient to crush him; even they were being daily increased. Most of his time, he had to work on his master's estate. Out of that which he earned in his few free hours, he had to pay tithes, dues, ground rents, war taxes, land taxes, imperial taxes, and other payments. He could neither marry nor die without paying the master. Aside from his regular work for the master, he had to gather litter, pick strawberries, collect snail-shells, drive the game for the hunting, chop wood, and so on. The peasant saw his crop destroyed by the wild game. The community meadows and woods of the peasants had almost everywhere been forcibly taken away by the masters. And in the same manner as the master reigned over the peasant's property, he extended his wilfulness over his person, his wife and daughters. He possessed the right of the first night. (*The Peasant War in Germany*, F. Engels, pp. 47-48).

Meanwhile the clergy was more and more ceasing to perform any real social function.

The invention of the art of printing, and the requirements of extended commerce robbed the clergy not only of its monopoly of reading and writing, but also of that of higher education... The newly arising class of jurists drove the clergy out of a series of influential positions. The clergy was also beginning to become largely superfluous, and it acknowledged this fact by growing lazier and more ignorant. The more superfluous it became, the more it grew in numbers, thanks to the enormous riches which it still kept on augmenting by fair means or foul. ... They (the high Church dignitaries) . . . not only exploited their subjects as recklessly as the knighthood and the princes, but they practised this in an even more shameful manner. They used not only brutal force, but all the intrigues of religion as well; not only the horrors of the rack, but also the horror of excommunication, or refusal of absolution; they used all the intricacies of the confessional in order to extract from their subjects the last penny, or to increase the estates of the church. Forging of documents was a widespread and beloved means of extortion in the hands of these worthy men. ... The manufacture of miracle-producing saints' effigies and relics, the organisation of praying-centres endowed with the power of salvation, the trade in indulgences was resorted to in order to squeeze more payments out of the people. (*The Peasant War in Germany*, pp. 40-41).

It was no wonder, then, that the Church dignitaries became an object of hatred not only to the peasantry, but even to the nobility who envied them their many fat livings.

The clergy were, however, divided into two distinct groups. The higher hierarchy—archbishops, bishops, abbots and priors—formed an aristocracy. They were either imperial princes themselves, or ruled as vassals over large areas with numerous serfs and bondsmen. Besides this wealthy hierarchy there were the rural and urban clergy who enjoyed none of the riches of the Church. They received modest prebends, and being of peasant or middle class origin they were nearer the life of the masses and sympathised largely with their aspirations, in much the same way as Wiklif's Poor Priests had sympathised with the English peasantry of their day.

While the participation of the monks in the movements of their time was the exception, that of the plebeian clergy was the rule. They gave the movement its theorists and ideologists, and many of them, representatives of the plebeians and peasants, died on the scaffold. (*The Peasant War in Germany*, Engels, p. 42.)

LUTHER AND THE PEASANTS

Martin Luther, with his vague declaration of human liberty and German brotherhood, found adherents both among the peasantry and the middle class; though this uneasy unity quickly vanished when the peasants took violent measures to carry into effect what they held to be the implications of Luther's teachings.

The Edict of Worms (1521) had denounced Luther as an opponent of law and a breeder of sedition, and there had been some justification for this view since the early Luther had not hesitated to preach the revolutionary use of violence.

"If the raging madness (of the Roman Church) were to continue," he wrote, "it seems to me no better counsel and remedy could be found against it than that kings and princes apply force, arm themselves, attack those evil people who have poisoned the entire world, and once for all make an end to this game, with arms, not with words. If thieves are being punished with swords, murderers with ropes, and heretics with fire, why do we not seize, with arms in hands, all those evil teachers of perdition, those popes, bishops, cardinals, and the entire crew of Roman Sodom? Why do we not wash our hands in their blood?"

It was a different thing, however, when the peasants acted on this advice, and began burning castles. Luther denounced them in unbridled language.

Dear Gentlemen, (he cried) hearken here, save there, stab, knock, strangle them at will, and if thou diest, thou art blessed; no better death canst thou ever attain.

It is true that at first he attacked the governments as well, declaring that the revolts had been provoked by oppression; also he advised both parties to come to a peaceful understanding.

I have told you, (he wrote) that you are both wrong and are fighting for the wrong. You nobles are not fighting against Christians, for Christians would not oppose you, but would suffer all. You are fighting against robbers and blasphemers of Christ's name; those that die among them shall be eternally damned. But neither are the peasants fighting Christians, but tyrants, enemies of God, and persecutors of men, murderers of the Holy Ghost. Those of them that die shall also be eternally damned.

But when he had to choose between prince and peasant, between defence of the established social order and social revolution, he never hesitated. The whole weight of his authority was flung into the scale against the peasantry. "The only way to make Herr Omnes (i.e. Mr. Everyman, his nickname for the peasants) do what he ought is to constrain him by law and the sword to a semblance of piety as one holds wild beasts by chains and cages," he said; and again: "Better the death of all the peasants than of the princes." He urged the princes to strangle the rebels "as you would mad dogs"; and when the insurrection was finally quelled he bragged that it was he who had killed the peasants because he had given the orders to kill. "All their blood is upon me," he said.

Luther's translation of the Bible had been a powerful weapon in the hands of those who demanded freedom and social justice; now he turned the same weapon against the peasants, and found a sanction for serfdom in it.

> There should be no serfs because Christ has freed us all! What is that we hear? That is to make Christian freedom wholly bodily. Did not Abraham and the other patriarchs and prophets have serfs? Read what St. Paul says of servants, who in all times have been serfs. So this article is straight against the gospel, and moreover it is robbery, since each man would take his person from his lord to whom it belongs. A serf can be a good Christian and enjoy Christian liberty, just as a prisoner or a sick man may be a Christian although he is not free. This article would make all men equal and convert the spiritual kingdom of Christ into an external worldly one; but that is impossible, for a worldly realm cannot stand where there is no inequality; some must be free, others bond; some rulers, others subjects. (Martin Luther on the *Twelve Articles*, May, 1525.)

THOMAS MÜNZER

Thomas Münzer was the ideologist of the Peasant War. He took Luther's proclamation of freedom for all men seriously, and when he discovered that Luther was, in fact, trying to limit this universal liberty to the princes and the middle class, he broke with him and denounced him as a deceiver of the people.

Münzer was in many respects a greater man than Luther, and he certainly possessed much more intellectual honesty. Born in Stolberg, in 1498, his scholarly attainments in the theology of the times gained him his doctor's degree, and the position of a chaplain in a Halle nunnery.

In 1520 he went to Zwickau, where he came into contact with the Anabaptists, whose leader was a cloth-maker named Nicholas Storch.* The Anabaptists preached that the Day of Judgment and the Millennium was at hand, and they had "visions, convulsions, and the spirit of prophecy." But beneath an appearance of humility and unconcern for worldly things, they concealed the growing opposition of the poorer classes to the existing social order, and they came into conflict with the Council of Zwickau. Münzer had influenced them considerably (although he had not joined them) and now he defended them. However, they were compelled to leave the city, and Münzer departed with them towards the end of 1521.

He went to Prague and attempted to join the remnant of the Hussite movement, but his unconventional opinions soon compelled him to flee from Bohemia, and in 1522 he became a preacher at Altstedt, in Thuringia. Here he ordered the entire Bible to be read to the people in their own tongue. Supporters flocked to him from all parts, and Altstedt soon became the centre of the popular anti-priest movement for the whole of Thuringia.

Up to this time Münzer was directing most of his attacks against the Roman priests, and appealing to the princes and people to rise in arms against them.

> If you wish to be the servants of God (he said), you must drive out and destroy the evil ones who stand in the way of the Gospel. . . . We must destroy those who stand in the way of God's revelation, we must do it mercilessly, as Hezekiah, Cyrus, Josiah, Daniel and Elias destroyed the priests of Baal, else the Christian Church will never come back to its origins. We must root the weeds in God's vineyard at the time when the crops are ripe. God said in the Fifth Book of Moses, 7, 'Thou shalt not show mercy unto the idolators, but ye shall break down their altars, dash in pieces their graven images and burn them with fire that I shall not be wroth at you'.

These appeals to the princes were of no avail; and Münzer turned to the peasants and workers who were already (as we have

---

*Zwickau was a centre of Anabaptism in Switzerland, where Nicholas Storch, a cloth-maker, preached a religious communism. Münzer came under his influence, and is reputed to have said that Storch knew the Bible better than all the priests combined. A whole community, including twelve apostles, gathered around him, and his disciples believed that the truth was revealed to him in divine revelations. In 1522 Storch settled in Thuringia, and he became one of the leaders of the Peasant War. In collaboration with Münzer, Pfeifer and others, he composed a programme of demands, which declared that property belonged to all alike since God had created all men equally bare, and had given to them everything on the land, in the water, and under the sky. Nicholas Storch died in Munich, in 1525.

seen) in a state of unrest and revolt. He "began to pick up the threads of the sporadic revolts of the last half-century and to or-ganise and co-ordinate them." (*The Sixteenth and Seventeenth Centuries,* P. C. Gordon Walker, p. 101.) At the same time his ideas became more definite, and, under cover of Christian phraseology, he preached a kind of pantheism: indeed, in some of his speeches and pamphlets he became practically an atheist. He denied that the Bible was the only infallible revelation. The only revelation (he said) was reason, which has existed among all peoples at all times. Christ (he taught) was not God, but a man— a prophet and a teacher; and his Lord's Supper nothing but a plain meal of commemoration during which bread and wine are consumed with mystic additions. Heaven was to be sought in this life, and not in some world after death; and, just as there is no Heaven in the beyond, so there is no Hell, and no damnation. Devils are but the evil desires and cravings of Man.

Münzer gave a direction to the vague gospel feeling for equality which he found among the peasantry and turned it into his own communism. Engels wrote of him:

> There is more than one communist sect of modern times which . . . did not possess a theoretical equipment as rich as that of Münzer of the Sixteenth Century. His programme [was] less a compilation of the demands of the then existing plebeians than a genius's anticipation of the conditions for the emancipation of the pro-letarian elements that had just begun to develop among the plebeians.   (*The Peasant War in Germany,* pp. 66-67.)

Thomas Münzer desired the immediate establishment of the Kingdom of God on Earth, by which he understood a free society without class differences or private property. He declared that all existing authorities which refused to join in the revolution must be overthrown, and work and property must be shared in common; and that in order to realise this programme a Union of the people was necessary throughout the whole of Christendom. Princes and nobles were to be invited to join this Union, and where they refused they were to be overthrown by force.

Münzer laboured with tireless energy to organise such a Union among the peasants of the south and south-west of Germany, seeing in them the class that could carry his ideals of liberty and equality into practice. He travelled widely, giving direction and conscious purpose to blind, spontaneous revolt, and his preaching assumed an ever more revolutionary character.

Clergy, princes, the nobility, and the patricians of the cities, were all denounced, and

> he pictured in burning colours the existing oppression, and contrasted it with the vision of the millennium of social republican equality which he created out of his imagination. (*The Peasant War in Germany*, p. 67.)

He wrote pamphlet after pamphlet, and sent out emissaries in all directions to preach his revolutionary doctrines. It was among the Anabaptists that

> he found invaluable agents. This sect, having no definite dogmas, held together by the common symbol of a second baptism, ascetic in their mode of living, untiring, fanatic and intrepid in propaganda, had grouped itself more closely around Münzer. Made homeless by constant persecutions, its members wandered over the length and breadth of Germany, announcing everywhere the new gospel wherein Münzer had made clear to them their own demands and wishes. Numberless Anabaptists were put on the rack, burned or otherwise executed. But the courage and endurance of these emissaries was unshaken, and the success of their activities amidst the rapidly rising agitation of the people was enormous.   (*The Peasant War in Germany*, p. 71.)

Some of Münzer's followers destroyed St. Mary's Chapel in Mellerbach, near Altstedt, claiming that they were carrying out the Biblical injunction "Ye shall break down their altars, and dash in pieces their pillars, and hew down their Asherim, and burn their graven images with fire." (*Deuteronomy*, vii, 5). When this happened the princes of Saxony came in person to Altstedt to quell the disturbances. They summoned Münzer before them, when he delivered a sermon the like of which they had never heard from "that easy-living flesh of Wittenberg", as Münzer called Luther. He told them that ungodly rulers, and especially priests and monks who treat the Gospel as heresy, must be killed, and he justified this drastic policy by reference to the New Testament. The sources of the evils of usury, thievery and robbery (he said) were the princes and masters who had taken all creatures into their private possession—the fishes in the water, the birds in the air, the plants in the soil. These usurers preached to the poor the commandment *Thou shalt not steal*, yet they robbed the peasant and artisan. If they (the lords and masters) did not remove the causes of discontent how could things improve? "Oh! dear gentlemen, (he cried) how the Lord will smite with an iron rod all these old pots! When I say so, I am considered rebellious. So be it!"

Münzer had this sermon printed in Altstedt; whereupon the printer was punished with banishment by Duke Johann of Saxony. Münzer's writings were now subject to censorship by the ducal government of Weimar, but he was not to be intimidated, and published in the city of Mühlhausen a provocative pamphlet which concluded with the words:

> All the world must suffer a big jolt . . . the ungodly will be thrown off their seats and the downtrodden will rise.

When Münzer published this Luther denounced him in his "Letter to the Princes of Saxony against the Rebellious Spirit", and declared him to be an instrument of Satan. Moreover, Union letters in Münzer's handwriting were intercepted wherein he called upon the subjects of Duke Georg of Saxony to offer armed resistance to the enemies of the Gospel, and the Duke demanded his extradition. Münzer was forced to leave Altstedt.

He went to Nürnberg, where he printed his reply to Luther, whom he charged with flattering the princes. "The people will free themselves in spite of everything," he wrote, "and then the fate of Dr. Luther will be that of a captive fox." The city council confiscated the paper, and Münzer was forced to quit the city.

He made a propaganda trip through Suabia to Alsace, and thence to Switzerland, and back to the Upper Black Forest. There is no doubt that this mission

> added much to the organisation of the people's party, to a clear formulation of its demands, and to the final general outbreak of the insurrection in April, 1525. It was through this trip that the dual nature of Münzer's activities became more and more pronounced—on the one hand, his propaganda among the people whom he approached in the only language then comprehensible to the masses, that of religious prophecy; on the other hand, his contact with the initiated, to whom he could disclose his ultimate aims. Even previous to this journey he had grouped around himself in Thuringia a circle of the most determined persons, not only from among the people, but also from among the lower clergy, a circle whom he had put at the head of a secret organisation.
> (*The Peasant War*, F. Engels, pp. 71-72.)

Münzer became the centre of a revolutionary movement which spread throughout south-west Germany, with connections between Saxony and Thuringia, through Franconia and Suabia up to Alsace and the Swiss frontier. Finally, when the general outbreak was at hand, he returned to Thuringia, where he wished to lead the movement personally.

THE MISTAKES OF THE PEASANTS

The revolt began on October 24th, 1525, with a rising in the Margraviate of Stühlinger. The peasants refused deliveries to the Landgrave, and, assembling in considerable numbers, they marched on Waldshut. Here they formed a Union with the city middle class, and emissaries were sent to rouse the peasants of the Moselle, the Upper Rhine, and Franconia. The aims of the Union were proclaimed to be the abolition of feudal power, the destruction of all castles and monasteries, and the elimination of all masters save the Emperor. The German tri-colour was the banner of the Union.

The rising spread rapidly, and at first the nobles of Upper Suabia (whose troops were fighting in Italy against Francis I of France) were paralyzed with fear and incapable of offering any real resistance. The peasants sacked and burned castles and monasteries ("priests' nests," as they called them), and they paid off many a long-standing debt of hatred, torturing and killing many of the nobles who fell into their hands. Count Ludwig von Helfenstein (who had given orders for the summary execution of all the rebels who fell into his hands) was himself put to death with fourteen of his knights. They were made to run the gauntlet under the blows and jeers of the peasants, that being the most humiliating death the rebels could devise for them.

Some interesting glimpses of the conduct of the insurgents during the spring of 1525 are given by Michael Eisenhart, a citizen of Rothenburg on the Tauber, where the rule of the honourables (or patricians)* was overthrown by the lower middle class and the plebeians who set up their own provisional government.

March 21. The working classes in the town now begin to revolt. They cease to obey the authorities and form a committee of thirty-six to manage affairs.

March 24. This evening . . . some one knocked off the head of Christ's image on a crucifix and struck off the arms.

---

*These patrician families controlled the city council and held all the city offices. They administered all the city revenues, and exploited both the poorer classes of the city and the peasants who came under their jurisdiction. They practised usury in money and grain, enjoyed various monopolies, and gradually deprived their fellow citizens of every right to use the city forests and meadows, and used them for their own private gain. They imposed road, bridge and gate payments and other duties; sold trade and guild privileges, and master and citizen rights. "The peasants of the city area were treated by them with no more consideration than by the nobility and the clergy. On the contrary, the city magistrates and bailiffs, mostly patricians, brought into the villages, together with aristocratic rigidity and avarice, a certain bureaucratic punctuality in collecting duties". (*The Peasant War in Germany*, pp. 43, F. Engels).

March 26. Chrischainz, the baker, knocked the missal out of the priest's hand in the chapel of Our Lady and drove away the priest from mass . . . The following Monday, while the priest was performing service in the parish church and chanting "Adjuva nos, Deus salutaris noster," Ernfried Kumpf addressed him rudely, saying that if he wished to save himself he would better leave the altar. Kumpf then knocked the missal on the floor, and drove the scholars out of the choir . . . On Friday . . . all the artisans were to lay all their complaints and demands before a committee. The taxes, wages and methods of weighing were discussed . . . *Friday, April 7,* Küplein, during the sermon, threw the lighted lamps about the church . . . On Holy Easter . . . in the night some millers attacked the church at Cobenzell and threw the pictures and images into the Tauber . . . Thursday after Easter, the women run up and down Hafengasse with forks and sticks, declaring they will plunder all the priests' houses, but are prevented. (From *Readings in European History,* James Harvey Robinson, pp. 288-289.)

But the peasants proved incapable of carrying through the revolutionary task which they had undertaken. Sectional interests divided them, and one district refused to help another, so that they were defeated in one battle after another by armies which were very much smaller than the total number of the rebels. They were jealous of the towns, and the towns of them; and it was only in the neighbourhood of Mühlhausen where Münzer's influence was strong, that any stable co-operation between the peasants and the city proletariat was achieved. There a primitive form of communism was attempted.

After their first panic the princes and nobles gained time by engaging in protracted negotiations with the rebels the while they collected their forces. The Suabian Union (which united the princes, nobles and the imperial cities of south-west Germany) promised the peasants a peaceful settlement of their grievances, and an investigation of their complaints; but when at last the promised court of enquiry met in December, it was composed entirely of nobles, and the proceedings dragged on interminably.

By February, 1525, even the peasants' slow patience was exhausted, and the storm really broke. The peasants gathered in a number of camps, and by the beginning of March some 30,000 or 40,000 were assembled in six camps in Upper Suabia.

The most outspoken and extreme section of the rebels were in the main Münzer's followers, and although they were everywhere in a minority they formed the backbone of the peasant armies. The mass of the peasantry were generally only too ready to make compacts with their masters. Moreover, as the struggle dragged

on many of the peasants became weary and went home. Added
to all these difficulties

> was the fact that the vagabond masses of the low grade proletariat
> had joined the (peasant) troops. This made discipline more diffi-
> cult and demoralised the peasants, as the vagabonds were an
> unreliable element, coming and going all the time. (*The Peasant
> War in Germany*, p. 105.)

But the greatest mistake which the peasants made was to
remain everywhere on the defensive and to enter into fruitless
negotiations with the ruling class, thus giving the princes time
to bring reinforcements from Italy where Charles V had just won
the battle of Pavia.

THE TWELVE ARTICLES

The peasants submitted their demands in the famous Twelve
Articles, the authorship of which was ascribed to Münzer by
contemporary historians, although actually they were not
composed by him. He had issued a much more revolutionary
manifesto to the insurgent peasants.

The demands made in the Twelve Articles were relatively
moderate. They demanded: (1) that the communities should have
the right to choose and appoint their own pastor, and should be
free to depose him "should he conduct himself improperly":
(2) the utilization of the great tithe for communal purposes
after payment from it of the pastor's maintenance. "What
remains over shall be given to the poor of the place, as the
circumstances and the general opinion demand. Should anything
farther remain, let it be kept lest anyone should leave the country
from poverty. Provision should also be made from this surplus
to avoid laying any land tax on the poor." The abolition of the
small tithes, whether ecclesiastical or lay, since "the Lord God
created cattle for the free use of man (and) we will not ... pay ...
an unseemly tithe which is of man's invention": (3) the abolition
of serfdom "unless it should be shown us from the Gospel that we
are serfs". "Not that we would wish to be absolutely free and
under no authority. . . . God does not teach us that we should
lead a disorderly life in the lusts of the flesh ... (and) we are ...
ready to yield obedience according to God's law to our elected
and regular authorities in all proper things becoming to a Christian": (4) the abolition of the lords' fishing and hunting rights.
For "in some places the authorities preserve the game to our great
annoyance and loss, recklessly permitting the unreasoning

imals to destroy to no purpose our crops which God suffers
grow for the use of man. . . . This is neither godly nor neigh-
urly. For when God created man he gave him dominion over
l the animals, over the birds of the air and over the fish in the
ater": (5) the freedom for "every member of the community
help himself to such firewood as he needs in his home. Also,
a man requires wood for carpentry purposes he should have it
ee, but with the knowledge of a person appointed by the
mmunity for that purpose" : (6) the limitation of excessive
nded labour "that we shall not continue to be oppressed . . .
nce our forefathers were required only to serve according to
e word of God": (7) the abolition of forced services or dues from
e peasant without payment: (8) the reduction of rents "so that
e peasants shall not work for nothing, since the labourer is
orthy of his hire": (9) justice in the administration of the law
ace "we are burdened with a great evil in the constant making
new laws . . . we should be judged according to the old written
w so that the case shall be decided according to its merits,
d not with partiality": (10) the restitution to the communities
meadows and fields which have been wrongfully appropriated
y individuals": (11) the abolition of the due called *Todfall*
eriot) since "we will no longer endure it, nor allow widows
d orphans to be thus shamefully robbed against God's will,
d in violation of justice and right": (12) "In the twelfth place
is our conclusion and final resolutiom, that if any one or more
the articles here set forth should not be in agreement with the
ord of God, as we think they are, such article we will willingly
cede from when it is proved really to be against the word of
od by a clear explanation of Scripture. Or if articles should
w be conceded to us that are hereafter discovered to be unjust,
om that hour they shall be dead and null and without force.
kewise, if more complaints should be discovered which are
sed upon truth and the Scriptures and relate to offences
ainst God and our neighbour, we have determined to reserve
e right to present these also, and to exercise ourselves in all
aristian teaching. For this we shall pray God, since He can
ant these, and He alone. The peace of Christ abide with us all".
The Twelve Articles were much less extreme than the demands
nich the radical section had formulated in an earlier programme,
e *Letter of Articles*. This was an open letter to all the peasantry
ging them to join "the Christian Alliance and Brotherhood"
the purpose of removing all burdens either by goodness,

"which will hardly happen", or by force, and threatening a those who refused to join with the "lay anathema", that expulsion from the society and from any intercourse with th Union membeis. All castles, monasteries and priests' endowmen were to be placed under lay anathema unless the nobilit priests and monks relinquished them of their own accord, move into ordinary houses, and joined the Christian Alliance.

THE REVOLT COLLAPSES

As soon as the princes and nobility felt themselves strong enou to take the field against the rebellious peasantry they wasted more time in words. They proceeded to the suppression of th rising, and destroyed the divided peasant forces in detail.

They took, too, a dreadful revenge for the fright they ha suffered. Thousands of wretched peasants were slaughtered cold blood, and scores of villages were burned to the groun "We played bowls in our turn with the heads of the peasants one of the princes grimly declared. Jäcklein Rohrbach, innkeeper who had been a prominent rebel leader, was chaine to a post, and slowly roasted to death, whilst his tormento feasted nearby and gloated over his sufferings.

Münzer had established his headquarters in the free imperi city of Mühlhausen, where whole masses of the lower middle cla had been won over to his doctrines. Mühlhausen had had revolution on March 17th, 1525, before the general uprising Southern Germany. The old patrician council had been ove thrown, and power had passed to a newly elected "Etern Council", with Pfeifer, a representative of the middle class, at head.

Münzer made heroic efforts to widen and organise the revo But

the worst thing that can befall a leader of an extreme party is to be compelled to take over a government in an epoch when the movement is not yet ripe for the domination of the class which he represents and for the realisation of the measures which that domination would imply . . . He finds himself in a dilemma. What he *can* do is in contrast to all his actions as hitherto practised; to all his principles and to the present interest of his party; what he *ought* to do cannot be achieved. In a word, he is compelled to represent not his party or his class, but the class for whom conditions are ripe for domination . . . he is compelled to defend the interests of an alien class, and to feed his own class with phrases and promises, with the assertion that the interests of that alien class are their own interests. Whoever puts himself in this awkward position is irrevocably lost. (*The Peasant War in Germany*, pp. 135-6, F. Engels.)

This was the weakness of Münzer's position.

Not only the movement of his time, but the whole century, was not ripe for the realisation of the ideas for which he himself had only begun to grope. The class which he represented not only was not developed enough and incapable of subduing and transforming the whole of society, but it was just beginning to come into existence. The social transformation that he pictured in his fantasy was so little grounded in the then existing economic conditions that the latter were a preparation for a social system diametrically opposed to that of which he dreamt. Nevertheless, he was bound to his preachings of Christian equality and evangelical community of possessions. He was at least compelled to make an attempt at their realization. Community of all possessions, universal and equal labour duty, and the abolition of all authority were proclaimed. In reality Mühlhausen remained a republican imperial city with a somewhat democratic constitution, with a senate elected by universal suffrage and under the control of a forum, and with the hastily improvised feeding of the poor. The social change, which so horrified the Protestant middle-class contemporaries, in reality never went beyond a feeble and unconscious attempt prematurely to establish the bourgeois society of a later period. (*The Peasant War in Germany*, pp. 136-7, F. Engels.)

Münzer, however, flung himself into the struggle with fanatical energy: his letters became more and more revolutionary.

Incessantly he fanned the flame of hatred against the ruling classes. He spurred the wildest passions, using forceful terms of expression the like of which religious and nationalist delirium had put into the mouths of the Old Testament prophets. (*The Peasant War in Germany*, p. 137.)

His efforts were in vain. The peasant revolt gradually collapsed, and the Landgrave Philipp of Hesse, together with Saxon troops, marched upon Mühlhausen. Münzer assembled his forces at Frankenhausen. He had several cannon, and some 8,000 men, but they counted few ex-soldiers among them, and sorely lacked military experience.

The tragic end came on the mountain which is still called Mount Battle (Schlachtberg). Münzer and his people entrenched themselves behind a barricade of wagons and awaited the assault of their enemies. The princes offered them an amnesty if they would betray Münzer alive into captivity, and Münzer gathered his followers into a circle that they might debate the offer. A priest and a knight were in favour of accepting it; but they were brought to the centre of the circle and beheaded as traitors.

Meanwhile, the princes' troops had encircled the mountain, and now they began to advance. The trained troops speedily broke through the barricade of wagons, and the peasant army fled in wild disorder. They had numbered, it is said, 8,000; and 5,000 were slaughtered in the pitiless pursuit which followed.

The survivors sought refuge in the town of Frankenhausen, but the city quickly fell to the princes' troops, and Münzer (who had been wounded in the head) was discovered in a house and taken prisoner. He was first racked in the presence of the princes, and then beheaded. He died with courage and dignity.

Thomas Münzer failed, but he occupies a significant place in the history of working class revolt. Throughout the Middle Ages there was a fairly continuous current of what may be called peasant-plebeian heresies, which denounced the privileges of the nobility and the city patricians, and sought the abolition of serfdom and (at least) the more flagrant inequalities of property. These social heresies found their theoretical justification in the Christian doctrine that all men are the children of God and equal in His sight.

During the feudal period these heresies were hardly to be distinguished from the body of heretical doctrine which represented in some measure the economic interest of the emergent middle-class, and which culminated in the Protestant Reformation. This was true, for instance, of the Albigenses. But in the 14th and 15th centuries the social heresies of the poor peasantry and town workers came more and more plainly to represent their hopes and interests, and went far beyond anything that the bourgeoisie desired in the way of social equality and freedom. This was true, as we have seen, of the teaching of John Ball and the poor priests, who voiced the aspirations of peasant and proletarian in the Lollard movement; and it was equally true of the Taborites in the Hussite movement. Finally, in Thomas Münzer's teachings communist ideas were definitely formulated as expressing the hope of an exploited class, and thereafter they were

> found in every great convulsion of the people, until gradually they merged with the modern proletarian movement. (*The Peasant War in Germany*, pp. 56).

CHAPTER 7

THE REIGN OF THE SAINTS

And I saw a new heaven and a new earth: for the
first heaven and the first earth were passed away.

REVELATION, xxi, I.

THE ANABAPTISTS

The history of the Anabaptists in the 16th and 17th centuries, and the hatred and horror with which their revolutionary doctrines filled the bourgeoisie of that period, invite comparison with the rather similar role of bogy man to capitalism which the Bolsheviks played in the years immediately succeeding the October Revolution. There were even the same charges of gross sexual immorality levelled against them; and in both cases the fearful imagination of the men of property saw their sinister influence in every social disturbance and in every expression of working class discontent.

It has already been pointed out (page 62) that Anabaptism was not an organised Church, but consisted rather of a number of small sects who held certain beliefs in common, and who took their generic name from the fact that they all denied the validity of infant baptism.

> The Anabaptist doctrine was but one of an endless variety of ideas, many of which had long been current. ... They denied the right of the secular magistrates to interfere in religious matters, and themselves withdrew in varying degrees from concern in the affairs of this world. Some, anticipating the Quakers, refused to bear arms; the Gartnerbrüder of Salzburg endeavoured to live in the pattern of primitive simplicity. One sect denied the humanity of Christ; another, of whom Ludwig Hetzer was the chief, began by regarding Jesus as a leader and teacher rather than an object of worship, and ended by denying his divinity. (*The Cambridge Modern History,* vol. II, p. 223).

Most of the Anabaptists indulged in Apocalyptic dreams of the Millennium; and again one is tempted to compare these chiliastic visions with the belief in the imminence of the World Revolution which the Bolsheviks held in the years immediately following their conquest of power in Russia.

Everywhere the Anabaptists were savagely persecuted.

Zwingli himself was hostile to them, and repressive measures were taken against their Swiss adherents; but in most parts of Germany they were condemned to wholesale death. Six hundred executions are said to have taken place at Ensisheim in Upper Elsass, a thousand in Tyrol and Gorz, and the Swabian League butchered whole bands of them without trial or sentence. Many were beheaded in Saxony with the express approbation of Luther, who regarded their heroism in the face of death as proof of diabolic possession. Duke William of Bavaria made a distinction between those who recanted and those who remained obdurate; the latter were burnt, the former were only beheaded. . . . Philip of Hesse was the only Prince of sufficient moderation to be content with the heretics' incarceration. (*The Cambridge Modern History*, Vol. II, p. 224).

Under these ruthless persecutions the Anabaptist doctrine of passive resistance to evil broke down. Their sufferings began "to set their hands as well as their minds in motion" (*Cambridge Modern History*, Vol. II, p. 224), and the conviction grew among them that it was their duty to assist in bringing in the Heavenly Kingdom on Earth which they believed to be imminent.

In Augsburg, Hans Hut proclaimed the necessity incumbent upon the saints to purify the world with a double-edged sword, and his disciple, Augustin Bader, prepared a crown, insignia, and jewels for his future kingdom in Israel. Melchior Hofmann told Frederick I of Denmark that he was one of the two sovereigns at whose hands all the firstborn of Egypt should be slain. (*Cambridge Modern History*, Vol. II, p. 224.)

JAN OF LEYDEN

From 1529 onwards there were Anabaptist outbreaks in a number of north German towns, including Minden, Herford, Lippstadt, and Soest; but it was at Münster that Anabaptism achieved a brief spell of political power.

Münster had longed witnessed a struggle between Catholics and Protestants. Bernard Rottman, the most prominent of the Reforming divines, had been expelled from the city, but had returned and established himself in the suburbs; and the Reformers had eventually obtained a majority in the City Council. Finally the Catholics were forced to accept an arrangement under which Lutheranism was to be tolerated in the six parish churches, and Catholicism in the Cathedral and the centre of the city.

But whilst Lutheranism suited the wealthier members of the
forming party, it no longer satisfied Rottman and the artisans
ho were his chief supporters, and in 1533 he resolved to streng-
en his position by inviting some Anabaptists from Holland to
ttle in the city. Chief among them were Jan Matthys, a baker
Haarlem, and Jan Beuckelssen or Bockelsohn, of Leyden
opularly known as Jan of Leyden). Matthys had declared
mself to be the Enoch of the New Dispensation, and had
pointed Twelve Apostles to proselytise the six neighbouring
ovinces; Beuckelssen was one of these. As a journeyman tailor
had travelled over Europe "from Lübeck to Lisbon" before he
as thirty, and had finally abandoned tailoring to become an
n-keeper at Leyden. There he came under the influence of the
nabaptists, and in January, 1534, he travelled to Münster as
atthys' representative.

Soon after his arrival in Münster civil war broke out, on
ebruary 9th; but for the time being the forces of conservatism
oved too strong for the revolutionaries. However, their
natical zeal made thousands of new converts, especially among
e women; besides which the legal immunities which the Ana-
aptists enjoyed in Münster attracted many of the sectaries from
olland and the neighbouring German towns. Presently Jan
atthys himself arrived in Münster; and at the next municipal
ection the Anabaptists secured a majority on the City Council.
ne of their members, Knipperdollinck, became burgomaster;
d six days later, at a great prayer meeting in the Town Hall,
atthys demanded the expulsion of all who refused to accept the
octrines of Anabaptism. This was done, and the Reign of the
aints began.

Like the earliest Christians they sought to have all things in
common, and as a commencement they confiscated the goods of
the exiles. To ensure primitive simplicity of worship they next
destroyed all images, pictures, manuscripts, and musical instruments on which they could lay their hands. Tailors and Shoe-
makers were enjoined to introduce no new fashions in wearing
apparel; gold and silver and jewels were surrendered to the
common use; and there was an idea of pushing the communistic
principle to its logical extreme by repudiating private property
in wives. The last was apparently offensive to public opinion . . .
and the nearest approach to it effected in practice was polygamy,
which was not introduced without some sanguinary opposition,
and did not probably extend far beyond the circle of Beuckelssen
and the leaders of the movement. (*The Cambridge Modern History*, Vol. II, p. 226).

The Anabaptists of Münster found their chief inspiration in the *Book of Revelation*, and all these measures were regarded as being a preparation for the second coming of Christ. Alarmed lest these subversive ideas should spread still more widely, the German princes laid siege to Münster, but the Anabaptists' fanatical conviction that they were doing the will of God, and their firm belief in the imminence of the Second Coming of Christ steeled them to hold out for eighteen months against all the force that their enemies could bring against them. Indeed, for a time it looked as though the movement might spread to the neighbouring towns of Liège, Köln, and Utrecht, and even to Amsterdam.

Jan Matthys was killed leading a sortie at Faster, and Jan of Leyden took his place. He dispensed with the Twelve Elders who had been the nominal rulers of the New Israel, and announced, by the mouth of his prophet Dusentschur, that it was the will of God that he should become King of all the world, and establish the Fifth Monarchy* of the Apocalypse.

On August 30th, 1534, he beat off the besiegers with heavy losses when they tried to storm the city; and in October of the same year he sent out 28 apostles to preach the New Kingdom to the neighbouring cities. Most of them were seized and put to death, among them being a young woman who attempted to "play the part of Judith to the Holofernes of the Bishop of Münster". (*The Cambridge Modern History*, Vol. II, p. 227.)

THE FALL OF MUNSTER

Jan of Leyden's attempt to rouse the thousands of Anabaptists who were scattered through North Germany and the Netherlands resulted only in sporadic risings, all of which were bloodily suppressed; but Münster was saved for a time by the mutual jealousies of the German princes, and by dissensions between Catholics and Protestants, together with the general fear that Charles V would exploit the opportunity to extend his Burgundian domains by annexing Münster.

In the end, however, their common hatred of the Anabaptists proved more powerful than their mutual suspicions, and a joint expedition was made against the Saints. Münster offered a desperate resistance, and in the end fell only through treachery, on

---

*The Fifth Monarchy was to be the last in the series of which Assyria, Persia, Greece and Rome were the preceding four.

the night of June 24th, 1535. A frightful slaughter followed, and Jan of Leyden and Knipperdollinck were tortured to death with red-hot pincers in the market-place. Jan's chief wife, Divara, was also executed. Münster was deprived of its privileges as an imperial city, and Catholicism was re-established. The Anabaptists were dispersed into many lands, and their doctrines exercised a powerful influence in England and America in the following century, being represented in this country by the Fifth Monarchy men who attempted two unsuccessful risings in 1657 and 1661.

CHAPTER 8

THE LEVELLERS

> These kind of Vermin swarm like Caterpillars And
> hold Conventicles in Barnes and Sellars. Some preach
> (or prate) in Woods, in fields, in stables In hollow
> trees, in tubs, on tops of tables. *A Swarme of Sectaries
> and Schismatiques; wherein is discovered the strange preaching
> (or prating) of such as are by their trades Coblers, Tinkers,
> Pedlers, Weavers, Sow-Gelders and Chymney-Sweepers.*
>
> John Taylor (1641).

THE GREAT REBELLION

The polemics of the English Revolution of the 17th century
were largely phrased in theological language. Fundamentally,
however, the struggle was between the royal absolutism which had
arisen upon the ruins of feudalism after the Wars of the Roses (and
which, for a time, had served the class interests of the bourgeoisie)
and an expanding capitalism which sought the political and
social conditions necessary for its growth. It was natural, therefore, that on the whole the old feudal aristocracy and the squire-
archy should support the King, whilst middle class traders and
manufacturers supported Parliament. London headed the opposition to the King, and largely financed the Parliamentary
forces, and the Eastern Counties ("the home of Lollardism,
where sectarians of all kinds abounded", *Cromwell and Communism,*
Eduard Bernstein, p. 48) were banded together in an Eastern
Association, of which Cromwell was soon to become the leading
spirit. The clothing towns of the West Riding (Bradford, Leeds
and Halifax) were centres of opposition to the Crown amidst
Royalist Yorkshire, and in Lancashire the clothing towns, "the
Genevas of Lancashire", were also islands of Parliamentary
opposition in a sea of Royalist sympathisers. In the west
Gloucester, Taunton and Exeter, centres of the west of England
textile industry, were all Parliamentary strongholds.

The Royalist faction included Anglicans, Roman Catholics,
and a few Presbyterians; whilst the supporters of Parliament can
be divided into two main groups, Presbyterians and Independents.
Of these the former, being in the main wealthy City merchants,
were the more conservative.

Social theories manifested themselves at that time in a religious form. Consequently the majority of comfortable citizens would be unconsciously biased in favour of that form of religion which was the most acceptable to the existing order, and the religion that met this requirement was in those days Presbyterian Puritanism. (*Cromwell and Communism*, Eduard Bernstein, pp. 51-52).

The Independents were the more radical section of the Parliamentary faction, and the name is used to describe a number of sects who (on a variety of grounds) were opposed to a centralized religious authority. They included such extremists as the Anabaptists, the Familists (who "would have all things common not onely goods and cattell but wife and children", if the author of *The Divisions of the Church of England* (1642), is to be believed), Fifth Monarchy Men, who aimed at the establishment of a monarchy of Christ as foreshadowed in the Book of Daniel; and the Ranters, some of whom were alleged to practise "free love".

There were, however, two broad tendencies among the Independents; the one represented by the "Gentlemen Independents" or "Grandees", as they came to be called, of whom Cromwell, Ireton and Fairfax were the outstanding personalities, and a left wing (if one may use modern jargon) known as the Levellers, of whom John Lilburne ("Freeborn John") was the leader. The Levellers were all agreed upon wanting more than a mere victory of the City of London over the King, but (and again one is reminded of the modern Socialist movement, and its endless capacity to produce left splinter groups) it had its own extreme wing, the True Levellers (or Diggers, as they were nicknamed) who held communist ideas far in advance of their day.

The economic issues behind the "Great Rebellion" are obvious enough: a struggle between the old decaying feudal order of society and the new, progressive capitalist economy. But it is easy to over-simplify what was happening. The middle class were chafing against what were essentially medieval conceptions of government which hindered their economic progress, and they were seeking a new political system more in consonance with their economic needs. They were, however, largely supported by the poor craftsmen and labourers of the towns and by the lesser peasantry, although the purely *economic* interests of these classes lay rather with the Crown which stood for the old traditional society, with its notion (for example) of a fair wage guaranteed by statute, and which had resisted with some measure of success the progress of the enclosures which bore so hardly upon the peasant.

It is at this point that religious controversies play such an important part in the struggle between King and Parliament, for the bourgeoisie could scarcely have dared challenge the Crown and the old order without the help of peasant and working class allies, and that help was secured by appealing not to their economic or material interests but to their religious sentiments.

> The close union of Church and State enabled the bourgeoisie to turn opposition to the former into revolt against the latter. Occasionally sincerely urged, as often as not skilfully and deliberately manipulated, the appeal to men's religious convictions obscured and distorted—for some years at any rate—the fundamental issues in conflict. Large sections of the population whose material interests should have allied them with the Crown were to rally to Parliament because they thought it was struggling to exorcise the devils the former had introduced into England . . . anti-Catholic sentiment . . . was fostered and aggravated by those opposed to the Crown in order to win the support of groups, particularly the peasants and labourers, who might otherwise have rallied behind the monarchy. . . Its success may be seen in the extent of the popular outcry against the alleged Catholic plots and sympathies of the Government during 1640-3. (*Left-Wing Democracy in the English Civil War*, David W. Petegorsky, pp. 43-46).

LEVELLERS AND DIGGERS

In matters of religion there was not much to distinguish the majority of the Levellers from the other Independents. A few, however, professed a rationalist deism, if not atheism. There was Richard Overton, for example, who wrote a pamphlet on the immortality of the soul, the first edition of which appeared anonymously in 1643. Twelve years later a revised edition appeared, bearing the title *Man wholly mortal, or a Treatise wherein 'tis proved, both Theologically and Philosophically, that as whole man sinned, so whole man died; contrary to that common distinction of Soul and Body; and that the present going of the Soul into Heaven or hell is a mere fiction: And that at the Resurrection is the beginning of our immortality; and then actual condemnation and Salvation and not before. With Doubts and Objections answered and resolved, both by Scripture and Reason; discovering the multitude of Blasphemies and Absurdities that arise from the Fancie of the Soul.*

Overton admits a resurrection at the end of time, but this was probably a concession to popular prejudice or in order to avoid a charge of atheism, for he treats this part of his subject superficially. The theological argument consists of a number of

blical texts referring to the complete perishing of the individual
ter death; and in his philosophical proof he compares Man
th animals, and argues that if the human soul survive the death
the body so too must the soul of an animal.

"It is interesting," comments Bernstein, "to recognise in Overton
the first representative of the school of thought which combined
systematic rationalism, or even materialism, with political and
social radicalism in England." (*Cromwell and Communism*, p. 90.)

Another of the Levellers who held advanced rationalist views
as Walwyn. No independent writings by him have survived,
ut he is said to have corrupted "young people" with his religious
nd political ideas, and to have asked them what better proof
ney had for the divine authorship of the Bible than the Turk
ad for the Koran. It was also his habit to take young people
n Sundays from one church to another that they might hear
arious preachers railing one against the other, and, having thus
own doubt in their minds, he would declare "the great mysteries
f life and salvation through Jesus Christ as well as the doctrine
f justification through His death, resurrection, sanctification,
nd condemnation by His spirit as mere fancies, as ridiculous,
onsensical, vapid and empty conception". Walwyn was
ccused of having said that the "Song of Songs" was a poem
/ritten by Solomon "about one of his whores", and that King
David and the patriarch Jacob had been a couple of sly foxes and
unning knaves: also that hell is nothing but the bad conscience
f evil men, and the only true religion to consist in helping the
oor.*

On social and political questions his opinions were no less
eterodox, for he is reputed as saying "What an inequitable
hing it is for one man to have thousands and another want
read". Also that "the world shall never be well until all things
e in common". Moreover, he expressed the revolutionary
pinion that "a very few diligent and valiant spirits may turn the
vorld upside down if they observe the seasons and shall with life
nd courage engage accordingly". To the objection that this
evolution would overturn all government, he is said to have
nswered that "there would then be less need of Government;
or then there would be no thieves, no covetous persons, no
leceiving and abuse of one another, and so no need of Government. If any difference do fall out, take a cobbler from his seat,

---

*A venomous exposition of these and similar charges is contained in a pamphlet
ublished in April, 1649, and entitled *Walwins Wiles: or The Manifestators Manifested.*

or any other tradesman that is an honest and just man, and
him hear the case and determine the same, and then beta
himself to his work again".

One of the most popular pamphlets issued by the Levell
(in 1648) bore the title: *Light Shining in Buckinghamshire, or*
Discovery of the main ground, original cause of all the slavery in
world but chiefly in England; presented by way of Declaration of many
the well-affected in the country, to all their poor, oppressed countrymen
England; and also to the consideration of the present army under
conduct of Lord Fairfax. *

This pamphlet took for its motto the text *Arise, O God, jua*
Thou the earth, and, in common with most Leveller literatur
it based its argument on the assertion that in creating Man G
had given him dominion over "inferior creatures" but had n
intended him to exercise arbitrary authority over his fellow-me
But whereas most Leveller pamphleteers reasoned from this th
men should have equal political rights *Light Shining in Buckingha*
shire maintained that it implied equality of property.

> All men being alike privileged by birth so all men were to enjoy
> the creatures alike without properties one more than the other . . .
> that is to say no man was to lord or command over his own kind;
> neither to enclose the creatures to his own use to the impoverishing
> of his neighbours.

By means of violence and murder (the argument continues) son
men robbed their fellows of their share of the earth, enclosin
land and setting themselves up as Lords of the Manors. The re
of the people, thus deprived of the means of life, were forced
become the slaves of those who had plundered them; since whe
the landlords have lived, not as God intended they should d
upon the fruits of their own labours, but by the servitude an
exploitation of those whom they have robbed. Moreover, i
order to secure their ill-gotten gains, they introduced tha
"heathenish innovation", the monarchy, and legalised the
robbery by charters, monopolies, tenures, patents, and enclosur
issued in the name of the King, and thus, "all tyranny shelte

---

*It has been assumed by Berens, James, Bernstein and others that *Light Shining*
Buckinghamshire was a Digger Tract, and that Winstanley, the leader of the Tr
Levellers or Diggers, was the author (or part author) of it. Petegorsky sugges
however, that it was the work of a number of peasants who had been affected b
Leveller propaganda, and he points out in support of this contention, that "its la
guage and argument are generally derived from Leveller literature", and that where
the Diggers held communist views, the tract "is essentially a plea for equal rath
than common ownership". (*Left-Wing Democracy in the English Civil War*, pp. 138-139
Light Shining in Buckinghamshire does, however, seem to have profoundly influence
Winstanley.

self under the King's wings". At the same time lawyers were
reated to help in this exploitation by complicating the legal
ystem; whilst the clergy was called into being to preach sub-
nission to the people. All these functionaries—lawyers, judges,
lergymen—have a vested interest in the maintenance of the
nonarchy, for to question it is to attack the very source of their
wn power and privileges. The common people (the pamphlet
oundly asserts) have no need of a king. What they need is
1) "a just portion for each man to live so that none need to beg
r steal for want but every man may live comfortably":
2) "a just rule for each man to go by, which rule is to be the
criptures": (3) government by "Judges called Elders", these
o be elected by the people: and (4) the confiscation of bishops'
ands and forest and Crown lands to provide a public fund for the
naintenance of the needy. For

> in Israel if a man were poor, then a publicke maintenance and
> stocks was to be provided to raise him again. So would all Bishops'
> Lands, Forrest Lands, and Crown Lands, do in our Land, which
> the apostate Parliament-men give one to another, and to maintain
> the needlesse thing called a king, and every seven years the whole
> Land was to the poor, the fatherless, widows and strangers,
> and at every crop a portion allowed them. Mark this, poor people,
> what the Levellers would do for you.

The pamphlet ends significantly with the biblical text:

> *What portion have we in David ? neither have we inheritance in the son
> of Jesse: to your tents, O Israel.* I KINGS, xii, 16.

A few months later a second pamphlet appeared entitled *More
of the Light Shining in Buckinghamshire*, which described how the
common people had been enslaved by the Norman Conquest,
and robbed by the usurpations of the lords and by the enclosure
of common lands.

Both these pamphlets are forthright in their denunciation of
the monarchy, the church, the nobility (who "come from the
outlandish Norman bastard"), and the rich. They are particularly
vehement in their attack on the lawyers, "these caterpillars of
society", as they call them. "O soldiers, you could never do a
better piece of service than to put down the lawyers", declares
More of the Light Shining in Buckinghamshire.

THE MECHANICK PREACHERS

After 1640 there was a tremendous outburst of sectarian activity.
"Sects bred and multiplied and seemed to fill the earth". (*Left-
Wing Democracy in the English Civil War*, David W. Petegorsky,

pp. 65-66). The economic depression of 1640, and a profoun
dissatisfaction among the poor with their conditions of lif

> impelled them to an effort to transcend their immediate selves
> and environment through a mystical union with God, to seek
> compensation for their suffering in a sense of nearness to their
> Maker. They gave expression to the hopes that the events of 1640-2
> had aroused—hopes to which they clung all the more desperately
> as their plight grew worse—by affirming that the millennium,
> and with it their deliverance from suffering was at hand. . . .
> Essentially, the sects were countering the inegalitarianism that was
> fundamental to Puritanism. Puritanism, by idéntifying worldly
> success with election, told the poor that they were damned. . . .
> The answer of those who were told that they were condemned to
> abject poverty in this world and to eternal damnation in the
> next was to assert the essential equality of all human beings
> before God by denying the doctrine of predestination and affirming
> in its stead, that the key to salvation was revelation. Puritanism
> had insisted that knowledge of God could come only through
> study and understanding of the Bible. By substituting the written
> word of the Scriptures for the hierarchy as the final authority in
> religious life, it took the effective direction of religious affairs
> from the hands of the prelates only to make it the monopoly of a
> literate, educated class. The reply of the poor—and hence, the
> illiterate and uneducated— was that not formal learning but an
> inner spiritual experience and inspiration were the true source
> of religious knowledge, that contact with God was not the exclusive
> privilege of a superior class, but could be attained by any man
> however humble his station. On the contrary, that inner spiritual
> experience by which alone men could be saved was far more
> likely to occur in those whom suffering had rendered meek and
> humble than in those whose wealth had made them haughty and
> proud. Salvation, they therefore affirmed in proclaiming the spiri-
> tual equality of mankind, was not a monopoly of a Chosen Elect,
> but possible for everyone; for every human being had within him
> a spark of divinity, an Inner Light that might at any moment
> be kindled. (*Left-Wing Democracy in the English Civil War,*
> pp. 64-65).

The activities of these "mechanick preachers" filled the men o
property with alarm, and the times are full of complaints b
middle class apologists of brewers and bakers, cobblers an
coopers, tinkers and tailors, saddlers and soap-boilers, button
makers and glovers, and the like, poor tradesmen and simpl
labourers, who

> inspired by the light of revelation that burned within them,
> mounted pulpit and platform to spread their message to their
> fellow-oppressed and downtrodden. (*Left-Wing Democracy in the
> English Civil War,* p. 66).

> These kind of Vermin swarm like Caterpillars and hold Conven-
> ticles in Barnes and Sellars. Some preach (or prate) in woods, in
> fields, in stables, in hollow trees, in tubs, on tops of tables,

is the angry protest of one of these bourgeois pamphleteers.
(*A Swarme of Sectaries and Schismatiques; wherein is discovered the
strange preaching (or prating) of such as are by their trades Cobblers,
Tinkers, Pedlers, Weavers, Sow-Gelders and Chymney-Sweepers*", John
Taylor, 1641); and Pagitt in his *Heresiography* (1645) complains
that these poor preachers come

> as one from a stable from currying his horses ; another from a
> stall from cobbling his shoes: and these sit down in Moses chair to
> mend all as Embassadours of Jesus Christ, as Heralds of the Most
> High God: these take upon them to reveale their secrets of
> Almighty God, to open and shut heaven, to save souls.

According to another indignant critic (*A Discovery of the Most
Dangerous and Damnable Tenets that have been spread within this few
yeares* (April 1647)), these mechanick preachers taught that the
immortality of the soul is a fiction, and "that all the Heaven there
is is here on Earth".

But the social implications of the teachings of these poor
sectaries alarmed the propertied classes more even than their
theological heresies scandalised them. Nor is that to be wondered
at, for the humble itinerant preachers (the 17th-century
equivalent of the "poor priests" of the 14th) emphasized the
essential equality of men, and denied that material possessions
had anything to do with salvation.

> The belief that all men are created spiritually equal has a habit
> of translating itself into an insistence that material inequality is a sin
> before the Lord because it is a perversion of His divine scheme;
> and the conviction that one is about to inherit the Kingdom of
> Heaven often leads to a demand for a commensurate share of the
> earth. . . It is difficult to speak with confidence on the degree to
> which that demand was explicitly asserted, because we must largely
> depend for our knowledge of what the preachers said on those who
> ridiculed them—and the fears of the latter impelled them to wild
> exaggeration. But this much is certain—that the early attacks on
> the sects were almost as much concerned with the social as with
> the religious aspects of their heresies. Many writers warned Eng-
> land of the dangerous and subversive social tenets the sects were
> propagating. (*Left-Wing Democracy in the English Civil War*, p. 68.)

Thus the author of *Heresiography* (1645) charges the Anabaptists
with teaching

> That a Christian may not with a safe conscience possesse anything
> proper to himselfe but whatsoever he hath he must make common ;

and the author of *Mercurius Rusticus or the Countries Complaint of the barbarous outrages Committed by the Sectaries of this late flourishing Kingdome* (1642), having asserted that Chelmsford was being governed by a tinker, two tailors, two cobblers, and two pedlars, declares that they teach

> That the relation of master and servant hath no ground or warrant in the New Testament but rather the contrary . . . that one man should have a thousand pounds a yeere and another not one pound perhaps not as much but must live by the sweat of his browes and labour before he eate, hath no ground neither in Nature or in Scripture. . . . That the common people heretofore kept under blindnesse and ignorance have a long time yeelded themselves servants, nay slaves to the nobility and gentry; but God hath now opened their eyes and discovered unto them their Christian liberty; and therefore it is now fit that the Nobility and Gentry should serve their servants or at least worke for their owne maintenance; and if they will not worke, they ought not to eate.

That Parliament was seriously concerned by the growth and activities of the sectaries is evidenced by the Ordinance of both Houses of February 4, 1647

> Concerning the growth and spreading of Errors, Heresies, and Blasphemies and for setting aside a day of Publike Humiliation to seeke God's assistance for the suppressing and preventing the same because of the perillouse condition that this Kingdome is in through the abominable blasphemies and damnable heresies vented and spread abroad therein.

THE AGITATORS

After the decisive defeat of King Charles at Naseby, on June 14th, 1645, there was increasing discontent in the army and widespread criticism of the aristocratic character of the House of Commons. In the counties the suffrage was limited to a minority of land-owners, and in many towns to the members of the corporations, or even to their officers alone, whilst many towns and boroughs which had remained stationary or had even declined in population and importance had the same parliamentary representation as important centres of commerce.

Moreover, the lower middle and working classes still smarted under economic grievances which Parliament (composed in the main of members of wealthy families) did nothing to remedy. The monopolies granted by the king had been cancelled, but the privileges of the great trading companies remained untouched.

Feudal obligations, such as the royal right to dispose of wardships (a right "oppressing to all the considerable families") had been abolished or fallen into desuetude, but the game laws, tithes and excise by which "inconsiderable" families were oppressed still remained, and the tradesmen, small business men and apprentices who formed the backbone of the Leveller movement were clamorous for some relief of their economic distress.

Oh that the cravings of our Stomacks could be heard by the Parliament and the city! they exclaim in *The Mournfull Cryes of many thousand poor Tradesmen, who are ready to famish through decay of Trade*. Oh that it were known that we sell our Beds and Cloaths for Bread! . . . O you Members of Parliament and rich men in the City, that are at ease, and drink Wine in Bowls, and stretch yourselves upon Beds of Down, you that grind our faces, and flay off our skins. Will no man amongst you regard, will no man behold our faces black with Sorrow and Famine?

Now there was no longer any reason to fear a Royalist victory, Parliament (in which the landowning and wealthy bourgeois interests were dominant) looked with waning enthusiasm upon the Army, which was mainly recruited from the peasantry and artisans, and officered (since the Self-Denying Ordinance had got rid of the aristocratic Presbyterian generals) partly by men promoted from the ranks and partly by the more radical members of the possessing classes. Differences were already arising within the Army itself, but for the time being these were held in check by the common antagonism to Parliament—an antagonism which was exacerbated by the fact that nearly a year's pay was owing to the Army, and that no provision was being made for the disabled and for widows and orphans of the men who had fallen in the Civil War.

Parliament sought to lessen the influence of the Army by trying to disband some of the regiments, and distributing the others in different places; but the rank-and-file countered this by creating a thoroughly democratic institution, the "Agitators". The name, (which is first met with in an address to General Fairfax, dated May 29th, 1647) had originally the same significance as the word "delegate" has today, for the Agitators were the agents or representatives of the common soldiers. The officers and general staff were forced to recognise them, and it was agreed that each regiment should elect two Agitators to be chosen from the ranks of the non-commissioned officers, who, with two officers appointed for each regiment, were to constitute the Council of the Army.

This Council held its first meeting in the church at Saffron Walden, in Essex, in May, 1647, to consider the proposals of the Commissioners of Disbandment sent down from Parliament, and negotiations proceeded between it and Parliament. These proving abortive, a great Convention was held on Newmarket Heath, on June 4th, 1647, when a manifesto was drawn up asserting that the Army was no troop of mercenaries, but "free commoners of England drawn together and continued in arms in judgment and conscience for defence of their own and the people's rights and liberties". Officers and men alike pledged themselves not to disband nor suffer themselves to be disbanded until they were assured that " we as private men, or other the freeborn people of England, shall not remain subject to the like oppression, injury, or abuse as has been attempted".

Six days later there was a still bigger demonstration on Triploe Heath, near Cambridge, at which over 20,000 were present; and finally, on August 7th, 1647, the Army occupied London "in order to protect Parliament". Eleven Presbyterians who had made themselves particularly obnoxious with resolutions against the Army were expelled from the House, and a number of others remained away from the sitting for some time. Thus the Independents became more and more dominant in Parliament.

But the Army was still riddled with discontent, and on September 10th, 1647, there appeared a pamphlet which expressed a

deep sense of the blood and confusion that threatens the Nation by reason of the delays of removing the people's burdens, and clearing and securing their Rights and Freedoms. (*The Resolution of the Agitators of the Army, concerning the prosecution of their late remonstrance and the protestation against the sitting of the late usurpers of parliamentary power in this parliament; with the reasons constraining them so resolutely to adhere to that their protestation; as they presented them to his Excellency Sir Thomas Fairfax.*)

Meanwhile Charles was exercising his not inconsiderable gift for intrigue by trying to play off Parliament against the Army, and negotiating in turn with the Presbyterians and the Independents. The sight of their leaders exchanging courtesies with the "Man of Blood" added fuel to the discontent of the rank-and-file of the Army, and it was about this time that the terms "Gentlemen Independents" and "Grandees" began to be applied to the high officers of the Army. The latter retorted by charging the Agitators with being destructive "Levellers". One Cromwellian newspaper (with a curiously modern gift for invective) referred to the Levellers as "these Switzerising anarchists".

THE AGREEMENT OF THE PEOPLE

The discontent which existed in the Army found expression in a manifesto entitled the *Agreement of the People, upon Grounds of Common Right, for uniting of all unprejudiced people therein*. This manifesto (which was further elaborated and published under the same title early in 1649) demanded that the supreme authority of the nation should be vested in a representative body of 400 members, to be elected by manhood suffrage. Those in receipt of wages or alms were, however, to be excluded from the suffrage. This restriction of the franchise is less undemocratic than appears at first sight since at that time

> an industrial proletariat in the modern sense of the word did not exist. The journeyman in the handicrafts were usually in the transition stage between apprentice and master. To extend the suffrage to the agricultural labourers would, in the then circumstances, have strengthened the reactionary party. (*Cromwell and Communism*, Eduard Bernstein, p. 87).

The *Agreement of the People* was a remarkable programme for the times in which it was formulated, and it anticipated most of the demands that were advanced two centuries later by the Chartists. It called for Annual Parliaments, the members of which were not to be eligible to sit in the two succeeding Parliaments; nor were salaried officials to be eligible for election, whilst lawyers sitting in Parliament were not to practise. There were to be no religious tests, and no coercive laws regarding religion; conscientious objection to military or naval service was to be respected, and a national militia was to take the place of the standing army. All polls, taxes and tithes were to be replaced by a direct tax on every pound's worth of real and personal estate. Each county was to elect its own officials, and measures were to be taken to ensure work and decent maintenance for the poor, the aged, and the sick.

Parliament declared the *Agreement* to be seditious and its authors liable to punishment; but the discontent grew. Some officers supported the *Agreement of the People*, and whole regiments were won over. Finally Cromwell decided to test the strength of the opposition by a series of meetings.

The first of these was held in the middle of November at Corkbush Fields, near Ware, in Hertfordshire, and a majority of the soldiers wore sea-green ribbons (the Levellers' colours) in their hats, together with copies of the *Agreement of the People*. Cromwell succeeded in winning over the more moderate regiments, and the men removed the Levellers' emblems from their hats. Others, however, met him with defiant shouts and taunts and in the end Cromwell arrested fourteen of the ringleaders as mutineers, and a court martial passed sentence of death on three of them. They drew lots, and two were reprieved; but the third, Richard Arnold, was executed. His memory was cherished by the Levellers as a martyr.

Two other meetings were held without untoward incident, and after that Cromwell proceeded to weed out the unruly elements from the Army.

Meanwhile the Scots had assembled an army of 40,000 to invade England; and there were Royalist risings in Kent, Essex and Wales. Fairfax crushed the Kentish and Essex rebels, whilst Cromwell marched first against the Welsh and then against the Scots. Having ruthlessly crushed the Welsh rising, he inflicted a signal defeat upon the Scottish army at Preston, on August 17th, 1648.

JOHN LILBURNE

Now that the Royalist cause was hopelessly lost the Levellers pressed more vigorously than ever for the *Agreement of the People* to be implemented, and eventually four representatives of each side met to discuss the matter. One of those chosen by the Levellers was John Lilburne, their greatest leader: a man of unyielding, tempestuous character, whose writings (it has been said) "read like the verbatim report of a man talking vehemently all night in an inn".

Born at Greenwich about the year 1615, he came to London in 1630 as an apprentice to a city merchant, a linendraper, named Thomas Hewson. He was soon drawn into the political life of the metropolis, and, at the age of twenty, fell foul of the Government for distributing literature which had been printed in Holland and smuggled into this country. At that time the Calvinists were in power in Holland, and many of their co-religionists who were persecuted in England, found refuge there. Thither now John Lilburne fled to avoid arrest.

In December, 1637 he thought it safe to return to this country, but he was arrested and charged with having caused to be printed in the towns of Rotterdam and Delft various "scandalous" pamphlets, and having smuggled them into England. He was condemned to a fine of £500, to be whipped from Fleet Bridge (Ludgate Circus) to Westminster, and then to stand in the pillory for an hour and a half, and thereafter to be imprisoned in the Fleet.

Lilburne lay in gaol for more than two years, and it was not until the victory of the Long Parliament over the King in the winter of 1640-41 that he was set at liberty.

Lilburne fought for Parliament in the Civil War, and was twice wounded; but in 1644 he refused to sign the Covenant which Parliament had made with the Scots, and left the Army rather than compromise his conscience.

On his return to civil life Lilburne became a regular frequenter of the meetings of the London Independents, which were held in City taverns, and where much criticism was heard of the aristocratic character of the House of Commons. He also took to writing, and was several times imprisoned because of pamphlets which Parliament declared to be "scurrilous, libellous, and seditious".

Lilburne was a natural choice when the Levellers were selecting their four representatives to meet the Grandees. One of his fellow delegates was the William Walwyn to whom reference has already been made; and when John Price, one of the Gentlemen Independents, objected to him, Lilburne retorted with characteristic vehemence that Walwyn had more honour and honesty in his little finger than Price had in his whole body, and that he would rather resign from the committee than serve on it without Walwyn. In the end both Price and Walwyn retired; and the Committee (now reduced to six members) agreed on November 15th that a Committee should be formed consisting of representatives of the Army and delegates of the "Well-affected" in the country (i.e. supporters of Parliament as against the disaffected Royalists) which should formulate a scheme for the "foundation of a just government", this scheme then to be submitted to and voted upon by all the well-affected throughout the country. Protracted negotiations followed, and eventually a new Committee of Levellers and Gentlemen Independents was set up to draft a fresh *Agreement*.

This mixed commission was still engaged on its task when matters moved to a dramatic climax. On December 6th, Colonel Pride expelled the Presbyterian members from the House of Commons, and on January 19th, 1649, Charles was brought before a Special Court (on which Lilburne was offered a seat, but refused to serve), and was sentenced to death, on January 27th. Three days later he was executed; and on February 6th a resolution was carried by Parliament abolishing the House of Lords as "useless and dangerous". On May 19th, by resolution of Parliament, England was declared a Free Commonwealth.

By this time the mixed Commission of Levellers and Gentlemen Independents had prepared the new *Agreement*; but difficulties arose with the General Staff, and the question of religious toleration was discussed at great length. Finally, on December 21st, a compromise was reached under which all Christian sects which did not disturb the public peace were not to be interfered with by the State, Roman Catholics and Episcopal State Churchmen alone being excepted.

However, the real stumbling-block was the dissolution of Parliament. Cromwell, realist that he was, opposed the idea of fixing an early date for this, and, though he was in a minority upon this point on the Council of Officers, he carried his point of view that the revised *Agreement* should not be sent to Parliament for signature and subsequent circulation, but should be further considered, and that only so much of the *Agreement* be circulated as Parliament might deem fit. From his own point of view Cromwell was acting soundly enough: the elements in the country hostile to the Independents and the Army were far too numerous to risk a new election. Even in such counties as Norfolk and Suffolk most of the middle class and the gentry were opposed to the Independents and the Army, and these classes set the example in most of the counties. Like the peasantry, they were anxious to get rid of the military burden, and elections might easily have resulted in a predominantly Royalist Parliament.

Lilburne and his friends retired from the commission about the middle of January, 1649; and on January 20th Parliament shelved the *Agreement of the People* by declaring that it would "take it into consideration as soon as the necessity of the present weighty and urgent affairs would permit."

It was during these acrimonious negotiations that the difference in aim between the Grandee Independents and the Levellers came most consciously to light. Apart from the Levellers the only member who had a clear and coherent view of the situation was Commissary-General Ireton . . . and his was consciously bourgeois to a remarkable degree. By saying that he was against the manhood suffrage desired by the Levellers because all Constitutions were primarily intended to safeguard property he somewhat nonplussed the Leveller members. (*The Levellers and the English Revolution*, Henry Holorenshaw, pp. 65-66).

The Levellers were very bitter in the reproaches which they

hurled at the Grandees, and at Cromwell in particular.

> Was there ever a generation of men so Apostate so false and so perjur'd as these? did ever men pretend an higher degree of Holinesse, Religion, and Zeal to God and their Country than these? these preach, these fast, these pray, these have nothing more frequent than the sentences of sacred Scripture, the name of God and of Christ in their mouthes: You shall scarce speak to *Cromwell* about any thing, but he will lay his hand on his breast, elevate his eyes, and call God to record, he will weep, howl and repent even while he doth smite you under the first rib. (*The Hunting of the Foxes.* Probably written by Richard Overton.)

To Lilburne and his friends Cromwell was a malevolent, self-seeking hypocrite; but the truth is that together with his ambition and class prejudices he had a practical cast of mind averse to abstract thinking. He was, above all else, a practical politician who shaped his policy according to the possibilities of the times. The "Levellers were the ideologues of the movement. They started from abstract political theories, and accordingly saw facts through the spectacles of these theories". (*Cromwell and Communism*, Eduard Bernstein, pp. 86-87). They were two centuries and more before their time. The class whose interests they championed was still too immature to win and hold political power.

THE REVOLT IN THE ARMY

Soon after the *Agreement* had been shelved, the new Council of War endeavoured to deal with the growing discontent in the Army by forbidding soldiers to address petitions to Parliament or to any one save their officers, or to correspond with any civilians on political matters. The Council further resolved to apply to Parliament for authority to try by court martial and to hang any one who incited the Army to mutiny.

Lilburne headed a deputation of London citizens who presented themselves at the House of Commons to petition against these measures, and protests were soon forthcoming from the Army itself. On March 1st, 1649, there appeared a *Letter to General Fairfax and his Council of Officers*, signed by eight soldiers, in which were set out the complaints of the Army against its leaders. It charged Cromwell with aspiring to royal dignity, called Parliament a mere reflector of the Council of War, and this latter a tool of Cromwell, Ireton, and Harrison.

> We are English soldiers engaged for the freedom of England (it declared) and not outlandish mercenaries to butcher the people for pay, to serve the pernicious ends of ambition and will in any person under Heaven.

The *Letter* demanded the immediate ratification of the *Agreement* of Newmarket Heath, and concluded by "freely and gladly" endorsing Lilburne's petition.

The authors of this protest were court-martialled, when three retracted and were pardoned. The remaining five stood firm, and were sentenced to be led past the heads of their detachments seated backward on a wooden horse, to have their swords broken over their heads, and to be expelled from the Army.

This sentence was carried out on March 6th, but failed to quell the revolt: rather it goaded the Levellers to more energetic action. A new pamphlet appeared denouncing the proceedings which had been taken against the five soldiers, and repeating the main charges against the Army chiefs.

> We have not the change of a Kingdome to a Commonwealth; we are onely the old cheat, the transmutation of names but with the addition of New Tyranies to the old. (*The Hunting of the Foxes from New-Market and Triploe-Heaths to Whitehall by Five Small Beagles (March, 1649)*).

On Sunday, March 25th, Lilburne read a scathing denunciation of Cromwell and his Staff to an enormous crowd which assembled in front of his house. Signed by Lilburne, Overton, Prince and Walwyn, it demanded the election of a new Parliament, and bore the title *The Second Part of England's New Chains Discovered*.

The Council of State attempted to persuade their Foreign Secretary, John Milton, to write an answer to this pamphlet; but Milton (who probably sympathised with the Levellers' defence of personal liberty) refused to do so, and the Council took other steps to deal with the malcontents. Lilburne and his co-signatories were committed to the Tower, and a petition to Parliament in favour of the arrested men (which is said to have been signed by 80,000 people, an extraordinarily high figure when the circumstances of the time are considered) was ignored. A deputation of citizens who spoke on their behalf met with a sharp rebuke from the Speaker for their "seditious proposals", and a deputation of women was dismissed with the brusque reply that the matter was beyond their understanding, and they had better return home and wash their dishes.

About this time Charles' son was proclaimed king in Ireland and Scotland, and in practically every continental court the Royalists were plotting against the young republic. In these circumstances that supreme realist, Cromwell, did not hesitate to suppress by sheer violence an agitation which threatened to disrupt the Army—the mainstay of the revolutionary bourgeoisie of the day. He did make a last attempt to win Lilburne over to his point of view, but without success.

As is usual when political agitation wins mass support, much of the dissatisfaction of the times was economic in origin. The poor harvest of 1648 sent prices rocketing to famine levels, and there "was a great dearth in the country." "Never was there in England so many in want of relief as now," the people of London complained in March 1649 (*The Humble Petition of Divers Inhabitants of the City of London and Places Adjacent in the behalfe of the Poore of this Nation*). Moreover, while Parliament was granting extraordinary salaries to the Grandees of the Army and the Council State, the soldiers' pay was constantly in arrears. Finally, the Government was making payment in paper notes, which soon fell to one-fourth of their nominal value.

Matters came to a head in April, 1649, when a detachment of dragoons belonging to Colonel Whalley's regiment refused to proceed to Ireland until their demands had been met. Cromwell, by intimidation and persuasion broke the mutiny, and five of the mutineers were sentenced to death. Only one man, Robert Lockyer (chosen by lot) was actually shot in April, and before his execution he is reported as saying to his comrades, "Let not this death of mine be a discouragement, but rather an encouragement, for never man died more comfortably than I do."

His funeral was the occasion of an imposing demonstration, for thousands of craftsmen and labourers, with their wives and daughters, followed the coffin, which was decked in rosemary, one bundle being dipped in the blood of the "Martyr of the Army". They wore sea-green and black ribbons, and outside the city they were joined by many more mourners who had not cared to demonstrate openly within its precincts.

But the revolt was far from being over; for even whilst Cromwell was winning over the troops quartered in London by his astute oratory, news came from Banbury that Captain Thompson, with 200 troopers from Colonel Whalley's regiment, had revolted, and issued a manifesto entitled *England's Standard Advanced*, in which they demanded the application of the revised *Agreement*.

On May 10th came even more ominous news. In Salisbury almost the whole of Colonel Scroope's regiment had also declared in favour of the *Agreement*, and had placed themselves under the command of Ensign Thompson, the brother of Captain

Thompson. The greater part of Ireton's regiment, which was stationed in the neighbourhood of Salisbury, together with Harrison's and Skippon's regiments were also in revolt; and the mutineers were intending to join forces and to resist being sent to Ireland until the long-promised reforms had been carried out. Nearly all the rebels were tried veterans of the Civil War, and they declared in a dignified manifesto that they had sold up their farms or given up their businesses in order to fight against the tyranny of king and bishops, and that they would not allow a new tyranny to arise.

Cromwell acted with characteristic energy. Collecting all the reliable troops that were available, he and Fairfax proceeded by forced marches towards Salisbury, and the mutineers (now some 1,200 strong) were surprised (by treachery it is said) and overwhelmed in a night attack at Burford. Over 400 of the mutineers surrendered; but despite the promises of clemency which had been made, four of them, including Ensign Thompson, were sentenced to be shot. Thompson and two corporals died courageously: the fourth man, Ensign Dean or Denne, was "very contrite", and was pardoned.

After the executions Cromwell delivered one of his half-religious, half-political addresses, as a result of which the remaining prisoners promised to abandon all further seditious attempts to enforce their desires. They were presently reinstated in their regiments, and the following summer were sent to Ireland.

In the afternoon of the day of the executions, Cromwell and Fairfax proceeded to Oxford, where the University conferred degrees upon them. Parliament also thanked them, and the great City merchants (who had execrated Cromwell often enough in the past) hailed him as their saviour, and entertained him to a splendid banquet on June 7th, 1649, in the Grocers' Hall, at which Cromwell and Fairfax were presented with gold dishes and plates. At the same time a frivolous attempt was made to remedy some of the economic grievances which nourished the Levellers' movement, by providing £400 to be distributed among the poor of London. The wealthy City merchants had been in a state of panic, and the most extravagant rumours were afoot concerning the plans of the Levellers. They were charged with atheism and denying the immortality of the soul: but what was even more frightening to men of property, it was said "they will have no man call anything his, for it is tyranny that a man should have any proper land; particular property is devillish". Thus declared

England's Discoverer, or the Levellers Creed, which was published a few days before the banquet in the Grocers' Hall. This pamphlet asseverated that

> their emissaries (are) specially sent to raise the servant against the master, the tenant against the landlord, the buyer against the seller, the borrower against the lender, the poor against the rich, for encouragement every beggar shall be set on horseback.

After Burford the Levellers steadily lost influence, though they still had friends in the Army, and many supporters among the London populace.

LILBURNE'S LAST DAYS

The closing years of Lilburne's life were no less stormy than his earlier days had been. In 1652 he was banished, and went to Holland, and when he returned to England in 1653 (after Cromwell had dismissed the "Rump" of the Long Parliament which had sentenced him to banishment) he was arrested and tried for "breach of exile". The hearing of his case at the Old Bailey Court of Assizes dragged on for weeks, but he was eventually acquitted; and after being kept in close custody by the Council of State for some time, he was sent to Jersey in March, 1654, and held there as a prisoner of state.

In the autumn of 1654 he was transferred to Dover Castle, and a few weeks later London newspapers received a report that he had joined the Quakers. He died on August 19th, 1657.

Lilburne was the protagonist of the poor peasants and the craftsmen and artisans of his day—the class from which the modern proletariat was presently to evolve. Cromwell, on the other hand, was devoted to the interests of the propertied classes. This comes out clearly in the speech which he made on the dissolution of Parliament on January 22nd, 1655, when he used the most violent language against the Levellers.

> It is some satisfaction (he said) if a Commonwealth must perish, that it perish by men and not by the hands of persons differing little from beasts! That if it must need suffer, it should rather suffer from rich men than from poor men, who, as Solomon says, " when they oppress leave nothing behind them, but are a sweeping rain."

After the collapse of the revolt in the Army many of the radical elements must have despaired of bringing about the social and political changes which they desired by their own powers, and turned to the Almighty to accomplish what they had failed to achieve. After 1649 there is a fresh outburst of mystical religion and sectarian activity; and "it is to this period that the origins of such groups as the Quakers and the Fifth Monarchy Men are to be traced". (*Left Wing Democracy in the Civil War*, p. 115.) With the failure of political agitation and the repressive measures that were taken by the government to crush the revolt,

> social aspirations . . . were translated into the terms of religious radicalism. The angels may enter where men may not venture to tread; and what political activity has failed to achieve, Divine intervention would surely effect. The rights of the individual which society should guarantee became the privileges of the Saints which God would assure; and a social order in which legislation was to abolish inequality and injustice became instead a world in which as a result of the inner spiritual regeneration of mankind, men would cease to oppress their fellows. (*Left-Wing Democracy in the English Civil War*, pp. 115-116)*

THE SIGNIFICANCE OF THE LEVELLERS

It is not easy to assess the real strength and influence of the Levellers' movement. Undoubtedly its main support was in and around London, although it appears that propagandists carried its doctrines to remote parts of the country, and that it found some adherents in the North of England. To what extent it was an organised movement it is difficult to say: the Levellers' own publications throw no light on this problem, and the accounts of their opponents are inaccurate and often contradictory. The term Leveller was not even a strict party appellation, but was applied indiscriminately to those taking part in civil commotions of a purely local character which had little to do with the political aims of Lilburne and his friends. Indeed, the Leveller leaders often protested against the nickname (which was applied to them by their enemies), and were at pains to explain that they did not wish to "levell mens Estates, destroy Propriety, or make all things common". (The second *Agreement of the People*, Dec. 15th, 1648): This unequivocal declaration was repeated in the third *Agreement* of May 1st, 1649, which represents the final development of their political and social theories.

From July, 1648, to the end of September, 1649, information about the movement is provided by a journal which was described as the organ of the Levellers, and which produced most of the

---

*Winstanley's mystical and theological writings (*see* following chapter) are a product of this period. He too, protests, that "sharp punishing laws were made to forbid fishermen, shepherds, husbandmen, and tradesmen for ever preaching of God any more but schollars bred up in humane letters only should do that worke". *The Breaking of the Day of God* (May, 1648).

proclamations and pamphlets which the Levellers published during that period. This paper was entitled *The Moderate*, the name being intended to indicate the calm impartiality of its style. In its issue of July 31st to August 7th, 1649, it comments upon the execution of some cattle thieves, and blames the institution of private property for the death of these criminals, arguing that if private property did not exist there would be no need for men to steal.

From the issue for the last week in August, 1649, we learn that the Leveller movement numbered many miners in its ranks, especially in Derbyshire, where they are reported to be in dispute with the Earl of Rutland, and determined, if Parliament fails to give them justice, to have recourse to "natural law". With their friends and sympathisers they were said to number twelve thousand, and they threatened "in default of a hearing to form a resolute army". The *Moderate* declared that "the Party of the Levellers in Town promises them assistance in the prosecution of their just demands". The strength of this discontent movement was possibly overrated: at any rate, a few days later a letter from the "Freeholders and Miners, etc." of the Derbyshire mining district published in a Cromwellian paper, states that the miners numbered at most four thousand, and that the Levellers did not have a dozen followers in Derbyshire.

The last issue of the *Moderate* appeared in September, 1649, when Parliament enacted a press law which re-established the system of licences, and prescribed heavy penalties for the publication of abusive and libellous matter.

Can we regard the Levellers as constituting a working class movement? Hardly, for at that period the industrial working class had barely begun to develop in this country. Britain was still in the main an agricultural country in spite of the growing importance of commerce and manufacture. According to Gregory King, who wrote at the end of the 17th century (*Natural and Political Observations*, 1694) about 30 per cent of the country population consisted of peasant freeholders and tenants, and no really formidable agrarian movement was possible on such a basis. Moreover, there was still a good deal of common land available for squatters, and this helped blur the sharp edges of discontent. It was not until after the Restoration (and especially after the "Glorious Revolution" of 1689) that conditions were created which might have resulted in a revolutionary agrarian movement.

The Levellers were the extreme left of the middle-class revolution. "Like all extreme parties, they tend here and there to overstep the boundary at which they stand, but they remain finally in the middle-class camp". (*Cromwell and Communism,* p. 171*).

---

*It is interesting to note that when the Chartists took up the struggle for adult suffrage two centuries later their demands were hardly more advanced than those of the Levellers.

CHAPTER 9

THE DIGGERS

> While men are gazing up to heaven, imagining after a
> happiness or fearing a hell after they are dead, their
> eyes are put out, that they see not what is their birth-
> right, and what is to be done by them here on earth
> while they are living.
> *The Law of Freedom in a Platform, or True Magistracy*
> *Restored.*   Gerrard Winstanley.

ERRARD WINSTANLEY

"The Digger Movement (says M. Beer) although small in the
umber of its adherents, was an agrarian revolt on a surprisingly
xtensive theoretical basis. It was as if all the Peasant Wars of
ie past had suddenly become articulate". (*A History of British
ocialism,* p. 60.) Though it lasted little more than a year—April
649 to Easter 1650—it produced a number of remarkable
aanifestoes and pamphlets, most of which were written by
errard Winstanley.

Little is known about the life of Winstanley. He was born
t Wigan, in 1609, and came to London at the age of twenty,
'here he served his apprenticeship under the widow of a member
f the Merchant Taylors Company. He became a freeman in
637, but gave up his business about a year after the outbreak of
ie Civil War "by reason of the badness of the times". Later he
ecame acquainted with William Everard, who seems to have
layed an important part in turning his thoughts to politics.
verard was one of the soldiers arrested in 1647 for promoting
ie first *Agreement of the People* in the "New Model", and in
)ecember of the same year he was cashiered from the Army.
Ie and Winstanley were acquainted with one another by the
utumn of 1648.

As was usual in the polemics of the day, Winstanley clothed
is ideas in Biblical phrase and language, and what Petegorsky
alls "a spiritual interpretation of history" (*Left-Wing Democracy
a the English Civil War,* p. 126) runs through his earlier tracts.*
'he history of the human race (he contends) is a record of God's

---

*For an excellent summary of the early writings of Winstanley *see Left-Wing
emocracy in the English Civil War* (Chap. 3-5), by David W. Petegorsky.

attempt to kill the spirit of selfishness in men by revealing Himself to them through Jesus Christ. Man is saved from the Beast within him through the power of Christ. The first Adam is

> the wisdom and the power of the flesh in every man, who indeed is the Beast . . . covetousness . . . pride and envy, lifting up himself above others, and seeking revenge upon all that crosses his selfish honours. And hypocrisy, subtlety, lying imagination, self-love. . . . This is the first Adam, lying, ruling and dwelling within mankind. (*The New Law of Righteousness*, January 1649*.)

But the divine revelation which enables Man to master this first Adam will come not primarily to men "of study, learning and actings", but rather to the "despised, the unlearned, the poor, the nothings of this world", and these shall serve as living witnesses of the salvation which God intends for all mankind. These Saints will be reviled and persecuted; but ultimately all mankind shall be redeemed and "Jesus Christ . . . will dwell in the whole creation, that is, in every man and woman without exception". (*The Mysterie of God Concerning the whole Creation Mankinde* (April-May 1648)).

History, for Winstanley, is

> the story of a continuous conflict between opposing forces. The arena of that struggle is primarily the hearts and souls of men; but the conflict finds reflection and objectification in the institutions and laws men create as instruments for its prosecution. Salvation and freedom for mankind will not come through some sudden miracle, but from the progressive revelation of Christ to every individual, through the triumph of love over selfishness and lust in every human being. (*Left-Wing Democracy in the English Civil War*, p. 130.)

Winstanley conceives of God not as a majestic Being dwelling aloof from men in a Heaven beyond this world, but as a spirit that dwells in all mankind. Thus he advises his readers not to

> look for a God now as formerly you did to be a place of glory beyond the Sun, Moon and Stars nor imagine a divine being you know not where but see him ruling within you . . . He that looks for a God without himself . . . is led away and deceived by the imaginations of his own heart. (*The Saint's Paradise or the Fathers Teaching the only Satisfaction to Waiting Souls*. June-September, 1648.)

A man becomes conscious of the presence of God within himself when he has conquered selfishness and greed, and no longer feels that he "cannot live without money, lands, help of men and creatures". (*The Saint's Paradise*.)

---

*Most of the quotations from Winstanley's writings are taken from *Gerrard Winstanley, Selections from his works*, Edited by Leonard Hamilton.

Sometimes Winstanley identifies God with Reason, contending that "though men esteem this word Reason to be too mean a name to set forth the Father by, yet it is the highest name that can be given him". (*The Saint's Paradise*). "It is reason that made all things and it is Reason that governs the whole Creation". (*The Saint's Paradise*). It is Reason, too, that makes a man deal justly with his fellows.

> Wouldest thou have another to come and take away thy Goods, thy liberties, thy life ? No, saith the Flesh, that I would not. Then, saith Reason, Do as you wouldest be done unto . . . (*The Saint's Paradise.*)

As time goes on the mystical element in Winstanley's writings decreases, and more and more he sees the struggle between good and evil not merely as a clash of spiritual forces within the individual man, but also as one between economic classes, with the wealthy striving to retain their wealth and privileges, and the poor seeking for social justice and equality. That he did not regard his social theories as a contradiction of his religious ideas, but rather as a logical development from them, is shown by the fact that he published a collected edition of his theological works early in 1650 at the very time he was giving effect to his social theories by carrying through the St. George's Hill experiment in practical communism.

WINSTANLEY'S SOCIAL THEORIES

Petegorsky suggests that

> an influence of decisive importance in Winstanley's rapid development from his rational theology of the autumn of 1648 to his practical communism of the spring of 1649 was the activity of a group of advanced country Levellers in Buckinghamshire. Winstanley living near the borders of that county, may have come into personal contact with some members of that group, but at any rate the influence of their first short tract, *Light Shining in Buckinghamshire* of December, 1648, is unmistakably reflected in his remarkable work *The New Law of Righteousness*, of the following month . . . (Winstanley) was able . . . to expand the suggestions of *Light Shining, etc.*, into a comprehensive social philosophy that so completely transferred his interests from man's spiritual difficulties to his social and economic problems. (*Left-Wing Democracy in the English Civil War*, pp. 138-142.)

The New Law of Righteousness Budding forth, in restoring the whole Creation from the bondage of the Curse Or A Glimpse of the new Heaven, and a New Earth wherein dwells Righteousness Giving an Alarm to silence all that preach or speak from hearsay or imagination (to give it its full title) was published in January 1649, and is a blend of the mystical and the practical. Winstanley is still concerned with the spiritual struggle within Man, and his argument is still fundamentally a religious one, but he now definitely recognises that private property is the source of all social misery and strife. "Self-propriety (he says) . . . is the curse and burden the creation groans under" (*The New Law of Righteousness*). And again, it is

> this particular propriety of mine and thine (that) hath brought in all misery upon people. For, first it hath occasioned people to steal from one another. Secondly it hath made laws to hang those that did steal. It tempts people to do an evil action and then kills them for doing of it. (*The New Law of Righteousness.*)

Winstanley's analysis is a remarkable one for the times in which he lived, and Petegorsky rightly says that

> in his argument for a system of common ownership he has already passed far beyond all other thinkers of the period. (*Left-Wing Democracy in the English Civil War*, p. 138.)

Man at his creation (he contends) was a perfect being; but selfishness arose within him, and became a desire for the exclusive possession and enjoyment of material things, and thus private property was born. As the earth became the private property of the few the rest of mankind were enslaved and forced to labour for them, although "the King of Righteousness did not make some men to be tyrants, and others to be slaves", but rather "The earth was made by the Lord to be a common treasury for all, not a particular treasury for some". (*The New Law of Righteousness*).

Winstanley sees that all tyranny arises out of this private ownership of the earth,

> for let men say what they will, so long as such are rulers as call the land theirs, upholding this particular property of mine and thine, the common people shall never have their liberty, nor the land ever freed from troubles, oppressions and complainings. (*The New Law of Righteousness.*)

Men would never be free and happy, he believed, until the means of life were held in common.

> When the earth becomes a common treasury as it was in the beginning, and the King of Righteousness come to rule in everyone's heart, then He kills the first Adam; for covetousness thereby is killed. A man shall have meat and drink and clothes by his labour in freedom, and what can be desired more in earth? Pride and envy likewise is killed thereby, for every one shall look upon each other as equal in the Creation; every man indeed being

a perfect creation of himself. And so this second Adam, Christ the restorer, stops or dams up the runnings of those stinking waters of self-interest, and causes the waters of life and liberty to run plentifully in and through the Creation, making the earth one storehouse, and every man and woman to live in the law of righteousness and peace as members of one household. (*The New Law of Righteousness.*)

God willed the common people ("the lowest and most despised sort of people, that are counted the dust of the earth, mankind that are trod under-foot") to work upon the common lands "without either giving or taking hire, looking upon the land as freely mine as anothers". But social change of this sort (Winstanley predicts) will be vigorously opposed by

covetous, proud, lazy, pampered flesh that would have the poor still to work for that devil (particular interest) to maintain his greatness that he may live at ease. (*The New Law of Righteousness.*)

He sees, too, that State and Church both exist primarily to defend the existing property relationships; and (when allowance is made for archaisms and the occasional use of theological modes of expression) there is something astonishingly modern in his analysis of the social relationships which arise on the economic foundation of private property in land and capital. Having seized the land by force, the landlords (he argues) created a system of law and government to protect their privileges; and to help in the enslavement of the people they also established a visible church which had no divine sanction. Religion is used to keep the common people content with their slavery; for "your false teachers" put this notion of an "outward heaven" into "your heads to please you while they pick your purses". (*The New Law of Righteousness*). And so he has scant patience with those who

seek for the new Jerusalem, the City of Zion, or heaven, to be above the skies, in a local place, wherein there is all glory, and . . . this not to be seen neither by the eyes of the body till the body be dead. (*The New Law of Righteousness.*)

"A strange conceit", he called it, and declared that this

outward heaven . . . is a fancy which your false teachers put into your heads to please you with, while they pick your purses, and betray your Christ into the hands of flesh, and hold Jacob under to be a servant still to Lord Esau. (*The New Law of Righteousness*).

For him (as for Thomas Münzer) the Kingdom of Heaven was to be here, on earth.

If you look for heaven, or for manifestation of the Father's love in you in any place, but within yourselves, you are deceived . . . if you look for any other hell or for sorrows in any other place, than what shall be made manifest within the bottomless pit, your very fleshly self, you are deceived, and you shall find that when this bottomless pit is opened to your view, it will be a torment sufficient. For from hence doth the curse spread, and all that misery you are or may be capable of, it is but the breakings forth of that stinking dunghill, that is seated within you, and is in that power of darkness that rules within the Creation, your body. (*The New Law of Righteousness*).

Winstanley develops the same ideas a few months later in *The True Levellers Standard Advanced or the State of Community opened and presented to the Sons of Men* (April, 1649). This pamphlet is a defence of the Diggers' attempts to set up a Communist colony at Cobham, and shows

the cause why the common people of England have begun, and gives consent to dig up, manure and sow corn upon George Hill, in Surrey; by those that have subscribed, and thousands more that gives consent.

It opens with a sentence which Bernstein suggests "savours of the 18th century rationalists" (*Cromwell and Communism*).

In the beginning of time the great creator Reason made the earth to be a common treasury . . . not one word was spoken in the beginning that one branch of mankind should rule over another.

Winstanley proceeds to charge the government with having failed to keep its promises to make "this people a free people".

Thou hast made many promises and protestations to make the land a free nation; and yet at this very day the same people to whom thou hast made such protestations of liberty are oppressed by thy courts, assizes, sessions, by thy justices and clerks of the peace, so called, bailiffs, committees, are imprisoned and forced to spend that bread that should save their lives from famine. (*The True Levellers Standard Advanced*).

The overthrow of the King has not brought freedom to the common people.

Take notice (he writes) that England is not a free people, till the poor that have no land have a free allowance to dig and labour the commons, and so live as comfortably as the landlords that live in their enclosures . . . not only this common or heath should be taken in and manured by the people, but all the commons and waste ground in England, and in the whole world, shall be taken in by the people in righteousness, not owning any property; but taking the earth to be a common treasury, as it was first made for all. (*The True Levellers Standard Advanced*).

He ends his plea for social justice by declaring that

> if any of you that are the great ones of the earth, that have been bred tenderly and cannot work, do bring in your stock into the common treasury, as an offering to the work of righteousness, we will work for you, and you shall receive as we receive.
>
> *(The True Levellers Standard Advanced.)*

Winstanley does not propose to seek justice "by force of arms".

> We abhor it; for that is the work of the Midianites to kill one another; but by obeying the Lord of Hosts, who hath revealed Himself in us and to us, by labouring the earth in righteousness together, we eat our bread with the sweat of our brows, neither giving hire nor taking hire, but working together and eating together, as one man, or as one house of Israel restored from bondage. And so by the power of reason, the law of righteousness in us, we endeavour to lift up the Creation from that bondage of civil property which it groans under. *(The True Levellers Standard Advanced).*

And again:

> He that delivered Israel from Pharoah of old, is the same power still, in whom we trust, and whom we serve. For this conquest over thee shall be got, not by the sword of weapon, but by my spirit, saith the Lord of Hosts. *(The True Levellers Standard Advanced.)* *

It is interesting to note that in spite of the pacifism which Winstanley preached and the Diggers practised in the face of considerable provocation, their enemies charged them with having seized a house and "put four guns into it", and declared that they were "Cavaliers" who "wait for an opportunity to bring in the prince" (Charles II). In the Calendar of State Papers there is a copy of a letter from Winstanley and John Palmer, on behalf of their associates, to the Council of State of the Commonwealth, in which they protest against these grotesque charges, and affirm that "we are peaceable men (who) do not resist our enemies, but pray God to quiet our hearts, and we desire to conquer by love".

Gross charges of immorality were also made against the Diggers (similar to those that were later to be levelled against Socialists), and they were not only accused of robbing others, but of holding women in common. Winstanley warmly repudiated this latter charge.

---

*The same opinion is expressed in *A New Year's Gift for the Parliament and Army* (1650), where he declares that "Victory that is gotten by the sword is a victory that slaves get one over another . . . But victory obtained by love, is a victory for a King."

However, by 1651, when Winstanley produced his blueprint for a model community (*The Law of Freedom in a Platform, or True Magistracy Restored*), he gave up his extreme pacifist views, and made provision in his Utopia for the use of violence both by an army and a police force.

For my part (he wrote) I declare against it. I own this to be a truth, that the earth ought to be common treasury to all; but as for women, let every man have his own wife, and every woman her own husband, and I know none of the Diggers that act in such an irrational excess of female community. If they should, I profess to have nothing to do with such people, but leave them to their own master, who will pay them with torment of mind and diseases in their bodies. (*A New Year's Gift for the Parliament and Army.* January 1650.)

But the dominant theme that runs through all Winstanley's later writings is that the land has been stolen from the people, and that with the victory over the King the land ought to return to the people,

or else what benefit shall the common people have (that have suffered most in these wars) by the victory that is got over the king ? (*A Letter to the Lord Fairfax and his Council of War with Divers Questions to the Lawyers and Ministers.*) (June, 1649.)

And again, everyone without exception . . . "ought to have the liberty to enjoy the earth for his livelihood, and to settle his dwelling in part of the commons of England, without buying or renting land of any, else there is no true freedom," for "if the common people have no more freedom in England but only to live among their elder brothers (i.e. the landowners), and work for them for hire, what freedom then have they in England, more than we have in Turkey or France ? " (*A Letter to Lord Fairfax.*)

There is something perennially modern, too, in Winstanley's complaint that

there are but few that act for freedom, and the actors for freedom are oppressed by the talkers and verbal professors of freedom. (*A Watchword to the City of London and the Army.* September, 1649.)

Winstanley's writings have a simple, forthright vigour, and he has a gift for coining descriptive phrases that stick in the reader's memory. For example, his contemptuous rejection of "the traditional, parrot-like speaking from the Universities and Colleges" (*A Declaration from the Poor Oppressed People of England.* May, 1649); or his biting denunciation of "caterpillar lawyers" and the law which is

a very good name to cover his knavery; for he is a mighty beast with great teeth, and is a mighty devourer of men. He eats up all that comes within his power. . . . The law is the fox, poor men are the geese; he pulls off their feathers, and feeds upon them.

Another memorable phrase is that lawyers

love money as dearly as a poor man's dog do his breakfast in a cold morning,

and they are

such neat workmen, that they can turn a cause which way those that have the biggest purse will have them. (*A New Year's Gift for the Parliament and Army.*)

O you Parliament-men of England (he cries), cast those whorish laws out of doors, that are so common, that pretend love to everyone, and is faithful to none. For truly, he that goes to law, as the proverb is, shall die a beggar. So that old whores, and old laws, picks men's pockets and undoes them . . . burn all your law books in Cheapside, and set up your government upon your own foundations. Do not put new wine into old bottles; but as your government must be new, so let the laws be new, or else you will run farther into the mud, where you stick already, as though you were fast in an Irish bog. (*A New Year's Gift for the Parliament and Army.*)

Winstanley was equally forthright in his denunciation of the clergy who "will serve on any side, like our ancient laws, that will serve any master". (*A New Year's Gift for the Parliament and the Army*). For

If the clergy can get tithes or money, they will turn as the ruling power turns, any way: to Popery, to Protestantism, for a king, against a king, for the monarchy, for state government. They cry who bids most wages, they will be on the strongest side, for an earthly maintenance. (*A New Year's Gift for the Parliament and Army.*)

Nor will the ministers

take 12d. a day as other labourers have, but they will compel £100 or more to be paid to them yearly. Secondly they lay claim to heaven after they are dead, and yet they require their heaven in this world too, and grumble mightily against the people that will not give them large temporal maintenance. (*An Appeal to All Englishmen to Judge between Bondage and Freedom.* March 1650.)

But

true religion and undefiled is this, to make restitution of the earth, which hath been taken and held from the common people by the power of conquests formerly, and so set the oppressed free. (*A New Year's Gift for the Parliament and Army.*)

THE DIGGERS OF COBHAM*

In *The New Law of Righteousness* (January 1649) Winstanley states that divine revelation came to him whilst he was in a trance. Texts darted at him from the sky.

Likewise I heard these words " Work together, Eat bread together, declare all this abroad." Likewise I heard these words:

---

*In its report of an incident at St. George's Hill on April 23rd, *The Kingdom's Faithfull and Impartiall Scout* refers to the "Diggers". This appears to be the first occasion on which the term was applied to them. Generally they referred to themselves as "True Levellers".

" Whosoever it is that labours in the earth for any person or persons that lifts up themselves as Lords and Rulers over others and that doth not look upon themselves equal to others in the creation, the hand of the Lord shall be upon the labourer. I the Lord have spoke it and I will do it.   Declare this all abroad."

He goes on to explain that

I have now obeyed the command of the Spirit that bid me declare all this abroad, I have delivered it and I will deliver it by word of mouth, I have now declared it by my pen. And when the Lord doth shew unto me the place and manner how he will have us that are called common people to manure and work upon the common lands, I will then go forth and declare it in my actions. (*The New Law of Righteousness.*)

Soon afterwards, early in April, 1649, Winstanley kept his promise to give practical effect to his communist theories. It was a time of acute social tension. The Levellers' revolt in the Army was coming to a head, and the whole country was in the throes of a political and economic crisis, with widespread unemployment and social discontent. In Winstanley's vivid phrase the old world was "running up like parchment in the fire". (*The True Levellers Standard Advanced or the State of Community opened and presented to the Sons of Men,* April, 1649).

With some twenty or thirty poor men Winstanley and William Everard* came to St. George's Hill, near Cobham, in Surrey, and began to dig some waste land, and sow it with corn, parsnips, carrots and beans. They explained to the local people that as yet they were few, but that in a little while their numbers would be four or five thousand; and they declared that it was

an undeniable equity that the common people ought to dig, plow, plant and dwell upon the Commons without hiring them or paying rent to any.

The local gentry took alarm, and Mr. Drake, lord of the manor of St. George's Hill (and a Member of Parliament), and Parson Platt, lord of the manor of Cobham, appealed to the Council of State for military assistance.

The Council of State sent two troop of horse to Cobham, and on April 20th Everard and Winstanley were brought before General Fairfax, when they refused to remove their hats since "he was but their fellow creature".† Everard defended their actions

---

*William Everard was regarded as the leader of the Digger movement until he left it in May, 1649, and his name headed the list of signatories to the first Digger manifesto The *True Levellers Standard Advanced.*

†John Lilburne had made the same gesture at his trial before the Star Chamber, in 1637. Later this symbolic assertion of human equality was adopted by the Quakers.

by declaring that ever since the coming of William the Conqueror the "people of God had lived under tyranny and oppression worse than that of our forefathers under the Egyptians". Lately (he said) he had seen a vision which bade him "Arise and dig and plough the Earth, and receive the fruit thereof"; and all that he and his fellows sought to do was to restore the "ancient Community of enjoying the fruits of the Earth", and to distribute the benefits thereof to the poor and needy, and to feed the hungry and clothe the naked. He went on to explain that they did not intend to break down fences, or to meddle with private property, but only to till the common land and "make it fruitful for the use of men", for they did not see why they should die while there was an abundance of common land lying idle. They would recruit the "poor, workless and oppressed into their ranks", and bring them from a "shiftless vagabondage into good citizenship". Finally (he said) the time would come when the present freeholders, the perpetrators of Norman tyranny, would pull down their fences, give up their landed property, and willingly join the community, thus ending all tyranny and slavery and establishing God's kingdom on earth.

Everard made it clear that they would not defend themselves by arms, but would "submit unto authority, and wait till the promised opportunity be offered", which they believed to be at hand.

With their notice by the Council of State and the appearance of their leaders before Fairfax, the Diggers enjoyed the spotlight of national attention for a brief period. Most of the news-sheets of the last weeks of April note their activities.... Some ... contented themselves with brief and factual accounts of the information which had reached the Council and the interview with Fairfax. Others, reporting the affair, dismissed it as the work of a few madmen; Everard, particularly, is described by most papers as " a mad prophet." (*Left-Wing Democracy in the English Civil War*, pp. 163-4).

According to one account "they are a distracted crack-brained people"; but *Mercurius Brittanicus* accuses the Royalists of having instigated the Digger venture in order to increase the general confusion and unrest so that the Royalists might have a chance to seize power; and *Mercurius Pragmaticus* gloomily remarks that

what the fanatical insurrection may grow into cannot be conceived for Mahomet had as small and despicable a beginning whose damnable infections have spread themselves many hundreds of years since over the face of half the universe.

Meanwhile the local gentry at Cobham organized a boycott of the Diggers "so that they could neither buy nor sell", and early in June several soldiers, under a Captain Stravie, came to St. George's Hill, and beat up a man and boy, seriously injuring the latter, and also burned a house. A few days later several men attacked four Diggers on the common. The Diggers, in accordance with their principle of refusing to use violence, offered no resistance, and were so brutally beaten one was not expected to live. A cart in which they were hauling wood to rebuild their house was smashed and the horse seriously injured.

Hooliganism failing to get rid of the Diggers, the law was invoked, and early in July Winstanley and fifteen of his companions were arrested on a charge of trespass, and brought to the manor court at Kingston. The Diggers refused to employ legal assistance, but were not allowed to plead their own case; and a jury of rich freeholders imposed fines which were deliberately made so heavy (£10 a man, plus twenty-one shillings and a penny costs), that they could not pay, whereupon their property was distrained. "Will Star and Ned Sutton, both freeholders, and others the snapsack boys and ammunition drabs" drove away four cows which Winstanley had either hired or borrowed, and

> beat them with their clubs, that the cows' heads and sides did swell, which grieved tender hearts to see. And yet those cows never were upon George Hill*, nor never digged upon that ground, and yet the poor beasts must suffer because they gave milk to feed me.
> (*A Watchword to the City of London and the Army.* Winstanley, September, 1649.)

The four cows were rescued "out of those devils' hands" by sympathisers; but other cows (Winstanley says) were killed to feed the "snapsack boys and the ammunition drabs" that helped to drive them away, "that they might be encouraged by a belly full of stolen goods to stick the closer to the business another time".

On August 24th, 1649, a meeting was held at the "White Lion" at Cobham, when "much sack and tobacco was consumed", and a mob was organised to raid the colony and dig up the seeds.

> Alas! you poor blind earth moles (Winstanley wrote of them), you strive to take away my livelihood, and the liberty of this poor weak frame my body of flesh, which is my house I dwell in for a time; but I strive to cast down your kingdom of darkness, and to open hell gates, and to break the devil's bonds asunder, wherewith you are tied, that you my enemies may live in peace, and that is all the harm I would have you to have. (*A Watchword to the City of London and the Army.*)

---

*St. George's Hill. Like the Quakers, the Diggers omitted the word "Saint".

even of Winstanley's cows and a bull were driven off during
the night, "some of the cows being a neighbour's that had hired
the pasture." However, "these cows (Winstanley relates) are
brought home again, and the heart of my enemies is put into the
bound of vexation because the cows are set free".

The persecution of the Diggers continued: not only were their
cows driven off, but hogs and cattle were "let into the standing
barley and other corn".

And when they had done this mischief, the bailiffs and other
Norman snapsack boys went hollowing and shouting, as if they
were dancing at a Whitsun Ale, so glad they are to do mischief
to the Diggers, that they might hinder the work of freedom.

Was it for this, Winstanley asks, that the King was overthrown.

You zealous preachers and professors of the City of London, and
you great officers and soldiery of the army, where are all your
victories over the Cavaliers, that you made such a blaze in the
land, in giving God thanks for, and which you begged in your
fasting days and morning exercises? Are they all sunk into the
Norman power again and must the old prerogative laws stand?
What freedom then did you give thanks for? Surely that you had
killed him that rode upon you, that you may get up into his saddle
to ride upon others. Oh, thou City, thou hypocritical City! Thou
blindfold, drowsy England, that sleeps and snorts in the bed of
covetousness, awake, awake! The enemy is upon thy back, he is
ready to scale the walls and enter possession, and wilt thou not
look out? (*A Watchword to the City of London and the Army.*)

And he cries that

all the rabble of the nations, lords, knights, gentlemen, lawyers,
bailiffs, priests and all the Norman snapsack boys and ammunition women to the old Norman camp, do all combine together
in the art of unrighteous fury, to drive the poor Diggers off from
their work that the name of community and freedom, which is
Christ, may not be known in earth.

In the winter the troops were called in again, but some of them
"were very moderate and rational men" Winstanley says, and
one of them

was very civil, and walked lovingly with the Diggers round their
corn which they had planted, and commended the work, and
would do no harm . . . and when he went his way he gave the
Diggers twelve pence to drink. (*A New Year's Gift for the
Parliament and Army,* Gerrard Winstanley.)

However, the soldiers stood by while the parson

caused a poor old man's house upon the common to be pulled
down in the evening of a cold day, and turned the old man and
his wife and daughter to lie in the open field, because he was a
Digger. (*A New Year's Gift for the Parliament and Army.*)

But Winstanley says of "the poor tenants that pulled down the house" that they did it "for fear they should be turned out of service of their livings", and he asks "Can the Turkish Bashaws hold their slaves in more bondage than these Gospel-professing lords of manors do their poor tenants?"

> And when the poor enforced slaves had pulled down the house, then their lords gave them ten shillings to drink, and there they smiled one upon another, being fearful, like a dog that is kept in awe, when his master gives him a bone and stands over him with a whip. He will eat, and look up, and twinch his tail. (*A New Year's Gift for the Parliament and Army*.)

But Winstanley was convinced that "in their hearts they are Diggers".

As for the Diggers themselves they "were mighty cheerful, and their spirits resolve to wait upon God, to see what He will do".

And they took

> the spoiling of their goods cheerfully, counting it a great happiness to be persecuted for righteousness' sake by the priests and professors, that are the successors of Judas, and the bitter-spirited Pharisees that put the Man Christ Jesus to death. (*A New Year's Gift for the Parliament and Army*.)

In this pamphlet Winstanley sets out

> A bill of account of the most remarkable sufferings that the Diggers have met with from the great red Dragon's power since April 1, 1649, which was the first day that they began to dig and to take possession of the commons for the poor on George Hill in Surrey. (*A New Year's Gift for the Parliament and Army*).

Among other persecutions he relates how

> divers of the Diggers were beaten . . . by William Star and John Taylor and by men in women's apparel, and so sore wounded that some of them were fetched home in a cart. (*A New Year's Gift for the Parliament and Army*).

Elsewhere (*An Humble Request to All the Ministers of both Universities and to all Lawyers of every Inns-a-Court*, April, 1650), Winstanley declares that Parson Platt's men kicked and struck a woman "so that she miscarried of her child, and by the blows and abuses they gave her she kept her bed a week".

In the end this constant savage persecution proved too much even for the courage and endurance of the Diggers, and before Easter, 1650, the Cobham colony had ceased to exist. Prior to that, however, the Diggers had sent missionaries to several counties to urge the poor to follow the St. George's Hill example, and also to collect funds for their own little community. They visited more than thirty towns and villages in Buckinghamshire,

Surrey, Hertfordshire, Middlesex, Berkshire, Huntingdonshire and Northamptonshire. These delegates carried a letter from Winstanley, which was also signed by 25 other Diggers, declaring their intention to persist in their plans despite all opposition, but adding that their crops having been destroyed, dire necessity might force them to give up their venture unless help was forthcoming.

This mission must have met with some success, for in March, 1650, the "poor inhabitants" of Wellingborough in Northamptonshire had begun to dig upon the "common and waste-ground called Bareshank". However, they were speedily suppressed, and the Council of State wrote to Mr. Pentlow, the justice of the peace for Northampton, congratulating him on the prompt measures he had taken against the "Levellers in those parts". Another colony was established at Coxhall, in Kent; and it appears that similar attempts were made in Gloucestershire, for we hear of "rude multitudes levelling the enclosures". But all these communities failed, and the movement died out.

WINSTANLEY'S UTOPIA

With the collapse of the Cobham experiment Winstanley appears to have devoted himself to the task of trying to win converts to his communist ideas by reason and persuasion rather than by example. In February, 1652, there appeared the fullest and most closely reasoned exposition of his ideas that he ever published, *The Law of Freedom in a Platform, or True Magistracy Restored*. In this he outlines in considerable detail his conception of an ideal community. The work is humbly presented to Oliver Cromwell, with the plea that

> it may be here are some things inserted which you may not like, yet other things you may like. Therefore I pray you read it, and be as the industrious bee, suck out the honey and cast away the weeds.

He declares that Cromwell has "the power of the land in your hand", and must

> either set the land free to the oppressed commoners, who assisted you, and paid the Army their wages; and then you will fulfil the Scriptures and you own engagements, and so take possession of your deserved honour. Or secondly, your must only remove the Conqueror's power out of the King's hand into other men's, maintaining the old laws still; and then your wisdom and honour is blasted for ever; and you will either lose yourself, or lay the foundation of greater slavery to posterity than you ever knew.

I

His appeal, of course, was in vain: Cromwell had not the slightest sympathy with Winstanley's levelling, communist theories. He represented the triumphant bourgeoisie of his day, and could but choose one policy; the consolidation of their power. The fight against priestcraft and the divine right of kings (in which the poorer peasantry and the poor artisans of the towns had played a not inconsiderable part) did not mean liberty for the common people, but the enthronement of the divine right of property. After the English Revolution, British capitalism went its triumphant way, building a world empire, turning the English peasant into a pauper, and accumulating (by commerce, the slave trade, the loot of India, and the theft of the common lands) the capital that made possible the Industrial Revolution which began in the second half of the eighteenth century and which ushered in the most dreadful age of exploitation that the English worker has ever known. Winstanley prophesied with more truth than he knew when he declared that Cromwell must either "set the land free to the oppressed commoners" or "lay the foundation of a greater slavery to posterity than you ever knew."

In a preamble to his proposals Winstanley enumerates the popular grievances of the times:

(1) Lack of religious toleration. The "burdens of the clergy remain still upon us," he says, and

> if any man declares his judgment in the things of God, contrary to the clergy's report or the mind of some high officers, they are cashiered, imprisoned, crushed, and undone, and made sinners for a word, as they were in the popes' and bishops' days.

(2) In many parishes the "old formal ignorant episcopal priests" remain, many of whom

> "are bitter enemies to the Commonwealth's freedom, and friends to monarchy . . . and are continually buzzing their subtle principles into the minds of the people," thereby " causing a disaffection of spirit."

(3) The burden of tithes still remains.

(4) The administration of justice is still arbitrary.

> In many courts and cases of law, the will of a judge and lawyer rules above the letter of the law.

(5) The laws remain the same as in the King's day;

> only the name is altered ; as if the commoners of England had paid their taxes, free-quarter, and shed their blood, not to reform, but to baptize the law into a new name, from kingly law, to state law.

(6) The old feudal dues and obligations still oppress the common people, the lords of the manors "requiring fines and heriots" and driving the people off the common land unless they will pay rent "as much as they did, and more, when the King was in power". Moreover, in parishes where common land remains

the rich Norman freeholders, or the new (more covetous) gentry overstock the commons with sheep and cattle; so that inferior tenants and poor labourers can hardly keep a cow, but half starve her.

In many parishes, too, there is injustice in the assessment of taxes due to the influence of "two or three of the great ones", whilst the

country people cannot sell any corn or other fruits of the earth in a market town, but they must pay toll,

and are oppressed by high duties and market dues.

This statement of popular grievances is followed by an attack upon the titles to landed property. Winstanley argues that the land belongs to the landowner "either by Creation right, or by right of conquest". If the owner bases his claim on "Creation right" then the land "is mine as well as his; for the Spirit of the whole Creation, who made us both, is no respecter of persons"; and if he claims the earth by right of conquest "the kings are beaten and cast out, and that title is undone". Since the common people helped win a victory over the King they have an equal right to a share in the earth.

Winstanley then goes on to develop his communist theories, and explains that in his "True Commonwealth" there will be no buying and selling, for

when mankind began to buy and sell, then he did fall from his innocency; for then they began to oppress and cozen one another of their Creation birthright.

He anticipates the modern Marxist theory of the economic origin of war when he declares that

this buying and selling did bring in, and still doth bring in dis-contents and wars. . . . And the nations will never beat their swords into ploughshares and their spears into pruning hooks, and leave off warring, until this cheating device of buying and selling be cast out among the rubbish of kingly power.

He anticipates modern Socialist criticism, too, when he argues that great wealth is not the result of the thrift and industry of the owner but is the result of the exploitation of the workers.

> If a man have no help from his neighbours he shall never gather an estate of hundreds of thousands a year. If other men help him to work, then are those riches his neighbour's as well as his own.

And again "all rich men live at ease, feeding and clothing themselves by the labours of other men."

Winstanley is a throughgoing Leveller, for he will have no titles or honours in his ideal Commonwealth, save those which are the mark of some great service to society.

> He who finds out any secret in nature shall have a title of honour given him . . . But no man shall have any title of honour till he win it by industry, or come to it by age or office-bearing.

And the "highest nobility" is "to be a faithful Commonwealth man in a Parliament house".

Nor will there be any need of lawyers in his Utopia, "for there is to be no buying and selling".

Winstanley stresses that while in his ideal state the earth and storehouses are to be common property, "every family shall live apart as they do now"; nor shall any one be compelled to enter this Commonwealth against his will. All that he asks is

> that the Commonwealth's land, which is the ancient commons and waste lands, and the lands newly got in, by the Army's victories, out of the oppressor's hands, as parks, forests, chases and the like, may be set free to all that have lent assistance either of person or purse to obtain it, and to all that are willing to come in . . . and be obedient to the laws of the new Commonwealth.

The long preamble is followed by Chapter I, in which Winstanley discusses the meaning of freedom. Once again there is something astonishingly modern about his views. Freedom does not consist (he argues) in the removal of restrictions on trade, or in "freedom to have community with all women", or in religious freedom. "True freedom lies where a man receives his nourishment and preservation, and that is in the use of the earth".

> Surely then, oppressing lords of manors, exacting landlords, and tithe-takers, may as well say their brethren shall not breathe in the air nor enjoy warmth in their bodies, not have the moist waters to fall upon them in showers, unless they will pay rent for it; as to say, their brethren shall not work upon the earth, nor eat the fruits thereof, unless they will hire that liberty of them.

Having thus insisted that men cannot be truly free without economic freedom, Winstanley goes on in Chapter 2 to discuss the government of the country. He distinguishes between what he calls "a kingly government, and a Commonwealth government". The former (he says) "governs the earth by that cheating art of buying and selling", whereby every man's hand is against his fellows. This government can only rest on force, for "if it had not a club law to support it there would be no order in it". Moreover, this kingly government produces war, for it "beats pruning hooks and ploughs into spears, guns, swords and instruments of war", that the wealthy man may

> live idle and at ease by his brother's labours. Indeed this government may well be called the government of highwaymen, who hath stolen the earth from the younger brethren (i.e. common people) by force, and holds it from them by force. . . . This kingly power is the old heaven and the old earth that must pass away.

On the other hand "Commonwealth's government governs the earth without buying and selling", and thereby restores "ancient peace and freedom".

In Chapter 3 Winstanley explains that in his ideal Commonwealth all officers would be chosen annually, for

> nature tells us that if water stands long it corrupts; whereas running water keeps sweet and is fit for common use.

> Have we not (he asks) experience in these days, that some officers of the Commonwealth are grown so mossy for want of removing, that they will hardly speak to an old acquaintance, if he be an inferior man, though they were very familiar before these wars began ? "

Winstanley's Utopia is thoroughly democratic, with manhood suffrage for all over twenty, although

> uncivil livers, as drunkards, quarrellers, fearful ignorant men, who dare not speak truth lest they anger other men; likewise all who are wholly given to pleasure and sport, or men who are full of talk, are "not fit to be chosen officers in a Commonwealth."

Yet even these "uncivil livers" may "have a voice in the choosing". Those, however, who fought for the king or lent him money are neither to be eligible for office nor to have the franchise.

Above all (says Winstanley) men of courage are needed for public office.

> Men who are not afraid to speak the truth; for this is the shame of many in England at this day: they are drowned in the dunghill mud of slavish fear of men; these are covetous men, not fearing God, and their portion is to be cast without the city of peace among the dogs.

Winstanley also believes that officers should be

above forty years of age,* for they are most likely to be experienced men; and all these are likely to be men of courage, dealing truly and hating covetousness.

If poor men are elected to public office they are to have

a yearly maintenance from the common stock until such time as a Commonwealth's freedom is established, for then there will be no need of such allowance.

In Chapter 5 Winstanley enumerates the officers who will be necessary in his ideal Commonwealth. In each town or parish "peace officers" are to be chosen to form a council to order the affairs of the parish, and to administer justice.

Overseers are also to be chosen yearly for every town and parish,

to preserve peace, in case of any quarrels that may fall out between man and man. For though the earth with her fruits be a common treasury, and is to be planted and reaped by common assistance of every family, yet every house and all the furniture for ornament therein is a property of the indwellers ; and when any family hath fetched in from the storehouses or shops either clothes, food, or any ornament necessary for their use, it is all a property of that family. And if any other family or man come to disturb them, and endeavour to take away furniture, which is the ornament of his neighbour's house, or to burn, break, or spoil wilfully any part of his neighbour's house, or endeavour to take away either food or clothing which his neighbour hath provided for his use, by reason whereof quarrels and provoking words arise; this office of overseers is to prevent disturbances, and is an assistance to the peacemaker.

Other overseers are to be appointed whose duty it is

to see that young people be put to masters, to be instructed in some labour, trade, science, or to be waiters (i.e. shop assistants) in storehouses, that none may be idly brought up.

Overseers are also to be chosen

for every trade . . . this overseer to go from house to house to view the works of the people of every house belonging to his trade and circuit, and to give directions as he sees cause. . . . And . . . there are to be overseers . . . in the country parishes, to see the earth planted.

It was inevitable in the circumstances of the times in which Winstanley lived that he should conceive of his Utopia as founded upon small-scale production. Thus most of the production

---

*Winstanley was forty-two when he wrote *The Law of Freedom*. He further justifies this choosing of officers from those who are over forty by arguing that "by this time man hath learned experience to govern himself and others. For when young wits are set to govern they wax wanton". (*The Law of Freedom*, Chap. 5).

is to be carried on in the people's homes, although the community is to maintain public workshops wherein boys who do not wish to follow their father's trade, may be trained in some other craft.

> Every tradesman shall fetch materials, as leather, wool, flax, corn and the like, from the public storehouses to work upon them without buying and selling ; and when particular works are made, as cloth, shoes, hats and the like, the tradesmen shall bring these particular works to particular shops without buying and selling. And every family, as they want such things as they cannot make, they shall go to these shops and fetch without money.

Overseers are to be appointed to see that the various tradesmen bring their work to the storehouses and shops in this way.

Besides these overseers, "all ancient men, above sixty years of age " are to be general overseers or elders,

> And wheresoever they go, and see things amiss in an officer or tradesman, they shall call any officer or others to account for their neglect of duty.

In addition to these overseers, the community is to choose a chief soldier (i.e. chief constable) with assistants under him, to execute justice, arrest offenders against the law, and to maintain law and order: a taskmaster, who is to see that those who are sentenced to lose their freedom shall do their appointed work: and an executioner to whip, behead, hang or shoot offenders " according to the sentence of the law".

There are to be annual Parliaments; and Parliament's first concern "is to . . . give out orders for the free planting and reaping of the Commonwealth's land", which will consist of all crown and church lands "recovered out of the hands of the Pope's power by the blood of the commoners of England", together with the commons and wastes which have been seized by the lords of the manors. Parliament is also " to abolish all old oppressive laws, and to enact new laws for the ease and freedom of the people"; and it is to raise an army to wage war abroad if occasion demand, or to suppress insurrection at home. (It can be seen that Winstanley has modified his earlier pacifist ideas).

Winstanley sets great store by science and education. On the weekly day of rest the chosen minister for the year is to read reports of "the affairs of the whole land, as it is brought in by the postmaster"; lectures are to be given "in all arts and sciences . . . as in physics, surgery, astrology, astronomy, navigation, husbandry, and such like" or upon "the nature of mankind, of his

Men and women are to be free to marry whom they love, "and for portion, the common storehouses are every man's and maid's portion, as free to one as to another". Marriage is to be a civil ceremony, without the need of a priest.

When any man or woman are consented to live together in marriage, they shall acquaint all the overseers in their circuit therewith, and some other neighbours. And being all met together, the man shall declare by his own mouth before them all that he takes that woman to be his wife, and the woman shall say the same and desire the overseers to be witnesses.

THE SIGNIFICANCE OF WINSTANLEY

As we have seen, communist theories were far older than Winstanley, but while the

communism of the medieval movements . . . is generally a vague and mystical affair, and does not derive from a reasoned examination of social and historical forces, with Winstanley . . . the demand for common ownership was rooted . . . in a comprehensive social philosophy that became the basis of a political programme. It emerged as the result of a reasoned analysis of the role of private property in history and of the results of social division. Unlike the medieval varieties, it proposes communism not only in distribution, but in production as well. (*Left-Wing Democracy in the English Civil War*, pp. 150-151.)

Winstanley in his power of economic analysis and his understanding of class forces is halfway to scientific socialism. And in the influence which his writing later exerted on John Bellers, and through him upon Robert Owen, he is linked with the modern Socialist and Co-operative movements.

CHAPTER 10

THE QUAKERS

Oh! Foolish People . . . are not these the choicest
of thy Worthies . . . now in power? Hath it not
been the top of thy desires and labors to see it in their
hands, and are not they now become weak as other
men, and the land still in travail but nothing brought
forth but wind?

James Naylor.

THE CHILDREN OF LIGHT

After the collapse of the Digger movement some of the Diggers
appear to have joined the Quakers. Bernstein (*Cromwell and
Communism*) and Dr. G. P. Gooch (*English Democratic Ideas in the
Seventeenth Century*) have both asserted that Winstanley himself
became a Quaker, and most historians have followed their
example; largely basing their assertion on Winstanley's pamphlet
*The Saints' Paradise; or the Fathers Teaching the only Satisfaction to
Waiting Souls,* which contains ideas that bear a striking resemblance to those of the Friends. However, Petegorsky (*Left-Wing
Democracy in the English Civil War*) adduces evidence which throws
considerable doubt on the belief that Winstanley ended his life
as a Quaker.

The similarity of the argument of the tract to Quaker concepts
(he says) must be considered rather the result of the general environment of the period than of any direct contact between Winstanley and George Fox and his followers—for which there is no
evidence whatever. (*Left-Wing Democracy in the English Civil War,*
Appendix I.)

Quakerism can trace its spiritual descent from the Anabaptists.
Like them the Quakers relied less upon tradition and the Bible,
and more upon the "inner light" for the revelation of God's
will, and the very name by which they called themselves, the
"Children of Light", forms a connecting link between them and
many of the German Anabaptists.

The name which they eventually took, the Society of Friends,
is derived from 3 *John, i.* 14: "Our friends salute thee; Greet
the friends by name".

The more popular name of Quakers has been explained in a
number of ways. According to one account it was derived from

the fact that members of the sect at their prayer meetings frequently fell into religious ecstasies, with trembling and convulsions; but the more generally accepted explanation is that
when George Fox, the founder of the movement, was arraigned
before Justice Bennet of Derby on a charge of brawling, he
admonished the judge and the assembled company to "quake
at the name of the Lord".

The period was one in which all religious dogmas were being
questioned, and the various Christian sects were busy denouncing
one another.

> These disputes were carried on in the streets and open places,
> the public joining in, as in the case of modern political meetings.
> The result was that scepticism spread among the people, many
> of whom turned their backs on religion altogether. Judging
> from the reports of Quaker missionaries, there were in England
> at that time a considerable number of people who denied the truth
> of the Biblical story of the creation. . . . Others attached themselves
> to obscure sects, brooding on the mysteries of creation (the so-
> called " seekers "), or waiting for a sign from heaven which was
> to solve their doubts (the so-called " waiters "). (*Cromwell and
> Communism*, Eduard Bernstein, p. 227.)

One of these "seekers" was George Fox, the son of a Leicestershire
silk weaver. Born in 1624, and bred during the period of Puritan
persecutions, he developed a strong religious bent at a very
early age. When he was nineteen he began to go from place to
place, preaching and disputing upon religious questions. None
of the existing churches satisfied him: he found them all too
worldly, and none of them seemed to correspond to primitive
Christianity.

Eventually he reached a state of mind which Bernstein calls
"a compound of rationalism and mysticism, of democracy and
political abstention". (*Cromwell and Communism*, pp. 227-8.)
All the misery and sacrifices of the Civil War seemed to him to
have been without profitable result. Men who had been looked
upon as liberators had themselves become oppressors once they
were raised to power. The conclusion seemed to be that evil lay
not in social or political systems but rather in man himself, in the
frailty of human nature.

Because of their doctrine of the "inward light", of the possibility
of God communicating His will by direct revelation to the
individual, the Quakers denied the need for a professional clergy
paid by the State; and because of this they consistently refused
to pay tithes. Every one, they maintained, should say what they

ner voice prompts him to say: and we read in Fox's *Journal*
at the priests "trade" or "sell" their gospel, that the bells of
eir "steeple-houses" resemble market-bells, which call the
ople together that the priest may "spread out his wares for
le". There were frequent instances in which Quakers entered
church during a service and interrupted the preacher, crying:
Come down, thou false prophet, thou impostor, thou blind
ader of the blind, thou hireling!" Sometimes they preached
eir own doctrine after the regular church service was finished,
d not infrequently they were stoned or beaten up by a hostile
owd, and left lying unconscious on the ground, unless some
aritable soul took pity on them. They suffered a legal
rsecution that was hardly less violent, many of them being
ed, imprisoned, or whipped, and they provided more
artyrs of this sort than all the other sects of their time put
gether.

In a memorial addressed to Parliament in 1657, it is shown
at between the years 1651 and 1656, no less than 1,900
uakers were sent to prison, and that 21 died in prison. It
as been further estimated that between 1661 and 1697,
3,562 Quakers were imprisoned, and that 338 died in prison
from the effects of ill-treatment, and that 198 were trans-
orted.

The Quakers accepted the full implications of the Sermon
n the Mount, and repudiated war and forcible resistance
evil.

Men who had helped to fight Cromwell's battles bore quietly
the worst brutalities from excited ruffians, and risked death rather
than defend themselves. (*Cromwell and Communism*, Eduard
Bernstein, pp. 233-34.)

urthermore, the Quakers would suffer any penalties rather than
ke an oath, and it was their rule to address every one as "thou",
ecause they considered it tantamount to a lie to address an
dividual as though he represented a plural number; nor
ould they doff their hats to anyone, because equal respect was
ue to all men, high or low, rich or poor.

HE MYSTICS

Up to the proclamation of the Commonwealth in 1649 George
ox had been like the "voice of one crying in the wilderness";
ut after 1650 he made converts in increasing numbers in all
arts of the country.

The aftermath of revolution is usally a period of disappoin
ment and disillusionment on the part of many of those who on
set their hopes upon it, and the English Revolution was n
exception to this rule. Though the Leveller movement had bee
crushed there was widespread discontent with the course
events under Cromwell's dictatorship.

Army agitation, Leveller propaganda, Digger activity, the impact
of events had imparted to the people an acute awareness of their
class interests. After 1649 and 1650 that social consciousness could
no longer be given direct political expression. Instead, it found its
voice in the tremendous revival of mystical enthusiasm and
millenary fervour that dates from those years. If the price of political agitation was persecution and imprisonment, it was much
more convenient to shift the initiative for social change to the
Lord who could risk with impunity the wrath of dictators. And
if the practical efforts of mortals had failed to achieve the
desired results, surely God, in His time, would bring the eagerly
awaited millennium.

Radical activity, then, was channelised into religious fervour ;
and the growth of the Quakers, the Fifth Monarchists, the Ranters
and hundreds of other varieties that defy classification testifies
to its intensity. . . . The Levellers and the Diggers had given to
the common people the vision of a better world ; and that vision
had been sketched in full and attractive detail. They had sought
to persuade their fellows that it was a world that was not set ın a
distant heaven, but that could be achieved immediately on
earth. They had imparted to the people the recognition that the
privileges of the wealthy were fashioned of the blood and sweat
of the poor. And they had constantly emphasized that the people
could expect no relief through the charity or humanitarianism
of their oppressors and that the delay of the social reforms that
had been promised was the result not so much of the political
incapacity of their rulers as of deliberate and conscious purpose.
A profound understanding of those perceptions is present, in one
form or another, in all the mystical sects in the several years after
1650. As the sects moved farther away from their origins, those
social perceptions were modified and finally distorted beyond
recognition by the extreme religious fanaticism and abstract
spiritual symbolism in which they were expressed. That
this class consciousness, however, was a dominant factor in shap-
ing the early development of those mystical movements is, I
believe, indisputable.

The forms in which that consciousness was expressed, let me
repeat, were infinitely varied and fantastic. To the Fifth Monarchists, the millennium, which they interpreted with a rigid
faithfulness to the Scriptural description, would be ushered in
by the Saints, most likely by force, when God would indicate the
propitious moment. The Quakers believed that the new era in
human history would be inaugurated only when all men recog-

nized the Inner Light within them, when the power of love had triumphed in mankind. The Ranters,* the wildest and most eccentric of all sects, were so convinced of the omnipresence and imminent revelation of God that they felt that every impulse, every urge, every sign of activity or motion, was a manifestation of His Being. Two things, however, are of vital significance in all of this seeming confusion—the nature of the millennium all sects envisaged and the dogmatic affirmation that only the poor, the downtrodden, the despised, could be chosen as the Saints, as the first Children of Light, as those in whom God would first manifest himself—in other words, that the poor would be the instruments through which the millennium would be established on earth. (*Left-Wing Democracy in the English Civil War*, pp. 235-6.)

One hears the echoes of the class struggle in the fulminations of the sectaries against the rich and privileged.

" Go ye workers of iniquity into everlasting punishment," Fox threatened the rich. " Howl and weep, misery is coming upon you, enemies of God, adversaries of righteousness. (*Newes Coming Out of the Northe Sounding Towards the South or a Blast Out of the North Up into the South.* 1656).

Iubberthorn thundered against

all who live in pride and idlenesse and fulnesse of bread by whom the creation is devoured and many made poor by your meanes and you (who) live upon the labours of the poor and lay heavie burthens upon them, grievous to be borne. (*The Immediate Call*, 1654.)

And George Foster declared that God had announced to him that He will

come to destroy all things besides myself and will suddenly take from man his goods and pictures of gold and silver and will make them for fear of me give them away, for I come to take vengeance on those that have afflicted the poor. (*The Pouring Forth of the Seventh and Last Vial upon all Flesh and Fleshliness which will be a Terror to the Men that have Great Possessions*—1650.)

QUAKERISM AND COMMUNISM

Some of the disaffected soldiers who obtained their discharge or were dismissed from the Army joined the Quakers, and during the first years of the Commonwealth Fox was overshadowed by men who were better-known than himself, and who led the revolutionary religious opposition to Cromwell. They "marched

---

*The Ranters made the common ownership of all goods one of their cardinal tenets. "They taught (according to one of their former members) that it was quite contrary to the end of the Creation to appropriate anything to any man or woman but that there ought to be community of all things". (*The Ranters Last Sermon*, by J. M. *deluded brother lately escaped out of their snare* (1654).

through the streets of London, denouncing with uplifted voic
Cromwell's Government, and predicting its downfall"; and wher
representatives of the Army (in April 1659) presented a petitior
to Parliament in favour of the "good old cause" of liberty and o
the republic, Quakers supported it by a memorial which added
further demands to the petition. It was not until after the
Restoration that Fox's doctrine of abstention from politics wa
generally adopted by the Quakers.

The writings of Fox and the better-known advocates of early
Quakerism reveal no peculiar social or economic trends; but some
sections, at least, of the sect tried to spread communist ideas
and in 1653 an influx of Fifth Monarchy men

> brought revolutionary ideas into the extremist section of the
> new society. (*The Protestant Churches*, Leslie F. Church, p. 111.)

The Reverend Thomas Hancock in an article entitled "Early
Quaker Politics" (published in the *Weekly Times & Echo*, fo.
Feb. 1896) states that there exist a number of Quaker pamphlet
which "show a distinctly socialistic tone of thinking"; and there
is considerable evidence that Quakers declaimed in their meeting
against private property. At a very early period they sent ou
apostles of the new faith to the Continent and to America; and
Pringsheim relates that in 1657 some Quakers caused grea
excitement in Zeeland and Rotterdam by preaching that al
goods ought to be held in common. He quotes a bourgeois paper
the *Hollandse Mercurius*, of 1657, where the Communist teaching
of the Quakers is ascribed to the fact that they are "mostly
thieves and paupers".

JAMES NAYLOR THE KING OF ISRAEL

Among the Quakers who were prominent in opposition to Cromwell was an ex-quartermaster of the Army, James Naylor. The
son of a well-to-do farmer near Wakefield, he joined the Parliamentary Army in 1642, when he was about twenty-four years of
age. While serving in the Army he went over to the Independents, and gave religious addresses which had the power to
move men strongly. An officer who heard him preach after the
bloody battle of Dunbar wrote that "he had been inspired with
greater fear by Naylor's sermon than he had felt in the battle".

Soon after Dunbar Naylor obtained his discharge on account
of illness, and returned home to his farm. In 1651 he heard
George Fox preach, and speedily embraced his ideas; and in the

 pring of 1652, while following the plough, he suddenly felt
ithin himself the call to become an itinerant missionary of the
ew doctrine. He at once set off on his travels, during the
ourse of which he met Fox in London.

In the autumn of the year Naylor was arrested at Orton, in
Westmorland, for preaching a "blasphemous" sermon, in the
ourse of which he had declared that the body of Christ after the
esurrection was "not carnal but spiritual"; and, refusing to
ecant, he was kept in prison for nearly six months. Whilst he
as in gaol a Quakeress, Margaret Fell, sent him £5 for his
maintenance, but Naylor accepted only the twentieth part of it,
or, like many Quakers, he followed an ascetic life.

Some idea of his teachings at this time may be gathered from
pamphlet which he published the same year (1652). It bears
he title: "*A Lamentacion (By one of England's Prophets) Over the
Ruines of this Oppressed Nacion, To be deeply layd to heart by Parlia-
ent and Army, and all sorts of People, lest they be swept away with the
Broom of Destruction, in the Day of the Lord's fierce wrath and Indigna-
on, which is near at hand. Written by the Movings of the Lord in James
Naylor*".

Naylor's political disillusionment is revealed in the opening
assage:

> Oh England! how is thy expectation failed now after all thy
> travails! The people to whom Oppression and Unrighteousness
> hath been a Burden, have long waited for Deliverance, from one
> year to another, but none comes, from one sort of men to another
> . . . For as power hath come into the hands of men, it hath been
> turned into violence, and the will of men is brought forth instead of
> Equity . . . He that turns from iniquity is made a prey to the wicked
> and none lays it to heart through the nation, for all hearts are full
> of oppression, and all hands are full of violence, their houses
> are filled with oppression, their streets and markets abound with it,
> their Courts which should afford remedy against it are wholly
> made up of iniquity and injustice. . . . Oh! Foolish People . . .
> are not these the choicest of thy Worthies, who are now in power?
> Hath it not been the top of thy desires and labors to see it in their
> hands, and are not they now become weak as other men, and the
> Land still in travail but nothing brought forth but wind?

He declares that no reliance can be placed in men, nor is anything
o be hoped for from a change of government: improvement can
ome only from the cultivation of the right spirit.

Upon his release from prison Naylor resumed his mission,
nd early in the year 1655 he came to London, where a fairly
rong Quaker community existed. His fervent preaching soon

K

made him a popular speaker, and he became famous even outsi
Quaker circles. He came into contact with prominent opponer
of Cromwell such as Bradshaw and Sir Henry Vane, and eve
members of Cromwell's "Court" attended his meetings. Som
thing like a Naylor cult grew up, "especially among the fema
members of the Quaker community". (*Cromwell and Communis*
p. 239, Eduard Bernstein). At first Naylor resisted this adulato
tendency; but in the end it seems to have been too much for hi

In the summer of 1656 he set out for Launceston to visit F
in prison in order that they might discuss the differences whi
had arisen in London, and which probably had reference
the attitude to be adopted towards contemporary politi
Several of his admirers accompanied him, and "his journ
tended to assume a Messianic aspect". (*Cromwell and Communis*
Eduard Bernstein, p. 239).

> The Quaker gospel, with its mystical idea of the inner light, did
> not preclude this. The inner light, the divine illumination, varied
> in the strength of its manifestations. Why should not James Naylor
> with his enthralling eloquence be called to perform a special
> work ? Why should not the Spirit manifest itself in him with the
> same power as in the Son of Mary ? (*Cromwell and Communism,*
> Eduard Bernstein, p. 239).

In the west of England, in the centres of the cloth industr
Quakerism had made rapid strides, and as early as 1654, it
reported that Quaker meetings in Bristol were always attend
by from three to four thousand people. In a town of little ov
30,000 they had, in 1658, over 700 members, most of whom we
mechanics, though they also had many adherents among t
soldiers of the garrison.

When Naylor passed through Bristol on his way to Launcest
demonstrations took place, and even some disturbances, and
his arrival in Exeter he was arrested as an agitator and a d
turber of the peace. This, however, only increased his populari
and more and more his admirers tended to treat him as a Messia
This was particularly true of the women. He was referred to
the "only son of God", and one, Stranger, wrote: "Thy nar
shall no longer be James but Jesus." Another Quaker, Thom
Simmonds, called him "Thou Lamb of God". His devote
visited him in prison, where the women (we are told) fell dov
before him and kissed his feet: and a certain Dorcas Ebury ev
went to the length of proclaiming that Naylor had brought k
back to life after she had been dead for two days.

Towards the end of October, Naylor was released from prison,
and began his return journey, mounted on horseback, and accompanied by followers on foot and on horse. At Glastonbury and
Wells people spread their garments on the road before him; and
when he reached Bristol his entry into that city became an
imitation of Jesus's entry into Jerusalem, with Naylor's companions singing such hymns as "Hosannah in the Highest", and
"Holy, Holy, Holy".

The rain poured down in torrents as the strange cavalcade
entered Bristol, and the roads were like quagmires. The weather
may have dampened the ardour of Naylor's supporters: at any
rate, though considerable crowds assembled to meet him, he was
arrested without any trouble. Nevertheless, the local authorities
were loath to bring him to trial in Bristol, and after a first hearing,
he and six of his companions were sent to London on November
10th.

After a Committee of 55 members of Parliament had made an
inquiry into his case, Naylor was tried at the bar of the House;
and though he declared that the homage done to him was not
meant to apply to his mortal self but to God speaking through him,
he was found guilty on December 8th of "abominable blasphemy".
For seven days the House of Commons debated whether sentence
of death should be imposed upon him; and finally, on December
16th, it was decided by 96 votes to 82 that Naylor should stand
in the pillory for two hours, then be whipped through the streets
of London by the hangman, after which he was to be pilloried
again, his tongue perforated with a hot iron and the letter B
(for blasphemer) to be branded on his forehead. Thereafter he
was to be taken to Bristol and conducted through the city seated
backwards on a horse, and whipped again. This savage punishment having been inflicted upon him, he was to be kept in solitary
confinement during the pleasure of Parliament.

Naylor endured this ferocious punishment with stoicism;
but the first whipping was so severe the execution of the rest
of the sentence had to be postponed. Meanwhile petitions in his
favour poured in upon Parliament, some from people of considerable influence such as Colonel Scrope. Cromwell himself was
prompted to ask Parliament the grounds for their verdict, and his
question led to another debate in the House. This debate was
still in progress when a further part of the sentence was inflicted
upon Naylor, his tongue being perforated and the letter B
branded on his forehead. Whilst this mutilation was taking place

his followers stood around the scaffold in great numbers, an
one of them, Robert Rich, a merchant, tried to hold a placar
over his head bearing the words *This is the King of the Jews*
It was, however, torn up by the hangman's assistants. Afte
the branding was complete his adherents kissed his hands an
feet; and later, during his shameful ride through Bristol, Rober
Rich and other Quakers rode in front of him singing hymns

At this distance of time it is not easy to guess what was in th
minds of Naylor's supporters. Certainly religious ecstasy and
chiliastic dreams played a big part in producing the extra
ordinary demonstrations just described: but it was probably mor
than religious frenzy which made the movement so dangerou
that the House of Commons was prepared to spend weeks dis
cussing it. The general discontent and disillusionment of th
times was sharpened by the growing despotism of Cromwell
who had just appointed his Major-Generals to administer th
country. Possibly the demonstrations in Bristol when Naylo
made his spectacular entry, were to be the prelude to a revolt
Certainly it is improbable that Parliament would have spen
months investigating the affair unless they had supposed tha
some movement hostile to the existing regime was being fostere
under the cover of religion; and in this connection it is significan
that Naylor was expressly deprived of pen and paper during hi
imprisonment.

Some historians have dismissed Naylor as a madman, bu
his writings and letters show no trace of mental derangement
and even after his discharge from solitary confinement (which
was hardly calculated to cure mental disorder) he remained a
powerful and logical debater.

Naylor was released from prison in 1659, and died the following
year; but though the extreme wing of Quakerism thus lost
its most powerful representative, it continued to exist for a
considerable time after his death, and this despite the fact that
the government took stern measures to suppress the sect, as is
evidenced by the fact that from 1656 to 1658 3,000 Quakers were
imprisoned. It was not until after the Restoration that Quakerism
became non-political.

Moreover, in spite of continued persecution under Charles II
the Quakers continued to increase, and at the time of the Great
Plague (1665) it is said that in London alone there were 10,000
of them, "chiefly recruited from the lower classes", and their
numbers mounted steadily until about the year 1680.

But from the moment when they enjoyed official recognition as a
religious community, their numbers began to fall. . . . Among
all the more important religious communities of the epoch of the
Revolution, none has so bravely borne persecutions as the
Quakers. While Baptists and Independents temporised, the
Quakers practised passive resistance in such a manner as to have,
we may well say, tired and worn out their persecutors. But to none
of those Churches of the Revolution has the toleration obtained,
and the equality of rights subsequently gained, proved so fatal
as to the Quakers. (*Cromwell and Communism*, p. 245).

HN BELLERS

A more sober attempt at social reform is associated with the
ime of another Quaker, John Bellers (1654-1725), "a phenomen-
figure in the history of political economy", as Marx calls him.
apital, Vol. I, Everyman edition, p. 257).

Bellers was born of well-to-do Quaker parents, and numbered
nong his friends William Penn, the founder of Pennsylvania.
1695 he wrote an essay entitled "*Proposals for Raising a Colledge
Industry of all usefull Trades and Husbandry with Profit for the Rich,
plentiful living for the Poor and a good education for Youth, which will
advantage to the government by the Increase of the People and
eir riches. Motto: Industry brings Plenty.—The Sluggard shall
cloathed with Raggs. He that will not work shall not eat*".

Bellers dedicated the first edition of this work to his co-religion-
s, the "Children of Light named in scorn Quakers", declaring
at

The consideration of your great Industry . . . Hath induced me to
Dedicate these following Proposals to your serious Consideration,
whilst I think you a very regular Body, willing and capable
of such an Undertaking.

iefly, what Bellers proposed, was a communal colony or
sociation, wherein labour and not money was to be the standard
which necessaries would be valued. By labour he plainly
eans labour-time. As early as 1662 Sir William Petty had
cribed the value of commodities to the labour embodied in
em; but Bellers was the first to suggest putting this idea into
actice, and thus he

anticipated Robert Owen and John Gray who in the years from
1820-1850 advocated labour-time notes as a means of exchange
instead of money tokens. (*A History of British Socialism*, M. Beer,
p. 174).

here was nothing vague or visionary about Bellers' scheme;
was thoroughly sober and worked out in practical detail.

He estimated that for a colony of 300 persons, combining manu facture and agriculture, a capital of £15,000 would be require and he proposed to raise this sum by loans from interested peop —mainly from Quakers in the first instance. Every contributic of £50 was to entitle the patron to one vote on the Administrativ Council; but no one was to have more than five votes no matte how much he invested. The profit was to be credited each yea to the shareholders according to their investments, and migl be drawn out or added to the principal; but no kind of stoc jobbing was to be allowed with the shares, because this "w ruin any good thing". Moreover, no surplus was to be distribute in the shape of profits until all the material and cultural needs of th workers in the College had been amply provided for in ever respect.

Bellers realized that a considerable sum of money would needed to start the College, and he argued that "a thousan Pound is easier raised where there is Profit, than one hundre Pound only upon Charity". He also remarked, with a kind innocent slyness, that "the Rich have no other way of living b by the Labour of others; as the Landlord by the Labour of h Tenants, and the Merchants and Tradesmen by the Labour the Mechanicks", and used that as a justification for payir interest on the money raised for his project.

Bellers explained that he preferred to call his colony a Colle rather than a Workhouse, which savours too much of th "Bridewell"; and also because all kinds of useful instructio would be imparted to the members. Working conditions wer to be as good as those enjoyed by the best situated apprentic in London, and the normal working day was to be observec except that as the workers

> grow in years in the college, they may be allowed to abate an Hour in a Day of their Work, and when they come to Sixty years old (if Merit prefer them not sooner) they may be made Overseers; which for ease and pleasant life, will equal what the Hoards of a private purse can give.

Managers and overseers or officials were to be paid (lik the workers) in kind and not in cash; and all meals were to b taken together.

Although he described a community of 300 persons in ord to illustrate how his scheme would work, Bellers pointed out tha the college might be considerably larger, and might number 3,00 members, especially in districts where staple manufactures wer carried on. Even seafaring men might be members of it: in short, it should be "an epitome of the world".

He argued very cogently that such a community would effect a big saving by dispensing with shops, and cutting out middlemen and other useless trades, and by savings on lawyers' fees and bad debts. Moreover, there would be a further saving in communal cooking and heating, and in the cost of provisions bought in bulk, and many women would be set free from domestic duties to become productive workers. Nor would there be wastage of labour power due to unemployment. Finally, (and here again he anticipates Marx, cp. *Capital*, Vol. I, Chapter 25), the College would benefit by the proper combination of industry and agriculture: the fields would be better cultivated, more cattle would be kept, and more manure would be available for the fields.

Bellers set a high value on labour which is

as proper for the body's health as eating is for its living; for what gains a man saves by Ease, he will find in Disease. . . . Labour adds Oyl to the Lamp of Life when thinking Inflames it.

At the same time, however, he attached great importance to education; and here again there is something astonishingly modern about his views. Thus, in his model community, children were to learn by practice and experience rather than by rote, and work and learning were to go hand in hand, "an Idle learning being little better than the learning of Idleness".

Bellers recognised that he had to begin the practice of his ideas with the young. "Old people", he says in the Introduction to his *Proposals*,

are like earthen vessels, not so easily to be new moulded, yet children are more like clay out of the Pit, and easy to take any form they are put into.

Hence if the poor should perchance at first "prove brittle", the patrons who had found the money for the College should not lose patience. "Seven or fourteen years may bring up young ones that Life will be more natural to". And so he proposed to make a start with some trustworthy workers who would set a good example to others: the rest, at first, would consist largely of apprentices.

Bellers made his proposals sound very practical: there was nothing of the dreamy spinner of impossible utopias about him. Nevertheless, it does not appear that he got the support which he had hoped to get from the "Children of Light." Possibly this was due less to lack of sympathy than to lack of means. However, whatever the explanation, the second edition of his pamphlet, issued in 1696, was not dedicated to the Quakers, but to the Lords and Commons of Parliament and to the thoughtful and those concerned for the public weal. Parliament is requested to examine his proposals and to carry them out for the benefit of the nation: the "thoughtful" are requested to deposit subscriptions and contributions for the projected enterprise with two London citizens mentioned by name, one a merchant, the other a lawyer.

A year later (1697) at the conclusion of another pamphlet issued by Bellers, *An Epistle to Friends Concerning the Education of Children*, there is an appeal to the Friends signed by about 45 Quakers, in favour of giving the College of Industry a trial.

ROBERT OWEN AND BELLERS

John Bellers' College of Industry inevitably provokes comparison with Robert Owen's Villages of Unity and Co-operation: but although the two proposals have many features in common, Owen appears to have developed his idea quite independently of Bellers. He records in his autobiography that a copy of the second edition of the *Proposals* was accidentally found, about 1817, by Francis Place when the latter was sorting out some useless books from his library. Place wrote to Owen saying: "I have made a great discovery—of a work advocating your social views a century and a half ago".

Owen told Place he would have a thousand copies printed for distribution, and would acknowledge that the author deserved the credit of being the parent of the idea of co-operative communities,

> although mine had been forced upon me by the practice of observing facts, reflecting upon them, and trying how far they were useful for the every-day business of life.

Owen kept his word, and thus Bellers' pamphlet was rescued from the obscurity in which it had been buried for more than a hundred years.

CHAPTER 11

CHRISTIANITY AND THE INDUSTRIAL REVOLUTION

> A stranger would think our churches were built, as
> indeed they are, only for the rich. Under such an
> arrangement where are the lower classes to . . . learn
> the doctrines of that truly excellent religion which
> exhorts to content and to submission to the higher
> powers ?
> *An Inquiry into the State of Mind amongst the Lower Classes.*
> Arthur Young (1798).

> What the millions should generally know is this: that
> no rich man believes in religion of any sort except as
> a political engine to keep the useful classes in subjection
> to the rich.
> Bronterre O'Brien, in the *Poor Man's Guardian*,
> December 12, 1835.

RELIGION AND SOCIAL UNREST

In no age perhaps was the use of Christianity as an antidote to
social unrest more blatant than during the Industrial Revolution
which began in this country in the second half of the 18th century.
No slave or servile class was ever more brutally exploited than
the industrial proletariat whom this "Revolution" called into
being. Men and women worked for sixteen or seventeen hours
a day, and children of five were employed underground in the
mines as trappers, where they might sit in darkness for twelve
hours at a stretch, unless a good-natured collier gave them a bit
of candle. "Sometimes I sing when I've light, but not in the dark:
I dare not sing then", one of these pitiful little victims told the
Children's Employment Commission which issued its Report in
1842. Parish authorities got rid of little pauper children by selling
them to millowners who (in at least one authenticated case) agreed
to take one idiot child with every twenty normal children. It was
an age which saw the creation of vast, sprawling slum cities,
which, in the memorable phrase of J. L. and Barbara Hammond,
"were not so much towns as barracks: not the refuge of a civilization but the barracks of an industry". (*The Town Labourer,
1760-1832.*)

Some measure of the savage exploitation of the working class is to be found in the fact that, in the course of four years, Robert Owen showed a profit of £160,000 on the New Lanark Mills, besides paying 5 per cent. on the capital employed, and raising the selling value of the factory 50 per cent. And Owen, be it remembered, was a model employer, for whom his business contemporaries predicted speedy bankruptcy when he reduced the hours of labour from seventeen to ten a day, and refused to employ children under ten years of age. Never were such profits wrung from the blood and sweat and tears of the common people: never was there such misery and degradation for the workers.

They were a helot class, denied all political power, for an oligarchy of landed gentry had a monopoly of Parliamentary and Local Government, until the Reform Act of 1832 was wrung from them under threat of a violent revolution. The workers played an important part in the agitation for political reform; but they were tricked by their middle class allies when the Reform Bill was won; and it was not until 1867 that the town worker got the vote, and not until 1884 that the village labourer was enfranchized.

Meanwhile the Combination Acts forbade the formation of trade unions; and even with their repeal, in 1825, ways and means could often be found to make trade union organisation impossible. There is the famous case of the Six Dorset Labourers (the Tolpuddle Martyrs) who, in 1834, were transported for seven years for combining to raise their wages (which were 7/- a week).

The ruling class were constantly haunted by a dread that these wretched slaves might revolt; and the modern mind is a little startled at times by the astonishing candour with which religion was urged as an opiate for social unrest.

One philanthropic organisation, passably progressive as the nineteenth century goes, had the honest candour to claim a deep interest in the morals of the poor on the grounds that 'as in every country they are numerous and a threat to our personal security, we are obliged on innumerable occasions to trust them with our property and, what is more, the minds of our children may be influenced by the good or bad qualities of the servants in whose care they spend so much of their time. The higher ranks are thus deeply interested in providing a moral and religious education for the whole of the poor. As these are enabled to rise in the scale of civilization they will feel more repugnance to the degradation of parish relief and the enormous sums extracted from the industrious part of the community will be saved.'

(Quoted from *Adult Education Committee Final Report*, 1900, by Ernest Green, M.A., J.P., in *Education for a New Society*, p. 5.)

Arthur Young even went to the length of suggesting the building of a great number of churches in the form of theatres, with benches and thick mats for the poor, and galleries and boxes for the well-to-do, so that the "lower classes" might be given a chance to learn "the doctrines of that truly excellent religion which exhorts to content and to submission to the higher powers". (*An Inquiry into the State of Mind amongst the Lower Classes*, 1798).

> Twenty years later, one Englishman out of seven being at that time a pauper, Parliament voted a million of public money for the construction of churches to preach submission to the higher powers.   (*The Town Labourer, 1760-1832*, J. L. & Barbara Hammond, p. 235.)

Even as late as 1843, on the eve of the collapse of the Chartist movement, the Earl of Shaftesbury moved in the House

> the need for instant and serious consideration of the best means of promoting the blessings of a moral and religious education among the working classes. (*Education for a New Society*, Ernest Green, M.A., J.P., pp. 14-15.)

Hannah More ("that prime old primate in petticoats", as Cobbett calls her), exemplifies the philanthropic mind of the period. With her sister Martha she undertook the moral reclamation of the poverty-scourged workers in the Mendip villages. They started Sunday-schools and Women's Benefit Clubs in several villages.

> These they managed despotically, and they used to pay periodical visits to see that their teachers and pupils had not lapsed from virtue and Bible reading, and to address the villages in a series of charges. (*The Town Labourer, 1760-1832*, J. L. & Barbara Hammond, p. 226.)

> The condition of these villages was such that one of them was popularly known as Botany Bay or Little Hell. In one place Hannah More mentions that the wages are a shilling a day; in another two hundred people are crammed into nineteen hovels. . . . The sisters More were benevolent women who put themselves to great trouble and discomfort out of pity for these villages, and yet from the beginning to the end of the *Mendip Annals* (in which they describe their " Charitable Labours ") there is not a single reflection on the persons or system responsible for these conditions. It never seems to have crossed the minds of these philanthropists that it was desirable that men and women should have decent wages, or decent homes, or that there was something wrong with the arrangements of a society that left the mass of people in this plight. (*The Town Labourer*, pp. 226-227).

Their prudish comment upon the 200 glassworkers who were huddled in the nineteen hovels is: "Both sexes and all ages

herding together: voluptuous beyond belief"; and they are
shocked that "the work of a glasshouse is an irregular thing . . .
not only infringing upon a man's rest, but constantly intruding
upon the privileges of the Sabbath". They seem equally shocked
that "the wages are high, the eating and drinking luxurious—the
body scarcely covered, but fed with dainties of a shameful
description".

> Thus the guilty in this scheme of civilization are not the persons
> who neglect to provide the decencies of life and housing and
> education for the men and women by whose labour they become
> rich, but the voluptuous glassworkers who feed their bodies on
> shameful dainties. . . . The employers and gentry are sometimes
> blamed, it is true, in these pages, but they are only blamed for
> their want of sympathy with the efforts of the More sisters to
> teach religion. They are nowhere blamed for ill-treating their
> dependents, or told that they have any duties to them except
> the duty of encouraging them to listen to Hannah More on the
> importance of obedience, and on the claims to their regard and
> gratitude of a Providence that had lavished such attention upon
> them. (*The Town Labourer*, p. 227.)

There was an occasion when a Blagdon woman was condemned
to death for attempting to begin a riot and stealing some butter
from a man who demanded an unreasonable price for it. As the
Hammonds caustically remark:

> It would seem to most people that much as the village might need
> a Sunday-school, the judges who were responsible for this piece of
> barbarity needed one a great deal more, but the philanthropic
> sisters, both of whom refer to the case, have no complaint to make
> of the sentence. The More sisters took the parish in hand, with
> the gratifying result that they were able to report a few months
> later that many of the pupils 'understood tolerably well the
> first twenty chapters of Genesis.' (*The Town Labourer*, p. 228.)

On another occasion, during a famine, when wheat was at
134 shillings a quarter and labourers were living on a shilling
a day, Hannah More offers the wretched victims of slow starvation
the consolation that

> in suffering by the scarcity you have but shared in the common
> lot, with the pleasure of knowing the advantage you have had
> over many villages in your having suffered no scarcity of religious
> instruction.

And again, addressing the women of Shipham in 1801 on the
same topic:

> Let me remind you that probably that very scarcity had been
> permitted by an all-wise and gracious Providence to unite all
> ranks of people together, to show the poor how immediately they
> are dependent upon the rich, and to show both rich and poor that

they are all dependent on Himself. It has also enabled you to
see more clearly the advantages you derive from the government
and constitution of this country—to observe the benefits flowing
from the distinction of rank and fortune, which has enabled the
high so liberally to assist the low : for I leave you to judge what
would have been the state of the poor of this country in this long
distressing scarcity had it not been for your superiors. . . . We
trust the poor in general, especially those that are well instructed,
have received what has been done for them as a matter of favour,
not of right—if so, the same kindness will, I doubt not, always
be extended to them whenever it shall please God so to afflict
the land.

Wilberforce played a big part in winning personal freedom
for black slaves, but his writings and speeches show
that the tendency to regard Christianity in politics as only one of
the sanctions of the existing order was no accident, but an essential
part of its spirit. He was . . . largely responsible for the degradation
of industrial life due to the savage measures taken by the upper
classes to prevent working men from protecting their standard of
living by defensive organisation. If any one event can be singled
out as having led more than any other to that degradation, it is
the enactment of the Combination Laws of 1799 and 1800 in
which Wilberforce took a leading part. It is particularly interesting,
therefore, to turn to the pages of his *Practical View of the System of
Christianity*, a work that attained an immense popularity, in which
he has something to say on the relation of religion to the economic
circumstances of society. There he explains that Christianity makes
the inequalities of the social scale less galling to the lower orders,
that it teaches them to be diligent, humble, patient, that it re-
minds them "that their more lowly path has been allotted to them
by the hand of God; that it is their part faithfully to discharge
its duties, and contentedly to bear its inconveniences ; that the
present state of things is very short; that the objects about which
worldly men conflict so eagerly are not worth the contest; that the
peace of mind, which Religion offers indiscriminately to all ranks,
affords more true satisfaction than all the expensive pleasures
which are beyond the poor man's reach; that in this view the poor
have the advantage; that, if their superiors enjoy more abundant
comforts, they are also exposed to many temptations from which
the inferior classes are happily exempted; that, ' having food and
raiment, they should be therewith content,' since their situation
in life, with all its evils, is better than they have deserved at the
hand of God; finally, that all human distinctions will soon be
done away, and the true followers of Christ will all, as children of
the same Father, be alike admitted to the possession of the same
heavenly inheritance." (*The Town Labourer*, pp. 231-232.)

Palay, in his *Reasons for Contentment addressed to the Labouring
Part of the British Public* (1793), made a similar claim for religion
that it "smooths all inequalities because it unfolds a prospect

which makes all earthly distinctions nothing". Indeed, he even seems to have persuaded himself that there was scarcely any respect in which the poor were not more fortunate than the rich. "Some of the necessities which poverty ... imposes" he says, "are not hardships but pleasures. Frugality itself is a pleasure".

> A yet more serious advantage (he says) which persons in inferior stations possess, is the ease with which they provide for their children. All the provision which a poor man's child requires is contained in two words, ' industry and innocence.' With these qualities, though without a shilling to set him forwards, he goes into the world prepared to become a useful, virtuous, and happy man.

This theme, that the poor are just as well off as the rich in Christian England under the British Constitution, was developed with even greater gusto by Hannah More in a series of political tracts that had an immense vogue.

> She published a great number of dialogues and jingles to illustrate the theme that the most modest attempt to reform or relax the ferocious laws that held society together would inflict great suffering upon the poor. (*The Town Labourer*, p. 234.)

But if it was the policy of the Church of England to "indulge the rich and keep down the poor", this was not true of the Evangelicals, whose "greatest ornament was Lord Shaftesbury, famous for his leadership of the Ten Hours Movement". Mr. S. Maccoby remarks very truly in his *English Radicalism, 1832-1852* that "it was a peculiarity of the Ten Hour Movement, that though manned by plebeian Radicals . . . it was led by religious philanthropists from the opposite political camp." (*English Radicalism 1832-1852*, S. Maccoby, Ph.D., p. 34).

Lord Ashley (as he was then) was no democrat, but a Tory. In his opinion Socialism and Chartism were "the two great demons in morals and politics", and he confessed that "from the first hour of my movement to the last I had ever before me and never lost sight of it, the issue of a restoration of a good understanding between employer and employed". In 1833, when he undertook the leadership of the Ten Hours Bill movement, he made it clear to the workers

> that all should be carried on in a most conciliatory manner, that there should be a careful abstinence from all approach to questions of wages and capital; that the labours of children and young persons should alone be touched; that there should be no strikes, no intimidation and no strong language against their employers either within or without the walls of Parliament. (*Life and Work of the Seventh Earl of Shaftesbury*, Edwin Hodder, pp. 155-156.)

It would be grossly unfair to him to suggest that he was a conscious humbug who advocated social reform to avoid social revolution; nevertheless, he records in his diary that

> I may rejoice and heartily thank God that the operatives of Lancashire and Yorkshire, suffering as they are, remain perfectly tranquil. Such, under God, is the fruit of many years of sympathy and generous legislation.

Rothstein may be exaggerating when he suggests that in 1848 the factory movement "may be said to have saved the country from a revolution which seemed likely to break out at any moment" (*From Chartism to Labourism*, Th. Rothstein, p. 78); but the movement which Lord Ashley led certainly offered vent for the angry temper of the working class of that period, and gave them enough hope to continue to struggle for an improvement in their lot by peaceful and constitutional methods; moreover, the Ten Hours Act of 1847 (and, for that matter, the repeal of the Corn Laws and the easing of the infamous Poor Law) "were secured under the pressure of torchlight meetings, the riots, insurrectionary plots and strikes of Chartism". (*The Common People 1746-1938*, G. D. H. Cole and Raymond Postgate, p. 309). Without the explosive pressure of mass working class discontent it is doubtful whether Ashley's philanthropic concern for the workers would have extorted any serious concessions from the ruling class.

THE METHODISTS

Methodism played an even more important part in the new industrial civilization than the philanthropic activities of the Church of England. On a population

> partly neglected, partly dragooned by the Church, there descended a religion that happened to supply almost everything that it wanted. The Church offered no function to the poor man: his place was on a rude bench or a mat, listening to sermons on the importance of the subordination of the lower classes to the grand family worshipping amid the spacious cushions of the squire's pew. The Chapel invited him to take a hand in the management of the affairs of his religious society: perhaps to help in choosing a minister, to feel that he had a share in its life, responsibility for its risks and undertakings, pride in its successes and reputation. As a mere exercise in self-government and social life, the Chapel occupied a central place in the affections and the thoughts of people who had very little to do with the government of anything else. . . . The men and women who were drawn into the brisk, alert, and

ardent life of the new religion found plenty to occupy their minds and to stimulate faculties and interests that were otherwise left neglected. (*The Town Labourer*, J. L. & Barbara Hammond, pp. 270-271.)

No wonder, then, that

it was in the new industrial districts that the Evangelical revival had the most rapid and lasting influence in building up a religious life outside the Established Church. (*The Town Labourer*, J. L. & Barbara Hammond, p. 268).

In Yorkshire one person out of 23 was a Methodist, in Lancashire one out of 51, whereas in Surrey the proportion was one in 249 and in Sussex one in 211. (Table published in the *Annual Register* for 1824). The millions of pounds of public money voted by Parliament for the building of churches in 1818 (see p. 155) were justified on the grounds that it was unwise to leave the new industrial districts to the Methodists.

Methodism brought colour and excitement to a people living drab, dull lives.

The old Jewish civilization became actual and vivid to men and women who listened to the rhetoric of the new type of preacher. The Sunday-schools, that spread rapidly over the north of England and the industrial districts, were primarily institutions for interpreting this civilization to children brought up in the factories and mines. . . . A Revival fed the imagination of the new population on the exciting history of a fierce and warlike race living under conditions very unlike those of Manchester or Leeds, leaving a literature rich in metaphor and image, which awakened amid the bare and colourless life of the new civilization dreams and reveries and visions full of awe and splendour. It is significant that this religion spread most quickly, and in its extreme form, among the workers living in the deepest gloom, for the miners were particularly given to Methodism. Perhaps the very dangers of their employment prompted them to seek this special and miraculous sense of protection, just as the belief in the miraculous salvation of religion is particularly strong among the deep-sea fishermen of Brittany. This religion did for the working class what Greek and Roman literature did for the ruling class: drawing aside the curtain from a remote and interesting world, seeming thus to make their own world more intelligible. . . . For the miner or weaver the Chapel with its summons to the emotions, its music and singing, took the place that theatres, picture galleries, operas, occupied in the lives of others. (*The Town Labourer*, pp. 272-3.)

Many magistrates wrote to the Home Office complaining that Methodism helped to make the working class discontented and strengthened the forces of working class organisation.

Other magistrates, particularly parsons, thought the Government ought to watch them. Indeed,

> the term Methodist served as well as the very different term Jacobin for a description of the disreputable. . . . Those who read more closely will observe that whenever any particular person is mentioned as seditious, he generally turns out to be a Baptist or Presbyterian. The Dissenters had always been more or less radical, and a parson magistrate had a quick sense for sedition in those quarters. (*The Town Labourer*, pp. 277-78).

In fact, however,

> the official attitude of the Methodist leaders seems to have been quite clearly conservative in the years of crisis, 1817 and 1819. (*The Town Labourer*, pp. 279-280.)

An example of their moderation and anxiety not to run foul of the civil authorities is to be found in an Address adopted at a Conference of Methodist Ministers at Bristol, and sent to the Home Office in August 1819 by one of the secretaries of the Wesleyan Missionary Society. The text is as follows:

> We deeply sympathise with those of you, dear Brethren, who, from the pressure of the times, and the suspension of an active commerce, are, in common with thousands of your countrymen, involved in various and deep afflictions. We offer up our prayers to God for you in this dark season of your distress, " that you may not be tempted above what you are able to bear "; and that he who " comforteth the distressed ", may comfort you. " Cast all your care on God, for he careth for you": and fail not to remember, and to comfort one another with these words, "that in heaven, you have a better and enduring substance". In the present changeful scene of things, one event happeneth to the righteous and the wicked; but you are nevertheless still under the care and the eye of your Father in heaven. Such afflictive events he will sanctify to those who trust in him:—his promises cannot fail because he changeth not. "*He knoweth the way you take, and when he hath tried you, he will bring you forth as gold*". Never fail, dear brethren, to commit your cause to him, who has a thousand ways to "deliver the godly out of temptation", or to render their temptations the over-ruled instruments of putting them in possession of a good which shall remain their portion and their joy, when their spirits shall be for ever beyond the reach of the joys or sorrows of this present state. "*In patience possess ye your souls*". And remember him who hath said, "*I will never leave you, nor forsake you*".
>
> As many of you to whom this measure of national suffering has been appointed reside in places where attempts are making by "unreasonable and wicked men", to render the privations of the poor the instruments of their own designs against the peace and the government of our beloved country, we are affectionately anxious to guard all of you against being led astray from your

L

civil and religious duties by their dangerous artifices. Remember you are Christians, and are called by your profession to exemplify the power and influence of religion by your patience in suffering, and by *"living peaceably with all men"*. Remember that you belong to a Religious Society which has, from the beginning, explicitly recognised as high and essential parts of Christian duty, to *"Fear God and honour the King; to submit to magistrates for conscience' sake, and not to speak evil of dignities"*. You are surrounded with persons to whom these duties are the objects of contempt and ridicule: show your regard for them because they are the doctrines of your Saviour. Abhor those publications in which they are assailed, along with every other doctrine of your holy religion; and judge of the spirit and objects of those who would deceive you into political parties and associations, by the vices of their lives, and the infidel malignity of their words and writings. *"Who can bring a clean thing out of an unclean?"* (Quoted in *The Town Labourer,* pp. 280-1.)

The official attitude of the Methodists is well exemplified in this manifesto: namely, that the meek and righteous would be compensated for their sufferings in this world in an after-life, and that to attempt to change existing inequalities was "infidel and irreligious". No wonder that Cobbett called them in his forthright way the "nasty, canting, lousy Methodists". In the *Political Register* for June 12th, 1813, he says "There are, I know, persons, who look upon the Methodists . . . as *friends of freedom.* It is impossible they should be. They are either fools or tricksters". A few years later (in 1824) he called them "the bitterest foes of freedom in England", and accused them of having "served as spies and blood-money men" amongst the people of the north.

Cobbett may have been over harsh; nevertheless, it is true to say, that on the whole Methodism was unfavourable to the growth of the Trade Union movement or a spirit of revolt among the workers. The Hammonds in their acute and intensely interesting study of the effects of Methodism on the new industrial working class, very truly remark that

> The Methodist movement was a call not for citizens, but for saints: not for the vigorous, still less the violent redress of injustice, but for the ecstatic vision: the perfect peace of expectation. The brutal inequalities of life, the wrongs inflicted on man by man, the hardships of poverty and suffering, these vexations of a passing world were merely trials of faith for the true Christian, who could escape from them and sustain his soul with dreams of a noble and confidential companionship in this world and of radiant happiness hereafter. The reforms that he wanted had nothing to do with Parliament or Corn Laws or Combination Laws. (*The Town Labourer,* p. 282.)

nd again:

In so far as this religion touched on the affairs of this world, it tended to reflect the conservative spirit of its first missionary. The spirit of its teaching was just the opposite to the spirit of the Trade Union movement of the time. It taught patience where the Trade Unions taught impatience. The Trade Union movement taught that men and women should use their powers to destroy the supremacy of wealth in a world made by men; the Methodist that they should learn resignation amid the painful chaos of a world so made, for good reasons of His own, by God. The trade unionist taught that men were not so helpless as they seemed, for combination could give them some control over the conditions of their lives. The Methodist taught that men were not so helpless as they seemed, for religion could make them independent of the conditions of their lives. Further, the Trade Union movement made loyalty to a class a virtue, teaching men and women to think of themselves as the citizens of a community struggling to be free. The Methodist movement had just the opposite effect. It preached an intense spiritual individualism. It taught men and women to think of themselves, not as members of a society with common interests, common hopes, common wrongs, but as individual and separate souls, certain to suffer eternal damnation unless they could attain by a sudden spring of the heart a victorious sense of pardon and escape from sin. . . . The Methodist move-ment . . . softened the sense of class and it soothed the grievances of the poor, for it created new affinities and sympathies, and brought reconciling dreams into their lives of hardship. It set up a rival to the ideal of civic freedom. It diverted energy from the class struggle at a time when wise energy was scarce, and money when money was still scarcer. (*The Town Labourer*, pp. 283-285.)

The same point of view is expressed by G. D. H. Cole in *A Century of Co-operation*, when he points out that the new type of employer

and his workpeople attended the same places of worship, and after the church had driven them forth against Wesley's will came to be united in their hostility to the claims of the Establishment". This "served to mitigate for many the class antagonisms which were inherent in the economic confrontation of the two classes of millowner and factory hand. The workmen who could not stomach this community were driven forth from the main dissenting connexions as well as from Mother Church. They found refuge in little chapels of their own under preachers who had also been driven forth, or they were impelled into complete revolt. But a complete severance from religion was tolerable to but few except in the biggest towns. It meant too much isolation, and too much deprivation of consolations which were sorely needed. Any religion that held men in communion with their fellows seemed to be better than none; and only the few who could make a religion of Chartism—which had its own churches—or Co-operation—which had its "rational religion" and its Social Halls—could bear to break wholly away from the more theological brands of worship. The times were terrible for the poor—terrible for their drabness as well as for the physical privations which they required. Religion administered some comfort, and consequently the chapels were well filled. This was one great factor in breaking the spirit of working-class revolt and impelling the leaders of the workers into more sober courses of economic and political thought. Politically it led them towards union with the Liberal manufacturers who were the mainstay of the dissenting congregations. Economically it led them from revolutionary Trade Unionism and Chartism to the 'New Model' Trade Unionism of the 'fifties' and to the new forms of Co-operation which were developed under the inspiration of the Rochdale Pioneers." (*A Century of Co-operation*, G. D. H. Cole, pp. 55-56.)

Yet, in spite of itself, Methodism helped the working class struggle of the period.

Methodism was in a very real sense a school, and when men and women go to school they may learn more lessons than those taught on the blackboard. Moreover the early Methodists had the credit of introducing the teaching of writing in the Sunday-schools. . . . The teaching of writing was an enormous boon to the working class. And there were other important arts that might be acquired in this school. The upper class could learn to speak at Eton: the working class in the little Bethel. The Methodist Sunday-schools would attract men and women with the gifts of oratory, leadership, organisation: they gave scope, experience, and training. . . . The teaching of Methodism was unfavourable to working-class movements; its leaders were hostile and its ideals perhaps increasingly hostile; but by the life and energy and awakening that it brought to this oppressed society it must, in spite of itself, have made many men better citizens, and some even better rebels.   (*The Town Labourer*, pp. 286-287.)

NONCONFORMITY AND REVOLT

Certainly many significant leaders of working class revolt were Methodists. Several of the Rochdale Pioneers were prominently connected with local religious Nonconformity. G. D. H. Cole says of Rochdale at this period:

I doubt if any other town of its size was equally prolific in religious controversies and foundations. New churches and chapels were continually being built, and among the dissenting congregations there were constant shifts, secessions, and foundations of new sects. The Unitarians were first in the field, their meeting going back to the exclusion of Robert

Bath in 1688. The Wesleyans came next, founding their first Society in 1760, and building their first chapel in Toad Lane (where now stands the central store of the Pioneers) ten years later. The Baptists followed with their first meeting house in 1773; and the earliest Sunday Schools were begun in 1782. In 1806, as we have seen, came the Cookites, or Methodist Unitarians, as the sequel to Joseph Cooke's exclusion from the Methodist Connexion. The Friends built their meeting house in 1808, the Particular Baptists their Hope Chapel in 1810, the followers of the Countess of Huntingdon their St. Stephen's Church in 1811, and the Methodist New Connexion, which had started services in 1814, its own chapel in 1822. The Roman Catholics built themselves St. John's Church by public subscription in 1829; and the Established Church built new places of worship in 1820 (St. James's) and 1835 (St. Clement's)—the latter out of the "Million Grant" voted by Parliament for the erection of new churches in the growing industrial towns. These are only a few out of many new places of worship built in the late eighteenth and early nineteenth century. The dissenters especially were continually outgrowing their spiritual homes, and were aided by the benefactions of devout manufacturers to erect new ones— usually of surpassing ugliness. Rochdale was the home of all the sects; and among them was the little sect of the Owenite Socialists, with their "rational religion" based on a rejection of all theological dogmas, from whom the original inspiration, though by no means all the original membership, of the Equitable Pioneers was drawn. (*A Century of Co-operation,* by G. D. H. Cole, pp. 54-55.)

One of the best known of the "Pioneers" was James Wilkinson, he shoe-maker preacher known in Rochdale as the Reverend James Wilkinson. He was a "Cookite", "a brand of Methodist Unitarianism indigenous to Rochdale". (*A Century of Co-operation,* G. D. H. Cole, p. 72). The "Cookites" were the followers of Joseph Cooke, originally a Wesleyan Methodist minister who was expelled by the Methodist Conference in 1806 on account of his unorthodox opinions. Cooke's followers built a new chapel— Providence Chapel in the High Street—for him, and he continued to preach there until his death in 1811. Later there was a secession under the leadership of James Wilkinson, John Ashworth, and James Taylor,* and by 1818 the secessionists had built themselves a new chapel in Clover Street the congregation of which "contributed a substantial membership both to the Chartist body and to the Society of Equitable Pioneers" (*A Century of*

---

*James Taylor had gone as a delegate from Rochdale to the Chartist Convention of 1839 and to the National Conference of 1840. He was also the Rochdale delegate to the Manchester Conference of 1840, at which was formed the National Charter Association. In 1842 he was arrested and tried at Lancaster for his part in the great strike movement of that year. He was acquitted.

Co-operation, p. 49). John Garside, another of the pioneers, wa
also well-known as a local preacher; and two others, John
Kershaw and John Scowcroft, were Swedenborgians also
associated with the Unitarians.

> I cannot find that the others had any religious affiliations (says
> Cole). It was only at a later stage that recruits came in from the
> Established Church, the Wesleyan Methodists, and other well-
> established bodies. (*A Century of Co-operation*, p. 72.)

On the other hand, George Jacob Holyoake, in his *History o*
the Rochdale Pioneers, declares that at least half of the origina
Pioneers were associated with the Clover Street Chapel.

There is, of course, considerable doubt as to who should b
included among the famous twenty-eight Pioneers (if there *wer*
twenty-eight of them*), but in spite of controversy it is beyond
doubt that a number of the famous Twenty-eight were actively
connected with the religious life of Rochdale.†

Among the wretchedly paid and oppressed village labourer
of the period religious Nonconformity was also found to go often
hand-in-hand with political nonconformity. George Loveless
the leader of the Tolpuddle Martyrs, was a local preacher
of the Wesleyan Methodists. Nonconformity was particularly
important in the country districts, where

> the country parson had none of the characteristics of the village
> priest of the Middle Ages. He was, indeed, in his social status
> above even the leaseholding farmers, and, as a rule, squires and
> parsons ranked together, meeting on terms of social equality.
> The poorer parsons, and there were many very poor benefices,
> were tied to their homes, and here they devoted their spare
> time to some attractive hobby such as archaeology or natural
> history. But the men with private property or richer benefices
> took an active part in country life. They attended the social
> functions of the gentry, often shot and sometimes hunted with
> them, and took part in other forms of sport. Some sat on the
> Boards of Guardians, many were magistrates. Such men belonged
> to the governing class, and many indeed held what was called the
> " family living ". Sometimes the parson was himself the squire,

---

*For a very thorough study of this problem see the Appendix to Mr. Cole
A Century of Co-operation.

†It was probably due to the multiplicity of strongly-held religious views that th
Co-operative Movement declared itself neutral in religious matters. As early as 183
when the Third Co-operative Congress was held, in London, a resolution was carrie
declaring that "Whereas, the co-operative world contains persons of all religiou
sects, and of all political parties, it is unanimously resolved, that Co-operators, *as suc*
are not identified with any 'religious, irreligious, or political tenets whatever; neithe
those of Mr. Owen, nor of any other individual". *See* Holyoake's *History of t*
Rochdale Pioneers, p. 20.

and so earned the nickname of "squarson". The typical country parson of the 19th century was above all things a "gentleman". In religious matters he kept clear of the controversies of the time, avoiding fervour and adopting the moderate view, whilst in political life he supported, as a rule, the squire's party. Thus inspired, he took a friendly interest in the farmers, their wives and families, and in a kindly if somewhat patronizing spirit did something by the administration of doles to alleviate the miserable condition of the impoverished labourers. But when the labourers showed independence and made a struggle for better conditions, the parsons rarely actively supported them.

The influence of the Nonconformists was of a distinctly different character. The chapels of the more important sects, the Congregationalists, the Baptists and Methodists, were as a rule in the country towns or the big villages, and had the support of a section of the shopkeepers, a few of the more broad-minded farmers, and some of the village artisans and more intelligent labourers. Amongst these people the minister moved, definitely cut off by his religious views from the houses of the gentry, the clergy and the orthodox farmers. Such of the labourers as took an independent line in religion tended, if the opportunity offered, to attach themselves to the Primitive Methodists—the Ranters as they were often called. This offshoot of Methodism, founded early in the 19th century, was, from its beginning, a movement led by rough, uneducated men, who made their appeal to the poor. Its preachers, like the medieval friars, were to be found tramping through the country districts preaching, in face of much persecution, a gospel of simple Christianity. Many labourers became "Primitives", and their little chapels, built in the last century, are still common in some counties, especially in the East of England, where they had a strong following. The "Primitives" have always shown sympathy with the labouring population. In 1830 they took an active part in the risings of that time, and in common with other Nonconformists did much to help the Trade Union movement in the seventies. Many of the Leaders of the latter movement had, indeed, obtained their power of speaking through the practice they had obtained as local preachers. (*A Short History of English Rural Life*, Montague Fordham, M.A., pp. 153-154.)

That was true of Joseph Arch the Warwickshire farm labourer who, in February 1872, formed the National Agricultural Labourers' Union. A moving speaker, he had got his early training in that art as a Primitive Methodist preacher. "Through the eloquence, the revivalist fervour, and the untiring energy of Joseph Arch*, the movement spread like wildfire among the

---

*Joseph Arch writes feelingly of the autocratic rule of the parson in his native Warwickshire village, when he was a boy. See his autobiography, *Joseph Arch: The Story of his Life.*

rural labourers of the central and eastern counties" (*The History of Trade Unionism,* Sidney and Beatrice Webb, pp.331-332), and at its peak had 80,000 (some estimates put it as high as 100,000) members. The union conducted a campaign throughout the country, demanding a wage of 16s. a week for labourers, and actually secured a general rise of about 4s. a week.

This revolt of men whom their masters had been used to think of almost as serfs filled the employers with surprise and fury "as if the dumb had spoken and the the crippled walked" (*The Common People,* G. D. H. Cole & Raymond Postgate, p. 389), and the farmers ruthlessly victimized any man who joined the Union.

> It is needless to say that they received the cordial support of the rural magistracy. In aid of a lock-out near Chipping Norton, two justices, who happened both to be clergymen, sent 16 labourers' wives, some with infants at the breast, to prison with hard labour, for 'intimidating' non-Union men. (*The History of Trade Unionism,* pp. 331-332.)

The Church was openly partisan, and

> the spirit in which the rural clergy viewed this social upheaval is not unfairly typified by the utterance of a learned bishop. On September 2, 1872, Dr. Ellicott, the Bishop of Gloucester, speaking at a meeting of the Gloucester Agricultural Society, significantly suggested the village horsepond as a fit destination for the 'agitators' or delegates sent by the Union to open new branches. (*The History of Trade Unionism,* p. 332.)

The Anti-Poor-Law movement of the eighteen-thirties (which was later absorbed into the Chartist movement), provides further instances of working class leaders whose hatred of social injustice flowed from their religious beliefs.

> The leaders of the movement drew their inspiration from the Bible, from a belief that the Act (of 1834) was a violation of Christian principles . . . This tendency to hark back to the Bible and to Christianity as a basis of political and social practice is the most interesting phase of the whole Chartist movement. (*The Chartist Movement,* Mark Hovell, M.A., p. 85.)

The infamous Poor Law of 1834 was based on the principle that out-relief should never be given to able-bodied males, and that when the wretched victims of capitalism were admitted to the new workhouses—Bastilles, as they were soon named— existence should be more unpleasant than the worst possible way of earning a living outside. Paupers were to be kept in "a contrite frame of mind by means of a low diet, a severe discipline, and a rigid segregation of the sexes which separated man and wife" on

ιe sound Malthusian principle that surplus workers should not
ε allowed to breed.

The most prominent leaders of the agitation against this
ιameful measure were Richard Oastler and Joseph Rayner
tephens.* Oastler was a member of the Established Church,
lthough his father had been a Methodist and a personal friend
f John Wesley. Stephens was the son of a Wesleyan minister,
nd entered the Wesleyan ministry himself, in 1825, to be
xpelled when he became an active Chartist.

> It may be safely said that Stephens went a long way towards
> making the factory and poor law movement into a kind of religious
> revival.... With Stephens and Oastler alike the Bible was the source
> of all political and religious teaching. Says Oastler : "I take the
> Bible, the simple Bible with me, without either note or comment,
> and in spite of all that men or devils may devise against me,
> I will have the Bill." . . . Stephens' special gift was denunciation.
> He conceived himself as a successor of Bishop Latimer or of those
> Old Testament prophets, summoned by the Almighty to chastise
> the Jeroboams and Ahabs of their time, prophets "who told
> kings what they were to do and the people likewise, who told
> senates and legislatures what kind of laws they were to make and
> what laws they should not make." He imagined himself at war
> with Satan, whose reality and vitality, already an established dog-
> ma of the Wesleyan community, was vouched for by the existence
> of such persons as Malthus and the Poor Law Commissioners.
> These he compared to Pharaoh who ordered a massacre of inno-
> cents, but unfavourably, as Pharaoh was frank about the matter
> whilst the Commissioners were hypocritical. (*The Chartist Move-
> ment*, Hovell, p. 89.)

At a meeting at Newcastle-on-Tyne, called in 1838 to demand
he repeal of the Poor Law Amendment Act, he declared that

> If this damnable law, which violated all the laws of God, was
> continued, and all means of peaceably putting an end to it had
> been made in vain, then, in the words of their banner, "For
> children and wife we'll war to the knife". If the people who pro-
> duce all wealth could not be allowed, according to God's Word,
> to have the kindly fruits of the earth which they had, in obedience
> to God's Word, raised by the sweat of their brow, then war to
> the knife with their enemies, who were the enemies of God. If
> the musket and the pistol, the sword, and the pike were of no

---

*Oastler and Stephens also took a prominent part in the struggle for the Ten
Hours Bill. Lord Shaftesbury is usually given the chief credit for the Ten Hours Act
of 1847, but Oastler's forceful propaganda and years of agitation by a host of humble
working men whose names are unknown to us, made that piece of social legislation
possible. The Bradford workers knew that and placed on record their "heartfelt
gratitude to that noble of Nature Richard Oastler, Esq., the originator of, and persevering advocate of, the greatest boon to the factory working population of this
country". (Bradford, June 16, 1847).

avail, let the women take the scissors, the child the pin or needle. If all failed, then the firebrand—aye, the firebrand, I repeat. The palace shall be in flames. I pause, my friends. If the cottage is not permitted to be the abode of man and wife, and if the smiling infant is to be dragged from a father's arms and a mother's bosom, it is because these hell-hounds of commissioners have set up the command of their master the devil, against our God.

And again, at Glasgow, in January 1838:

> If they will not reform this, aye uproot it all, they shall have the revolution they so much dread. We shall destroy their abodes of guilt, which they have reared to violate all law and God's book. If they will not learn to act as law prescribes and God ordains, so that every man shall by his labour find comfortable food and clothing—not for himself only, but for his wife and babes—then we swear by the love of our brothers—by our God who made us all for happiness—by the earth He gave us for our support—by the Heaven He designs for those who love each other here, and by the hell which is the portion of those who, violating His book, have consigned their fellowmen . . . to hunger, nakedness, and death ; we have sworn by our God, by heaven, earth, and hell, that from the East, the West, the North and the South, we shall wrap in one awful sheet of devouring flame, which no arm can resist, the manufactories of the cotton tyrants, and the places of those who raised them by rapine and murder.

MESSIANIC RELIGION

In some instances religion took on forms that recall the chiliastic dreams of the Middle Ages. Many of the sects tended to forget "the new Manchester in the New Jerusalem", and

> the early history of the Primitive Methodist connection reads like the history of the early Christians in its isolation from the world and its expectation of an imminent day of judgment. (*The Town Labourer, 1760-1832*, J. L. & Barbara Hammond, p. 283).

It was a time of millennial hopes, and Robert Owen convinced himself that within a brief space, possibly no more than five years, the Trade Unions would transfer society into a Socialist community by taking over industry and running it co-operatively.* In November 1833 he addressed the Annual Meeting of the Operative Builders' Union—the Builders' Parliament, as it was called—which had been formed in the previous year, and which united all the building crafts into one body, with a probable

---

*This period witnessed the formation of the Grand National Consolidated Trades Union of Great Britain and Ireland, and its mushroom growth in the twelve months October 1833 to October 1834 to half-a-million members, and its equally rapid disintegration. Owen played a great part in the formation and fortunes of the Grand National.

membership at one time of some 60,000. Owen persuaded it to form itself into a Builders' Guild for the co-operative erection of buildings, and in a public lecture which he delivered soon afterwards, he announced the form which the new society was to take, by saying: "I now give you a short outline of the great changes which are in contemplation, and which shall come suddenly upon society like a thief in the night".

Commenting upon these excited years, G. D. H. Cole and Raymond Postgate remark that

> Psychologically, the great majority of the British working class was in those years, and for fifteen more years to come, diseased: as it had indeed always been in a greater or lesser degree since the eighteenth-century equilibrium had been broken up. Unable to find any rational methods of escape, it turned to irrational. It demanded a sure promise of happiness—of food, of rest from overwork, clothing and what delights it could imagine—within its own lifetime. It found this in prophetic religions; one of the legitimate ways of regarding Owenism is to class it among the Messianic religions which arose in the early nineteenth century. (*The Common People, 1746-1938*, G. D. H. Cole and Raymond Postgate, pp. 264-5).

Owen himself was often called the "revered father". James Morrison,* whom Postgate calls "one of the most level-headed leaders of this time", wrote to him:

> I hope you will not hesitate to tell me of my errors, my prejudices and my natural discrepancies. Your doctrines have made me a *better* and a *happier* being. Before I knew the great truths which you have developed I was a rough and irritable stickler for vulgar Liberty—since my personal intercourse with *you* I have become better—but I do not feel satisfied. I have not that *charity* which beareth all things—which endureth long and is patient of suffering. Need I tell you I have been trained to be *hasty, impassioned* and prone to sudden bursts of feeling. You must have perceived my prejudices, my ambition, my weaknesses. Be, then, my Physician —I put my case in your hands. Give me your counsel—your practice inspires my perfect confidence. . . . I shall look upon you as a Father and try to become a faithful Son. May circumstances be auspicious to my Baptism and make me worthy to be
> yours truly,
JAMES MORRISON.
> (Quoted by Raymond Postgate in his *The Builders' History*, pp. 83-84.)

As for Owen

his mind was already, indeed, partially withdrawn from the

---

*Morrison, a bricklayer, was the editor of the semi-official journal of the Builder's Union, the *PIONEER*, which later transferred its allegiance and became the official organ of the Grand National Consolidated Trades Union of Great Britain & Ireland.

outside world. He had begun to live among the fantasies in which he ended his life. He had, for example, previously announced that the millennium had commenced on May 1, 1833. What he meant by this, what it meant to him or to his followers it is impossible to conceive. (*The Common People*, p. 263.)

Presently he fell out with his two chief assistants, James Morrison, and J. F. Smith, a lecturer and "a sort of clergyman" who was editor of Owen's own journal *The Crisis*.

These two men, far more clear-headed than those who surrounded them, had for several issues been preaching what today would be called the strategy and tactics of the class-struggle. They urged reform of the Union structure, abstention from trivial conflicts, consolidation and conservation of energy for one well-considered attack—"a long strike, a strong strike, and a strike all together"—and generally an informed and directed hostility to the employers. Smith's economic analyses (signed "Senex") are astonishingly modern and intelligent: reading them torn from their context, few critics would believe that they antedated Marx. But though this advice corresponded to economic reality, it increasingly vexed Robert Owen. . . . All the objective facts were on their side, but Owen's disapproval was enough to close down THE CRISIS, which Smith edited, and expel Morrison's PIONEER from its position in favour of a new official journal of the Consolidated. . . . All arguments must have been in favour of the propaganda of Smith and Morrison. Yet the disapproval of Owen was enough to extinguish them. This was, as has already been suggested, directly because of the apocalyptic nature of his speeches. He announced with absolute conviction that the millennium was about to arrive—with a minimum of exertion by his listeners—or even that it had arrived. Because of their economic conditions . . . the working class of Great Britain was prepared to accept this affirmation. (*The Common People*, pp. 262-264.)

The causes which gave to Owenism its messianic qualities, bred even more monstrous forms of religion, all of which depended for their popular appeal upon "the promise of a heaven which could be secured by merely believing the prescribed set of propositions, and which would shortly appear on this earth." (*The Common People*, p. 226).

As late as 1851 the Mormons had 222 churches with 30,000 sittings. George Turner, one of the most successful prophets, not only promised immediate rewards to his followers, but actually announced the date on which the Lord would take over the government of the world and reward the faithful. The date was 1817, the Cabinet was named, its salaries fixed, and one of the advantages of the new regime was to be that the power of men and women to enjoy each other was to be increased "and that an hundredfold". The date passed uneventfully, but the new Church was undismayed. John Ward succeeded to Turner, and the Church extended as far as Australia, where its practices became demonstrably pathological. Joanna Southcott, still unforgotten, and perhaps the most important, announced that she was pregnant with Shiloh, the new Messiah. She died of dropsy, but her followers were unaffected by such external facts: they continued numerous and certain of the imminent coming of the Kingdom of Heaven up till 1885, when the last prophet J. J. Jezreel died. (*The Common People*, pp. 265-266.)*

---

*The founder of the Jezreelites (as they were popularly called) was one James White, a soldier, who gave the society the title of the "New and Latter House of Israel", and to himself the alliterative name of James Jershom Jezreel. He commenced his mission in October 1875, and addressed himself chiefly to members of the old Christian Israelite Church at Gillingham and elsewhere. He claimed to be divinely inspired, and in due course produced a "Flying Roll", the idea having been suggested to him by *Zechariah*, v. i ("Then I turned, and lifted up mine eyes, and looked, and behold a flying roll"). "The work, if such an exalted term can be applied to it, is a wretched jumble of texts and prophecies, and consists largely of a re-hash of the writings of the late John Wroe, the leader of the Christian Israelite Church". (*The Jezreelites and their Famous Tower*, reprinted from *Chats About Gillingham*, by permission of the author, Mr. C. S. Leeds, p. 1.)

The sect made considerable progress, and many members of the old Israelite Church accepted Jezreel as "God's last messenger to man", in what was mysteriously termed "the third and last watch". "The tenets were not new to old members of the Christian Israelite Church, many of whom 'gathered' at Gillingham from various parts of England and Scotland and the United States of America, and, what is more, gave proof of their faith in Jezreel and his teachings by selling all their goods and casting the proceeds into the 'treasury'. The sect, it was understood, was to be run on family lines, and all things were to be 'in common' ". (*The Jezreelites and their Famous Tower*, p. 2).

The sect began the erection of a "four-square" building, and over £30,000 was spent on this "temple" before work was suspended for lack of funds. The Jezreelites' Tower still stands on Chatham Hill.

CHAPTER 12

THE CHRISTIAN SOCIALISTS (1848-1854)

> We have used the Bible as if it were a mere special
> constable's handbook, an opium dose for keeping
> beasts of burden patient while they are being over-
> loaded.
>
> *Charles Kingsley.*

THE YEAR OF REVOLUTIONS

In February, 1848 the French king was driven from his throne
by the people of Paris, and a republic was proclaimed. The effect
of the February revolution was as if the key-stone of an arch had
been withdrawn: the whole political structure of Europe began
to collapse. In one country after another the ruling dynasty was
tumbled over by popular insurrections. The Elector of Hesse
and other German princelings were compelled to grant a
constitution to their people, and on March 13th the populace of
Vienna rose in revolt, and Metternich fled to England. Before the
end of the month the Austrian emperor had been forced to grant
constitutions to the kingdoms of Hungary and Bohemia, incorpor-
ating long-desired reforms. In Italy, the Milanese, in five days
of fighting, drove out the Austrian garrison, and the Venetians
followed this example, and Venetia and Lombardy declared
their independence of Austria. The greater part of Italy flared in
revolt: constitutions were granted to Naples, Rome, Tuscany and
Piedmont by their rulers. Florence declared herself a republic,
and the Pope fled from Rome and put himself under the protection
of the King of Naples. In February, 1849, a constitutional
assembly declared the temporal power of the Pope abolished,
and proclaimed a Roman republic. Even the King of Prussia
was forced to promise a constitution, and to stand bareheaded
whilst the funeral of the revolutionary dead passed before his
balcony; and a national assembly was convoked at Frankfurt
to draft a constitution for a united Germany.

The whole of Europe seemed threatened by a revolutionary
tidal wave; and in this country there was a revival of the Chartist
movement.

The successive Continental revolutions, the news of which strangely
unsettled even the most prosaic of the middle class, had a much

deeper effect on working men still suffering extensively from the industrial results of the financial shocks of 1847. On March 2nd, an enthusiastic London meeting of the Chartists sent a congratulatory deputation to the Republican Government at Paris, and very soon Stepney Green, Bethnal Green, and Clerkenwell Green, the principal meeting-places of the working-class politicians of the Metropolis, were the scenes of "immense gatherings." That the provincial towns were also overcome by the same excitement became evident from the events of the week beginning on Monday, March 6th. Glasgow especially was for a time in the hands of a mob pillaging provision shops and shouting "Bread or Revolution" and "Vive la République". But it was London's West End which saw the most remarkable Chartist manifestations. For three successive days there were Chartist hostilities with the police in connection with the ban placed upon meetings in Trafalgar Square, and on one occasion a movement was attempted upon Buckingham Palace.

After this explosive intimation of its revival Chartism engaged in several weeks of mass meetings, sometimes in halls, sometimes on town greens, and sometimes on the waste ground outside or between populous places. Chartists were once more listening to inflammatory oratory, signing yet another National Petition, and electing yet another Convention. (*English Radicalism, 1832-52*, S. Maccoby, Ph.D. pp. 279-280.)

HE END OF CHARTISM

The revolutionary Chartist hopes of 1839, and the threats of rmed insurrection which had accompanied them had faded ut in the ill-fated Monmouthshire rising of November 3-4, when ohn Frost and some 4,000 colliers and iron-workers tried to free Ienry Vincent from gaol and fought a pitched battle in the streets f Newport with the military. The Chartist losses in that battle ave been estimated at various figures between 11 and 53. One esult of the disturbances of that period was that most of the utstanding Chartist leaders were gaoled, and the movement was ft for a time leaderless and dispirited.

But Chartism revived. Various schemes for Chartist education nd propaganda were putforward, and in July, 1840, the National harter Association was founded, and the attempt was made to reate a nation-wide party, organised in towns and wards, with a veekly membership subscription of a penny.

The National Charter Association was the first serious attempt t the creation of a mass working class political party in this ountry, and the organisers faced colossal difficulties, including he fact that the Corresponding Act of 1817 made it illegal to und a national organisation with branch societies. The N.C.A.

was a notable achievement therefore, even if it is true that "it was only the exceptional Chartist who religiously renewed his twopenny membership card every quarter and paid his weekly subscription besides". (*English Radicalism 1832-52*, p. 214).

At first the Association enrolled members slowly, and by the end of 1841 had 13,000 members in 282 localities. By the summer of 1842, when it appears to have reached its maximum strength, the Association claimed a membership of 48,000 organised in 400 localities.

That year saw the second Chartist Petition, which was signed by 3,317,702 persons and was over six miles long. It excited the wildest hopes among the Chartists, not least in the mind of Feargus O'Connor.

August saw a strike in Ashton-under-Lyne which was turned into a strike for the Charter. It spread over Lancashire, Yorkshire, Staffordshire, Cheshire, the Potteries and Warwickshire into Wales, and the Scottish miners also came out. It is reported that when Campbell, the secretary of the Association, saw the smokeless chimneys of Manchester from the train he declared "Something must come out of this, and something serious".

But, at the best, most of the Chartist leaders were very vague as to what their next move should be, and at worst frankly alarmed at the storm which they had helped to provoke. On August 27th, at the very time when trades as far north as Aberdeen were considering joining in the strike, O'Connor denounced it in the *Northern Star* as an Anti-Corn-Law League plot. The strike was already beginning to weaken at the centre, and O'Connor's weak denunciation helped to wreck it completely, and to inflict a defeat upon Chartism from which it never fully recovered. With the collapse of the great strike the ruling class took their revenge for the fright which they had suffered by arresting 1,500 of the strikers, and transporting 79 of them to Australia.

The two high tides of Chartism in 1839 and 1842 were largely the result of trade depression which inflicted intolerable suffering upon the working class of the industrial north. 1847 and 1848 were also years of bad trade and heavy unemployment, and these economic factors making for mass discontent were aggravated by the dramatic events on the Continent. Once again fantastic hopes were raised, and O'Connor drafted a constitution for a British republic, with himself as President. A new Petition was drafted, another National Assembly convened, and a mass meeting called for April 10th, 1848 to present the petition

This meeting was arranged to take place on Kennington Common, whence it was to march to Parliament; and the ruling class (already shaken by the events in Europe) had horrific fears of an English revolution. 150,000 or more special constables were sworn in, and the Duke of Wellington massed an army in London, and "made preparations as though for Waterloo".

Kennington Common was packed on April 10th, the attendance being stated at various figures between 25,000 and 250,000, these estimates being coloured, no doubt, by the author's political opinions. One thing is certain: there was no revolutionary upheaval. O'Connor's threats proved to be wind as usual, and when the procession to the House of Commons was banned he implored the people not to be provoked. The great meeting from which so much had been hoped (and feared) fizzled out tamely, the Petition being conveyed to Parliament in three cabs. Later, when the signatures were counted, the fiasco was complete, for the numbers were announced as slightly less than 2,000,000 instead of the 5,700,000 which the Chartists had claimed, and many of these were obviously fictitious and somewhat risible.

THE CHRISTIAN SOCIALISTS

Chartism never recovered from the fiasco of April 10th, and thereafter dwindled both in the numbers of its adherents and in its power to sway the masses.

> Some such startling defeat of the Chartists was inevitable, even if the leadership had been wiser. The enemy, the capitalistic class, which the Chartists were attacking, was enormously stronger than they believed. It was nothing like the feeble landowners who had surrounded George IV. So far from being in decay, it had during this period and the immediately subsequent years, begun to use fully its economic powers of expansion for the first time, and provided itself with legal instruments which enabled its progress to astonish the world. (*The Common People 1746-1938*, by G. D. H. Cole and Raymond Postgate, p. 285.)

However, the events that culminated in the Kennington meeting had frightened the capitalist class, and along with the customary savage persecution of the working class rebels, there was a growing realization that some amelioration of working-class conditions were desirable. It is at this stage that the small group of middle class reformers (mostly parsons and barristers) known as the Christian Socialists appear on the scene.

On the morning of the Kennington Common demonstration Charles Kingsley, a young country parson, came up to London,

M

and went to see the Reverend Frederick Denison Maurice, then a professor at King's College, London, and leader of the "Broad Church" party in the Church of England. Maurice gave him a letter of introduction to a young barrister named Ludlow, and that afternoon the two of them set off for Kennington, and had got as far as Waterloo Bridge when they met the remnants of the great mass meeting trudging homewards through the rain. The same evening Kingsley and Ludlow discussed the exciting events of the day with Maurice, and conferred on the best means to "save the country from disturbances, and the people from harmful utopias".

The next day Kingsley wrote that "Maurice is in great excitement. . . . We are getting out placards for the walls, to speak a word for God. . . . I am helping in a glorious work". The same evening he adds: "I was up till four this morning, writing posting placards under Maurice's auspices".

The following day posters appeared on the London hoardings signed "A Working Parson" (Kingsley's nom-de-plume), which assured the workers that "almost all men who have heads and hearts" know their wrongs and the patience they have shown. They implored the workers not to "mean licence when you cry liberty", since "the Almighty God, and Jesus Christ, the poor Man who died for poor men, will bring freedom for you, though all the Mammonites on earth were against you". The workers are asked, will the Charter free them from "slavery to gin and beer?"; and the homily concludes: "There will be no true freedom without virtue, no true science without religion, no true industry without the fear of God and love to your fellow-citizens. Workers of England, be wise, and then you *must* be free, for you will be *fit* to be free".

Other posters appeared in due course, all of them critical of Chartism, and urging the need for individual regeneration if social amelioration was to be achieved.

> I am a radical reformer (runs a typical passage). I am not one of those who laugh at your petition of April 10th; I have no patience with those who do. . . . But my quarrel with the Charter is that it does not go far enough in reform. I want to see you free, but I don't see how what you ask will give you what you want. I think you have fallen into just the same mistake as the rich of whom you complain—the very mistake which has been our curse and our nightmare—I mean the mistake of fancying that legislative reform is social reform, or that men's hearts can be changed by Acts of Parliament. If anyone will tell me of a country where a

charter made rogues honest or the idle industrious, I shall alter
my opinion of the Charter, but not till then. . . . Be fit to be free
and God himself will set you free.

This linking of Christianity with a demand for social reform
had little in common with the earlier revolutionary movements
of which I have written, in which the demand for social justice
was based upon Biblical sanction. The Christian Socialists were
no revolutionaries: their approach to the working class was one
of condescending (though quite honest) benevolence. They came
to them as middle-class philanthropists* who were quite genuinely
shocked by the wretched conditions under which masses of poor
people lived and worked; but whilst they were anxious to improve
working class conditions they deplored the class struggle, and
deprecated any manifestation of working class militancy. Maurice
expressed their basic idea in these words:

> The question is, how to eliminate Owenism and Chartism? Re-
> pression has proved powerless; but the Queen, in a conversation
> with Lord Melbourne, has indicated the proper way, to wit, edu-
> cation. But what sort of education will be capable of doing away
> with Chartism? The one that will point out to him (to the worker)
> his unjust claims and will satisfy his just demands. (*The Life of
> F. D. Maurice*, by G. F. Maurice, Vol. ii, p. 269.)

And though their first series of tracts made a special appeal
to Chartists, they sought "to convince them of the folly and wrong
of open violence", and gloried "in the success of the householder
constables". (*Charles Kingsley and Christian Socialism*, by Colwyn
E. Vulliamy, p. 10).

They were largely ignorant of the Trade Union and Co-operative movements, and Max Beer has described them, not unfairly,
as "leaders and officers, but without any army behind them".
History of British Socialism, Vol. ii, p. 184). Not only did they
regard Owenite and Chartist ideas as dangerous, but Maurice

---

*Of the best known members of the group Maurice and Kingsley were clergy-
men; Ludlow, Furnivall, Brickdale, and Thomas Hughes (better known, perhaps, as
the author of *Tom Brown's Schooldays*), were barristers; Walsh was a doctor; Campbell
and Penrose were architects; and Mansfield a trained scientist. Several of them
were queer almost to the point of being cranks. "There was Mansfield with his
cotton-cloth shoes, and Campbell with his 'fonetic nuts', and Furnivall, vegetarian
and non-smoker and teetotaler, with a spelling all his own . . . and even the leaders
were a couple of parsons and a strange fellow who had spent half his life in France.
They were admittedly on their own showing a queer collection . . . And to them
had come Tom Hughes, the "blue", with the healthy mind and the healthy body,
whom no one could accuse of madness or vice, who was the ideal hero of the British
public and the sporting press. . . . Here was something to give their critics pause . . .
they could not be so bad after all if a man like that was among them". (*Christian
Socialism 1848-1854*, by Charles E. Raven, M.A., pp. 130-131).

(whom Ludlow has described as "towering spiritually by head and shoulders over the rest" (*Economic Review*, Oct. 1893)), was "no democrat and condemned the doctrine of the sovereignty of the people as atheistic and subversive". (*History of British Socialism* M. Beer, Vol. ii, p. 182.) Quite naturally he had offered his services as a special constable on April 10th, 1848, but had been excused on account of his clerical rank. For him

> the church was a visible society ordained by Christ for bringing about the Kingdom of God. This Kingdom was at all times more truly real, more genuine, than the "kingdoms of this age" because it existed in the Divine mind. (*The Common People 1746-1938*, G. D. H. Cole and Raymond Postgate, p. 315).

The events of 1848 seemed to him a direct manifestation of Divine power. "Do you really think", he wrote,

> that the invasion of Palestine by Sennacherib was a greater event than the overthrowing of nearly all the greatest powers, civil and ecclesiastical, in Christendom ?

His conception of Socialism was inextricably mingled with a religious mysticism.

> We want the Church (he said) fully to understand her own foundation, fully to work out the communism which is implied in her existence.   Church reformation, therefore, in its highest sense, involves *theologically* the reassertion of these truths in their fullness, apart from their Calvinistical and Tractarian limitations and dilutions; *socially* the assertion on the grounds of these truths of an actually living community under Christ, in which no man has a right to call anything that he has his own, but in which there is spiritual fellowship and practical co-operation. (*Life of F. D. Maurice*, J. Maurice, p. 10.)

Ludlow, of whom General Sir Frederick, then Colonel, Maurice later wrote (December 21st, 1889), that "John Malcolm Ludlow was the founder of the movement; and he brought in my father by the force of his strong will",* declared that he (Maurice)

> never understood the meaning of democracy . . . and Maurice himself in the most elaborate of his letters on this topic admits that he does not believe democracy to be possible except upon a basis of slavery.   Athens had been a slave-state. Modern experiments, in France and America, had only led to chaos and military despotism, or to corruption and negro-servitude. With these examples before him his view is that there must always be some visible embodiment of the principle of authority, and that this is to be obtained better by monarchy and aristocracy, wherein certain persons are elevated above the normal

---

*Quoted by Charles Raven in *Christian Socialism, 1848-1854*, p. 55.

level, than by democracy and slavery, wherein the same differentiation is reached by depressing one class below the others. . . . 'I
must have Monarchy, Aristocracy, and Socialism, or rather
Humanity, recognised as necessary elements or conditions of an
organic Christian society,' he writes. (*Christian Socialism 1848-1854,*
Charles E. Raven, p. 91).

Ludlow† himself

was equally exalted, but more practical, his insistence on working-
class self-government and the practical details of workshop management seemed to Maurice unwise and more than a little
worldly. (*The Common People 1746-1938* by G. D. H. Cole and
Raymond Postgate, pp. 315-316.)

Like Maurice, Ludlow also wondered on April 10th "whether
he should not enlist to defend the city against an orgy of blood-
shed". (*Christian Socialism 1848-1854,* p. 106).

Charles Kingsley was at one with Maurice in setting a high
value on aristocracy; to him the House of Lords "represented all
that was noble and permanent in the national character".
(*Charles Kingsley and Christian Socialism,* Colwyn F. Vulliamy).

In his "First Letter" as Parson Lot, he wrote:

God will only reform society on condition of our reforming every
man his own self—while the devil is quite ready to help us to
mend the laws and the parliament, earth and heaven, without
ever starting such an impertinent and " personal " request.

Mr. Vulliamy in his little pamphlet *Charles Kingsley and Christian
Socialism* (pp. 10-11) recounts a significant incident which
occurred at the Cranbourne Coffee Tavern where Maurice
addressed Chartist leaders and other working men.

On one occasion (he writes) the National Anthem was hissed.
Hughes, like an evangelical Desmoulins, sprang on a chair, vowed
that any man who insulted the Queen would have an account to
settle with him personally (he was a proficient pugilist), ordered
the pianist to play on loudly, and himself led the singing of the
Anthem, which was continued so vociferously that interruption
was either quelled or was drowned by mere tumult.

Nor is it without significance that three copies of Kingsley's
most famous pamphlet, *Cheap Clothes and Nasty,* are reported on
one occasion as "lying on the Guards' Club table!" (Letter to
Mrs. Kingsley, June 1850, cf. *Life of Kingsley,* i. p. 236. Quoted
in Charles Raven's, *Christian Socialism 1848-1854,* p. 195.)

---

†Furnivall, one of the earliest recruits, also described Ludlow as "the true main-
spring of our Christian Socialist movement" (*Christian Socialism 1848-1854,* p. 55).

THE BEGINNING OF THE MOVEMENT

On April 12th, 1848, Maurice, Ludlow and Kingsley met agai
and decided to start a penny weekly, which they called *Politic
for the People*. Seventeen numbers were issued, and then lack c
funds forced them to suspend publication. Ludlow, who wrot
over the signature of "John Townsend", or, more generally
"J.T.", was responsible for about a third of the total matte
published in the paper. Maurice, whose work was either ur
signed or signed "A Clergyman", wrote an introductory articl
on "Fraternity", and also contributed several dialogues, a story
and a number of other articles; whilst Charles Kingsley ser
several contributions, including the three famous "Letters c
Parson Lot", and some short poems. William Lovett (who ha
founded the London Working Men's Association in 1836, an
had drafted the famous Charter in 1838) sent an address whic
Maurice reviewed. "One or two working men sent letters, bu
their number was disappointingly small". (*Christian Socialis
1848-1854*, p. 111).

> The objects of the paper were explained in the first issue
> Politics (it was said) have been separated from Christianity;
> religious men have supposed that their only business was with
> the world to come; political men have declared that the present
> world is governed on entirely different principles. . . . But Politics
> for the people cannot be separated from Religion. They must
> start from atheism or from the acknowledgment that a Living
> and Righteous God is ruling in human society not less than in the
> natural world. . . . The world is governed by God; this is the rich
> man's warning; this is the poor man's comfort; this is the real
> hope in the consideration of all questions, let them be as hard of
> solution as they may; this is the pledge that Liberty, Fraternity,
> Unity, under some conditions or other, are intended for every
> people under heaven.

Politics for the People put Ludlow in touch with a number c
working class leaders. Among them was Walter Cooper (brothe
of Thomas Cooper the well-known Chartist poet). Cooper, wh
was working at that time as a tailor in Fetter Lane, was a promi
nent Chartist and a capable speaker. He was impressed b
Politics for the People, and agreed to help Ludlow to get together
meeting at which members of the Christian Socialist grou
might discuss social problems with working men. The "Cra
bourne Coffee Tavern" was chosen as a meeting place, and th
first meeting was held there on April 23rd, 1849. Thereaft
weekly meetings were held at which lectures or addresses wei
delivered, or debates took place.

The first of these meetings "began in a somewhat frigid fashion", and

the general embarrassment was not diminished by the first speakers, who were men with grievances that they were glad to air. They said many hard things of their social superiors, and made the group feel distinctly uncomfortable. The clergymen came in, as usual, for a good deal of plain speech. Then up rose Charles Kingsley; and with the stammer which marked his utterance until he lost himself in his subject blurted out "I am a Church of England clergyman", and then, after a pause, and with folded arms, "And I am a Chartist". After which he spoke with some frankness, and the meeting became friendly". (*Christian Socialism 1848-1854*, p. 139.)

It was at the "Cranbourne" meetings that the Christian Socialists made contact with the Owenite Socialist, Lloyd Jones, who was in touch with all the surviving Owenite and Co-operative groups. Despite his religious scepticism, Lloyd Jones threw himself whole-heartedly into the plans of the Christian Socialists.

Other recruits were the watch finishers, Joseph Millbank and Thomas Shorter, both of whom were Chartists, and who subsequently succeeded Charles Sully as joint secretaries of the Society for Promoting Working Men's Associations. Sully, who also came to the "Cranbourne" meetings, was a bookbinder from Paris, and had an extensive knowledge of the French movement for Co-operative Production. He

had taken a full share in the revolutionary outbreaks of the two past years. Becoming convinced of the futility of physical force as an instrument of reform, he left France and came to London with a strong recommendation from a friend of Ludlow's. The group were delighted to have found one who knew the French Associations at first hand, and who was honest, energetic, competent, and experienced. (*Christian Socialism 1848-1854*, p. 184.)

Another French recruit was A. L. Jules Le Chevalier, who in May, 1850, adopted the name St. André. He professed to be a follower of St. Simon, and was expelled from France in June, 1849. He met Ludlow and other members of the group in November, and his

plausible address, wide knowledge, and ready enthusiasm gave him at once a prominent position in their counsels. At the beginning possibly he was sincere . . . but after a time their suspicions were aroused . . . and in March 1852, he severed his connection with the Society. . . . Maurice, the most charitable of men, refers to him, years afterwards and not unjustly, in a letter to Ludlow as a "clever sharper". After the fall of the French Empire and the exposure of Napoleon's intrigues "Le Chevalier" was discovered to have served for some years as a paid secret agent! (*Christian Socialism 1848-1854,* pp. 143-144.)

It was at these "Cranbourne" meetings that Ludlow found support for his plans to start self-governing workshops on the model of those established in France. Ludlow had been brought up in France, and he "was at once intimately acquainted with French Socialist and Co-operative ideas and almost entirely ignorant of their British equivalent". (*A Century of Co-operation,* G. D. H. Cole, p. 97). He had inspected several of the Paris workshops where the French workers were carrying out the ideas of Buchez and Louis Blanc by forming self-governing Producers' Associations, and he had

> collected a large bundle of papers containing their constitutions, conditions of membership, and regulations, and a full account of the results of his research was published in 1850 as the fourth in the series of *Tracts on Christian Socialism.* This really magnificent work, he wrote, seemed to meet the very mischiefs we are anxious to deal with. (*Christian Socialism 1848-1854,* p. 143.)

PRODUCERS' CO-OPERATION IN GREAT BRITAIN

> It is a curious fact (says G. D. H. Cole) that the Christian Socialists, when they first launched out on their attempt to foster Producers' Co-operative Societies of working men, seem to have known practically nothing about all the previous attempts that had been made in Great Britain to achieve this very thing. They soon learnt about these earlier movements and discovered that they were still in being; but at the outset they derived their inspiration to form such Societies entirely from France. (*A Century of Co-operation,* G. D. H. Cole, p. 97.)

If the Christian Socialists had not been so aloof from the working class movement of their day they would have known that the movement for Co-operative Production in Great Britain had experienced a revival in the second half of the 'forties after the failure of the Owenite colony at Queenwood (1846). Even before this failure the Trade Unions had taken a renewed interest in schemes for Co-operative Production which had been prevalent in the days of the Grand National Consolidated Trades Union of 1834. In 1845, just before a trade depression set in, a Trade Union Conference (the first national conference of this kind since the collapse of the Grand National in 1834) assembled in London, and formed a National Association of United Trades for the Protection of Labour. This was intended to help to co-ordinate working class action in trade disputes and to represent the general claims of the working class before Parliament and the public.

The National Association of United Trades did not set out with the millennial ideas of the Grand National, and it declared its willingness to negotiate with the employers and its desire to avoid having recourse to strike action by the setting up of mutually agreed "Boards of Trade", or conciliation courts. At the same time, however, it prepared for possible strikes and lock-outs by setting up another body, the National United Trades Association for the Employment of Labour, which revived the Union Shop and Co-operative Production projects of the eighteen-thirties. The proposal was to raise a £50,000 Employment Fund to be "devoted to the formation of self-supporting industrial colonies", which could employ members during industrial disputes.

At the next yearly conference it was announced that the National United Trades Association for the Employment of Labour had 123 men at work under its auspices, mainly in boot-making and other hand trades which required very little capital. But hardly had the new movement taken shape when the economic depression of 1846-47 began; and in 1848 the two Associations were merged into a single body.

As the funds of the National Association of United Trades for the Protection of Labour became exhausted many societies which had joined it fell away ; but the Association survived for several more years. Then, in 1849, it became involved in a strike of the Wolverhampton tinplate workers. The employers met this strike by a prosecution of both strikers and leaders for incitement to breach of contract and for other offences. The trials dragged on until 1851; and this protracted legal struggle greatly weakened the Association. After that it steadily declined, and gave up the attempt to develop Co-operative Production. It finally disappeared in 1867.

About the same time as the National Association of United Trades for the Protection of Labour was being formed, a group of old Owenites formed the Leeds Redemption Society, in 1846.

The aim of the Redemptionists was to persuade workmen to subscribe a penny a week to a fund which was to be used for the "Redemption of Labour" by setting the members to work both on the land and in self-governing workshops. . . . In the following year the Redemptionists took a leading part in the establishment of the Leeds Co-operative Corn Mill, out of which sprang the Leeds Co-operative Society. They also had presented to them an estate at Garnlwyd, in Carmarthenshire, on condition that it should be returned to the donor if they failed to put it to Co-operative use. On this estate a small number of the Redemptionists settled down in 1848 and proceeded to erect workshops as well as till the land, supplying their products to the Co-operative Societies at Leeds and elsewhere. . . . The venture . . . lasted until 1854, when the estate was given up and handed back to the donor, and the Leeds Redemption Society ended in the following year. . . . The Bury Redemptionists started in 1850 a Co-operative Store which ran for four years, and in 1851 they helped the local bootmakers to win a strike by establishing Co-operative Production. The movement also spread to Liverpool, where in 1851 there was a project afoot for the newly founded Amalgamated Society of Engineers to buy the Windsor Foundry, which had just failed, and restart it as a Co-operative Workshop. . . . [It] came to nothing, because before it could be completed all the funds of the A.S.F. were swallowed up in the great engineers' lock-out of 1852. (*A Century of Co-operation*, G. D. H. Cole, p. 101.)

Thus the Redemption Society movement was in full swing in the north of England at the very time when the Christian Socialists were becoming interested in Co-operative Production; but they seem to have known nothing about it.

THE TAILORS' ASSOCIATION

During the summer of 1849 Henry Mayhew published his *London Labour and the London Poor,* and his dreadful revelations about slum conditions and the sweating systems (revelations which were based on first-hand investigation) made a tremendous impression upon the reading public. As if to underline his indictment there was an outbreak of cholera during August and September.

The Christian Socialists

plunged into practical relief-work. Mansfield with his scientific training went down to investigate sanitary conditions in the plague-areas. Walsh lost the support of his wealthy patients by accepting a post as inspector in Bermondsey. Kingsley came up from Eversley to join the crusade, and from his experiences on Jacob's Island got the material for one of his most lurid chapters in *Alton Locke*. (*Christian Socialism 1848-1854,* p. 145.)

He was also impelled to write his first and most famous pamphlet, *Cheap Clothes and Nasty,* in which he exposed the London sweatshops. It was published in January, 1850. Finally, he set about writing *Alton Locke*.

Mansfield conceived a scheme for a Health League, "for uniting all classes of society in the promotion of the Public

Health, and the removal of all causes of disease which unnecessarily abridge men's right to live", but nothing came of it. Instead the group devoted themselves to setting up a Tailors' Association. Maurice entered heartily into the venture; and wrote a typical letter to Kingsley on the subject, declaring that

> Competition is put forth as the law of the universe. That is a lie. The time is come for us to declare that it is a lie by word and deed. I see no way but associating for work instead of for strikes. I do not say, or think we feel, that the relation of employer and employed is not a true relation. I do not determine that wages may not be a righteous mode of expressing that relation. But at present it is clear that that relation is destroyed, that the payment of wages is nothing but a deception. We may restore the whole state of things: we may bring in a new one. God will decide that. His voice has gone forth clearly bidding us come forward to fight against the present state of things; to call men to repentance first of all, but then also, as it seems to me, to give them an opportunity of showing their repentance and bringing forth fruits worthy of it. This is my notion of a Tailors' Association. (Quoted by Charles Raven, *Christian Socialism 1848-1854*, pp. 149-150.)

On January 8th, 1850, a meeting of the promoters of the scheme with several working men and one or two master-tailors—about twenty persons in all—was held in Maurice's house, and adopted a constitution based upon those of the Paris associations. Walter Cooper was appointed manager at a salary of £2 a week, and shortly afterwards a shop and workrooms were found at 34 Castle Street, and a three-years lease was signed on January 18th.

Meanwhile a public meeting of journeymen tailors was held at the Mechanics Institute, Chancery Lane, and a motion was carried declaring that

> individual selfishness as embodied in the competitive system, lies at the root of the evils under which English industry now suffers: the remedy for the evils of competition lies in the brotherly and Christian principle of Co-operation—that is, of joint work, with shared or common profits: this principle might be widely and readily applied in the formation of Tailors' Working Associations.

Twelve men undertook to join, and work began on February 11th. Within two months the number of men employed had risen to a couple of dozen. An account of this Association was written by Hughes, and was published in the spring as the second of the *Tracts on Christian Socialism*. Maurice in a letter to Daniel Macmillan, dated February 7th, refers to the venture, and makes the typical confession that "our great desire is to Christianize Socialism".

The Association prospered at first. Trade was brisk, and Cooper, when giving evidence before the Slaney Commission in May, 1850, declared that during the first three months of their existence the number of Associates rose from 12 to 34, that they had done business to the tune of £250, and had made a profit of £77.

> Besides their wealthier customers, whose clothes were made to measure, they had found a large demand from their fellow artisans for ready-made goods, and it was hoped that by turning attention to these in the slack seasons they could keep their members fully employed all the year round. Wages were being paid at an average rate of 24s. a week, the skilled workmen getting as much as 33s.—rates which compared favourably with those paid elsewhere in the best houses in the trade. (*Christian Socialism 1848-1854*, p. 195.)

LITERARY ACTIVITIES

On February 19th Maurice published a tract entitled *Dialogue between Somebody (a person of respectability) and Nobody (the writer)*, in which the general ideas of Christian Socialism were expounded. Within the next nine months six more *Tracts on Christian Socialism* followed. (2) *A History of the Working Tailors' Association*, by Hughes; (3) *What Christian Socialism has to do with the question at present agitating the Church*, by Maurice; (4) *The Working Associations of Paris*, by Ludlow; (5) *The Society for Promoting Working-men's Associations*, by Ludlow and Sully; (6) *Prevailing idolatries or hints for political economists*, by Ludlow; (7) *Dialogue between A. and B., two clergymen, on the doctrine of circumstances*, by Maurice; After a year's interval yet another *Tract* was added to the series, *A Clergyman's answer to the question "on what grounds can you associate with men generally,"* by Maurice. Ludlow writing of the *Tracts* in January 1851, says:

> The Tracts have been circulated to the extent of thousands, and have been favourably noticed in the most unforeseen quarters by men perhaps whose candour the authors were presumptuous enough to distrust. (*Christian Socialism 1848-1854*, p. 157.)

On November 2nd, 1850, there appeared the first number of *The Christian Socialist, a Journal of Association, conducted by several of the Promoters of the London Working Men's Associations*. It was priced at a penny, and Ludlow undertook the editorial work. The object of the paper was stated to be "to diffuse the principles of co-operation as the practical application of Christianity to the purposes of trade and industry". In each weekly issue a

Gazette was inserted, containing a record of the various Associations, both in London and the provinces, and abroad.

The paper reached a circulation of 1,500 copies almost immediately, and this was doubled within a year. However, it required a circulation of at least 5,000 to pay its way, and it had eventually to be discontinued after the promoters had lost about £400 on the venture.

Meanwhile, a fresh series of *Tracts by Christian Socialists* was issued. The first was by Maurice, and was published in May 1851. It was intended to be Number One in a *Series of English History by a Clergyman*, but the series was not, in fact, continued. The next tract was Kingsley's *Cheap Clothes and Nasty*, reprinted as a second edition, and priced at 2d. instead of the original 4d. The third and fourth contained another reprint,—Ludlow's article on *Labour and the Poor*, which had originally appeared in *Fraser's Magazine*, and was now revised and issued in two parts. There the series ended, though another series of *Tracts for Priests and People* was launched in January 1854. This series was confined almost entirely to religion and theology.

In addition to these tracts the Christian Socialists were responsible for publishing a large number of other pamphlets. Most of these contained reports of lectures, or the sermons and addresses of Maurice and Kingsley. The last of them appears to have been issued in 1853, under the title of *Strikes Suspended by Self-employment*.

Finally, mention should be made of Charles Kingsley's *Alton Locke*, which appeared in August 1850, and ran into three editions in little over a year.

THE SOCIETY FOR PROMOTING WORKING MEN'S ASSOCIATIONS

It was in June, 1850, that the Society for Promoting Working Men's Associations was established, and the Christian Socialists set to work to advocate "with an almost apostolic fervour the formation of associations of producers, in which groups of working men were to become their own employers". (*The History of Trade Unionism*, by Sidney and Beatrice Webb, p. 225). Sully prepared the first draft constitution for the Society, and after this had been drastically revised by Ludlow, and amended by the other Promoters it was issued as a tract in June.

The Society was to work through two bodies, the Council of Promoters (consisting of the Christian Socialists who advanced the initial capital, with Maurice as President) and the Central Board, consisting of the managers of all the Associations together with a rank-and-file representative from each of them, and a secretary appointed and paid by the Council. The duties of the Central Board were to regulate the relations of the various Associations one with another and with the public, subject to the consent of the Council, and to co-operate with the Council in the formation of new Associations. In the beginning the meetings of the Council and the Central Board were held separately; but in April, 1852, they began to meet jointly.

The Associations themselves were controlled each by its own Council of Administration, which consisted of the manager, a chairman, treasurer, and secretary, and a specified number of Associates. This Council had the right to be consulted by the manager in the conduct of the business; and it could also fix prices for the goods produced by the Association, subject to the control of the Central Board. However, executive authority remained in the manager's hands: he alone took orders, gave out the work, directed the preparation of the material, and sold and received payment for the goods produced. The chairman, however, was recognised as head of the workshop, and had the right to enforce fines for breaches of duty there. It was intended that the appointment of the manager should eventually be in the hands of the Associates (who would thus become self-governing); but at the start it was provided that so long as money was owing to the Promoters they should retain the right to veto any manager whom the Associates might appoint, and should also define his powers and duties. The capital advanced by the Promoters was to be gradually repaid out of the profits of the Associations.

New Associates were required to serve a probationary period, during which time they were to be paid at the same rates as full members, and were to receive in addition a fixed sum in lieu of a share in the profits; but they were to take no part in the control of the Association.

The most elaborate part of the Constitution was that which dealt with the division of profits. The principle of an equal wage for all was rejected, and it was agreed that an allowance be paid to each Associate, "which shall be a fair day's remuneration for a fair day's work whether by time or piece according to the custom of the trade", and that this allowance should be in proportion to the skill and energy of the individual concerned. The net profit or surplus (after deducting expenses, setting aside

proportion for repaying loans or for paying interest on them,
and reserving a portion to increase the capital and extend the
business) was to be divided every six months between all the
Associates "in proportion to the time they have severally worked".

There was to be no Sunday work, and the working day was not
to exceed ten hours, excluding meal-time, unless with the consent
of the Board and the Council. No Association was to be used for
political agitation (although individual members were free to
hold what views they liked); and all disputes between members,
or between members and the manager were to be settled by
arbitrators chosen by each party. Disputes between Associations
were to be settled by the Central Board, subject to the right of
appeal to the Council.

The Society promoted (or helped to promote) Working Associations in a number of trades. The early Associations were formed
by accepting any one who cared to join, up to the number who
could be given work, and disputes soon arose between the
managers and the workers. Even the original Association, the
Castle Street Working Tailors, made scarcely any inquiry into
the record and character of intending Associates.

> We called together large bodies of tailors, and told them what we
> intended to do, and then accepted the first that put down their
> names. (*First Report* of the Society, issued in 1852, p. 6.)

To make matters worse in the case of the Castle Street Tailors,
Walter Cooper, the paid secretary, preferred public speaking
to the mundane job of managing the shop, and when he went off
on a lecturing tour in September, and the Tailors' Council of
Administration took over his work, they found his accounts were
in a hopeless confusion. No definite charge of dishonesty was
made; but the Council wrote to him on September 12th, urging
him to return, and commenting upon his book-keeping in a way
which he resented as insulting. He returned, and a long wrangle
ensued, during the course of which Cooper tried to dismiss the
Council, and found that the whole body of Associates supported
them. Eventually the Promoters intervened, a full enquiry was
held, and the Association was virtually dissolved, and when it
was re-constituted eleven of the original members were refused
admission.

After that the Tailors' Association was relatively successful;
and on March 7th, 1851, Cooper reported that they were in a
position to pay off the whole loan of £300, and still have another
£300 in hand. "They were . . . apparently free from the discords

and suspicions which had produced the crisis six months before. . . . Their prices were well able to stand comparison with those of other firms". (*Christian Socialism 1848-1854*, p. 198).

In April 1852 a branch, specially intended to cater for the needs of the lower and middle classes, and consisting of Associates drawn from tailors who had been reduced to slop-work, was opened at 68 Westminster Bridge Road, and was known as the Borough Branch of the Working Tailors' Association. By this time the Castle Street Group had 19 members.

Of the eight original Associations three were of Boot and Shoe-makers, "a business which seemed to lend itself admirably to the methods of the Christian Socialists", (*Christian Socialism 1848-1854*, p. 200), but of all the Associations none proved more disappointing than these.

Two of the three were set up in April, 1860. One, the Ladies' and Gentlemen's Working Boot and Shoemakers Association, was established in part of a large house and shop at 11B Tottenham Court Road, and began work with a loan of £165; but the cost of these premises (about £160 per annum) proved a too heavy burden, and within a couple of months the Association had to be re-constituted. In this way they lost the summer trade in light shoes, and in September, when the demand was for heavier foot-wear, the Association found itself with a "large and useless stock of light shoes on hand and neither money nor materials". (*Christian Socialism 1848-1854*, p. 201). The Promoters advanced a further loan of £65, and prospects seemed brighter. But fresh dissensions broke out; the manager found it impossible to keep the confidence of the Associates; and it became hopeless to try to carry on. One of the causes of failure appears to have been the fact that none of the members were high-class workmen.

Meanwhile, the "Gentlemen's Working Boot and Shoe and Strong Shoemakers Association" had been set up in business at 151 High Holborn; but they also were soon beset by difficulties. As with the Ladies' Shoemakers, they had trouble with their managers, and

> the best craftsmen would not consent to join an Association which made it a condition of membership that work should be done on the premises. Cobblers have always had a bad reputation for sociability, and it is possible that the rule of the Society, forbidding speculative arguments in the shops, may have pressed hardly upon them. (*Christian Socialism 1848-1854*, p. 202).

Eventually, in July the Holborn premises were closed down and

he two Associations were combined. The men who had been
esponsible for the disagreements were got rid of; but matters
howed little improvement. Early in the following spring there
vas fresh squabbling between the manager and the members;
nd the Council of Promoters decided that the Associates should
orfeit all rights of self-government during a probationary period.
They appointed a new manager to act under their instructions.
After this things went a little better (though the Association did
ot return to full self-government), and by July, 1852 it had 24
members and eight women binders at work.

The third Cobblers' Association, which was founded in June
850, was even less successful than the two we have just consid-
red. There were innumerable quarrels between the members and
he first two managers; and matters came to a head when the
Associates selected for their third manager "a man who could
either read nor write, and drew upon themselves a strong protest
om the Central Board". (*Christian Socialism 1848-1854*, p. 203).
The Association was finally dissolved in December.

It was in the building trade that the Christian Socialists
met with the greatest success, although they

> had often to complain that the Builders were adopting the
> outlook and policy of a joint-stock company owing to their
> expressed desire to admit to Associateship persons not engaged in
> the trade, provided they contributed to the funds. (*Christian
> Socialism 1848-1854*, p. 206.)

The Working Builders' Association was started in May 1850,
n December they were able to take premises at 4 All Saints Place,
Caledonian Road, and they not only paid off the money loaned
hem by the Promoters, but showed a balance on the credit side.
However, the usual trouble about managerial authority cropped
p, and in February 1851 the Associates quarrelled violently and
issolved the Association. Five of them applied for re-admission
nto the Society, and made a fresh start as the North London
Working Builders' Association. This time they were more
uccessful, and by the end of 1851 they were employing from 20 to
5 Associates.

On July 4th, 1850, a second Builders' Association (the Pimlico
uilders) was founded as the outcome of a strike, and commenced
ork the following October. On April 16th, 1851

> they were able to celebrate the building of their first entire house,
> and the owner of it, himself a working man, expressed himself as
> delighted with the quality of their work. (*Christian Socialism 1848-
> 1854*, p. 207.)

N

By July 1852 they had 46 members, had built some 20 houses and owned property to the value of £4,700, in addition to more than £1,000 worth of stock.

Of the remaining two original Associations, one was the Working Printers' Association, which consisted of four friends who were provided with a printing press by the Society, and with quarters in a house, 4A Johnson's Court, Gough Square, at a cost of about £44. They never did much business outside printing the Society's periodicals, tracts, pamphlets and catalogues, but they managed to pay their way, and increase their numbers to six, and on occasion to employ 12 to 14 workmen.

Finally, there was the Working Bakers' Association, founded in April, 1850, with 10 members, and a manager, James Clarkson, who supplied the initial capital. In June a disagreement occurred, Clarkson resigned, and thereafter the Association consisted of three members, and did practically no business beyond what the Promoters were able to put in its way. "Eventually they were absorbed into the service of the Co-operative stores, as the London Co-operative Bakery". (*Christian Socialism 1848-1854*, p. 209-210.

One other venture is worth notice. On February 18th, 1850 the North London Needlewoman's Association was founded. I was not affiliated to the Society, but was managed by a separate committee of eight ladies, of whom Mrs. Maurice was the secretary. It rented 31 Red Lion Square (the Maurices making themselves responsible for the rent) and £500 was collected for the purchase of furniture and materials. Besides workrooms and a shop, there were lodging-rooms, where single women could live at a cost of 1s. 6d. a week. Twenty women workers from the London sweat-shops worked in this establishment, under a superintendent, who was paid a fixed salary, and acted directly under the Managing Committee. It was arranged that part of any profits should go to repay the loan and interest on it, and the remainder should be divided among the needlewomen quarterly. This Association, of course, was little more than a charitable organisation. It survived until the autumn of 1853, when it was wound up. The house in Red Lion Square was afterwards used for a time by the Working Men's College.

Some twelve months after the foundation of the original eight Associations two more were set going. One was the Working Pianoforte Makers' Association (February 1851), which eventually opened premises at 5 Charles Street, Drury Lane, in the October. These premises and the plant and goodwill had been bought from the men's employer by Neale. There were for some time 14 Associates and 3 non-Associates, and they had a market for four or five pianos a week. The other Association was the City Working Tailors', of 23 Cullum Street, Fenchurch Street. Their first effort failed, but they started again, in May, 1852, with six Associates, Neale advancing them money for their initial expenses. By 1853 the group had failed altogether as a Working Association, and was trading as Bowen, Brown & Co. It finally disappeared completely in 1857.

The last Association to be founded under the direct auspices of the Christian Socialists was the Working Smiths'. A start was made in July, 1852, in premises in Pimlico, and though the Association was never very large it lasted for some years.

Two more charitable organisations were also set on foot: the East London Needlewomen's Home and Workshop, started in the autumn of 1851, at 51 Wellclose Square, Whitechapel, and the Ladies Guild, started at 4 Russell Place, Fitzroy Square, early in 1852. The first was similar to the Needlewomen of Red Lion Square, and was intended to help the poorest of all the sweated women workers. Lord Shaftesbury and several other prominent philanthropists agreed to serve on the Committee, together with some of the Promoters; but "the big folk, with the exception of one City Missionary, took no trouble whatever in the matter", (*Life of Maurice*, ii, p. 65), and the "Home" did not long survive. The Ladies Guild was intended to assist "distressed gentlewomen" and the Guild was presented with the patent rights of a new method of painting on glass. Much time was spent in teaching this to the members, and by July it was reported that 27 were at work. The Guild appears to have survived until 1856.

Two Associations which got going in the provinces associated themselves with the Society, though they were not directly sponsored by it. The first was the Southampton Tailors' Association, which was first mooted in April, 1850. It was formed by a group of journeymen, who raised the necessary capital by means of 5s. shares, and reported their intentions to the Society of Promoters in November. They were recognised as an Association connected with the Society in June, 1851, and a circular, which they sent out in April 1852, speaks confidently of their "most unequivocal success". The second provincial Association which associated itself with the Society applied for recognition in September 1851. This was the Hatters of Salford. They had hoped for help from their Trade Union, and when this was refused they subscribed equally to a fund for the purchase of tools and materials, and managed to collect £40. Arrangements were made with Co-operative stores in Glasgow, Bradford, Halifax and London to sell their goods on a commission basis (of 10 per cent.). Eventually they joined forces with the Manchester Working Tailors' Association, and the two set up a shop at 83 Bridge Street. This Association was one of the longest-lived: in 1864 there was a very favourable account of it printed in the *Westminster Review*. It carried on until 1873, and only ceased after the tailors had been compelled to disband for want of sales.

All over the country similar experiments were undertaken. "We are only a very small stream of the great flood", says the *First Report* of the Promoters' Society. In the pages of the *Christian Socialist* and the *Journal of Association**

> we find a continuous stream of enquiries, proposals, reports and discussions coming in from sympathisers and imitators everywhere. The Silk-weavers of Bethnal Green, the Plush-weavers of Salford, the Saw-makers of Sheffield, the Stone-masons of Sunderland— these are some of the Associations which, though not formally connected with the Society, yet worked in close contact with it. And in several towns organisations parallel in scope to the Society of Promoters had been set up, such as the General Labour Redemp- tion Society of Bury, whose first object, as set out in its constitu- tion, was to unite labourers "by forming associations". This was founded on September 16th, 1850, by the "Central Committee of the Iron Trades of Bury," made the *Christian Socialist* its official organ in November, and on New Year's Day mustered nearly eight hundred members to meet Maurice, Hughes and Neale when they visited the north. Somewhat similar was the Halifax Working Men's Co-operative Society, founded in January, 1851, which sent its reports and balance-sheets regularly to the *Christian Socialist*, and at its first anniversary meeting made a deputation from the Council of Promoters the guests of the evening. As for Tailors' Associations they grew like mushrooms under the spell of Cooper's eloquence: in Edinburgh, Glasgow, Liverpool and Newcastle-on-Tyne, Associations were formed . . . and others were mooted, and sometimes even started at Doncaster, Norwich, Sunderland, Aberdeen and Dublin. (*Christian Socialism 1848-1854*, pp. 222-223.)

CHRISTIAN SOCIALISM AND THE TRADE UNIONS

The formation of the first Working Tailors' Association was responsible for bringing into the Christian Socialist movement

---

*In January, 1852, *The Christian Socialist* was replaced as the organ of the Co- operators by *The Journal of Association*—a change indicative of the passing of control from the "promoters" to the Societies which they had set on foot.

man of whom George Jacob Holyoake has said, "His monument n the Co-operative Movement". This was Edward Vansittart Neale. Having seen an advertisement of the Association he isited Castle Street, and got into touch with the Society of Promoters, who speedily invited him to join their council.

Neale was a barrister with chambers in Lincoln's Inn. Unlike he other Christian Socialists he was a really wealthy man, with house in Mayfair and a "place" in Warwickshire, and now

> at last, they had a well-filled purse placed at their disposal with a lavish and unsparing enthusiasm. It would have been quite beyond the power of the others to do more than start the Tailors and such Associations as required hardly any plant or costly materials. The campaign in the provinces would have been impossible. . . . The movement could never have been more tentative and local; and the losses of the first few weeks would have put an end to the whole adventure. But Neale . . . made it evident that he was prepared to sacrifice everything for the cause. At his instigation and with his support schemes of far-reaching importance became practicable. . . . Even Hughes, his closest comrade in the movement, never knew the extent of his losses, but only that they involved the sale of his house in Hill Street and of an estate in Warwickshire, and constrained him for many years to live with strict economy and to accept a salary for his work.*
> (*Christian Socialism 1848-54*, p. 229.)

After Neale joined the Council attempts were made to interest he trade unions in the plans of the Christian Socialists. In the utumn of 1850 Lloyd Jones and Walter Cooper were sent out to undertake propaganda work in the Midlands and in Lancashire. They also signed a circular letter which was sent to all the London Trade Societies urging them to support plans for Co-operative Production on the model of the Working Associations which the Society of Promoters had established, and asking them to grant an interview. "We are anxious", they said,

> to explain to you, as men holding official positions in your trade, the nature of the operations in which we are engaged.

Two interviews were granted, both with societies of Cabinetmakers, beyond which there seems to have been no response to the circular.

Thus far the Working Associations formed directly under the auspices of the Christian Socialists had been set up for the most part in badly organised trades, and the Trade Unions had had little to do with them. It was not until after the merging of a

---

*Greening estimates Neale's losses at £60,000.

number of small societies of engineers and ironworkers to form the Amalgamated Society of Engineers, Machinists, Smiths, Millwrights and Patternmakers, in January, 1851, that any impression was made by the Christian Socialists on an important trade union.

The Amalgamated Society of Engineers created a new type of Trade Union organisation, which was speedily copied by the Carpenters and others.

> From 1852 to 1889 the elaborate constitution of the Amalgamated Society of Engineers served as the model for all new national trade societies, whilst old organisations found themselves gradually incorporating its leading features. (*The History of Trade Unionism*, by Sidney & Beatrice Webb, p. 217.)

These "New Model" Unions were quite unlike the small, local craft societies of earlier days, or the cumbrous "all-in" Unions which had been attempted in the early decades of the 19th century. They catered in the main for the "aristocracy of labour", the highly skilled craftsmen, and they had high subscription rates which made them still more exclusive. Unlike the loosely-organised General Unions such as the "General Union of Trades (or Philanthropic Hercules) of 1818, or the Grand National Consolidated Trades Union of Great Britain and Ireland, of 1833-34, the new amalgamated societies no longer entertained revolutionary or chiliastic dreams of overturning capitalism and building a new social order. Instead they were increasingly concerned with providing friendly society benefits for their members (out-of-work pay, funeral benefits, disablement benefits, travelling allowances, even old age pensions to superannuated members), and they combined "the functions of a trade protection society with those of a permanent insurance society". (*The History of Trade Unionism*, Sidney & Beatrice Webb, p. 218). They also became more and more adverse to risking their funds in strike action, and the Stonemasons' Central Committee, for instance, repeatedly caution their members "against the dangerous practice of striking. . . . Keep from it", they urge, "as you would from a ferocious animal that you know would destroy you". (*History of Trade Unionism*, p. 199). The Portsmouth Lodge of this society even went to the length of suggesting that not only should strikes cease, but that the very word "strike" should be abolished.

> The minutes and circulars of the larger Unions abound in impressive warnings against aggressive action. (*History of Trade Unionism*, p. 198.)

low often have disputes been averted by a few timely words with
e employers!" say the Ironmoulders (*Address of Delegate Meeting*,
ptember 26, 1846): whilst in 1854 the Flint Glass Makers, on
e proposition of their Central Committee, abolished the allow-
ice of "strike money" by a vote of the whole of the members.
Many unions sought to make their labour scarce, and thus
ney hoped) to raise the rate of wages, by establishing an
nigration fund for their members. Thus the Flint Glass Makers
eclare in 1857 (*Address of Executive*) that "It is simply a question
' supply and demand, and we all know that if we supply a
·eater quantity of an article than what is actually demanded
iat the cheapening of that article, whether it be labour or any
ther commodity is a natural result". "In this application of
ie doctrine of Supply and Demand the Flint Glass Makers were
)ined by Compositors, Bookbinders, Ironmoulders, Potters,
nd . . . the Engineers. For the next ten years an Emigration
und becomes a constant feature of many of the large societies".
The History of Trade Unionism, p. 201).

The avoidance of aggressive strike action, and the search for
ther means of improving the conditions of their members had
een characteristic of many Trade Unions before the Amalgamated
ociety of Engineers was formed, and all that the Engineers'
eaders did was to continue this policy with greater vigour and
bility. It was in keeping with their preference for a "constructive"
olicy that they should send their General Secretary, William
Allan, and William Newton (the two men who had been mainly
esponsible for the creation of the A.S.E.) to discuss with the
ociety for Promoting Working Men's Associations the possibility
f devoting some of their funds to the development of Associations
n the engineering trades. Up till then the only Associations
which the Christian Socialists had succeeded in forming had been
n the "ill-organised trades where the work was done under
lomestic conditions" (*Christian Socialism 1848-54*, p. 235), and, not
innaturally, the Promoters were delighted with this new and
promising development. They suggested that the Windsor
fronworks, a foundry in Liverpool which had recently failed and
was now for sale, should be bought and run as a self-governing
Association.

Accordingly six trustees were appointed, including Hughes,
Ludlow and Neale, and a prospectus was issued with a covering
letter from the Executive Council of the A.S.E. inviting the public
(and especially members of the Iron Trades and of the Co-

operative movement) to subscribe to the £50,000 (which it was estimated was needed) by taking up £1 shares to be paid for in monthly instalments. On January 6th the membership of the Union endorsed by an overwhelming majority in a ballot vote the proposal of their Executive to invest £10,000 in the venture, and definite plans were prepared for starting such an Association. It was decided that the workmen employed in the concern were to be members of the A.S.E., and that wages were to be paid at the standard rates fixed by the A.S.E. Profits were to be devoted to the payment of interest on capital at 5 per cent., to providing an unemployment fund, to improving the condition of the Associates and other workers employed, and to extending the business or forming similar establishments: in other words, no part of the profits was to be divisible except in the shape of unemployment benefit and collective benefits.

Unfortunately for these ambitious plans the great engineering lockout began in 1852, when the London and Lancashire employers set out deliberately to smash the new amalgamated society. The Engineers had been seeking an end to piecework and to systematic overtime, and the employers had threatened a general lockout of the industry if a strike took place at any one establishment. On January 1st, 1852, the members of the A.S.E. refused to work overtime, and on the 10th of that month the masters kept their threat to close every important engineering works in London and Lancashire.

A three-months struggle followed, in which the Christian Socialists helped by letters to the press, pamphlets, and lectures, and also by liberal donations. (According to the Webbs Lord Goderich, afterwards the Marquis of Ripon, gave the Engineers' Executive £500, and Charles Raven puts his total help at double that figure). Meanwhile the employers insisted not only on the unconditional withdrawal of the men's demands—only 16 out of the 11,800 members of the A.S.E. had declared against the abolition of overtime and piecework when a vote had been taken in the preceding August—but also presented the men with the hated "document", i.e. demanded that they should give a written promise to leave the Union.

The A.S.E. had a fund of £25,000 when the struggle began, and other trade societies donated another £5,000, whilst the general public subscribed £4,000 to their strike funds. Nevertheless these financial resources became exhausted, and in April the men were forced to resume work on the employers' terms. Almost all the masters insisted upon their men signing the "document", but as they did this under duress the men had no compunction about remaining members of the Union, and the A.S.E. remained substantially intact. But their funds were now exhausted, and they had no longer the means for financing a venture in Co-operative Production on the scale suggested by the Christian Socialists.

However, two less ambitious schemes were financed by Neale and his cousin, A. A. Vansittart, who was also a man of considerable means. In January John Musto (brother of Joseph Musto, President of the A.S.E.), persuaded his fellow employees to form the Southwark Working Engineers' Association, and Vansittart secured a factory for them in Cambridge Road, Mile End. The constitution which they adopted was modelled on that which had been drafted for the Windsor Ironworks. The A.S.E. was represented at the first meeting of the shareholders (March 6th) by Newton and Joseph Musto, who expressed warm approval of the venture.

About the same time Neale bought a small factory, the Atlas Works, in Emerson Street, near Southwark Bridge, and started another Association, also modelled on the plan for the Windsor Ironworks. The venture was launched on March 25th, and once more the A.S.E. blessed the undertaking.

As late as April 29th the A.S.E. were still willing to support Neale's venture, and on that date there appeared in *The Times* an address from their Executive Council to their members and to the trades in general, reporting five resolutions which they had adopted on April 22nd. The last of these is worth quoting in full:

> That in the opinion of this meeting hostile resistance of labour against Capital is not calculated to enhance the condition of the labourer. We therefore advise that all our future operations should be directed in promoting the system of self-employment in associative workshops, as the best means of effectually regulating the conditions of labour, and that this resolution be submitted to our next delegate meeting.

Appended to this resolution was a letter signed by William Allan, the General Secretary, on behalf of the Executive Council, and dated April 26th. This was even more enthusiastic in its advocacy of Co-operative Production.

> How shall we set about the work of preparation for a coming time ? (it asked). There is but one way—we must co-operate for production. The events of the last few months have directed the attention of working men to co-operation, and inclined them to

it more decidedly than years of prosperous industry could have done. Perhaps a greater good is to come out of present evil than could have been in any other way brought about. We have learned that it is not sufficient to accumulate funds, that it is necessary also to use them reproductively, and if this lesson does not fail in its effects a few years will see the land studded with workshops belonging to the workers—workshops where the profits shall cheer and not oppress labour, where tyranny cannot post an abominable declaration on the gates ; where the opportunity of working is secured without the sacrifice of all that makes work dignified and honourable.   Then, indeed, the artisan may successfully assert his claim to be treated as a man with thoughts and feelings instead of a machine.   And if the employers, seeking to wrong him, close the gates of the factories, he will not then stand in forced idleness, consuming the accumulations of the past years, but with double energy he will turn to the factory, and there do the work of the country, without the unneeded help of others. . . . Assisted as we have been by the advice of men who take a deep interest in the promotion of Working Men's Associations, and have counselled the abandonment of all attempts to deal with the capitalists in a spirit of hostility—and given it as their opinion that nothing but creating a new relationship between capital and labour can effectually elevate the condition of the toilers of society, we must progress in these principles, and we hope that our next delegate meeting will lay down the basis of our future permanent prosperity. Immediately on receipt of this circular each secretary is instructed to convene a meeting of the members of his branch, so that its contents may be made generally known to the members.*

But the brutal fact was that the Amalgamated Engineers had no funds with which to back these brave words, and the Engineering Associations had to depend on what Neale and Vansittart advanced. Disaster soon overtook them. The Mile End Ironworks lost heavily through taking on a large contract at too low a price, and had to close down in 1854. The Atlas Works lasted a year or two longer before they were wrecked by quarrels among the Associates. Some small ventures also disappeared.

By 1855 the A.S.E. was becoming hostile to the idea of Co-operative Production, for experience had convinced them that when workmen became managers or secretaries of these undertakings they usually ceased to be energetic members of their Unions.

We have found, say the Engineers' Executive in their Annual Report of 1855, that when a few of our own members have

---

*The Christian Socialists were further encouraged by a declaration on June 2nd, by the National Association of United Trades that "the time has come for the entire abandonment of strikes and turn-outs as a means of protecting labour", and that "the only thing left is to organise and carry out a self-supporting co-operative reproductive system of employment."

commenced business hitherto they have abandoned the society, and conducted the workshops even worse than other employers. (*The History of Trade Unionism*, by Sidney and Beatrice Webb, p. 226.)

THE CHRISTIAN SOCIALISTS AND CONSUMERS' CO-OPERATION

The experiments which the Christian Socialists conducted in Co-operative Production had no permanent results and are of comparatively little importance to the development of the British working class movement. As we have seen, there was nothing original in their notion of self-governing workshops, and many such ventures were undertaken in this country by working men who were entirely uninfluenced by anything that Ludlow and his friends thought or did. Their real claim to be gratefully remembered by the working class is the help they gave to Consumers' Co-operation. There is a certain irony in that, for the majority of the Christian Socialists did not rate Consumers' Co-operation nearly so highly as Producers' Co-operation.

> For the Christian Socialists proper, Producers' Co-operation, on a basis of high moral principles, was the objective; and Consumers' Co-operation was valued only to the extent that it helped to provide an outlet for goods made by Producers' Societies. For the Co-operators of the North, even if they strongly favoured Producers' Co-operation, as many of them did, Consumers' Co-operation came first. Neale and Lloyd Jones stood midway between the two points of view, trying to combine them into a single unified movement. (*A Century of Co-operation*, G. D. H. Cole, p. 132.)

Neale had been greatly influenced by Lloyd Jones and the Chevalier St. André, "neither of whom was principally interested in the religious aims of the Christian Socialist group or in the tiny Working Men's Associations which the group were so painfully nursing" (*A Century of Co-operation*, p. 130). In June, 1850, St. André proposed a plan for a Co-operative Agency which could act as a general centre for Co-operative trade and as a federal organ of the whole movement. Neale was impressed by this suggestion, and drew up a scheme of his own, which included the proposal for a "General Union" of Co-operative societies, which would link the individual societies together so that the more successful could help the less successful out of a common fund. He also proposed that this "General Union" should have as an auxiliary a General Co-operative Agency along the lines which St. André had suggested.

As a first step towards realizing these ideas, Neale put up the capital, in October 1850, for opening the London Co-operative Stores, at 76 Charlotte Street, Fitzroy Square (the old head-quarters of the Owenite Equitable Labour Exchange). This store (says G. D. H. Cole) "seems to have provided for dividend on purchases in a rudimentary form". (*A Century of Co-operation*, p. 130). Lloyd Jones was appointed manager, and St. André supervisor, and a prospectus was issued stating that the object of the Stores was to "enable members of the Associations and other persons who might desire it, to obtain articles of daily use free from adulteration, of the best quality and at the lowest charge, after defraying the necessary expense of management, distribution, and providing for a reserve fund". After these administrative expenses had been met, all subscribers of not less than five shillings were to receive back the profits upon their purchases. Members of Working Associations were offered special terms even if they did not become subscribers.

Neale's proposals for a "General Union" to unite all the Working Associations and the Co-operative Stores into one body was discussed at a special conference of the Promoters' Society, and the scheme was referred to the Central Board. There it seems to have been dropped, for although the Board resolved to form themselves into a General Industrial Association (thereby securing legal status) there is no record of any action being taken to implement this decision.

Meanwhile Lloyd Jones left for the north, and succeeded in getting a conference of Co-operative Societies to meet in Manchester over Christmas. The main business of this conference was a discussion of the proposed Industrial and Provident Societies' Act; but Lloyd Jones used the opportunity which the gathering of co-operators afforded to establish a Northern Store in Manchester on similar lines to those of the London Co-operative Stores. In April, 1851, he persuaded another Co-operative Conference, in Bury, to carry a resolution in favour of the establishment of a "Central Trading Department", and to appoint a committee to report on the matter to a further conference.

The following month (May, 1851) Neale converted his London Co-operative Stores into a Central Co-operative Agency, which he hoped to make a Co-operative Wholesale agency for the whole Co-operative movement of the country, at the same time supplying the Working Associations with a market for their products.

Then in June a representative Co-operative Conference (which included the important Yorkshire and Lancashire societies) met in Manchester, and received the Report of the committee which had been appointed at the Bury Conference. This Report stressed the need for measures to combat the sale of adulterated food and to give the local Co-operative Societies the advantages of bulk purchases in the wholesale markets; and it proposed to raise a capital of £3,000 in £5 shares, these to be taken up in the first instance by Co-operative Societies, and thereafter to whatever extent might be necessary by individual sympathisers. Interest at 5 per cent. was to be paid on this capital, and the remaining profits to be divided into four equal parts. One was to go to a reserve fund, until this fund equalled the paid-up capital; one was to be used in promoting Working Men's Co-operative Associations; and the remaining two quarters were to be used for the payment of dividends to Co-operative Societies in proportion to their purchases. The

> scheme is in most respects practically identical with the plan adopted by Neale for his Central Co-operative Agency. There are, however, two differences, and one of them is highly significant. Neale's plan did not specifically give Societies the priority over individuals in subscribing the capital required; nor did it provide for dividend on purchases, allocating the "two-fourths" instead to payment of a bonus on wages to the employees of the Agency. (*A Century of Co-operation*, G. D. H. Cole, p. 131.)

This rival plan did not deter Neale from persevering with his own scheme, and a circular was sent to the Trades Societies of the kingdom asking for their support of the Central Co-operative Agency. A Committee was appointed to follow up this appeal, and an address was printed in the *Christian Socialist* for November 15th, 1851, which proposed (among other things) that a Model Association be formed in each trade to employ members of the Trade Society who might be unemployed. It also suggested that Co-operative Stores should be organised to supply articles of domestic consumption and raw materials for the Productive Associations, and to provide them with a market for the goods which they produced. The Central Co-operative Agency should assist (it suggested) by supplying goods and raw materials at wholesale prices, and in warehousing, displaying and selling the manufactured products of the Working Associations.

The Society for Promoting Working Men's Associations was not consulted about the Address, and Ludlow, when he returned from a tour in the north, criticised it as an appeal to the commercial instincts and as being false to the moral principles of Christian Socialism, and a breach threatened between himself and Neale. More and more there was a divergence of views between the two men.

> Ludlow was an enthusiast for Co-operative Production; but, with Maurice and Kingsley, he stressed the need for individual moral and religious conversion as an indispensable basis for the success of the Co-operative principle, and he had become convinced by the growing pains of the Working Associations that he and his fellow-promoters had made a mistake in not selecting carefully enough, on moral and Christian principles, those who were allowed to become working associates. The promoters therefore wished to go slow, and to limit their practical efforts to tried supporters who could be relied upon to act in the spirit of Christian Socialism. . . . Neale . . . though a churchman, did not share Ludlow's view. He wanted to join hands, on a secular basis, with Trade Unions and Co-operative Stores in order to create a nation-wide movement of Producers and Consumers; and the Central Co-operative Agency, backed by his money, rested on this wider basis, and was in no way subject to the Christian Socialist 'Council of Promoters'. (*A Century of Co-operation*, G. D. H. Cole, p. 110).

One result of this clash of opinion was that the offices of the Society for Promoting Working Men's Associations were removed from the rooms which it had occupied at Charlotte Street. On February 5th, 1852, Penrose, a member of the Council, prepared plans for the construction of a hall to seat 300 people, together with offices for the Society under the workshops of the Tailors' Association, at 34 Castle Street. The work was entrusted to the North London Working Builders.

Meanwhile two branch stores had been founded by the London Co-operative Stores. One, which opened at 18 Newnham Street, Edgware Road, in April 1851, had to be wound up after a year owing to internal quarrels; the other, opened at 13 Swan Street, Manchester, as a result of the conference of December, 1850 (see page 204), was more successful, and served the Central Co-operative Agency as a northern agent for wholesale business.

Before long, however, Neale's Agency had to face the competition of a rival "Wholesale"; for St. André, whom G. D. H. Cole describes as "a genial scoundrel of considerable force and personality" (*A Century of Co-operation*, p. 103), left the Central Co-operative Agency, and set up, in December 1852, the Universal Supply and Demand Establishment (shortened to the Universal Provider), at 159 Fenchurch Street. It got some Co-operative

support, the Rochdale Pioneers dealing with it as well as with
Neale's Agency; nevertheless it failed and was dissolved on April
27th, 1855.

For a while the Central Co-operative Agency seemed to thrive.
and in the spring of 1855 it removed to "a fine block of buildings,
comprising showrooms, factory and warehouse" at 356 Oxford
Street, its old Charlotte Street premises having become too small
for it.

Another of Neale's activities about this time was the founding,
in January, 1852, of a Co-operative League for the discussion
of Co-operative problems; whilst in June of the same year he
brought forward proposals for a Co-operative Investment Society,
which could receive deposits from individuals or from Trade and
Benefit Societies, and make advances, after the manner of a Building Society, to bodies of working men who needed capital for
Co-operative ventures. Neale got the support of the National
Association of United Trades for the Protection of Labour for
his scheme, but nothing ever came of it.

Meanwhile, the Society for Promoting Working Men's Associations having by this time completed its Castle Street head-
quarters, a series of debates and lectures took place there, at
which many prominent people spoke, among them Bronterre
O'Brien, perhaps the ablest theoretician that the Chartist Movement produced.

These meetings paved the way for summoning a general
conference of Co-operators. Since the abandonment of the
Owenite Congresses no serious attempt had been made to get
together a representative body to which the whole Co-operative
movement could look for guidance. Now the Society of Promoters called a national conference to consider the new Industrial
and Provident Societies Act, which had become law on June 30th,
1852. The conference met in the Castle Street Hall, on July
26th and 27th, and delegates were invited from all known
Co-operative organisations. Twenty-eight organisations were
represented by 25 delegates, those unable to send a delegate
being allowed a proxy. Hughes gave an account of the scope
and value of the new Act, and a Committee was appointed to
arrange a similar conference in Manchester, the following year.

However, the chief value of this conference was that it asked
the Council of the Society for Promoting Working Men's Associations to prepare a memorandum explaining the advantages
which Co-operative Societies could secure by registering under

the new Act. In September such a memorandum was circularised, together with a set of *Model Rules for Industrial Societies,* as necessitated by the Act. These Model Rules were approved by the Registrar, J. Tidd Pratt, on September 16th, and were of very considerable help to Co-operative Societies.

THE INDUSTRIAL AND PROVIDENT SOCIETIES ACT

The great service which the Christian Socialists did for the Co-operative Movement was to secure the passing of the Industrial and Provident Societies Act of 1852. Mr. G. D. H. Cole has produced an excellent summary of the legal position of the Co-operative Societies before the passing of this Act (*A Century of Co-operation*) and this section owes much to his account.

Co-operation (he points out) never suffered under legal disabilities as severe as those which beset the Trade Unions. No one was ever put in prison for belonging to a Co-operative Society, and no one ever suggested that it was unlawful to form such a body, or for it to engage in trade or production. The difficulty was not that Co-operative Societies were under the ban of the courts, but rather that no special provision had been made for them, so that they were unable to enlist the positive protection of the law when it was needed either to secure them against fraudulent or negligent officials or to enable them to carry on trade in such a way as to enter into firm contracts, to sue or be sued as collective bodies, or to enjoy any reasonable security for their funds. . . . The Co-operative Societies of the Owenite period mostly did without any sort of legal status, though a few which sprang directly out of Friendly Societies may have been registered under the Friendly Societies Acts. These Acts, however, were not designed to cover trading enterprises, and before 1834 the recognition accorded by the state even to Friendly Societies was very narrowly limited. They had been first recognized under George Rose's Act of 1793, which was designed to foster Friendly Societies under the patronage of members of the upper classes rather than as bodies created by the workers for mutual self-help. . . . Thus things remained until 1834, when an amending Act widened the scope allowed Societies by extending legal recognition to Friendly Societies formed "for any purpose not contrary to law". Trading Societies were thus for the first time made eligible to apply; but there was still no special provision for them. The Act of 1846 went considerably further, including what came to be known as the "frugal investment" clause, which authorised the establishment of Societies "for the frugal investment of the savings of the members, for better enabling them to purchase food, clothes, or other necessaries, or the tools or implements of their trade or calling, or to provide for the education of their children or kindred". (*A Century of Co-operation,* pp. 114-118.)

The Act of 1846 established the Friendly Societies Registry, and gave full powers of enrolment to the Registrar, and it was no longer necessary for societies to submit their rules at enrolment to Quarter Sessions (as it had been, for instance, when the Rochdale Pioneers founded their society in 1844).

However, "the Act of 1846 remained seriously defective from the standpoint of the Co-operative Movement. Trading Societies were dealt with only in the "frugal investment" clause, and under this the Societies were empowered to trade only with their own members. . . . The position of Producers' Co-operatives which had to seek markets outside their membership was left very uncertain. Moreover, the Societies . . . could hold personal property only through trustees, and landed property not at all: they were restricted to investing any accumulated funds through the National Debt Commissioners, and there was no power for Societies to federate or join together in any way. (*A Century of Co-operation*, pp. 117-118).

This, then, was the position when the Christian Socialists took up the question, and began to seek a modification of the law. As a first step Hughes approached a Member of Parliament by the name of Robert Aglionby Slaney, "a gentleman upon whose name as the promoter of Slaney's Act Christian Socialism has conferred an undeserved immortality". (*Christian Socialism 1848-54*, p. 289). Slaney was completely ignorant of the subject which he undertook to champion in the House, but the Christian Socialists "coached him carefully", and in the spring of 1850 he moved for the appointment of a Select Committee of the House to report upon "Investments for the Savings of the Middle and Working Classes".

Ludlow, Neale, Hughes and Lloyd Jones, and several working men, including Cooper, gave evidence before this Committee; and the Christian Socialists also induced H. Bellenden Ker (Counsel to the Board of Trade and an acknowledged authority on Company Law) to appear. "On the whole his testimony was disappointing" (*Christian Socialism 1848-54*, p. 292); but John Stuart Mill, who was also persuaded to give evidence, "filled the Christian Socialists with delight" (*Christian Socialism 1848-54*, p. 295) by his approval both of Co-operative stores and of Associations for Co-operative Production.

There was a further Committee the following year; and eventually in 1852 the Industrial and Provident Societies' Act*

---

*It is an interesting point that it was a Conservative Government which put this Act on the Statute Book, after a Liberal Government had refused facilities, apparently because it had been alarmed during the Engineers' lock-out of 1852 by the attempt which the men had made to defeat their employers by embarking on Co-operative production.

O

received the royal assent on June 30th, and the "Co-operative Movement was at last given an assured, though not yet a fully satisfactory, legal status" (*A Century of Co-operation*, p. 110).

The new Act carried with it very real advantages. Under it the Co-operative Societies, while retaining all their privileges under the Friendly Societies Acts, were given for the first time an Act of Parliament specifically designed to meet the needs of both Producers' and Consumers Co-operation. They were set free from the provisions of the Act of 1844 compelling partnerships of more than 25 persons to register as joint stock companies in order to secure trading protection. . . . Under Company Law as it then stood it was an essential requirement that companies should allow free transfer of their shares. This rule, applied to Co-operative Societies, would have meant that control might have passed right out of the hands of those trading at the Stores—or in the case of Producers' Societies out of the hands of the employees or of other shareholders concerned to keep them working on truly Co-operative lines. Indeed this loss of control did actually occur in the case of the bodies (the "Working-class Limiteds") which became registered as joint stock companies. . . . The Act of 1852 restricted the transference of shares (called in the Act "subscriptions") in Industrial and Provident Societies so as to require holders who wished to dispose of their "subscriptions" either to sell them back to the Society or at any rate to secure the consent of the Board of Management to the transfer to a particular person. Industrial and Provident Societies were further differentiated from joint stock companies in that no one could hold more than £100 in the subscribed capital . . . but the Societies were free . . . to accept loans from their members up to an amount equal to four times the subscribed capital. . . . The Societies were, moreover, freed from the restrictions imposed on Friendly Societies in respect of the investment of their funds, and were thus enabled to invest their resources freely in the development of their operations. (*A Century of Co-operation*, pp. 118-119.)

But despite the vastly improved status which the Co-operatives enjoyed as a result of the 1852 Act they did not get all that they wanted.

The privilege of limited liability was still refused, and this remained as a serious deterrent to working-class investment, though the difficulty could be to some extent got round . . . by the device of vesting property absolutely in the hands of trustees. This was the method adopted by the Christian Socialists for their Working Associations. . . . Moreover the Act of 1852 contained no provision for joint or federal action by Co-operative Societies, and it was therefore impossible for Neale to organise his Central Co-operative Agency on a federal basis. He had to resort to the old device of trustees to hold the property and to constitute a joint stock company—Jones, Woodin, and Co.—to carry on the actual trading operations, and he could not give the Societies which agreed to deal with the Agency any effective control over its affairs. This was undoubtedly one reason for its failure. (*A Century of Co-operation*, pp. 119-120.)

THE END OF THE CHRISTIAN SOCIALIST MOVEMENT

In the year 1853 the Co-operative Societies held a National Conference at Manchester. At this conference the Northern Consumers' Societies (which had been formed on the Rochdale model) played the leading role, and the Society for Promoting Working Men's Associations transformed itself into the Society for Promoting Industrial and Provident Societies under the new Act. The next year (1854) when the Co-operative Conference met at Leeds, the Christian Socialists definitely dropped out as an organised body. They wound up their Society, leaving the Co-operative Conference (which it was intended to make an annual affair) to take over its functions, and Neale to bear the remaining responsibility through the Central Co-operative Agency.

By this time many of the Working Associations had failed. As already related the Mile End Ironworks had been wound up in 1854 (see page 202); and the Atlas Works only lasted a year or two longer. The Amalgamated Shoemakers' Association had also been deprived of self-government, and was still in difficulties; and in the end the manager, Thomas Christmas, took over the business and conducted it as a private firm.

The Printers, too, became a private firm; and the Pimlico Builders incurred serious losses and had to be wound up in 1853. The North London Builders survived until 1860, when it became a private business. Even the Castle Street Tailors (which had been the pioneer, and the model for all the Associations) came to grief in 1860, when it was discovered that Walter Cooper had been misapplying the profits and falsifying the books.

Nor was the Central Co-operative Agency any more long-lived than the Working Associations. The Manchester branch which had been established by Lloyd Jones in 1850 had faded out by 1852 or 1853, and in 1857 even Neale was forced to accept the fact of failure. The Central Co-operative Agency ceased to exist as a Co-operative concern, and what was left of it was carried on as an ordinary company under James Woodin, its former business manager. One reason for its failure was that London was too far off to act as a Wholesale Society for the Yorkshire and

Lancashire stores, whilst Consumers' Co-operation in the metropolis was still too embryonic to keep a Wholesale going.*

After the Christian Socialists wound up their Society, they devoted much of their time to the cause of popular education, and founded the Working Men's College (1853-54). This was originally housed in the premises vacated by the defunct Needlewomen's Association at 31 Red Lion Square. Later the College was transferred to Crowndale Road, Camden Town.

Maurice became principal of the Working Men's College and lectured on literature and theology; whilst Ludlow gave lectures on law, and Furnivall taught English Grammar. There were also courses in Public Health, Geometry, Algebra, Arithmetic and Geography. Later French, Latin, German and Greek were added to the syllabus; and Hughes conducted sparring classes, whilst Ruskin offered to take a drawing class, and actually taught in the College until 1860.

Some of the Christian Socialists, however, retained a lifelong interest in Co-operation, notably Neale, who became secretary to the Co-operative Union and retained that position during "its formative years" (*A Century of Co-operation*, p. 113), and Ludlow, who was appointed Chief Registrar of Friendly Societies in 1875, an office which he held until 1891. Thomas Hughes also remained interested in the movement, and in the 'sixties and 'seventies he ventured and lost money in Co-operative productive concerns formed on a profit-sharing basis. He continued, also, to be a good friend to trade unionism, and in 1867, when the Unions suddenly found themselves "deprived of the legal status which they imagined they had acquired, and saw themselves once more destitute of any legal protection for their accumulated funds" (*The History of Trade Unionism*, Sidney & Beatrice Webb, p. 262) Thomas Hughes was almost their only spokesman in Parliament.

The Boilermakers' Society had proceeded against the treasurer of their Bradford branch for wrongfully withholding the sum of £24; but the magistrates, to the general surprise of all concerned, held that the Society could not proceed under the Friendly Societies Act, since Trade Unions were outside its scope.

---

*It was left to the Consumers' Societies of the north to develop a Co-operative Wholesale. For a while the Rochdale Pioneers' Equitable Society acted in that capacity, and "from the establishment of the Rochdale Pioneers' wholesale department in 1850 to the creation of the North of England Wholesale Society in 1863 there is a quite continuous record of development", (*A Century of Co-operation*, G. D. H. Cole, p. 133) though the story "is at certain points difficult to piece together aright".

The Court of Queen's Bench upheld this decision, giving the additional reason that the objects of the Union if not actually criminal (since the repeal of the Combination Acts in 1825) were yet so far in restraint of trade as to render the Society an illegal association.

> Trade Unionism was now at bay. . . . It was easy to foresee that the employers and their allies would make a determined attempt to . . . suppress Trade Unionism by the criminal law. On the other hand, the hard-earned accumulations of the larger societies, by this time amounting to an aggregate of over a quarter of a million sterling, were at the mercy of their whole army of branch secretaries and treasurers, any one of whom might embezzle the funds with impunity. (*The History of Trade Unionism*, Sidney & Beatrice Webb, pp. 262-263.)

The first action of the Junta (as the Webbs have named the little group of Trade Union leaders who at that time dominated the new amalgamated societies, and through them the London Trades Council)

> was to call to their councils those middle-class allies upon whose assistance and advice they had learned to rely. (*The History of Trade Unionism*, p. 263.)

Thomas Hughes and Frederic Harrison helped them to present their case to the Royal Commission which had been appointed in 1867 to inquire into what were known as the "Sheffield outrages" (where blacklegs had been terrorized by the explosions of cans of gunpowder in the troughs of their grinding wheels or by having cans of gunpowder thrown down their chimneys. In some cases these explosions had caused serious injuries). As a result of their skilful handling of the Unions' case "the official report of the Commission, from which the enemies of Trade Unionism had hoped so much, contained no recommendation which would have made the position of any single Union worse than it was before". (*The History of Trade Unionism*, p. 269).

> Harrison and Hughes had not restricted themselves to casting out all dangerous proposals from the majority report. Their minority report, which was signed also by the Earl of Lichfield . . . advocated the removal of all special legislation relating to labour contracts, on the principle, first, that no act should be illegal if committed by a workman unless it was equally illegal if committed by any other person; and secondly, that no act by a combination of workmen should be regarded as criminal if it would not have been criminal in a single person. (*The History of Trade Unionism*, p. 270.)

After a long campaign the Conspiracy and Protection of Property and the Employers and Workmen Acts of 1875 gave the Trade Unions most of what they demanded.

> Henceforth master and servant became, as employer and employee, two equal parties to a civil contract. Imprisonment for breach of engagement was abolished. The legalisation of Trade Unions was completed by the legal recognition of their methods. Peaceful picketing was expressly permitted. The old words "coerce" and "molest" which had, in the hands of prejudiced magistrates, proved such instruments of oppression, were omitted from the new law, and violence and intimidation were dealt with as part of the general criminal law. No act committed by a group of workmen was henceforth to be punishable unless the same act by an individual was itself a criminal offence. Collective bargaining, in short, with all its necessary accompaniments, was, after fifty years of legislative struggle, finally recognised by the law of the land. (*The History of Trade Unionism*, p. 291.)

THE FUNCTION OF CHRISTIAN SOCIALISM

"The corruption of Chartism", wrote Th. Rothstein, "was the special task entrusted to a group of people—mostly clergymen—who were the founders of Christian Socialism". (*From Chartism to Labourism*, p. 354). Such a verdict is to attribute an improbable degree of conscious malevolence and cunning to the capitalist class of that period. It is also grossly unfair to the Christian Socialists, for, whilst it is true that they were pained by working class militancy, and sought (in the words of Kingsley's biographer) "to promote a more brotherly spirit between rich and poor", they were quite sincere in their desire to help the working class. G. D. H. Cole and Raymond Postgate offer a more balanced judgment when they declare that

> together with Radical dissenting ministers they (the Christian Socialists) were responsible for preventing that hostility between the organised working class and organised religion which became universal on the Continent. There was, henceforward, always a small percentage of persons with a genuine sympathy with Socialism and the misery of the working class, whose influence prevented the Church and the Chapels being counted wholly as enemies: similarly a strain of religiosity and pietism ran powerfully in the Labour movement and was later to be an effective obstacle to the spread of Marxian philosophy. (*The Common People 1746-1938*, by G. D. H. Cole & Raymond Postgate, p. 316.)

Moreover, it is undeniable that the Christian Socialists put the working class deeply in their debt by the invaluable help which they rendered in the struggle to win a legal status for the Co-operative and Trade Union movements.* The Rochdale Pioneers recognised that when they in 1855 publicly declared that

> They were convinced that the Society for Promoting Working Men's Associations had, during the period of its active existence, conferred great benefits on the Co-operative cause by gathering all sorts of valuable information, and spreading it throughout the country amongst the various Co-operative bodies; by urging on the attention of Parliament, through members favourable to the cause, the legal hindrances to the movement; and by helping to procure such alterations to the laws relating to Friendly Societies as to give freer action and greater security to the men who have embarked in the Co-operative undertaking. Not only have they done these things, but they have likewise drawn up model laws suitable for either distributive or productive associations, so as to facilitate the safe enrolment of all Co-operative bodies, and to secure the highest degree of legal accuracy with the smallest possible cost; in addition to which, they have at all times given legal advice freely to such of the Societies as stood in need of it—a matter, it must be acknowledged, of great value to bodies of working men.
>
> The Rochdale Equitable Pioneers feel deeply the value of the services rendered to Co-operation by the Council of the Society for Promoting Working Men's Associations; and, as the fullest and most acceptable acknowledgment, they considered that the best thing they could do would be to attempt to continue the work which the Society for Promoting Working Men's Associations had begun, and perfect, if possible, the design which they were unable to complete. (Quoted by George Jacob Holyoake in *The History of the Rochdale Pioneers*, p. 52.)

From their own point of view the Christian Socialists failed, for they were much more concerned with their utopian plans for self-governing workshops than with fostering Consumers' Co-operation: indeed, many of them were critical of the Consumers' Co-operative movement for being mercenary and lacking in high Christian idealism.

There were many reasons why their Working Associations failed: indeed, they were bound to fail, even as Owen's equally utopian "Villages of Unity and Co-operation" were foredoomed to failure. The fundamental reason for their lack of success was that the Working Associations ran counter to the whole economic

---

*"The Christian Socialists performed a vitally important service to the whole Co-operative Movement by helping to place on the Statute Book the Industrial and Provident Societies Act of 1852—the law which first gave Co-operative Societies a recognised legal status and a reasonably satisfactory measure of protection for their funds". *A Century of Co-operation*, G. D. H. Cole, p. 97.

trends of their day: tiny colonies of Co-operative producers could not function within the structure of a capitalist society. Especially a capitalist society which was still economically progressive, and had before it a century of development, during which it was to develop enormously the productive forces of society, and thus create the technical basis not for little, isolated self-governing communist utopias, but a world-wide Socialist order.

But even apart from this basic contradiction between their ideals and the economic realities of their day, there were many detailed reasons why the Working Men's Associations came so speedily to grief.

The Christian Socialists aspired to convert the working classes to an impossibly high moral code, and to a theological approach to industrial problems which most working men were quite unprepared to accept. Moreover, they made the mistake of supposing that real Co-operative Societies could be created from above with capital supplied by wealthy idealists, and that the workers would submit to a position of tutelage under the middle-class promoters until this capital had been repaid. Trouble between managers responsible to the promoters and working associates wanting self-government was unavoidable, and there were in addition disputes about the principles on which the Associations were working. The promoters adopted the principle of paying the standard wages of each trade and limiting the working hours to ten, including meal times, and of apportioning the surplus after payment of wages and interest on capital one-third to a reserve fund, one-third to repayment of capital, and the remaining third to a bonus on wages. There were disputes about the basis of this bonus. Was it to be equal for all associates, or proportionate to hours worked, or proportionate to wages paid? The promoters favoured the second alternative; but some of the Associations preferred the third, while minorities in them favoured the first. There was, furthermore, the question whether each Working Association was to be regarded as a financially independent body. The promoters insisted that prices charged must be controlled by the Central Board representing all the Associations, with an appeal to themselves as long as capital was owed them. This was accepted, but the Associations would have none of the proposal of Neale and some others that they should be treated as parts of a "General Union", with pooling of profits and reserve funds over the whole body. When they made profits they wanted to keep them: when others made losses they were not prepared to shoulder the burden. In practice each Association remained a separate financial entity, and they failed, not all together, but one by one. (*A Century of Co-operation*, pp. 112-113).

CHAPTER 13

THE RISE OF THE MODERN SOCIALIST MOVEMENT IN GREAT BRITAIN

> There are derelict churches in the Strand . . . and
> there are slums hard by. There are thieves in the
> Strand, and prowling vagrants, and gaunt hawkers,
> and touts, and gamblers, and loitering failures, with
> tragic eyes and wilted garments; and prostitutes plying
> for hire. . . . As London is, so is England. This is a
> Christian country. What would Christ think of Park
> Lane and the slums, and the hooligans ? What would
> He think of the Stock Exchange, and the Music Hall,
> and the racecourse ? What would He think of our
> national ideals ? What would He think of the House
> of Peers, and the Bench of Bishops, and the Yellow
> Press ?
>
> *God and My Neighbour*, Preface, by Robert Blatchford.

THE GUILD OF ST. MATTHEW

The modern Socialist movement in this country dates from the widespread social discontent and the great industrial struggles of the eighteen-eighties: but it is significant that the first attempt to create a Socialist organisation came not from working men but from a group of Anglican clergymen, headed by Stewart Headlam, a young London curate. In 1877 Headlam founded the Guild of St. Matthew which expounded a Socialist interpretation of Christianity, and played a not inconsiderable part in the spread of Socialist ideas. Stewart Headlam later became a prominent member of the Fabian Society, and served on the London School Board.

Several years after the formation of the Guild of St. Matthew the propagandist activities of the Stratford Radical Club resulted in the foundation (in 1881) of the Labour Emancipation League, which was essentially a working class body, and "the real pioneer of proletarian Socialism in the 'eighties'." (*British Working Class Politics, 1832-1914,* G. D. H. Cole, p. 85.) The Labour Emancipation League arose out of a series of open-air meetings held in 1881 on the Mile End Waste, and had as its object "the establishment of a free social condition of society, based on the principle of political equality, with equal social rights for all." The same year

(1881) saw the formation of the Democratic Federation.   The Federation was a Radical rather than a Socialist body, and it was not until 1883 that it adopted a Socialist policy, and issued it as a pamphlet *Socialism Made Plain*.   The following year (1884) it changed its name to the Social Democratic Federation.   The Fabian Society was founded in 1883 by a little group of intellectuals; and in 1893 the Independent Labour Party was formed. Thus the Guild of St. Matthew was in existence before the foundation of any of the Socialist societies which helped create the modern Labour Party.

The Guild published a monthly newspaper, *The Church Reformer,* which Sidney Webb described as being "a frankly Socialist medium of great ability", (*Socialism in England,* p. 64) and it recruited several hundred lay and clerical members.   The Guild's social philosophy can be gauged from a memorial which it presented to the Pan-Anglican Conference of Bishops in 1888.

Our present social system—if the words 'social system' can be used of that which is largely the outcome of anarchic competition— is cruel and dishonest, and needs drastic reform and radical reorganisation. The startling contrast between the hovels of the poor and the houses of the rich within the same city, between the pitiful wage of the labourer and the vast income of the idler, between the poverty of the tenant and the luxury of the landlord, especially in our large towns, has been put before English society with startling vividness*. A wave of Socialist thought has swept over England. The older party divisions are becoming less and less distinct. Socialism seems destined to produce in the near future a perfectly new moral 'line of cleavage' in English Society. "Herein, we respectfully submit to your Grace, are great moral questions with which it is the plain duty of the Church to deal. It has long been conceded by many Churchmen that the housing and feeding of 'Christ's poor' are pre-eminently matters with which the followers of Him who fed the hungry and healed the sick should concern themselves. Under the 'Housing' question lies the Land question, as surely as the house stands on the land. Mr. George denounces our present land system as one that robs the many for the benefit of the few. His opponents retort with a charge of 'plunder', and describe the movement for restoring to the people the value which they give to the land as one of 'robbery plus cant'. Shall the Church of Christ be dumb when men turn to her for guidance in this matter ? Her priests, in the name of God, from the altars of His Church, proclaim, 'Thou shalt not steal'. What is it to steal ?   Again, the Socialist objects to the competitive commercial system under which we live that it 'robs the poor

---

*A reference to the revelations of a recent Royal Commission on the Housing of the Poor.

because he is poor'; that it enables and encourages the capitalist to 'build his house by unrighteousness and his chambers by wrong', inasmuch as it gives him the power, by taking advantage of the competition for a mere livelihood, to 'use (a large part of) his neighbour's service without wages, and give him nought for his work'. The differences between political party programmes sink into insignificance beside the moral question here involved. Churchmen are beginning to ask, 'Is it *true* that the landlord and capitalist are able, independently of any work done by themselves, to appropriate a large share of the results of the labour of their unprivileged brethren? If it be true that this is so, is it *just*?' " (Quoted by Sidney Webb in *Socialism in England*, pp. 66-67).

The Memorial enumerates two Christian principles:

First, *Every man should work*. There should be no idle class; no class of those who consume but do not produce, no privileged body allowed to live upon the produce of others' labour without rendering a due equivalent.

Secondly, *The produce of labour must be distributed on a much more equitable system than at present*. The landlord and the capitalist, say the Socialists, secure far too great a share of the wealth created by labour. They take the first and often the largest share with an acknowledged tendency to increase their takings till no more than a bare subsistence is left to the labourer. The Socialist claim may not be orthodox economy from the stand-point of *laissez faire*, but it sounds strangely like an echo of St. Paul's dictum, 'The husbandman that laboureth must be the first to partake of the fruits.' 'He that plougheth ought to plough in *hope*, and he that thresheth thresh in hope of partaking'. And yet it has needed almost a revolution within the last generation to bring 'hope' within the life of the English husbandman.' (*Socialism in England*, pp. 67-68).

The final conclusion of the memorialists is that "with the main contentions of the Socialist, the Christian is not only able but bound to agree".

THE CLARION

Perhaps Robert Blatchford* and *The Clarion* did more to stimulate interest in Socialism in those early days than any of the organisations we have just named. Certainly the British Socialist Movement has produced no more effective and influential weekly paper than *The Clarion* even though (in the expressive phrase of Mr. Cole) it "stank in the nostrils of the 'unco guid' as a

---

*Blatchford's famous pamphlet *Merrie England* had an enormous influence in spreading Socialist ideas. It was published originally at a shilling, and 20,000 copies were soon sold. Pete Curran suggested a penny edition, and in less than a year the sales rose to over a million, in addition to which many pirated editions were sold in the U.S.A.

wicked, roystering, atheistical, impudent, blasphemous, god-forsaken horror of a paper".

But Blatchford's atheism was no mere negation of God and religion: rather it was provoked by the belief that religion tends to distract men from the real task of busying themselves with the job of making this world a fit place for all men to live in.

> In such a world as this, friend Christian (he wrote), a man has no business reading the Bible, singing hymns, and attending divine worship. He has not *time*. All the strength and pluck and wit he possesses are needed in the work of real religion, of real salvation. The rest is all "dreams out of the ivory gate, and visions before midnight". (*God and My Neighbour*, p. 194.)

And again, in another typical passage :

> I know nothing about Gods and heavens. But I know a good deal about Manchester and London, and about men and women; and if I did not feel the shames and wrongs of the world more keenly, and if I did not try more earnestly and strenuously to rescue my fellow-creatures from ignorance, and sorrow, and injustice, than most Christians did, I should blush to look death in the face or call myself a man.
> I choose my words deliberately again when I say that to me the most besotted and degraded outcast tramp or harlot matters more than all the Gods and angels that humanity ever conjured up out of its imagination. (*God and My Neighbour*, p. 191.)

Blatchford was (to use his own description) a Humanist: that word aptly summed up his whole social philosophy, which was a protest against injustice and needless suffering.

> Truly we should love all men (he wrote). Let us, then, begin by loving the weakest and the worst, for they have so little love and counsel, while the rich and the good have so much. (*Britain for the British*, p. 43.)

In the main a humanist* rather than a Marxist approach to Socialism was typical of the working class movement in Great Britain in the nineties of the last century.

> In the "eighties" (writes G. D. H. Cole) the Social Democratic Federation and the Socialist League had sought to capture the masses by converting them to Socialism as a doctrine of class-war. Blatchford and also, to a great extent, Hardie appealed to them rather in the name of human fellowship and decent feeling. In Great Britain the "nineties" were above all else the age of an ethical Socialism full of warm feelings of sympathy for the poor, and somewhat scornful of doctrines that could not be cast into the

---

*"I am an Agnostic, or Rationalist, and I am a Determinist, and I am a Socialist. But if I were asked to describe myself in a single word, I should call myself a Humanist."
(*God and My Neighbour*, p. 189).

form of moral imperatives. "Scientific" Socialism did not appeal to Blatchford or to Hardie. They wanted to make converts on the basis of human brotherhood rather than of the class-war—even though they recognized the class-war as a fact.*

Undoubtedly, this appeal was at that time the most likely to bring over large sections of the British workers from their traditional allegiance to Gladstonian Liberalism. As followers of the great Mr. Gladstone, they had been nourished on moral inspirations and high-sounding phrases; and they were gradually finding out that these phrases meant nothing in terms of their everyday material needs. They were ready to be weaned from a Liberalism that had discarded Chamberlain's social Radicalism together with its author; they were not ready to do without the feeling of virtue with which Gladstone had held them comforted for the lack of more substantial advantages. They were in many cases still closely attached to one or another Nonconformist congregation; and even when they became sceptical of the dogmas of the Churches they were apt to feel cold and uncomforted unless they could find some spiritual substitue. (*British Working Class Politics, 1832-1914,* pp. 134-5.)

The same spiritual cravings accounted for the success of John Trevor's Labour Church movement, which became organised in the Union of Labour Churches, in 1893.

KEIR HARDIE

Keir Hardie, like so many other early members of the Independent Labour Party, received his training as a public speaker in the church and in the Temperance and Brotherhood movements. Writing of his early days in Ayrshire, William Stewart says that

he became Grand Worthy chief of the local Good Templars' Lodge. He took his share of the church work and filled the pulpit on occasions . . . and frequently his voice was to be heard at the street corners in Cumnock and in some of the neighbouring villages preaching the Gospel of Christ as he understood it. (*J. Keir Hardie,* William Stewart, p. 20.)

Later, it was natural for him to turn

most of his economic arguments into moral discourses in which the capitalist class was cast for the part of Satan. This was not affectation, or calculated for effect: it came natural to him. And that it did so was highly opportune at a time when the advocates of Socialism and Labour representation were trying to win over a

---

*Blatchford gave practical recognition to the fact of the class struggle when he advised his working class readers that "if you wish the interests of the working class to be attended to, you will . . . form a working-class party". (*Britain for the British,* p. 148.) Hardie of course, took the same line as a practical politician, and played a notable part in persuading the British Trade Unions to create their own independent political party.

working class still largely tied to Nonconformity, and held fast to Liberalism by the close alliance between the Chapel and the Liberal electoral machine. The "Lib-Labs" were mostly lay preachers as well as Trade Union officials; and the task of winning over their followers needed a man such as Hardie who could speak a language they could readily understand. . . . Hardie, despite his public reputation for wildness, did not sound at all wild to a gathering of miners or iron-workers or factory operatives who had been brought up on the Bible, and were much readier to accept Socialism when it came to them clothed in the garments of morality than when it was presented in economic terms or by means of slogans of class-war. (*British Working Class Politics, 1832-1914,* pp. 119-120.)

And thus it was natural that the "New Unionists", when they began to turn their attention to politics, looked to Keir Hardie rather than to Mann, or Burns, or Tillett for leadership.

CHAPEL INFLUENCES

But if many of the early propagandists of Socialism in this country found inspiration and guidance in the Christian teachings of their youth, religious Nonconformity also exercised a baneful influence on the political education of the working class, and helped delay the formation of an independent political party of their own long after economic conditions were ripe for such a development. This was true of both those mass working class movements, the Co-operatives and the Trade Unions.

Close links between Store and chapel . . . existed in many parts of the North, and tended to keep leading Co-operators on the Liberal side as long as Liberalism and Nonconformity walked hand in hand. (*A Century of Co-operation,* G. D. H. Cole. p. 312.)

Within the Trade Union movement the same thing happened. Many of the Lib-Labs who used their influence within the Trades Union Congress and the Trade Unions to oppose the formation of an independent Labour Party were "pious

---

*The following excerpt from an article in *The Miner,* written when Hardie was in the thirties, is a good example of how he identified Socialism and Christianity. "The world today is sick and weary at heart. Even our clergy are for the most part dumb dogs who dare not bark. So it was in the days of Christ. They who proclaimed a God-given gospel to the world were the poor and the comparatively unlettered. We need today a return to the principles of that Gospel which, by proclaiming all men sons of God and brethren one with another, makes it impossible for one, Shylock-like, to insist on his rights at the expense of another". (Quoted by William Stewart in *J. Keir Hardie,* pp. 32-33.)   In a penny pamphlet, *The I.L.P.—All About it,* Hardie wrote that "To some, Socialism comes in the form of an intellectual conviction, to others it can be stated in the terms of a proposition in political economy ; to ninety-nine per cent of the members of the I.L.P. Socialism comes with all the emotional power of a great religious truth."

Methodists and local preachers", to use the phrase which Elie Halévy (*A History of the English People, 1895-1905,* Book ii., p. 134) applies to Burt and Fenwick, representative Trade Union leaders of the period. Thomas Burt was the leader of the North-umberland miners, and won Morpeth in the General Election of 1874: he shares with Alexander Macdonald (who won a Stafford seat in the same election) the honour of being what the Webbs call the first "Labour members" of the House of Commons. (*History of Trade Unionism,* p. 290.) Charles Fenwick succeeded Henry Broadhurst as Secretary to the Trades Union Congress. Both Burt and Fenwick were Lib-Labs.

This Nonconformist strain in the British working class move-ment has continued down to the present day. The late Arthur Henderson (who more than any other man was the architect of the Labour Party's electoral machine) was a Dissenter, a teetotaller, and a leading figure in the Brotherhood Movement; and in our own day the Right Hon. A. V. Alexander is proud of the fact that he is a Baptist preacher*.

THE GENERAL STRIKE

There has never been in the British working class movement anything comparable with the anti-clericalism which has been characteristic of a good deal of European Socialism. That significant fact was curiously illustrated in the General Strike of 1926—when this country came nearer to violent revolution than at any time within the memory of living man.

Foreign Socialists were unable to understand the part played by religion in the strike. Some of the strongest fighting centres proved to be also the most religious. Poplar (*Lansbury's Bulletin*) on the 8th wrote, "To-morrow is Sunday. You will come to our meetings at night, but I would like you to attend the Church Services nearest your home. . . . It is Christ's gospel of passive resistance which you are practising to-day". Preston carried, from Canon Donaldson of Westminster, a message which might have shamed the "negotiators":—

"I earnestly beg that the workers will stand firm. If they stand firm, they will win; but if they begin to doubt and quaver and to blackleg—all will be lost for a generation."

In Wigan, where the railwaymen carried the burden of the

---

*Mr. Joseph Bradshaw, J.P., in his presidential address to the Co-operative Congress in 1946, said that "after 2,000 years, they must still go back to the Sermon on the Mount for the only reliable basis on which to build their new democratic world. Whatever their achievements in science, industry or culture, it was only when we learned to acknowledge the Divine truth of that message that they wou attain universal happiness and peace". *The Co-operative News, 15.6.1946.*

strike on their backs, the editor appointed by them, on being chosen "knelt by my chair, acknowledged our weakness and asked for Divine guidance", and on Sunday he produced the curious bulletin reproduced here,* inexplicable in any other country. All St. Albans railway strikers formed into a procession on one day and marched to the Abbey for a special service. And it was the same railwaymen who on the 13th refused to go back and wired to the General Council, cursing it and telling it to reimpose the strike. Shrewsbury's official time-table one day began:—

9-45 a.m.   Intercession service at . . . Chapel.
10-45 a.m. Strike Committee meets. All strikers may attend and listen.
12.0 Noon. Service at St. Mary's.

(*A Workers' History of the Great Strike*, by R. W. Postgate, Ellen Wilkinson, M.P., and J. F. Horrabin, pp. 41-43.)

Socialists may approve or disapprove of the religious strain which runs through the British working class movement: but its influence, even today, cannot be denied, even though it may be true that the majority of workers are now largely indifferent to all forms of organised Christianity.

---

*WIGAN JOINT STRIKE COMMITTEE. LEGS OF MAN ASSEMBLY ROOMS.

No. 2. Sixth day of strike. Sunday, May 9th, 1926.

MY DEAR PUBLIC,
　　　　　Remember the Sabbath Day to keep it Holy.

Thou shalt love the Lord thy God with
All thy heart, soul, mind and strength and
Thy neighbour as thyself.

Daily bulletin.
News from all points.
Situation magnificent.
Everywhere solid.

Public meetings well supported by eminent men of all shades of thought and from all stations of life.

Facsimile of the Wigan Strike Bulletin, Sunday, May 9th. (Reproduced in *A Workers' History of the Great Strike*, p. 42).

CHAPTER 14

FASCISM, BOLSHEVISM AND SOCIALISM

*The aim of Socialists should be the founding of a
religion, towards which end compromise is no use.*
William Morris.

MODERN INDUSTRY AND RELIGION

Modern industrial society, with large-scale commodity production based on giant factories and power-driven machinery, the whole depending upon a vast and growing accumulation of scientific knowledge, engenders a temper altogether alien to traditional religion. In a less complex civilization, in which the great majority of men were engaged in agriculture, and were largely at the mercy of all the vagaries of nature, the notion of a personal God (or gods) who arbitrarily intervened in human affairs, was natural enough. In the illuminated missals of the Middle Ages one finds the figure of Christ with vines growing out of his wounds, whilst bishops and abbesses devour the grapes which are growing on these vines. Such a conception of God could have occurred only in a backward agrarian society possessed of little of our modern knowledge of the universe. To such a community grossly anthropomorphic conceptions of the Deity did not seem absurd or irreverent. Herbert Spencer, in his *Study of Sociology,* gives an amusing example of the anthropomorphic conceptions which were common at that period.

> God, having one day gone out with the saints and the apostles for a walk, left Peter at the door of heaven with strict orders to admit no one. Soon after a tailor came and pleaded to be let in. But Peter said that God had forbidden any one to be admitted; besides, the tailor was a bad character, and 'cabbaged' the cloth he used. The tailor said the pieces he had taken were small, and had fallen into his basket; and he was willing to make himself useful— he would carry the babies, and wash or mend the clothes. Peter at last let him in, but made him sit down in a corner, behind the door. Taking advantage of Peter's going outside for a minute or two, the tailor left his seat and looked about him. He soon came to a place where there were many stools, and a chair of massive gold and a golden footstool, which were God's. Climbing up on the chair, he could see all that was happening on earth; and he saw an old woman, who was washing clothes in a stream, making away with some of the linen. In his anger, he took up the footstool and

threw it at her. As he could not get it back, he thought it best to return to his place behind the door, where he sat down, putting on an air of innocence. God now re-entered, without observing the tailor. Finding his footstool gone, he asked Peter what had become of it—had he let anyone in ? The apostle at first evaded the question, but confessed that he had let in one—only, however, a poor limping tailor. The tailor was then called, and asked what he had done with the footstool. When he had told, God said to him: "O you knave, if I judged like you, how long do you think *you* could have escaped ? For long ago I should not have had a chair or even a poker left in the place, but should have hurled every thing at the sinners." (*The Study of Sociology*, pp. 137-138.)

Such gross anthropomorphism is unthinkable to the modern industrial worker whose labour

in the great industries has removed him . . . from the influences of the environment of nature which in the peasant keep up the belief in ghosts, in sorceries, in witchcraft and other superstitious ideas. . . . Drought, excessive rains, hail, cyclones, etc. never make him think of their action on nature and her harvests. His urban life shelters him from the anxieties and the troublesome cares which assail the mind of the farmer. Nature has no hold on his imagination.

The labour of the mechanical factory puts the wage-worker in touch with terrible natural forces unknown to the peasant, but instead of being mastered by them, he controls them. The gigantic mechanism of iron and steel which fills the factories, which makes him move like an automaton, which sometimes clutches him, mutilates him, bruises him, does not engender in him a superstitious terror as the thunder does in the peasant, but leaves him unmoved, for he knows that the limbs of the mechanical monster were fashioned and mounted by his comrades, and that he has but to push a lever to set it in motion or stop it. The machine, in spite of its miraculous power and productiveness, has no mystery for him. The labourer in the electric works, who has but to turn a crank on a dial to send miles of motive power to tramways or light to the lamps of a city, has but to say, like the God of Genesis, "Let there be light," and there is light. Never sorcery more fantastic was imagined, yet for him this sorcery is a simple and natural thing. He would be greatly surprised if one were to come and tell him that a certain God might if he chose stop the machines and extinguish the lights when the electricity had been turned on; he would reply that this anarchistic God would be simply a misplaced gearing or a broken wire, and that it would be easy for him to seek and find this disturbing God. The practice of the modern workshop teaches the wage-worker scientific determinism, without his needing to pass through the theoretical study of the sciences. (*Social and Philosophical Studies*, Paul Lafargue, pp. 49-50.)

As long ago as 1909 C. F. G. Masterman wrote that

the world of today . . . is not becoming atheist. It is ceasing to believe, without being conscious of the process, until it suddenly wakes up to the fact that the process is complete. (*The Condition of England*, p. 223.)

Suburban London (he asserted) is losing its old religions. It still builds churches and chapels of a twentieth-century Gothic architecture: St. Aloysius, reputed to be dangerously "High" because its curates wear coloured scarves; the Baptist Chapel, where the minister maintains the old doctrines of hell and heaven, and wrestles with the sinner for his immortal soul; the Congregational Church, where the minister is abreast with modern culture, and proclaims a less exacting gospel, and faintly trusts the larger hope. But the whole apparatus of worship seems archaic and unreal. . . . The old lights have fallen from the sky, existence has become too complex and crowded for the influences of wider spaces reaching to a far horizon. (*The Condition of England*, p. 69).

And yet again:

The Churches are extraordinarily active, endeavouring in this way and in that to influence the lives of the people. Their humanitarian and social efforts are widely appreciated. Their definite dogmatic teachings seem to count for little at all. They labour on steadily amid a huge indifference. The very material of their appeal is vanishing. Fear which is the beginning of wisdom no longer terrifies a society which sees orderly arrangements everywhere accepting the secure as the normal. It cannot believe that, even if any future world exists at all—of which existence it is becoming increasingly doubtful—that future world will not in essence re-establish the decencies and commonplaces of the modern city state. There is less material therefore to-day for the appeal—to the general—of the revivalist preacher, with which Wesley and Whitefield changed the face of eighteenth-century England. The fleeing from the city of Destruction, the crying out against the "burden" of sin, the vision of the flames of hell flaring close to the Celestial City, represents an apparatus of experience that is alien to the present. "Religion", was Dolling's testimony from Poplar, "has, so to speak, gone to pieces. There is no opposition. We do not care enough to oppose. God is not in any of our thoughts: we do not even fear Him. We face death with perfect composure, for we have nothing to give up, and nothing to look forward to. Heaven has no attraction, because we should be out of place there. And hell has no terrors". (*The Condition of England*, pp. 220-221.)

Masterman in his profoundly despondent book further gave it as his opinion that

there can be no doubt that apart from any question of future revival, present belief in religion, as a conception of life dependent upon supernatural sanctions or as a revelation of a purpose and meaning beyond the actual business of the day, is slowly but steadily fading from the modern city race. Tolerance, kindliness, sympathy, civilization continually improve. Affirmation of any responsibility beyond that to self and to humanity, continually declines. Life therefore gradually ceases to be influenced or coloured by any atmosphere of "other-worldliness". Present disabilities find no compensation in the hope of a future redress, which makes the present endurable. (*The Condition of England*, pp. 219-220.)

Élie Halévy reaches the same conclusion about the (seemingly) secure world in the years just before the First World War.

The characteristic feature of the age (he wrote) was not the irreligion (the term would be too strong) but the religious indifference of the masses. (*A History of the English People, Epilogue Vol. i.*, 1895-1905, *Book III*, Pelican Books Edition, pp. 133-134. Élie Halévy.)

Referring to the inquiry into the condition of the chief religious denominations in London which Cadbury conducted from May, 1902 to June, 1903, he says:

If the Nonconformists could find consolation in the fact that the decline of their sects had been perhaps less marked than the decline of the Anglican Church, the results of the inquiry were none the less disquieting to a sincere Christian. While the population of the area to which the inquiry related had increased by half a million in about 15 years, the number of practising Christians not only failed to show a corresponding increase but had actually fallen by 150,000; and . . . it was found that of every hundred inhabitants of London only 16 were practising Christians. (*A History of the English People, Epilogue Vol. i.*, 1895-1905, *Book III*, Pelican Books Edition, p. 133.)

NAZISM AND COMMUNISM

Today it is more than ever true that the great mass of people in this country are indifferent to traditional religion; that at the most they pay an occasional conventional respect to it, such as using the services of the Church for marriages and burials.

But it is not only belief in organised Christianity which has declined. Socialism, too, has lost much of the fervour and idealism of its pioneer days. Men and women who espoused the unpopular cause in the closing decades of the last century were often sustained by a profound sense of serving a great human movement which moved to inevitable and not far distant triumph. Whether they came to Socialism emotionally, or whether they prided themselves on being materialists, and expounded "Scientific Socialism" (often with as sharp a nose for heresy as any Father of the Early Church) they saw in it much more than political manoeuvring or even economic planning for a world of material plenty and security. It is not too much to say that many of them found in Socialism the same emotional satisfaction that men found in religion in earlier ages. Not infrequently they sacrificed their own interests to the movement: and they were sustained in face of ridicule and persecution by the knowledge that they served something bigger than themselves, something that gave a meaning and a dignity to their own brief and trivial lives. And (particularly in the case of the devout Marxist) their faith gave them the same certain promise of ultimate victory over the forces of evil, even though the Kingdom of God was not in some future state of blessedness, but was the classless society which was shortly to come into being, and a personal Deity was replaced by impersonal economic forces. The seventeenth-century Calvinists had known that the Gates of Hell should not prevail against the Chosen of the Lord (which usually meant against the rising middle class): the Marxist was apt to turn the Materialistic Conception of History into something curiously like a theological dogma, and to feel the same comforting assurance that the Proletariat was inevitably destined to be the grave-digger of Capitalism, and to usher in the millennium of Communism.

It was inevitable, no doubt, that Socialism should shed this chiliastic idealism as it grew from a small unpopular sect into a mass movement that played an increasing part in the administration of the capitalist state. It ceased, of necessity, to recruit mainly the exceptional man and woman: its appeal was more and more to everyday people. And everyday people are not in the habit of living with visions of the New Jerusalem, whether such visions be of this world or of the next.

Yet it remains true that the normal man is never happy unless he can give his loyalty to something bigger than himself; to an ideology which simultaneously provides him with an explanation of the world in which he finds himself, and calls upon him to serve the common good of some social group with which he is associated. In short, the average man is religious: he is not the self-seeking, rational being imagined by the cruder forms of Victorian rationalism. And so, of course, the decline of the old faiths, and the weakening of the hold of the Christian churches over men's imaginations and loyalties has not produced the rational world which the Victorian Secularist so confidently predicted. Masses of men no longer have any belief in Christian mythology (or in Christian ethics, for that matter); but they have given blind, unreasoning allegiance to Nazism or to the dogmas of the Communist International. For both Nazism in

Germany and Communism in Russia have had many of the characteristics of an organised church. Both demanded that the neophyte accept once for all certain fundamental dogmas that must never be questioned on pain of damnation. Both required their followers to lose their identity in the Party (the Church), and to accept with cheerful, blind devotion the infallibility of the Party leadership, no matter how that leadership might twist and turn, and contradict its own *ex cathedra* assertions of yesterday. Both practised the Jesuitical policy that the end justifies the means, even though the means be systematic lying, persecution of former members, and mass murder. Both have shown themselves as militant and intolerant as Islam in the heyday of its career as a conquering faith, or the Society of Jesus at the time of the Spanish conquests in the New World. And both (despite much in their doctrine which is manifestly irrational) have succeeded in winning the fanatical loyalty of great numbers of men and women—and particularly of young men and women.

> The means (says Professor Laski) by which Fascist leadership in Germany and Italy, especially in the former country, has sought to obtain its psychological hold upon the masses . . . is built upon the religious impulse—worship of, and utter surrender to, the leader is made into a cult comparable in its outward expression of intensity only to the fanaticism of the historic religions. Hitler, for instance, is the especially chosen of God; he is infallible; he is omniscient; he is the father of his people. He is not bound by the laws of men; special insights are communicated to him. . . . He becomes a semi-sacred person, not to be judged by ordinary standards. He is half-ruler, half-priest, deified in his own lifetime, spoken of in terms of an adoring adulation it is sacrilege to doubt. It is not, I think, blasphemous to suggest that it has been the deliberate effort of the Nazi party to make of Hitler in a real sense a god to the people. (*Reflections on the Revolution of Our Time*, Harold J. Laski, p. 119.)

> In Russia (writes Borkenau) the Bolshevik party had really been, to a great extent, what Lenin wanted it to be: a select community, a sort of religious order of professional revolutionaries, crusaders of a materialistic faith. (*The Communist International*, F. Borkenau, p. 419.)

And again, referring to Lenin's *Materialism and Empirio-Criticism,*

> That which makes the work so important is Lenin's complete unawareness of the fact that he himself, with his absolute belief in materialism, is just as religious as those 'fideists', in other words those Christians, whom he fights, and much nearer, in psychology and method, to an Eastern ascetic than to the thorough religious indifference of a Poincaré or a Mach; he does not even

suspect the paradox and defends materialism with the fury of an inquisitor. (*The Communist International*, p. 49.)

And

Naive religious beliefs are a strong and constructive force in history . . . This religious belief, this implicit acceptance of Marxism, not as a method of research but as a creed, responded to an urgent practical necessity. Without it, Lenin might have been a better student of social problems; but without this firm conviction he could not have been the man with an iron will and a single purpose, 'the revolution'. Again, in this narrow dedication of everything to one single aim, the true religious fanaticism of an early civilization reveals itself a mentality which, if realized in its true character, can only provoke among men of the West the wonder which the early Christians provoked among the Greeks. It is no less a tremendous practical force for all its intellectual limitations. (*The Communist International*, pp. 50-51.)

Since Lenin's death the tendency for Bolshevism to grow into a new religion has been in no wise checked, but rather the contrary.

The cult of Stalin, indeed, has become a veritable religion, with the Politbureau as a college of Cardinals, and the secret police acting as inquisitors for a Bolshevik Pope. Deviation from orthodoxy is, as in a militant religion, punished by imprisonment or death. (*Reflections on the Revolution of Our Time*, p. 69.)

and

the Puritan's citations of Scripture are the precise equivalent of the Bolshevik's citations of Marx. (*Reflections on the Revolution of Our Time*, p. 73.)

Moreover,

the average Russian citizen . . . has been educated both by experience and propaganda, to think of the Soviet Union as the land of the socialist revolution, beset by enemies, internal and external, on all sides. He believes in its achievement and its prospects as firmly as the early Christians believed in the certainty of the Second Coming. (*Reflections on the Revolution of Our Time*, p. 70.)

A NEW HUMANISM

If Socialism is to generate the dynamic to create a new and worthwhile civilization it has got to be able to inspire an equally profound, but more rational devotion among its adherents. It will not do that by a cautious insistence upon being "practical"; nor will it do it by the lavish use of Marxist jargon, or by seeking to appeal to men's minds alone. Of course, the Socialist movement needs its blue-prints of the new society which it seeks to build. Equally it needs a scientific theory and analysis for an understanding of what is happening in the world of economics and politics. But men are not moved to action by masses of detailed plans for social reform, or by the sweet reasonableness of Fabianism: nor are they activated by scientific reasoning about the laws of social development. They are impelled, in the main, to strive against social injustice, and to sacrifice their personal interests (maybe their lives) in a struggle for a better world not by reason but by deep social emotions.

If Socialism is to win and hold power to make a new social order that shall be something better than a totalitarian state able to give material security only at the price of personal freedom and the degradation of human individuality, it must recapture something of the passion and enthusiasm of its pioneers, who saw a noble vision of the world that shall be ; a world from which poverty, crime, and war have been banished ; a world in which free men and women can love truth, and justice, and beauty. It needs to re-discover the dynamic energy with which William Morris hated all the ugliness, and meanness, and dull stupidity of our machine civilization: but it must denounce not only shoddy, mass-produced clothes and furniture, and houses and amusements, but also mass-produced, shabby little ideals, and all the pitiful waste of individuality and all the frustration which is part of our modern world.

Above all Socialism must recapture the sense which many of the pioneers had of serving a great impersonal end which gives a meaning and a dignity to our own brief, petty lives ; a sense of being part of a great fellowship of men who have striven, in many ages, and in all lands, to make the Brotherhood of Man a living reality, and not a cant phrase on the lips of insipid priests or slick politicians.

> For fellowship is heaven, and lack of fellowship is hell: fellowship is life, and lack of fellowship is death: and the deeds that ye do upon the earth, it is for fellowship's sake that ye do them, and the life that is in it, that shall live on and on for ever, and each one of you part of it, while many a man's life upon the earth from the earth shall wane.

THE END

BIBLIOGRAPHY

Social Struggles in the Middle Ages, by M. Beer
Guilds in the Middle Ages, by Georges Renard
A Short History of the English People, by J. R. Green
A History of British Socialism, by M. Beer
Six Centuries of Work and Wages, by Thorold Rogers
The Great Revolt of 1381, by Charles Oman
A Short History of English Rural Life, by Montague Fordham
The Medieval Village, by G. G. Coulton
Man's Worldly Goods, by Leo Huberman
Socialism Utopian and Scientific, by F. Engels
The Critique of Political Economy, by K. Marx
An Outline of Man's History, by P. Gordon Walker
Early British Economics, by M. Beer
Religion and the Rise of Capitalism, by R. H. Tawney
The Sixteenth and Seventeenth Centuries, by P. Gordon Walker
Left-Wing Democracy in the English Civil War, by David W. Petegorsky
The Peasant War in Germany, by F. Engels
Readings in European History, by James Harvey Robinson
The Rise and Fall of the Anabaptists, by E. Belfort Bax
The Cambridge Modern History
Medieval and Modern Times, by James Harvey Robinson
Cromwell and Communism, by Edouard Bernstein
The Levellers and the English Revolution, by Henry Holorenshaw
The Leveller Tracts, 1647-1653, by W. Haller & G. Davies
Levellers' Manifestoes of the Puritan Revolution, by D. M. Wolfe
History of the Great Civil War, by S. R. Gardiner
Gerrard Winstanley, Selections from his works, by L. Hamilton
The Protestant Churches, by L. F. Church
The Town Labourer, 1760-1832, by J. L. & B. Hammond
The Village Labourer, 1760-1832, by J. L. & B. Hammond
Capital, vol. i. by Karl Marx
Education for a New Society, by Ernest Green
English Radicalism, 1832-1852, by S. Maccoby
Life and Work of the Seventh Earl of Shaftesbury, by E. Hodder
Lord Shaftesbury, by J. L. & B. Hammond
Son to Susanna, by G. E. Harrison
The Opinions of William Cobbett, by G. D. H. & M. Cole
A History of the English People in 1815, by Elie Halévy
From Chartism to Labourism, by Th. Rothstein
The Common People, 1746-1938, by G. D. H. Cole & R. Postgate
A Century of Co-operation, by G. D. H. Cole
History of the Rochdale Pioneers, by G. J. Holyoake
The History of Trade Unionism, by Sidney & Beatrice Webb

The Chartist Movement, by Mark Hovell
The Builders' History, by R. Postgate
Charles Kingsley and Christian Socialism, by C. F. Vulliamy
Christian Socialism, 1848-1854, by C. E. Raven
God and My Neighbour, by Robert Blatchford
Merrie England, by Robert Blatchford
Britain for the British, by Robert Blatchford
British Working Class Politics, 1832-1914, by G. D. H. Cole
Socialism in England, by Sidney Webb
J. Keir Hardie, by Wm. Stewart
A History of the English People, 1895-1905, by Élie Halévy
The History of the Fabian Society, by E. R. Pease
A Workers' History of the Great Strike, by Postgate, Wilkinson & Horrabin
Social and Philosophical Studies, by Paul Lafargue
The Condition of England, by C. F. G. Masterman
Reflections on the Revolution of Our Time, by H. J. Laski
Faith, Reason and Civilization, by H. J. Laski
The Communist International, by F. Borkenau
Conrad Noel. An Autobiography, by Conrad Noel
Joseph Arch. The Story of his Life, by Joseph Arch
The Concern for Social Justice in the Puritan Revolution, by W. Schenk

INDEX

235

Taus, Battle of, 48
Tawney, R. H., quoted, 56-9, 61, 65
Taylor, James, 165
Taylor, John, quoted, 98-9
Ten Hours' Act, 158-9, 169 n.
Tertiaries, Franciscan, 16
Thomas Aquinas, St., 40
Thompson, Capt., 109
Thompson, Ensign, 109-10
Tillett, Ben, 222
Toledo, Council of, 41
Tolpuddle Martyrs, 154, 166
Trade Unions, 154, 198 ff., 212-13
Trevor, John, 221
Triploe Heath, 102
Turks, 16
Twelve Articles, 82-4

Ulrich of Württemberg, Duke, 71
Union of Labour Churches, 221
Union Shoe Movement, see Bundschuh
"Universal Provider", 206
Urban II, 41
Usury, 55-60
Utraquists, 45

Valens, 11
Vane, Sir Henry, 146
Vansittart, A. A., 201
Verona, Councils of, 18, 22
Vincent, Henry, 175
Vulliamy, C. F., quoted, 179, 181

Waldensians, 14, 21 ff. 27 n., 46
Waldus, Peter, 21
Waldshut, 80
Walker, P. C. Gordon, quoted, 55, 60, 62-4, 77
Walsh, 179 n., 186
Walwyn, W., 95, 105, 108
Webb, S. & B., quoted, 167-8, 189, 198-9, 202-3, 212-4, 218-9, 223
Wellingborough, 129
Wellington, Duke of, 177
Wenzel, King, 46
White, James, 173
White, William, 37
Wigan, 224
Wiklif, John, 25 ff., 44
Wilberforce, W., 157
Wilkinson, James, 165
Winstanley, G., 111 n., 115 ff., 139
Woodin, James, 211
Woollen Industry, mediaeval, 17-18
Working Men's College, 212
Worms, Edict of (1521), 74

Young, Arthur, quoted, 155

Zealots, Franciscan, 16-17
Zebello, Monte, 21
Ziska, John, 46-8
Zwickau, 76
Zwingli, 61